THE EARLY CLOCKMAKERS OF GREAT BRITAIN

BRIAN LOOMES, BA, FSG

N.A.G. PRESS LTD
LONDON

Published 1981

Author's additional works
Watchmakers and Clockmakers of the World, Volume 2
County Clocks and their London Origins
Yorkshire Clockmakers
Lancashire Clocks and Clockmakers
Westmorland Clocks and Clockmakers
The White Dial Clock
Complete British Clocks

ISBN 7198 0200 8

Typeset in Great Britain by The Grange Press, Southwick, Sussex.
Printed by Anchor Press, and bound by William Brendon Ltd, both of
Tiptree, Essex.

CONTENTS

Preface

I have compiled, in this book, as many details as I have found on each clockmaker and clock worker who was operating before 1700. Something like 5,000 makers of watches, clocks and mathematical instruments are included from all parts of Great Britain, although the bulk of them worked in London, and London makers probably account for four-fifths of the entries. What I have *not* done is simply to copy out names of this period from other books. Readers of this book will probably be familiar with the lists in Baillie and Britten, and I want to make it clear that I have tried in virtually every instance to go to the original source record. In many cases this will have been the same source which Baillie and Britten used, in particular the Clockmakers' Company archives. I adopted this method not only because there is no merit in copying out someone else's work, but because there are errors in both Baillie and Britten, especially in the latter.

I do not know how Britten compiled his lists of Clockmakers' Company members. He almost certainly used some of their indexed records but these records themselves contain several errors. Also, the original seventeenth-century documents are very difficult to read unless one is experienced with the script and, as I understand it, Baillie employed an experienced record-searcher to overcome this problem. While this sounds like an admirable idea, it did mean that mistakes and misinterpretations crept in simply because the researcher did not understand clockmaking.

Set out below is a facsimile of an original script taken from the Clockmakers' Company archives for 1632. This is comparatively neatly-written and in a clear hand, which may give some indication of the problems presented by a badly-written section.

A facsimile of an original script, in a comparatively clear hand, from The Clockmakers' Company archives, dated April, 1632. See facing page for transcription.

This daye Lewes Cooke appeared at the Court but
would not come in Court (before the Mr., Wardens and (Mr. = Master)
Assistants) without command the which was pformed by
the Clarke of the Companie. And upon his appearance
in Court he was demannded his fine for setting a
forreyner at work such as the (?) of the
lawe doe allow of, but denied to pay any And was
likewise asked if he had brought his apprentice to
be riegestred for the tyme he had to serve he replied
he had not, neither would he, And likewise for the
40s. he had subscribed to pay towards the p'rement (= procurement)
of the Corporation he answered also he would pay
none, and in a very abusive and scornfull manner with
much ill Language left the Court, for all which his
misdemeanour he is to be taken course withall by the
Mr. and Wardens as cause shall require.

I have been through the Clockmakers' Company archives, word by word, in both the rough (working) books and the neat books, where both survive, up to the year 1720. This task alone took six years. The Company was kind enough to allow me to microfilm its records for this purpose and I have presented it with a copy of the microfilm to help save future wear and tear on its documents. This microfilm record of the Company archives has been a permanent fixture on my desk since 1975.

Where there is a discrepancy between my facts and those of Britten and Baillie, it is nearly always (I hope) because I have found an error in their work. There are bound to be occasions, however, where mistakes have crept in to my work, and I would be most grateful for any drawn to my attention. I hope, at least, to have avoided the more obvious pitfalls – for two beautiful howlers see under the surnames Forgat and Master. Britten often gives the name of the master whom an apprentice served, but it seems to me that he did not understand the procedure of 'turning over' (explained on page 38) and his master's name might sometimes be the teacher, sometimes the nominee. I am not trying to belittle the work of either Britten or Baillie, because they did cover three centuries where I have covered only one, and even then there were times when I almost abandoned the task!

Occasionally, I have included an entry which I am unsure about – there are various reasons why this has happened. If a correspondent reports a clock that he has dated too early, or a name or a town has been misread, or a clock is an outright fake, or a clock's authenticity is in doubt, then I have played safe by including the entry. If the information turns out to be correct it will serve its purpose; if wrong then it will probably do no harm.

I had perhaps best point out that the entry of a name in this directory in no way should be taken as evidence of the authenticity of any clock that happens to be seen bearing that name. Likewise, the absence of a name should not be taken to assume that such a maker was somehow 'inferior' or that such a clock might be 'wrong' (although both could apply in certain instances).

It is hoped that this information will be useful in a variety of ways to those who wish to look up the makers of their clocks, but it is all too easy for the information presented here to be misunderstood and misinterpreted, and I am most anxious to avoid that happening. It must be appreciated that much of the information comes from records which are three centuries old and which may be incomplete, inaccurate or illegible, and which may have been deliberately falsified for reasons we may not understand. So, if there are apparent contradictions within the directory, it is because there are contradictions within the records themselves.

In order to understand these entries the reader must know how the system of apprenticeship worked and how an apprentice might progress to become a Freeman or a Free Brother of a guild (the Company of Clockmakers of London is the one most commonly referred to). Readers must also know how a member of the Company progressed to the higher offices in that Company – Steward, Assistant, Warden and Master.

Interpretation of the details in the directory is not, as might first be imagined, a matter of commonsense, and readers who assume these details are self-explanatory will almost certainly fall into the trap of misinterpreting them. The following chapters attempt to explain the systems and procedures of the day.

The details of a man's life are given, where possible, up until his death, even if he did not die until 1750 or even later. I am, however, more concerned with events which occurred before 1720, and after this date I do not list a man's apprentices. My detailed search of the Clockmakers' Company archives ended at 1720 and post-1720 information is less detailed. The year 1700 is the final cut-off point and a maker who made his first clock in 1701 (or finished his apprenticeship in 1701) is *not* included, even though he was obviously apprenticed in the seventeenth century. If he made his first clock in 1700 or before, then he *is* included.

Throughout this book I have used the dating system of the day, which must, at times, involve the use of double-dating. In British dating the old Julian Calendar system was used until 1752, and the new year began on 25th March, not on 1st January. To avoid confusion today we usually express dates between 1st January and 25th March of any year before 1752 in double form, so that what was then styled 4th February 1670 (known as Old Style) and what we would today, in retrospect, regard as 4th February 1671 (known as New Style), is written as 4th February 1670/71. On occasions a date might be used in single dating, for example, March 1680, and this refers to a date after the 25th March and before 1st April of the new year.

After each entry I have mentioned 'work known'. This denotes work which I know to have survived, but not necessarily work which I have examined personally. It also includes work which I am advised has survived. I have made no attempt to study the working methods of the 5,000 clockmakers nor do I have any additional information as to whether a certain clock is the one sold in such-and-such a saleroom in the 1930s. Everything I know about the clockworkers in the period up to 1700 is in the pages that follow.

An entry which records, for example, a longcase clock by a certain maker should not be taken to mean that 'only one is known to have survived.' People do sometimes misinterpret information in this way and can assume that their own clock can be described in terms of 'one of only two known to survive.' I mention known types of work simply to indicate the type of work produced by that clockmaker. If you come across work by a certain maker of a type different to that described, I would be happy to hear about it, and similarly about clocks signed in a different manner from that described, or with a different 'address', or by a maker who is not listed.

It is impossible for me to acknowledge the kind assistance given to me in compiling this work by numerous people over the years. I can only say that of all the authors and researchers of the various aspects of clock-making, not a single one has proved unhelpful, and all have willingly allowed me to quote facts from their books or have supplied me with seventeenth-century facts from their researches. This is, perhaps, a sign of the generosity of most clock researchers who will spend years trying to unravel facts about a maker, and then willingly pass that information along for the price of a mere word of thanks. Having myself sometimes been in the situation of having had large chunks of my own research quoted in other books, not only without permission but with no acknowledgement (and in one case having seen an entire book appear based on my own research into one particular clockmaking family with neither a by-your-leave nor a thank-you), I am always anxious to acknowledge help from others. I cannot here list each person by name, but a list of their books is to be found in the bibliography, and if a reader wants to pursue a provincial maker he should consult these works. I must, however, give special thanks to Alan Treherne, E. J. Tyler and Roy Gault, whose as yet unpublished researches are continuing at the time I write this, and to Peter Nutt who helped, as always, with the research.

Beverley,   **Brian Loomes**
North Yorkshire.   **1981**

CHAPTER 1

The Apprenticeship System

A youngster who was given formal training in the craft of clock and watchmaking (which, in this book, includes the related trades of locksmith, blacksmith, whitesmith, instrument maker, engraver, and so on) signed a legal contract called an indenture of apprenticeship drawn up between himself (and his parents or guardians) and the master he was to work under. The indenture set out the basic terms of the contract on behalf of both parties. So, a youngster is often said to have been 'bound' to a master, or set 'to serve' a master, and these words are often used in old records to mean the same thing as 'apprenticed'. In fact these words are taken from the text of the apprenticeship indenture (sometimes called a bond), an example of which we shall see below.

Unfortunately, nothing about these old records is simple and sometimes the words 'bound' and 'serve' are used in the same context but with a very different meaning, which is examined more fully in the business of 'turning over' discussed later. It was possible for a boy to be 'bound' to one master, but 'to serve' (ie work under) a different master. Fortunately, it is usually obvious from the text where this applies.

Set out below is a transcription of a surviving apprenticeship indenture, preserved in the archives of the Worshipful Company of Clockmakers.

This indenture witnesseth that Richard Allen
son of John Allen of Pangborne in the county
of Berks, Gent: --
doth put himself apprentice to Henry Harper, Citizen
and Clockmaker of London, to learn his art: and with him (after
the manner of an apprentice) to serve from the day of the date
hereof. --

unto the full end and term of seaven years, from thence next following to be fully compleat and ended. During which term the said apprentice his said Master faithfully shall serve, his Secrets keep, his lawful commandments every where gladly do. He shall do no damage to his said Master, nor see to be done of others but that he to his power shall lett or forthwith give warning to his said Master of the same. He shall not waste the goods of his said Master, nor lend them unlawfully to any: He shall not commit fornication nor contract matrimony within the said term. He shall not play at cards, dice, tables, or any other unlawful games, whereby his said Master may have any loss. With his own goods or others during the said term without licence of his said Master he shall neither buy nor sell. He shall not haunt taverns or play-houses, nor absent himself from his said Master's service day or night unlawfully: But in all things as a faithful apprentice he shall behave him self towards his said Master and all his during the said term. And the said Master his said apprentice in the same art which he useth, by the best means that he can, shall teach and instruct, or cause to be taught and instructed, finding to his said apprentice, meat, drink, apparel, lodging, and all other necessaries, according to the custom of the City of London during the said term. And for the true performance of all and every the said covenants and agreements either of the said parties bindeth himself unto the other by these presents. In witness whereof the parties abovenamed to these indentures interchangeably have put their hands and seals the eighteenth day of August in the eighth year of the reign of our Sovereign Lord King William the third of England, etc. Anno.Dm. 1696.
Francis Speidell.   Richard Allen.
Both the apprentice and master signed this document, but, surprising as it may seem, there were quite a few masters and apprentices who were unable to write and so they signed with a cross.

Not all youngsters were trained under a formal apprenticeship. For instance, a working clockmaker might very well train his own son or sons in the trade without feeling there was any need for such an agreement – though some fathers did formally bind their sons, perhaps mostly those who were under the close scrutiny of the Clockmakers' Company. Cases of youngsters who never served a proper apprenticeship must account for some of the entries where I have been unable to discover with whom a boy learned his trade. Probably a good many more of these cases are accounted for by the fact that apprenticeship details just have not survived or because the relevant documents have yet to be discovered.

Some makers, amongst them some highly-skilled craftsmen, had never received any training and were often proud of the fact that they were self-taught. One such clockmaker was Thomas Peirce of Berkeley, Gloucestershire, who died in 1665 and whose epitaph begins:

'Here lyeth Thomas Peirce, whom no man taught,
Yet he iron, brass and silver wrought;
He jacks and clocks and watches made . . .'

These 'untrained' men were a bit of a problem to the authorities who often insisted on evidence of training, and we will come back to this point later.

A youngster normally served a term of seven years, being bound at the age of fourteen and completing his service at the age of majority (twenty-one). We can therefore calculate the boy's approximate year of birth by deducting fourteen from his apprenticeship year, and in many of the directory entries this has been done to give an approximate year of birth (b.c. 1665 means born circa 1665). Sometimes boys were bound at a younger age than fourteen although they were still unable to complete their training until the age of twenty-one, perhaps because it was felt they were not yet mature enough. It is usually safe to assume that an apprenticeship term of eight years indicated that a boy was bound at thirteen, nine years indicating twelve, and there are rare instances of ten year apprenticeships, where a child would have been bound at eleven. Instances of very young boys being bound are infrequent and occurred more often during the early years of the Clockmakers' Company, and in some instances might have been a result of a child being orphaned. However, it seems that apprenticeship under the age of fourteen was not encouraged and as time went by it became increasingly frowned upon, so that eventually there are instances on record where the Clockmakers' Company cancelled the apprenticeship of an under-age child, or made him rebind himself again a year or two later. This apparently confusing practice of a child being apprenticed for a second time (sometimes to a different master) a year or two after his first binding, has sometimes led past writers to assume there were two different boys each having the same name, a situation further complicated when only one eventually became free.

After an apprentice had completed his period of training he was then officially passed out as being 'free' of his apprenticeship. This was normally signified by his appearing before the guild concerned (in London, the Clockmakers' Company) and being enrolled and sworn in as

13

a member, confirmation then being set in the records. Just to confuse matters some clockmakers deliberately delayed 'taking up their freedom', as this was called, for reasons which I will explain later.

The Clockmakers' Company specified that an apprentice who had completed his term must then work for two years as a 'journeyman', ie as a workman under a master clockmaker (though it need not be under the man he had served his apprenticeship with), before he could set up in business on his own account. This two-year period was sometimes reduced to one year on payment of a penalty 'fine', but I doubt whether this fine was always enforced. When it was enforced it was often through the selfish motives of some third party who 'ratted' on a rival, or through maliciousness on the part of a hostile member of the Company administration. The Company administration would often turn a blind eye to unofficial practices, but were usually obliged to act if such practices were officially reported to them. Sometimes they were motivated by jealousy – the constant prosecutions and persecutions of the Fromanteel family group were mostly motivated by envy on the part of the less-talented Company administrators and Fromanteel succeeded despite the constant hostility from his 'protective' guild.

A freed apprentice was required to produce, at the end of his journeyman period, an example of his workmanship – rather like sitting the practical part of an examination. This work was often called a 'masterpiece', in other words a piece proving his worthiness to become a master (the word has acquired a very different meaning today). The Clockmakers' Company seldom seems to have insisted on a masterpiece. By contrast the Edinburgh guild, known as the Guild of Hammermen and covering all metalworkers, always insisted on a test piece or 'essay piece' as they called it, and in the case of clockmakers it usually required a clock and a lock. In most provincial towns the testimony that the lad had finished his apprenticeship was usually taken as adequate proof of his ability and he was normally allowed freedom of the town (ie freedom to trade in the town) on that basis – although a good number seemed to think it might help if they made a gesture of goodwill by making a present of the clock to the town.

A master did not take on an apprentice out of the kindness of his heart, but for a fee paid by the boy's parents or guardians; the size of the fee depended on the stature of the clockmaker. It could range from about £5 upwards, but Ahasuerus Fromanteel senior stated in 1666 that he had never accepted less than £20 for taking an apprentice (a sum that at this same period was almost a year's wages to a journeyman). In the case of orphans the fee was often reduced or in some instances waived altogether, especially if the master was a relative, though sometimes other relatives or guardians would agree to buy the boy's clothing. An interesting example of one kind of orphan, a foundling, can be seen in the case of Samuel Lebow who was apprenticed to Richard George in 1705. He was obviously an abandoned baby who had been brought up by the parish and was named after the parish. The Clockmakers' Company records describe him as 'a child in the care of the parish of St. Mary Lebow'. For his part the master taught the boy clockmaking. If he was a provincial clockmaker this may well have involved making a clock with the engraving, though engraving was always a specialised facet and was often carried out by separate workmen. Sometimes a master clockmaker employed one or more specialist engravers in his work force. In the case of London makers they were very often specialists in a way their rural counterparts were not and, while the apprentice may well have been shown all aspects of the work, he was probably not expected to become proficient in every one of these aspects. The early provincial maker was always more of an all-rounder than his London counterpart – indeed he had to be. The master's duty was to give the boy a good general grounding to the point where he was capable of going out into the world to earn his living from his craft.

An example of extreme specialization comes to mind with Richard Morgan whose speciality was making springs for watches and clocks, work which, even as early as the seventeenth century, most clockmakers would never have attempted. Morgan was warned on a couple of occasions by the Clockmakers' Company that his apprentices must be given at least as much experience in clock and watchmaking as in spring-making to prevent them from becoming over-specialised.

Apprentices were not allowed to marry. Often they married as soon as their apprenticeship was over, so that the date of freedom from apprenticeship coincides with the start of married life and the start of an independent career. Sometimes, however, an apprentice did marry before his time was up but marriage during apprenticeship was very much frowned upon by the authorities, so much so that in London such an offender was automatically disqualified from being able to take up his freedom of the city by servitude. When John Bayes, the watchmaker, applied for his freedom of the City of London in 1649, he was obliged to purchase his freedom being 'debarred from freedom by service as he married before the expiration of his apprenticeship'. The important criterion was the date of completion of apprenticeship. Edward Banger, for example, completed his service in September 1694, married his master's niece (Margaret Kent, Tompion's niece) in December 1694 and took up his freedom in the Clockmakers' Company in July 1695.

Quakers were not willing to swear oaths and so they were sometimes allowed to take a 'covenant servant', a term coined for just such an occasion and apparently first used for Daniel Quare's apprentice in 1673.

Apprentices were not always as conscientious as one might suppose. Francis Robinson, for instance, had been in some sort of trouble, was punished and then returned to his master who, though he wanted to get rid of him, was unable to get any other master to take him off his hands. One Robert Beale had served only three years of his term when, in 1680, his master reported that 'being afflicted with the King's Evil he hath bin gone with his friends about half a year and not likely ever to return' (supposedly, the King's Evil could only to be cured by the touch of a King). In 1682 Edward Orton was said to have 'gone from' his master, being 'not able to do him any service by some infirmities in his limbs', but he seems to have recovered and went on to become a regular clock-maker. In 1672 William Bulstrode was only four years into his appren-ticeship when found to be 'incapable of learning his trade and to be put away'. The same thing happened to Thomas Drew in the same year.

Female 'apprentices' need to be mentioned since, as far as I can establish, girls were not apprenticed in the trade, even though the names of some girls appear in this directory as being apprenticed through the Clockmakers' Company. One or two 'girls' were in fact boys – Faith Leake, for example, was male. Girls' names appear in the records for two reasons. First, a clockmaker who was a freeman of the Clockmakers' Company had a right to bind his children through the Company, and some bound their daughters as well as their sons, even though there is nothing to show that these girls worked in the trade. Second, some members of the Clockmakers' Company took up trades which had nothing whatsoever to do with clockmaking (how this came about is explained later) – such as Henry Jevon, a lawyer, who bound several girls, probably to train as clerks. A number of girls were bound to a member 'for' his wife, which meant to follow the wife's trade. Women did play a part in the Clock and Watch trade, especially when they carried on trading as widows after their husbands died, but so far as I can see they were not formally apprenticed into the trade.

The number of apprentices permitted to any member varied over the years is difficult to pin down, and in any case was frequently exceeded either with official consent or without it. A member of the Clockmakers' Company was limited to one apprentice for the first five years of his Freedom, and to two when the first one had completed his five years. However, it was quite possible to break this rule so long as a fine was paid – you could do almost anything with official approval if you agreed to pay a big enough fine. The alternative was to go ahead and do it anyway, but if you were found out then you would still have to pay a fine. Sometimes second apprentices were allowed within the five-year term; later a third one or even more. In 1691 the rules were changed to allow a second apprentice to be employed after the first had completed only two years, and they were changed again in 1700 to waive the condition that the second apprentice could not be taken until the first had served two years, but the overall guide was to be that no-one was to have more than two apprentices at any one time. Of course, it was not observed. At most periods the Master, Wardens and Assistants were usually allowed at least one apprentice more than a common member. There were always ways round this problem. Once an apprentice was out of his time and became a journeyman, then he could take on his own quota of apprentices, and so a workmaster with perhaps five journeymen, could soon build up as large a workforce as wanted.

It was often a problem to get time-served apprentices to take up their freedoms in the Clockmakers' Company, because once they did so they had to pay the entrance fee and the regular subscriptions (called quarter-age because it was payable quarterly at each of the four major Quarter Court meetings). Many apprentices kept a low profile to try and get away without paying, even long after their period of service had ended. In the directory which follows the term 'apprenticed till . . .' is often used and the date given is the date on which the term of service was due to end. However, the date of his being 'free' which follows shows the date when the man actually took up his freedom in the Company, and in theory these two dates would be the same – Edmund East, for example, was apprenticed until 1696 and freed in July 1696.

Often a man delayed taking up his freedom until the year after his term ended, but sometimes this delay was much longer. Henry Bradley, for example, ended his apprenticeship in 1674 but did not take up his freedom until 1681, although still working in London, since he claimed he could not afford to do so any sooner. Sometimes freedom was delayed for quite exceptional lengths of time, as happened to John Bowen, whose term ended in 1684 but who delayed his freedom until 1710 and then 'upon his earnest request being poor was admitted gratis'.

Many youngsters never did take up their freedoms in the Clockmakers' Company, and this is conveyed in the directory by the term 'not freed'. There could be many reasons for this, death is an obvious one, moving away from London another, sometimes both, as with young Ezekiel Andrews, who died whilst on a voyage to the East Indies, his apprenticeship still not formally completed. The implication behind 'not freed' must be that an apprentice did not stay on to work in London, but we must be a little cautious about inferring this in each case because some got away with long-delayed freedoms.

There are many examples in the directory of youngsters who were apprenticed in London but who were not freed, and of men of the same name who spring up in provincial towns within a few years – in most cases it seems safe to assume they were one and the same. Normally, it would be essential for such a tradesman to take up his freedom in the town to which he had moved, but he would only need his Clockmakers' Company freedom if he wanted to work in London. Some eventually had to take up their Clockmakers' Company freedoms when they wished to return to work there later. Abraham Fromanteel, for example, was apprenticed to his father in London in 1662, but never took up his freedom in 1669, perhaps because they had then moved from London. When in 1680 he wanted to return to work in London, having been working in Newcastle-upon-Tyne, his father made a plea to the Clockmakers' Company to grant Abraham's freedom as soon as was possible, which they did.

The question of delaying taking up freedom was always a problem to the authorities. The Clockmakers' Company repeatedly warned that no members must employ foreigners or unfree men or deal with them, but obviously many did (including members of the administration themselves). A flagrant case came to light in July 1691 for Andrew Strachan, 'a Scot between thirty and forty years and no freeman for several years past has worked here without consent and avoided prosecution by moving from place to place – hath this July bound himself for seven years to Thomas Warden (a Free Haberdasher) to avoid redress'. But the Company was not having any of this, and it cancelled his apprenticeship. Strachan's case shows how it was possible to work in London for several years without being caught, even when not a freeman of any Company.

CHAPTER 2

The Worshipful Company of Clockmakers

In the late sixteenth and early seventeenth centuries the clockmaking trade in Britain was confined to a few specialists because making domestic clocks and watches was a new skill. Church clocks and tower clocks had been made for over a century, but usually by a few specialised itinerant clockmakers, mostly, if not entirely, from France, Germany and the Low Countries. Once installed, these turret clocks were usually maintained by local blacksmiths and other metalworkers who, in time, often blossomed into rural clockmaking families.

Domestic clocks tended to be of two main types. Watches, tiny examples of highly-skilled intricacy in gold and silver, much bejewelled, made to entertain and amuse their wealthy owners, and house clocks (often built on the same principles as a large watch), spring-driven, housed in gold and silver caskets, and often designed to show the ingenuity of the maker in recording not simply the hours, but calendars, planetary conjunctions and astrological information, sometimes incorporating automated figures or automated scenes. Such a clock was a 'magic box' designed to amaze and impress a small, wealthy market. This highly-exclusive craft was hardly a separate trade but more of a side-branch of the work of the goldsmith, silversmith and jeweller. In the century up to about 1620 it is doubtful whether we can record twenty names of exponents of the craft in Britain, and the ones we do know of were almost entirely foreign. Nicholas Kratzer, Nicholas Urseau, Bartholomew Newsam, Anthony Risby, Randolph Bull, John Vallin and his son, Nicholas, and David Ramsay – are the well-known few, but their output seems to have been small judging by the few surviving examples of their work, and this despite the fact that a king's or a lord's treasures had a far better chance of survival than prized possessions of the common man.

The lantern clock began to be made from about 1600 and was the first domestic clock which had a chance of being sold in a much wider market. Foreigners dominated the trade and this caused a lot of ill-feeling within the craft, small though it was. Its members wished to protect their emerging market from overseas competition and whilst many of the exponents were foreigners, or of foreign extraction, they apparently saw no inconsistency in wishing to ban foreigners from their marketplace. In 1622 sixteen of these so-called British craftsmen petitioned James I for a charter to form their own Company of Clockmakers so as to keep out foreigners, mainly Frenchmen, who they accused of peddling cheap wares over here which, though seemingly very attractive, were of poor workmanship. They named certain offenders currently working in London, and from this list we can see that the total work strength, 'British' and foreign, including apprentices, journeymen and masters, numbered less than sixty. The 'British' petitioners (sometimes called the 'original petitioners' to distinguish them from the later petitioners of 1629) were Robert Grinkin (the elder), Henry Archer, Ferdinando Garret, James Vautrolier, Edmund Bull, George Bull, Francis Foreman, Isaac Simes, John Smith, John Wellowe (or Willow), Anthony Risby, William Yate, Nicholas Walters, Cornelius Yate, Daniel Saunders and John Harris. This petition came to nothing.

In 1629 a new petition was submitted to the new King, Charles I, by the now larger group of London clockmakers, which by this time included some of the men formerly complained about because they were foreigners. This petition was successful and resulted in a charter from Charles on 22nd August 1631, and the Worshipful Company of Clockmakers was duly formed. It had powers to control the trade and its exponents in London and within a ten mile radius, but not beyond that as is sometimes believed. Theoretically, no-one was allowed to trade unless he joined the Company. The Company controlled the making not only of clocks and watches (with associated parts such as watch cases, springs, chains, etc.) but also such items as sundials and measures (ie rulers). Measures were normally sold by what were known as cane-sellers (who might also be iron-mongers) but were usually made by clockmakers, particularly those who specialised as 'mathematical instrument makers'.

The Company controlled the training of apprentices and the numbers allowed to each master, and, in furthering its aim of preventing the sale of poor-quality work which might bring the trade into disrepute, was authorised to search any premises, by force if necessary, where there might be illicit or inadequate work. The members were required to pay a subscription, called 'quarterage' since it was paid at the major Quarter Court meetings, held four times a year. The subscription was normally four pence a quarter.

The Company seem to have been easily able to frighten off the unqualified. Francis Starley (or perhaps Sturley) was caught in 1641 and when tackled he confessed that he had not served any apprenticeship but had only spent six weeks training under a Mr. Stillinger. He was banned from trading. In 1671 David Davis, a pinmaker, was ordered to stop calling himself a clockmaker but to stick to pinmaking. In 1680 one 'Hatly, a sword cutler in New Street near Shoe Lane, who maketh pin cases and tradeth in watches and clocks' was banned for not having served an apprenticeship. In 1697 William Ginn worked 'in the Little Old Bayly using the Art of a Boxmaker (ie a watch case maker) but is by trade a Turner, given one month's warning to cease the trade' – but he was admitted into the Clockmakers' Company two years later. Perhaps the biggest difficulty for the Company throughout the seventeenth century (and no doubt later too) was that of dealing with those whose living was in the clock trade but who were Freemen of other City Companies. The Clockmakers' Company wanted all clock workers to become its members, pay their quarterage and observe its rulings. That, after all, was the whole point of the Company's existence. But for all kinds of reasons a lot of clockworkers already belonged to other companies, principally the Blacksmiths' Company. Quite often a Freeman of another company, who was paying his quarterage and observing its rules and otherwise going peaceably about his own business, was suddenly told by this new Company that he was to observe its rules and pay his quarterage to the Clockmakers.

John Drake was a Blacksmiths' Company member from 1605, and one who after almost thirty years in the trade was not at all pleased to have this new company attempt to regulate his life. He was made to submit a written apology in 1633 for his 'intemperate and disgraceful speeches' which he had uttered to the Clockmakers' Company, 'rashly and in my haste and passion – I am sorry, they granting me that after the expiration of my eldest apprentice, that I may take another in the middle time, before the expiration of my youngest apprentice'. But the emnity did not end there. In 1654 he was reported to the Lord Mayor, who usually settled these inter-company disputes, because he was fifteen years in arrears with his Clockmakers' Company quarterage – hardly an oversight, one might imagine. The Lord Mayor made him pay up, which he did in July, but not exactly graciously and 'did use revilling language against the Master, calling (him a) Turd and shitten fellow and using other (illegible) words to the disparagement of the Company'. He was summoned to appear again to account for his rugged language and no doubt to eat humble pie.

The case of Andrew Strachan shows how it was possible to escape detection by the Clockmakers' Company whilst working in London – perhaps by moving house regularly, and a few men whose names appear on surviving clocks today probably fall into this category – see Thomas Bridge of London, several of whose clocks still survive. Some names are noted in the directory as being 'not known to CC', which is a term I have coined to indicate that this person's name does not appear in the Company records at that time. I explain this to avoid any misinterpretation of this term, which does not mean that an enquiry *today* to the Clockmakers' Company would fail to produce any information. It means that such a person apparently worked either without being detected by the Company or else that it turned a blind eye towards his activities. We do not always know which, but sometimes we do.

The Company was assiduous in searching out non-member clockworkers and those they did discover were usually pressed into joining or badgered to stop trading or moved on elsewhere, and in any of these instances the offending names were duly recorded in the archives. But a number, such as Thomas Bridge, appear to have escaped notice altogether.

John Saville senior was a Freeman of the Vintners' Company but also of the Clockmakers' Company, in which he served up to the rank of Assistant (he was excused Wardenship however, which might have been on account of conflicting duties within the Vintners' Company). In complying with Clockmakers' Company rules he pointed out in 1678 that if he so wished he could have made his son, John junior, a Freeman of the Vintners' Company by patrimony (ie a son's automatic right to freedom in the same Company of which his father is a Freeman). The implication is that while Saville said he would comply, he let them know that he was not obliged to – and the Clockmakers' Company had no reply to that.

This brings us back to the time when the Clockmakers' Company began, for many clockmakers were already under allegiance to other Companies – an arrangement that could not easily be broken by Clockmakers' Company legislation. In 1680 mention is made of 'controlling the many abuses that have grown up of those who do not come into the Company', such as the 'Great church clockmakers of iron' (makers of large iron turret clocks), some of whom still remained within the Blacksmiths' Company. But this problem of double allegiance did not only affect the Blacksmiths' Company. Right through the seventeenth century and into the eighteenth there were occasions (not always recorded in the Clockmakers' Company archives) when clockmakers traded under the freedom rights of other Companies and never did join the Clockmakers' Company. The Clockmakers' Company could threaten people, but it had no powers to force them to join it.

In 1694 the Clockmakers' Company pressed for an Act to force anyone working in the trade and Free of the City to take up the Freedom of the Clockmakers' Company and to bind their apprentices through that Company. In January 1698 Mr. Tompion reported that he knew of several people who were free of other Companies who were willing to become Clockmakers' Company Freemen if this could be arranged without cost to them. In July 1698 it was ordered that 'all who practice the Art and who are Free of the City' (and of other Companies) be admitted free of charge into the Clockmakers' Company. In other words, where it was impossible to force them to join they tried to entice them – but some still avoided joining the Clockmakers' Company.

The Company seems to have been far more competent at searching out deficient work, which it dealt with by confiscation, by defacement, or by smashing the defective parts and ordering replacements of the correct quality to be made. This it did by making regular inspection tours of the various workshops which were known as 'Searches', sometimes called the 'Walks' or the 'Four Walks'. The area was split into sections, sometimes three, at other periods four, and a tour was made of each circuit by several senior officers who dealt with deficient work on the spot and who also took this as a convenient opportunity for collecting unpaid quarterage moneys.

In 1653 William Almond was ordered to hand in to the Clockmakers' Club a good, substantial 'house clock' to replace an imperfect one he had sold someone (this must have been a lantern clock). In 1652 Samuel Davis' house in Lothbury was searched and a chamber clock, thought to be of poor quality, was seized and broken, 'that it might not be put to sale to defraud or deceive the people of the Common Wealth', and he was fined forty shillings. In 1656 John Wyeth showed them a 'spelter metal' boxed watch, which the Company 'disliked', considering it deceitful 'being in

Imitation of Gould' and it ordered that no more should be made. In 1658 'This search day a contrat, second wheel and a dyal wheel being taken from Thomas Battin, was viewed by the said Company and adjudged to be so bad as not fitting to be put into any work, and (he) was fined according to the orders of the said Company. The defective wheels were broken up.' In 1658 Bernard Gernon had some of his work defaced.

In March 1682/83 a 'view' of some poor watches of Robert Halstead was postponed as 'it was late and candle light', and this was deferred until 'some more convenient time by open day light'. In fact two inadequate movements were smashed though he denied they were his own work but claimed to have taken them in part exchange. In 1688 they searched the workrooms of Samuel Rosse and confiscated certain inadequate watch movements. His wife not only refused to pay the search fee but 'gave them very evil words'. The movements were later returned to him with the defective parts removed. In January 1682/83 they confiscated from John Cotsworth a very 'unworkmanlike and insufficient' watch movement which he was finishing and which bore an invented name (John Rouden, London) – he was fined, though he claimed it was made by 'a little crookback man in Shoe Lane'! There were many more such instances, but not all members took it lying down. In 1633 Lewis Cooke was made to apologize in writing for 'uncivil words' he had spoken to John Harris, one of the Wardens – 'he having found fault with some work I had made. I did give the said John Harris the lye, and told him that he was a botcher and that he never made so good a piece of work in his life as that was which he found fault withall. These words being rashly and unadvisedly spoken, I am heartily sorry . . .'

The Company was strict with the measure-sellers too. In February 1671 it 'seized at the same time from Mr. Anthony Poole, Ironmonger in Foster Lane 2 plain joynt 2-foot rules & 5 plaine 2 foot rules, 4 being tipped & 1 untipt', and others too. One two-foot rule confiscated in March 1672/73 from Mr. Harris, an ironmonger, was one tenth of an inch too long. The Company kept the 'standard measures' of length which were actual measuring sticks such as yardsticks – in 1690, for instance, there is a note that two brass standards for yards were put into the Company chest (probably replacement measures). In 1688 Hilkiah Bedford carried the Standard Measure on a search. There are extant copies of the Wardens' accounts for some years, and these show the payments made at each stop on the search, and one records a humiliating moment for Warden Samuel Horne – 'In Chancery Lane Warden Horne

24

lost the search paper when there had been rec'd 13s 6d whereof it was remembered that there was rec'd of Mr. John Harris 3s 4d and of Mr. Barlow Rooks 3s 4d. But it was forgotten of whom was the other 6s 10d.' Warden Horne had probably made too many unscheduled stops along the way for liquid refreshment.

Apart from the four Quarter Court meetings, a meeting of the administrators could be called at any time, as thought fit – and this was sometimes done at intervals of only a few days when urgent business was on hand. The Company had no hall of its own and meetings were usually held in taverns and, occasionally, in the house of a member or in the hall of some other City Company by special arrangement. The place and time were generally chosen by the Master, and it was the duty of all senior officers to attend. Indeed, occasional latecomers or non-attenders were threatened and even fined on rare occasions. The occasional, determined attempt like this to tighten up discipline only reveals how lax it really was, and these attempts seldom influenced the determined rebel.

Courts were held – sometimes once, sometimes repeatedly – at Northumberland House, the White Lion near Guildhall, the Master's House (S. Hacket – 1647), Mr. Nicasius' shop in Fleet Street in 1648, the Horns Tavern in Fleet Street, the St. John Head in Ludgate, the Red Lion at Nicholas Shambles End, the Master's house in Fleet Street (Edward East – 1653), Broiderers Hall, the Rose Tavern, Newgate Market, Salters' Hall, Plasterers' Hall, the house of Thomas Claxton in Guildhall Yard 1661-63, the Feathers Tavern in St. Paul's Churchyard, the Miter Tavern in Wood Street, the Three Sugar Loaves in Loathbury, the George in Ivy Lane, the Dolphin in Abchurch Lane, the Castle Tavern in Fleet Street, the Crown Tavern in Smithfield, the Roe Buck in Queen Street, the Cat in Long Lane, the George in Ironmonger Lane, the Cooks' Hall Aldersgate Street, the Castle Tavern in Cornhill, the Beket Tavern in Old Change, Founders' Hall and Goldsmiths' Hall. This is by no means a complete list, but it does show the variety of meeting places. The meetings could be at any time of day, and were sometimes held as early as 7.00 a.m., usually at the whim of the administration, which consisted of a Master, three Wardens and a group of several Assistants (generally about ten, but of no fixed number).

The Company had the ability to keep a tight control over the quality of work produced by its members, but it was a major problem to force outsiders to join. This proved very difficult if an offender was particularly obstinate or elusive or if he felt he had just reason to refuse. There were a handful of men during the seventeenth century whom the Company never attempted to coerce, yet who openly practiced the trade without belonging to the Clockmakers' Company. Another problem was that prejudiced officers tended to bend the rules to their own advantage which may not have been in the best interests of the trade or its members.

The first Master was named as David Ramsay (not surprisingly, being the King's Clockmaker) though he scarcely ever bothered to attend meetings. The first Wardens were Henry Archer, John Willow and Sampson Shelton. The first Assistants were also named. The senior offices were held for a year at a time in rotation by appointing an Assistant, usually on the basis of seniority, to the office of Junior Warden, Middle (or Renter) Warden, and Senior Warden and then Master. After his year as Master he reverted to being an ordinary Assistant again. Once appointed Assistant he held that office for life, apart from his year's spell in each of the four senior offices. Once an ordinary member had joined the Company as a Freeman or Brother it was not necessary for him to attend meetings unless he was specially summoned, probably to account for his transgressions. Often he would attend 'to present' his new apprentice, ie to have him officially accepted and recorded, and perhaps to attend when his apprentice took up his freedom. We must remember, however, that an apprentice may not have taken up his freedom until after his master's death, and whilst this is sometimes made clear in the records it is not always specified. It should by no means be automatically assumed that a master was still alive at the time of his apprentice's freedom unless we have confirmation of this from some other source.

Only members could be appointmented to a Company office (with the exception of the Clerk), but there is a widely-held misconception about this, just as there is about membership. It was not, as is sometimes suggested, an honour to be 'invited' to join the Company – joining was compulsory and non-compliers were harrassed and even fined. Likewise the holding of more senior positions within the Company was usually a matter of compulsary promotion according to seniority. The first Company duty which a member would be eligible to perform was to hold the post of Steward, two were usually appointed each year until 1672, after which it became four per year. Stewards served for one year only and were chosen according to seniority. Apparently, they had only one function, which was to pay for and organise the Annual Feast, sometimes called the Stewards' Feast. Needless to say, very few held this office willingly. Usually those eligible to serve came up with an excuse, probably pleading financial hardship. In 1718 Claude du Chesne was excused stewardship 'because he has five children and pleads inability' (ie to pay).

The standard practice was to fine those unwilling to perform the task, though occasionally members were excused without a fine (as all were in 1668-69, perhaps because of the enormous rebuilding costs after the Great Fire). Those entitled to attend the Annual Feast were the Stewards and those of the rank of Assistant and above, and their wives. However, it seems clear that some senior members would tend to abuse the priviledge by bringing along extra guests and occasional reminders were issued as to just who was entitled to a free meal.

So often did members avoid Stewardship that in 1682 those chosen were ordered to serve, but it was never possible to enforce this ruling, even though the fine for refusal rose to £6. 10s. 0d. per person by 1683, £10 by 1700 and in 1713 to £12. 12s. 0d., plus a quarter of the cost of the Feast, but not to exceed £15. 15s. 0d. In 1686 all those called upon to serve elected to pay a fine instead and with the £40 thus raised the Feast was organised by the Master and Wardens. The Feast could be cancelled in a bad year, as happened in 1690/91. In 1695 an order was issued that no Frenchmen be allowed to dine at the Feast unless specially invited, which suggests someone had been handing out unauthorised invitations. In 1695 all the Stewards rebelled, led by Daniel Beckman, and they refused to pay for the Feast, despite the Lord Mayor's order, but they eventually agreed to treat the Master, Wardens and Assistants only. As these were the only people supposed to be attending anyway, this is further evidence of the abuses which had crept in.

A typical response on being called to serve as Steward is that of Jonathan Jones who, in 1712, 'appeared, and being acquainted therewith, he was very rude, being in drinke, and would not give any direct answers whether he would hold' (the office). He later apologized. Apart from the Annual Stewards' Feast it seems that a special feast was held when new Assistants were appointed, when there was 'an handsome entertainment provided for dinner according to custom' (1716). This usually took place at irregular intervals several years apart. One last comment about the Feast is worth making, from the records for 1717 when 'Davies (a Quaker) performed the cookery thereof, but very indifferently'!

The next rank within the Clockmakers' Company officers was that of Assistant. The Assistants were chosen from among those who had already reached the rank of Steward. In 1720 a rule was passed that Assistants should henceforth be chosen from those Company Freemen who were Free of the City (ie had the right to trade on their own account) but the very passing of this rule suggests that this had not previously been the case when selection had been made from any Company Freeman of adequate seniority. When a member entered as an Assistant he had to pay an entrance fee of £6. 13s. 4d., which was no doubt a further reason why some members were very reluctant to become Assistants. (The reason for fees of peculiar amounts like this one stems from the ancient coin, the old Noble or Mark, which was worth 6s. 8d., and ancient fees were often in multiples of 6s. 8d.)

Assistants were chosen according to seniority, and not on merit, but in 1676 a ruling was passed to select Assistants by voting and not by seniority of Stewardship, but in practice those on the short list would have passed the rank of Steward anyway. As with most other company offices one could buy exemption on payment of a large enough fine, and some of the more rebellious members (the Fromanteels for example) paid fines rather than hold *any* office.

Assistants were usually appointed in groups of three or four at a time whenever deaths began to reduce the numbers of senior Assistants. Occasionally a man was excused on the grounds of poverty. Some were very reluctant attenders and despite threats of punishment for non-attendance there were a few determined objectors who refused to attend for years, usually men who were trapped between two companies. Edward East had the good fortune to be very wealthy and powerful, and he was not easily browbeaten into submission.

The next rank of Warden was filled by the most senior Assistant. Again some refused, Edward East, for instance, completely refused to serve as Warden until forced to do so in 1638 by the Lord Mayor, but even then he seldom attended. The Wardens controlled the Clockmakers' Company finances and supervised the account books, investment funds and so on. When one had served for three successive years as Warden, one year in each of the three levels of Wardenship, one then served as Master of the Company in the fourth year.

The Company appointed members to positions of responsibility according to their length of service, not on account of their popularity or through merit. Appointment to Warden and Master was made in the autumn of each year and hence a man serving, for example, from 1681-82 served only the one year.

There were one or two instances in the early years of the Company when, by abusing the system, certain Masters did manage to get themselves reappointed for a second term of office – Sampson Shelton did this and so did John Harris, Edward East, Simon Hacket, Robert Grinkin, John Nicasius, Jeremy Gregory, John Pennock, Nicholas Coxeter and perhaps others whom I have failed to note. This happened mostly during the Civil War when normal continuity may have been broken, but probably also occurred as a result of deliberate manipulation when a clique of associates felt there was some advantage to be obtained. The idea that a Master who held that office more than once must have been doubly meritorious is quite false – in fact it is perhaps an indication that he was less than scrupulous. In 1683 a rule was passed to forbid a former Master being re-elected and to reaffirm the seniority principle. In 1701 the policy was adopted whereby the name of one former Master was allowed to go into the electoral hat each year for possible re-election. This was almost certainly done as a sop to Charles Gretton who had just ended his year's term as Master by donating £50 to the Company, and the chance of re-election as Master was the Company's way of expressing gratitude. In fact no Master was appointed for a second term, at least until 1720, ignoring the 'manipulators' during the Civil War.

Another office in the Company was that of Clerk, whose responsibility was that of keeping the minutes and writing them up. Occasionally this office would be combined with that of the Beadle, whose duties are a little difficult to understand. The Beadle's main function appears to have been along the lines of liaison officer or administrator looking after Company business, and in the case of the Clockmakers' Company this was probably something of a sinecure. This office was almost always given by the Court of the Company to a very poor member as a means of supplementing his income. This was a kind gesture but it transpired that a penniless administrator was not always the most efficient for this task, and in any case poverty was often accompanied by illness, which involved the regular appointment of new Beadles to replace deceased ones. Samuel Davis was dismissed from this office in 1680 'being charged with negligence and unfittness for the place, and he not much desirous to keep it, unless he might have an augmentation of allowance . . .' Poor he might be, but he was unlikely to get any richer as Beadle, it seems. Daniel Stevens held the office until he died in 1697, then Richard George until his death 1712, then John Drew who died in 1713, Christopher Gould who died in 1718 and Charles Tolley who died in 1720. In the very early days they do not seem to have had a Beadle, but at that time two or three particular members fulfilled the Beadle's main duty, which was concerned with binding apprentices.

The Beadle appears to have bound apprentices 'through' himself when they were to serve some member of the Clockmakers' Company who was also a Freeman of some other Company (and therefore was usually only a Brother of the Clockmakers' Company – see next chapter for a full explanation of Brothers and Freemen). In the early days this task was apparently shared between Oswald Durant, Thomas Dawson and Richard Masterson, and they (and all the Beadles later) seem to have taken an unduly high number of apprentices, most of whom were to serve other masters. The position is slightly confused by the fact that a Beadle was himself a practising clockmaker and would also bind his own apprentices in the normal way; it is sometimes difficult to recognise which ones were bound 'through' him and which were bound *to* him.

Poverty was often the result of illness or old age and the Company took pains to try to give financial aid to unfortunate members – even on rare occasions to poverty-striken non-members if they were in the clock trade. Help, unfortunately, came too late for Widow East, who was granted a payment of ten shillings in January 1676/77, but when the Master called to deliver it he found that she had died 'but the daughter, being in great need, he gave 5s. of it to her and put the rest in the poor box.' In January 1648/49 John Surmoire was given charity, 'being a poore decayed member of this Company.' In January 1672/73 they gave ten shillings towards the burial of Paul Lowell senior, 'being a very indigent member of the Company.' James Seaburne was evidently a poor man, having just failed in 1674/75 to get the job as Beadle, coming runner-up. In 1689 the Company gave him ten shillings 'wherewith to but him tooles', but this was not a regular hand out. Robert Whitwell was given ten shillings charity in 1673/74 'for relief in his sickness', but he died not long after. In 1669 John Thorpe received six shillings charity from the poor box being 'a poor member of the Company who is blind', though he was later referred to as 'almost blind' and he later received regular hand outs until his death more than ten years later. Failing eyesight was one penalty often paid by men who worked at intricate tasks (such as engraving) in poor candle light. Edward Hunt had to have 'care for his eyes which are very weak.'

Sickness was not always synonymous with poverty. Henry Perry could not serve as Steward in 1718, but 'sent word by his maid that he was going to Bath for his health'. Isaac Daniell had long spells of illness from 1672 for the last ten years of his life having 'bin longe under great infirmity and inability of body' and 'grievously afflicted with the Gout'. John Seller also suffered with gout. The Company paid a kind of pension scheme to those too ill or too old to work, which was intended only for those (and their widows) who had been fee-paying members, though they did bend the rules sometimes out of compassion. John Glover's widow was left with 'five poor fatherless children' and the Company paid the apprenticeship fee for one of them. Longserving members also, like Thomas Hancorne, were cared for – he was 'sick and in want' in 1709 and was given a regular charity until his death, and after that it was paid to his widow. Numerous members got quarterly payments in times of hardship, and numerous widows were dealt with similarly.

Ironically, some of these poor members who lived out their final days in abject poverty have since become famous for producing exceptional work. Christopher Gould is one example, Claude du Chesne another and John Midnall who was arrested for debt. Indeed several members spent time in prison, mostly for debt, including John Saville, William Thorowgood and John Short's widow. William Davenport was supposedly accused of counterfeiting and William Newbon was sentenced to death for stealing watches, but he got a last minute reprieve. Davenport and Newbon are not particularly famous but it is surprising to find Christopher Gould's name amongst those receiving regular charities, and perhaps saddest and most surprising is to find William Clement among them. He was old and may well have been infirm in 1697 when he was excused attendance on account of his age, though he still put in occasional appearances. But in 1704 the great man, perhaps the one recognised by his own circle more than any other in his time, was in such reduced circumstances that he was given a regular pension, the telling phrase 'if he will accept it' being added to the entry, suggesting that his pride might cause him to decline the offer. It is extremely sad that men who had once been among the finest clockmakers should have died in such poverty, relying in some instances on hand outs from the Company to get by.

CHAPTER 3

Freemen, Brothers and Citizens

Generally speaking, a tradesman was not allowed to set up shop in a town unless he was accepted into the business community as a qualified person. This usually meant satisfying those concerned of his ability, and the easiest way of doing that was probably by producing his apprenticeship indenture to prove that he had served his time in the trade. Sometimes, however, petty jealousies amongst rival tradesmen could still mean his request to trade was rejected. The right to trade was called Freedom.

In a village or small country town there was probably no official body to whom one could present evidence of training. In a larger town or city, more so in London, you had to have the freedom of the town to trade. Some larger towns might have a guild of members of related crafts, and normally one had first to satisfy the appropriate guild in order to satisfy the town's governing authority. The Clockmakers' Company was a rather special case of a trade guild controlling practitioners of that trade in London and the immediate surrounds. In London, and perhaps also in the larger provincial cities, a tradesman had to obtain two freedoms – first, freedom of the appropriate Company in order to establish his competence in the craft and second, freedom of the City in order to establish his right to set up shop. So, to become a master clockmaker in London, ie one running his own shop, a man needed to be a Freeman of the Clockmakers' Company and also a Freeman of the City of London (Freemen of the City were often known by the title 'Citizen of London' – all those who lived there were inhabitants, but only those free of the City were Citizens). To become a Freeman of the City it was essential that a man first become a Freeman of a Company (some rare exceptions will be given later), but not all those who obtained the first wanted to obtain the

Lantern clock with balance-wheel control and alarmwork,
signed 'Solomon Wasson of Bristoll', dating from the
middle-seventeenth century. (*F. Küng, Luzern.*)

I

Winged lantern clock, signed 'John Holloway Devizes Fecit' and dated 1682 with what is probably the original owner's name, Daniel Dike, engraved alongside. *(F. Küng, Luzern.)*

II

Lantern clock with alarmwork signed 'William Sellwood at ye mermayde in Lothbury', dating perhaps from the 1640s. (*Dusty Miller Gallery, Harrogate.*)

III

Balance-wheel lantern clock, c. 1650, signed 'Thomas
Knifton in Lothbury Londini'. (*F. Küng, Luzern.*)

IV

Watch with calendar feature by John Smeaton
of York, c. 1660. (*British Museum, London.*)

Lantern clock, c. 1660, signed 'Thomas Loomes at ye
Mermayd in Lothebury fecit'. (*Dusty Miller Gallery,
Harrogate.*)

Ebony eight-day striking and pull repeating bracket clock,
c. 1720. Signed 'Cha Gretton London'. *(Eric Bruton.)*

Ebonised bracket clock signed 'P. D. Bradford, London',
a maker about whom nothing is known, but dating from
c. 1690. (*F. Küng, Luzern.*)

Ebony eight-day striking bracket clock, c. 1680, by
Richard Jarrett of London, *(Eric Bruton.)*

VIII

Ebony and tortoiseshell veneered eight-day striking clock
with date aperture, c. 1670. 'Robert Seignior Londini' is
signed along the bottom edge of the dial plate. (*Eric
Bruton.*)

Ebony eight-day three train quarter striking bracket
clock, c. 1670. Signed 'Edward Stanton Londini' along the
bottom of the dial plate. (*Eric Bruton.*)

Above: Detail of face of eight-day longcase clock, c. 1685, signed 'William Holloway at Stroud'.

Right: An unusually early example of a lacquered longcase clock, in blue, dating from c. 1685, by William Holloway of Stroud. (*Dusty Miller Gallery, Harrogate.*)

Left: Ebonised longcase clock with bolt and shutter maintaining power, c. 1670, by Ahasuerus Fromanteel (senior) of London. (*G. Marsh, Winchester.*)

Above: Detail of face of the Fromanteel clock (*left*), showing eight-inch dial.

Right: Ebonised provincial longcase clock, c. 1690, by John Greenbanck, place unknown. (*Dusty Miller Gallery, Harrogate.*)

Far right: Marquetry longcase clock, c. 1700, by John Williamson of Leeds. (*Brighton Museum and Art Gallery.*)

XII

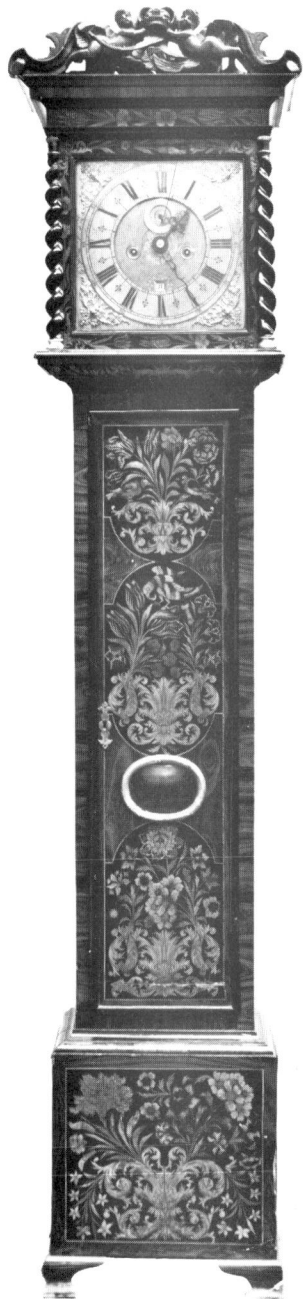

XIII

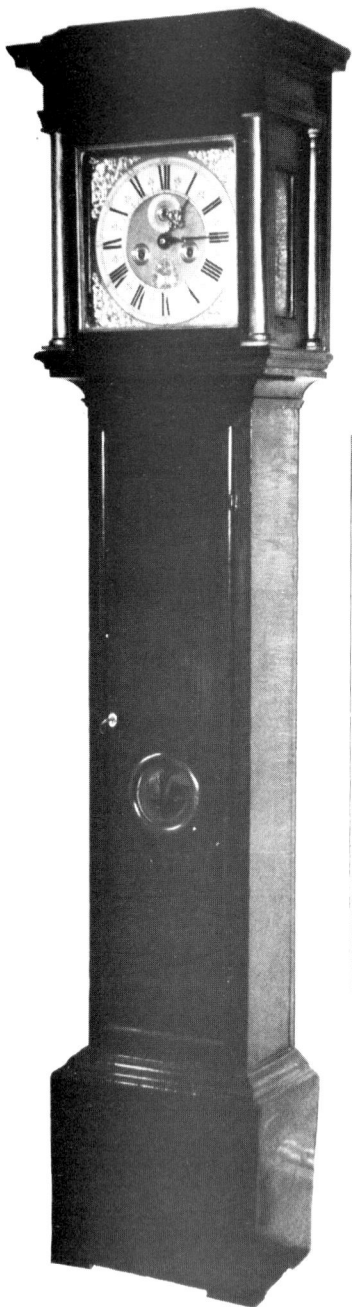

Left: Ebonised longcase clock, c. 1700, by James Jordan of Chatham. *(Dusty Miller Gallery, Harrogate.)*

Above: Detail of face of eight-day longcase clock, c. 1700, signed 'Jams Jordan Chatham fecit'.

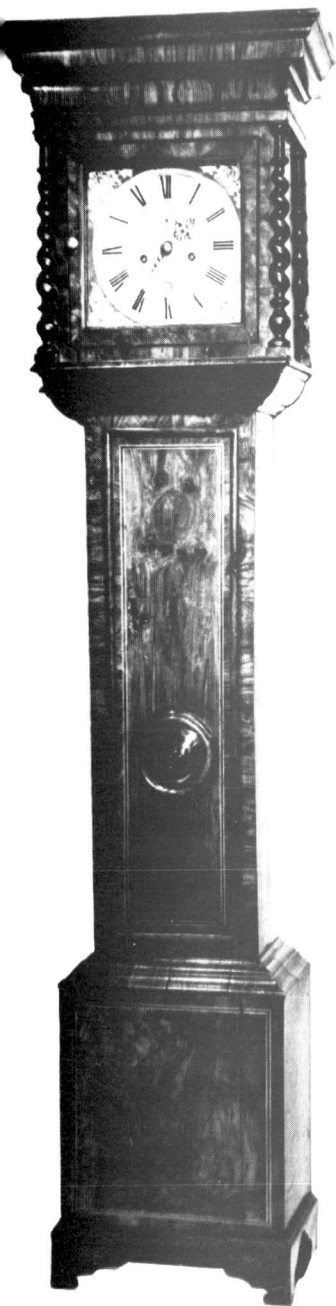

Left: Walnut case of a clock by Peter Stretch illustrating the contrast of the heavier provincial style with that of London. (*Dusty Miller Gallery, Harrogate.*)

Above: Detail of face of eight-day longcase clock, c. 1700, signed 'Peter Stretch Leek'.

Above: Detail of face of eight-day longcase clock signed 'Henry Elliott Londini fecit', c. 1690. (*Dusty Miller Gallery, Harrogate.*)

Right: Detail of face of eight-day longcase clock signed 'Tho. Bridge Londini fecit', c. 1690. (*Dusty Miller Gallery, Harrogate.*)

second. For instance a journeyman, ie a man working under a master clockmaker as an assistant, or 'servant' as they were sometimes called, did not need to be a Freeman of the City, since he did not wish to set up his own shop to trade.

Let us take the example of a clockmaker in London who, having served his apprenticeship of seven years, intended to carry on working as a journeyman, either under his present or another master, but who had no thoughts of setting up on his own. Such a man often felt he had nothing to gain by taking up his official freedom in the Company. Furthermore, once he did so he had to pay the entry fee and a regular quarterly subscription. Some felt they were better off keeping a low profile and hoped their need for official freedom in the Company would be forgotten about.

This is one reason why a number of entries in the directory section give apprenticeship details and then state 'not free', which means that freedom was not taken up as it should have been. We do not always know today whether they were 'not freed' because they moved out of the Company jurisdiction (to another town for instance) or whether they remained there quietly working as journeymen forgoing their options to become free. In January 1680/81 the Clockmakers' Company passed a resolution that 'those who are out of their time (ie have completed their apprenticeships) and practice the trade, whether for themselves or for a master, shall be prosecuted unless they take up their freedoms', and a list of half a dozen known offenders was drawn up. Normal procedure must have been flouted to quite an extent for the Company to decide to prosecute offenders.

One snag was that until a man had taken up his freedom in the Company he was not allowed to take an apprentice. It therefore follows that some of the ones who kept a low profile and avoided taking up their freedom for some time did suddenly apply for their freedoms when they wanted to take apprentices. The records often show late freedom and first apprentice binding taking place on the same day.

In January 1681/82 a resolution was passed to stipulate that those who applied for freedom in the Clockmakers' Company must show a master-piece before admission (a masterpiece was a piece of work that revealed a man's competence at his craft). Now though this had been the theory for a long time, it had rarely been enforced, and the passing of the resolution did little to alter this.

Some of the attempts at enforcing stricter control of Company freedoms seem to have been short-lived. In 1717 it was stipulated that no-one was to enroll an apprentice, 'turn one over' or make one free, until the master had also shown proof of his own freedom. I doubt whether that was ever enforced but it may have been thought convenient to have it on the rulebook in case it was ever needed. (The complicated business of 'turning over' will be explained later.)

A clockmaker who had been apprenticed through the Clockmakers' Company would usually take up his freedom as a Freeman of the Company, at which time his name would be put forward by the Company to the Chamberlain's Court, who would grant him Freedom of the City of London. He was then officially a Citizen of London and would style himself as 'Citizen and Clockmaker of London'. Likewise, a man apprenticed through the Haberdashers' Company and taking up his City Freedom would be styled 'Citizen and Haberdasher of London', but just as 'Haberdasher' denoted the trading Company, which was not necessarily the same trade as the one he practised, so a person described as a 'Citizen and Clockmaker of London' may not necessarily have followed the trade of clockmaking. Similarly, men styled as 'Citizen and (any other trading guild) of London' could well have followed a trade quite different from that of the named trading Company, and all of those recorded in the directory are believed to have been connected with the clock trade while being members of quite different trading companies.

Why would a man who had trained as a clockmaker become a member of the Haberdashers' Company (or any other company) and take the confusing title of 'Citizen and Haberdasher'? There were several reasons. One might be that a man's father had been a member of that Company (eg a Free Haberdasher), and so his son would automatically have the right, in time, to be a Freeman of that same Company, a practice known as Freedom by Patrimony. So the description 'Citizen and Haberdasher' may not have meant the same thing at all as 'citizen and haberdasher'.

If this all seems confusing to us today, it was also confusing and very frustrating to the tradesmen of the time, and the constant problem of rival Companies each competing for a man's membership, allegiance and quarterage, was the main concern of Company business. The London Companies were so numerous and so keen to operate their respective 'closed shop' practices that there was constant bickering between them, and the unfortunate individuals caught in between two companies often did not know which way to turn. For a variety of reasons craftsmen who practised the art of clock and watch making in London (including all its minor related branches) included members not only of the Clockmakers' Company, but of the Companies of Goldsmiths, Blacksmiths, Haberdashers, Tobacco Pipe Makers, Merchant Taylors, Plumbers, Barber Chirurgeons, Waxchandlers, Weavers, Loriners, Salters, Grocers, Shipwrights, Clothworkers, Vintners, Fishmongers, Stationers, Leathersellers, Joyners, Cutlers, Carpenters, Pewterers, and so on.

Probably the reason why so many men (whose allegiance clearly belonged to the Clockmakers' Company by virtue of their trade) also belonged to other Companies is that the Clockmakers' Company was formed later than most others, and so sons had already joined the same companies as their fathers or even grandfathers, although they had learned an entirely different trade. The number of men who had allegiance to two Companies was naturally greater in the early years of the Clockmakers' Company (founded 1631) when all trading clockmakers, of necessity, would have belonged to other Companies. By the end of the seventeenth century, however, dual allegiance had almost become a thing of the past.

In the Clockmakers' Company the Freeman, as we have seen, was someone who had served his time as an apprentice and who had been bound under the Company auspices to a Company member. But a member of the Company might not himself be a full Freeman, because membership consisted of two categories – the Freeman and the Brother, a less important position basically for anyone who was acceptable as a member but who was not apprenticed through the Company.

In 1631 when the Company began, there were no Freemen in the true sense of the word, since no-one could have served an apprenticeship under the Clockmakers' Company. The first true Freemen were those apprenticed in 1632 and freed from 1639 onwards. But to avoid the nonesense of all Clockmakers' Company members being second-class persons in the form of 'Brothers', the Company often cheated a little in these early years and termed members Freemen when they were really only Brothers. But these two terms were not simply different ways of saying the same thing.

A member would join as a Brother if he had not been trained under a Company member – so, for instance, a member who was trained in the provinces had to join as a Brother. So did a member who was already a full Freeman in some other City Company. When the Clockmakers' Company was founded, many of the clockmakers already practising the craft were members of the Blacksmiths' Company, but as from 1631, when all clock workers were required to join the new Company, all those who were Free Blacksmiths were supposed to join the Clockmakers' Company in this secondary capacity as a Brother. Naturally they did not like this idea at all because in their own Company they had full status as Freemen. Many refused to join or ignored the new Company as long as they could. The select few who formed the administration of the newly-formed Clockmakers' Company discreetly gave themselves the full title of Freemen.

Basically, a Brother was not allowed to sign his work with his own name and it follows therefore that he could not set up his own shop to trade in, but he had to work as a journeyman under another master. Those who already worked as journeymen (and in 1631 that was the majority of those in the trade) probably had nothing to lose by changing companies. But what about those who were full Freemen of another Company and perhaps also Freeman of the City of London with automatic right to be allowed to trade as masters? They were still Brothers in the new Company, but retained their right to trading status.

The system was so complicated and so full of inconsistencies that it is very difficult for us to come to too many conclusions about a man's background simply on the basis of his status in the Clockmakers' Company, whether he be a Freeman or a Brother. But, basically, to trade as a Master a man had to be either a Freeman of the Clockmakers' Company or a Freeman of the City of London (perhaps through some other city company) or both. Generally speaking, once the Clockmakers' Company was established a clockmaker could not become a Freeman of the City unless sponsored by his trading company, which by that time had to be the Clockmakers' (but there were even exceptions to this!).

Let us look at an example or two of how the system worked for a Brother. In January 1630/31 Ahasuerus Fromanteel joined the Black-smiths' Company as a Brother, having come down to London from Norwich. In 1632 he joined the newly-formed Clockmakers' Company, also as a Brother, and he was almost always at loggerheads with the administration about the unfair practices of the Company, as he saw them. In January 1655/56 he became a Freeman of the City of London, not in the usual way by sponsorship from the Clockmakers' Company, but by personal letter of recommendation from Oliver Cromwell, a 'recommendation' few would have been bold enough to reject. Thereupon he was admitted as a Free Clockmaker in the Clockmakers'

Company (another term for a full Freeman). The implication is that Fromanteel needed to become a full Freeman and that it was very important to him, and the only reason that seems likely is that he needed Freedom before he could open his own shop. By obtaining City Freedom he forced the Clockmakers' Company into granting him full status there too. After all he had been a Brother for twenty-three years and the implication is that throughout this time he had worked either as a journeyman under some other master or, perhaps, as an outworker making movements for others in the trade. It would seem that he was not supposed to sign his own work or sell it in a shop until he had City Freedom and, once he had obtained that City Freedom, the Clockmakers' Company were powerless to stop him and could hardly refuse to pass his full Company Freedom. Fromanteel may well have been a special case because of his bad relationship with the Company, so we will look at one or two other examples.

Thomas Tompion, whose apprenticeship is unknown, was born in Bedfordshire and worked either there or in Buckinghamshire before moving to London in 1671, when he joined the Clockmakers' Company as a Brother (he could not join as a full Freeman as he was not Company trained). However, in April 1674 he became a full Freeman 'by redemption', which means on payment of a fee (achieving full Company Freedom by payment in this manner became more common from the later years of the century). Again the implication is that he needed to be a full Freeman to be able to sell his goods, a fact which may help us to date his work.

The case of Peter Garon was unusual because, although he had served Richard Baker and had been apprenticed through the Clockmakers' Company he was, on completion of his time, refused entry as a Freeman 'being an alien'. This seems to have been extremely unfair since many aliens had been already admitted and when he applied for Freedom of the City he was granted it, and within a month the Company was obliged to make him a full Freeman of the Company.

Samuel Knibb came to work in London in 1662 and bought his entry into the Clockmakers' Company in 1663 as a full Freeman, by redemption as it is called, but this was an unusual practice. In 1682 Jeremy Gazuet, a watch-chain maker from Geneva, was made a Free Brother in the Clockmakers' Company. In 1685 he had goods confiscated because he had sold watches bearing his name 'being a Brother but not a Freeman nor Free of the City.'

In the seventeenth century the entry fee for taking up Freedom in the Clockmakers' Company was twenty shillings, as it was for a Brotherhood, but an alien had to pay thirty shillings. After 1712 any free denizen or naturalised person was charged double the usual entry fee. Francis Dinnis was admitted as a free Brother in 1667 and, presumably after he had been refused full Freedom, went to complain to the Lord Mayor in 1672/73 and was allowed full Freedom by redemption by order of the Lord Mayor. It certainly seems that it was difficult for an 'unwelcome' Brother to obtain his full Company Freedom, whilst for some it could be really quite easy. To some extent it was a matter of whether a person fitted in, and for much of its history the Clockmakers' Company was run according to the political bias of its administrators. Political connections, family relationships and religious prejudices played a very important part. The more I begin to understand these relationships the more it is obvious that more lies beneath the surface than above it. The tremendous hostilities and bitter conflicts that occasionally burst through to the surface, through what we must remember is a series of records that were edited very much in favour of the controlling group, did not spring up simply on account of an ill-chosen word that slipped out one night at the Castle Tavern in Fleet Street. These were deep and bitter conflicts.

As I mentioned earlier a Brother was of lower status in the Clockmakers' Company than a Freeman, and one of the ways in which this inferiority showed itself was in the inability of a Brother to bind an apprentice directly to himself. Instead he had to take an apprentice 'through' a full Freeman and then have the boy transferred to himself, a process known as 'turning over' an apprentice. A quick glance at the directory section shows how this is denoted. Sometimes the apprentice was said to be 'bound' to Freeman A, 'to serve' Brother B. The lad actually worked from the outset with the person whom he 'served' or, to put it another way, the person to whom he was 'turned over'. He did not physically move from one master to another but directly served the Brother concerned. For brevity the directory shows apprentices as bound 'through' (abbreviated to 'thro'') whichever Freeman it was. The reason I have bothered to list those 'through' whom boys were bound is because in some cases there was a working relationship between the Brother whom a boy served and the Freeman through whom he was bound, and such 'turning over' can help to bring such relationships to light. For instance, a master who employed several Brothers as journeymen or outworkers might well act as the nominee through whom their apprentices would be officially bound.

That is the principle of 'turning over' but in these old records nothing is that simple, for the term 'turning over' has several other meanings. When a boy's master died and the lad was passed on to another master the same term could still be used, as it could when a boy changed masters, for whatever reason and no matter how many times. It is therefore very difficult and sometimes impossible to know from the Company records whether a boy actually served part of his time with master A before serving master B or whether master A was simply a nominee Freeman used when binding a boy to a Brother. Where I have been able to distinguish which I have made this clear in the directory. If it is not clear, it is because I have not been able to clarify the relationship.

Once the job of Company Beadle had been established the Beadle often took on the tedious duty of acting as nominee in the binding process. But even though the name of the Beadle appeared in such a binding it did not establish a working relationship with a Brother.

We know that a Clockmakers' Company Brother might well be a full Freeman of some other City Company. And we know what a Clockmakers' Company apprentice might never have taken up his Freedom. There were occasions when these two factors came together, so that a clock-maker who was perhaps a Freeman in the Weavers' Company and also a Brother in the Clockmakers' Company might well have decided to make his apprentice a Freeman not of the Clockmakers but of the Weavers. The Clockmakers' Company were very keen to prevent this happening, but it did happen, and of course not just with the Weavers' Company but with many other companies. This circumstance may well explain why a lot of apprentices in the directory appear never to have become free, for their Freedoms may lie undiscovered in the archives of some other City Company.

Freedom was usually obtained through apprenticeship and was known as Freedom by servitude. A clockmaker who entered as a Brother obviously could not qualify as a full Freeman by servitude, but had to buy his Freedom, known as Freedom by redemption – we have already seen that Tompion did this. The third method of obtaining full Company Freedom was by patrimony, that is by right of the boy's father being a full Freeman, but this method did not come into effect until later on in the history of the Clockmakers' Company, simply because the Company was formed later than many others.

In 1678 John Saville senior explained to the Clockmakers' Company that he could, if he so wished, have his son made a Freeman by patrimony in the Vintners' Company, of which he himself was a Freeman, and in the face of this threat the Clockmakers' Company allowed him to bend their rules a little – in other words, better let a member bend the rules than lose him altogether. One of the earliest Freedoms by patrimony in the Clockmakers' Company was that of Edward Eays junior in 1684/85.

I mentioned earlier how a man did not always follow the trade of the trading Company to which he belonged, and patrimony Freedom is one cause of this. A father who was a Clockmakers' Company Freeman had the right to make each of his children free in that Company, even if they followed trades as varied as butcher, baker or candlestickmaker, and some did use that right, not only for their sons but also for their daughters. This accounts for those girls who were made free in the Clockmakers' Company. The girls were not working in the clock trade, but had simply taken up their right to Freedom by patrimony.

As time went by, of course, ever-increasing numbers of children had the right of patrimony, and by the eighteenth century this meant that numerous Clockmakers' Company Freemen followed trades widely different from their parents, including such diverse trades as druggist, attorney, stable-keeper, snuffboxmaker, hatter, cheesemonger, cider merchant banker, writing-master, undertaker, and many more. In the seventeenth century such instances were less common.

There were, however, even more ways a non-clockmaker might be allowed into the Clockmakers' Company apart from the patrimony rule, namely by virtue of special dispensations for special reasons, usually involving a written permit from the Lord Mayor. One reason was that in order to encourage people to move back into the rebuilt part of the City, following the Great Fire of London, such newcomers were offered Freeman status as an incentive. So, Thomas Coxeter, who was a bricklayer by trade and who had helped in the rebuilding, was allowed Freedom of the Clockmakers' Company by redemption in February 1673/74 because he had taken a house in the rebuilt zone. Henry Jevon, a lawyer, was admitted for the same reason, as was Thomas Gregory, a tallow chandler. But why such men could not have been admitted to Companies more relevant to their trades, I do not know.

Such men who followed these 'stray' trades might also bind apprentices in their Company and they would be trained not in clockwork but in their masters' trades. So when, for example, the attorney Henry Jevon took girls as apprentices they were not being apprenticed into clock-working but were presumably trainee clerical workers. Another instance of a special dispensation being given to enable someone to enter the Clockmakers' Company can be found in the case of John Briggs, who was allowed in as a Brother under the special rules to help former soldiers return to civilian life, though in his case his trade as a watchglass-cutter *was* akin to clockmaking.

The intention of these preliminary notes is to prevent the reader from misinterpreting the information in the directory. Apart from the fact that I would like to think this book is geared to the pursuit of knowledge rather than ignorance, there is nothing more annoying to me than to hear my own painstakingly-researched data misused or mis-quoted. But there still remain some aspects of the subject which I have been unable to unravel. Occasionally, the record of a member's (usually a Brother's) entry into the Clockmakers' Company gives his trade in more detail than just 'clock' or 'watchmaker'. Some were described as 'Great' clockmakers. In the past writers have often taken this to mean 'important, famous and highly-skilled', but this interpretation is quite incorrect. It is illogical because when someone like Tompion, who was said to be 'Great', joined the Company in 1671 he was a nobody, and did not become great in the sense of being famous until much later.

So what does the term 'Great Clockmaker' mean in an admission entry? I am afraid I do not know. Most members were entered simply as a clock or watchmaker. But quite a number were 'Great clockmakers' and some, albeit a few, were 'small clockmakers', but what did that distinction mean? I have tried to test several interpretations but without any success.

A 'small clockmaker', for example, could not have meant a maker of watches. I have applied the term 'small clockmaker' to bracket clocks, lantern clocks, and longcase clocks but without any success. I have applied 'Great Clockmaker' to turret clocks and longcase clocks (ie tall clocks) also with only partial success. In short, I was unable to draw any firm conclusions as to what these terms did signify, though we still know for certain that 'Great' did not mean famous.

The only clue I did find was in a 1680 reference to certain clockmakers who had remained within the Blacksmiths' Company and who were described as 'great church clockmakers of iron'. This suggests that a 'Great' clockmaker might have been a turret clockmaker, but it must be pointed out that a good number of those so described have no surviving turret clock work to their credit (at least no recorded example).

It would have been particularly satisfying to have been able to establish just what was meant by 'Great' in the admission entries because these men were obviously entered as specialists and some of them did become famous later on (though not necessarily in turret clockmaking). The clockmakers described as 'Great' included Tompion, Clement, the Clowes, Gould, Williamson and Windmills, and, if we are able to say for certain that these men were recognised as specialists in turret clockmaking when they entered the Company, then this could have a considerable bearing on our assessment of their work and status. This applies especially to Clement because of the possibility that he was the inventor of the anchor escapement.

THE DIRECTORY
OF MAKERS

LIST OF ABBREVIATIONS
AND EXPLANATIONS

acc.	according
apr.	apprentice(d)
aprs.	apprentices
Apr	April (all other months are similarly abbreviated)
b.	born
b.c.	born circa
bap.	baptised
c.	circa
CC	the Clockmakers' Company
Co.	company
co.	county
cf	compare
gent.	gentleman
incl.	including
inst.	instrument
mat.	mathematical
nr.	near
poss.	possibly
prob.	probably
qv	see under
sic	as printed
succ.	succeeded
thro'	through
till	until

NOTE. A 'boxmaker' was a watch-case maker

I have kept to the original language and spellings of the Clockmakers' Company records wherever possible. Parish names have not been altered (eg 'St. Andrew Holborn' has not been altered to St. Andrew's, Holborn), nor have references to counties no longer in existence. Various other antique phrases have been kept (eg 'over against') and, in order to condense as much information as possible into one volume, I have on occasions forsaken the use of single quotation marks inside double "quotes" simply by running the original phrases together.   B.L.

A

ABARGEYN, Hans **London**
Servant (ie journeyman) of Lewis Billiard in St. Clement Danes parish in 1549. Prob. a foreigner.

ABBOTT, Richard **London**
B.c. 1654. Apr. Jun 1668 to Hilkiah Bedford, mat. inst. maker till 1675 but not freed.

ABERLEY, Joseph **London**
B.c. 1650. Apr. Jan 1664/65 to Sutton Isaac till 1671 but not freed.

ACASTLE, Robert **Taunton (Somerset)**
Watchmaker, died 1667. At least one watch known.

ACASTLE, Thomas **Taunton**
Recorded as watchmaker c. 1670 (Baillie). Nothing else known.

ACEY, Jonathan **York**
Son of Peter. B. 1635, freed 1656. Uncertain whether he was a clockmaker.

ACEY, Peter **York**
Clockmaker. Married 1633 Joan Leckenby. Died 1639. Son, Jonathan, b. 1635, *qv*.

ACHURCH, William **London**
B.c. 1677. Apr. Aug 1691 to William Jacques till 1698. Free Sep 1699.

Took as aprs.: Oct 1716 his son, **William Achurch**; Aug 1719 **Edward Cox**; Nov 1719 **Richard Bignell** (taken from Tudor Smith). Worked till at least 1719.

ACTON, Abraham   **London**
Recorded by some authorities as apr. in 1691, but this actually took place in 1694 and he is excluded from this present volume.

ACTON, Edward   **London**
B.c. 1672. Apr. Jan 1686/87 to Edmund Appley, *qv*, but not freed.

ACTON, John   **London**
Recorded by some authorities as CC 1677, but I cannot trace him and this is prob. an error for Thomas, *qv*.

ACTON, Thomas   **London**
'Worketh in clock work'. Free Brother of CC Jan 1677/78.

ADAM, Elias   **England**
Recorded by some authorities as dial maker in 1627. Possible error for Elias Allen, *qv*.

ADAMS, Edward   **Youghal (Co. Cork)**
Clockmaker 1628-29.

ADAMS, John   **Crediton (Devon)**
Believed died 1639.

ADAMS, Thomas   **Oxford**
Smith, locksmith and TC maker. Apr. to John Bates, blacksmith. Freed Oct 1613. Worked 1630-63 on various town clocks. In 1640 assisted John Raye to install new clock in St. Mary's and he maintained this 1650-52. Also made hour glasses. Died late 1664.

ADAMS, Thomas   **Plymouth**
Short pendulum lantern clock known, c. 1685.

ADAMSON, ----   **London**
Late 17th century bracket clocks signed thus are prob. by John Adamson, *qv*.

ADAMSON, Anna   **London**
Watch, 1696. Prob. widow of John Adamson, *qv*.

ADAMSON, Humfrey   **London**
Made a clock for Whitehall Chapel in 1668 for £19.7.0. This man was not a member of CC, nor was he known to them – a very puzzling factor if he was a regular clockmaker. Several clocks signed by surname only and somtimes ascribed to him, may have been the work of John, *qv*.

ADAMSON, John   **London**
Clockmaker, admitted as a Brother in CC Sept 1686. A record from later in 1686 of a lost watch, 'a gold minute watch lately made by Mr. Adamson over against the Blue Boar in Holborn', suggests that this was John's place of work, not Humfrey's. There is no evidence to suggest the two were related. He had little contact with CC and seems to have had a short working life. He was dead before 1698, prob. by 1693. Anna Adamson, recorded in 1696, is prob. his widow. Longcase clocks and bracket clocks are known signed: 'John Adamson, London'. Some signed by surname only may be his or Humfrey's, *qv*.

ADAMSON, Thomas   **Burnley (Lancashire)**
Watchmaker. Died 1699.

ADDISON, Edmund   **London**
B.c. 1665. Apr. Jul 1678 to Joseph Ashby till 1686, but was not freed.

ADEANE, George   **London**
see Dean, George.

ADEANE, Henry   **London**
B.c. 1654. Apr. Aug 1667 to Richard Scrivener till 1675. Freed Sep 1675. Aprs.: Nov 1675 **Josiah Simcox**; Apr 1677 **Matthew Marshall**; Jun 1680 **Nicholas Warne**; Jul 1691 **Joseph Howes** – free Sep 1698; Mar 1694/95 **William Cripple** (son of William Cripple) – freed Apr 1702; Sep 1699 **Henry Complin** (son of Philo Complin of London); May 1704 **John Newman** (son of William Newman of parish of St. Olave, Southwark, butcher); his son, **Henry Adeane**, freed Aug 1706 by patrimony. References after 1704 could be to the son. Work known – at least one watch. May have worked mainly as an engraver, which his master was.

AILLEWARD, John (see also Aylward)   **Great Yarmouth**
Free as locksmith 1455. TC maker.

ALCOCK, Elias   **London**
Recorded by some authorities 1650-75, but this seems to me to be a clerical error and I doubt his existence.

ALCOCK, Edward   **Leicester**
Freed Sep 1692, apr. of John Wilkins, clock and watchmaker.

ALCOCK, John   **London**
Recorded by some authorities 1650-70, but this seems to me to be a clerical error and I doubt his existence.

ALCOCK, Thomas   **London**
Watchmaker, working by 1630. Entered CC Oct 1632 (as a Brother ?), became Assistant in 1638, Warden 1645-46, after which he would normally have become Master but he ceased to attend meetings. Took as his own apr. Feb 1637/38 **Copley Wirral** (bound thro' Oswald Durant) – freed Feb 1647/48. However, he acted as an intermediary in binding altogether 26 other aprs. for other masters – as the Beadle often did, though Alcock did not officially hold this office. These were, two aprs. each to J. Selwood, E. Allen, P. Closon, R. Smith, H. Child; one each to T. Land, J. Nicasius, S. Bartram, D. Fletcher, R. Ash, W. Bowyer, W. Selwood, E. East, I. Law, W. North, S. Betts, R. Morgan, W. Rogers, S. Shelton, R. Scrivener, T. Reeve. A study of his association with these numerous other Masters fails to reveal any working relationship, and he was probably an independent Master watchmaker. He was still living in 1649, after which nothing more is known of him. Work known – watches, one signed 'Thomas Alcock fecit'.

ALCORNE, Richard   **Edinburgh**
B.c. 1680, son of Henry Alcorne (who died 1733) and his wife, Margaret (Henderson), assay master of the Edinburgh Mint. Apr. Nov 1694 to Andrew Brown. Freed Sep 1703. For his test piece he made a pendulum alarm clock, short swing (ie long pendulum?) and a lock and key for its door. He made it in the shop of Richard Mills, *qv*. In Nov 1704 he took **William Sutor** as apr. – freed 1712. He died in 1735, when son, James, served heir general.

ALDRED, John **London**
B.c. 1672/73 (poss. son of Leonard Aldred?). Apr. Mar 1686/87 to
Henry Reeve (thro' Edward Bridgman) till 1693/94 but not freed.

ALDRED, Leonard **London**
Free Brother in CC Apr 1671 as a Great Clockmaker. Still working in
May 1685 when threatened with prosecution for arrears of quarterage.

ALDRIDGE, Daniel **London**
B.c. 1666. Apr. Dec 1680 to Henry Young till 1687, but not freed. He is
believed to have died before 1711, when widow Aldridge (presumably *his*
widow) received charitable payment from CC.

ALDWORTH, Samuel **Oxford and London**
B.c. 1659, son of John Aldworth of Childrey, Bucks. Apr. to John Knibb
at Oxford 1673 to 1680, but worked with him till 1689, when he set up on
his own. Moved to London in 1697, when Joseph Knibb sold his London
business, and was admitted into the CC as a Free Brother (watchmaker)
in Dec 1697. In 1703 he married Elizabeth Knibb aged 23 of Collingtree
nr. Northampton (thought to be the daughter of John). By 1720 he had
returned to Childrey. Work known – lantern, bracket and longcase
clocks and a watch. Some signed 'Samuel Aldworth' (without place),
some 'Samuel Aldworth, Oxon.', some 'Samuel Aldworth in the Strand'.
At least one longcase is signed as at Childrey.

ALEXANDER, John **Edinburgh**
Son of Alexander Alexander of Cannongate. Apr. Dec 1667 to Robert
Smith, clockmaker. Freed Aug 1671 having made as test piece one clock
and one sundial.

ALISON, James **Cupar (Fife)**
Clockmaker from Cupar. Made Magdalen Chapel (Edinburgh) TC in
1641/42. Repaired Dundee church clock 1648.

ALKINS, ---- **London**
Watch recorded as 1666 (Baillie). I cannot trace this maker.

ALLAM, Andrew (sometimes also Allum and Allen) **London**
B.c. 1642, apr. Jan 1655/56 to Nicholas Coxeter till 1663. Free Jun 1664.
Took **Thomas Davis** as apr. in Oct 1667 and in Jul 1669 **John Carter**.
However, Allam died before 1674 and Davis was transferred to

Coxeter to finish his term, which he did in Oct 1674. He worked in Grub Street. Known work – lantern and longcase clocks.

ALLATT, George London
(sometimes Allet(t) and even Alliatt, but he signed himself Allatt) B.c. 1669. Apr. Dec 1683 to Thomas Tompion (thro' Solomon Bouquet) till 1690. Freed Jul 1691. Took as aprs.: Apr 1696 **Edward Watson** – freed Sep 1704; Apr 1700 **William Davison** (son of Nicholas Davison, late of Woburne (?), Bucks, gardener, deceased); Apr 1706 **Humfrey Forster** (son of John Forster of Oxford, musician); Sep 1706 **John Parry** (thro' Richard George). Not heard of after 1706. Work known – bracket and longcase clocks signed 'George Allatt (*sic*) – London'.

ALLAWAY, John London
B.c. 1667. Apr. May 1681 to Bernard Rainsford till 1688. Not freed till May 1695. (His master prob. died soon after 1681.) Took as aprs.: May 1695 **Robert Sanderson** – free Oct 1704; Jul 1695 **Joseph Bleeke** (thro' John Smith); Sep 1699 **Joseph Million** or **Millison** (son of Joseph Million of St. Mary Magdalen, Bermondsey, barber, deceased). Still alive 1704.

ALLEN, Andrew (see Allam)

ALLEN, Elias London
Mat. Inst. Maker and 'mathematician'. Never officially admitted into CC, but became Assistant 1633, Warden 1635-36, Master 1637, and attended till 1652. Prob. died shortly after – reputedly in 1654. Took as aprs.: Mar 1639/40 **Ralph Greatorex** (thro' T. Dawson) – freed Nov 1653; Mar 1640 **Edward Grimes** (thro' R. Masterson), about whom a dispute arose in Jun 1651; Apr 1646 **Withers Cheney** (thro' T. Alcock) – freed Apr 1657; May 1646 **John Prigeon** (thro' T. Alcock). Known work – sundials, one of which, said to have been formerly in Ashurst churchyard, was inscribed: 'Elias Allen made this diall and gave it to the parish of Ashurst, Ano. Domini 1644'.

ALLEN, James London
Never officially admitted to CC. In Jun 1637 took as apr. **John Major** (thro' T. Dawson). Died before 1663. Known work – watch recorded, made in 1644.

ALLEN, John   London
Free Brother in CC Mar 1653. Nothing else known.

ALLEN, John   London
B.c. 1657. Apr. Jan 1671/72 to Richard Ames till 1678, but by Jul 1673 he had left Ames and nothing else is known of him.

ALLEN, Nathaniel   London
Prob. worked throughout as journeyman to William Bowyer, to whom he had been apr., dates not recorded. In Apr 1658 he applied to enter the CC 'next Michaelmas', though there is no actual record of his entry. He took over apr. **Edward Stanton** from Francis Bowen (another Bowyer journeyman) – Stanton was freed Jan 1662/63. Allen prob. died shortly after 1663. Work known – none in his name.

ALLEN, Thomas   London
B.c. 1650. Apr. Jan 1663/64 to Robert Whitwell till 1671 but never completed the term.

ALLETT, George (see Allatt)

ALLMAN, Andrew   London
Listed by some authorities as CC 1664 but this is a clerical error for Andrew Allam, *qv*.

ALLSOP, John   London
Longcase clock recorded, East Smithfield. c. 1715. Prob. error for Joshua, *qv*.

ALLSOP, Joshua   London
Sep 1689 admitted to CC as a Free Brother, 'Great Clockmaker who served his time in Northamptonshire'. In Dec 1693 he took apr. **George Barnes** (thro' H. Kilminster). Known to have been alive till 1705, perhaps later. Longcase clocks are known signed 'Joshua Allsop, East Smithfield', and 'Josh. Alsope, East Smithfield'. His handwritten signature was 'Allsop'. At least one watch is known.

ALLUM, Andrew (see Allam)

ALMAN (T) (see Almond)

ALMOND, John   **London**
Prob. already working by 1663, when he appears on CC lists, though not as a member. Sep 1671 freed in CC by patrimony, being the eldest son of Ralph Almond, *qv*. In 1680 he received £50 under his father's will.

ALMOND, Ralph   **London**
B.c. 1623, younger brother of William Almond, *qv*. Apr. Aug 1637 to Oswald Durant till 1644. Free Dec 1645. Took as aprs.: Dec 1651 **John Watts**; Sep 1659 **James Fothergaile**; May 1661 **James Farmer**. Additionally he took four aprs. on behalf of his brother, William, whom they served, and another for William's journeyman, Richard Lyons. This suggests he may well have worked for his brother William until the latter's death about 1669. Became Assistant in CC from 1668, Warden 1674-77, and Master 1678 (despite being warned for abusing the Master in 1677). He died in 1680, described as a clockmaker, of St. Catherine Creechurch parish, and left bequests to his son, John, *qv*, son, Joseph, daughter, Ellenor and wife, Ellenor. He also mentions monies due to him from the Exchequer (?).

ALMOND, William   **London**
B. pre-1613. In Apr 1633 he became a free Brother in CC, which he seems to have regarded with hostility, being repeatedly warned for arrears of quarterage. In 1653/54 they seized a house clock of his as faulty, which may have encouraged him in becoming a 1656 rebel against the administration. In 1662 his place of work was Lothbury. Aprs.: Nov 1637 **Edward Taylor** (thro' Oswald Durant); about 1646 **Charles Bell**; Nov 1649 **Charles Rogers** – freed Dec 1657; Nov 1649 **Richard Lyons** – free Dec 1656; Nov 1653 **William Raynes** – free Jan 1660/61. All these latter were taken thro' brother, Ralph, *qv*. In Aug 1656 took **Ralph Ludford** (thro' Samuel Davis); Nov 1658 **Thomas Parker** (thro' David Moody) – freed Apr 1669. He is last known to have been alive in Apr 1669, when brother Ralph paid off his serious arrears of quarterage, and he prob. died not long after that. At least one lantern clock is known to survive, a balance-wheel example signed 'William Almond in Lothbury fecit'.

ALSOP (see Allsop)

ALWOOD or **ALWORDE, William**   Tiverton (Devon)
Worked on church clock 1607-12.

AMBROSE, David   **London**
Free Brother in CC Jul 1669. Paid quarterage till at least 1671.

AMBROSE, Edward   **London**
In Oct 1634 the CC ordered him to finish the watch he had been working
on in the service of Josias Cuper before transferring to work under Elias
Volant. Made a Free Brother in CC May 1637. The 1634 and 1637 entries
refer to one man, not two as Baillie suggests.

AMES, Katherine   **London**
Widow of Richard, *qv*. In Dec 1684 she took **Robert Browne** apr. till
1692, but was not freed.

AMES, Richard   **London**
B.c. 1634. Apr. Feb 1648/49 to Peter Closon (thro' R. Masterson) till
1655. Freed Jan 1656/57. Aprs.: Feb 1657/58 **John Ebsworth** – free Apr
1665; Dec 1662 **Christopher Ebsworth** – free Jan 1669-70; Apr 1667
Thomas Grice – free May 1675; Oct 1667 **Richard Richardson** – free
Sep 1675; Apr 1670 **Simon Jarvis**; Jan 1671/72 **John Allen**; Jul 1673
William Newton; Sep 1675 his son, **William Ames** – free Jan 1682/83;
Feb 1677/78 **Nicholas Hitchman**; Jul 1679 **Joseph Kenton** – free Sep
1686. Also took an apr. in Sep 1670 for James Atkinson. Made Assistant
1669, Warden 1676-81, elected Master in Sep 1682 but died soon after –
Thursday 12 Oct. Widow Katherine continued the business. Work
known – at least one lantern clock survives signed 'Richard Ames nr. St.
Andrews Church in Holburn Fecit'.

AMES, William   **London**
B.c. 1659, son of Richard Ames, *qv*. Apr. Sep 1675 to his father till 1682,
freed Jan 1682/83. In Jun 1686 took **William Wilson** as apr. – freed Dec
1693. In Nov 1687 he described himself in his marriage licence as a clockmaker, bachelor, aged 28 of the parish of St. Andrew Holborn, to marry
Mrs. Anne Shaw of St. Bottolph's Aldgate parish, spinster, aged 22 – at
St. Bottolph's Aldgate or St. Bottolph's Bishopgate. Still living in 1693
when he last paid CC quarterage and prob. died soon after, certainly
before 1697/98. Prob. worked mostly for his father and no work is known
in his own name.

AMYOT, Peter   **Norwich**
Lantern clocks and watches are recorded from c. 1660 to c. 1720. This is
a Huguenot surname, but nothing is known of his origin.

ANDERSON, Charles   **Aberdeen**
1699. Nothing else known.

ANDERSON, David junior   **Aberdeen**
Made town sundial in 1597.

ANDERSON, Robert   **London**
B.c. 1677. Apr. May 1691 to Thomas Tompion (thro' Michael Knight)
till 1698 but not freed.

ANDERSON, William   **London**
B.c. 1632. Apr. Feb 1646/47 to Simon Bartram (thro' Lionel Wythe) till
1653; Some authorities record a maker of this name as free in CC 1649,
but this is a clerical error.

ANDREWS, Ezekiel   **London**
B.c. 1661. Apr. Sep 1674 to Edward Fowell, a clockmaker of Whitechapel but a Freeman of the Merchant Taylors' Co. (thro' Roger
Nicholls) till 1682. He was never freed, however, as he died on a voyage
to the East Indies. His will, dated 12 Nov 1684 – 'I, Ezekiel Andrews of
London, clockmaker, now outward bound upon a voyage to East India in
and with the good ship or vessel called *Loyal Adventure*, Captain William
Goodlad commander, do make my will . . . .', appointing Will Longland
(maybe father of his fellow-apprentice, John Longland, *qv*) his attorney
in London. Proved Jun 1690. He died at Fort George in the East
Indies. Doubtful whether he ever made any clocks in his own name –
none are known.

ANDREWS, Isaac   **London**
Recorded by some authorities as apr. 1674 but this is an error for Ezekiel.

ANDREWS, James   **London**
B.c. 1672, apr. Jan 1686/87 to Joshua Hutchin (thro' Lawrence Sindry)
till 1693 but never freed.

ANDREWS, John   **London**
B.c. 1666, apr. Apr 1680 to Nathaniel Pyne, later transferred to Samuel
Stanton (which is strange as the latter was not a known clockmaker) till
1687. Freed Sep 1688. Took as aprs.: Sep 1692 **Samuel Guy**; May 1695
Samuel Harris – free Apr 1708; Mar 1697/98 **Joseph Smallwood** (later
transferred to Thomas Player); Jul 1701 **Christopher Parker** (son of the

late John Parker, Citizen and Clockmaker, deceased); Sep 1705 **Benjamin Claridge** (son of Thomas Claridge of Hanwell, Co. Oxon, farmer); May 1708, his son **William Andrews** – free Jul 1719; Jul 1712 **William Baseley;** Mar 1715/16 **Joseph Fenn.** Nothing is known about him after 1715. Worked in Leadenhall Street. Longcase clocks and at least one lantern clock and one watch are known, some signed 'John Andrews, Londini fecit', 'John Andrews, Leadenhall Street, London' and 'John Andrews, London'.

ANDREWS, Robert   **London**
B.c. 1649. Apr. Nov 1661 to John Nicasius till 1670, but never made free. No work known. Some authorities state free in CC 1709, but this refers to a later man of the same name.

ANDREWS, Thomas   **London**
B.c. 1674, apr. Nov 1688 to William Slough (thro' John Jackson) till 1695. Freed Sep 1705. In Sep 1705 he took as apr. **Henry Ladbrooke** (son of John Ladbrooke of Lilbourne, Co. Northampton, Gent.). Longcase clocks are known by this maker. Bailie gives Leadenhall Street as his address but I cannot confirm this. Some authorities list a second Thomas Andrews as apr. in 1686 to Joshua Hutchin but this is an error originating in the CC records for James, *qv.*

ANDREWS, Thomas   **Woodbridge (Suffolk)**
Repaired church clock of St. Clement's, Ipswich, in 1594 and 1597.

ANGEL, Richard   **Wigtoft (Lincolnshire)**
Paid in 1484 for keeping church clock.

ANIS, ----   **London**
Mentioned by Robert Hooke in his diary in 1674. First – 'At Anis and Tompion's'. Second 'With Anis to Mr. Godfrey. Paid Anis £25 in full of all work about the turret'. This might be a previously unrecorded maker, might not refer to a clockmaker at all, or might perhaps refer to Edward Enys, whose unusual name was much abused.

ANNATT, Nicholas   **London**
B.c. 1659, apr. Sep 1673 to Henry Jones till 1680 but not freed. Prob. related to Charles Annott, *qv.*

ANNOTT, Charles   **London**
B.c. 1659, apr. Sep 1673 to James Ellis till 1680, but not freed. Prob.
connected with Nicholas Annatt.

ANSELL. Richard (sometimes **Anselme**)   **London**
B.c. 1658, apr. Nov 1672 to Jeffrey Bayley till 1679. Freed Jul 1680.

ANSTEY, John   **London**
B.c. 1669, apr. Dec 1683 to George Nau, jeweller and watch case maker,
till 1690, but not freed in CC.

ANTHONY, James   **Truro**
In 1698 was discharged from keeping the town clock, but was reinstated
in 1699 and converted it to a pendulum at his own cost.

ANTONEY, Walter   **Ashburton (Devon)**
Said to have made church clock 1499-1500.

APERYS, John   **London**
Servant of Lewis Billiard in 1549 in St. Clement Danes parish. Prob.
French.

APJOHN, Henry   **London**
B.c. 1635, apr. Dec 1649 to Robert Whitwell (thro' James Seabourne) till
1656 but not freed.

APPLEBY, Edward   **London**
Recorded by some authorities as CC 1681 but this appears to be an error
for Edmund Appley.

APPLEGARTH, Thomas   **London**
B.c. 1650, apr. Sep 1664 to Hugh Cooper on whose death he was
transferred to Jeffrey Bayley till 1672. Freed Jul 1674. In Mar 1680/81
took as apr. **Thomas Bradford** – freed Jul 1692. In Jan 1680/81 he
received charity from CC of 5 shillings, but by Apr 1681 he had died and
his widow received the charity.

APPLEY, Edmund (also Applay)   **London**
B.c. 1656, son of Humfrey Appley, a weaver of Westmoreland county.
Apr. July 1670 to Jeffrey Bayley till 1677. Freed Jan 1677/78. In Sep
1681 he took as apr. **William Smith**; Jan 1686/87 took **Edward Acton**;

Aug 1687 took **Joshua Roe** (thro' Jeffrey Bayley). Died whilst on a business visit to Edinburgh and was buried there 11 Aug 1688. Andrew Brown, clockmaker there, paid for the church bells to be rung at his funeral. His will describes him as a watchmaker at Charing Cross, London, 'having come to Scotland about necessary affairs and here falling sick and fearing that my sickness be unto death,' and mentions his father and sister's son, Joseph Dowglas. Appears to have worked initially for Bayley but bracket and lantern clocks are known signed with his own name – eg 'Edmund Appley, Charing Cross'. (See also Loomes: *Complete British Clocks*.)

APSEY, William   Monksilver (Somerset)
Made TC 1699.

ARCHER, Henry   London
Was a 1622 petitioner for CC and became the first Warden in 1632, acting as deputy to the Master, David Ramsay, who scarcely ever attended. Said to have been formerly in the Blacksmiths' Co. In Jan 1633/34 he took **Thomas Laxton** as apr. (later transferred to Richard Lord). He is believed to have died in 1649. Known work includes a drum-shaped table clock and two or three watches, and has a distinctly French influence.

ARCHER, John   Henley-on-Thames (Oxfordshire)
Smith and TC maker. Repaired chimes of Henley church clock in 1532 and 1535-41.

ARCHER, John   London
Said to have been journeyman of Nicholas Vallin and to have died in 1603.

ARCHER, John   London
B.c. 1637, apr. Apr 1650 to James Starnill (thro' R. Masterson, who is believed to have been an engraver) till 1658. Freed Nov 1660. In Feb 1660/61 took **Robert Brewton** apr; Aug 1681 took **John Dawson** apr. later transferred to Daniel Beckman (also an engraver) and freed Sep 1688. Widow Archer received a single charitable payment from CC in Sep 1690, so John prob. died not long before. He is known to have been an engraver and examples of his work are either unknown or, more likely, unrecognised. However a lantern clock reputedly by Jonathan Archer c. 1670 may be by him.

ARCHER, Walter   place not known
Several clocks noted c.1700 – c.1715, longcase, lantern and 30-hour hook-and-spike wall clocks. No details are known about him nor his place of work, but this is prob. in the Southern English provinces.

ARCHER, William   Stratton (Cornwall)
Kept church clock 1590.

ARDEN, ----   London
Paid CC search fee 1671. Prob. a measure seller.

ARLANDY, John   London
Made a free Brother in CC Apr 1682, 'a chain maker who married the widow Tomaguez', ie a maker of watch chains who had married the widow of Abraham Thomaguez, *qv*. Prob. French. Working till at least 1705. Examples of his work would be unidentifiable.

Arlaud, Benjamin   London (?)
Watches known c. 1680 but this is a well-known family of Swiss watch-makers and the work is prob. Swiss.

ARLAUD, Henry   London (?)
Watches known c.1630 – c.1685, thought to have been made in England. Nothing is known about him in this country. Not known to CC. Maybe Swiss?

ARMIGER, Joseph   London
Apr. Jun 1677 in the Weavers' Co. to James Graves, an engraver. Free Sep 1688 in the CC by order of the Lord Mayor, being the apr. of James Graves, 'Citizen and Weaver, but professing a branch of the art of clockmaking'. In Oct 1688 took **Henry Richards** apr., later transferred to George Cawdron (also a James Graves apr.). Armiger was prob. a journeyman working in the Graves engraving business.

ARNOLD, Richard I.   Bodmin
Paid for mending town clock 1692-1700. Died 1724 leaving tools to son, Richard II, who succeeded him.

ARNOLD, Thomas   London
B.c. 1673. Apr. Sep 1687 to Nathaniel Chamberlain (senior or junior?) till 1694 – freed Sep 1703. A watch by him is recorded.

ARNOT, James   **Ards (Co. Down)**
1622.

ARONDELL, Laurence   **London**
Frenchman, 1568 (Ballie). No further details.

ARTHUR, William   **London**
B.c. 1655. Apr. Jun 1669 to Nicholas Coxeter till 1676. Free Dec 1676.
In Dec 1681 took as apr. **Daniel Robinson** – not freed.

ASH(E), ----   **London**
Subscriber in 1630 towards incorporation of CC. Almost certainly Ralph
Ash, *qv.*

ASH(E), Ralph   **London**
Free in CC (as a Brother?) Feb 1646-67 (but see previous entry?). Aug
1641 took **John North** as apr. (thro' O. Durant) – freed May 1650. In Jul
1648 took as apr. **Thomas Chapman** (thro' T. Alcock); May 1650 took
Edward Swan (thro' John Bayes); Feb 1652-53 took **Richard Craggs**
(thro' John North) – later transferred to Humfrey Pierce; Jul 1654 took
William Bayley (thro' Humfrey Pierce) later transferred to Samuel
Vernon; Aug 1656 took **Joshua Short** (thro' John North) later transferred to Lancelot Meredith. In 1656 he joined the rebels against the CC
administration. Prob. died before 1660.

ASHBOURNE, James   **London**
B.c. 1649, apr. Jan 1663/64 to Thomas Wilson 'for a basket maker' – an
expression open to several possible interpretations. Not freed. No
recognisable work known by him.

ASHBROOKE, John   **London**
B.c. 1672, apr. Jul 1686 to Zachariah Mountfort till 1693, but not freed.
Work known – longcase clock.

ASHBROOKE, Thomas   **London**
B.c. 1671, apr. Jun 1685 to Cuthbert Lee till 1692 but not freed. No work
known.

ASHBY, Joseph   **London**
B.c. 1650, apr. Feb 1663/64 to Matthew Crockford till 1671. Freed Apr
1674. In May 1676 took as apr. **Charles Tolley** – said in Jul 1678 to have

'gone to be a soldier' but in fact later transferred to John Brewer, another Crockford journeyman. In Jul 1678 took **Edmund Addison.** In Sep 1687 took an apr. for T. Tompion. In 1687 he was much in arrears of quarterage and in 1698 these amounted to eight years' arrears, which he never paid and he prob. died soon after 1698. It seems likely that he worked always as journeyman to Crockford and no work is known signed in his own name.

ASHLEY, James   London
B.c. 1634, apr. Jun 1647 to Robert Smith (thro' T. Alcock) till 1655. Smith however died in Oct 1652 and Ashley was never freed. He was prob. dead by 1662/63.

ASHTON, Charles   Chester
Watchmaker, freed 1682/83.

ASHTON, Edward   Dublin
Watchmaker apr. to G. Southwark, free in 1671 in Dublin Goldsmiths' Co. In 1673 had **Walter Bingham** as apr. Died 1674.

ASHTON, John   London
B.c. 1657, apr. Dec 1671 to John Savill (thro' L. Wythe) till 1678 but not freed.

ASHTON, Miles   London
B.c. 1650, apr. Oct 1663 to Benjamin Wolverstone till 1671, but not freed.

ASHTON, Thomas   London
1654. This is Thomas Eston or Eyston, *qv.*

ASHTON, Thomas   London
B.c. 1673, apr. Aug 1687 to Thomas Bradford till 1694 but not freed.

ASHURST, William   London
In CC 1699 according to some authorities, but I cannot trace him.

ASHWELL, Josiah   Leicester
B.c. 1680, apr. to John Wilkins till freed 1702. Believed worked till mid-century. Two lantern clocks and a longcase are known.

ASHWELL, Nicholas   **London**
B.c. 1629, apr. 1642/43 to Robert Grinkin (thro' O. Durant) till 1650.
Free Dec 1649. In Jun 1650 took **John Hiccock** – free Jul 1657.

ASKE, Henry   **London**
B.c. 1655, apr. Jan 1669/70 to Edward Norris till 1676. Free Jan
1676/77. In 1688 lived in the parish of St. Martin Ludgate. It is
interesting to note that he signed both the freedom oath and the 1697
oath of allegiance with his mark, as he could not write! Took for aprs.:
Jul 1688 **George Graham** – free Sep 1695; Sep 1697 **George Maddins**.
Also took an apr. for Isaac Lowndes and one for Jonathan Lowndes.
Work known – lantern clocks signed 'Henry Aske London fecit'.

ASPINALL, J.   place not known
Watch hallmarked 1720. Leicester. Perhaps the next maker, *qv*.

ASPINALL, Josiah (also Aspinwall)   **London**
Clockmaker, Free Brother in CC Jan 1675/76. Work known thro'
watches. In a play, *The Lancashire Witches*, produced in 1681, in a
discussion on watches one character asks; 'Is yours Aspenwolds?' and
gets the answer: 'No, Tompions'. Presumably this refers to Josiah
Aspinall, but see next entry.

ASPINALL, Peter   **Ashton in Makerfield**
Maker of guns, spurs and prob. clocks. Free 1664. Repaired TC
1666-72. Died 1677. Left three sons who prob. succeeded him.

ASPIN(W)ALL, Samuel   place not known
Mid-17th century watch and clock-watch known, one signed 'S. Aspinall
fecit'. This is a Lancashire surname.

ASPIN(W)ALL, Thomas   place not known
Watch recorded c. 1605.

ASSELIN, ----   **London**
Bracket and longcase clocks known c. 1700 signed by surname only
could be by Francis or Stephen – prob. Stephen.

ASSELIN, Francis (also **Asselinne** and **Asselynne**)   **London**
Admitted to CC as a free Brother Nov 1687, a Frenchman, an engraver
and a free Denizen. Was a Freeman of the Haberdashers' Co. In Jan

1692/93 he took as apr. **Richard Vick** (thro' W. Speakman) later transferred to Daniel Quare. Worked till at least 1704 and prob. till 1717. Work known – see last and next entry.

ASSELIN, Stephen   **London**
Bracket clocks, watches and longcase clocks from c.1700 – c.1720 are recorded signed 'Stephen Asselin, London'. He seems to have been unknown to the CC. See previous two entries.

ASTWOOD, Joseph   **London**
B.c. 1645, Apr 1659 to Benjamin Bell till 1666, but not freed.

ATKINS, Jonathan   **London**
B.c. 1675, apr. Apr 1689 to Samuel Clay till 1696 but not freed.

ATKINS, Joseph   **London**
B.c. 1640, apr. Apr 1654 to Robert Fowler (thro' J. Bayley) till 1661, but not freed.

ATKINSON, James   **London**
Mat. inst. maker and a freeman of the Joyners' Co. Admitted to CC as a free Brother Feb 1667/68. Took as aprs.: Jul 1670 **George Flower** (thro' Lionel Wythe) – freed Jul 1682; Sep 1670 **Eysum Perkins** (thro' R. Ames); May 1672 **Cornelius Beard,** transferred from E. Thorowgood; Jan 1679/80 **Peter Collins** (thro' H. Wynne) – freed Sep 1687; Sep 1686 **Edward Daniell** (thro' D. Stevens). Became Assistant from 1697 but did not attend meetings after 1700, hence neither became Warden nor Master. Working till at least 1704. Work known – none recognised.

ATKINSON, John   **Cockermouth (Cumberland)**
Repaired church clock 1668-74, prob. a smith.

ATKINSON, Joseph   **London**
Recorded as 1687 CC by some authorities, but this arises from a clerical error in CC records for James, *qv.*

ATLEE, Henry   **London**
Apr. Jul 1662 to Charles Rogers. Free Jul 1672.

ATLEE, John (Atte Lee)   **Henley-on-Thames (Oxfordshire)**
Repaired church clock 1412-1448.

ATLEE, Roger   **London**
B.c. 1651, apr. Nov 1664 to Job Betts (thro' R. Pierce) till 1672 but not freed.

ATTERBURY, Francis   **Warwick**
Clocksmith. Repaired church clock 1592.

AUDLEY, Joseph   **London**
B.c. 1669, apr. Dec 1683 to Thomas Tompion till 1690, but not freed. Not in his service in 1695.

AVERILL, John   **London**
see D'Averill.

AXFORD, John   **Bristol**
Clock and watchmaker. Married 12 May 1687 and 21 Feb 1690/91. No work known. Was marriage counter-productive?

AYERS, Henry   place unknown
Lantern clock dated 1628.

AYLOFFE, Elizabeth   **London**
Apr. Mar 1678/79 to Joan Wythe, widow, till 1685, but not freed. Prob. not trained in clock work anyway.

AYLWARD, John (also Ailleward)   **Aylesbury**
Made church clock for Aylesbury in 1691 and agreed to maintain it free for 31 years in return for lease of two cottages. Prob. the Guildford man.

AYLWARD, John   **Guildford**
Watch and lantern clocks known – late 17th century to about 1720. Also recorded as of 'Braintford'.

AYNSWORTH, John   **London**
Longcase and lantern clocks known from c.1680 – c.1710, some signed 'Aynsworth-London', some 'J. Aynsworth-Westminster'.

AYRES, Richard (also Ayers and Ayeres)   **London**
B.c. 1656, apr. Jul 1670 to Henry Jones till 1677. Free Sep 1680. Took as

aprs.: Sep 1681 **Edward Trickey;** Apr 1683 **Samuel Cambridge** – free Apr 1698. Died c. 1696-98.

AYRES, Samuel   **London**
B.c. 1650, apr. Dec 1664 to Edward Norris till 1671 but not freed.

B

BACHLATT, Matthew   England
Denizen clockmaker 1544.

BACKWELL, Thomas (see Bakewell)

BACON, John   London
Free Brother in CC Jul 1639.

BACON, William   Colchester
Working c.1648 – c.1680. Lantern clocks are known, including a
balance-wheel one, and an eight-day longcase clock. Signed: 'Gulielmus
Bacon, Colcestria fecit' and 'William Bacon, Colchester'.

BADDELEY, Phineas   London
Apr. Jul 1652 to Evan Jones (thro' D. Moody). Free Jan 1661-62.

BADDSTON, John   Ipswich
Thought to be a blacksmith. Repaired church clocks 1625, 1628, 1636.
Maintained Old Westgate Gaol clock in 1629, then newly built. Died
1666. Succeeded by son, Edmund.

BADGER, Henry   London
B.c. 1658, apr. Sep 1672 to John Harris till 1679 but in Dec 1672 he was
dismissed by his master and his indenture was cancelled.

BAGGELEY, William   Chester
Repaired church clock 1637-38.

BAGLEY, Thomas senior   **London**
B.c. 1636, apr. Oct 1650 to Richard Morgan (thro' N. Tomlins) till 1657. Freed Nov 1658. Took apr. **Richard Fennell** over from Matthew Crockford – freed Nov 1679, by which time Bagley had died. It is impossible to identify his aprs. from those of Thomas junior.

BAGLEY, Thomas junior   **London**
Apr. May 1656 to Thomas Loomes – freed Oct 1664. Though sometimes described as Thomas Bagley junior, his relationship to Thomas senior is unknown. Thomas I or II took as aprs.: Jun 1666 **John Plydell; William Lucas** (from Robert Robinson) – freed Apr 1669; Apr 1669 **Richard Thomlinson; John White** (taken over from Thomas Loomes) – freed Sep 1670; Nov 1677 **Ralph Panck.**

BAGSHAW, Edward   **London**
B.c. 1668, apr. Dec 1681 to Thomas Wheeler till 1689. Freed Sep 1691. Took as apr. Jul 1695 **Thomas Temple** – freed Aug 1720. Still alive 1696 but prob. dead by 1697.

BAILY (see under Bayley)

BAKER, Richard   **London**
Apr. to John Chatfield through the Blacksmiths' Co., then transferred Jun 1683 to Richard Browne, clockmaker, thro' the CC. Made a freeman in CC Jun 1685 by redemption by the order of the Lord Mayor – a Great Clockmaker. This prob. means that having served a partial apprenticeship under each Company the Lord Mayor decided he had served a long enough period in order to justify his freedom. Took as aprs.: Sep 1685 **John Hunt** (thro' John Wise junior); Apr 1687 **Peter Garon** – freed Jul 1694 by order of the Lord Mayor, at which time Baker was fined by the CC for having trained an alien in Garon; Aug 1689 **Silvester Law;** Nov 1691 **Daniel Vinio; Robert Batterson** (taken over from W. Davison) – freed Feb 1693/94; Jun 1695 **Robert Andrews** – free May 1710; Sep 1697 **John Jacob;** Apr 1699 **Thomas Chambers** (son of Thomas Chambers of North Mimms, Herts, yeoman); Aug 1700 **Thomas Draper** (son of James Draper late of Hackney, Middlesex, gardener, deceased). He died about the end of the year 1700. In May 1710 his widow, Jane, still evidently carrying on the business, took **Thomas Evans** apr. – free Apr 1718. Work known – several longcase clocks including a month clock, also bracket clocks and watches. Some

signed 'Richard Baker, Exchange Alley', some 'Richard Baker, London'. Baillie gives Lombard Street as his address, which I cannot confirm.

BAKER, Thomas   **Blandford (Dorset)**
Marquetry longcase clock known, apparently late 17th century, but nothing known of this maker.

BAKEWELL, Thomas (sometimes Backwell)   **London**
Free Brother in CC Apr 1654. In Oct 1664 he was threatened with prosecution for arrears of quarterage. In Apr 1665 he paid off the arrears and promised to re-bind thro' the CC his apr. currently bound thro' the Clothworkers' Co. – though in fact he did not and is not heard of again. Work known – a lantern clock is recorded signed 'Thomas Bakewell on Tower Hill fecit'.

BALDWIN, Christopher   **London**
B.c. 1642, apr. Sep 1656 to John Freeman till 1663, but not freed.

BALDWIN, John   **London**
B.c. 1677, apr. May 1691 to Stephen Rayner till 1698, but not freed.

BALDWIN, Robert   **London**
B.c. 1668, apr. Jul 1682 to Thomas Virgoe till 1689, but not freed (Virgoe died 1685).

BALDWIN, Thomas   **London**
B.c. 1664, apr. Sep 1678 thro' N. Coxeter to John Benson, an engraver and a freeman of the Weavers' Co., till 1685. Freed Sep 1685. Took as apr. Feb 1687/88 **Ambrose Willis**. I have no record of him after 1687 and he was dead by 1697-98. Work known – a watch is recorded. (Another Thomas Baldwyn was a freeman from 1706).

BALL, John   **Liverpool**
Clockmaker. Married 1699. Children born up to 1715 include three sons. He and his wife, Catherine, both died in 1716. He lived at Hackins Hey.

BALL, John   **London**
B.c. 1611, son of William Ball of London. Apr. Nov 1624 in Merchant Taylors' Co. to Simon Bartram, watchmaker, of Blackfriars till 1632. Free in CC May 1637.

BALL, Victor   **London**
In 1647 when challenged by the CC he confessed he was not learned in the trade but was trained as a tailor and he was forbidden the trade. In Jun 1652 however he was again warned by the CC for practising the trade without having served an apprenticeship. He was prob. dead by 1662/63.

BALLARD, John (see Bellard)

BANBURY, John   **London**
B.c. 1661, apr. May 1675 to Robert Wood, a boxmaker, till 1682. Free Apr 1686. Took as aprs.: Oct 1693 **Valantine Jones** – free Jan 1705/05; Nov 1695 **Richard Stephens** – free Jul 1715; Apr 1700 **John Shirt** (son of Edward Shirt of St. Bottolph Aldersgate, labourer); Jul 1702 **George Hall** (son of William Hall, late of the parish of St. Sepulchre, London, baker, deceased) – free Feb 1710-11. Last known to be alive in 1704. May well have been a boxmaker.

BANCKS, Austin   **London**
Clockmaker? Inherited worktools of Robert Grinkin junior in his 1660 will.

BANGER, Edward   **London**
B.c. 1668, son of Edward Banger, joiner, of North Petherton, Somerset. Apr. Sep 1687 to Thomas Tompion (thro' Joseph Ashby) till 1694. Married Dec 1694 Margaret Kent (Tompion's niece). Freed Jul 1695. Took as aprs.: Nov 1696 **Richard Elmes** – free Sep 1708; Nov 1703 **George Whitlock**. He is believed to have worked throughout this time for Tompion (whose nephew he was) but left Tompion's service about 1708, supposedly under a cloud. There is a gap until Oct 1715 before Banger took his next apr., named **Banger Higgins** (apparently named after the master), who was turned over in Apr 1720 to William Wild a freeman of the Leathersellers' Co., but 'of the same trade' as Banger himself – there is some doubt whether his trade at that time was still in clockmaking. Banger died in 1720 – hence the turnover of Banger Higgins. Work known – his name appears apparently only on clocks and watches signed jointly by Tompion and himself. For further reading see R. W. Symonds: *Thomas Tompion, his life and work* and J. B. Penfold's article: *Whatever became of Banger; Antiquarian Horology*, Dec 1971. At least one bracket clock known – signed 'E. Banger – London'.

BANKS, ----   **Nottingham**
Late 17th century watch recorded – Baillie.

BANKS, Austin (see Bancks)

BANK(E)S, George   **Stoke on Trent**
Repaired church clock 1658.

BANKS, John   **Chester**
Free 1682. Nothing else known.

BANKES, William   **London**
B.c 1676, apr. Mar 1690 to Benjamin Bell, later (on Bell's death in 1691?) transferred to John Higginson till 1697. Freed Sep 1698. Believed died soon after.

BANK(E)S, William   **Sheffield**
Late 17th century lantern clock recorded, signed 'William Bankes in Sheffield'. Might just be the previous maker? Also longcase clock.

BANTING, William   **London**
Recorded by some authorities as 1646 CC. Error for William Bunting, *qv*.

BARACHIN, Stephen   **London**
A French watchmaker. Made a Free Brother in CC Sep 1687. Prob. a member of the Huguenot family of goldsmiths of this name who settled in London at this time. Prob. died c. 1697/98.

BARBER, Jonas   **Otley (Yorks) and London**
B. Otley, Yorkshire in 1652, son of Thomas and Jane Barber. In Jun 1672 he was already working in London, but prob. at that time not at clock work. An entry in the CC accounts records payment of a search fee by Samuel Weedon, ironmonger, 'Jonas Barber's man'. He was admitted a free Brother in CC Dec 1682 (at the same court as John Williamson, also believed to be a Yorkshireman and later at Leeds, *qv*). Lived in Painters' Rents in Ratcliffe Hamlet. Died in the summer of 1698. In his will made in 1695 he mentions his brothers and sister back in Yorkshire. He prob. died a bachelor. His work is known through longcase clocks, including a month longcase, and lantern clocks, signed 'Jonas Barber, Ratcliffe Cross'. For further information see B. Loomes: *Westmorland Clocks and Clockmakers*, where the Barber family is covered in detail.

BARCLAY, William   **Aberdeen**
Kept town clock. Died 1560.

BARCOLE, John (also Barcoll)   **London**
Apr. May 1638 to William Bowyer (thro' R. Masterson). Free Mar
1647/48. Prob. died before 1662.

BARFORD, Thomas (and Berford)   **London**
B.c. 1643, apr. Nov 1656 to Thomas Daniell (thro' Simon Dudson) till
1664, but not freed. In 1672 Mr. Berford paid quarterage, which might
have been him.

BARJON, John   **London**
Some authorities record him as CC 1685. Prob. a clerical error for
Barton.

BARKER, George (or Barkham?)   **London**
Sep 1653 agreed to join CC at next court – but did not. In Apr 1655
widow Barker received charity from CC.

BARKER, William   **London**
Free in CC 1632 (as Brother?). Paid quarterage 1635-39.

BARKHAM (see Barker)

BARLOW, Edward   **Lancashire**
B. 1639 at Warrington as Edward Booth, but took the name Barlow after
his godfather. Entered the English College at Lisbon in 1659 and was
ordained as a Catholic priest there in 1664. Returned to England 1670 as
chaplain to the Langdale family in Yorkshire. From 1672 was at
Charnock Richard, Lancashire, till his death there in 1719. It is
sometimes stated that he served as steward of the CC in 1677, which is
incorrect – he was not even a member of the CC. He is sometimes
credited with the invention of rack striking work about 1676. This prob.
arises from a misunderstanding of his application to the King in 1687 for
sole patent to make 'pulling repeating clocks and watches' – what we
would now usually call 'pull-repeating'. This application was
strenuously opposed by the CC at the expense of £25 in legal fees and was
rejected by the King, on the grounds that it was already common
practice, 'the same being now made by several clockmakers'. In 1695 he
is said to have patented (with Thomas Tompion and William Houghton

of Chorley, Lancashire, gent.) the pre-cursor of the cylinder escapement. He was not an actual maker of clocks or watches and no work is known to survive in his name.

BARLOW, Thomas London
Recorded by some authorities as CC 1692. Error for Thomas Darlow, *qv*.

BARLOW, William Kings Lynn
Not of Lyme Regis as is sometimes stated. Lantern clock c. 1700.

BARNARD, Francis London
B.c. 1661, apr. May 1675 to Roger Nichols who transferred him illegally in Jul 1675 to serve Isaac Puzy, who was fined. Presumably remained with Puzy till 1682 but was not freed.

BARNARD, John London
B.c. 1661, apr. Sep 1675 to Francis Dinnis till 1682. Free Jan 1682-83. Took as aprs.: Mar 1684/85 **William Small**; Dec 1687 **John Smith**; Aug 1689 **Thomas Shepherd** (thro' John Smart); Jul 1696 **John Sumers**. Still alive 1697 but prob. died soon after – see Mary Barnard. Baillie lists him at St. John Street but I don't know his source for this address. He was prob. an engraver, as Dinnis was.

BARNARD, Mary London
In Aug 1698 took **Benjamin Thrip** apr. She was prob. the widow of John carrying on his business.

BARNARD, Nicholas (see also Bernard) London
B.c. 1648, apr. May 1662 to Peter Bellune (thro' T. Claxton) till 1669 but not freed. Was prob. a boxmaker, as Bellune was, but see N. Bernard.

BARNARD, Ralph London
B.c. 1664, apr. May 1678 to John Cotsworth till 1685, but not freed. In Jul 1682 his apprentice had 'gone from him and not likely to return'.

BARNES, George London
B.c. 1679, apr. Dec 1693 to Joshua Alsop (thro' Henry Kilminster) till 1700, but not freed. Prob. died before Apr 1697, when widow Barnes received charity from CC.

BARNES, Matthew Northampton
1663-85.

71

BARNES, Richard **Worcester**
Watches known c.1600 – c.1610.

BARNETT, John **London**
B.c. 1662, apr. Jun 1675 to John Ebsworth till 1682. Free Sep 1682. In Jun 1692 John Barnett, clockmaker, widower, aged 30, of St. Margaret's parish Lothbury, married Hannah Stavely of St. Bottolph Bishopsgate, spinster aged 22. Took as aprs.: Oct 1684 **George Clent**; Aug 1691 **Benjamin Hume**; Feb 1694/95 **James Hagger**; Mar 1701/02 **William Webster** (son of Daniel Webster, late of St. Mary Matfellan (alias Whitechapel), Middlesex, clothworker, deceased) – free Jul 1710. Worked at the sign of the Peacock in Lothbury. Appears to have died early in 1702 when his quarterage payments cease. A number of his clocks are known – longcase ones including one quarter-striking on six bells and a three-month one; also bracket clocks and lantern clocks. Some (lanterns) are signed 'John Barnett at Ye Peacock in Lothbury, Londini fecit'. Others signed 'John Barnett Londini fecit'.

BARON, Edmund **London**
B.c. 1679, apr. May 1693 to Thomas Feilder till 1700 but not freed.

BARR, Thomas **Lewes**
Listed by some authorities as lantern clockmaker c. 1700. Prob. error for Thomas Barrett, *qv*.

BARRAUD, Henry (see Berraud)

BARRETT, Edward **Lewes**
At Headborough from 1656, married 1659, died 1718.

BARRETT, Henry **London**
B.c. 1670, apr. May 1684 to Charles Gretton. Free Apr 1692. Still alive 1697 but prob. died soon after.

BARRETT, James **Manchester**
Watchmaker. Had son, Micah, b. 1678.

BARRETT, Robert **London**
Watchmaker. Free Brother in CC Feb 1687/88. There till c. 1693 after which nothing more known.

BARRETT, Simon   **London**
B.c. 1654, apr. Jul 1668 to Joseph Wells, a mat. inst. maker and freeman of the Joyners' Co. (bound thro' Thomas Claxton) till 1675. Freed Apr 1678. In Apr 1682 took **Caleb Burge** apr. – not freed. Prob. mat. inst. maker like his master.

BARRETT, Thomas   **Canterbury**
Late 17th century watch known. Maybe the Lewes man, *qv.*

BARRETT, Thomas   **Lewes**
Clockmaker, working 1690, married 1691. Several longcase clocks known.

BARRIDGE, John   **London**
B.c. 1640, apr. Mar 1654 to Hugh Cooper till 1661 but not freed. Prob. died pre 1662.

BARRINGTON, Benjamin   **Limerick**
Clockmaker 1693-1724, son of Samuel.

BARRINGTON, Samuel   **Dublin/Limerick**
Clockmaker c. 1660. Died 1693.

BARRINGTON, Urian (see Berrington)

BARROW, James   **Edinburgh**
B.c. 1679. The Edinburgh Gazette of 1699 wrote: 'James Barrow, aged about twenty, of a low stature, a little pock-marked, speaks the English accent, had on when he went away a short flaxen coll cut wig, in an ordinary habit, run away from his master (Andrew Brown of Edinburgh) the nineteenth instant, with a plain gold watch without a christal, with an enambiled dial, the emembling on the figures is broken off, a silver pendulum watch with a minute hand made by W. Young at Charing Cross, London . . . whoever can secure the said youth and give notice thereof to Captain Andrew Brown, watchmaker in Edinburgh, shall have two guineas reward'. It is not known what became of him but a watchmaker of this name is known in London in the early 18th century.

BARROW, John   **Halifax**
Watchmaker. His wife (or daughter?) died there in 1728. Maybe connected with the London family of this name.

BARROW, John London

B.c. 1657, apr. Jul 1671 to Francis Ireland till 1678. Free Jul 1681. Took as aprs.: May 1683 **Joseph Moore** – free Sep 1690; Jul 1688 **Samuel Barrow** – free Apr 1696; Apr 1693 **Samuel Holliard** – free Apr 1705; Jan 1697/98 **William Franklin** – free 1712; Jul 1700 **John Gill** (son of the late Edward Gill of St. Andrew Holborn, Middlesex, blacksmith, deceased) – free Dec 1707; Jan 1700/01 his son, **William Barrow** – free Jul 1710; May 1706 **George Barrow** (son of William Barrow, late of ? Charton, co. Chester, farmer, deceased); May 1710 **John Mason** – free Nov 1719; Apr 1713 **John Burch;** Oct 1717 **Andrew Fleming** (transferred in Jul 1719 to William Barrow after master's death); **John Thompson** transferred Sep 1719 to George Clarke. Made Assistant 1705, Warden from 1710, Master 1714. Last attended 1718. Died 1719 (before Jul). Prob. had North Country connections – Francis Ireland was from Lancashire and George Barrow from Cheshire. Address at the Hermitage suggests close association and prob. relationship with Samuel Barrow, *qv* who also worked there. Work known – at least one watch as well as longcase clocks. Signed 'John Barrow, Hermitage, London' and 'John Barrow, Londini fecit'.

BARROW, Nathaniel London

B.c. 1639, apr. Jan 1653-54 to Job Betts (thro' N. Payne) till 1660. Free Jan 1660/61. Aprs.: Nov 1664 **Thomas Smith;** Apr 1667 **Daniel Finch** – not freed; Oct 1668 **John Finch** – free Jan 1675/76; Sep 1672 **Henry Hammond** – free Jul 1680; Aug 1677 **Thomas Bates** – free Nov 1684; Oct 1680 **John Frearson** – free Aug 1689; Oct 1686 **William Weedon** – free Jul 1695. In 1688 he was left a bequest in the will of William Seabourne, *qv* as his 'loving friend' – 'my black vest and the breeches that belong to them'. In 1668 he stood as a bondsman for Samuel Horne, *qv* for whom Seabourne worked as journeyman. In May 1679 he helped John Layton to pay his CC arrears of quarterage by lending him the money, to be repaid by deducting a sum from 'each movement that Leighton makes for him'. Became CC Assistant from 1676, Warden from 1685, Master 1689. Last attended in 1700 though from 1698 he was excused regular attendance on account of his age (about 59?). He seems to have died late in the year 1700. He could well be the father of John and/or Samuel, but this is not known. Work known – several watches but also longcase clocks, including a month one and bracket clocks.

BARROW, Samuel London

B.c. 1674, apr. Jul 1688 to John Barrow (relationship, if any, unknown) till 1695. Free Apr 1696. Took as aprs.: Feb 1698/99 **Matthew Jackson** (son of the late Matthew Jackson deceased, citizen and Wheelwright of London) – free Sep 1715; Jun 1704 **John Stanley** (son of Gabriel Stanley of Blackfor…(?), Leicestershire, labourer) – not free, working till at least 1704, perhaps later. Worked 'at the sign of the Spring Clock in East Smithfield near Hermitage Bridge'. Work known – longcase clocks signed 'Samuel Barrow at the Hermitage'.

BARTHOLOMEW, John　　　　　　　　　　　　　　**London**
B.c. 1655, apr. Oct 1668 to John North, then transferred to Benjamin Wolverston, then to Robert Smith till 1676. Free Dec 1675. Took as aprs.: Dec 1675 **Daniel Fitton** (thro' Robert Smith); Jul 1676 **Joseph Hussey** (later transferred to Francis Hussey). Not heard of after 1676.

BARTLETT, John　　　　　　　　　　　　　　　　**Chester**
1642 dial (Baillie).

BARTLETT, Moses　　　　　　　　　　　　　　　**Exeter**
Died 1709. Sundial recorded.

BARTON, Jacobus　　　　　　　　　　　　　　　**Norwich**
Son of Jacques van Barton (also **Berthen**), claspmaker. Freed Feb 1629-30 as a clockmaker, having been apr. to his father.

BARTON, Jacques van (also Berthen)　　　　　　**Norwich**
Claspmaker and merchant. Father and master of Samuel and Jacobus 1616-29, whom he taught clockmaking. May well have been the master of Ahasuerus Fromanteel.

BARTON, James　　　　　　　　　　　　　　　　**Chester**
Clockmaker. Refused freedom at Chester 1696 (being from Ormskirk). Married 1698 Martha Seddon at Ormskirk, where he worked till he died in 1718.

BARTON, James　　　　　　　　**Ormskirk (Lancashire)**
Clockmaker. Died 1718 (according to Baillie).

BARTON, John　　　　**Henley-on-Thames (Oxfordshire)**
B.c. 1659. Clock and watchmaker. Married Oct 1685 aged 26 to Mary Day, widow of Henley, at Bix, Oxfordshire.

BARTON, John　　　　　　　　　　　　　　　　**London**
B.c. 1644, apr. Nov 1657 to David Parry and was fraudulently kept by him and James Gregory – prob. contrary to CC rules.

BARTON, Samuel (also van Berthen)   **Norwich**
Son of Jacques van Barton, to whom he was apr. in 1616 for 7 years.
Freed as clockmaker Nov 1628. Work known – none. Quite possibly the
same man as in the next entry.

BARTON, Samuel   **London**
Free Brother in CC Oct 1640. Possibly the man from Norwich, *qv*. Baillie
records him at Manchester and records a watch by him. I can confirm
neither.

BARTRAM, Simon   **London**
B.c. 1598, son of Robert Bartram of London, feltmaker. Apr. Feb
1611-12 thro' the Merchant Taylors' Co. to John Jelly of Barnard Castle
ward till 1619. Took as apr. in Nov 1624 thro' the Merchant Taylors' Co.
John Ball, *qv*. Became Assistant in CC 1632, Warden from 1638, Master
1650-51. Took as aprs. in CC: Nov 1637 **Henry Strigg** (thro' O. Durant);
Feb 1646/47 **William Anderson** (thro' L. Wythe); Mar 1646-47
Christopher Hall (thro' T. Alcock) – free Nov 1655; **Ahasuerus
Fromanteel** junior – free Jul 1663; Aug 1657 **Joseph Romney** (thro'
L. Wythe) – freed Oct 1664; Mar 1664-65 **John Curtis** (thro' S. Horne) –
on Bartram's death in 1667 he was passed to Jeremy Gregory. He had
close links with Jeremy Gregory and Robert Grinkin, with whom in Oct
1655 he shared journeyman **Stephen Jarrey**. Married Oct 1663 Mary
Ascoll. He worked at least till 1662 in Blackfriars (in the parish of St.
Bartholomew the Less). His will, dated Jul 1665, mentions his wife
Mary, who was to have the house they lived in, which was hers before
marriage. He mentions a shop occupied by John Hicks at Pauls Wharfe
in the parish of St. Bennett Pauls Wharfe, but we do not know whether
this was his own shop. Also mentions his daughter Mary Bartram,
spinster, and daughter, Martha, wife of William Darby, cutler of
London. Bequeathed to 'my loving friend Jeremy Gregory, Citizen and
Goldsmith' £5. Also bequeathed 40 shillings to 'my loving friend
Nicholas Coxeter, Citizen and Clockmaker, to buy him a ring to weare in
remembrance of me and my love to him'. The will was proved in Nov
1667. Work known – one or two watches, which seems surprisingly little
and it is possible he may have worked for Gregory at some time.

BARTRAM, William (also **Bertram**)   **London**
B.c. 1663, apr. May 1677 to Samuel Horne, transferred after Jun 1681
till 1684 to Samuel Bowtell, another Samuel Horne journeyman. Freed

Sep 1684. Took as aprs.: Jul 1686 **Edward Jones;** Dec 1691 **David Boulanger;** Aug 1699 **John Winsmore** (son of John Winsmore of Burford, Oxon, mercer) – free 1712; took over **John Bayley** from Edward Hunt – free Jul 1700; Apr 1702 **Margaret Cary** (daughter of the late Christopher Cary of St. Mary Rotherhithe, Surrey, deceased) to serve his wife in the trade of mantuamaking; Apr 1708 **William Cooper.** In 1708 he was excused CC stewardship as he was at present busy 'on the Queen's business'. A William Bertram, Master of the CC in 1732, is believed to be a different man. Work known – watch with six-hour dial signed: 'Will Bertram, London'. He was a goldsmith.

BASELEY (see under Beseley)

BASSET, Thomas London
B.c. 1654, apr. Jan 1668-69 to Isaac Webb, mat. inst. maker (thro' L. Wythe) till 1675, but not freed. See next entry?

BASSETT, Thomas Bath/Wells
Watchmaker, married 10 Aug 1675. Maybe from London – see previous entry.

BASTIEN, ---- London
Kept Westminster clock 1547. 'Haurologier' to Cromwell (Baillie).

BATES, Henry London (?)
Longcase clock c. 1695 – place not known.

BATES, Joseph London
B.c. 1660, apr. Jan 1678/79 to William Standish till 1685. Free Apr 1687. In May 1683, then a clockmaker of St. Andrew's parish, Holborn, a bachelor aged 23, he married Anne Coleman of the same parish, 23, a spinster at St. Dunstans in the West. Took as aprs.: Jun 1687 **Robert Carleton** (thro' T. Elton); Jan 1706/07 **George Stevens.** Not heard of after 1706. Said to have worked in White Alley, Holborn, which seems correct.

BATES, Thomas London
B.c. 1663, apr. Aug 1677 to Nathaniel Barrow, a known maker of watches, till 1684. Freed Nov 1684. Took as aprs.: Nov 1691 **James Lloyd** – free Sep 1700; ?1686 **John Silvester** later transferred to Henry Jones; Aug 1696 **John Ord;** Sep 1699 **Zachariah Findlow** (son of

Richard Findlow of the parish of St. Andrew Holborn, gentleman); **Morris Hughes** (taken over from Henry Hammond) – freed Mar 1699/1700. Working till at least 1704.

BATES, William　　　　　　　　　　　　　　　　**Leicester**
Clock and watchmaker, free Sep 1692, having been apr. to John Wilkins. One of this name at Dublin in 1720s, and one in London 1727.

BATTEN, Edward　　　　　　　　　　　　　　　　**London**
B.c. 1656, apr. Jan 1670/71 to John Marke (thro' L. Wythe) – till 1677 but not freed.

BATTEN, John　　　　　　　　　　　　　　　　**London**
Admitted to CC as free Brother Jan 1668/69, a clockmaker. Died 1686 leaving bequests to brother Richard, Peter Southworth and his wife, *qv* and Thomas Jenkins and wife, *qv*. Prob. a bachelor.

BATTERSBY, George　　　　　　　　　　　　　**Manchester**
Clockmaker. Married 1694 Mary Oakes.

BATTERSON, Robert　　　　　　　　　　　　　**London**
B.c. 1672, apr. Dec 1686 to William Davison, later transferred to Richard Baker till 1693. Freed Feb 1693/94. Took as aprs.: Sep 1696 **James Batterson; Dec 1701 Robert White** (son of Jeremiah White, late of the parish of St. John Wapping, shipwright, deceased). Not heard of after 1701. Work known – longcased clocks.

BATTIN, Thomas　　　　　　　　　　　　　　　**London**
Son of Thomas Battin. Apr. May 1654 to Edward Ward (thro' Thomas Loomes) till 1661. Free Jul 1661. In Mar 1657/58 the CC seized some badly made clock wheels from him and fined him for poor workmanship – which seems unusually harsh treatment for one still an apprentice. 24 Mar 1657/58 'This search day a contrat, second wheel & a dyal wheel being taken from Thomas Battin was viewed by the said Company and adjudged to be so bad as not fitting to be put into any work, and was fined acc. to the orders of the said Company. The wheels were broken up.' In Jul 1663 he took **William Halley** apr.

BAVIN, Thomas　　　　　　　　　　　　　　　**Chester**
Serviced church clock 1696.

BAVIS, George   **London**
Recorded by some authorities as CC 1687. Error for George Beavis, *qv*.

BAWDYSON, Alan (Allaine)   **London**
'Stranger' (foreigner) in Strand Parish, Westminster, in 1540 with Lewis
Billiard his servant. Clockmaker to Edward VI. French?

BAXTER, Charles   **London**
B.c. 1659, apr. Sep 1673 to Erasmus Micklewright till 1680. Freed Apr
1681. In Jun 1683 took **Robert Rouse** apr. Prob. died before 1697-98.
Work known – watches. Baillie says also St. Neots, but I do not know
where he found this information.

BAXTER, William   **London**
Never actually admitted into CC but was known to them. In 1639 paid
quarterage (as Backster). Worked in Lothbury when in Aug 1662 he took
as apr. **Samuel Enwood.**

BAYER, William   **London**
Recorded by some authorities as a lantern clockmaker in 1623. Prob.
error for Bowyer, *qv*.

BAYES, Benjamin   **London**
Apr. Nov 1661 to his brother John Bayes – freed Aug 1675. Prob.
worked purely for John, *qv*.

BAYES, John   **London**
Free Brother in CC Nov 1646. Free of the City of London Jul 1649
by redemption in CC, John Bayes being 'debarred from freedom by
service as he married before expiration of his apprenticeship'. One surety
was given by Onisephorus Helden, goldsmith, who may have been his
master. Took as his own aprs.: **Francis Matthews,** taken over from
Sampson Shelton on his death (1648) – freed Jul 1656; Jun 1652 **Richard
Boyle** – free Oct 1660; Mar 1659/60 **John Park;** Jun 1660 **Thomas
Pidgeon;** Nov 1661 **Benjamin Bayes** his brother – free Aug 1675; Jan
1662/63 **Isaac Wilmot.** Also acted as intermediary in binding 11 other
aprs. for other masters: S. Hacket – 3, J. Gregory – 2, H. Child – 2, and
one each to J. Betts, N. Parke, O. Helden, R. Ash. Several of these are
known members of the Goldsmiths' Co. In 1656 he was amongst the
rebels against the CC administration. In 1660 he was a beneficiary under
the will of Robert Grinkin as a 'very loving friend'. In 1662 he worked in

Cornhill. He became CC Assistant 1653, Warden from 1658, when he ceased to attend meetings – he might otherwise have been Master. He died between 1664 and 1666. His widow received a regular pension from the CC and despite being 'sick and in great want' in 1670, she continued to draw her pension till 1679. Work known – three watches and a lantern clock signed 'Johannes Bayes Londini'.

BAYFORD, George   **London**
B.c. 1667, apr. Jul 1682 to Richard Colston. In May 1692 he was described as a watchmaker, bachelor, aged 25, of St. Paul's Shadwell, Middlesex, when he married Anna Archer, spinster aged 17 of Woodford, Essex.

BAYLEY, Edward (also Bail(e)y)   **London**
Freeman of the Goldsmiths' Co. His apr. **George Crouch** (son of George Crouch of Holborn) was transferred to William Raynes and freed Jan 1668/69. He seems not to have been a member of CC. Work known – lantern clock signed 'Edward Bayley, London'. Known to have made watches.

BAYLEY, Edward   **Uttoxeter (Staffordshire)**
Set up clock for Alstonfield church Dec 1682. Maybe the Londoner above?

BAYLEY, Jeffery (also Bailey, Baylie, etc)   **London**
B.c. 1623, apr. Sep 1637 to Thomas Pace (thro' O. Durant) till 1644. Free Mar 1646. There was a serious dispute between master and apr. for which they were brought before the CC in 1642 and again in 1646, but neither man would supply details of their quarrel(?). Took as aprs.: Mar 1653 **Daniel Stephens** – free Apr 1661; Aug 1654 **William Smith;** Apr 1657 **John Wheatley** – freed May 1668; **William Standish** – freed Jan 1668/69; 1664 or later took over **Thomas Applegarth** from Hugh Cooper on death of latter – freed Jul 1674; Feb 1668/69 **Edward Lee;** Jul 1670 **Edmund Appley** – free Jan 1677/78; Nov 1672 **Richard Ansell** – free Jul 1680; post 1674 took over **Joseph Page** from Nicholas Coxeter (prob. when latter died in 1679) – freed Apr 1683; Sep 1680 **Sebastian Porter;** Jul 1683 **Edward Drew** – free Jul 1692; Jun 1687 **Samuel Lee** – free Mar 1694/95. Additionally he acted as intermediary in binding 11 aprs. for other masters: two for F. Stephens, one each for J. White, J. Cowpe, W. Pettit, R. Fowler, I. Daniell, J. Puller, E. Appley, J. Waters, E. Lambe. No obvious connection is known with any of these men

except that Appley was his own journeyman. In 1662 he worked in Westminster. Became CC Assistant 1665, Warden from 1670, Master 1675/76, last attended 1693. Prob. died c. 1696 (before 1697-98). Work known – two or three lantern clocks signed 'Jeffrey Bayley at the Turn Stile in Holburne'.

BAYLEY, John   **London**
B.c. 1668, apr. Jul 1681 to Nicasius Russell till 1689, but not freed.

BAYLEY, John   **London**
B.c. 1678, apr. Jun 1692 to Edward Hunt, watchmaker, till 1699. Freed Jul 1700, having been transferred to William Bartram (prob. because Hunt was going blind). Took as aprs.: Sep 1701 **Hugh Richards** (son of Evan Richards late of (T?)esatherwyn, County Montgomery) – free Aug 1709; Nov 1705 **Jacob Hughs** (son of David Hughs of parish of St. Margaret's Westminster, victualler); Jun 1708 **John Godfrey**; Jun 1709 **Thomas Yorke** (son of Edward Yorke late of parish of St. George, Southwark, goldb(eater?), deceased) – freed Oct 1716; Jan 1713/14 **Thomas Potts; Isaac Edwards** (from H. Kilminster) – free Oct 1719; Nov 1719 **Peter Daniel Cornu** (from John Lewis). Nothing known of him after 1719. Work known – gold watch hallmarked 1712.

BAYLEY, Michael (or Miles?) (also Baily)   **London**
Miles Bayley paid CC quarterage in 1672/73. Michael Bayley, a scale-maker in Bartholomew Lane in 1674, had three faulty sundials confiscated by CC.

BAYLEY, Robert (also Bayly)   **Wells (Somerset)**
Repaired TC 1683-84.

BAYLEY, William   **London**
Apr. Jul 1654 to Ralph Ash (thro' Humfrey Pierce), later transferred to Samuel Vernon (on death of Ash?), then transferred again to Benjamin Wolverston. Freed Apr 1663. In Sep 1680 applied unsuccessfully for job as CC Beadle (usually given to a poor member).

BAYLIFFE, ----   place not known
Carlisle Cathedral records show payments to 'Mr. Bayliffe the clock-maker' in 1687 for work on the clock and bells. Maybe Robert Bilcliffe from York?

BAYLIS, J. Tewkesbury
Lantern clock recorded as c. 1700 but I have no data on him.

BAYSE, Thomas London
Recorded as CC 1695 by some authorities. I cannot trace him.

BAYLY (see Bayley)

BEACHING (see Benching)

BEADLE, William London
B.c. 1653, apr. Jan 1667/68 to William Raynes till 1674, but not freed.

BEALE, John London
B.c. 1645, apr. Jan 1658/59 to Nicholas Coxeter till 1666 but not freed.

BEALE, Robert London
B.c. 1664, apr. Dec 1677 to Bernard Rainsford till 1685 but never freed because in Nov 1680 his master reported that 'being afflicted with the King's Evil* he hath bin gone with his friends about half a year and not likely ever to return'. (*A disease popularly supposed to be cured by the touch of a King.)

BEARD, Christopher London
Recorded by some authorities. Error for Cornelius Beard, *qv*.

BEARD, Cornelius London
B.c. 1656, apr. Oct 1670 to Edward Thorowgood (thro' L. Wythe) but transferred May 1672 (perhaps on death of E.T.) to James Atkinson, mat. inst. maker till 1677, but never freed.

BEARD, Thomas (see Boad)

BEARD, William London
B.c. 1653, apr. Oct 1667 to James Ellis till 1674 but not freed.

BEASELEY (see under Beseley)

BEAUMONT, Philip London
B.c. 1675, apr. Aug 1689 to Withers Cheney till 1696, but not freed.

BEAUVAIS, Simon   **London**
Admitted to CC Apr 1690 as free Brother, a watchmaker. Prob. French
Huguenot. One of this name worked in Paris in 1675. In Aug 1694 he was
summoned before the CC regarding his aprs., of which, he admitted, he
had three (one bound in France, another bound for five years, and the
third his son – all aliens). In Jul 1695 he was fined for having alien aprs.,
but refused to pay. Still working in 1704 and prob. later. Work known –
watches. Also watches signed 'Simon and Paul Beauvais'. Maybe Paul
was his son.

BEAVIS, George (also Bavis)   **London**
Admitted to CC as free Brother Sep 1687, a chainmaker and a freeman of
the Loryners' Co. and of the City of London. Working till 1705 at least.
Work known – prob. not recognisable.

BECK(E), John   **London**
B.c. 1659, apr. Jun 1673 to Daniel Quare (thro' John White) till 1681.
Fred Sep 1681. Some records give Richard in error for John.

BECK, Nicholas   **London**
Apr. Sep 1660 to Thomas Webb, later transferred, perhaps on Webb's
death, to John North – freed Jul 1669. Took as aprs.: Apr 1673 **Edward
Millett** (who had been deserted by master George Kingsmill) – freed Nov
1680; Sep 1674 took over **John Waters** from John North – freed Jan
1682/83; Sep 1680 **Philip Browne,** later transferred to Cuthbert Lee; Jun
1686 **John Ring** later transferred to Thomas Martin. He died before
1694, when his widow received CC charity until she died in 1706. His son
Joseph was admitted by patrimony in Aug 1701. May have worked for
John North as journeyman.

BECK, Richard   **London**
Apr. May 1646 to John Selwood (thro' T. Alcock), transferred Jan
1651/52 following Selwood's death to Thomas Loomes his successor.
Freed May 1653 on the same day that Loomes was fined for allowing him
to sign his work prematurely. Took as aprs.: Jun 1653 **Thomas Browne;**
Jul 1653 **Anthony Freeman** transferred to widow Fletcher; May 1658
took over **John Tymms** from Nicholas Tomlins, who had died.
Additionally he acted as intermediary in binding two aprs. for Jeremy
Gregory and one for William Comfort. In 1656 he joined the rebels
against the CC administration. He is not heard of after 1658 and was

prob. removed or dead by 1662. Work known – lantern clock signed 'Richard Beck at the French Church' and a watch.

BECK, Richard London
Apr. 1673 – this is an error for John, *qv*.

BECKETT, Gilbert London
Baillie records a watch in 1678. He had a son, John, apr. in CC in 1698, Gilbert then being a freeman of the Leathersellers' Co. and of the City of London.

BECKMAN, Daniel (signed Beeckman) London
B.c. 1658, apr. Jul 1671 to Charles Bonner till 1679. Freed May 1680. Took as aprs.: Mar 1680/81 **Peter Lodwick** – free Jul 1689; May 1686 **William Dixon; John Dawson** (from John Archer) – free Sep 1688; Sep 1688 **Nathaniel Green** (thro' Thomas Hancorne) – free Sep 1695; Jun 1691 **Charles Bonner** junior (apparently he was too young and he was re-bound to him May 1693) – free Sep 1705; Dec 1699 **Thomas Whittingham** (son of William Whittingham of Middlewich, County Chester, surgeon). Additionally he bound an apr. for Jonathan Jones. Before 1684 he had married Mary, daughter of Thomas Taylor senior (of Essex House Gate?), *qv*. In Mar 1680-81 he with others did seize goods of J. Gazuett *qv*, a foreigner, whom he accused of signing his name on goods when not a freeman but a mere brother. In Jul 1694 he refused 'in very unbecoming language' to become a CC Steward, but the next year he agreed to hold the post. In fact he organised a rebellion by all the stewards, despite the Lord Mayor's order to refuse to treat anyone but the CC administration at the annual stewards' feast. In Jun 1695 he was paid 40 shillings for engraving the CC Coat of Arms on a new copper plate (prob. for the Feast invitation tickets!) His son Daniel is said to have been a CC freeman in 1726. Still alive in 1705, after which I have nothing further on him. Work known – watches. May well have worked principally as an engraver.

BECKMAN, John (also Beeckman) London
Freeman in CC Jul 1695 having been apr. of Samuel Lowndes, who was not a CC member nor a known clockmaker. In Jul 1695 he took as apr. **Robert Simkins** (son of Robert Simkins) – freed 1709. Still working in 1697 but not heard of thereafter. Work known – a bracket clock is recorded signed 'John Beckman in the Pall Mall' (the Lowndes family of clockmakers worked in Pall Mall Court).

BECKNER, Abraham   **London**
In Jun 1652 he was challenged by CC for practising without having
served an apprenticeship, but he must have satisfied them for he was
admitted as a Brother in Oct 1652. Took as aprs.: Nov 1653 **Richard
Houghton** (thro' Nicholas Payne); Dec 1654 was made to return the
unnamed apr. of widow Masterson; Jul 1660 took **Jeremy Johnson**
(thro' Nicholas Payne) – transferred (on his death in 1667?) to Ahasuerus
Fromanteel junior and freed 1668. Became CC Assistant 1660, Warden
from 1664, was still alive in Oct 1666 but had died by the following Jan
(1666-67), leaving his widow, Mary. By 1662 he was working in Pope's
Head Alley, Cornhill. Work known – watches.

BEDDELL, Joseph (see Biddle)

BEDFORD, Hilkiah (sometimes Helkiah)   **London**
Mat. inst. maker and a freeman of another Co., but was made a free
Brother in CC in Feb 1667-68, though he refused to take the oath. This
suggests he was a Quaker as they would not swear oaths. Took as aprs.:
Jun 1668 **Richard Abbot** (thro' B. Wolverston senior); Jun 1671 **James
Benbrick** (thro' Thomas Taylor); Jul 1672 **Anthony Billinghurst** (thro'
L. Wythe). In 1671/72 he worked in Fleet Street ('not far from Charles
Danley at the sign of the Grape'). He was still working in 1680 when his
name was put forward for steward, but is not heard of later. Work known
– obviously he was primarily a maker of measures and instruments – in
Apr 1668 he carried the Standard Measure on a CC search. However one
or two clocks are known by him including a bracket clock and a lantern
clock.

BEDFORD, Samuel   **London**
B.c. 1677, apr. Jul 1691 to Joseph Windmills till 1698 but not freed.
Baillie says he married in 1698, which I cannot confirm.

BEECKMAN (see Beckman)

BEEFORTH, John   **York**
Watchmaker, b. 1656, son of George Beeforth, Merchant Taylor. Free
there in 1680.

BEEFORTH, Robert   **York**
Locksmith and clocksmith. Appointed keeper of Minster clock 23 Jun
1658.

BEEG, Christianos   **London**
Watchmaker. Free Brother in CC Sep 1698. This was a man not a woman
– some authorities have Christian*a* in error. Believed died later in 1698.

BEGULAY, John   **Swanton Morley (Norfolk)**
Made church clock at Ludham in 1676. Nothing else known.

BELL, ----   **Cambusnethan (Scotland)**
Listed as 1700 by Baillie. Nothing else known.

BELL, Benjamin   **London**
B.c. 1636, apr. Aug 1649 to Thomas Claxton till 1657. Freed Apr 1657.
Took as aprs.: Apr 1659 **Joseph Astwood**; Jul 1667 **Thomas Warren;
James Ellis** (transferred from John Frowd) – freed Oct 1667; Feb
1670/71 **Robert Dent** – free Jul 1681; Jan 1671/72 **William May** – freed
Mar 1679; **Richard Clempson** (transferred from Jeremy Gregory) –
freed Jul 1673; 1674 **Thomas Broad** – freed Jan 1682/83; (in Dec 1678
Broad had been ill six months and away with friends in the country and
Bell was allowed to take over **Richard Gilkes** from William Hancorne
('who absenteth') – freed Jul 1686); Aug 1676 **William Slough** – free Aug
1687; Mar 1681/82 **Benjamin Brandon** (later transferred to Cuthbert
Lee); Dec 1682 **Ebenezer Harris;** Aug 1683 **John Sudell;** Mar 1685/86
Alexander Hewett; Jul 1688 **John Blackmore** (thro' or from Nicasius
Russell); Mar 1690 **William Bankes** (later transferred to John
Higginson, prob. on Bell's death). Additionally he bound two aprs. on
behalf of Jeremy Gregory. Appointed Assistant in CC 1670, Warden
from 1678, Master 1682. Last attended 1691, in which year he died,
prob. a bachelor. In his will, in which he is said to be of the parish of St.
Benet Fink, he mentions his house in Cornhill, where he prob. worked,
which he left to his brother, Samuel Bell. Another property at Little
Moorfields and one at the lower end of Broad Street, and his houses at
Hatton Garden he left to his brother John Bell, *qv*. He also mentions
John Withers, *qv*, Joseph Bell, *qv*, and the widow of Thomas Bell. He left
his tools to Thomas Bell, *qv* and to Alexander Hewett, *qv*. He released
Francis Stamper, *qv*, from a debt of £25.

An entry in the diary of the physicist Robert Hooke for 20 Mar 1673-74
reads: 'borrowed Bell's engine for cutting wheels. He told me of one he
had to perfect them, but would not show it.' If this Bell was a maker, then
it seems more than likely that it would be Benjamin Bell, and this is prob.
the earliest documented record of such a machine. The one 'to perfect

them' prob. refers to a separate machine for 'rounding up' the teeth after they had been cut.

Work known – one or two watches. Several notices regarding lost watches by him, both silver and gold, appear in the *London Gazette*.

BELL, Charles   **London**
B.c. 1633, apr. 1646 to William Almond (thro' Ralph Almond) – not freed.

BELL, Daniel   **London**
B.c. 1669, apr. Sep 1683 to John Pepys – not freed.

BELL, Henry   **Edinburgh**
Working in Cannongate in 1660. Work known – none, but see next entry.

BELL, Henry   **London**
Late 17th century bracket clock signed 'Henry Bell, Lothbury' recorded by Baillie. I cannot trace this maker, but see previous entry.

BELL, John   **London**
Mat. inst. maker, a freeman of another Co. but admitted to CC as a free Brother in Feb 1667/68. He was constantly in arrears with his quarterage payments till at least 1698. May have been brother of Benjamin Bell, *qv*, and mentioned in his 1691 will. Work known – brass sundial signed 'John Bell – London 1710'.

BELL, John   **London**
B.c. 1656, apr. 1671 to Robert Halstead till 1679 but not freed.

BELL, Joseph   **London**
B.c. 1670, apr. Jun 1684 to Robert Halstead, later transferred to John Trubshaw. Freed Nov 1691. Mentioned in will of Benjamin Bell *qv*, in 1691. Paid no CC quarterage after 1692. Gone or dead by 1697.

BELL, Matthew   **Edinburgh**
Apr. 1680 to Richard Mills, *qv*.

BELL, Thomas   **London**
B.c. 1677, apr. Jun 1691 to Samuel Mather (thro' John Norcott) till 1698, but not freed. Was left the work tools of Benjamin Bell in his will in 1691.

BELLARD, John (also Ballard)   **London**
Made a free Brother in CC Sep 1674. Took as aprs.: Sep 1674 **Thomas Prince** (thro' L. Wythe); Nov 1677 **Richard Richardson** (thro' S. Davis); Oct 1683 **Michael Parkhurst** (thro' D. Stevens); Sep 1688 **John Moncrief** (thro' A. Winch). In Jul 1689 he was said to be 'beyond the sea'. Work known – watch recorded.

BELLINGCAME, Christopher   **Bristol**
Repaired turret clock in 1557.

BELLINGER, Charles   **London**
B.c. 1672, apr. Jun 1687 to John Bellinger, effective from Sep 1686 as he had then been bound to a non-member, 'which indenture is now cancelled'. Not freed.

BELLINGER, John   **London**
B.c. 1663, apr. Aug 1677 to Robert Starr, mat. inst. maker and a freeman of the Stationers' Co. (bound thro' Nicholas Coxeter) till 1684. Freed Jul 1686. Took as aprs.: Sep 1686 **Charles Bellinger**; Dec 1695 **Edmond Biggs;** Jul 1704 **Stephen Coleman** (son of Stephen Coleman, Citizen and Draper); Mar 1706/07 his son, **John Bellinger** – free 1725; Oct 1715 **James Jones**. Still working 1715 and perhaps later.

BELLINGER, Richard   **London**
B.c. 1662, apr. Dec 1676 to Edward East till 1683, but not freed.

BELLOM(E) (slip for Bellune, *qv*)

BELLO(O)N (see under Bellune)

BELLUNE, Peter   **London**
(also misspelt as Bellon, Belloon and Bellome)
A Pierre Belon or Le Belon is recorded in Paris as clockmaker to the Queen from 1635 to 1649, which may be the same man. In 1635 and 1638 the CC fined him for non-payment of quarterage, though no actual date of his admittance seems to be recorded. Took as aprs.: May 1647 **Samuel Horne** (thro' J. Quash) – free May 1654; Feb 1649 **Samuel Griell;** Jan 1653 **Richard Nau** (thro' S. Bouquet) – free Apr 1661; Jul 1657 **Stephen Howlett;** Nov 1658 **Robert Mason** (thro' David Moody): May 1662 **Nicholas Barnard** (thro' T. Claxton); Jul 1664 **Edward Morris** (thro' R. Nau) – free Jan 1672/73. Believed married Jane, the daughter of Josias

Cuper, before 1659. By 1661 he is referred to as Captain Bellon, presumably a Royalist soldier. In 1662 he worked in Fleet Street as a boxmaker. Became CC Assistant 1656. Last attended in 1662. He was obviously of French extraction. In Sep 1673 CC paid a charity of 20 shillings to his widow/successor, 'he being lately deceased'.

BELSON, Thomas   London
Never actually admitted to CC but known to them. Took as aprs.: 1652 **William Thorowgood** (thro' W. Petty) – free Jan 1660; Nov 1654 **Thomas Waldegrave** (thro' W. Petty). Prob. dead by 1662-63.

BENBRICK, James   London
B.c. 1657, apr. June 1671 to Hilkiah Bedford (thro' T. Taylor) till 1678, but not freed.

BENBRIDGE, Thomas   London
B.c. 1655, apr. Aug 1669 to Robert Starr, mat. inst. maker (thro' T. Claxton) – till 1676. Freed May 1683. Prob. died c. 1698.

BENCHING, Edward (perhaps Beaching?)   London
B.c. 1645, apr. Sep 1659 to Robert Robinson till 1666, but not freed.

BENN, John   London
Listed by some as CC 1678 – error for Bennett, *qv*.

BENN, Thomas   London
B.c. 1646, apr. Mar 1660-61 to Benjamin Hill till 1667 – not freed.

BENNETT, John   Dublin
Watchmaker. Apr. to J. Popkins 1675. Brother in Dublin Goldsmiths' Co. 1694.

BENNETT, John   London
B.c. 1657, apr. Apr 1670 to Thomas Taylor of Holborn till 1678. Freed Jul 1678. Married as bachelor aged 30 of St. James Clerkenwell, a clockmaker, Nov 1687 to Margaret Blaxley of same parish, spinster, 30, at Allhallows in the Wall. Dead by 1697/98.

BENNETT, John   London
Made a free Brother, a clockmaker, Apr 1677. In Jul 1677 took as apr. **John Chatborne** (thro' S. Davis). Not heard of again.

BENNETT, John   **London**
In Apr 1685 one John Bennett was to be prosecuted for working when
not free in CC. Can hardly refer to either of the previous two men of this
name.

BENNETT, Mansell   **London**
Made a free Brother in CC as a clockmaker Jul 1688. Was a member till
1711 when he was called for steward but was 'out of towne'. Not heard of
later. Strangely, he seems to have taken no aprs. (thro' the CC anyway).
Work known – watches and longcase clocks signed 'Mansell Bennett,
Charing Cross' and 'Mansell Bennett at the Dial and Three Crowns,
Charing Cross'.

BENNETT, Matthew   **Dorchester**
1650 – according to Baillie, nothing else known.

BENNETT, Richard   **London**
B.c. 1657, apr. Jan 1671/72 to William Lloyd – till 1678. Not freed.

BENNETT, Samuel   **London**
B.c. 1660, apr. Sep 1673 to Edward Whitfield till 1681 but not freed.

BENNETT, Thomas   **London**
B.c. 1654, apr. 1667 to Henry Harper till 1675, but not freed. In May
1677 had a faulty watch confiscated by CC. Work known – none, but
obviously made watches.

BENNETT, Thomas   **Tiverton (Devon)**
Kept Blundell's school clock 1610.

BENNETT, William   **London**
B.c. 1663, apr. Apr 1677 to John Browne, mat. inst. maker (thro'
S. Davis) till 1684. Freed Sep 1687. Took as apr.: Oct 1687 **Edward
Bushel.** Dead or gone by 1697-98.

BENNETT, William   **London**
B.c. 1661, apr. Apr 1675 to Robert Lynch till 1682. Threatened with
prosecution in Apr 1685 for working when not a freeman of CC. Freed
Jul 1692. Took as aprs.: Jun 1694 **Richard Hutchinson** – freed Jul 1702;
Feb 1697/98 **George Arcutt;** Oct 1702 his son, **John Bennett** – freed Sep
1712 by patrimony; **Thomas Bale** transferred to Michael Bowles,

Haberdasher and freed Oct 1704; Sep 1707 his son, **Richard Bennett** – free Jul 1715; Apr 1709 **John Nash** (son of John Nash of Henley-on-Thames, Oxford, bargemaster) – free Oct 1717; Oct 1714 **William Bussy**; May 1718 **Francis Briggs.**

BENSON, John   London

B.c. 1639, apr. 1652 to James Starnell (thro' Richard Masterson) till 1660. In Robert Grinkin's will of 1660 he features as a witness and is mentioned as a 'loving friend'. By 1662 he was recognised by CC as an engraver but did not become a free Brother till Jan 1669/70, being already a freeman of the Weavers' Co. Took as aprs.: in Weavers' Co. Aug 1662 **Elisha Dodd** – free in CC Jan 1670/71; in CC Sep 1678 **Thomas Baldwin** (thro' Nicholas Coxeter) – free Sep 1685; Aug 1681 **Robert Thacke** (thro' E. Norris) – free Jan 1689/90; Jun 1685 **Thomas Munday** – free Nov 1692; Dec 1687 **John Berry** – free Apr 1697; Mar 1689-90 **Matthew Bunce** – freed Jul 1698; Sep 1692 (his son?) **Samuel Benson** – free Jan 1700/01; Mar 1693/94 **John Ives;** Nov 1698 **John Coppin** (son of Richard Coppin, late of Margate in the Isle of Thanet, mariner), later transferred to Samuel Stevens; Dec 1698 **John Charles** (son of Thomas Charles, labourer, deceased, late of St. Andrew Holborn parish); Apr 1700 **Richard Peckover** (son of John Peckover, Citizen and Carpenter of London). His wife, Martha, died Nov 1690 – buried St. Albans Wood Street. He was buried there 20 Dec 1700. Daughter Hannah died 1707-08, a spinster. Daughter, Martha, married in 1695 John Berry, *qv*. Work known – longcase clock c. 1690 signed 'Johannes Benson – Londini'. Britten records one dated 1709 which seems unlikely. No doubt worked mostly as an engraver.

BENSON, Samuel   London

Apr. Sep 1692 to John Benson, who was prob. his father. Free Jan 1700-01. Married Jan 1701/02 at St. Albans Wood Street to Sarah Walmsley. Issue: 1702 Mary, died 1703; 1703 Samuel; 1705 George; 1706 Ann; 1714 Marcey. Work known – watch recorded c. 1730(?).

BERAUD, Henry (also Berraud and Barraud)   London

Never actually admitted to CC but accepted by them. In 1633 he presented his apr. through CC and in 1635 he made a gift to them. Prob. dead before 1662/63. Work known – a watch recorded.

BERAUD, James   London

In Apr 1632 he became journeyman to John Charlton (not apr. as Baillie says). Never actually admitted into CC but known to them and tolerated by them without membership. Prob. dead by 1662-63.

BERAUD, Stephen London
Listed as 1670 CC by some authorities. I cannot trace such a person.

BERAULT, John London
B.c. 1677, apr. Nov 1691 to Thomas Jones till 1698, but not freed.

BERAU, widow (also Beraw) London
Received regular CC charities from Apr 1671 to Apr 1681 'as her husband did give the CC a silver spoon'. Maybe widow of John Berrow or maybe even Henry Beraud?

BERFORD (see Barford)

BERJON, John London
Watch and chain maker. Free Brother in CC Apr 1685.

BERKELEY, Thomas London
B.c. 1663, apr. Nov 1676 to William Dobson (thro' S. Davis) till 1684, but not freed.

BERNARD, Nicholas Paris
Late 17th century watches known. Maybe Nicholas Barnard, *qv.*

BERRINGTON, John London
B.c. 1667, apr. Jul 1681 to Henry Hester till 1688 but not freed.

BERRINGTON, Urian London
(sometimes Barrington, also Urin and Vrin)
B.c. 1663, apr. Sep 1677 to Nathan Delander till 1684. Freed Dec 1684. Signed Berrington. Took as aprs.: Jul 1691 **Timothy Bristow;** Dec 1695 **Philip Gyfford;** Apr 1700 **George Pickering** (son of Thomas Pickering of Hunton (also Huntington), Kent, Gent.); Aug 1701 **John Love** (taken over from William Finch) – free May 1707; Apr 1705 his son, **Urian Berrington;** Jul 1708 **Solomon Gibbs** – free May 1716. In 1711 he received CC charity 'being in necessity', and again in 1716, after which I have no record of him.

BERRISFORD, Edward   **London**
B.c. 1650, apr. Apr 1663 to Benjamin Wolverston till 1671, but not freed.

BERROW, John (see also Berau?)   **London**
B.c. 1661, apr. Jun 1675 to John Buckenhill, watchmaker, till 1682, but not freed.

BERRY, Francis   **Hitchin (Hertfordshire)**
Repaired clocks at Quixwood, nr. Baldock in 1692. Longcase and lantern clocks recorded c. 1700 – c. 1710, signed 'Fran: Berry – Hitchin'.

BERRY, John   **London**
B.c. 1660, apr. Dec 1674 to Richard Pepys till 1681. Freed Jul 1688. Believed alive till c. 1707, but very hard to distinguish him from next men, *qv*. One of them was a goldsmith.

BERRY, John   **London**
B.c. 1670, apr. Aug 1684 to John Ebsworth till 1691. Free Apr 1692. Believed still in Ebsworth's employ till at least 1703. Later (by 1705) at the Dial in St. Clement's Lane, Lombard Street, where he was still in 1748 along with his son, John junior. Believed married Oct 1696 Elizabeth Mallett. Took as aprs.: Apr 1697 **Samuel Vosmore**; Oct 1698 **John Wragg**; Sep 1699 **William Tripet** – free 1706; May 1703 **John Allen** (son of Thomas Allen, late of Canterbury, butcher, deceased) – free Apr 1720; Sep 1704 **John Walford** (son of Uriah Walford of parish of St. Giles without Cripplegate, Middlesex, taylor) – free Jun 1717; Dec 1709 **John Paradice** – free Mar 1718/19. Became Assistant 1717, Warden from 1720, Master 1723. Work known – longcase clocks, bracket clocks and watches.

BERRY, John   **London**
B.c. 1674, apr. Dec 1687 to John Benson, engraver, till 1695. Freed Apr 1697. Was himself an engraver. Married Oct 1695 Martha daughter of John Benson, and had issue born 1697 Elizabeth (died 1701); 1698 John, 1699 Henry. Difficult to know which J.B. took all the aprs. but this one certainly took: **Samuel Bridges** (from Joseph Hechstetter) – freed Aug 1704. Died 1708. In Sep 1711 his widow was excused his arrears but had to pay quarterage for the period since his death. Work known – prob. not identifiable.

BERRY, Samuel   **London**
B.c. 1616, apr. Mar 1631 to Thomas Howse, 'brown baker' till 1639, but not freed. Although Howse was a watchmaker, he was a member of the Bakers Co.

BERSON, John Cola   **London**
In 1677 he was an apr. of Abraham Thomeguez, clockmaker, and agreed to become a Brother in CC when his service ended – but he did not.

BERTRAM, William (see Bartram, William)   **London**

BESELEY, Nathaniel (also Baseley, etc.)   **London**
B.c. 1672, apr. Mar 1686/87 to Henry Hammond, later transferred to John Willoughby till 1693. Freed Mar 1694/95. Working till at least 1704. Took as aprs.: Apr 1696 **William Toothaker** – free Oct 1703; Jun 1698 **James Desesar** – free Apr 1707.

BESELEY, Thomas (also Baseley and Beasley, etc.) **London**
B.c. 1662, apr. Dec 1676 to Isaac Daniel, watch case maker (thro' J. Bayley) till 1683. Freed Jan 1683-84, though master had died by 1682. Married as bachelor, 22, watch case maker of St. Bride's parish, Jan 1684 to Mrs. Elizabeth Griffith, widow, 30, at St. Martin's Outwich. Took as aprs.: Jan 1685-86 **William Warburton** – freed Nov 1693; Feb 1692/93 **Samuel Sedgwick**; Sep 1696 **Abel Jarvis** – free Jul 1704; Jan 1704/05 **Richard Luck** (son of Henry Luck of Bishop Oakland (Aukland), Co. Durham, apothecary); Nov 1711 **Charles Bacon,** later transferred to Abel Jarvis. Still alive in 1711 but may have died before 1719. Work known – longcase clock signed 'Thomas Beasley – London'.

BESHOLT (error for Beshott, *qv*)

BESHOTT, Peter   **London**
Alien in 1622 at St. Olave's in Hart Street.

BESTWICK, Henry   **London**
B.c. 1664, son of Richard Bestwick, *qv*, and Katherine. Apr. Jan 1678/79 to Thomas Stead (thro' S. Davis) till 1685. Free Sep 1686 having been transferred to his mother (Stead may have died before 1686). Believed died c. 1697/98. Widow Bestwick who received CC charity in 1714-15 was prob. his widow.

BESTWICK, Katherine
Widow of Richard, *qv*.

BESTWICK, Richard   London
A freeman of the Cutlers' Co. but a springmaker. Working in Shoe Lane by 1662 and known to CC but never officially admitted into the Co. Took as apr. Jun 1666 **Erasmus Micklewright** (thro' L. Wythe) – freed Aug 1673. By Mar 1672/73 he had died and his widow, Katherine, then took: **John Dearmer** (thro' H. Hester) – free 1680; Jun 1674 **Rowland Thompson** (thro' L. Wythe); Sep 1678 her son, **Henry Bestwick** (thro' S. Davis) – free Sep 1686. Work known – none, but prob. not identifiable.

BETTS, Job   London
No record of his official entry into CC. Took as aprs.: Nov 1653 **Francis Bicknell** (thro' N. Payne) – freed Jun 1665; Nov 1653 **Francis Witness** (thro' N. Payne); Jan 1653/54 **Nathaniel Barrow** (thro' N. Payne) – free Jan 1660; Oct 1655 **John Kidd** (thro' N. Payne); Jan 1656-57 **William Kennon** (thro' J. Bayes) – free Mar 1674/75; Nov 1664 **Roger Atlee** (thro' R. Peirce); Oct 1675 **Samuel Betts** (thro' S. Davis). In 1656 joined rebels against CC administration. In 1662 he is erroneously listed as Joseph Betts. Work known – none, but his loss of a gold watch is recorded in the *London Gazette*.

BETTS, Joseph   London
1662 – error for Job Betts, *qv*.

BETTS, Samuel   London
No records of his official entry into CC. Took as aprs.: Oct 1648 **James Lello** (thro' T. Alcock) – free Apr 1656; Sep 1656 **Peter Walker** (thro' N. Payne) – freed Oct 1663. A watch by 'Mr. Betts in Lumbard Street' lost in 1664 may have been by Samuel or Job. In 1675 he was succ. by Markwick 'at the back of Royal Exchange' and Betts' old stock of watches was to be sold off. He died about 1673/74. Both Samuel and Job seem to have had close connections with Nicholas Payne and neither seem to have been official members of the CC.

BETTS, Samuel   London
B.c. 1661, apr. Oct 1675 to Job Betts (thro' S. Davis) till 1682 but not freed. Work known – watches and bracket clocks may be by him or the earlier Samuel. Some authorities give CC 1682 – but I cannot trace this.

BEVAN, ----   **London**
Baillie has CC, died before 1680. This is an error for Berau (widow), *qv*.

BEVERLEY, James   **London**
B.c. 1670, apr. Jun 1684 to Robert Doore till 1691 but not freed. Work known – watches and bracket clocks signed 'Ja. Beverley – London'.

BEZAR(D), Stephen (see also Beraud)   **London**
Free Brother in CC Jan 1647/48. Paid his quarterage till at least 1673. Steward 1670.

BICKERSTAFFE, William   **Longton**
Son of Robert Bickerstaffe, also of Longton, yeoman. Apr. 1663 to Thomas Wright of Chester, clockmaker.

BICKNELL, Francis   **London**
Apr. Nov 1653 to Job Betts (thro' N. Payne). Free Jun 1665. Took as aprs.: Jun 1665 **Richard Randell; Ellis Langford** (transferred from Gowen Langford) later passed over to Morgan Cave; took over **George Tipping** on death of Samuel Knibb (post-Jan 1665) – freed Jun 1674.

BIDDLE, Joseph (sometimes Beddell)   **London**
B.c. 1662, apr. Aug 1676 to Cuthbert Lee till 1683. Free Apr 1684. Took as aprs.: Mar 1686/87 **Noe Hurt** – free Dec 1695; Nov 1694 **Thomas Browne** – free Jul 1703. Paid quarterage till late 1704. In Aug 1705 he was excused Assistantship for a small fine as he was 'indisposed' and 'retiring in to the country'.

BIDDLECOMBE, John   **Sturton Caundle (Dorset)**
30-hour longcase clock recorded dated 1705. Nothing else known.

BIGG, Benjamin   **London**
B.c. 1664, apr. Feb 1678/79 to Robert Cooke, mat. inst. maker (thro' S. Davis).

BILBIE, Thomas   **Chew Stoke (Somerset)**
Clockmaker (and bellfounder?) working 1660.

BILCLIFFE, John   **York**
Clocksmith. Free 1617. Chamberlain 1626-27. Believed still alive in 1639 when son, John, junior, freed, *qv*.

BILCLIFFE, John junior   **York**
Watchmaker, son of John, senior. Free 1639.

BILCLIFFE, Robert   **York**
Watchmaker. Free 1627. Believed married 1630 Elizabeth Ellis. Died 1641.

BILCLIFFE, Robert junior   **York**
Clockmaker. Son of Robert Bilcliffe senior. Free 1653. *cf* Baycliffe.

BILLE, John (sometimes Billey, signed Jean)   **London**
Presumably of French extraction. Watchmaker. In Feb 1686/87 promised to become a Brother in CC, which he did in Jul. In Sep 1699 he was guilty of some misdemeanour but was to be treated gently on account of his poverty.

BILLIARD, Lewis (sometimes Balearde)   **London**
A Huguenot, b. in Gascony. In 1540 was servant (journeyman) to Alan Bawdyson, clockmaker to Edward VI at Strande parish, Westminster. Then in St. Clement Danes parish till 1568 as a crossbow-maker. In 1561 made clock for Rye church at a cost of £30.

BILLINGE, John   **Wigan**
Watchmaker. Free 1671.

BILLINGES, John   **London**
Free Brother in CC Jan 1637-38.

BILLINGHURST, Anthony   **London**
B.c. 1658, apr. Jul 1672 to Hilkiah Bedford (thro' L. Wythe) till 1679 but not freed.

BILLINGHURST, William   **London**
B.c. 1655, apr. Nov 1668 to Thomas Fenn till 1676 but not freed.

BILLINGTON, Joseph   **Chester**
Clockmaker. Free 1669/70.

BILLOP, William   **London**
B.c. 1667, apr. 1681 to Henry Merryman till 1688. Free Sep 1688. Prob.

died or left soon after. Listed in CC quarterage book in 1698 but had paid no quarterage for last ten years. Work known – longcase clock.

BILSB(O)ROUGH, William   Gargrave? (Yorkshire)
Repaired Long Preston church clock 1707-09. Married at Burnsall 1727 (W.B. of Gargrave, clockmaker and architect) to Francis Lund of Kirkby Malham. At least two clockmakers in succession bore this name. Work known – marquetry longcase signed 'William Bilsbrough fecit'.

BINDLEY, Joseph (see also Bingley)   **London**
B.c. 1660, apr. Sep 1674 to Richard Prince ('when R.P. has taken up his freedom') (thro' L. Wythe) till 1681, but not freed.

BINGHAM, Walter   **Dublin**
Apr. 1673 to Edward Ashton. Free as clockmaker/goldsmith 1680. Had as aprs.: 1681 **Thomas Meeking**; 1693 **Edward Fitzgerald**. Warden 1694/97, Master 1700-01, 1704 and 1720. Died 1727. Work known – walnut bracket clock signed 'Bingham – Dublin'.

BINGLEY, Giles   **London**
B.c. 1678, apr. Jun 1692 to Edward Eyston till 1699, but not freed.

BINGLEY, John   **London**
Advertised in 1696 for a watchmaker. (See Bindley?).

BINNS, Robert   **Halifax**
Clockmaker. Buried there 1 Dec 1729. Work known – longcase clock c. 1710 signed 'Robert Binns in Halifax fecit'.

BIRCH, Thomas senior   **London**
B.c. 1636, apr. Feb 1649 to Thomas Mills (thro' N. Coxeter) till 1657. Freed Apr 1658. Took as aprs.: Jan 1663/64 **William Nash**; Apr 1669 **Benjamin Smith**; Dec 1674 **Ruth Smith** (bound to his wife, Jane, to learn her trade, which was unspecified); May 1682 **James Christmas**; Nov 1684 **Richard Westwood** – free Jan 1691/92. Seems to have been a poor man. In Feb 1665/66 he was given charity of five shillings by CC. He was excused Stewardship in 1673 and again in 1686 on grounds of poverty. Prob. died c. 1696/97. Work known – lantern clocks signed 'Thomas Birch in the longe walke Neere Christ Church, Londini, fecit' prob. by him though could be by his son.

BIRCH, Thomas junior   **London**
B.c. 1661, apr. Aug 1675 to Samuel Clyatt till 1682 – free Jan 1682/83.
Difficult to distinguish him from Thomas senior (they were prob. father
and son). Took as aprs.: Oct 1687 **Benjamin Jacob** (thro' W. Fuller) –
free Sep 1706; Nov 1691 **Lewis Holland** – free Dec 1698; Dec 1694
Robert Halhead; Dec 1698 **Jacob Thomas** (son of David Thomas of
parish of Allhallows in the Wall, London, joiner). Also bound an apr. for
Richard Medhurst of Croydon. Received CC charity from 1711-16, after
which he is not heard of again. Had son, Samuel, who was given CC grant
towards apprenticeship with Moses Meigh in Apr 1715. Work known –
none, but see Thomas Birch senior.

BIRCHALL, John   **Liverpool**
Watchmaker. Died 1686.

BIRCHMORE, William   **London**
Ironmonger without Newgate. Had faulty rulers confiscated by CC in
1672.

BIRD, Edward   **London**
One or two longcase clocks are recorded by him, usually signed Edward
Bird Londini fecit' c. 1700-c. 1710. (Baillie has 1684 apparently in error
for Luke Bird, *qv*). A clock by Thomas Grimes bears Bird's nameplate on
the dial. No maker of this name seems to have been known to CC.

BIRD, John   **Belfast**
Clockmaker, working 1654-67. Free there in 1667. Made a coffin clock
in 1664. Work known (today) – none.

BIRD, Luke   **London**
B.c. 1662, apr. Sep 1675 to James Delaunder (thro' Jeremiah Johnson)
till 1683. Free Sep 1683. Took as aprs.: Jul 1684 **David Jackson** (thro'
W. Simcox); Jun 1687 **John Ewer; John Higgs** (transferred from John
Fort) – freed Nov 1688. Working till at least 1701 (at Old Bailey?).

BIRD, Michael senior   **London/Oxford**
B.c. 1634, son of John Bird, mercer, of Oxford. Apr. Oct 1648 to
Edmund Gilpin, watchmaker, in CC (thro' Thomas Taylor) till 1654, but
not freed there. Freed at Oxford 1654. Took as aprs. there: 1656 **Robert
Heyten; 1664 Anthony Hodges** – freed 1672; 1668 **John Harris;** 1672

99

his son, **Michael Bird**; 1674 **Richard Saunders**; 1676 **Wright Lane**; 1678 his son, **Nathaniel Bird**; 1682 his son, **Wright Bird**; 1688 **Greenaway Curtice**. Worked there till his death in 1689, leaving widow, Sarah, and sons, *qv*. Work known – watches, longcase clocks, bracket clocks and also token coins issued at Oxford in 1688. Work signed 'Michael Bird – Oxon'.

BIRD, Michael junior   **Oxford/London**
B.c. 1658, son of Michael Bird senior of Oxford, *qv*. Apr. to father in 1672 till 1679. Admitted into CC as Brother Mar 1682-83. Was administrator to father's estate in 1690. In 1685 he was to be prosecuted for not binding aprs. through CC. Jan 1686/87 he 'hath taken his freedom of the City of London by Redemption and has committed himself to the Blacksmiths' Company' and having thus changed companies he should be fined £20. In Jun 1687 he submitted to their jurisdiction and agreed to bind his apr. **Charles Mason** thro' CC, whom he had formerly bound through the Blacksmiths' Co. He took over apr. **Samuel Mather** from ---- Smith of the Haberdashers' Co. – freed in CC Jun 1691. Not heard of again till 1701, when he was warned to pay his quarterage arrears lest he be prosecuted. In Jan 1703-04 he claimed to have been out of the country during part of the period and refused to pay. Not heard of again after that. Work known – bracket clock signed 'Michael Bird – London'.

BIRD, Nathaniel   **London**
Son of Michael Bird, senior, of Oxford. Apr. to father there 1678 till 1685.In Jan 1692/93 he took **Thomas Cawcutt** apr. in CC (thro' J. Ebsworth), although Bird was himself not free of the CC. Work known – longcase clock.

BIRD, William   **London**
B.c. 1653, apr. Jan 1667/68 to Henry Crump, a clockmaker but free of the Vintners' Co. (thro' L. Wythe) till 1674 but not freed in CC.

BIRD, Wright   **Oxford**
Son of Michael Bird senior, apr. 1682 to father till 1689, but apprenticeship cancelled Jun 1686. Perhaps because he died?

BIRDWHISSELL
(see under Birdwhistle).

BIRDWHISTLE, Francis   **London**
B.c. 1661, apr. Dec 1675 to Edward Jackson till 1682. Freed Sep 1687.
In Jul 1693 his brother, Thomas, was made a free Brother of CC, having
served him for seven years, though never officially bound. Alive 1693 but
dead by 1697/98.

BIRDWHISTLE, Isaac (signed Birdwhissell)   **London**
B.c. 1668, apr. May 1682 to Thomas Jenkins till 1689. Free Aug 1692.
Still working 1702. Work known – watch.

BIRDWHISTLE, James   **London**
Name written in CC records as James, but this is an obvious error for
Isaac.

BIRDWHISTLE, Thomas   **London**
Brother of Francis. Made a free Brother in CC 1693 having served
Francis for seven years, though never officially bound to him. Working
till late in 1700 at least. Took as aprs.: 1694 **William Lovett** – free Mar
1702/03; Aug 1700 **Solomon Lacy** (son of Solomon Lacy of parish of St.
John Wapping, Middlesex, mariner) – parish of St. Peter Poor in Bread
Street erased from records.

BIRLEY, John   **Sheffield (Yorkshire)**
Watches recorded made c.1690 – c.1705. Nothing known but see John
Brierley.

BISHOP, John   **Maidstone (Kent)**
Lantern clock known, c. 1650.

BISSE, Edward (sometimes Bysse)   **London**
Unlikely to have been working before Mar 1625 when he was made a
freeman of the City of London by redemption thro' the Coopers' Co.
(presented by Robert Tompson, founder (= Founders' Co.)). In Oct
1632 he was 'forbidden the trade' by CC, but in Nov he was admitted as a
free Brother. In 1637 he took as apr. **Thomas Hamlyn** (thro' Thomas
Dawson). Work known – a table clock and three or four watches, signed
'Edward Bisse fecit'.

BLACKFORD, Anthony   **Exhill (Exhall?) (Warwickshire)**
Watchmaker, free at Warwick 1669.

BLACKMORE, John   **London/Exeter (Devon)**
B.c. 1674, apr. Jul 1688 to Benjamin Bell (thro' N. Russell) till 1695 but
not freed. Bell had died in 1691, however. A watchmaker of this name
was made a freeman at Exeter in Feb 1698-99 (being the son of John
Blackmore, apothecary) and must surely be the same person. By Mar
1701/02 the Exeter maker had absconded leaving his apr. destitute.

BLACKWELL, Thomas   **London**
Recorded as CC 1654 by some authorities – error for Bakewell, *qv*.

BLICK, ----   **London**
Cane-seller, 'over against ye Grayhound Taverne nr. Charing Cross'.
Paid CC search fee 1671-72.

BLISS, Ambrose   **Canterbury/London**
A watchmaker of this name was made a freeman of Canterbury in 1647 by
redemption. In Jan 1653/54 he was made a free Brother in CC. Took as
aprs.: Jul 1654 **John Cornish** (thro' H. Erbury); Jan 1655/56 **Judah
Cann**; Mar 1657 **David Lloyd** (thro' J. Cooke) – freed Jan 1677/78. In
1656 he supported the CC administration against the rebellious
members. In Nov 1661 he was to appear before the Lord Mayor
concerning irregularities in binding aprs. In 1662 he worked in Cornhill.

BLOCK, Francis   **London**
B.c. 1675, apr. Jul 1689 to John Bellinger till 1696 but not freed.

BLOWERS, Isaac senior   **Beccles (Suffolk)**
B. 1660, son of Edward Blowers. Married c. 1690 Alice X. Issue b. 1693
Isaac; 1695 Benjamin; 1701 Edward – of the three Isaac and Edward
followed his trade. Believed to have made Beccles church clock c. 1690
and made Lowestoft Town Hall clock in 1698 at a cost of £20. Died
11 Aug 1719. Succ. by son Isaac to whom he left his work tools in his will,
where he describes himself as a locksmith. Work known – turret clocks,
longcase and lantern clocks.

BLUNDELL, John   **London/Horley (Oxfordshire)**
B.c. 1665, apr. Dec 1678 to George Nau, watch case maker, till 1686 but
not freed. One of this name worked at Horley, Oxfordshire, by 1700,
who may be the same man. Work known – longcase and bracket clocks
known by the Londoner. 30-hour longcase known signed 'Jno. Blundell
– Horly, 1700'.

BLUNDELL, Richard   **London**
In Apr 1682 he was the servant (journeyman?) of George Nau, watch case maker, and was threatened with prosecution by CC unless he took up his freedom. Became a free Brother in Jul 1682. Took as aprs.: Jan 1684-85 **Edward Metcalfe** (thro' N. Russell); Jan 1692-93 **William Harrison** (thro' F. Raynsford) – free Nov 1700; Jun 1696 **Henry Rawlins** – free Sep 1706; Sep 1699 **Robert Higgs** (son of Peter Higgs of Waddleton*, Oxfordshire, taylor) – free Sep 1714; Mar 1706/07 **William Blundell** – free Jul 1716; Mar 1707/08 **Robert Sly** – free Aug 1720; Oct 1717 **Jonathan Mingo**. Not heard of after 1717.

(*Waddleton is not traceable and may be Wardington, which is very close to Horley and suggests a connection c. 1699-1700 with John Blundell.)

BLUNT, Morris   **London**
Not a member of CC but known to them. In Aug 1641 took apr. **Richard Coulton** (thro' O. Durant) in CC. Prob. dead by 1662/63. Work known – none (but Baillie records a watch lost pre-1744 signed Blunt – London, and no other Blunt is recorded this early).

BOAD, Thomas   **London**
(sometimes erroneously recorded as Beard, but signed clearly Boad) B.c. 1670, apr. Nov 1684 to Robert Nemes, a founder and free of the Founders' Co. till 1691. Free Apr 1692. Took as aprs.: Jul 1693 **James Cooper**; Nov 1694 **Peter Skinner**. Working till 1704 but not heard of later. Work known – none, but may have been a founder and work would be unrecognisable.

BOAK, Samuel   **London**
Recorded by Britten at the Golden Spread Eagle without Aldgate, 1692. I cannot trace him.

BODHAM, Stephen   **London**
B.c. 1667, apr. Sep 1680 to Edward Enys till 1688 but not free.

BODDILY, Elizabeth   **London**
Apr. Jun 1683 to Margaret Gardner (prob. widow of John, qv) thro' L. Wythe. Free Jun 1692. Listed in quarterage book in 1698 but had not paid for three years. Trade not known, maybe not to do with clocks.

BOGUET, F.   London
Recorded by Britten as c. 1640. Prob. error for S. Bouquet.

BOLLAND, John (sometimes Bollard)   Halifax
Repaired church clock 1664-91.

BOND, Thomas   London
B.c. 1671, apr. Apr 1685 to Wither Cheney till 1692, but not freed.

BONNER, Charles   London
Apr. Dec 1650 to Nicholas Parke (thro' J. Cooke) later transferred to
Parke's widow. Freed Mar 1659. Believed to have been mainly an
engraver. In 1662 he worked in Chancery Lane. Took as aprs.: **John
Lucie** (taken over from N. Parke, prob. after Parke's death) – freed Oct
1663; Aug 1662 **George Dean** – free Jul 1671; Jul 1668 **Henry Jones;** Jul
1671 **Daniel Beckman** – free May 1680; Jul 1674 **Richard George** – free
Nov 1681; Aug 1678 **Roger Burton.** Also bound an apr. for Isaac Ploveir,
two for George Hambleton, two for Robert Webster (including his own
son, Jasper Bonner apr. 1681), one for A. Warfield, and four for Edward
Clough, for whom he may have worked at one time. He died 1681/82.
His widow received occasional CC charities till 1694. Work known –
watches and at least one longcase clock.

BONNER, Charles junior   London
May well have been son of Charles senior. Apr. Jun 1691, but may have
been under age for he was bound to him again in May 1693 – till 1698.
Free Sep 1705. Took as aprs.: Jun 1715 **Thomas Gilbert;** Oct 1717
Hugh Egan.

BONNER, Jasper   London
B.c. 1667, son of Charles Bonner senior, apr. Jun 1681 to Robert
Webster (thro' his father) till 1688, but not freed.

BOOKER, Richard   London
Listed by some authorities as CC 1694-99. Error for Richard Rooker, *qv.*

BOOLE, Jonathan   London
B.c. 1662, apr. Apr 1676 to Sarah, widow of Nicholas Payne, till 1683 –
not freed.

BOONE, Edward London
B.c. 1668, apr. Jul 1681 to Robert Dent, later transferred to Thomas Tompion till 1689. Freed Jul 1691. Took as apr. May 1693 **Thomas Mullinex.** Working till 1697, but prob. not long after. Work known – watch.

BOORD, John Wells (Somerset)
Repaired TC 1675-6.

BOOTH, Edward (see Barlow, Edward)

BOOTH, Joshua Manchester
Baillie lists him as c. 1700.

BORGIN, Henry (also Burgin) London
'Without Bishopsgate'. Token coin bearing a clock dial and his name c. 1677. May not be a clockmaker.

BOSCH, Ulrich London
A stranger (foreigner), admitted to CC as a free Brother and a free Journeyman Jul 1652. Born in the city of Cullen (Cologne). Not known who he worked for. Work prob. would not bear his name.

BOTELER, Henry Exeter
Repaired cathedral clock 1405-29.

BOULANGER, David London
B.c. 1677, apr. Dec 1691 to William Bartram till 1698 but not freed.

BOULTON, Job London
'At the Bolt & Tunn, Lombard Street'. Had a gold and a silver watch and other items stolen in 1683. Not a known maker but other makers are known to have worked at the Bolt & Tunn and Boulton is obviously derived from this. Maybe an invented name(?) James Tunn may be linked, and also George Graham worked at one time opposite the Bolt & Tunn, and James Tunn clocks are said to be from the Graham workshop. There is a mystery here that has not yet been solved.

BOUQUET, David senior London
(sometimes written as Bowkett or Bowker)
A Frenchman. Supposed member of Blacksmiths' Co. In 1622 listed

105

as an alien journeyman at Mr. Sampson's house in Blackfriars with two aprs. (No maker named Sampson is known unless this is a slip for Sampson Shelton?). He apparently worked in Blackfriars till 1662. In Oct 1632 he was admitted to CC as a free Brother. In early 1633 he was in France ('as Mr. Paul Lowell states') but was back by Oct 1633. Had Isaac Plovier as journeyman, who was made a Brother in Dec 1637. Took as aprs.: Apr 1637 **William Fawcett** (thro' T. Dawson); May 1641 his son, **Solomon Bouquet** (thro' O. Durant) – freed Dec 1651; Nov 1646 **Jacob Harris** (thro' J. Quash); Aug 1648 **Abraham Herbert**; Jun 1657 **Hugh Roberts** (thro' S. Bouquet) – free June 1664. In Apr 1653 took **James Fonnereau** as journeyman (whilst he was in England) and in Oct 1655 took **Guillaume Grebaunal** as journeyman. Also he bound an apr. for Thomas Weekes. Was CC Assistant 1634-65, in which year he is said to have died. Work known – lantern clocks, but mainly watches, some signed 'D. Bouquett, London', some 'David Bouquet à Londres'.

BOUQUET, David junior   **London**
B.c. 1638, son of David senior. Apr. 1652 to Solomon Bouquet (his brother) till 1659 but not freed.

BOUQUET, Dorcas   **London**
Widow of Solomon Bouquet senior. Took as aprs.: Apr 1681 **William Verback**; Jun 1686 **Thomas Knight**. Also from 1676 bound several aprs. for other masters, mostly jewellers, namely for D. Megrett, John Martins, N. Mobert and her son, Solomon Bouquet (junior). Received charities from CC from 1690 to 1694 and usually got more than other widow pensioners.

BOUQUET, Hector   **London**
B.c. 1642 (prob. son of David Bouquet) apr. Oct 1656 thro' Solomon Bouquet to Isaac Mebert or Mobert, diamond-cutter till 1663, but not freed. Prob. worked in jewellery trade.

BOUQUET, Solomon senior   **London**
Son of David Bouquet, apr. May 1641 to father (thro' O. Durant) – freed Dec 1651. Took as aprs.: Apr 1652 brother **David Bouquet**; May 1671 **Thomas Spencer** – free Nov 1685; Mar 1671/72 **John Sowter** – free June 1683. Also bound aprs. for D. Bouquet, Peter Bellune, Isaac Roumyeu, Isaac Mebert (all French and mostly with jewellery trade connections). Not heard of during period 1656-70 and may have been abroad then. Made CC Assistant 1674 but never seems to have attended. May have

died soon after 1674 and certainly before Apr 1676, after which his widow, Dorcas *qv*, continued to pay his quarterage.

BOUQUET, Solomon junior   **London**
Son of Solomon senior. Already serving in Jan 1675-76 as apr. of Samuel Drossate having been bound thro' the Shipwrights' Co., but was rebound to him thro' CC. Freed Mar 1682-83 by patrimony. Took as aprs.: Dec 1683 **George Allatt** – later transferred to Thomas Tompion; Apr 1687 **Ebenezer Fisher** (thro' N. Russell); Thomas Walkden (thro' Dorcas Bouquet); Jul 1695 **Daniel Tookie;** Dec 1697 **John Somers;** May 1700 **Peter Laurent** ('son of Moses Laurent, late of Issondun in province of Berry, France, Gent., deceased and made a denizen Mar 1699/1700'). In Aug 1685 as a watchmaker of Hackney, Middlesex, aged 26, bachelor, he was married to Deborah Graves of St. Giles Cripplegate, spinster, aged 19 – at St. Mary Savoy, Middlesex. Work known – a watch.

BOWDINGIS, Adrian (also Bowdowingis)   **Edinborough**
Working 1595.

BOWEN, Francis   **London**
B.c. 1633, apr. Feb 1647 to William Bowyer (thro' T. Alcock) till 1654. Free Apr 1655. Took as apr. Dec 1655 **Edward Stanton** – free Jan 1662. In 1656 he rebelled with others against CC administration. Not heard of after 1662. Prob. successor to Bowyer in Leadenhall Street, Work known – lantern clocks, signed 'Francis Bowen in Leaden Hall Streete, Londini'.

BOWEN, John   **London**
B.c. 1663, son of Richard Bowen senior. Apr. Jan 1677-78 to his widowed mother, Mary, till 1684 but not freed until Jul 1710 when 'upon his earnest request being poor was admitted gratis'. Work known – a watch is recorded and a lantern clock.

BOWEN, Mary   **London**
Widow of Richard Bowen senior, carrying on after his death. In Jan 1677/78 she took her son, **John,** as apr. – not freed till Jul 1710. In Jan 1684/85 she bound her son **Thomas** apr. for Henry Bridgen. She received CC charity from 1683 to 1687 after which she is not heard of again.

BOWEN, Richard senior   **London**
B.c. 1636, apr. Sep 1650 to Robert Smith (thro' N. Payne) till 1657.
Freed Oct 1657. Took as aprs.: Feb 1659/60 **Richard Warren** – free May
1668; Dec 1660 he and wife, Mary, took **Sarah Tory**; Jan 1667/68 **Henry
Merryman** – free Feb 1674/75; **William Lloyd** (taken from T. Daniel) –
free Apr 1671; **Robert Doore** (taken from Edward Enys) – free Jul 1671;
Feb 1670/71 his son **Richard Bowen** – freed 1678. Additionally he bound
an apr. for Thomas Holland, Joseph Webb, William Watmore and Evan
Jones. Died about 1677. Work known – watch.

BOWEN, Richard junior   **London**
B.c. 1657, son of Richard Bowen senior. Apr. Feb 1670-71 to father till
1678. Free Jan 1678/89. Work known – watch signed 'Richard Bowen
Londini fecit'.

BOWEN, Thomas   **London**
B.c. 1671, son of Richard Bowen senior. Apr. Jan 1684/85 to Henry
Bridgen (thro' his mother) till 1692 but not freed.

BOWTELL, Samuel   **London**
B.c. 1660, apr. Apr 1674 to Samuel Horne till 1681. Free Jun 1681. Took
as aprs.: **William Bartram** (from Samuel Horne, maybe after Horne's
death) – free Sep 1684; Apr 1683 **William Finch** – free Jan 1691-92; Jul
1685 **John Hicks** (thro' G. Heady) – free Jul 1694; Nov 1691 **George
Tapp;** Jun 1694 **William Bowtell** – free Oct 1704; Jun 1701 **Thomas
Jelley or Jelles** (son of James Jelley of Weston, Hunts, farmer) – free Apr
1720; Sep 1707 **William Noyes.** Made CC Assistant 1710 but never
attended and prob. died c. 1710.

BOWYER, John   **London**
A late 17th century ten-bell musical lantern clock is known signed 'John
Bowyer Londini fecit'. Nothing is known about him and he was not a
member of CC nor apparently known to them.

BOWYER, William (sometimes Boyear and even Bayer)   **London**
Believed working as early as 1620s. Member of CC by 1632. Took as
aprs.: **Nathaniel Allen** – freed before 1658; **John Barcole** (from
R. Masterson) – free Mar 1647; Mar 1638 **Joseph Jackson** (thro'
T. Dawson) – free Mar 1646; Feb 1647 **Francis Bowen** (thro' T. Alcock)
– free Apr 1655. Was asked to be CC Assistant 1640. In Jul 1642 he gave a
'great chamber clock' for excusal from all future offices. Nevertheless

became an Assistant in 1651, Warden 1653, when he last attended. In Feb 1650 he was complained against for not binding his son-in-law (name not known) thro' CC. Seems to have been always a reluctant member and prob. belonged to another Company. Prob. died about 1653 and certainly before 1662/63. Work known – several lantern clocks, some dated (1623 & 1626), signed 'William Bowyer in Leadenhall Street fecit', 'William Bowyer fecit', 'William Bowyer in London fecit' and one said to be signed as Boyear.

BOYCE, Abraham (also Boice and Boys?)   **London**
Son of Henry Boyce of Bowe, Essex, hempdresser. Apr. 1607 in Blacksmiths' Co. to John ? Birost. Took as aprs. in Blacksmiths' Co.: Jun 1631 **Abraham Fromanteel**; Aug 1632 **Andrew Prime** – freed 1641. Not sure whether he was a clockmaker but his aprs. seem to have been. Work known – a large clock-watch is recorded signed 'A. Boys & Jacques Duduict' – perhaps by this man.

BOYCE, James (also Boyse)   **London**
B.c. 1671, apr. Apr 1685 to Erasmus Micklewright till 1692. Freed Jul 1692. Took as aprs.: Feb 1693/94 **Theophilus Maund** or **Mound**; Feb 1695/96 **Richard Lee**; Apr 1698 **Thomas Alexander**; Apr 1701 **William Camden** (son of John Camden of Stanlake, co. Oxon, wheelwright) – free 1708. Still working in 1709 but when called for stewardship in Jul 1712 he was 'out of town' and was not heard of thereafter. Work known – longcase and bracket clocks, signed 'James Boyce, London'.

BOYCE, Thomas   **London**
B.c. 1673 (could be brother of James?). Apr. Aug 1687 thro' Erasmus Micklewright to an unnamed clockmaker who was a member of the Haberdashers' Co. till 1694. Freed Jan 1695-96. (Master was prob. James Metcalfe or Thomas Overbury or Thomas Warden, *qv*). Took as aprs.: May 1699 **John Arding** (son of John Arding of parish of St. Giles Cripplegate, London, grocer); May 1702 **John Smith** (son of John Smith of St. Giles Cripplegate, founder). Working till at least 1705.

BOYLE, Richard   **London**
Apr. Jun 1652 to John Bayes. Freed Oct 1660. Prob. dead or gone by 1662.

BOYS, A. (see Boyce)

BRACKL(E)Y, George London
B.c. 1655, apr. Mar 1669/70 to Philip Buckner till 1676. Freed Apr 1677. In May 1682 took **Thomas Farmer** as apr., later transferred to Edward Massey. Prob. left or died before 1696/97.

BRADFORD, John London
Lantern clock recorded signed 'John Bradford London'. Maybe error for Thomas? No John is known.

BRADFORD, P. D. London
Bracket clock c. 1690 recorded. No details of this man are known.

BRADFORD, Robert London
Watch recorded c. 1700. Again nothing known of his life.

BRADFORD, Thomas senior London
B.c. 1659, apr. Sep 1673 to Joseph Windmills (thro' William Speakman) till 1680. Free Sep 1680. Took as aprs.: Jun 1683 **Bryan Thornhill**; Aug 1687 **Thomas Ashton**; Apr 1693 **William Sims**; Mar 1694/95 **William Hornblower** – free Jul 1714; Jul 1700 **Thomas Taylor** (son of Richard Taylor of Puckeridge, co. Herts, innholder); May 1707 **Francis Speed**. Working till at least 1705. Widow Bradford got CC charities from 1710 to 1716. Work known – longcase clocks signed 'Thomas Bradford London' and 'Thomas Bradford Londini fecit'. Also a watch.

BRADFORD, Thomas junior London
Not known if related to Thomas senior. B.c. 1667, apr. Mar 1680 to Thomas Applegarth till 1688. Freed Jul 1692. Took as aprs.: Nov 1713 **Francis Franklin**; Aug 1716 **John Anderton**; Oct 1719 **Walter Bowen** (from Samuel Glover). Work known – confusion with work of Thomas senior makes identification uncertain.

BRADLEY, Henry London
B.c. 1653/56, apr. Oct 1667 to William Robinson till 1674. Free Jun 1681. In Feb 1674/75 he was working for Charles Gretton though not yet a freeman. Robinson complained but Bradley said he could not afford to take up his freedom yet. Took as aprs.: Jun 1683 **John Pecket**, later transferred to H. Merryman; Sep 1691 **Hugh Richardson**. In Aug 1691 as a clockmaker and widower of St. Mary Woolnoth parish aged about 35 he married Dorothy Antrobus of St. Stephens Walbrooke, a spinster

aged 23 – at St. Mary Woolnoth. Prob. dead or gone by 1696/97. Work known – longcase clocks signed 'Henry Bradley, Exchange Alley'.

BRADLEY, John London
B.c. 1658 (could be brother of Henry?). Apr. Jan 1671/72 to Edmund Gilpin (thro' J. Markwick) till 1679 but not freed.

BRADLEY, Langley London
B.c. 1663, apr. Feb 1687/88 to Joseph Wise till 1694. Free Apr 1695. Took as aprs.: May 1695 **Thomas Norwood** (thro' R. Knight); Aug 1700 **Joseph Mountford** (son of Bartholomew Mountford of Southampton co., clerk); Feb 1708/09 **John Paybody** (son of John Paybody of St. Mary Magdalen Bermondsey, hairdresser, deceased); Nov 1713 **John Wood;** Apr 1719 **Edward Roberts;** and perhaps others after 1720. Worked at the Minute Dial in Fenchurch Street, but in 1748 was at Mile End. CC Assistant from 1720, Master 1726. Work known: best known for turret clocks esp. the famous one for St. Paul's with two figures striking the quarters built in 1707. For many years there were disputes about its performance and pamphlets were published about the dispute. Other turret clocks known include St. Giles Edinburgh and Cripplegate Church, London. Also known for longcase and bracket clock and watches. For further reading see *Clocks Magazine*, Feb and Mar 1979 issues.

BRADSHAW, Ellis Shrewsbury
Watchmaker there 1695.

BRADSHAW, John London
Apr. Jan 1651/52 to Lancelot Meredith (thro' William Petty) – free Dec 1658. Prob. gone by 1662. Work known – none but could be same man as next entry.

BRADSHAW, John Shrewsbury
Watchmaker there 1695. Maybe the Londoner above?

BRADSHAW, Henry London
B.c. 1673, apr. Aug 1687 to William Slough till 1694. Free Sep 1695. Took as aprs.: Sep 1696 **Thomas Rennolds** – free Apr 1706; Apr 1702 **Thomas Gawthorne** (son of Jonathan Gawthorne late Citizen and Plasterer of London); Jul 1704 **Dilkes Barnett** (son of Daniel Barnett late

111

of Coleshill, co. Warwicks, apothecary, deceased); Sep 1711 **Thomas Bower;** Apr 1715 **Edward Chollwell;** Jul 1719 **Roger Jennings;** perhaps others later.

BRAFIELD, Thomas (sometimes Brayfield)   **London**
B.c. 1660, believed son of John Brafield. Apr. Mar 1674/75 to Erasmus Micklewright till 1681. Free Sep 1682. Took as aprs.: Nov 1685 **George Vicary;** Jul 1691 **Richard Hutton; Robert Gideon** (taken from William Young) freed Mar 1691/92; Sep 1692 **Charles Browne;** Jul 1693 **Richard Harris;** Aug 1695 **Philip Hill;** Jan 1696/97 **James Brown;** Sep 1711 **John Pattenden;** Mar 1714/15 **Daniel Constable.** In Sep 1688 an inadequate gold watch case was seized by CC in the shop of Benoni Tebbatt, said to belong to Brafield, but later William Brafield confessed he had made it. Work known – longcase clock recorded.

BRAFIELD, William (and Brayfield)   **London**
B.c. 1657 (could be brother of Thomas?). Apr. Jun 1671 to Thomas Williamson till 1678. Free Sep 1678. In 1688 he confessed he had made the faulty gold watch case for which Thomas Brafield was being held responsible. Took as apr. Jul 1683 **Thomas Goldsmith** – free Apr 1692. Working till 1705 at least. Work known – lost watch recorded.

BRAND, Basil   **London**
B.c. 1648, apr. Oct 1660 to John Matchett till 1669, but not freed. One of the same name, the son of William Brand, Gent. of London, was apr. in Blacksmiths' Co. Oct 1658 to John Drake, and free of the City in 1668. Maybe Matchett took him over from Drake?

BRAND, Henry   **London**
Signed a CC document in 1637 but maybe not a clockmaker.

BRANDON, Benjamin   **London**
B.c. 1667, apr. Mar 1681/82 to Benjamin Bell later transferred to Cuthbert Lee till 1689. Free Dec 1689. Paid no quarterage and prob. died or left soon after.

BRANT, Richard (see Brent)

BRANT, Richard   **London**
B.c. 1678, apr. Jul 1692 to John Dickens, later transferred to Thomas Cattell till 1699. Free Sep 1700. Working till at least 1703.

BRASSINGTON, George　　　　Stoke-on-Trent (Staffordshire)
Repaired church clock 1687-89.

BRAYFIELD (see Brafield)

BRAZIER, ----　　　　London
Working c. 1700. Nothing else known. Work known – watch.

BRE(A)MES, Leonard　　　　London
Admitted to CC as free Brother Apr 1633.

BREBANT, Peter (also Brebent)　　　　London
Watch and clock recorded c.1710 – c.1730. Nothing else known.

BRENT, Richard　　　　London
(Some authorities have Nicholas in error). B.c. 1635, apr. Dec 1649 to
Samuel Davis till 1656 but not freed. Prob. dead by 1662/63.

BRETON, Henry (also Britton)　　　　London
Kept Westminster clock 1413.

BRETT, James　　　　place not known
Lantern clock recorded c. 1695. No other data.

BRETT, Robert　　　　London
Paid CC quarterage 1639. (One of this name was free of the City c. 1585
by redemption in the Bricklayers' Co. – maybe him?).

BREWER, Edward　　　　London
B.c. 1652, apr. Apr 1665 to Stafford Freeman till 1673 but not freed.

BREWER, John　　　　London
B.c. 1656, apr. Jan 1670/71 to Matthew Crockford till 1677. Free Mar
1677/78. In Jan 1683/84 took over apr. **Charles Tolley** from Joseph
Ashby, another Crockford journeyman. Prob. worked for Crockford.

BREWER, Jonathan　　　　Norwich
Free, was watchmaker there Nov 1640, though apparently not apr.
there.

BREWER, William (also Bruer) **London**
B.c. 1640, apr. Nov 1654 to Onisephorus Helden (thro' L. Wythe) till 1661, but not freed. Prob. dead or gone by 1662.

BREWTON, Robert **London**
Apr. Feb 1660/61 to John Archer, engraver, but not freed.

BREYNTON, Vaughan **London**
B.c. 1667, apr. May 1681 to Jeremiah Johnson till 1688. Freed Sep 1693. Paid no quarterage after 1694 and prob. dead or gone by 1697.

BRIAN, ---- (see Bryan)

BRICE, Clement **London**
B.c. 1675, apr. Jan 1689/90 to Jeremiah Martin till 1696 but not freed.

BRICKENDEN, Nathaniel **London**
B.c. 1638, apr. Apr 1651 to Robert Whitwell till 1659, but not freed.

BRICKHILL, James **London**
B.c. 1655, apr. Oct 1668 (not 1648 as some say) to Robert Jole, mat. inst. maker, and a freeman of the Stationers' Co. (thro' L. Wythe) till 1676 but not freed.

BRIDGE, Thomas (see also Bridges) **London**
Half a dozen longcase clocks, eight-day and 30-hour, are known signed 'Thomas Bridge Londini fecit' and 'Thomas Bridge London fecit'. These apparently date from c. 1690 to c. 1710. He was not a CC member and was apparently unknown to them. Maybe same man as in next entry, but see Thomas Bridges too.

BRIDGE, Thomas (see also Bridges) **Bolton (Lancashire)**
Clockmaker. Died there 1717 leaving widow, Elizabeth. May be the London man above?

BRIDGE, Thomas **Wigan**
Clockmaker. Free there 1712. Married 1716 Ellen Winstanley. Repaired church clock several times till 1745. Wife died 1727. Work known – longcase clocks signed 'T. Bridge de Wigan'. Could be related to the London and Bolton namesakes above.

BRIDGE, William   London
Blacksmiths' Co. member. In Sep 1674 he took **Samuel Capper** as apr. in CC (thro' Thomas Morgan). 'Mr. Bridge' who paid CC search fee in 1674-75 may have been him – or Thomas?

BRIDGEMAN, Edward   London
Apr. Jul 1655 to John Matchett. Free Oct 1662. Bound an apr. for H. Reeve and one for T. Williamson. Paid CC quarterage to end of 1698. Said to have worked at Russell Street, Covent Garden.

BRIDGEN, Henry (also Brigden)   London
B.c. 1661, apr. May 1675 to Richard Warren till 1682. Free May 1682. Took as aprs.: Dec 1684 **William Wright**; Jan 1684-85 **Thomas Bowen** (thro' Mary Bowen, his mother).

BRIDGES, Thomas   Edinburgh
An Englishman who became journeyman to Andrew Brown in Sep 1691. Work known – none, but compare Thomas Bridge (?).

BRIERLEY, John   Sheffield
Watchmaker at Upperthorne who died in 1711. See also Birley.

BRIGGS, John   London
Made a free Brother in CC Sep 1669. 'John Briggs a cutter of glasses for watches, formerly a soldier under the Duke of Albermarle when the King was restored, produced the Act of Parl. 12 Car. 2, enabling soldiers of the army then to be disbanded to exercise trades and a certificate according to the said Act, and prayed to be admitted a Brother of the Company . . .' In Dec 1675 he received five shillings charity from CC 'being in great poverty''.

BRIGGS, Robert   Doncaster (Yorkshire)
Clock keeper. Died 1621. Prob. not a maker.

BRIGGS, Robert   Doncaster (Yorkshire)
Repaired church clock 1663 and was paid £4 yearly to maintain it. Prob. not a maker.

BRIGHTWELL, ----   London
Paid CC search fee 1671-74. Prob. a measure-seller.

BRISBOROUGH, John London
Denizen clockmaker 1544.

BRISTOW, John London
B.c. 1640, apr. Mar 1653 to Richard Craile (thro' W. Petty) till 1661 but not freed.

BRISTOW, Timothy London
B.c. 1677, apr. Jul 1691 to Urian Berrington till 1698 but not freed.

BRITTAINE, Boaz London
B.c. 1656, apr. Aug 1670 to William Speakman till 1677. Free Mar 1679.

BRITTAINE, Stephen London
B.c. 1670, apr. Apr 1684 thro' J. Herbert to Sarah Payne, widow (Herbert was prob. her journeyman) till 1691. Freed Apr 1692. Died sometime before 1715 when his widow, Barbara, asked CC for a grant to help apr. her son, Langford Brittaine, to James Tolley, a framework-knitter, which she did in Feb 1716/17. In Nov 1720 she asked for a grant to help bind her son, Stephen, to Henry Harris, clockmaker.

BROAD, Thomas London
B.c. 1661, apr. from late 1674-1682 to Benjamin Bell. In Dec 1678 he had been sick for more than six months and staying with friends in the country and Bell was allowed a new apr. in his stead. Freed Jan 1682/83, which suggests he returned later.

BROADWATER, Hugh Oxford/London
Son of John Broadwater (alias Griffin) of Iffley, Oxfordshire, fisherman. Apr. Dec 1680 at Oxford to John Harris till 1687. Made a free Brother in CC Jul 1692 as a watchmaker. (Baillie says he moved there 1689-?). Alive 1697 but listed as dead by 1698. Work known – at least one watch.

BROADWAY, Thomas London
B.c. 1635, apr. Jul 1648 to Humphrey Downing (thro' L. Wythe) till 1656, but not freed.

BROCKE, Samuel London
Watches recorded c. 1620. Nothing known about him.

BROCK, W. Charterhouse
Recorded as 1650 (Britten). No other details.

BROCKHURST, Benjamin Coventry/London
Longcase clocks known from the late 17th century to about 1740. No details known about him.

BROE, Henry (Henri) (sometimes Bron) London
A Frenchman 'at a Joyners at Broad street end at London wall' in 1622. John Averill worked in same house. Still working in 1662.

BROMLEY, ---- Staindrop (Co. Durham)
Two marquetry longcase clocks recorded believed c. 1700. Nothing else known.

BRON, Henri (see Broe)

BRONNE, Peter England, place not known
Longcase clock recorded c. 1700. Nothing else known.

BROOKE, Edward London
B.c. 1667, apr. Sep 1681 to William Robinson till 1689. Not freed.

BROOKE, George London
B.c. 1657, apr. Sep 1670 to Robert Cosby till 1678. Freed Sep 1681. Took as aprs.: Mar 1681/82 **William Simpson**; Aug 1694 **John Weller** – free Jan 1713/14; Sep 1701 **William Spearing** (son of Richard Spearing of Winchester, gent.) – free Feb 1719/20. Not heard of after 1701. Work known – watch and longcase clock signed 'George Brooke London'.

BROOK, John London
Free Brother Oct 1632. Paid dues till 1635. Mrs. Brookes, who in 1646 was given a charitable payment by CC, maybe his widow.

BROOK(E)S, Edward London
B.c. 1669, apr. Sep 1683 to Edward Whitfield, later transferred to Robert Gregory then to James Stedman till 1690. Free Dec 1690. Prob. dead or gone by 1692, after which date he paid no quarterage. Work known – bracket clock.

BROOK(E)S, Edward   London
B.c. 1680, apr. Apr 1693 to John Martin till 1701, not freed.

BROOKES, John   London
B.c. 1671, apr. Nov 1685 to William Clement (thro' D. Stevens) till 1692. Not freed.

BROOKS, John   London
B.c. 1679, apr. Jul 1693 to Mathew Crockford junior till 1700. Not freed.

BROOKS, Samuel   London
B.c 1666, apr. Apr 1680 to Joseph Windmills till 1687, but not freed.

BROOKSTED, John   London
B.c 1657, apr. Sep 1671 to John White till 1678, but not freed.

BROOME, Thomas (he spelled it Brome)   London
Free Brother in CC Jan 1652/53 'a worker on gold and silver boxes for watches, having been apr. to a goldsmith'. In 1662 he was listed as an 'outlier', an ambiguous term which may refer to his specialised trade or his residential district. In Jun 1665 he took as apr. (thro' H. Cooper) **Robert Vaughan.**

BROSY, Abbot   London
Baillie has 1680. Nothing known.

BROSY, Michael   London
Watch recorded c. 1640. Nothing else known.

BROWN, Andrew   Edinburgh
B.c. 1651, son of the late John Brown of Lang Newton. Apr. Feb 1665-66 to Humphrey Milne, clockmaker. Freed Aug 1675. For his test-piece he made a clock in the house (shop) of John Alexander. Took as aprs.: **John Brown** – freed 1689; 1679 **David Johnstoun**; 1688 **Thomas Gordon** – freed 1703; 1688 **Alexander Johnstoun**; 1694 **Richard Alcorne** – freed 1703; Nov 1696 **William Pen**; 1698 **Thomas Hog**; 1703 **Thomas Ancrum**; Dec 1710 **James Dunbar** from Aberdeen. His apr. or journeyman, **James Barrow**, ran away in 1699 stealing some watches. In Sep 1691 he took as journeyman **Thomas Bridges**, in Feb 1702 **Robert Brown**, and in 1703 **John Groom**. He became Captain of the City Guard in 1685, Master of the Hammermen's Guild in 1689. In

1688 he paid for the bells to be rung at the funeral of Edmund Appley, *qv*. In 1696/97 he made a new clock for Magdalen Chapel for £35 and maintained it till his death about 1711. By Apr 1712 he had died and his son, Andrew, applied to the Guild for financial help to move to London. This was granted as he was 'in great want'. The father was apparently another example of a highly capable maker who died almost penniless. He may have been related to Humphrey Milne, as he was in some way involved with rents from Mylne's land at the New Well. Work known – watches and longcase clocks, at least two of them in marquetry cases, one a month clock.

BROWNE, Charles   **London**
B.c. 1678, apr. Sep 1692 to Thomas Brafield till 1699 but not freed.

BROWNE, Edward   **Bristol**
Clockmaker. Married there Nov 1689.

BROWNE, Elias   **Norwich**
B. 1604, son of John Browne, cutler, apr. 1619 to Edward Wright, goldsmith there. Freed Jun 1633 as a clockmaker, but was also a goldsmith. At one time was High Sheriff. Died 1660 aged 56.

BROWNE, James   **Bristol**
Apr. to his father, James Browne, blacksmith. Freed there 1679.

BROWNE, James   **Croydon**
Made a free Brother in CC Sep 1687 as a watchmaker. May even be the Oxford man below. Dead or gone by 1697.

BROWNE, James   **Oxford**
B.c. 1650, son of James Browne, printer of Oxford. Apr. May 1663 to Richard Quelch, watchmaker there, till 1671 but not freed. May have succ. Quelch by 1696.

BROWNE, John   **Bristol**
Clockmaker, working 1689.

BROWN, John   **Dundee**
Formerly a Gray Friar. Kept church clock 1564-73.

BROWN, John   **Edinburgh**
Son of Andrew Brown of Edinburgh, tailor. Apr. to Andrew Brown, clockmaker. Freed Aug 1689, making a clock as his test-piece. Died 1710 or a little before. His widow, Grisel (née Dalrymple) was given charity by the guild in Jul 1710. His son, John, was freed there in 1720.

BROWN(E), John   **London**
Mat. inst. maker, free of another Co. but made a free Brother in CC Feb 1667-68. Took as aprs.: Apr 1669 his son, **Thomas Browne** (thro' L. Wythe) – free 1676; Aug 1675 **Daniel Thomas** (thro' S. Davis) – free Aug 1682; Apr 1677 **William Bennett** (thro' S. Davis) – free Sep 1689; Nov 1682 **Edward Kyffin** (thro' S. Davis); May 1684 **Thomas Pollycott** (thro' D. Stevens); Aug 1687 **James Crosse**. Became Assistant in CC 1669, Warden from 1677, Master 1681. From 1690 he was excused attendance 'in regard to his age and inability of going much' (ie walking). In 1701 he received charitable payments from CC.

BROWN, John   **London**
B.c. 1673, apr. Nov 1687 to Richard Fennell till 1694 but not freed.

BROWN, Matthew   **Dublin**
Clockmaker there 1651 (maybe from London?).

BROWNE, Matthew   **London**
Brother in CC Apr 1633 but not heard of thereafter.

BROWNE, Moses   **London**
B.c. 1673, apr. Oct 1687 to Robert Nemes till 1694 but not freed.

BROWN, Philip   **London**
B.c. 1666, apr. Sep 1680 to Nicholas Beck, transferred later to Cuthbert Lee and then John Harris of the Old Bailey till 1687. Freed Apr 1688. Took as apr. Nov 1689 **Thomas Shrubb**. Prob. dead or gone by 1693.

BROWN, Richard   **London**
B.c. 1654, apr. Nov 1668 to Lawrence Sindry, later transferred to Edward Norris till 1675. Freed Jan 1675/76. Took as aprs.: Aug 1678 **Henry Mowtlow** – free Nov 1685; Jun 1683 took over **Richard Baker** from John Chatfield – freed Jun 1685; took **Richard Farmer** from Edward Norris – freed Jul 1683; Jul 1683 **Richard Chilcott** – free Sep 1690; Jul 1687 **Mark Washington** (thro' T. Evans). In 1693 he was much

in arrears with quarterage. Prob. dead by 1697. Prob. worked for some years as journeyman to Norris. Work known – lantern and longcase clocks and a watch. One lantern clock signed 'at ye Green Dragon in Cheapside'.

BROWNE, Richard   **London**
B.c. 1657, apr. Aug 1671 to John Fetters (thro' L. Wythe) till 1678 but not freed.

BROWNE, Richard   **Rumford/Romford (Essex)**
Lantern clock recorded c. 1695.

BROWNE, Robert   **London**
B.c. 1673, apr. Dec 1684 to Katherine Ames till 1692 but not freed.

BROWNE, Thomas   **Bristol**
Son of James Browne, blacksmith. Freed there 1643.

BROWNE, Thomas   **London**
B.c. 1639, apr. Jun 1653 to Richard Beck till 1660 but not freed. Work known – lantern clock which could be by him or next man.

BROWNE, Thomas   **London**
B.c. 1655, son of John Browne, mat. inst. maker. Apr. Apr 1669 to father (thro' L. Wythe) till 1676. Free Jul 1676. Took as apr. May 1679 **Thomas Meades** – free Apr 1687.

BROWNE, Thomas   **Warwick**
Repaired church clock 1606-07.

BROWNING, James   **London**
B.c. 1636, apr. Nov 1650 to Thomas Platt (thro' Henry Erbury) till 1657 but not freed.

BROWNSCOMBE, Joseph (Joshua?)   **Exeter (Devon)**
Free 1648. Repaired cathedral clock 1647.

BRUCE, David   **Aberdeen**
Kept town clock 1538.

BRUCE, Thomas   **London**
B.c. 1633, apr. Aug 1645 to Simon Hacket (thro' R. Masterson) till 1654, but not freed.

BRUER (see Brewer)

BRULEFUR, Jean (Brulefer?)   **London**
Longcase clock c. 1690 known, but nothing known of the maker.

BRUL(E)FER, Louis   **London**
Bracket and longcase clocks known from the late 17th century, one signed 'Louis Brulefer à Londres'. A clockmaking family of this name worked in Paris at that time.

BRUNSLEY, Will   **London**
Recorded by Baillie as c. 1670 – perhaps an error for c. 1760?

BRUSH, Thomas   **London**
On CC list of 1662. Prob. a corruption of Thomas Birch, *qv*.

BRYAN, Richard   **London**
B.c. 1669, apr. Jun 1683 to William Speakman till 1690. Freed Apr 1696. Took as apr. Dec 1696 **William Bird**. Working 1697 but not heard of thereafter.

BRYAN, Robert (also Brian and Brain)   **London**
B.c. 1649, apr. Apr 1662 to William Seaburne till 1670 but not freed. (Seaburne died in 1668).

BRYAN, Samuel   **London**
B.c. 1671, apr. May 1685 to James Hassenius (thro' D. Stevens) till 1692 but not freed.

BRYANT, George   **London**
B.c. 1644, apr. Apr 1657 to William Smith (thro' N. Tomlins) till 1665 but not freed.

BRYCE (see Brice)

BUCK, Edward   **London**
B.c. 1618, apr. 1632 for seven years in CC, master not named, but not freed.

BUCK, John Chester
Clockmaker at Foregate Street in 1663. Steward of Chester Goldsmiths 1664. Still working 1670. Work known – at least one lantern clock signed 'John Buck in Chester'.

BUCKENHILL, Edward London
B.c. 1658, apr. Sep 1672 to James Delander (thro' W. Thorowgood) till 1679. Free Feb 1687/88. Prob. dead or gone by 1697.

BUCKENHILL, John London (and **Worcester?**)
B.c. 1650, apr. Jun 1664 to William Thorowgood, later transferred to John Smith then back to Thorowgood again. Took as aprs.: Jun 1675 **John Berrow; Aug 1685 George Cheriton**. In 1685 he received a charitable payment from CC. One by this name worked at Worcester as a watchmaker in 1719. Work known – watches.

BUCKINGHAM James London
Watch reported c. 1700 – error for Joseph?

BUCKINGHAM, Joseph London
Not a CC member nor apparently known to them but several watches and longcase clocks are recorded c.1685 – c.1720. Some signed 'Joseph Buckingham in ye Minories', some 'Joseph Buckingham, London'. Believed worked at the Blackmoor's Head and Dial, Minories.

BUCKNELL, James Crediton (Devon)
Longcase clock and watch known from c. 1690.

BUCKNER, Philip London
Apr. May 1660 to Peter Closen (thro' N. Coxeter), free Jan 1667-68. Took as aprs.: Mar 1669/70 **George Brackley** – free Apr 1677; Mar 1676 **James Hancorne**. Got CC charities in 1681 but he died late in 1681 or early 1682 after which his widow received a regular pension until 1712. Their son, Richard, was free in CC in 1701.

BUL(C)KE, Jacques de London
Repaired royal clocks in 1599. Believed also worked in Paris. Work known – drum watch and two oval watches.

BULL, Edmund London
Son of *a* John Bull (maybe John Bull, goldsmith?). Apr. in Blacksmiths'

Co. to Robert Grinkin and freed Mar 1607/08. Was a 1622 petitioner for
CC. Work known – several watches, at least one signed 'Edm. Bull In
Fleetstreet Fecit'.

BULL, Emanuel London
Son of Randolph Bull. Said to have been clock keeper to Prince Henry in
1610. Mentioned as a watchmaker in his father's will in 1617. Work
known – two watches.

BULL, George London
Blacksmiths' Co. member from 1617. Petitioner for CC in 1622.

BULL, John London
Goldsmith and perhaps clock/watchmaker. Brother of Randolph, whom
he had as journeyman for 12 years up to about 1580. One of this name was
a goldsmith in St. Michael Cornhill parish from 1557 till his death in
1589.

BULL, John London
Must be a different person to the above. Subscriber to CC in 1630. Freed
Oct 1632. Cautioned 1646 for not observing the rules. In 1662 he worked
at Temple Bar.

BULL, John London
B.c. 1667, apr. Sep 1691 to Benjamin Graves (thro' C. Maynard) till 1698
but not freed.

BULL, Nicholas London
B.c. 1665, apr. Jun 1679 to Nathaniel Chamberlain till 1686 but not
freed.

BULL, Randolph (also Rainulph) London
Goldsmith, clock and watchmaker. Brother of John Bull, goldsmith,
whom he served as journeyman for over 12 years up to approx. 1580.
Free of the City of London as a member of the Goldsmiths' Co. In 1591
was appointed Clockmaker to the Queen at a salary of a shilling a day plus
£3. 6s. 8d. livery (a year). He was later (1617) demoted to keeper of
Westminster Palace clock as David Ramsay took over the more senior
post. He died in late 1617 in St. Gregory parish, leaving a widow, Jane,
four daughters and a son, watchmaker Emanuel Bull, qv. He left
property at Fulham. An overseer to the will was Anthony Risby, qv. In

1612 he supplied the first Earl of Salisbury with a watch, price £8. Work known – three or four watches, one dated 1590. Believed to be from France. (For more information see *Country Clocks* by B. Loomes).

BULL, Thomas   Oxford
Clock and watchmaker and smith. Free there in 1592.

BULL, William   London
An alien working in 1622 for Cornelius Mellin in Blackfriars, prob. as journeyman.

BULLBY, John (see Bulpy)

BULLIMORE, Henry   London
B.c. 1673, apr. May 1687 to John Fitter (thro' E. Micklewright) till 1694, but not freed.

BULLMAN, Thomas   Liverpool/London
Clockmaker. Had issue baptised there: 1701 Robert, 1702 Sarah, 1704 Rebecca. Lived at Dale Street. Must surely be the man by whom a longcase clock is recorded signed 'Thomas Bullman, Swan Alley, London'.

BULLOCK, Ezekiel (and **Isaac**)   Lurgan (Co. Armagh)
Born 1650, son of George Bullock of Shankhill, co. Armagh, who is believed to have come from England. Married 1684, in Belfast, Ruth Allison. Was a Quaker. At Lurgan 1689-1714. He was a master millwright by trade but also made clocks. His son Isaac, also helped him. Work known – an eight-day longcase clock.

BULLOCK, Richard   Ellesmere
Longcase clock recorded c. 1700. Other members of this clockmaking family are recorded there later.

BULLBY, John   Stirling
Parish clerk there. In 1519/20 he was appointed to keep the town clock, which he later admitted he was not qualified to do.

BULPY, John (also Bullby)   London
Free Brother in CC Oct 1632. John Bull was also free then, and one wonders whether this is a clerical error.

BULSTRODE, William London
B.c 1657, apr. Apr 1671 to Henry Hester till 1678 but in Nov 1672 he was described as 'incapable of learning his trade and to be put away'.

BULTE, Daniel London
(neither Bulty nor Bultry as is sometimes recorded)
Apr. Mar 1655 to Ralph Greatorix, freed Apr 1663.

BUNBERY, Dutton Chester
Free 1636, apr. of Thomas Wright, clockmaker.

BUNCE, Matthew London
Apr. Feb 1684-85 to William May but not freed. May died not long after and perhaps Bunce was rebound as below.

BUNCE, Matthew London
Apr. Mar 1689-90 to John Benson till 1696. Freed Jul 1698. In Jan 1697-98 he married Denise Watts. Took as apr. Apr 1699 **William Ley** (son of Samuel Ley, clerk, deceased, late of Flyver, co. of Worcester) – free 1711. Not heard of after 1699.

BUNNET, Lewis (perhaps Buimett) London
An illicit workman of James Girod summoned to CC court in April 1695 but failed to appear.

BUNTING, Joshua London
Apr. Mar 1648 to William Bunting, but rebound (maybe too young?) Feb 1651 to Thomas Wolverston (thro' William Bunting) till 1658, but not freed.

BUNTING, William London
B.c. 1624, apr. Sep 1637 to Thomas Dawson till 1645, freed Feb 1645-46. Took as aprs.: Feb 1647 **Nathan Smith;** Jul 1647 **John Cann** – free 1649; Aug 1647 **Thomas Fenn** – transferred Jun 1650 to John Cann; Mar 1648 **Joshua Bunting**. Also bound an apr. for Thomas Knifton, John Cann, Henry Ireland, Edward Taylor, Thomas Wolverston and two for Jeremy Gregory. Believed died c. 1650-54. Thought to have worked in Popes Head Alley, Cornhill. Work known – a watch inscribed 'Joanni Miltoni 1631' (which would seem to be odd if intended as a date).

BURBIDGE, ----   **Edinburgh**
1673.

BURGE, Caleb   **London**
B.c. 1668, apr. Apr 1682 to Simon Barrett till 1689 but not freed.

BURGE(S) (see also Burgis(s))

BURGES, Charles Edward   **London**
B.c. 1664, apr. Apr 1678 to James Clowes till 1685 but not freed.

BURGES, Elias   **London**
B.c. 1667, apr. May 1673 to Edward Enys till 1680. Freed Jul 1681.
Took as aprs.: Sep 1702 his son, **Charles Burges**. Also bound an apr. for
Edward Stanton and one for James Hatchman. Not heard of after 1702.
Work known – longcase clocks.

BURGES, Henry   **London (?)**
Late 17th century lantern clock known, signed 'Henry Burges fecit' –
place unknown. But see Henry Burgin?

BURGESS, John   **Liverpool**
Watchmaker at Toxteth Park. Died 1716. Maybe John Burgis of
London?

BURGES, William   **London (?)**
In Mar 1682-83 a watch signed 'William Burges fecit', suspected of being
an invented name, was seized by CC in the shop of Jasper Harmar.

BURGIN, Henry (or Borgin?, but see also Burgess?)   **London**
Token coin of c.1677 gives his address as 'without Bishopsgate'.
Clockmaker or seller?

BURGIS, Edward   **London**
Clocks known by him include longcase, lantern, and bracket clocks,
some signed 'Edward Burgis – London'. Nothing much known about
him and was not a member of CC. In Apr 1670 he married at St. Saviour's
Southwark to Patience Clement, sister of Francis Clement, *qv*. He and
his wife were both still alive in 1713. In Jan 1698/99 a 'Mr.' Burgis and
Mr. Watson asked the CC to give an opinion on the clockmaking contest

between Prevost and Threlkeld, but they refused to get involved – this *may* have been him.

BURGIS, John   London
Subscriber to CC in 1630, entered as a Brother in 1632. Took as aprs.: Aug 1641 **William Izod** (thro' O. Durant) – free May 1649; Jan 1646 **Thomas Jackson** (thro' J. Quash). Not heard of after 1646. Work known – a watch.

BURGIS, John   London
B.c. 1659, apr. Dec 1673 to Samuel Davis junior (thro' Samuel Davis senior) till 1680 but not freed.

BURGIS, Thomas   London
B.c. 1633, apr. Jan 1647/48 to Thomas Knifton (thro' W. Bunting) but not freed. Dead or gone by 1662.

BURK, ----   London
Fined by CC 1633. Never admitted as a member. Dead or gone by 1662.

BURLEIGH, Ninyan   London (and **Durham?**)
Free Brother in CC Jul 1692. Not heard of after 1693. Work known – none, but a bracket clock and a watch are known signed 'Ninyan Burleigh-Durham' c. 1730.

BURPUN, John (also Burpur)   London (?)
Longcase clock c. 1705 known. Place not stated but prob. London. Lost watch advertised in 1705 by 'Burpur'.

BURRELLS, John and **Harry**   Dunfermline (Scotland)
Repaired church clock 1605.

BURSCOUGH, Thomas   London
B.c. 1679, apr. Dec 1693 to John Sowter till 1700 but not freed.

BURTON, Abraham   London
B.c. 1636, apr. May 1650 to Richard Masterson, transferred in 1653 to his widow. Freed Oct 1657. A watch of 'c. 1700' might be by him.

BURTON, John   London
B.c. 1659, apr. Sep 1672 to Richard Warren till 1680 but not freed.

BURTON, Roger London
B.c. 1664, apr. Aug 1678 to Charles Bonner till 1685, but not freed.

BURTON, Samuel and **Thomas** Hawkshead (Westmorland)
Listed as c. 1690 but this is much too early a dating of mid-18th century clocks.

BURTON, William London
B.c. 1667, apr. Sep 1681 to Francis Dennis till 1688 but not freed.

BUSBY, Nicholas London
Never actually admitted to CC but was known to them. Prob. dead by 1663.

BUSCHMANN, John (also Bushman) London
B.c. 1661, a High German watchmaker. Made a Brother in CC Sep 1692. Married in Dec 1690, then aged 29 a bachelor of the parish of St. Margaret Westminster, to Mary Wyatt, 23, spinster, at Christ Church, London (as Johannes Busshman). Assistant in CC 1720. Believed working till 1725. Work known – several longcase clocks, several watches, bracket clocks and a hexagonal table clock and a lantern clock signed 'John Bushman – London'.

BUSHEL, Edward London
B.c. 1673, apr. Oct 1687 to William Bennett till 1694 but not freed.

BUSHELL, Samuel London
B.c. 1676, apr. Jul 1690 to Withers Cheney till 1697 but not freed.

BUSHELL, Timothy London
Recorded as a clockmaker in 1681 but not a member of CC and not known to them.

BUSHMAN (see Buschman)

BUSHNELLS, Thomas London
Supposedly at 'the Dial in East Smithfield' in 1692 but I cannot confirm this. Not a member of CC.

BUTLIN, ----   **London**
Ironmonger at the Cross Keys within Newgate. Had faulty measures confiscated by CC in 1672 and 1673.

BUTTERBAY, John   **Horsham (Sussex)**
Lantern clock recorded, supposedly c. 1700. No other details.

BYSSE (see Bisse)

C

CABOT, Guillaume (or **William**)   **London**
In Sep 1654 he was taken as journeyman to Thomas Eyston through CC
for one year only. Maybe the person of this name who married at Rouen
in 1657.

CABRIER, Charles   **London**
Admitted into CC Feb 1697/98 as a Freeman by redemption, a
watchmaker. In 1717 took his son, **Charles Cabrier** junior, as apr. –
freed 1726. In 1700 he was threatened with a lawsuit by a customer
concerning poor watches. Said by Baillie to have worked in Lombard
Street. Was at the Dial, Tokenhouse Yard, in parish of St. Margaret
Lothbury, in 1730. One of this name at Monkwell Street, parish of St.
Olave Silver Street, in 1731 as a watchmaker. Maybe him or his son; the
latter was in Broad Street in 1743, at number 79. Work known – several
watches signed 'C. Cabrier – London', also longcase clock signed
'Carolus Cabrier Londini fecit' and bracket clock.

CABRIER, Charles   **Stepney**
Britten says CC 1692, but I cannot trace such an entry.

CADE, Simon   **London**
B.c. 1666, apr. Apr 1680 to Henry Wynne till 1687. Freed Apr 1688, but
paid no quarterage thereafter. Work known – a barometer signed 'Simon
Cade, Charing Cross'.

CADGELL, Thomas   **London**
B.c. 1669, apr. Jul 1682 to William Elmes till 1690 but not freed. Maybe
the Mr. Cadell who lodged in 1699 with John Hicks, *qv.*

CAKEBREAD, Richard (alias **Richard Tayler**)   **Oxford**
Blacksmith, freed Sep 1566. Worked on St. Martin's church clock 1579
and Christ Church Cathedral clock in 1583. Had as aprs.: **Thomas
Rolewright** – freed 1584; **Thomas Rysson** – freed 1587; **John Slatford** –
freed 1592, by which year Cakebread had died.

CALBECK, John   **London**
B.c. 1658, apr. Jul 1672 in CC to James Field (of the Woodchandlers'
Co.) thro' L. Wythe – not freed.

CALCOTT, Tobias   **London**
Apr. Jun 1664 to George Johnson – not freed.

CALLE, Samuel   **Exeter**
Clockmaker there in 1685.

CALLOT, Henry (also Callowe and *cf* Collo?)   **London**
Working for Tompion in 1695 though not registered thro' CC.

CALLOWE, Harry (also **Callot** above)   **London**
An ebonised bracket clock from the Tompion workshop bears the name
'Harry Callowe Londini fecit'. See Callot above.

CALVERT, Nicholas   **London**
B.c. 1641, apr. Jun 1655 to Robert Grinkin (thro' B. Hill) till 1662 but
not freed.

CAM, William   **London**
Supposedly free in CC 1686 (obviously confused with William Cann, *qv*).
Paid quarterage till about 1696, dead by 1698. In Mar 1690 took
Timothy Law as apr. Work known – a lantern clock is recorded signed
'William Cam Londini fecit'.

CAMBRIDGE, Samuel   **London**
B.c. 1669, apr. Apr 1683 to Richard Ayres till 1690. Free Apr 1698. In
Apr 1703 took **Thomas Onion** (son of John Onion, late of Berkeley,

Gloucestershire, surgeon) as apr. (The records have master as John Cambridge in error). Paid quarterage till at least 1704, after which nothing known.

CAMPE, Thomas London
B.c. 1658, apr. May 1672 to Cornelius Harbottle till 1679 – not freed.

CANBY, George Selby (Yorkshire)
A Quaker clockmaker. Married 1665 Elizabeth Turner. Lived at Summercroft, nr. Selby. Issue b. 1667 Zacheus; 1669 Elizabeth, who married 1691 Marmaduke Storr, whose children became clockmakers. George died at Summercroft in 1705, his widow in 1718. Work known – a lantern clock signed 'Geo. Canby fecit in Selby'.

CANCHE, James (also **Jacques**) London
French watchmaker. Free Brother in CC Apr 1692. Paid quarterage till late 1701. Work known – at least one watch survives.

CANCHER, James – error for Canche, *qv*.

CANN, John London
Apr. Jul 1647 to William Bunting till 1654 but in fact was made a free Brother in CC Oct 1649 (suggesting he must have served at least five years' apprenticeship elsewhere before joining Bunting). Took as aprs.: Jun 1650 **Thomas Fenn** (transferred in 1652 to Gowen Langford); Aug 1650 **Judah Cann**. (Both bound thro' W. Bunting.) He prob. died about 1654. His widow claimed in Apr 1656 that she should be recompensed for the time her servant Judah Cann should have spent with her 'he being now with Mr. Blisse'. Work known – none, prob. worked as journeyman to Bunting.

CANN, Judah (erroniously Judith) London
Apr. Aug 1650 to John Cann (a relative?) thro' W. Bunting. Transferred Apr 1654 (on John's death?) to Ahasuerus Fromanteel, transferred again Jan 1655-56 to Ambrose Blisse. In Apr 1656 William Bunting's widow claimed that she should be recompensed for the time he should have spent as her servant. Judah was not freed in CC and no work of his is known. Prob. dead or gone by 1662.

CANN, William   **London**
Clockmaker, made a free Brother in CC Sep 1686 and was summoned for 'transgressions' before them in Jul 1687. There is some confusion with William Cam, *qv*.

CANNINGE, John   **London**
Alien 'behind St. Clement's church' in 1622. Had Godrone working with him, prob. as journeyman. He maybe the same person as John Kennett, *qv*.

CAPPER, Samuel   **London**
B.c. 1660, apr. Sep 1674 (thro' T. Morgan) to William Bridge, 'blacksmith' (which prob. means of the Blacksmith's Co.) till 1681 – not freed.

CARD, Edmund   **London**
B.c. 1659, apr. Jan 1672-73 to James Clowes (thro' T. Morgan) till 1679. Free Apr 1680. Paid quarterage till 1688 and prob. died soon after and certainly before 1698.

CAREY (see Cary)

CARLETON, Robert   **London**
B.c. 1673, apr. Jun 1687 to Joseph Bates (thro' T. Elton) till 1694, but not freed.

CARMICHAEL, John   **Edinburgh**
Kept Magdalen Tower clock in 1644.

CARPENTER, Edward   **London**
Son of (Richard?) Carpenter, late of St. Martins in the Field, Middlesex. Apr. to John Whitlack Jan 1639 (thro' Mr. Dawson) – not freed.

CARRON, Samuel   **London**
Supposedly free in CC 1689 (I cannot confirm this). Certainly a member in 1697, but not on quarterage list.

CARTE, John   **Coventry/London**
From Coventry. Free Brother in CC Sep 1695. Paid quarterage till 1702 but prob. not later. In Oct 1696 'John Carte watchmaker from Coventry and lately lived at the Dial & Crown nr. Essex Street in the Strand is now

removed to the corner of Lombard Street'. Work known – supposedly sold a world time-dial clock to Peter the Great. Watch recorded signed: 'John Carte in Garden Court in the Middle Temple'.

CARTER, Christopher   **Galby (Leicestershire)**
B. 1676. Lantern clock signed 'Christopher Carter Galby' c. 1700. No other work known.

CARTER, Francis   **London**
B.c. 1656, apr. Nov 1670 to Robert Dingley till 1677 but not freed.

CARTER, John   **London**
B.c. 1655, apr. Jul 1669 to Andrew Allum till 1676 but not freed. Longcase clock signed 'John Carter, London'.

CARTER, Phillip (see also Charter?)   **Huntington**
Two marquetry longcase clocks known, believed c. 1685 but prob. later.

CARTER, Samuel   **London**
B.c. 1669, apr. Sep 1683 to William Fuller till 1690 but not freed.

CARTER, Thomas   **London**
B.c. 1638, apr. Dec 1651 to Isaac Law (thro' J. Cooke). Freed Dec 1659.

CARTER, Thomas   **London**
B.c. 1660, apr. Jun 1674 to George Tomlinson (thro' L. Wythe) till 1681 but not freed.

CARTER, Thomas   **London**
B.c. 1676, apr. Sep 1690 to Joanna May, widow (thro' J. Herbert) till 1697. Freed Jul 1699. Took as apr. Dec 1700 **Thomas Hughes** (son of late Herbert Hughes of Oswick, co. Glamorgan, deceased) – free Nov 1712. Paid quarterage till mid 1704 when died. Work known – at least one lantern clock and a month walnut longcase, both signed 'Thomas Carter, London'.

CARTIER, Jacques   **London (?)**
Said to be maker of a watch which belonged to Oliver Cromwell and at least one other late 17th century watch is known, signed 'Cartier – London'. A maker of this name worked at Montaubon in 1650 and Toulouse in 1688. Not recorded in CC.

CARTWRIGHT, Benjamin London
Recorded at 18 West Smithfield 1669-72, but I cannot confirm this. Longcase clock recorded c. 1710 signed 'Benjamin Cartwright junior, London'. Not known to CC.

CARTWRIGHT, Thomas London
B.c. 1679, Dec 1693 to Christopher Gould (thro' R. Watts) till 1700 (but not freed?). May have belonged to Masons' Co. Took as apr. in CC Sep 1705 **Richard Packe** (son of Christopher Packe of St. Giles Cripplegate, physician) thro' B. Graves – freed May 1713. Reputedly died in 1741. Work known – several longcase clocks including a month one and also watches, signed 'Thomas Cartwright Londini' and 'Tho. Cartwright Royal Exchange Londini fecit', and also 'Thomas Cartwright watchmaker to the Prince'.

CARVER, Isaac London
Mat. inst. maker and freeman of another Co., not known which one. Free Brother in CC Feb 1667-68, 'though refused to take the oath' (maybe a Quaker?). Took as aprs.: Mar 1671/72 **Charles Saunders**; Jun 1676 **Jonathan Wells** (both thro' H. Wynne); May 1680 **Nathan Smith** (thro' S. Davis) – free Jul 1689; Apr 1686 **Jacob Finch** (thro' H. Wynne) – not free; Oct 1688 **William Hargrove** (thro' J. Weekes). Paid no quarterage after 1691 but still alive in 1697. Work known includes a watch.

CARY, George London
B.c. 1658, apr. Mar 1671/72 to John Curtis till 1678. Free Sep 1679. Took as apr. Jun 1684 **John Martin**. Not heard of thereafter.

CARY, Thomas (sometimes **Carey**) London
B.c. 1678, apr. Feb 1691/92 to John Northcott till 1699. Freed Apr 1706. Took as apr. Jan 1710/11 **William Cawdron**. Not heard of thereafter.

CASINGHURST, Christopher London
B.c. 1677, apr. Mar 1690/91 to Robert Nemes till 1698 but not freed.

CASSWAY, Charles London
B.c. 1642, apr. Dec 1656 to Thomas Mills (thro' N. Coxeter) till 1663 but not freed.

CASTE, J. London
Watch c. 1690 recorded. Prob. error for Carte, *qv*.

CASTER, William **London**
B.c. 1676, apr. Jun 1690 to Joshua Hutchen (thro' D. Stevens) till 1697.
Freed Aug 1697, but paid no quarterage thereafter.

CATER (widow) **London**
Made sundials in Moorfields 1672. See Danley, also Frewen.

CATLIN, Daniel **Kings Lynn (Norfolk)** and **Godmanchester(?)**
Late 17th century and early 18th century lantern and longcase clocks
recorded. Believed family of Quakers. Maybe also at Godmanchester
(Hunts).

CATTELL, Thomas **London**
B.c. 1667, apr. Jul 1681 to William Cattell till 1688. Free Sep 1688. Took
as aprs.: Jul 1691 **Thomas Cattell;** Feb 1694/95 **Foulke Davis;** Aug
1700 **Richard Edey** (son of Thomas Edey of Luton, Bedfordshire,
innholder) – free May 1716; **Richard Brant** (from John Dickens) – free
Sep 1700; **John Shelton** (from John Dickens) – free Sep 1702; Sep 1704
John Allen (son of Henry Allen of Uxbridge, Middlesex, taylor) – free
Apr 1720; Nov 1708 **John Weeks;** May 1714 **Thomas Nightingale.**
Nothing known of him after 1714. Work known – bracket and longcase
clocks signed 'Thomas Cattell London'.

CATTELL, Thomas **London**
B.c. 1677, apr. 1691 to Thomas Cattell till 1698 but not freed.

CATTELL, William **London**
Apr. Jan 1664/65 to Edward Stanton. Freed Apr 1672. Took as aprs.:
Jan 1672/73 **Richard Chase;** Jul 1676 **John Rant** – freed Sep 1687; Jul
1681 **Thomas Cattell** – freed Sep 1688; Jun 1687 **Joseph Hechstetter** –
free Jan 1694-95; post 1680 **John Dickins** (from John Longland) – freed
Sep 1688. Cattell not heard of later than 1687. Prob. dead or gone by
1697. Work known – lantern clocks, marquetry longcase clocks,
including a month one, and bracket clock signed 'Wm. Cattell in Fleet
Street Londini fecit'.

CATTERALL, Benjamin **Chester**
Watchmaker, married there 1698.

CATTLE, John   **London**
Clockmaker in St. Saviour's parish, Southwark, in 1632 when son,
William, was born. Apparently not known to CC. Work known – lantern
clock signed 'John Cattle fecit 1633' beneath alarm disc.

CAVE, Morgan   **London**
A member of Blacksmiths' Co., apparently never officially admitted into
CC but took following aprs. thro' them: **Ellis Langford** (thro'
F. Bicknell) – freed Sep 1672; Jan 1675-76 **Joseph Sermon** (thro'
S. Davis) – not freed.

CAWDREY (see Corderoy)

CAWDRON, George   **London**
B.c. 1652, apr. Sep 1675 to James Graves (thro' S. Davis) but perhaps too
young for he was re-bound Aug 1676 to Graves (thro' J. Matchett) till
1683. Freed Jan 1684/85. Took as aprs.: Dec 1686 **William Matthews**;
Sep 1687 **Benjamin Light** (thro' R. Gilkes); Aug 1688 **William Mabb**;
Henry Richards (from J. Armiger) – freed Sep 1699. Paid quarterage till
1697; prob. dead by 1698. May have been an engraver like his master.

CAWKUTT, Thomas   **London**
B.c. 1678, apr. Jan 1692/93 to Nathaniel Bird (thro' J. Ebsworth) till
1699 – not freed. (Obadiah Cawkutt was a witness to the will of John
Ebsworth in 1699).

CAWNE, Robert   **London**
B.c. 1654, apr. Jul 1668 to Lionel Wythe till 1675. Freed Sep 1675, after
death of master. In Apr 1676 took **William Mayo** as apr.

CAYNE, Andrew   **London**
Working 'without Bishopsgate' 1696 – unconfirmed.

CHABENEX, John   **London**
Watch known, pre-1710.

CHABONER/CHALONER, Henry   **Dublin**
Clock and watchmaker, apr. 1678 to G. Southwark. Free 1685-1700.

CHAMBERLAINE, Daniel   **London**
B.c. 1646, apr. Jan 1660/61 to Thomas Chamberlaine (thro' B. Hill) –
not freed.

CHAMBERLAINE, John   **Bury St. Edmunds**
B.c 1643 (son of John Chamberlaine of Ipswich?). Supposedly free in CC
1687, but I cannot confirm this. Alderman at Bury 1700. Died there
11 Jan 1726/27 aged 83. Administration to widow, Frances. Work
known – watch c. 1670 signed 'John Chamberlaine St. Edmunds Bury'
and also lantern clocks.

CHAMBERLAINE, John   **Ipswich**
Had son b. there 1644 named John (John of Bury?) and daughters b.
1646 and 1653. Buried 31 May 1675. Work known – a watch recorded.

CHAMBERLAINE, John   **London**
B.c. 1677, apr. Sep 1691 to George Etherington (thro' D. Stevens) till
1698 – not freed.

CHAMBERLAINE, Joseph   **Norwich**
Lost watch by him recorded in 1687.

CHAMBERLAINE, Nathaniel senior   **London/Chelmsford**
B.c. 1637, maybe son of Thomas of Chelmsford. Apr. Mar 1651/52 to
Benjamin Hill (thro' L. Wythe) till 1658. Freed Jun 1659. Working in
Fleet Street in 1662. Took as aprs.: Nov 1661 **Richard Halstead** – free
Mar 1669-70; Nov 1671 **Samuel Phillips;** Jun 1679 **Nicholas Bull;** Sep
1681 **Samuel Glover** – freed Aug 1694; Sep 1687 **Thomas Arnold** – free
Sep 1703; later aprs. attributed to Nathaniel junior. In 1669-70 prob. still
worked for Hill, who offered to pay his quarterage arrears. In 1676/77
advertised: 'These are to give notice that Nathaniel Chamberlin, watchmaker (who hath lived several years at Chelmsford in Essex) hath . . .
taken a chamber at Mr. John Rust's in Angel Court in Lombard Street
where he doth intend, God willing, to attend the last fortnight in every
term for the mending of his own work and accommodating all persons
that shall have occasion for New'. Work known – watch signed 'Nat.
Chamberlaine in London'.

CHAMBERLAINE, Nathaniel junior   **London/Chelmsford(?)**
Son of Nathaniel senior, freed in CC by patrimony Nov 1685. Took as
aprs.: Aug 1709 **James Crocker** (son of John Crocker of Grougeth-in-
Cornely (?), Cornwall, gent.); Nov 1714 **Thomas Gape;** Mar 1715-16
John Hubbard. Made CC Assistant 1713, Warden from 1714, Master
1717. Work known – watches.

CHAMBERLAINE, Thomas   **Chelmsford and London(?)**
(see also Thos. Chambers)
Not officially a member of CC but was known to them and tolerated by them (perhaps outside their jurisdiction?). Working 1642-60. Took as aprs.: 1642 **Thomas Haven** – free 1652; Jan 1660/61 **Daniel Chamberlaine** (thro' B. Hill). Dead or gone from London by mid-1663. Work known – watches from c. 1630 signed 'Thomas Chamberlaine fecit'.

CHAMBERLAINE, Thomas   **London**
B.c. 1662, apr. Jul 1676 to Samuel Rosse, later transferred to Henry Harper till 1683. Freed Jan 1687/88, after which paid no quarterage, and prob. dead or gone by 1689.

CHAMBERS, Charles   **Deen** or **Dean**
Lantern clock c. 1700. I do not know if this is Dean or some long-forgotten place called Deen.

CHAMBERS, Edward   **London**
B.c. 1656, apr. Oct 1670 to Evan Jones (thro' S. Horne) till 1677 – not freed. Freed at Canterbury 1678.

CHAMBERS, James   **London**
Supposedly at 3 Squirrels, St. Dunstan's Church in 1690.

CHAMBERS, Jonathan   **London**
Longcase clock c. 1690 known. Lantern clock signed 'Jonathan Chambers fecit'.

CHAMBERS, Thomas   **London**
In 1662 listed by CC as working in Westminster. Maybe error for Thomas Chamberlaine.

CHAMPION, John   **London**
Brother in CC Mar 1640/41. Made a full Freeman Dec 1651. These two events relate to the same man, not two, as some authorities suggest. In Jun 1652 took **John Hendrickson** as journeyman for six months. Took as apr. Jan 1651/52 **Samuel Witte** – free Jan 1660-61. Made Assistant 1656 but never attended meetings. Prob. died soon after and before 1662.

CHAMPION, John   **Wells (Somerset)**
1641, supposedly brother of Robert, but I cannot confirm this.

CHAMPION, Robert   **Wells (Somerset)**
Lantern clock recorded signed 'Robert Champion, Wells fecit 1630'.

CHANTRELL, Roger   **Chester**
Repaired Holy Trinity clock 1624.

CHAPMAN, John   **London**
B.c. 1665, apr. Jan 1679-80 to William Herbert till 1686 but not freed.

CHAPMAN, Samuel   **London**
Recorded as 1676 (Baillie) but must be an error for Simon.

CHAPMAN, Simon   **London**
B.c. 1653, apr. Mar 1667 thro' N. Coxeter to John Nash, a mat. inst.
maker and freeman of the Grocers' Co., till 1674. Freed Mar 1675. Took
as aprs.: Jun 1676 **William Stiffe; George Ryley** (thro' J. Stanes) – freed
Jul 1686; Jul 1687 **Paul Dunston.** Called for Stewardship in 1688 but did
not appear and by Jul 1689 he was 'beyond the sea'.

CHAPMAN, Thomas   **London**
B.c. 1636, apr. Jul 1648 to Ralph Ash (thro' T. Alcock) till 1657, but not
freed. However a Thomas Chapman of the Blacksmiths' Co. took as apr.
in Mar 1656/57 **William Clement** and Oct 1657 **Francis Clement.** Not
listed as a clockmaker by CC in their 1662 list.

CHAPMAN, Thomas   **London**
B.c. 1645, apr. Jun 1659 to Withers Cheney till 1666, but not freed.

CHAPMAN, Titus   **London**
B.c. 1669, apr. Jun 1683 to Thomas Williamson till 1690 but not freed.
Work known – a watch is recorded.

CHARAS, Charles Samson   **London**
Clockmaker, French, made a free Brother in CC Jul 1692. Paid
quarterage till 1694 but not later, though still working 1697.

CHARLESWORTH, John   **London**
B.c. 1662, apr. Dec 1676 to Edward Clough (thro' William Speakman)
till 1683 but not freed. Work known – a watch.

CHARLTON, Daniel (or **Thomas**)   **London**
Apr. Nov 1637 to Mr. West (thro' T. Dawson) – not freed. Name
uncertain through faulty records.

CHARLTON, John   **London**
Working c. 1630. A petitioner for incorporation of CC and one of the first
Assistants in 1632, Warden 1635-36, Master 1640. Last attended 1651.
Took **James Beraud** as journeyman Apr 1632. Took as apr. Dec 1638
John Hamden. Work known – watch.

CHARNOCK, James   **London**
B.c. 1679, apr. Nov 1693 to Thomas Wheeler till 1700, but not freed.

CHARTER, Philip   **London**
Ordered by CC Jan 1655/56 to finish the work in hand for Benjamin Hill
and then to find a proper master. Not heard of again (but see Philip
Carter?).

CHASE, Richard   **London**
B.c 1659, apr. Jan 1672/73 to William Cattell till 1680 but not freed.

CHATBOURNE, John   **London**
B.c. 1663, apr. Jul 1677 to John Bennett (thro' S. Davis) till 1684 – not
freed.

CHATFIELD, John   **London**
Son of John Chatfield of Horsham, Sussex, clerk, late apr. of William
Craile (of Blacksmiths' Co.), sworn a freeman of the City of London
1655? Made a Brother in CC Jul 1675. May have died in 1683 in Jun of
which year his apr. **Richard Baker** was transferred to Richard Browne.
Work known – *London Gazette* of 1695 records a lost watch signed
'Chatfield – Londini'.

CHAVELL (see Chauvell)

CHAUVELL, James   **London**
(also found written Shovell, but he signed Chauvell)
B.c. 1677, apr. Oct 1691 to David Minuel (thro' D. Stevens) till 1698,
but not freed. However paid quarterage from 1699 and believed working
till c. 1720. Believed worked in Old Broad Street in 1699. Work known –
several watches c.1700 – c.1720, one signed 'James Chauvel, London'.

CHAUVELL, John (also **Shovell**) **London**
B.c. 1677, apr. Oct 1691 to Jeremie Gazuet (thro' D. Stevens) till 1698, but not freed. Maybe brother of James who was bound same day.

CHAVIN, James **London**
B.c. 1662, apr. Apr 1676 to Nicholas Mobert, diamond-cutter (thro' Dorcas, widow of Solomon Bouquet) till 1683, but not freed.

CHEAN(E)Y (see Cheney)

CHEESBROUGH, Aaron **Penrith (Cumberland)**
(also **Cheas(e)brough**)
Working there from about 1690, perhaps earlier, and his son, John, was b. about 1686, but perhaps not there. After death of first wife, Catherine, he remarried in 1706 to Jane Clement. He died in 1749. Work known – several 30 hour longcase clocks, usually with posted movements, and at least one eight-day of London style and quality.

CHEESEMAN, Daniel **London**
B.c. 1677, apr. Feb 1691/92 to Benjamin Wright till 1698. Free Sep 1699. Paid quarterage till at least 1704.

CHEESMAN, R. **Horsmunden**
Lantern clock recorded c. 1700.

CHENEVIÉRE, ---- **London**
Late 17th century watch recorded. Not known to CC.

CHENEY, Withers (also **Chean(e)y** and **Cheyne**) **London**
B.c. 1632, apr. Apr 1646 to Elias Allen, mat. inst. maker, (thro' T. Alcock) till 1653. Freed Apr 1657. In 1662 worked in Fleet Street, known as a 'waxchandler & free clockmaker'. If his trade was as a waxchandler, then it is surprising what an active part he took in the CC activities, yet no example of his clock work seems to be known today. Took as aprs.: Jun 1659 **Thomas Chapman;** then apparently a period without aprs. till: Mar 1674/75 **Isaac Nichol** – free Mar 1681/82; Sep 1678 **Thomas Feilder** – free Sep 1687; Jul 1682 **William Mount** – free Sep 1692; Apr 1685 **Thomas Bond;** Jan 1687/88 **Richard Eustace;** Aug 1689 **Philip Beaumont;** Jul 1690 **Samuel Bushell.** Also bound Jun 1682 **Elizabeth Boddily** for Margaret Gardner. Appointed Assistant 1682 (very reluctant attender at first), Warden 1691. In Oct 1695 he refused to

serve in office of Master and was excused 'considering his present residence out of towne', after which he never attended again and prob. died soon after, almost certainly before 1697/98.

CHERITON, George   London/Exeter
B.c. 1671, apr. Aug 1685 to John Buckenhill till 1692 but not freed. One of this name was at Exeter in Jul 1705, presumably same man.

CHETWOOD, John   London
B.c. 1678, apr. Sep 1692 to John Pitcher till 1699 but not freed.

CHIL(L)COTT, Richard (signed double 'l')   London
B.c. 1669, apr. Jul 1683 to Richard Browne till 1690. Freed Sep 1690. Took as apr. Sep 1692 **William Unett**. Paid no quarterage after 1693. Dead or gone by 1697/98. His son, John, was free in CC 1721. Work known – longcase clock signed 'Richard Chillcott, London'.

CHILD, Henry   London
Believed member of Goldsmiths' Co. In Aug 1640 CC warned him to join and he was admitted a Brother in Sep 1641. Took as aprs.: Apr 1647 **John Sharpe** (thro' T. Alcock); May 1648 **Abraham Savage** (thro' T. Alcock); May 1648 **Nehemiah Say** (thro' B. Hill) – free 1656; Sep 1649 **Henry Fulwell** (thro' J. Bayes); (period in 1650s without aprs.?); Jul 1663 **William Herbert** (thro' R. Pierce); Jan 1664-65 **Prittiman Sergeant** (thro' N. Payne). In 1664 Ralph Child, *qv* (a relative?) stood bond for him. Appointed CC Assistant 1653, Warden 1660, Master 1664-65, but died in office. In Jan 1664/65, after he had died, his widow attended CC to hand over the company papers. Work known – three-train lantern clock signed 'Henricus Childe, Londini'.

CHILDE, Henry   London
B.c. 1656 (perhaps son of Henry senior?), apr. Apr 1670, to Nicasius Russell till 1677. Freed Jan 1677/78. Took as apr. Jun 1688 **Tobias Doughty** – freed Jul 1696. Also bound an apr. for Philip Corderoy. From Mar 1694-95 he was in dispute with CC, the case against him being taken to the King's Bench. In Apr 1695 the CC paid 'the officers that arrested H. Child' and had to pay the debt to the Lord Mayor's Court and continued their case against him in Nov 1695 – prob. for non-payment of fines. Paid quarterage till at least 1705, perhaps later. Supposedly worked at Tower Royal, Budge Row. Work known – at least one watch.

CHILD, Ralph   **London**
Apr. Nov 1654 to Richard Peirce (thro' T. Wolverston, or perhaps transferred from him). Freed Jan 1661-62. Not heard of thereafter and not on CC list of 1662. In 1664 a Ralph Child of St. Bartholomew Close stood surety for Henry Child, which may have been this Ralph.

CHILD, Richard   **London**
One of this name, free of the City of London in 1617-18 may or may not have been him. Member of the Blacksmiths' Co. by 1629, steward 1634. Was admitted to CC as a Brother in 1632. Became CC Assistant 1637, Warden 1641-44, when last attended. Took as aprs. (in CC): Apr 1638 **James Wyther** (thro' R. Masterson); Nov 1638 **Thomas Goddard** (thro' R. Masterson); **James Seaborne** (thro' B. Hill) – freed May 1649. Supposedly worked in Fleet Street. Died between 1644 and 1650. In Nov 1650 CC made a grant to his widow and another in 1651 to buy her children 'hose and shoes', followed by occasional other grants till 1666.

CHIPP, Robert   **London**
B.c. 1655, apr. May 1679 to Robert Seignior till 1686 but not freed. Was a witness to Seignior's will in 1687.

CHRISTIAN, Evan or **Ewan**   **Isle of Man**
Maker of sundials variously dated 1666 and 1681.

CHRISTMAS, James   **London**
B.c. 1668, apr. May 1682 to Thomas Birch till 1689 but not freed.

CHURCH, Roger   **Bristol**
Maintained church clock 1583.

CHURCHMAN, Michael   **London**
B.c. 1672, apr. Nov 1685 to Thomas Spencer till 1693. Freed Nov 1694. Paid quarterage till at least 1702.

CHUTTER, Nathaniel   **London**
Baillie has 1683 – I cannot trace him.

CIPPRIAN, Michael   **London(?)**
Pre-1660.

CLAPPOT, Dennis (also **Claypot**)   York (and **London?**)
Watchmaker, free there 1697. One D. Clapot recorded as 18th century watchmaker in London.

CLAR(E)BURG, John de   York
Locksmith. Supposedly made clock for Minster in 1370. Free there 1387.

CLARK and **CLARKE** are listed together but distinction is made, where known. But see also Clerk(e).

CLARK(E), ----   London
In the Minories 1671/72, when had faulty rulers confiscated by CC. Prob. a measure-seller.

CLARK(E), Andrew   London
B.c. 1668, apr. May 1682 to Christopher Gould (thro' D. Stevens) till 1689 but not freed.

CLARKE, Christopher   Amsterdam/London
B.c. 1668 at 'Kelloby', England, which maybe Killerby, co. Durham, nr. Staindrop – if not then location not identified. Watchmaker who married in Amsterdam in 1694 Anna, daughter of Ahasuerus Fromanteel junior. Believed worked with his brother, John. He was the Clarke partner in 'Fromanteel and Clarke'. He inherited much of the Fromanteel fortune. His will, with bequests totalling several thousand pounds, was made in 1734, then being of New Ormond Street, parish of St. Andrew Holborn, Middlesex, mentioning widow, Ann, son John, and daughter, Ann, wife of James Clarke, and was proved in 1735. Work known – none under his own name but clocks and watches under the 'Fromanteel and Clarke' name, prob. manufactured in Amsterdam, but believed sold both there and in London. Later a partner with Roger Dunster in Amsterdam and products signed 'Clarke and Dunster'.

CLARKE and DUNSTER   London/Amsterdam
Partnership, starting from death of Ahasuerus Fromanteel junior c. 1703, between Christopher Clarke and Roger Dunster *qv*, and lasting till about 1725-30. Work known – watches, longcase and bracket clocks.

CLARK, Edmond   London
B.c. 1650, apr. Feb 1664/65 to Richard Granger, a butcher in Southwark (thro' William Petty) till 1671 but not freed.

CLARK, Elizabeth **London**
B.c. 1662, apr. Apr 1676 to Henry Jevon (a lawyer) and Christian his wife till 1683, but not freed.

CLARK, George **London**
Free Brother in CC Oct 1632. Supposedly at Whitechapel.

CLARK, Humphrey **London**
In 1632 CC told him to bring in proof of how long he had served as a clockmaker (ie apprenticeship proof). Must have been accepted as a Brother as he paid quarterage until 1641 at least.

CLARK, Humphrey **London/Hertford**
Apr. Sep 1657 to Peter Closon (thro' N. Coxeter), later transferred to Robert Robinson (perhaps after Closon's death). Freed Jan 1668/69. In 1669 was free of the City of London by aprship. (son of Thomas Clarke of Sp– (illegible), late apr. of Edward (error for Nicholas) Coxeter. Took as aprs.: May 1670 **John Parker** – free Apr 1678; Sep 1674 **Thomas Clark**; Sep 1681 **John Clarke**. Work known – at least one lantern clock signed 'Humphrey Clark of Hartford fecit', who is assumed to be the same man.

CLARKE, John senior **Bristol**
Watch recorded c. 1635.

CLARKE, John junior **Bristol**
Apr. Apr 1643 to Solomon Wasson. Free Feb 1650. Had as apr. **William Underwood** 1660 – free 1667.

CLARK, John **London**
B.c. 1661, apr. May 1675 to Peter Southworth till 1682. In Jun 1683 one such was involved in making watches for John Harman with invented names to be proceeded against by CC. Worked in his own house.

CLARKE, John **London**
B.c. 1667, apr. Sep 1681 to Humphrey Clarke till 1689 but not freed.

CLARKE, John **London**
B.c. 1669, apr. May 1682 to James Graves, an engraver and freeman of the Weavers' Co. (thro' N. Russell) till 1690. Freed Jul 1691. Took as apr. Oct 1695 **John Hawksbee** – free Sep 1709. Paid quarterage till 1696. Working 1697 but prob. not for long after. May well have been an engraver.

CLARKE, John   **Stamford**
Prob. error for John Stanford Clarke.

CLARK, John Stanford   **London**
B.c. 1672, apr. Apr 1686 to Thomas Jones till 1693. Freed Jan 1696-97.
Took as aprs.: Jan 1696/97 **John Tod** – free May 1707; Dec 1716 **Robert
Duncan;** Jan 1718/19 **Edward Clarke;** perhaps others later. Work
known – watch and prob. a lantern clock.

CLARKE, Jospeh   **Chester**
Watchmaker free there 1679.

CLARK, Mary   **London**
B.c. 1660, apr. Feb 1674/75 to Henry Jevon (a lawyer) and Christian his
wife till 1681 but not freed.

CLARK, Samuel   **London**
B.c. 1673, apr. Nov 1687 to John Martin till 1694 but not freed.

CLARKE, Thomas   **London**
B.c. 1660, apr. Sep 1674 to Humphrey Clarke till 1681 but not freed.

CLARKE, William   **London**
Apr. Feb 1647/48 to William Selwood (thro' S. Davis). Freed Nov 1654.
Selwood died Apr 1653 and left him a bequest of £6.00. Prob. dead or
gone by 1662.

CLARK, William   **London**
B.c. 1655, apr. Dec 1668 to Henry Crumpe till 1676 but not freed.

CLARK, William   **London**
B.c. 1674, apr. Jun 1688 to Thomas Clifton till 1675 but not freed. Work
known – bracket clock c. 1700 signed 'Wm. Clarke, Whitechaple'.

CLARKSON, John   **London**
B.c. 1635, apr. Apr 1649 to John Nicasius (thro' T. Alcock) till 1656.
Freed Jul 1657. Worked in Westminster in 1662. Took as aprs.: Oct
1659 **Richard Prince** (thro' T. Claxton) – freed Nov 1680; May 1664
Thomas Whethall. Not heard of after 1664.

CLAXTON, Richard   **London**
Apr. 1638, CC 1646. This is an error for Thomas, *qv*.

CLAXTON, Thomas   **London**
B.c. 1625, apr. Jan 1638/39 to Sampson Shelton (thro' O. Durant) till
1646. Freed Jun 1646. In 1656 rebelled against CC administration. In
1662 worked in Cornhill – his house was in Guildhall Yard where CC
court met several times from 1661-63. Took as aprs.: Aug 1649
Benjamin Bell – free Apr 1657; Aug 1650 **Richard Gorslow;** Jan 1653/54
John Wright – free Nov 1661; Oct 1663 **Christopher Rose;** Oct 1663
Michael Rose – free Jun 1676; **John Watts** (from John Norcott, later
passed over to T. Hollis) – freed 1664. Also bound aprs. for several other
masters including W. Elmes (two), John Savill, A. Prime, B. Bell,
I. Daniel (two), W. Bunting, H. Kent, W. Clay, P. Bellon, J. Wells
(two), J. Clarkson, R. Smith, J. Pennock, R. Starr. Made CC Assistant
1660, Warden 1668-69, Master 1670. Last attended in 1676, when prob.
died. Widow Jane received CC charity in 1680.

CLAY, Samuel   **London**
B.c. 1666, apr. May 1680 to Jeremy Gregory (thro' B. Bell) till 1688(?),
but freed Dec 1687. Took as aprs.: Sep 1689 **Jonathan Atkins;** Sep 1696
Richard Greene. Paid quarterage till about 1693, prob. died before
1697. His son, Jeremiah (b.c. 1691) was given CC charity to help bind
him as apr. in Feb 1706-07 (at which time his father was dead).

CLAY, Thomas   **Chelmsford (Essex)**
Lantern clocks recorded c. 1650.

CLAY, William   **London**
Never officially admitted into CC but was accepted by them. Took as
aprs.: Sep 1646 **Charles Duffa** (thro' T. Claxton); Aug 1649 **George
Fullum** (thro' L. Wythe); **Arthur Dove** – free Oct 1659. Supported the
CC administration in the 1656 dispute. Prob. dead by 1662. Work
known – lantern clocks and watches, one signed 'William Clay, King's
Street, Westminster'.

CLAYPOT (see Clappot)

CLAYTON, George   **Marple (Cheshire)**
Working about 1680 till death in 1716. Succ. by son, John. Work known
– longcase clock signed 'Georgius Clayton de Marple fecit'.

CLAYTON, Thomas   **London**
One such recorded as CC 1646 by some authorities is an error for Thomas Claxton, *qv*.

CLEAKE, Ezekiel   **Exeter**
Kept local TCs 1673 until death in 1709. Succ. by son of same name.

CLEARE, William   **London**
B.c. 1674, apr. Feb 1688/89 to Henry Jones till 1695 but not freed.

CLEAVE (see Cleeve)

CLEEVE, John (also **Cleave**)   **Belfast**
Repaired church clock 1665-66.

CLEEVE, William   **London**
Free Brother in CC Sep 1654. Not on 1662 list but received five shillings from poor box in Apr 1668.

CLEMENT and **CLEMENTS** are listed together but distinction is made, where known.

CLEMENTS, Abraham   **London**
Not a clockmaker but was the son of Robert Clements of Ausley(?), Warwickshire, farmer, and apr. in Blacksmiths' Co. to John Sayward from Sep 1634 till 1642, but not freed. Watch recorded as Allan Clements, 1641, maybe a misreading of Abm. or Abrm. or Allam and Clements.

CLEMENTS, Allen   **London**
Watch recorded dated 1641. Nothing known about him but see previous entry.

CLEMENT, Edward   **Exeter (Devon)**
Was there in 1688 as a clockmaker. Churchwarden at St. Lawrence 1691/92. Kept St. Johns church clock in 1690s. Believed buried there in 1720. This could well be Edward Clement from London – see next entry. Work known – at least one lantern clock signed 'Edward Clement Exon' and a 30-hour longcase signed 'Edwardus Clement Exon fecit'. One clock said to be signed 'Edward Clement, Devonshire'.

CLEMENT, Edward   **London**
Apr. Aug 1662 to Thomas Claxton, transferred to Andrew Prime. Freed
Apr 1671. Took as apr. Apr 1673 **Francis Harding** – freed Apr 1687 (and
one of this name recorded later at Portsmouth). Paid no quarterage after
1674 and may well have gone to Exeter between 1674 and 1688 – see
previous entry.

CLEMENT, Francis   **London**
Apr. in Blacksmiths' Co. Oct 1657 to Thomas Chapman (same master as
William Clement, whose brother he is thought to have been). Not freed?
Not a member of CC. Only two clocks are so far recorded by him, both
longcase signed 'Fra. Clement, London', one a 30-hour and both late,
dating from c. 1705. It may be that he worked as journeyman for William
and did not produce work in his own name until after William died in
1709, but this is speculation.

CLEMENT, Richard   **London**
A clockmaker working in parish of St. Saviour's Southwark in 1666,
when daughter Elizabeth was b. Believed brother of Francis, *qv*. Not in
CC.

CLEMENTS, Robert   **London**
B.c. 1665, apr. Sep 1679 to John Harris of Holborn Bridge till 1686.
Freed Sep 1686. Not, so far as is known, connected with William
Clement. Took as aprs.: Jun 1696 **John Hutchins** – free Sep 1703; Jan
1699/1700 **Goddard Doverdale** (son of Thomas Doverdale, late of
Castle Eaton, co. Wiltshire, clerk, deceased). Paid no quarterage after
1703 and not heard of thereafter. Work known – two or three longcase
clocks, some signed Clement, some Clements.

CLEMENT, William   **Bodmin (Cornwall)**
Was paid £5 in 1695 to repair turret clock. Prob. the Totnes man, *qv*.

CLEMENT, William (elder and younger?)   **London**
A very important clockmaker but his ancestry and life are still very much
uncharted. The only serious attempt at documenting his life appears to
be John B. Penfold's paper in *Antiquarian Horology* in Sep 1962, which
gives much useful information on the period after 1670. However, whilst
I believe that both the birth and death details, as set out by Penfold, are
incorrect, I am not yet able to document his true identity. It is almost
certain that there were *two* William Clements involved in clockmaking

(William Clement junior, as set out in the next entry, would therefore be the third of that name, though no work is recorded by him). Little is known of William the elder, indeed his existence has not yet been recognised. He was b. before 1622 (how long before is not known, and one of this name Free of the City in 1626 might, or might not, be him). He was a Freeman of the Blacksmiths' Co. in 1654, Livery 1664. He was still alive in 1675 (and possibly much later, though the 1697 Oath Roll is signed by only one person of this name – the Assistant) but later it becomes much harder to distinguish him from the younger William. He was not a member of the CC (but see also below). It was almost certainly this man who made the famous Kings College, Cambridge, turret clock in 1671 and prob. also a turret clock in 1667 documented in the Middle Temple archives. He was prob. the father of William the younger and Francis, *qv*, Patience (who married the clockmaker Edward Burgis in 1670) and Katherine (who married John Hatch, a cooper, in 1675) and prob. also Richard Clement, a clockmaker working in Southwark in 1666.

William the younger was b. about 1643, apr. in Blacksmiths' Co. 1656-57 to Thomas Chapman (the same master as his brother, Francis), was made a Free Brother in CC Dec 1677 as a 'great clockmaker'; his admission fee, most unusually, was excused. Some of the facts here quoted may of course refer to William the elder. He took as aprs. in CC: Dec 1677 **John Millett** (thro' S. Davis) – not freed; Nov 1684, his son, **William Clement** junior, *qv* thro' D. Stevens) – not freed; Nov 1685 **John Brookes** (thro' D. Stevens) – not freed; (and the elder or younger took) Sep 1694 **John Spring;** and also an apr. for John Westoby in 1694 and one for William Williamson in 1695. In Aug 1684 there was some trouble when John Millet and Edward Millett assaulted Clement (see Penfold). The CC evidently held Clement in very high esteem for reasons we cannot establish. In Sep 1678 they made him Assistant long before he should have been, according to seniority, 'by unanimous consent and approbation and for good reasons and especial esteem'. This *may* be thought of as evidence for the claim that he was the inventor of the anchor escapement at about this time – the matter is still unresolved, however. He became Warden in 1690, Master in 1694. In Sep 1697 he was excused attendance at CC meetings on account of his age (which seems unlikely since he was only 54, but it may refer to the elder William who would have been at least 75. This may seem an obvious interpretation but other evidence conflicts with this interpretation). Likewise the 1678 Assistantship *could* have been the elder man's. After the 1670s one William Clement lived in the parish of St. Saviours Southwark. William (the younger?) died in 1709, his wife, Katherine, having died in 1708-09. As from Apr 1704 the CC granted him a regular charity 'if he will accept it', which he did, the last payment being in Apr 1709 (he received the largest charity payment for each quarter). The whole Clement picture is very confused and I have only been able to set down some of the facts. The story has been confused however, and it now seems clear that the facts relate not to one man, but to two. Work known – at least one watch and several longcase clocks, some with considerable signs of innovation, including an eight-day single-handed clock and some with 1¼-second pendulums. Usually signed 'William Clement Londini fecit'.

CLEMENT, William junior   **London**
B.c. 1670, son of William senior. Apr. to father Nov 1684 (thro' D. Stevens) till 1691 but not freed. May have worked as journeyman for father. He died in Nov 1704 leaving a widow, Elizabeth.

CLEMENT, William   **St. Albans**
Longcase clock recorded signed 'William Clement, St. Albans' c. 1720. This is a single, unattached 'sighting', but it may form part of the William Clement mystery.

CLEMENT, William   **Totnes (Devon)**
Recorded there as churchwarden 1695, mayor 1711, died 1736. Wife, Mary, died 1732. Work known – a bracket clock signed 'Wm. Clement Totnes fecit', a 30-hour longcase signed 'William Clement Totnes' and a watch. No connection with the London namesake is known.

CLEM(P)SON, Richard   **London**
Apr. Nov 1661 to Thomas Claxton, later transferred to Benjamin Bell. Freed Jul 1673. Paid quarterage till 1674 but not later.

CLENT, George   **London**
B.c. 1670, apr. Oct 1684 to John Bennett till 1691 but not freed.

CLERK(E) (see under Clark(e))

CLEWES (see Clowes)

CLEWITT, Francis (*cf* Cluer?)   **London**
Cane-seller at the Blew Bell in the Strand nr. Charing Cross. Had faulty rulers confiscated by CC in 1671-72, allegedly obtained from Robert Jole.

CLIFT, William London
B.c. 1656, apr. Jul 1670 to Samuel Davis till 1677 but not freed.

CLIFTON, John London
In Lothbury in 1646 and infringing CC rules. Did not become a member so presumably moved on.

CLIFTON, Joseph London
The first known (ie recorded) maker of wooden cases for clocks. Left his trade token hidden in a purpose-made cavity in the base of an architectural ebonised longcase of a Fromanteel clock. On one side 'I.C. 1663', on the other 'Ioseph Clifton – his halfpenny, BVLL HEAD YARD, CHEPSIDE'. He married in Oct 1658 to Susan Tanfield and was certainly still there in 1664. He did not belong to the CC, nor to the Joyners' Co. nor Carpenters' Co.

CLIFTON, Thomas London
Supposedly free in CC 1651 – I cannot confirm this.

CLIFTON, Thomas London
Apr. Dec 1678 to Charles Gretton and freed Sep 1687. Took as apr. Jun 1688 **William Clark**. Paid quarterage till c. 1691 but not heard of thereafter. Prob. dead or gone by 1698-98.

CLOPTON, William London
B.c. 1644, apr. Aug 1655 to Onisephorus Helden till 1665 but not freed.

CLOSE, Samuel Belfast
c. 1700.

CLOSEN, Peter London
Freeman of another City Co. – perhaps Blacksmiths'. Subscriber to incorporation of CC in 1630. Took as aprs.: Jul 1638 **John Wise** (thro' T. Dawson) – free Oct 1646; May 1639 **Nicholas Tomlins** (thro' O. Durant) – free Oct 1646; May 1646 **Robert Cosby** (thro' T. Alcock) – free Jan 1653; Jun 1646 **Hugh Cooper** (thro' T. Alcock) – free Jun 1653; Feb 1648/49 **Richard Ames** (thro' R. Masterson) – free Jan 1656/57; Aug 1654 **William Speakman** (thro' N. Tomlins) – free Sep 1661; **William Fenkman** – free Sep 1661; **Philip Buckner** (thro' N. Coxeter) – freed Jan 1667-78; **Humphrey Clark** (thro' N. Coxeter later passed to Robert Robinson). He had a son living in 1642. Made Assistant in CC 1633

Warden 1637-38, when ceased to attend. Last known alive 1654 and prob. dead before 1662-63. Work known – lantern clocks including one quarter-striking three-train example. Signed 'Peter Closon near Hoburn Bridge fecit', 'Peter Closon Londini fecit' and 'Peter Closon Neare Holburne Bridge, Londini fecit', also supposedly 'Peter Closon at Holborne Bridge' and 'Peter Closon at London fecit'.

CLOUGH, Edward   **London**
Assessed by some authorities as c. 1630, which is much too early. Son of Humphrey Clough (a freeman of the Loriners' Co.). In 1668/69 he was granted freedom of the City of London 'being legitimate and born within the liberty'. He was a watchmaker and a freeman of the Loriners' Co. Took as aprs. in CC: Nov 1667 **Bernard Rainsford** (thro' C. Bonner) – free Jul 1677; Nov 1669 **John Baptist Hall** (thro' C. Bonner); Jan 1673-74 **Abel Gould** (thro' C. Bonner) – free Oct 1683; Sep 1674 **Nathan Greenhill** (thro' C. Bonner); Dec 1676 **John Charlesworth** (thro' W. Speakman). Supposedly worked at Fetter Lane and 'near Gray's Inn Gate in Holborn'. Work known – watches.

CLOUGHE, Thomas   **Colchester (Essex)**
Believed b. c.1565 – 75. In 1602 contracted to maintain Braintree church clock at 5 shillings a year. Buried 18 Sep 1626.

CLOWER, James – prob. error for Clowes, *qv.*

CLOWES, James (sometimes **Clewes**)   **London**
Admitted to CC as a free Brother in Apr 1671 as a 'Great Clockmaker'. Took as aprs.: Jan 1672/73 **Edmund Card** (thro' T. Morgan) – free Apr 1680; Apr 1678 **Charles Edward Burgess;** Sep 1687 **James Osmond** (thro' D. Stevens); Mar 1693-94 **Daniel Wint** (thro' T. Morgan); **John Johnson** – free Nov 1701. Paid quarterage till 1705, perhaps longer. Work known – longcase and bracket clocks signed 'James Clowes – London' and 'James Clowes Londini fecit', one reported as 'James Clower – London' may be mis-reading of dial or an engraving slip.

CLOWES, John   **London**
B.c. 1651, free Brother in CC Jan 1672/73 as a 'Great Clockmaker'. Married at St. James, Clerkenwell, Dec 1688, a clockmaker, widower, aged 37 to Tabitha Taylor of St. Andrew Holborn (maybe related to Thomas Taylor of Holborn, *qv*?) 23, spinster. Took as aprs.: May 1677 **Josiah Ridley** (thro' S. Davis) – free Jan 1685/86; Feb 1682/83 **William**

Sellars (thro' D. Stevens) – free Nov 1691; Jan 1685/86 **Richard Rooker** (thro' T. Wilson) – free Apr 1694; Jul 1688 **George Hanson** (thro' D. Stevens) – free Mar 1695/96; Sep 1691 **Francis Gregg** (thro' T. Morgan); Nov 1703 **Thomas Hill;** Jul 1709 his son, **John Clowes.** In Jul 1687 he was excused his term as Steward as it was vital for him to be 'in the country' at the time of the Feast. Became Assistant in 1708, was to serve as Warden in Oct 1713 but was indisposed and could not. He never attended again thereafter and prob. died 1713-14. Work known – several bracket and longcase clocks (incl. month longcase) and a lantern clock. Signed variously 'Jno. Clowes Russell Street, Covent Garden', 'John Clowes London fecit' and 'John Clowes London'.

CLOWES, Jonathan   London
Believed error for John since no such person traced.

CLUER, Obadiah (*cf* Clewitt?)   London
B.c. 1668, apr. Oct 1682 to Henry Evans till 1689. Freed Jul 1709. Took as apr. Feb 1709/10 **Joseph Taylor** – not freed. Not heard of after 1709. Baillie lists him at Lewisham but I don't know his source. Work known – longcase clock signed 'Obed. Cluer'.

CLYATT, Abraham   London
B.c. 1659, apr. Jul 1673 to Samuel Clyatt till 1680. Freed Jul 1680. In Sep 1682 was given permission to take a new apr. **Edward Orton** having left him (Orton was really **Samuel Clyatt's** apr.). Took as aprs.: Sep 1686 **Cornelius Russell;** Jun 1697 **James Nash.** Paid no quarterage after 1699.

CLYATT, Samuel senior   London
B.c. 1650, apr. May 1663 to Humphrey Peirce till 1671. Freed Apr 1672. Took as aprs.: Jul 1673 **Abraham Clyatt** – freed Jul 1680; Aug 1675 **Thomas Birch** – free Jan 1682/83; Aug 1680 **Edward Orton** (who left? – see Abraham Clyatt) – but freed Sep 1687; Nov 1682 **William Hill;** Nov 1686 **Samuel Harvey** – free Jul 1696; Mar 1688 **Edmund East** (from R. Lyons) – free Jul 1696; **James Jackson** (from R. Cosby) – freed Sep 1689; May 1695 **John Ashurst;** Jul 1698 his son, **John Clyatt;** Sep 1699 **John Brockhurst** (son of John Brockhurst of Coventry, scrivener, deceased); son, **Samuel Clyatt** junior, freed by patrimony Feb 1702/03; Aug 1707 **Hugh Swift;** son, **Abraham Clyatt** freed by patrimony Mar 1708/09; Sep 1714 **John Blaze.** Had a son, Erastus, b.c. 1690. Believed worked in Bell Alley, Coleman Street.

CLYMER, Richard **Bristol**
Clockmaker there 1675.

COASTFIELD (error for Coatsfield, *qv*)

COATES, Ralph **Darlington (Co. Durham)**
Made church clock in 1686 for £13.00.

COATSFIELD, John (not Coastfield) **London**
B.c. 1668, apr. May 1682 to Robert Starr (a freeman of the Stationers'
Co.) thro' T. Wheeler till 1689 – not freed.

COBB, John **London**
B.c. 1678, apr. Nov 1692 to Andrew Yeatman, then transferred to
Thomas Terrier till 1699. Freed Jul 1703. Not heard of after that and not
on CC quarterage list.

COBB, William **York**
Son of William Cobb of York. Free there as watchmaker in 1659. His
wife, Ann, died in 1673.

COBHAM, Joshua **Liverpool (Lancashire)**
Watch and watch case maker. Had children b. there between 1674 and
1681.

COCK, John **London**
Three longcase clocks and a watch are recorded c.1690 – c.1710, but
nothing seems to be known of this man and he was not known to CC.
Maybe the signature of one of the several John Cookes at this time?

CO(C)KEY (there are several spellings; Cockey is the commonest)

COCKEY, Edward senior **Warminster (Wiltshire)**
Watch and longcase clock known c.1690 – c.1710. A second Edward was
b. in 1701, but nothing seems to be known about the elder one.

COCKEY, Lewis (and **William**) **Frome (Somerset)**
A bellfounder from Bristol 1680. Died 1703. May also have made clocks.
Believed made chiming barrel for Wesbury church clock in late 17th
century.

COCKEY, William Warminster/Wincanton and **Frome**
Believed repaired church clock c.1700 – 21 at Wincanton and a longcase clock is known signed by him there. One of this name also at Warminster c.1680 – c.1700 and one of this name was churchwarden at Frome 1692-1700, where he also made bells till 1751. Whether all this refers to one, two, or three different men is not known.

COKE, William (error for Cooke, *qv*)

COLA, Berson John (see Berson)

COLE, Humphrey London
Supposedly working 1568-97, maker of portable sundials and compasses, and rules, one dated 1575, another 1582. In 1584 was referred to as 'old Humphrey Cole'.

COL(E)MAN, Francis senior Ipswich
Believed married there 1668 to Elizabeth Armond. Perhaps died 1709. Difficult to establish if the man of this name *was* the clockmaker. Work known – a lantern clock supposedly dated 1665.

COL(E)MAN, Francis junior(?) Ipswich
B. 1667, son of Joseph and Deborah Coleman, grocers. Married 1st 1689 Elizabeth Wade, 2nd 1709 Elizabeth Phillips. Was also a goldsmith. Died 8 May 1738. Work known – several watches on record.

COLLARD, Leonard London
B.c. 1661, apr. Feb 1675/76 to John Delander (thro' N. Delander) till 1682, not freed.

COLLEBER, John Exeter
Watchmaker there 1711. See Colliber.

COLLES, Christopher London(?)
Clocks recorded c. 1685 and c. 1700. Nothing else known.

COLLIBER, John London
B.c. 1676, apr. Oct 1690 to William Slough (thro' J. Wise junior) till 1697. Free Apr 1703. Took as aprs.: May 1703 **Edward Jones** (son of Thomas Jones, late of Bristol, gent.) later transferred to John Eyre.

COLLIER, Benjamin (sometimes Collyer)   **London**
B.c. 1670, apr. Jun 1684 to Stephen Wilmott till 1691. Freed Jul 1693.
Took as aprs.: May 1694 **Thomas Planner** – free Jul 1701; Jul 1696
Benjamin Jackson; Dec 1700 **John Norgate** (son of William Norgate,
late Citizen and Grocer of London) – free Dec 1712. Work known –
several watches and longcase clocks. An Act of Parliament clock signed
'Collyer in Leadenhall Street' was stolen in 1726.

COLLINS, John   **Tiverton (Devon)**
Repaired church clock in 1668.

COLLINS, John   **London**
B.c. 1680, apr. Jul 1693 to Thomas Gardner till 1701. Freed Sep 1701. In
Jan 1716-17 took son, **John Collins** apr., later transferred to John
Wilson. Worked at 'the White Horse and Black Boy in the Great Old
Bailey' in 1705. Work known – watch c. 1710 signed 'John Collins –
London'.

COLLINS, Peter   **London**
B.c. 1661(/65?), apr. Jan 1679/80 (thro' H. Wynne) to James Atkinson, a
mat. inst. maker and freeman of the Joyners' Co., till 1686. Freed Sep
1687. In Aug 1687 he was a clockmaker, a bachelor, aged 26 of Stepney,
Middlesex, when he was to marry Mary Robertson, spinster, aged 20 at
Hackney. Took as aprs.: Oct 1687 **John Dyson** (thro' J. North) – free
Apr 1695; Jul 1694 **Philip Gamage;** Oct 1699 **John Sanderlin** (son of
John Sanderlin, late of — (illegible), Middlesex. Paid quarterage till
1701 but not thereafter.

COLLINS, Robert   **London**
B.c. 1632, apr. Aug 1646 to Ahasuerus Fromanteel (thro' J. Quash) till
1653 but not freed.

COLLO, Dedie   **London**
French, a denizen clockmaker in 1544. *Cf* Callot later – perhaps same
family?

COLLYER (see Collier)

COL(L)OMBIER/COL(L)OMBY, Jacques/Jacob   **London**
Watches recorded c.1660 – c.1700. Nothing known. Prob. French.

COLOR, ----   **London**
Known to CC but not a member. Prob. dead by 1663.

COLS(T)ON, John (signed Coulstone)   **London**
B.c. 1625, apr. Sep 1637 to James Vautrollier till 1646. Free Nov 1646 (as
a free Brother).

COLSTON, John (signed Coulston)   **London**
Free Brother in CC 1653/54. Had son, Richard, freed by patrimony Jul
1682. Took as apr. Jul 1682 **Emanuel Jennings**. Prob. dead by 1693.
Work known – longcase clock.

COLSTON, Richard   **London**
Son of John Colston, freed Jul 1682 by patrimony. Took as aprs.: Jul
1682 **George Bayford**; Aug 1685 **Thomas Kewell**; Jan 1691/92 **Henry
Lawrence** – freed Apr 1704; Nov 1697 **Richard Scrivener**; Oct 1702
Thomas Colston. Paid no quarterage after 1702 and prob. died soon
after. From 1715 to 1720 his widow (Hester?) received charities from
CC. Work known – several longcase clocks and watches signed 'Richard
Colston, London'.

COMFORT, William (also Comford)   **London**
Free Brother in CC Nov 1646. Gave funds towards the 1656 rebellion
against the CC administration. Took as aprs.: Oct 1647 **Simon Scott**
(thro' L. Wythe); Oct 1653 **George Nevill** (thro' R. Beck); Oct 1658
Henry Reeve (thro' B. Hill) – freed Mar 1682. Not heard of after 1658
and prob. dead by 1662-63.

COMPTON, ----   **London**
Goldsmith in Duke Street, nr. Lincolns Inn Fields in 1695. Believed sold
watches, eg by Tompion.

COMPTON, Walter   **London**
Supposedly in Vere Street in 1692.

CONDUITT, Samuel   **London**
B.c. 1657, apr. Feb 1671/72 to Robert Halstead till 1678 but not freed.

CONDY, Thomas   **London**
B.c. 1670, apr. Mar 1684/85 to Cornelius Jenkins till 1691. Freed Jun
1692. Took as aprs.: Aug 1696 **Daniel Cesar** – free Sep 1703; May 1700

William Gibbs (son of John Gibbs of St. Bottolph Bishopsgate, London, labourer) – free Nov 1707; Aug 1707 **Charles Guy** – free Jan 1714/15. Not heard of after 1707.

CONNOCKE, Gilliam   London
Clockmaker from Holland 1583 – according to Baillie.

CONNY, John   London
Supposed apr. in 1630 in Blacksmiths' Co. Free Brother in CC Nov 1640.

CONSTABLE, Thomas   Dublin
Watchmaker there in 1660.

CONSTANTIN(E), John   London
A clockmaker who promised in Jul 1688 to join CC at next Quarter Court, but did not. Work known – bracket and longcase clocks signed 'John Constantine, London' and 'Constantin, London', but see next entry too.

CONSTANTIN, Philippe Girardel   London
Watchmaker at Spitalfields Market 1702/04.

CONYERS, Richard   London
B.c. 1658, apr. Sep 1672 to John Cooke till 1679. Freed Nov 1689. Took as aprs.: Nov 1689 **Gervas Wawen**; Apr 1693 **Thomas Lashbrooke** – free Sep 1701; Dec 1698 **John Beckett** (son of Gilbert Beckett, Citizen and Leatherseller); Apr 1700 **Henry Austin** (son of James Austen of Stepney, victualler) – free Sep 1712. Paid quarterage till late in 1701 and prob. died soon after. In May 1708 his widow, Susanna, and son, Richard (aged 14) asked CC for a grant towards his apprenticeship and received £5. Richard was bound to Richard George and freed Dec 1716.

COOK and **COOKE** are listed together with different spellings shown when known.

COOKE, Edward   London
B.c. 1673, apr. Jul 1687 to William Kenning (thro' D. Stevens) till 1694 but not freed.

COOKE, John   London
In 1622 was an alien and an apr. working with Cornelius Mellin in

161

Blackfriars. Work known – a watch is recorded but this might be by the next man, *qv*.

COOKE, John   **London**
Apr. Aug 1641 to Isaac Lawe (thro' J. Hopkins). Freed Apr 1649. Took as apr. May 1651 **Richard Wood** – not freed. Took several aprs. for other makers – one for Nicholas Parke, one for Ambrose Blise, one for Peter Delawne and two for Isaac Lawe, for whom he prob. worked as journeyman. In 1656 he supported the administration in the CC rebellion. Still alive as John Cooke senior in 1687 when he was in arrears with quarterage. Prob. dead by 1697/98.

COOKE, John junior   **London**
Apr. Nov 1655 to William Dobb (thro' T. Wolverston). Freed Dec 1662. Took as apr. Sep 1672 **Richard Conyers** – freed Nov 1689. Believed still alive as John Cooke junior in 1682 but nothing known thereafter. Work known – a longcase clock.

COOKE, John   **London**
B.c. 1670, apr. Apr 1684 to George Nau till 1691 but not freed.

COOK, Jonathan   **London**
Baillie has 1684. Prob. an error for John above, *qv*.

COOKE, Lewis   **York/London**
Made clock for York Corporation and free there in 1614. Had daughter, Thomasine, b. 1615, died 1616. In London in Apr. 1632 was fined by CC for employing a foreigner (John Daverill). Was also asked for proof of his own apprenticeship which he refused to show and left 'with much ill language'. Later he entered CC as a Brother. In Mar 1633/34 he apologised for insulting John Harris who had found fault with his work: 'I did give the said John Harris the lye and told him that he was a botcher and that he never made so good a peece of work in his life as that was which he found fault with all; these words being rashly and inadvisedly spoken I am heartily sorry . . .'.

COOKE, Richard   **London**
Apr. Aug 1659 in Weavers' Co. to Walter Henshaw, *qv*. Free in Weavers' Co. Sep 1675. He was a mat. inst. maker, free Brother in CC Feb 1667/68. Took as aprs.: Jun 1671 **Johnson Weeks** (thro' L. Wythe) – free Dec 1683; Feb 1678/79 **Benjamin Bigg** (thro' S. Davis).

COOKE, Thomas London
B.c 1636, apr. Jan 1649/50 to William Petty till 1657, but not freed. On CC list of 1662, not heard of thereafter.

COOKE, Thomas London
B.c. 1668, apr. Jan 1682-83 to Thomas Hicks till 1689. Freed Aug 1699 (having been transferred to William May). Took as apr. Apr 1702 **William Willes** (son of Isaac Willes late of St. Stephens Coleman Street, London, mariner, deceased). Paid quarterage till 1704, not heard of thereafter.

COOKE, Thomas London
Baillie has 1669/1702 CC – error for 1699, same man as above.

COOK, William Aberdeen
Kept town clocks with Patrick Wanhagan in 1651.

COOKE, William London
B.c. 1659, Apr. Mar 1673/74 to William Glazier till 1680. Freed Apr 1681. Paid no quarterage after about 1687. Dead by 1698. Supposedly 'escaped from prison' in 1697(?). His son, William, was freed in CC by patrimony Jan 1708/09. Longcase clock signed 'William Cooke Londini, Fecit'.

COOMBES, William London
B.c. 1675, apr. Sep 1689 to Isaac Lowndes (thro' H. Aske) till 1696 but not freed.

COOPER, Hugh (also **Hew**) London
Apr. Jun 1646 to Peter Closon (thro' T. Alcock). Freed Jun 1653. Took as aprs.: Mar 1654/55 **John Barridge; John Fletcher** (from J. Saville); Aug 1660 **John Edmondson; Thomas Simmonds,** freed Apr 1661; Sep 1664 **Thomas Applegarth** (who was transferred to Jeffrey Bailey on Cooper's death) – freed Jul 1674. Also bound an apr. for Peter Delawne and one for Thomas Broome. In 1662 worked in Fleet Street. Died post 1664 and pre 1674.

COOPER, James London
B.c. 1679, apr. Jul 1693 to Thomas Boad till 1700 but not freed.

COOPER, John   **Cardiff**
Watch c. 1700 and another c. 1705 with portrait of Queen Anne.

COOPER, John   **Warrington**
Quaker, clockmaker. His illegitimate child, Joseph, was baptised Oct 1698 'at the sine of the Swann at Boughton'.

COOPER, Stephen   **London**
B.c. 1661, apr. Jul 1675 to Thomas Morgan till 1682 but not freed.

COOPER, William (see Cowper)

COPE, Peter junior   **London**
Admitted to CC as a free Brother Jul 1638 – not heard of thereafter.

COPES, James (see Cowpe)

COPLEY, ----   **London**
In 1635 Mrs. Copley came to CC and asked for money for her husband, despite what they had already done for him. (?).

COPPING, George   **London**
B.c. 1642, apr. Nov 1654 to Richard Copping (thro' W. Petty) till 1663 but not freed. A George Copping senior was witness to the 1667 will of William Seabourne, *qv*.

COPPING(E), Richard   **Bury St. Edmunds (Suffolk)**
Believed b. 1615, married 1662, died 1689. Work known – longcase clock signed 'Richard Copping at St. Edmunds Bury in Suffolke'; lantern clock signed 'Richard Copping St. Edmunds Bury'. In Nov 1654 one of this name took as apr. in CC **George Copping** (thro' W. Petty). Not actually a member of CC himself. (The Richard Copping, mariner, deceased, of Marget in the Isle of Thanet, whose son, John, was apr. Nov 1698 to John Benson, seems unlikely to be the same man.)

COPPLESTONE, William   **London**
B.c. 1669, apr. Aug 1683 to William Robinson till 1690 but not freed. A clockmaker of this name supposedly worked at Plymouth c. 1790, but perhaps earlier?

CORBET, Hugh   Oxford
Locksmith, gunsmith and TC. Freed 1589. Repaired St. Martin's clock
c. 1592-1600. His apr. **Thomas Lane** was freed 1604 and another one in
1614. Kept St. John's College clock 1598-1603 and St. Mary Magdalene
clock 1604-16.

CORBET, Nathaniel   London
Lost watch recorded in 1693.

CORBITT, Benjamin   London
B.c. 1669, apr. Jan 1682/83 to Thomas Snelling till 1690 but not freed.

CORDER, William   Derby
Watch recorded pre-1689.

CORDEROY, Phillip   London
B.c. 1658, apr. Jul 1672 to Robert Seigniour till 1679. Freed Jul 1679. In
Nov 1680 as a clockmaker aged 22 of St. Mary Abchurch parish, a
bachelor, he married Mary Bagley of St. Clement's Lane, spinster, aged
24, at St. Martins in the Fields (she was prob. a relative of Thomas
Bagley, *qv*). Took as aprs.: Feb 1680-81 **William Morelley** (thro'
H. Child) later transferred to Thomas Tompion and freed Dec 1688; Jul
1686 **Samuel Motteux** – free Aug 1697; Sep 1691 **Richard Quarrel;** Jan
1691/92 **John Harvey** (thro' E. Norris); Aug 1695 **John Summers.** Still
alive 1697 but listed as dead 1698.

CORDREY, Thomas (also **Corderoy** and **Coudrey**)   London
B.c. 1649, apr. Jan 1663/64 to Nicholas Coxeter till 1670 but not freed.

CORDEROY, Walter (also **Cawdrey**)   London
B.c. 1678, apr. Apr 1692 to Thomas Taylor till 1699 but not freed.

CORDWELL, Robert   London
Believed married 1625, CC 1632. Took as apr. May 1637 **Gowen
Langford** (thro' O. Durant) – free 1651 or 1652. Assistant 1637, still
attending 1649. Not heard of thereafter and prob. dead by 1662.

CORNELIUS, Jacob   London
Believed working c. 1620. Never officially admitted into CC but was
known to them and was fined for non-payment of quarterage several
times between 1635 and 1646. Last mentioned 1649. Work known – a
table clock and a watch.

CORNISH, John   **London**
B.c. 1640, apr. Jul 1654 to Ambrose Bliss (thro' H. Erbury) till 1661 but
not freed.

CORNISH, Michael   **London**
Apr. to Benjamin Hill and freed in CC Oct 1661. Working in Fleet Street
1662. Took as aprs.: Aug 1670 **Richard Lloyd** – free Sep 1681; Apr 1672
John Parker; Apr 1678 **Jonadab Walker** – free Jan 1687/88; Jun 1686
Thomas Stapleton (later transferred to Richard Watts) – freed Jan
1693/94. Prob. dead by 1697 (maybe between 1686 and 1693).

CORNISH, Robert   **Battle (Sussex)**
Repaired turret clock 1685-86.

CORNISH, William   **London**
B.c. 1646, apr. Jun 1659 to Robert Hanslope till 1667 – not freed.

COSB(E)Y, Robert   **London**
B.c. 1632, apr. May 1646 to Peter Closon (thro' T. Alcock) till 1653. Free
Jan 1653-55 (as a Brother?). Took as aprs.: Sep 1655 **Charles Fox** (thro'
J. Pennock) – free Oct 1662; Sep 1670 **George Brooke** – free Sep 1681;
Apr 1676 **John Peers;** Nov 1681 **James Jackson** (later transferred to
Samual Clyatt and freed Sep 1689). Also took an apr. in Aug 1685 for
John Wheeler. In 1672 he was fined for refusing to be CC Steward.
Became Assistant in 1674. By Sep 1685 he had been overlooked for the
position of Warden, but in any event he did not wish to be and in fact
never attended again after 1685, and maybe died soon after. Work
known – lantern clocks signed 'Robert Cosbey at the Dyall in Rood
Lane, London'.

COSENS/CUSSANS, Nicholas   **York**
Hourglass maker. Free 1638. Married firstly 1639 Elizabeth Waid, with
issue 1640-50. First wife died 1652. Married secondly 1653 Jane
Barnard. He died 1654.

COSINE, Alexander   **London**
Alien working 1622 'with his brother', which prob. refers to John, *qv*.

COSINE, John   **London**
Alien working in 1622 with two aprs. 'in St. Bride's parish by the
Conduit in ffleet street'. Prob. brother of Alexander, *qv*.

COSSWORTH, John **London**
Recorded by Baillie as CC 1678 engraver. Prob. error for Cotsworth, *qv*.

COSTER, Robert **London**
B.c. 1633, apr. Nov 1647 to John Freeman till 1654. Freed Jan 1655/56.
Took as apr. May 1656 **Thomas Gilbert**. Prob. dead or gone by 1662.
Work known – none, but a lantern clock is known signed 'Robert Coster
– Newbury', which may however be by one of this name who was apr. in
London in 1695.

COSTER, William **London**
Supposedly in CC 1660 but I cannot confirm this.

COTHER, John **London**
B.c. 1653, son of William Cother, *qv*. Apr. Apr 1667 to Joseph Webb, a
freeman of the Clothworkers' Co. (thro' L. Wythe) but not freed.

COTHER, William **London**
A clockmaker and father of John Cother, *qv*, who was apr. in 1667. Was
not a member of CC but in Jul 1668 as a 'clockmaker of parish of St.
Paul's Covent Garden' he promised to join next Christmas and became a
free Brother in Jan 1668/69. Still alive in 1672 but not heard of thereafter.
Work known – winged lantern clock signed 'Gulielmus de Cother,
Covent Garden, London' and one signed 'William de Cother, Covent
Garden, London', another signed 'Gulielmus Cother de Covent Garden'.

COTSWORTH, John (also Cossworth) **London**
Apr. to Jeremy Gregory (thro' N. Coxeter), freed Jul 1669. Took as
aprs.: Apr 1673 **William Garfoot**, free May 1680; May 1678 **Ralph
Barnard;** Jul 1682 **Edward Crouch** (supposedly to replace his earlier apr.
Ralph Barnard who had 'gone from him') – freed Jul 1691; Apr 1687
Robert Porter; Jun 1694 **John Taylor** – free Sep 1702. In Jan 1682/83
the CC confiscated from him a very 'unworkmanlike and insufficient'
watch movement bearing an invented name (John Rouden – London),
which he was in the process of finishing. He was fined. He claimed it was
made by 'a little crookback man in Shoe Lane' and not by Francis
Dinnis, who was suspected. Seems not to have paid quarterage after
1702. Work known – bracket clock and month longcase signed 'John
Cotsworth, London'.

COTTEL, John   **London(?)**
Lantern clock recorded signed 'John Cottel fecit 1653'. Maybe London, but I cannot trace this man. *Cf* John Cottey?

COTTERELL (see Cottrill)

COTTEY, Abel   **Crediton (Devon)/Philadelphia (USA)**
A Quaker clockmaker b. c. 1655. Worked in Crediton. Emigrated to Philadelphia 1682 to become the first clockmaker there. He died there in 1711 leaving a widow, Mary, a son, John (then absent). Mary died 1713. His inventory is witnessed by Peter Stretch of Philadelphia, *qv*. Had **Benjamin Chandlee** as apr., who married in 1710 Sarah Cottey (Abel's daughter?). Work known – lantern clock signed 'Abel Cottey Crediton'. A longcase clock is known made in Philadelphia.

COTTEY, John   **Exeter (Devon)**
A clockmaker who was accused of entering the house of his father, Abel, and stealing a document in 1698. Presumably related to the Abel above, maybe his son John?

COTTISWOLD, Thomas   **Thame (Oxfordshire)**
A smith who repaired St. Mary's church clock 1458 and later.

COTTON, John   **London**
B.c. 1669, apr. Sep 1683 to Charles Lowndes till 1690. Free Jul 1695. Paid quarterage till about 1697 but prob. dead or gone by 1698. Work known – watches.

COTTRILL, William (also **Cotterell**)   **London**
B.c. 1673, apr. Jul 1687 to Edward Stanton till 1694. Freed Sep 1694. Had son, **John Cottrill,** apr. to him (date not specified) and freed Dec 1721. William paid no quarterage after c. 1696/97 and may have died soon after.

COULTON, Francis   **London**
Made a free Brother in CC Sep 1690 as a 'Great Clockmaker'. Ceased to appear in CC records by 1697/98, but in 1700 listed 'in St. Ann's'.

COULTON, Richard   **London**
B.c. 1627, apr. Aug 1641 to Morris Blunt (thro' O. Durant) till 1648 but not freed.

COUPE (see Cowpe and Copes)

COVELL, Richard   **London**
B.c. 1658, apr. Dec 1671 to Christopher Maynard till 1679 but not freed.

COVENTRY, Carr   **London**
B.c. 1636, apr. Dec 1649 to Samuel Davis till 1657. Freed Jul 1657. May
have been a Quaker. Took as apr. Jul 1660 **Thomas Tennant** – freed Apr
1668. Working in 1662 but not heard of thereafter.

COVERDALL, Daniel   **London**
B.c. 1669, apr. Apr 1683 to Thomas Rudkin till 1690 but not freed.

COWARD, William   **London**
B.c. 1659, apr. Dec 1673 to John Fromanteel till 1680. Freed 1681. Took
as aprs.: Jun 1684 **John Walthall; John Clarke** – freed May 1701. Not
heard of after 1685 when he last paid quarterage.

COWPE, ----   **Paris**
Bracket clock c. 1685 describing maker as 'Horlogier Anglais du Roi a
Paris'. May be one of the following.

COWPE, Edward (signed thus, but also Coupé?)   **London**
Free Brother in CC Jan 1687/88. Paid no quarterage after 1688. Work
known – late 17th century bracket clock signed 'Edward Coupé', prob.
by him.

COWPE, James (also **Coupe, Coope** and **Copes**)   **London**
Free Brother in CC Sep 1654. Took as apr. Sep 1655 **Edward
Worthington** (thro' J. Bayley). Last heard of 1656. Prob. dead or gone
by 1662. (Appears on quarterage list in 1698 but had not paid for last 39
years!). May have gone to Paris. Work known – watches supposedly
dating from 1663; bracket clock signed 'James Cowpe, fox Hall'
(Vauxhall).

COWPER, William (or **Cooper**)   **London**
Freeman of the Vintners' Co. Took as apr. thro' CC Aug 1677 **Charles
Rogers** junior (thro' S. Davis), later transferred to his father, Charles
Rogers senior.

COX, William London

Made a free Brother in CC Nov 1636 (already a freeman of the Silkweavers' Co.). Not heard of thereafter.

COXETER, John London

Listed by some authorities as apr. 1638, CC 1646-63. This is an error for Nicholas Coxeter, *qv* – there was no such person as John.

COXETER, Nicholas (also Coxetre and Coxeater) London

B.c. 1625, apr. Oct 1638 to John Pennock (thro' R. Masterson) till 1646. Freed Mar 1646/47. Took as aprs.: Aug 1647 **William Coxeter** – free Sep 1654; Jan 1647/48 **Thomas Wheeler** – free Feb 1655/56; Apr 1650 **Henry Smith** – free Apr 1658; May 1653 **Faustin Gilbert** – free Apr 1661; May 1655 **Edmund Wansell**; Jan 1655/56 **Andrew Allam** – free Jun 1664; Jan 1658/59 **John Beale**; Mar 1661/62 **Richard Tracy**; Jan 1663-64 **Thomas Corderoy** – free Feb 1670-71; took over **Thomas Davis** on death of his master, Andrew Allam – free Oct 1674; Sep 1668 **Isaac Hurst** – free Apr 1677; Jun 1669 **William Arthur** – free Dec 1676.

Additionally he bound many aprs. *for* other masters, much as the Beadle did, but as he was not Beadle, it may be interesting to list them. These included men with whom he obviously had working connections. Five for T. Mills, two each for J. Pennock, J. Benson, F. Munden, P. Closon, three for J. Gregory, and one each for T. Knifton, R. Scrivener, G. Poole, J. Nash, T. Daniel, D. Le Conte, J. Miller, J. Savill, J. Bayley, W. Elmes.

He worked in Lothbury. In 1667 was left 40/- for a gold ring in the will of his 'loving friend' Simon Bartram, *qv*. Became a Captain in the army, which one not known but prob. Royalist, and was frequently referred to as Captain Coxeter. Became CC Assistant 1651, Warden 1655, Master 1661-62 and 1671 and 1677, but in Mar 1677-78 he was indisposed and could not serve as Master. He died about Oct 1679. In Dec 1679 his widow gave over the CC papers which had been in his charge. Work known – several lantern clocks signed 'at ye 3 chaires in Lothbury' and also 'Neer Gould Smiths Hall, Londini'. At least one longcase clock is known.

COXETER, Thomas London

In Feb 1673/74 he was sworn a freeman of CC by redemption by order of the Lord Mayor, but was a bricklayer, having been employed in the re-building of the city and also having taken a house in the re-built part of the city. Signed with his mark.

COXETER, William   **London**
B.c. 1633, apr. Aug 1647 to Nicholas Coxeter till 1654. Freed Sep 1654.
Prob. dead or gone by 1662.

CRAGG, Samuel   **London**
B.c. 1676, apr. Mar 1690/91 to John Northcott till 1697 but not freed.
Maybe free in Leathersellers' Co.?

CRAGGS, Richard   **London**
Apr. Feb 1652/53 to Ralph Ash (thro' John North), later transferred to
Humphrey Peirce. Freed Oct 1660. Working 1662 but not heard of
thereafter.

CRAILE, Richard (sometimes **Crayle**)   **London**
Believed member of Blacksmiths' Co. In 1626 was witness to will of
Robert Grinkin senior. Original petitioner for CC but never officially
admitted. In 1646 was warned for not conforming to rules. Took as apr.
Mar 1653/54 **John Bristow** (thro' W. Petty). Prob. dead or gone by 1662.
Work known – watch signed 'Richard Crayle Londini fecit'.

CRANE, Thomas   **London**
B.c. 1668, apr. May 1682 to Thomas Hollis, later transferred to Isaac
Nicholl till 1689 but not freed.

CRATHORN, Jonathan   **Beverley (Yorkshire)**
Watch c. 1700. Nothing known about him.

CRAVEN, Thomas   **London**
Free Brother in CC Sep 1688 as a watchmaker. Paid quarterage till 1697
but not later.

CRAWLEY, Thomas   **London**
Already working as apr. of Richard Morgan in Jan 1655/56 when Morgan
was ordered to teach him springmaking and clock/watchmaking in
alternate months (to give the boy a more varied training than spring-
making alone). However in March the boy's father complained again of
this same fault and it was decided he should stay with Morgan till a new
master could be found to teach him clock and watchmaking. He was
freed in Oct 1660 having served with Davis Mell. In 1662 he worked at
Westminster. Paid CC quarterage till about 1680 but not thereafter.

Work known – none but his name appears on the base of a carillon lantern clock by Davis Mell.

CRAWSHAW, Edward   Worsborough (Yorkshire)
Ropemaker but also cared for church clock by 1704. He was the first of a long line of clockmakers which began with his son, William, b. 1694. He died in 1724.

CRAYLE, William (sometimes **Craile**)   **London**
Watchmaker, believed member of Blacksmiths' Co. 1651. Never actually admitted into CC but was known to them. Working in Fleet Street in 1662; later (1676) 'at the Black Boy in the Strand near the Savoy'. In Nov 1683 his daughter, Frances, aged 21, of parish of St. Mary Savoy married to William Rymer. Work known – one or two watches survive, one signed 'William Crayle in Fleete Street, London'.

CREED, Robert   **London**
B.c. 1675, apr. May 1689 to Thomas Tompion till 1696. Freed Mar 1699/1700. Took as aprs.: Apr 1700 **Thomas Bradford** (son of Richard Bradford, Citizen and Vintner of London) – free Oct 1710; Jun 1701 **Benjamin Sidey** (thro' E. Hill) – free May 1711; Jan 1702/03 **George Gray** (son of late George Gray of Clerkenwell, Gent, deceased). Said to have worked in Fleet Street, on whose authority I do not know. Paid no quarterage after 1702. Had a son, Robert, who joined CC in 1733. Work known – early 18th century watch signed 'Robert Creed' without town is prob. by him.

CREED, Thomas   Oxford/London
B.c. 1644, son of Henry Creed, husbandman, of Gloucestershire. Apr. at Oxford Sep 1657 to Richard Quelch, watchmaker, till 1665 but not freed there. One of this name (surely same man?) was made a free Brother in CC in Jan 1668/69. In May 1674 he was admitted as a full freeman in CC by redemption by order of the Lord Mayor. Took as aprs.: Jan 1669-70 **William Hillier** (thro' N. Russell) – freed Sep 1679; Aug 1676 **George Walker** – freed Apr 1684; Nov 1683 **Henry Smith**. May have belonged to the Loriners' Co. as in 1677 he was accused of binding an apr. thro' them. He may well have been a Quaker as he did not sign the 1697 Oath of Allegiance. He paid no quarterage after about 1685, was in arrears in 1687, and is not heard of after that date except concerning an incident in Jul 1699, when a watch was seized 'in his hand' at the premises of Samuel Stokes, bearing the name William Davison. Creed was ordered to break

the defective parts and renew them. This prob. means that he was working for Stokes in 1699. Work known – lantern clocks, one winged version with alarm signed 'Thomas Creed London'.

CREED, Thomas (II)   **London**
A second person of this name is recorded by some authorities as CC 1674, but this is an error and refers to the full freedom of the man recorded above.

CREITH, Robert (also **Creych**)   **Leith**
Repaired Edinburgh turret clock in 1554 and again in 1570.

CREEKE, Henry (see also **Crop**)   **London**
An Apr. 1655 he was fined by CC for practising the trade when not a member, but the fine was reduced 'as he is a poor man' and promises to make them a 'new house clock and larum' and Thomas Loomes promises to see it done. In Oct 1655 he was admitted as a Free Brother. Still alive in 1657 when he transferred an apr. to Thomas Loomes without permission. Prob. dead or gone by 1662, but see Crop. Work known – none. Prob. worked as journeyman to Thomas Loomes.

CRESSNER, Robert   **London**
Britten records him as 1690-1730 but I cannot trace any such person and he was not known to the CC.

CROCKETT, John   **London**
Not known to CC but a late 17th century plate-framed 30-hour clock is known. In 1695 a John Crockett lived in Christchurch parish with Elizabeth his wife. This may be him, and if so he must have escaped the attentions of the CC.

CROCKFORD, Matthew senior   **London**
B.c. 1636, apr. Mar 1650 to Thomas Mills (thro' N. Coxeter) till 1657. Took as apr. Apr 1661 **George Green;** Feb 1663/64 **Joseph Ashby** – free Apr 1674; Sep 1669 **Richard Fennell** (transferred before Nov 1679 to Thomas Bagley); Jan 1670-71 **John Brewer** – free Mar 1677-78. Worked in Chancery Lane in 1662 and prob. later 'at Royal Exchange'. Was excused stewardship in 1673 for a year or two due to 'difficulties'. In 1693 his son, Matthew, was freed by patrimony. Received charity from CC from late 1697 till Apr 1698 and he prob. died soon after that. Listed as 'dead' in 1698 quarterage book, having paid no quarterage for the past

23 years. Was presumably a very poor man to be excused in this way. Work known – at least one lantern clock is recorded signed 'Matthew Crockford at the Royal Exchange'.

CROCKFORD, Matthew junior   **London**
Son of Matthew senior and freed in CC by patrimony Jul 1693. Took as aprs.: Jul 1693 **John Brooks;** Jun 1718 **John Mobbs.** He paid no quarterage after about 1696, but was obviously still working in 1718. Nothing else known about him.

CROFT, John   **London**
Apr. Oct 1658 to Benjamin Hill. Freed Feb 1665-66.

CROME, Edmund   **London**
B.c. 1632, apr. Oct 1644 to Sampson Shelton (thro' O. Durant) till 1653 but not freed.

CROME, Robert   **London**
B.c. 1642, apr. Aug 1655 to John Pennock (thro' B. Hill) till 1663 but not freed.

CR(OP?), Henry   **London**
Name indecipherable. A boxmaker in Westminster in 1662. Maybe Creeke?

CROOKE, Isaac   **London**
B.c. 1661, apr. Jul 1675 to Nicasius Russell till 1682. Not freed.

CROOKE, Sampson   **London**
Apr. May 1661 to Samuel Horne. Prob. son of William Crook, yeoman, and free of the City of London in 1669. Free Jul 1668 in CC. Took as apr. Feb 1671/72 **Henry Pigott** – free Sep 1689.

CROSB(E)Y, Robert   **London**
In Apr 1685 he was to be prosecuted by CC for working when not a member. Work known – at least two longcase clocks, one signed 'Robert Crosbey in King Street near the Sqr.'.

CROSS(E), James   **London**
B.c. 1673, apr. Aug 1687 to John Browne till 1694 but not freed.

CROSS, Richard   **London**
In 1632 he complained to CC about (Richard) Masterson's malpractice, but not clear whether he was himself a maker.

CROSSE, Edmund   **Exeter**
Locksmith who repaired local TCs 1654.

CROUCH, Edward   **London**
B.c. 1669, apr. Jul 1682 to John Cotsworth till 1690. Freed Jul 1691. Took as aprs.: Jun 1694 **John James**; Sep 1698 **George Cartwright,** transferred Jan 1698-99 to Edward Hill; Nov 1709 **John Burges**; Aug 1713 **William Hayward**; Aug 1716 **Gervass Reeve**; Oct 1716 **Edward Wakeman.** In 1697 he traded as a watchmaker 'under St. Dunstan's church in Fleet Street'. Became CC Assistant 1713, Warden 1716-18, Master 1719, after which I have no information about him. Work known – longcase clocks, signed 'Edward Crouch – London'.

CROUCH, George   **London**
Son of George Crouch of Holborn. Apr. to Edward Baily and later William Raynes, freed Jan 1668-69. Free of the City of London 1669. Took as apr. effective Nov 1668 **John Kirk,** later transferred to E. Stanton. Still alive 1671 but not heard of thereafter.

CROW(E), Nathaniel   **London**
Apr. Jul 1654 to William Petty. Freed May 1661.

CROWLE, John   **St. Austell (Cornwall)**
Repaired town clock in 1679.

CRUCIFEX, John (also **Crucefix**)   **London**
Clocks by him supposedly c. 1680 are prob. later, and this is no doubt the maker who was free in CC in 1712.

CRUCIFEX, Robert (signed Crucefix)   **London**
Watchmaker, entered CC Dec 1689 as a Free Brother. In arrears with quarterage in 1701. In 1708 fined for refusing Stewardship – not heard of thereafter (though Baillie lists him up to 1747?). Supposedly working in Sweetings Alley. Work known – longcase and bracket clocks and watches.

CRUKSHANKS, John Aberdeen
Kept town clock in 1453.

CRUMPE, Henry London
Clockmaker but a freeman of the Vintners' Co. Freed as a Brother in CC
Jan 1667-68. Took as aprs.: Jan 1667-68 **William Bird** (thro' L. Wythe);
Dec 1668 **William Clarke; Jul 1670 Robert Gregory** (thro' E. Stanton) –
freed Apr 1678. Not heard of after 1670. Work known – none (may well
have worked as journeyman for Stanton).

CRUTTENDEN, Thomas London/York
B.c. 1657, apr. Mar 1667-68 to Robert Seignior (but this aprship prob.
cancelled on account of his extreme youth). Apr. afresh Apr 1670 to John
Fromanteel till 1678, but freed in Nov 1677. Went to York where free
1679 and had a shop in Coney Street. Married firstly Mary X, who died
1683. Married secondly 1684 Elizabeth Martin: issue 1688 Thomas,
Mary (died 1691), 1690 Henry, 1692 Margaret, 1693 John (died 1694),
1696 Sidney (became a butcher), 1697 Ruth (died 1697), 1698
Katherine. He died himself in 1698. Work known – several longcase
clocks, some signed 'Thomas Cruttenden York', and a lantern clock.
The double aprship has led some authorities to believe in error that there
were two makers of this name.

CUE, William London
B.c. 1665, apr. Sep 1679 to Thomas Morgan till 1686. Freed Jan
1691/92. Paid no quarterage after about 1693. Dead by 1698.

CUFF, James London
A watchmaker, Free Brother in CC Mar 1698/99. Took as aprs.: Oct
1711 **Charles Hoare; John Cuffe** (a relative?) – freed Mar 1718-19.
Work known – at least one longcase clock.

CULLIFORD, John (see Gulliford?) Bristol
Free there 1692. Repaired church clock 1706-18 when believed died. His
daughters maintained it in 1719. Work known – one or two longcase
clocks.

CULPEPPER, Edmund London?
Sundial bearing his name and dated 1666 also carries the name of Evan
Christian, *qv* but no place name. It was at one time in the Isle of Man, but
place of manufacture uncertain.

CUPER, Abel   **London**
Recorded as late 17th century, but nothing else known.

CUPER, Josias   **London**
Working by 1622, an alien, supposedly from Blois – 'the Lord Dorset's page'. Free in Blacksmiths' Co. 1628. Subscriber for CC in 1631. Admitted as a Free Brother in 1632. In 1634 he got his apr. **Edward Ambrose** back from Elias Voland till be finished the watch he had already begun work on. He died in 1660. His will, dated 1659, describes him as a clockmaker of Chelsey, and mentions his married daughter, Susan, wife of Robert Castle, and married daughter Jane Bellon (prob. the wife of Bellon the clockmaker, *qv*) who was to receive monies 'without the consent of her husband'(?). Work known – at least one watch survives.

CUPER, Lewis (Loys)   **London**
In 1622 working as 'alien without temple bar with Mr. Vautroler'. Supposedly from Blois. Admitted to CC (as Brother?) 1632. Believed later returned to Blois.

CURTIS, Greenaway (also **Curtice**)   **Oxford/London**
Son of Thomas Curtis, joiner of Oxford. Apr. to Michael Bird, an Oxford watchmaker for seven years but this was cancelled in 1689 when Bird died and he was transferred to Wright Lane. In Dec 1694 he was bound afresh to Joseph Foster thro' CC in London, but was not freed there. In 1699 on death of his father, he returned to Oxford where he worked till his death in 1702. Work known – a lantern clock.

CURTIS, John   **London**
B.c. 1651, apr. Apr 1664 to Simon Bartram (thro' S. Horne) till 1672. When Bartram died (1667) he was transferred to Jeremy Gregory – freed Apr 1671. Took as aprs.: Mar 1671/72 **George Cary** – freed Sep 1679; Jul 1679 **Henry Theodrricke**. Also bound an apr. for E. Fage. In May 1682 'being sick and in want' he was given ten shillings charity by CC. In Jul 1694 'widow Curtis' received charity from them. Work known – at least one lantern clock.

CURTIS, Joseph   **Chew Magna** (and **Axbridge?**)
Lantern clock recorded c. 1680. One 'Curtis of Axbridge', a jackmaker in 1705, may be same man. Joseph said to be still working in 1720.

CUSIN (see Cosine)

CUTHBERT, Amariah   London
B.c. 1673, apr. Apr 1687 to Thomas Ellis till 1694. Freed Sep 1694. Took
as apr. Nov 1697 **Daniel Scott.** Did not sign 1697 Oath of Allegiance and
may have been a Quaker. Paid quarterage till early in 1699 when he died.

CUTLER, George   London
B.c. 1678, apr. 1692/93 to William Jaques but not freed.

CUTTING, Christopher   London
A goldsmith. B.c. 1673, Sep 1687 to John Delander, watch case maker
(thro' Nathan Delander), till 1694. Freed Apr 1695. In Apr 1697 he
pleaded guilty to keeping **William Wren,** a foreigner, as his partner and
agreed to dismiss him by next month. Took as aprs.: Jun 1697 **Thomas
Jemmett** (transferred to J. Willoughby); Jul 1700 **Thomas Osmond** (son
of Richard Osmond, Citizen and Carpenter of London); Dec 1711 **John
Russell;** May 1715 **Isaac Telforth.**

D

D, G.   place unknown
Engraver of Robertus Harvie clock, place not known, c. 1600 was monogrammed 'G.D.'.

DADSWELL, Edward (also Dodswell)   **Rotherfield, Sussex**
B. 1659, son of Robert Dadswell. Married 1677 Elizabeth Elliott. Died 12 Aug 1736. Was a clocksmith and yeoman. Had nine children incl. Thomas (b. 1688).

DALLAM, Thomas   **London**
Made organs and an organ-clock in 1599 for Sultan of Constantinople – see *Clocks Magazine* Nov 1978.

DAND/DAUD/DANE, Tobias   **London**
In CC lists of 1662, indecipherable. Prob. Tobias Davis, *qv*.

DANIEL(L)(S). All variant spellings are listed together but distinction is made where possible.

DANIELL, Edward   **London**
Free Brother in CC Oct 1647. Took as apr. Nov 1647 **John Smith** (thro' L. Wythe) – free Nov 1654. Prob. dead or gone by 1662.

DANIELL, Edward   **London**
B.c. 1672, apr. Sep 1686 to James Atkinson, a freeman of the Joyners' Co. and a mat. inst. maker (thro' D. Stevens) till 1693, but not freed. Prob. freed in master's company.

DANIELL, Henry   London
B.c. 1633, apr. Jul 1647 to Henry Kent (thro' T. Claxton) till 1654 but
not freed.

DANIELL, Isaac   London
Believed to have been a watch case maker. Entered CC as a Free Brother
in 1646. Supported the administration in the rebellion of 1656. In 1662
worked in Chancery Lane. Took as aprs.: Jul 1647 **Cave Underhill** (thro'
T. Claxton) – free Oct 1655; Jan 1655 **Michael Lueb** (thro' T. Claxton);
Jun 1655 **John Powell** (thro' H. Smith); **Robert Halstead** (thro' R. Nau)
– freed Jul 1668; Aug 1669 **John Eman** (thro' S. Horne); Jun 1671
Cornelius Jenkins (thro' T. Fenn) – freed Sep 1678; Dec 1676 **Thomas
Baseley** (thro' J. Bailey) – freed Jan 1683-84. Became Assistant 1665,
Warden 1762-75 but illness prevented his regular attendance. In Nov
1672 he was absent 'by reason of his infirmity'. In Sep 1674 he has 'bin
longe under great infirmity and inability of body', but not to be excused
wardenship. In Sep 1677 he was not nominated for Mastership as he was
'grievously afflicted with the Gout'. By Aug 1682 he had died, his widow,
Anne, took **Samuel Marshall** as her apr. – freed Feb 1689/90.

DANIEL, Ralph   Stockport
Clockmaker. Married at Manchester, January 1697/98, Margaret Smith
of Moss Side.

DANIEL, Stephen   London
Watchmaker, freed Sep 1698 as a Brother but never paid quarterage and
prob. left London soon after or died.

DANIEL, Thomas   London
B.c. 1632, apr. Jan 1646-47 to Daniel Fletcher (thro' T. Alcock) till
1653. Freed Dec 1656. Was a rebel in 1656 uprising against CC. Took as
aprs.: Nov 1656 **Thomas Barford** (thro' S. Dudson); Dec 1658 **William
Lloyd** (thro' N. Coxeter) later transferred to R. Bowen – freed 1671.

DANIEL, William   London
Free Brother in CC Oct 1632. Took as apr. Apr 1641 **Nicholas Payne**
(thro' O. Durant) – free Apr 1648. Prob. dead or gone by 1662.

DANLEY, Charles   London
Caneseller 'at the Sign of the Grape in Fleet Street over against

Mr. Bedford' (*qv*). Had sundials confiscated by CC 1671-72, supposedly made by Widow Cater, *qv*.

DANSON, Robert   **London**
B.c. 1656, apr. Sep 1670 to William Standish till 1677. Freed Jul 1678. Paid quarterage till 1681 but not later.

DANTON, Robert (error for Danson, *qv*)

DARBYSHIRE, Henry   **Pemberton (Lanchashire)**
Watchmaker. Married 1697 Jane Knight.

DARBYSHIRE, Roger   **Wigan (Lanchashire)**
Watchmaker, free 1662. Took as apr. c. 1667-74 **Oliver Platt**. Died 1690. (Hawkes.)

DARGENT, James   **London**
(One Jacques Dargent, goldsmith, a Huguenot from Sancerre in Berri was in London in 1695 – prob. same man.) Jun 1700 free in CC by order of the Alderman's Court. Took as aprs.: Dec 1702 **Timothy Lenoir** (son of Timothy Lenoir of Long Acre, co. Middlesex, taylor; Aug 1706 **James Dibon** (son of James Dibon of St. Dunstans Stepney, co. Middlesex, weaver) – free Sep 1713; Jul 1712 **Peter Bailleu;** May 1714 his daughter, **Mary Anne Dargent;** Jun 1714 **Joseph Bailhon;** Apr 1718 **Charles Lapeu.**

DARLO(W), Thomas (signed Darlow, erroniously Darls)   **London**
Prob. an engraver. B.c. 1671, apr. Apr 1685 to George Deane till 1692. Freed May 1692. Took as aprs.: May 1693 **Dove Rayner** (thro' R. Williamson) – freed Jul 1701; Aug 1696 **Daniel Weatherhill;** his son, **Jeremiah Darlow** – freed Sep 1698; Jun 1699 **John Stafford** (son of Jonathan Stafford of Woollston, co. Warwick, clerk) – free Jan 1708-09; Jan 1706-07 **Samuel Stanley; John Jones** – freed Jan 1716-17.

DARY, Bartholomew   **London**
B.c. 1663, apr. Mar 1677-78 to Henry Dunn, a freeman of the Merchant Taylors' Co. (thro' S. Davis senior) till 1684 but not freed.

DAUNTENEY, Lawrence   **London**
Baillie records him as 1576, but I do not know his source.

DAVALL, John (sometimes Devall and Duval)　　　**London**
B.c. 1656, apr. Apr 1670 to Andrew Prime (thro' N. Payne) till 1677.
Free Nov 1677.

DAVENPORT, William　　　**London**
B.c. 1655, apr. Apr 1669 to Robert Smith (thro' T. Claxton) till 1676 but
not freed. Supposedly accused of counterfeiting in 1679.

DAVENPORT, William　　　**Nantwich**
Clockmaker. Buried Feb 1691/92.

DAVENPORT, William　　　**London**
B.c. 1670, apr. Nov 1684 to Thomas Whittle till 1691 – not freed.

DAVERILL, John (d'Averil)　　　**London**
In 1622 worked as an alien in the same house as Henry Broe, *qv*, 'at a
Joyner's at Broadstreet end at London wall'. In Nov 1632 had been
working half a year already (as journeyman?) for Lewis Cooke without
CC permission. Freed as Brother in CC Nov 1636. Last heard of 1641.

DAVETT, Abraham　　　**London**
Baillie has 1662 but I can't trace him. Prob. a misreading from 1662 list.

DAVIS and **DAVIES** are listed together but distinguished where
possible.

DAVIS, Aubrey (Awbery)　　　**London**
B.c. 1665, apr. Oct 1679 to Robert Nemes till 1686 but not freed. Work
known – a longcase clock is recorded.

DAVIS, Benjamin　　　**London**
Son of Samuel Davis. Free Brother in CC Apr 1678. Took as apr. Nov.
1680 **William Davis**. Recorded as at Thames Street – source unknown.
Work known – a longcase clock is on record.

DAVIS, David　　　**London**
Sep 1671 a pinmaker who had put on his cards of pins 'clockmaker and
pinmaker'. He promised not to do so in future.

DAVIS, James (or Joseph – records unclear)　　　**London**
In Sep 1700 was accused of following the trade of watchmaker at Ratcliffe

with aprs. not bound through CC. His father appeared for him and promised his son would take up his Freedom when he comes of age.

DAVIS, Jeffrey London
B.c. 1669, apr. May 1683 to John Sweby till 1690. Freed Jul 1690, but paid no quarterage after 1691 and prob. dead or gone by 1697-98.

DAVIS, John London
B.c. 1671, apr. Jul 1685 to Daniel Quare till 1692. Free Aug 1697. Prob. a Quaker like his master. Took as aprs.: Aug 1697 **John Hoddle** – free Jan 1704/05; May 1700 **John Cooke** (son of John Cooke late of Newport Pagnell, Bucks, (Clerk?)) – free Jul 1713; Aug 1702 **Francis Britten** (son of Francis Britten late of Newport Pagnell, Bucks, pattern drawer, deceased); Nov 1709 **Richard Scoope**. Work known – at least one watch. Maybe same as next entry.

DAVI(E)S, John Windsor
Recorded as 1678-89 (source unknown). Maker of Carillon Clock in Curfew Tower Windsor Castle and several longcase clocks and at least one lantern clock known, signed 'John Davi(e)s – Windsor'. Could be same man as previous entry.

DAVIS, Samuel senior London
B.c. 1626, apr. Feb 1640/41 to William Selwood (thro' R. Masterson) till 1647. Freed 1647-48. Worked in Lothbury 'at ye Golden Ball' (Francis Stamper worked there later). Took as aprs.: Jul 1648 **Thomas Evans** – free Sep 1673; Dec 1649 **Carr Coventry** – free Jul 1657; Dec 1649 **Richard Brent**; Sep 1651 **Philip Whinfield**; Jun 1655 **Thomas Langley** – free Oct 1664; May 1656 **Richard Perry**; Mar 1662/63 **Robert Moone**; Apr 1669 **Nicholas Towell**; Jul 1670 **William Clift**; Jan 1674-75 **Thomas Virgoe** – free Jun 1682; Aug 1676 **Francis Drummond**. In Jan 1674/75 he was appointed Beadle and in this capacity bound many aprs. (35 in fact) for other masters, many of them Quakers, and some of the above aprs. may have been bound for other masters too. In Sep 1680 he was discharged from the office of Beadle 'being charged with negligence and unfittness for the place, and he not much desirous to keep it, unless he might have an augmentation of allowance . . .'

In 1652 he had a faulty clock destroyed by CC and was fined 40 shillings for poor workmanship. He paid no quarterage after 1684 and prob. died in that year and certainly before 1698. Prob. succ. by Francis Stamper – his own sons, Benjamin and Samuel prob. dying before him.

Work known – a longcase clock signed 'Samuel Davis Londini fecit' and a lantern clock (balance wheel).

DAVIS, Samuel junior   London
Eldest son of Samuel Davis senior. Admitted as a free Brother into CC Dec 1673. Prob. a Quaker. Took as aprs.: (thro' father) Dec 1673 **John Burgis**; Aug 1675 **Francis Stamper** – free Nov 1682. Paid no quarterage after about 1683 and prob. died about then. Work known – none, unless it is mistaken for that of his father.

DAVIS, Thomas   London
B.c. 1653, apr. Oct 1667 to Andrew Allum on whose death he was transferred to Nicholas Coxeter (Allum's employer) till 1674. Freed Oct 1674. Took as aprs.: Aug 1682 **Edward Greene**; Jul 1687 **Joseph Mann**; Sep 1692 his son, **William Davis,** transferred to Jonathan Puller and freed Sep 1699; Jun 1695 **Edward Harper;** Jun 1698 **Samuel Weston.** Paid quarterage till late in 1699 when prob. died.

DAVI(E)S, Tobias (sometimes Toby)   London
Apr. May 1646 to William Selwood (thro' T. Alcock). Free May 1653. Selwood died Apr 1653 and left him a bequest of £6. Took as aprs.: Nov 1654 **Henry Ellis;** Aug 1656 **Gregory Julian** – free Jun 1664. Also bound an apr. for Charles Fox. Last heard of in 1670 when his name came up for Stewardship, but prob. died or left about that time. Maybe connected with Samuel Davis senior.

DAVIS, William   Boston (USA)
The first immigrant clockmaker who arrived in 1683. Origin not known but must be British and perhaps the first-listed Londoner below.

DAVIS, William   London
B.c. 1666, apr. Nov 1680 to Benjamin Davis till 1687 but not free.

DAVIS, William   London
One of this name in CC took as apr. Apr 1696 **Jonathan Spencer** – freed Jan 1704/05. He did not sign the 1697 Oath of Allegiance however. Work known – a bracket clock of c. 1700 could be by him or next maker. A maker of this name made the church clock at Kirkby Muxloe, Leicestershire in 1720, which may or may not be him.

DAVIS, William London
B.c. 1678, apr. 1692 to father, Thomas Davis, *qv*, till 1699. Freed Sep 1699 (having been transferred to Jonathan Puller). Paid quarterage till 1705 at least.

DAVISON, John Darlington (Co. Durham)
Said to have made town clock in 1638 for £5.00.

DAVISON, William London
A 'Great Clockmaker' and freeman of the Pewterers' Co. Was summoned to take up his CC freedom in Jul 1686 and was made a free Brother in Dec 1686. Took as aprs.: Dec 1686 **Robert Batterson** (later transferred to R. Baker and freed Feb 1693/94); Mar 1691-92 **Richard Spittle** – free May 1699; Apr 1694 **Henry Batterson** (transferred Oct 1696 to Jonathan Puller); Jul 1700 **Cornelius Langley** (son of Cornelius Langley of St. Katherine (?), victualler) – free Jul 1707; Apr 1704 **Gareth Mead** (son of John Mead of St. Andrew, Holborne, co. Middsx, painter); **Jonathan Spencer** – freed Feb 1704-05; Jan 1708/09 **Joseph Shelley** (son of Michael Shelley of Cheshunt, co. Herts). Received charity from CC 1710-15, when prob. died. Work known – none, but a defective watch by him is mentioned in CC archives, in the hands of Thomas Creed, *qv*.

DAVYES, John Exeter
Clockmaker there 1683.

DAWSON, John London
B.c. 1666, apr. Aug 1681 to John Archer, later transferred to Daniel Beckman (both were engravers) till 1688. Freed Sep 1688. Married Jul 1689, then a clockmaker, bachelor, aged 23 of St. Brides, London, to Mary Rowley spinster, 19, of Bridewell Precinct, at St. Nicholas Cole Abbey. Took as aprs.: Nov 1690 **William Wheatley,** later transferred to John Stevens and freed Jul 1698; Dec 1700 **Thomas Spencer** (son of John Spencer of St. Saviour's Southwark, gent., deceased); Sep 1702 **John Tench** (son of Thomas Tench of Hastings, Sussex, clerk); Dec 1709 **Thomas Smith** – free May 1719; Nov 1714 **John Kilby;** Sep 1716 **Thomas Priest;** Oct 1718 **William Smart.** Work known – at least one longcase clock is recorded but may have worked mainly as an engraver.

DAWSON, Robert Alford (?)
Recorded as CC 1678 (Britten) but I can find no such person.

DAWSON, Thomas (sometimes Dasson)   **London**
A petitioner for incorporation of CC. Free Brother 1632. In Feb 1636-37 was transferred as a full Freeman from the Imbroaderers' Co. Took as aprs.: Sep 1637 **William Bunting** – free Feb 1645/46. His name occurs often in CC archives as he acted as intermediary in binding many aprs. (16 or so) for other masters, much as the Beadle did later. These masters included: J. Whitlach, T. Pace, D. Bouquet, E. Allen, T. Land (Lamb?), West, R. Parkinson, J. Charlton, E. Bisse, A. Fromanteel, W. Bowyer, J. Allen, R. Grinkin, T. Howes, P. Closon, ---- Threlkell. Last heard of Mar 1639. Work known – none.

DAWSON, William   **London**
B.c. 1645, apr. Sep 1659 to Benjamin Wolverston till 1666 but not freed.

DAY, Edmund   **London**
Watch recorded as c. 1600. Maybe the following person.

DAY, Edmund   **London**
B.c. 1670, apr. Sep 1684 to Richard Jarrett till 1691. Freed Apr. 1692. Took as aprs.: Mar 1698/99 **James Hollyer** (son of James Hollyer, Barber Surgeon of London). Also erroneously listed as taking Mar 1698/99 **Michael Cheltenham** (son of Peter Cheltenham senior, Citizen and Joiner of London) who was in fact bound to Robert Williamson. Paid quarterage till 1700, when prob. left or died. Work known – watches and longcase clocks.

DAY, Isaac   **London**
Maker of watch cases. B.c. 1657, apr. in CC Apr 1670 to Barlow Rookes till 1678, but from Aug 1675 was transferred to Ahasuerus Fromanteel junior to serve till 1683. However Fromanteel is believed to have moved to Holland c. 1675/76 and in Sep 1676 he was bound thro' Weavers' Co. to serve Benjamin Graves, who in Jan 1676-77 promised to make him free in CC in due course, and he was freed in CC May 1679. Had as aprs.: Jan 1680-81 **David Jones** (transferred from H. Hickman) – freed Sep 1687; **Joseph Tanner** (transferred from Benjamin Graves) – freed Apr 1684; Nov 1682 **Richard Parsons** – freed Apr 1690; Aug 1685 **James Terrier** – free Sep 1694; Sep 1689 **Thomas Williams;** Apr 1694 his son, **Isaac Day** (some records say Jacob?); Jun 1695 **William Morgan** – free Dec 1704; Jul 1697 **George Bennett** – free Dec 1704; Dec 1704 **John Pittman** (son of Daniel Pittman of St. Bottolph Aldgate, gent.) – free Jan 1714/15; Jun 1706 **William Wilkinson** (son of Robert Wilkinson Citizen and Poulterer

of London) – free Oct 1718; Jul 1712 **William Rowland;** Apr 1715 **John Cates.** In Jun 1701 his wife received £5 charity from CC. Work known – none. Prob. specialised in casemaking and engraving work, prob. initially as journeyman to Graves.

DAY, Thomas London
B.c. 1669, apr. Feb 1682/83 to Michael Knight till 1690. Freed Apr 1691. Took as apr. Feb 1692/93 **John Williamson.** Paid no quarterage after c. 1693 and prob. died or left then.

DEACLE, Joan (or Dearle?) London
B.c. 1658, apr. Jun 1672 to Elizabeth, widow of Thomas Webb. Not freed.

DEANE, George (sometimes written Adeane) London
An engraver. B.c. 1650, apr. Aug 1662 to Charles Bonner till 1671. Freed Sep 1671. Took as aprs.: Sep 1673 **Richard Ellis** (transferred to J. Wolverston and freed Jul 1683); Jul 1680 **John Taylor** – freed Sep 1687; Apr 1685 **Thomas Darlow** – freed May 1692 (after Deane's death); May 1688 **Jeremiah Mison.** In Sep 1677 he presented to CC a copperplate engraving of the Company Arms for use in printing, etc. Must have died between 1688 and 1692.

DEANE, John Chester
Watch recorded 1696. Took as aprs. his sons **Joshua,** Jan 1697/98 and **John** 1699.

DEARLE (see Deacle)

DEARMER, Abraham London
B.c. 1678, apr. Sep 1692 to Thomas East till 1700. Freed Sep 1703. Took as aprs.: Dec 1709 **Peter Abbott** – free Mar 1719/20; Sep 1713 **Ralph Yeomans;** Mar 1716/17 **George Willis.**

DEARMER, John London
B.c. 1658, apr. Mar 1672/73 thro' H. Hester to Katherine, widow of Richard Bestwick till 1679. Freed Jul 1680, but as a Free Brother, a springmaker, being free of the Salters' Co. Took as aprs.: Jul 1680 **Morris Randall** (thro' S. Davis); May 1705 **William Battle** (son of James Battle of parish of St. James Clerkenwell, victualler); Aug 1708 **Caleb**

Dearmer. In 1687 he was much in arrears with quarterage but in May 1698 he was excused all arrears.

DEBAUFRE, Pierre (Peter) **London**
Frenchman, believed from Paris. Free Brother in CC Jun 1689. Paid quarterage till at least 1704. In Dec 1704 he applied to Parliament together with Jacob Debaufre (said to be his brother and a clockmaker at the sign of the Pendulum in Frith Street) and with Nicholas Facio for a patent for jewelling clocks and watches, which they obtained despite opposition from the CC. In 1705 he was resident in St. Anne's parish, Westminster, when his son, James, was apr. to Roger Nicholls. Pierre is not known to have been in London later than 1705. Earlier he was reputedly at Church Street, Soho. He is credited with the invention of the club-footed verge escapement for watches. Work known – watches and bracket clocks. One watch signed 'Pie. De Baufre, Inglese, Roma' suggests that he may have worked in Rome later.

DEBENHAM, ---- **Long Melford (Suffolk)**
Lantern clock recorded supposedly c. 1690, but this is prob. much too early a dating of a mid-18th century one.

DE BURGESS, Jacob **Blois (France)**
Supposedly there 1591-1643 and of English origin.

DE CHARMES, David **London**
Watchmaker, Brother in CC Apr 1691. Paid dues till at least 1703, after which I have no record of him.

DE CHARMES, Simon **London**
Frenchman, a watchmaker. Made a Free Brother in CC Apr 1691. Believed father of David, *qv*. Working in London till at least 1704 at 'his House, the Sign of the Clock, the corner of Warwick St, Charing Cross'. One of this name worked in Paris c. 1720. Work known – watches, longcase and bracket clocks, usually signed 'S. de Charmes, London'.

DE CHOUDENS, (Jean?) **London**
At Rouen c. 1680. A watch of c. 1720 is signed De Choudens, London.

DE COTHER (see Cother)

DE FRETIS, Nicholas　　　　　　　　　　　**London**
Apr. 1685. Prosecuted by CC for working when not a member.

DE HECK, (Gerard?)　　　　　　　　　**London(?)**
Watch case of a six-pointed star watch by David Ramsay signed 'de Heck sculp'. Believed to refer to Gerard de Heck of Blois, active 1608-29, which suggests the case was imported.

DE LA CHANA, Daniel　　　　　　　　　　**London**
A Frenchman, engraver, admitted as Free Brother Nov 1687 (with F. Asseline). Paid no quarterage after c. 1693.

DE LA FOSSE, Samuel (sometimes La Fosse)　　**London**
Frenchman, clockmaker. Made a Free Brother in CC Jul 1692. A. Huguenot. Working as watchmaker in Mickle Alley, Soho, in 1702.

DELANDER and **DELAUNDER** and **DELANDRE** are sometimes confused with Delaune.

DE LANCE (see de Launce)

DELANDER, Daniel (also Delaunder)　　　　　**London**
B.c. 1678, apr. Apr 1692 to Charles Halstead but later transferred to T. Tompion. Freed Jul 1699. Took as aprs.: Mar 1699/1700 **Philip Silvester** from John Silvester to serve an extra 1½ years; Aug 1702 **Richard Howard** (son of Maurice Howard of City of Worcester, weaver) – free Jan 1718/19; Nov 1705 **John Jackson** (son of Abraham Jackson of Brentford, Middlesex); Jul 1709 **William Robinson** (son of Thomas Robinson of Oxford) – free Apr 1720; May 1714 **Nathaniel Bateman;** Jul 1716 **William Martin;** Jul 1718 **Joseph Smith;** perhaps others later. Moved in 1712 from Devereux Court to a house between the two Temple Gates. In 1714 styled 'within Temple Bar'. Believed died 1733. Work known – numerous examples of bracket clocks, longcase clocks and watches, usually signed 'Daniel Delander, London'.

DELANDER, David　　　　　　　　　　　　**London**
Prob. a misreading of Daniel, *qv*.

DELANDER, James (also Delaunder)　　　　　**London**
A goldsmith. Free Brother in CC Jan 1668-69. Took as aprs.: Sep 1672

Edward Buckenhill (thro' W. Thorowgood) – freed Feb 1687/88; Sep 1675 **Luke Bird** (thro' J. Johnson) – freed Sep 1683; Sep 1680 **James Shirley;** May 1686 **William Sherwood** – free Dec 1695; Mar 1691/92 **John Parker** – free Sep 1706; Aug 1698 **John** or **James Johnstone** (son of John Johnstone) – free Sep 1706. Additionally he bound an apr. for Ignatius Huggeford of the Haberdashers' Co, 'now beyond the seas' and for Thomas Overbury, also of the Haberdashers' Co. and later at Rotterdam. In Mar 1704/05 he was responsible for tracing a jewelled watch by Huggeford, which the CC used as evidence in opposing Debaufre's patent application.

DELANDER, John (sometimes Delaunder)　　　　　　　**London**
Watch casemaker, admitted to CC as Free Brother in Feb 1675-76. Took as aprs.: Feb 1675/76 **Leonard Collard** (thro' Nathan Delander); Sep 1687 **Christopher Cutting** (thro' N. Delander) – free Apr 1695. In 1675 he worked 'over against St. Clement Church'. Not heard of after 1687, though a later man of the same name worked from c. 1705.

DELANDER, Nathaniel (also Delaunder, and see Delawne)　**London**
Watch casemaker, admitted into CC as a Free Brother Jan 1668-69, but in Mar 1675 was admitted a full Freeman by redemption by order of the Lord Mayor as he had taken a house in the newly-built part of the city. Took as aprs.: Mar 1671-72 **Thomas How** (transferred from Isaac Roumyeu); Jul 1674 **Stephen Mitchell** (thro' R. Lyons) 'when he (ie Delander) has taken up his freedom of the city'; Sep 1677 **Urian Berrington** – free Dec 1684; Apr 1684 **Peter Lamude;** May 1686 **Cornelius Helden; Jonathan Jones** (taken from R. Smith) – free Sep 1687; **William Jaques** (taken from J. Wright) – free Sep 1687; Aug 1690 **George Hamilton.** Additionally he bound two aprs. for John Delander. In Nov 1682 he was summoned before the Goldsmiths' Co. in a dispute regarding the fineness of metal used in watch casemaking. Became CC Assistant 1689 and attended regularly till 1691 when he prob. died as he never attended again. He was deceased by Jan 1705/06 when his son, John, was admitted into CC. Work known – at least one watch is known, though no doubt his major output was watch cases.

DELANDER, Peter (also Delandre)　　　　　　　　　　**London**
Made a Free Brother in CC Aug 1641. In Sep 1654 he presented his servant (apr.?) **Thomas Tudner** or **Turner** to CC. Dead by 1695.

DELANE, Peter London
Working at Temple Bar 1662. This is prob. a misspelling of Delandre, ie the previous maker.

DE LA RUE, Jean Anthoine (also Delarve) London
B.c. 1655. In Feb 1681/82, a bachelor, watchmaker, about 27, of St. Mary Savoy parish, Middlesex, married Anne Susanne des Bours, spinster, 17, of same parish at St. Dunstan in the West. Apr 1683 summoned to become a Brother in CC, 'a small clockmaker'.

DELAUNCE, James Frome (Somerset)
Lantern clock c. 1690 signed 'James Delaunce, Froome fecit'. Late 17th century longcase signed similarly. 30-hour musical longcase c. 1720/30 also known. Nothing known of his life. May be the London man below.

DE LAUNCE, James Dounton (Downton?)
Longcase clocks known c.1695 – 1715. Prob. the same man as at Frome.

DELAUNCE, James London
Clockmaker, Free Brother in CC Jan 1677/78. Paid quarterage till 1685 but not later. Believed went to France.

DELA(U)NE, Peter London
Prob. same man as Delander above. Took as aprs.: Oct 1650 **George Andrew** (thro' John Cooke); Oct 1650 **Henry Harland** (thro' W. Godbed) – free Nov 1654; Sep 1654 **John Trevor** (thro' H. Cooper).

DELAVILLE, John London
B.c. 1648, apr. Jan 1662/63 to Evan Jones (thro' S. Horne) but not freed.

DELAVERSPIERRE and **DELAVRESPIERRE, William** (and other spellings) see Lavrespierre.

DELAWNE, Nathaniel London
In 1662 was an alien and apr. of Cornelius Mellin in Blackfriars. This name is a variant of Delander, *qv*.

DELLAMARE, Peter (see Mer)

DELLUNG, Paul London
B.c. 1645, apr. Apr 1659 to Paul Lowell till 1666 but not free.

DEMOLYN, Jean (also De Mellin, Dewmelane, etc. see under Mellin)

DE MOUCHIE, John London
In 1662 was an alien working as journeyman with Cornelius Mellin in Blackfriars.

DENETT, Abraham London
In Show Lane in 1662. Prob. a misspelling of some other name, but I cannot recognise it.

DENNIS, Francis (see Dinnis)

DENNIS, Thomas London/Canterbury
B.c. 1658, apr. Sep 1672 to James Wightman till 1679 but not freed. One of this name was free at Canterbury in 1684, sold property there in 1685 (in Week Street?).

DENT, Robert London
B.c. 1657, apr. Feb 1670/71 to Benjamin Bell till 1678. Freed Jul 1681. Took as apr.: Jul 1681 **Edward Boone,** later transferred to Thomas Tompion and freed Jul 1691. Also bound an apr. for H. Merriman. Not heard of after 1689 when he last paid quarterage. Prob. related to William Dent.

DENT, William London
'Great clockmaker', made Free Brother in CC Sep 1674. Took as aprs.: Apr 1680 **Jeremiah Martin,** later transferred to Thomas Tompion and freed Sep 1687; Apr 1685 **John Oakley;** Dec 1696 **John Mason** – free Feb 1703-04; Sep 1702 **William Dent** (son of John Dent of Barnard Castle, Durham, glazier). Not heard of after 1704, when last paid quarterage.

DE PASS, Simon London(?)
Engraver of watch by Onisephorus Helden, acc. to Baillie.

DEPREE (see Dupree)

DERBY, Aron London
B.c. 1674, apr. Jul 1687 to William Garfoot till 1695 but not freed. Work known – a watch.

DE RO, ---- London
From Flanders c. 1625. Supposedly made a perpetual motion clock (Baillie).

DESBOROUGH, Christopher London
Apr. Aug 1658 to Anthony Grosse. Freed Feb 1665/66.

DESBROW, Elizabeth (also Disbrowe) London
B.c. 1664, apr. Oct 1676 to Henry Jevon and Christian his wife till 1683 but not freed.

DESESSARS, Abraham London
Prob. French, a watch chainmaker. Free Brother in CC Apr 1682. In 1702 lived in parish of St. Leonard Shoreditch, when his son, George, was apr. to William Sherwood. A James Desesar, apr. in 1698 to Nathan Baseley, is prob. related. I have no record of him after 1702 but Baillie puts his death as 1739. Work known – prob. not identifiable.

DES FOUNTAINES, Jacobus London
Watch recorded pre-1692.

DE(S)TACHES, John (and Dutache) London (and Dublin?)
In 1646 warned by CC against working without being a member. Free in CC Aug 1661. Listed as an engraver in 1662. One of this name in Dublin Goldsmiths' Co. 1670-99 may be same man.

DEVALL (see Davall)

DE VREESE, John London
Listed as working 1683, but I cannot trace him.

DE WELLKE, Christian London
Believed working c. 1620-30, when he was a subscriber for incorporation of CC. One Dewell admitted to Blacksmiths' Co. in 1628, a 'Polander', may be same man. Work known – a table clock and a watch.

DEWHURST, William   **Ribchester (Lancashire)**
A shopkeeper who serviced church clock in 1670.

DICKENS, John (signed Dickins)   **London**
B.c. 1666, apr. Jul 1680 to John Longland, later transferred to William
Cattle till 1687. Freed Sep 1688. Took as aprs.: Jul 1692 **Richard Brant;**
Aug 1695 **John Shelton** (both later transferred to Thomas Cattell,
perhaps on death of Dickens, which was prob. between 1693 and 1697.
Work known – longcase clock signed 'Jno. Dickens, London'.

DICKIE, Stephen   **Glasgow**
Kept town clock 1583.

DIDE, Thomas (see Dyde)

DIGHTON, William   **London**
B.c. 1673, apr. Sep 1687 to Samuel Rosse till 1694 but not freed.

DIKE, Nathaniel (also Dyke)   **London**
Apr. Apr 1656 to Thomas Wheeler. Freed Jul 1663. Took as apr. Dec
1664 **Francis Hill** – free Sep 1672; also took **William Fuller** from Robert
Silke and later transferred him to John White. Believed worked in
Exchange Alley.

DIKESOON, Thomas   **Peebles (Scotland)**
Son of William Dikesoon of Winkstoun. Kept town clock 1564.

DINGLEY, Robert   **London**
B.c. 1647, son of Thomas Dingley of Ewell, Surrey. Apr. Oct 1661 to
Richard Peirce till 1668. Freed Dec 1668 and also free of the city. Took as
aprs.: Nov 1670 **Francis Carter;** Dec 1676 **Benjamin Willoughby;** Jul
1680 **Timothy Middleton** – free Nov 1687; May 1686 **William Winter;**
Dec 1687 **Nicholas Edwards;** Nov 1692 **George Tyler** – free Dec 1699;
Dec 1695 **Robert Griffith** – free Jan 1706/07. Still alive in 1697 but listed
as dead by 1698. Said to have worked at George Yard, Lombard Street,
in 1692. Work known – watches and longcase clocks.

DINGLEY, William   **London**
B.c. 1648, apr. Jul 1661 to Lionel Wythe till 1669 but not freed.

DINNIS, Francis (also Dennis)   **London**
An engraver, admitted into CC as a Free Brother Apr 1667, then admitted as a full Freeman by redemption by order of the Lord Mayor Jan 1672-73. Took as aprs.: Sep 1675 **John Barnard** – free Jan 1682/83; Aug 1676 **William Hawkins** – free Jun 1684; Sep 1681 **William Burton.** In Jan 1682-83 he was alleged to have engraved a fictitious name on a watch for John Cotsworth and to have often done so before. He denied this, though admitted having done so in the past. In Feb he was accused by James Greene of having done so again, which he denied but said his workman had re-engraved a worn name on an old watch. In Jan 1683/84 he took **John Rowden** apr. – freed Jan 1691/92. Rowden was one of the names he had illicitly engraved on watches earlier. Not heard of after 1692 and dead by 1698.

DITCHFIELD, Richard   **London**
B.c. 1649, son of John Ditchfield, ironmonger, of Warrington, Lancashire. Apr. Oct 1663 in Clockworkers' Co. to Richard Cockson till 1670. Freed Dec 1670. Was an engraver. Became Free Brother in CC Dec 1677/78. In 1687 he was much in arrears with his quarterage. Listed as dead by 1697/98.

DIXON, William   **London**
B.c. 1672, apr. May 1686 to Daniel Beckman (an engraver) till 1693 but not freed.

DOBB(E), William   **London**
B.c. 1626, apr. Apr 1639 to James Vautrollier (thro' R. Masterson) till 1647. Freed as a Brother Sep 1646. Took as aprs.: Nov 1655 **John Cooke** (thro' T. Wolverston) – freed Dec 1662; Aug 1660 **Henry Randolph.**

DOBSON, William   **London**
Admitted to CC as a free Brother, a 'Great Clockmaker' Sep 1670. Took as aprs.: Nov 1676 **Thomas Berkeley** (thro' S. Davis); May 1684 **Thomas Luntley.** In Sep 1694 his widow received charity from CC. Work known – at least one lantern clock, signed 'William Dobson in High Holbourne, Londini fecit'.

DODD, Elisha   **London**
An engraver, apr. Aug 1662 in Weavers' Co. to John Benson, an engraver. Free in Weavers' Co. Jan 1670/71. Took as apr. thro' Weavers'

Co. c. 1683 **Thomas Walford,** who was freed as a Brother in CC Apr 1690. Dodd himself became a free Brother in CC Apr 1690.

DODDINGTON, John   **London/Kilkenny**
B.c. 1671, apr. Oct 1685 to Benjamin Wright (thro' A. Prime) till 1692 but not freed. Went to Kilkenny c. 1692, died there 1699.

DODSON, John   **London**
Apr. Apr 1655 to Isaac Law (thro' J. Cooke) but not freed.

DODSWORTH, John   **London**
In 1646 he was warned by CC and joined as a Free Brother Dec 1648. Took as apr. Jan 1651 **James Greene** (from W. Gibbs) – free Dec 1664; Apr 1654 **Robert Lynch** (from Thomas Taylor) – freed Apr 1670. Not heard of after 1654 and prob. dead or gone by 1662.

DONNE, ----   **London**
Never actually admitted to CC but known to them c. 1650. Prob. dead or gone by 1662.

DOO, Thomas   **Yarmouth (Norfolk)**
Made Martham church clock in 1674.

DOORE, Robert   **London**
B.c. 1650, apr. Jul 1663 to Edward Enys, later transferred to Richard Bowen till 1671. Freed Jul 1671. Took as aprs.: Apr 1676 **Benjamin Tebbatt** – free Sep 1683; Apr 1681 **John Newell;** Jun 1684 **James Beverley.**

DORRELL, Francis (sometimes Darrel)   **London**
B.c. 1679, apr. Jul 1693 to Thomas Speakman till 1700. Freed Sep 1702. Took as aprs.: Oct 1706 **Hugh Mundy** (son of Francis Mundy of St. Olave, Southwark, weaver); Aug 1711 **William Whitebread;** May 1716 **Henry Adams.** Not heard of after 1716. Work known – a watch.

DORSETT, Gregory (also Dossett)   **London**
Apr. Jan 1651/52 to Robert Grinkin (thro' L. Wythe) transferred later, prob. on Grinkin's death in 1660, to William Rogers. (In Grinkin's will was mentioned as a friend Henry Dorsett, maybe father of Gregory?). Freed Apr 1662. Took as apr.: Oct 1663 **John Scardeville.** He worked in Fleet Street in 1662, prob. as journeyman to Rogers. Still working in

1671, but when summoned to CC in 1677 regarding stewardship, he failed to appear and was not heard of thereafter.

DOSSETT – see Dorsett and Dowsett.

DOUD, James place not known
Watch recorded c. 1600.

DOWLING, Mortagh Dublin
Watchmaker and goldsmith. Free in Goldsmiths there 1700. Died 1746.

DOUGHTY, Tobias London
B.c. 1674, apr. Jun 1688 to Henry Child till 1695. Freed Jul 1696. Paid no quarterage after 1697 and prob. dead or gone by 1698.

DOVE, Arthur London
Apr. to William Clay (who was not a CC member). Free in CC Oct 1659. Took as apr. Mar 1668-69 **Samuel Gascoigne,** who was later (after Dove's death) transferred by his widow, Katherine, to Robert Seigniour and freed Apr 1676. He was alive in 1671, so must have died within the 1671-76 period. Work known – a stolen watch by 'Arthur Dove of St. Martins' was recorded in 1681.

DOVE, Henry London
Free in CC Jul 1667 (as Brother?)

DOVE, Robert London
Recorded as CC 1671, but this is an error for Dore, *qv.*

DOWNES, Christopher London
Admitted into CC Oct 1632, prob. as a Brother.

DOWNES, Jeremiah London
B.c. 1675, apr. Jan 1689/90 to James Jackson, thro' Hugh Roberts, till 1696 but not freed.

DOWNING(E), Humphrey London
Reputedly free in Barber Surgeons Co. and to have served Grinkin in the Blacksmiths' Co., but can hardly have done both. One of this name was free (in Blacksmiths' Co.) Sep 1604, having been apr. to John Kerrill, but this seems rather early. In 1646 he was not in CC and was never

actually admitted, but by 1648 seems to have been treated as if he were a member. Took as aprs.: (all bound thro' L. Wythe) Jul 1648 **Thomas Broadway**; Oct 1651 **Nicholas Pantin**; Dec 1655 **Henry Latham**; Aug 1657 **Edward Herbert** – freed Oct 1664; Jun 1662 **Charles Gretton** – free Jun 1672. In 1662 worked in Chancery Lane. Prob. dead or gone by 1663. Work known – none – maybe an engraver.

DOWSE, Gabriel   **London**
B.c. 1635, apr. Jun 1649 to **William Godbed** till 1656 but not freed.

DOWSET, John (see also Dorset)   **London**
B.c. 1679, apr. Oct 1693 to **William Mason** till 1700 but not freed.

DRAKE, John   **London**
Free in Blacksmiths' Co. Jul 1605, being the apr. of Mr. Starkie, his proof piece being a plate lock. This prob. means he was b. c. 1584 and apr. c. 1598. An original subscriber to CC in 1630 but because of his first loyalty to the Blacksmiths' Co. he was always at odds with the CC administration, and, when forced to pay all his 15 years of quarterage arrears in 1654, referred to Warden Nicasius as a 'turd and a shitten fellow'. He was one of the 1656 rebels against the administration. Was several times warned (ineffectually) about binding his aprs. thro' the Blacksmiths' Co. Seems to have taken **Basil Brand** as apr. Oct 1658, free of the City 1668. In 1636 he refused to serve as CC Assistant. In 1661 he was summoned to answer CC complaints – but did not. Worked in Westminster in 1662, but prob. died or moved away soon after, as he was not heard of again. Work known – at least one watch survives. One J. Dracque at Nérac in the early 17th century may be the same man.

DRAPER, Simeon   **London**
B.c. 1675, apr. May 1688 to Samuel Drossatt till 1696 but not freed. Drossatt was in the Shipwrights' Co., and maybe Draper was freed there?

DRAYCOTT, Francis   **London**
B.c. 1657, apr. Aug 1671 to Samuel Vernon but later transferred secretly to Robert Seigniour till 1678. Freed Aug 1678. Paid quarterage till 1681. Dead or gone by 1697/98.

DREW, Edward   **London**
B.c. 1669, apr. Jul 1683 to Jeffrey Bailey till 1690. Freed Jul 1692. Paid quarterage till 1705 at least and maybe later.

DREW, John   **London**
B.c. 1663, apr. Sep 1676 to Joseph Knibb till 1684. Freed Sep 1684.
Took as aprs.: May 1689 **Thomas Sparkes;** Dec 1695-96 **Isaac Lowndes;** Jan 1699/1700 **Henry Kent** (son of Henry Kent of Ipswich, victualler); Dec 1702 **Henry Owens** (son of Henry Owens late of St. Asaph, co. Denbigh, deceased); Sep 1708 **Ambrose Thompson;** Sep 1712 **George Hughs;** Nov 1712 **George Wright;** Aug 1713 **James Murray.** In Apr 1712 he was appointed Beadle (to replace Richard George who had died), an office usually given to the poorest members as a source of part-time income. From Jan to Jul 1713 he received CC charity. He died in Aug or Sep 1713, when Christopher Gould was appointed Beadle to replace him. His widow received CC charity from 1713 to her death in 1715. Work known – several longcase clocks and a lantern clock. Usually signed 'John Drew London fecit' but one signed 'John Drew Johnson Court in Fleet Street'.

DREW, Robert   **Chester**
Free 1675/76, a clockmaker.

DREW, Thomas   **London**
B.c. 1657, apr. Apr 1671 to Cornelius Harbottle till 1678. However, in May 1672 Harbottle pleaded that 'he is incapable of learning his trade and therefore he must needs put him away' – and did.

DROESHOUT, John (also Drowset and Drussett)   **London**
Free Brother in CC 1632. Took as apr. Oct 1637 **Daniel Jolly** (thro' O. Durant). Paid quarterage till at least 1647; not heard of thereafter.

DROSSADE, Samuel (signed Drossart, also Drossat(t)(e))   **London**
In Nov 1675 promised to become a Brother in CC. He was admitted Jan 1675/76, being a clockmaker but a freeman in the Shipwrights' Co. His present (1675) apr., **Solomon Bouquet,** who was bound thro' the Shipwrights' Co., was to be rebound thro' CC, and freed by patrimony Mar 1682-83. Took further aprs.: Apr 1680 **Lionel Playters** (thro' S. Davis); **John Norcott** – freed Apr 1681; May 1688 **Simeon Draper;** May 1695 his son, **Robert Drossade.** In Jan 1699 his daughter, Sara Drossade, was free of the Shipwrights' Co. by patrimony. Paid quarterage till at least 1704. Work known – at least two watches.

DRULARDY (see Duclardg)

DRUMMOND, Francis   London
B.c. 1663, apr. Aug 1676 to Samuel Davis senior till 1684, but not freed.

DRURY, D.   London
Recorded as late 17th century but I cannot locate him.

DRURY, James   London
B.c 1673, apr. Dec 1687 to Francis Hill till 1694. Freed Apr 1695. One
CC record describes him as son of Joseph Drury, but has been crossed
through. Took as aprs.: Sep 1698 **John Sutton;** Apr 1701 **Henry
Stanbury** (son of Robert Stanbury of Backswell, co. Warwick, miller) –
free Jul 1709; Dec 1706 **Thomas Woods** – free Jul 1714; Apr 1708
Samuel Henry Smith – free Jan 1715/16; Oct 1713 **Thomas Ladbrooke;**
Apr 1717 **Peter Crook,** perhaps others later, incl. son, **James Drury** –
freed 1720. My data on him ends in 1720, but he is believed to have lived
on till 1740. Work known – watches and longcase clocks signed 'James
Drury London'.

DRUSSETT (see Droeshout)

DRYER, Samuel   London
Two late 17th century watches recorded but I have no data on him.

DUBBAR, Hugh   London
B.c. 1634, apr. Oct 1648 to John Freeman till 1655 but not freed.

DUBOURK, Abraham   London
Failed to pay CC quarterage in 1635.

DU CHESNE, Claude   London
Clockmaker from Paris. Free Brother in CC Sep 1693. Took as apr. Dec
1715 **Richard Bullock** – maybe others later. Often in arrears with
quarterage. In 1718 was excused stewardship 'because he has five
children and pleads inability' (ie to pay). Lived in St. Anne's,
Westminster in 1720, when his son, Antoine, was apr. as a goldsmith
(freed 1729). I have no details of him after 1720 but he is believed to have
worked till c. 1730. Work known – a good number of clocks, several of a
complex nature. Longcase clocks usually signed 'Claudius de Chesne,
Londini'. Also bracket clocks, some signed 'Claude du Chesne, Long
Aker', and 'Claude du Chesne, Dean Street, Soho, Londini'.

DUCKER, Charles   Chester
Repaired Holy Trinity clock 1624.

DUCKER, George   Chester
Repaired Holy Trinity clock 1599-1602.

DUCKET, ----   N. Elmham (Norfolk)
Made church clock there 1567.

DUCKWORTH, John   Halifax (Yorkshire)
Repaired church clock in 1652. Prob. not a maker.

DUCKWORTH, Richard   Halifax (Yorkshire)
Believed clockmaker. Wife, Mary, died 1674. He died in 1677.

DUCLARDG or **DUCLARDY** (also Drulardy)   London
A Frenchman who sold clocks to the King c. 1530-35. The spelling of his
name is uncertain.

DUDDLESTONE, Thomas   Warwick
Maintained St. Nicholas church clock 1623-29.

DUDSON, Simon (also Dutson)   London
Apr. Dec 1647 to John Selwood (thro' T. Alcock) then transferred Jan
1651/52 (on Selwood's death?) to Thomas Loomes. Freed Nov 1654.
Was amongst the 1656 rebels against the CC administration. Took as
aprs.: Nov 1655 **William Tovey**; Nov 1656 **Edward Sedwell**, prob.
transferred to Thomas Loomes after Dudson's death and freed Oct 1664.
In Nov 1656 also bound an apr. for T. Daniell. Prob. died between 1656
and 1662. Britten gives his work place as Tower Street, on what authority
I do not know.

DUDWITT, James (also Duduict, Jacques)   London
In 1622 was an alien (French?) working at Mr. Garrett's in St. Martins.
Two of this name worked at Blois about this time. Work known – a watch
by the Blois maker, late 16th century, but see also under A. Boys.

DUGAST, Stephen   Dublin
Watch casemaker there in 1683. Huguenot?

DUKE, John   **London**
Watch of c. 1650 recorded signed 'John Duke, Fleet Street'. Maybe error for Joseph, *qv.*

DUKE, Joseph   **London**
Some authorities record two of this name at this time, but there seems to be only one. B.c. 1652, apr. Aug 1666 to Edmund Gilpin (thro' J. Markwick) till 1673. Freed Apr 1682. Took as aprs.: Mar 1686/87 **Cornelius Johnson** – free Apr 1694; Dec 1698 **Edward Avenall** (son of Stephen Avenall, late of Highworth, co.Wiltshire, maltster, deceased) – free Jul 1706; May 1701 **John Johnson** (son of Cornelius Jenkins; error for Johnson?) deceased, late of the parish of St. Andrew Holborne, Middlesex, sword cutler). Paid quarterage till at least 1705.

DUKE, Nathaniel   **London**
Recorded by some authorities but this is an error for Nathaniel Dike, *qv.*

DUNN, Benony (not Benjamin)   **London**
B.c. 1677, apr. May 1691 to Thomas Whittle then transferred to Thomas Gibbs till 1698 but not freed.

DUN(N), Henry   **London**
B.c. 1610, son of John Dunn of Nottingham city deceased. Apr. in Merchant Taylors' Co. Aug 1621 to John Spittlehouse till 1631. Free May 1630. Admitted to CC as Free Brother Apr 1677. Took as apr. in CC Mar 1677-78 **Bartholomew Dary** or **Davy** (thro' S. Davis).

DUN(N), Richard (also Donn)   **London**
'Officer' to the CC in 1632. Perhaps the Clerk and maybe not a maker at all.

DUNNINGS, William   **Battle (Sussex)**
Repaired church clock 1673-74.

DUNSTER, Roger   **Amsterdam/London**
Working from c. 1700 prob. only in Amsterdam, living on the Dam. Apparently had no children. Will dated 1723 leaves all to his wife Catharina (Mullins), proved in London in 1747. His mother, unnamed, was still alive in 1723. One-time partner with the Clarke and Dunster concern, *qv.* Work known – several watches and at least one bracket clock are known, signed 'Roger Dunster, Amsterdam'.

DUNSTON, Paul **London**
B.c. 1674, apr. Jul 1687 to Simon Chapman till 1695 but not freed.

DUPPA, Charles **London**
B.c. 1632, apr. Sep 1646 to William Clay (thro' T. Claxton) till 1653 but
not freed.

DUPREE, Elias and **Elie** (sometimes Depree) **London**
Free Brother in CC Apr 1634. According to Britten he worked in 1635 for
Edward East, was a Dutchman, and had been then in London about 20
years. One of this name is recorded in Holland in 1635. One Depree paid
CC search fee in 1673 and 1674 – if same man, he must have been in
his 70s.

DU PUY, Jean Pierre **London**
Watchmaker in Spitalfields Market in 1703.

DURANT, Charles **London**
Denizen, clockmaker in 1544.

DURANT, John **London**
In Aug 1632 he was apr. to William Pettit for 2 years effective from Apr
1633, but not freed. A Jean Durand worked in Rouen in 1649 and a
watch of c. 1690 is known by 'J. L. Durant', which may be him.

DURANT, Oswald **London**
An original petitioner for incorporation of CC and a very well-known
name in CC archives, largely because he acted as intermediary in binding
aprs. in much the same way as the Beadle did later. Free Brother 1632,
full Freeman Feb 1636/37, being transferred from the Imbroaderers' Co.
Took as aprs.: Aug 1637 **Ralph Almond** – free Dec 1645; Sep 1637
Richard Eyre; Apr 1638 **James Nelson**. Additionally he bound many
aprs. (28) for other masters, incl. the following: R. Grinkin – 2, E. East –
2, S. Shelton – 3, and one each to T. Pace, J. Vautrollier, D. Bouquet,
W. Daniel, M. Blunt, T. Alcock, T. Howse, T. Platt, J. Burgess,
J. Nicasius, S. Hackett, J. Droeshout, R. Cordwell, J. Midnall, R. Ash,
G. Smith, J. Pennock, S. Bartram, W. Almond, J. Harris, P. Closon.
Became Warden 1645 but oddly enough was never an Assistant, nor
Master, and prob. died soon after 1645. Work known – at least one watch
survives.

DURDENT, Andrew London
Apr. Aug 1655 to Samuel Horne. Freed Sep 1662.

DURRANT, Charles (see Durant)

DUTACH, John (see Destaches)

DUVAL, John (see Davall)

DUXBURY, Edmond London
B.c. 1661, apr. Jul 1675 to Henry Hester till 1682 but not freed.

DYDE, John London
Freeman in Blacksmiths' Co. before Sep 1677 when his apr. **Benjamin Harris** was transferred thro' CC to T. Tompion.

DYDE, Thomas (also Dide) London
Never actually joined CC but was known to them and tolerated by them. Working by 1662. His will, dated 1686, proved 1687, describes him as a watchmaker and mentions the 'house where I now dwell' at Fortee Green, Enfield. He mentions his 'cosen' John Harris, watchmaker, *qv*, also William Dyde, son of my brother (Charles Dyde) and god-daughter Elizabeth Harris. Left his son, Charles, land at Sewardstone, Essex. Prob. related to John Dyde above, *qv*. Work known – lantern clocks and watches. Also month longcase signed 'Tho. Dyde – Exchange Alley'.

DYER, ---- Tredington (Warwickshire)
Blacksmith? Attended church clock 1683-1719. A Giles Dyer who attended town clock in Boston, USA, 1673-84 may be connected.

DYKE (see Dike)

DYMER, Thomas Norwich
Kept church clock of St. Peter Mancroft in 1619.

DYMMOCK, ---- Bristol
Kept church clock 1557.

DYSON, John London
B.c. 1673, apr. Oct 1687 to John North later transferred to Peter Collins till 1694. Freed Apr 1695, after which he paid no quarterage, so prob. dead or gone by 1696-97.

E

EAGLE, John London
B.c. 1669, apr. Jul 1683 to Stephen Wilmot, then transferred several times and lastly to John Wheeler till 1690. Freed Jul 1690. Took as apr.: Feb 1693/94 **Hildesley Gunter**. Supplied a new clock to the Earl of Salisbury in 1696. In that same year he was summoned to appear at CC court, but did not. Paid quarterage till at least 1705, perhaps later. Work known – a longcase clock.

EAGLESFIELD, (Richard?) Carlisle (Cumberland)
Kept church clock 1704. Son, Robert, entered school there 1699.

EARLES or ERYLES London
Said to have been a subscriber to incorporation of CC in 1630 but I cannot confirm this.

EAST, Daniel London
Died 1672 according to Baillie, but I do not know his source and he was not known to the CC.

EAST, Edward senior (sometimes Est) London
A very famous maker. B. 1602 at Southill, Bedfordshire, son of John East. Apr. Mar 1618 in Goldsmiths' Co. to Richard Rogers till 1626. Freed 1627. Made one of the first Assistants in CC in 1632 (against his will), Warden 1638 (Master 1645 and 1653). He very seldom attended meetings after about 1660. Supposedly worked in Pall Mall in 1632. Worked in Fleet Street by the 1640s, supposedly at 'the Musical Clock',

and when he was Master he held the CC court meetings there. Later (1690) he worked at 'the Sun outside Temple Bar'. He was brother to Jeremy East, *qv*.

Took as aprs.: (in CC) Sep 1643 **Thomas Wolverstone** (thro' O. Durant) – free Sep 1650; Oct 1646 **Robert Hanslapp** (thro' T. Alcock) – free Mar 1653; Oct 1639 **Walter Gibbs** (thro' O. Durant) – free May 1648; Jan 1650 **Edward Wagstaffe** (thro' R. Masterson); Aug 1654 **Henry Jones** – free Jul 1663; Dec 1654 **John East** (thro' D. Moody); Jun 1657 **Adam Pearce** (thro' D. Moody) – free Jun 1664; Dec 1676 **Richard Bellinger**. There seems to be a large gap in his life as far as the CC records reveal it in the 1660s and early 1670s. He is said to have employed **Elias Dupree**, a Dutchman, in 1635, though I cannot confirm this. It seems likely that **Evan Jones** worked for him. In 1656 he supported the CC administration against the rebels.

In his will, dated 1688, proved Feb 1696/97, he mentions his residence at Hampton, Middlesex. He left 'the Swann with two necks', in Ladd Lane to his daughter, Anne Saunders. He mentioned his wife, Sarah, son, Edward, and Edward's son, Edmund. Also his son, James, and daughter, Elizabeth. His son, Edward, had already received his inheritance. The odd phrase 'It is my express will that my executrix bury me privately in the night time and that she give nothing but Rosemary att my funerall' suggests he may well have been a Catholic. In Oct 1692 he gave to CC £100, the interest to be used for payments to poor members. In Nov 1660 he was appointed Chief Clockmaker to the King (but was not Clockmaker to Charles I as is sometimes stated).

The East concern prob. had a very large workforce, which prob. included the following masters and their numerous aprs., many of whom were known or suspected Catholics/Royalists: Peter Bellon; David Moody; Benjamin Hill; Michael Cornish; Jeremy East and prob. all the other Easts, John Matchett, William Partridge, Evan Jones, and prob. others whose connection seems less obvious. A good number of these had French origins/connections. The East business house, with its French/Catholic/Royalist leanings, seems to have been in direct opposition to the Fromanteel business with its Anglo/Dutch/Protestant/Cromwellian inclinations. This large workforce could account for the comparatively large number of 'his' works which survive, compared to the very small number (if any) surviving by his associates.

EAST, Edward junior   London

Son of Edward senior and father of Edmund. Mentioned in 1688 will of Edward, though not specified as a clockmaker. Apparently not known to

CC. Work known – an early Georgian lacquer longcase signed 'Edward East London' may perhaps be by him?

East, Edmund London
Grandson of Edward senior, son of Edward junior. B.c. 1675, apr. May 1688 to Samuel Clyatt (thro' R. Lyon) till 1696. Freed Jul 1696. Paid quarterage till at least 1700 but not heard of thereafter. Work known – a watch and a longcase clock are recorded.

EAST, James London
Son of Edward senior and mentioned in his 1688 will. Clockmaker to the Queen from Apr 1662. Apparently not a member of CC.

EAST, Jeremy senior (sometimes Est) London
Brother of Edward senior. A man of this name married in 1637 to Catharine Davyes. Free Brother in CC Oct 1640, but said to be a member of the Goldsmiths' Co. before this (and master of **Jeremy Gregory**). Supported the CC administration in the 1656 rebellion. Worked in Fleet Street in 1662, prob. with Edward. Took as aprs.: Nov 1658 **Nathaniel Wilson** (thro' D. Moody); **Peter Southworth** (from J. Palfrey) – free Jan 1664/65; Jul 1667 **Charles Enou** (thro' L. Wythe). Not heard of after 1667. Work known – several watches said to date from c.1600 – c.1620 seem rather early for him. Some signed 'Jeremie East fecit', others 'Jeremy East Londini'.

EAST, Jeremiah junior London
B.c. 1640, apr. in CC Jan 1653/54 to **James Seaburne** till 1661 but not freed. Not known whether he completed his training, and post-1661 references to the previous maker may perhaps refer to this man.

EAST, John London
B.c. 1640, apr. Dec 1654 to Edward East (thro' D. Moody) till 1661 but not freed.

EAST, John Dublin
Said to be son of John East of London, watchmaker (but this can hardly have been the John East above and I know no other of this name). Apr. 1656 to Daniel Bellingham.

EAST, Nathaniel London
According to Baillie worked for the Court in 1670, but I do not know his source of this information.

EAST, Peter London
Admitted to CC as a clockmaker and a Free Brother Apr 1692. Paid quarterage till 1693. Still alive 1697 but prob. dead or left soon after and marked as dead by 1698. Work known – at least one longcase clock.

EAST, Thomas London
B.c. 1656, apr. May 1670 to John Harris till 1677. Freed Jul 1677. Took as aprs.: Jan 1679-80 **George Snell** – free Sep 1688; Mar 1681-82 **William Herris** (thro' H. Roberts); Sep 1689 **Francis William Harris;** Sep 1692 **Abraham Dearmer** – free Sep 1703; Jan 1699/1700 his son, **Edward East** – free Jul 1710; **John Hill** – free Apr 1706; Oct 1707 **John Wheatley.**

EAST, 'widow' London
Granted ten shillings CC charity in Jan 1676-77. Maybe widow of Jeremy? When the Master delivered it, he found that she too was dead 'but the daughter, being in great need, he gave five shillings of it to her and put the rest in the poor box'.

EAST, William (see Este)

EATON, Thomas Chester
Blacksmith. Repaired Holy Trinity clock 1599-1624.

EBSWORTH, Christopher London
B.c. 1648, apr. Dec 1662 to Richard Ames till 1669. Freed Jan 1669-70. Maybe brother of John Ebsworth, who had same master.

EBSWORTH, John London
Apr. Feb 1657 to Richard Ames. Freed Apr 1665. Took as aprs.: Jul 1667 **Bryan Lake** – free Oct 1674; Jul 1672 **William Sharpe** – free Jul 1681; Jun 1675 **John Barnett** – free Sep 1682; Aug 1684 **John Berry** – free Apr 1692; Dec 1684 **Jonathan Woodford;** Jul 1696 **Joseph Hutchin** – free Aug 1703. Additionally he bound an apr. for Nathaniel Bird. In May 1674 two faulty sundials were confiscated from his 'shop in Lothbury'. Worked at the Cross Keys in Lothbury but is said to have worked later at 'New Cheep Side' (but see also Thomas Knifton who worked at the Cross Keys in Lothbury earlier – maybe Ebsworth succ. him there). Was CC Assistant from 1682, Warden 1694-96, Master 1697. His will, dated May 1699, was proved in Sep 1699 and appointed Edward Stanton (*qv*) overseer, though there is no apparent business connection

between them. He mentions his wife, Susanna, and one Thomas Walker who may be the clockmaker of that name. Work known – several lantern clocks, usually signed 'John Ebsworth at ye Crossed Keys in Lothbury, Londini fecit' or 'John Ebsworth in Lothbury Londini fecit', but also 'John Ebsworth London'. Also several longcase clocks signed 'John Ebsworth Londini fecit' and 'John Ebsworth London'.

EDLIN, John London
B.c. 1662, apr. May 1676 to Robert Webster (thro' C. Bonner) till 1683. Freed Sep 1687. Took as aprs.: Feb 1688-89 **Thomas Weast** – free Aug 1698; Apr 1699 **Charles Viccaridge** (son of Charles Viccaridge, fishmonger, and citizen of St. Bridget and St. Bride's, London). This apprenticeship was repeated in May 1700 (perhaps the boy was under age in 1699). Paid quarterage till 1700, when believed to have died.

EDMONDS, Elizabeth London
B.c. 1665, apr. Jun 1679 to Henry Jevon and Christian his wife till 1686, but not freed.

EDMONDSON, John London
B.c. 1646, apr. Aug 1660 to Hugh Cooper till 1667 but not freed.

EDWARD, Clement Devonshire
Recorded as 1671 by Baillie but this is an error for Edward Clements, *qv*.

EDWARDS, Benjamin Bungay (Suffolk)
Repaired Metfield church clock in 1690.

EDWARDS, Gulielmus (see John and William Edwards)

EDWARDS, John (or William or John William) York
Clockmaker, free there 1654. Supposedly made clock for a church in Ousebridge in 1658. A turret clock signed 'Gulielmus Edwardus Cambria Brittania' and dated 1658 survives – maybe the same man?

EDWARDS, Joseph London
Apr. c. 1654 to John Nicasius but not freed.

EDWARDS, Nicholas London
B.c. 1673, apr. Dec 1687 to Robert Dingley till 1694 but not freed.

EDWARDS, Thomas   **London**
B.c. 1667, apr. Feb 1680/81 (thro' D. Stephens) to Robert Player, a freeman of the Joyners' Co. and a clock casemaker till 1688, but not freed.

EDWARDS, William   **London**
Supposedly in Blacksmiths' Co. 1630, but see Gulielmus and John.

EELES (see Ellis)

EGERSLEY, James   **London**
B.c. 1646, apr. Oct 1660 to William Godbed till 1667 but not freed.

EGLES, Henry (prob. misreading of Ellis, *qv*)

EGLETON, Christopher   **London**
B.c. 1669, apr. Jun 1683 to Charles Halstead, later transferred to Cuthbert Lee till 1690. Freed Nov 1695. Took as apr. Dec 1695 **William Shelton**. Paid no quarterage and prob. died or left soon after and before 1697-98. (Baillie records him till 1730, I don't know why). Work known – a watch.

EKINS, Charles   **London**
B.c. 1663, apr. Aug 1677 (thro' N. Coxeter) to Daniel Le Conte, a freeman of the Haberdashers' Co. till 1684, but not freed.

ELDRIDGE, John   **London (and Alresford, Hampshire?)**
B.c. 1656, apr. Mar 1669/70 to Lawrence Sindry till 1677. Free Mar 1677-78. On CC list of 1698 but had paid no quarterage for 20 years. Work known – an early 18th century longcase clock is recorded signed 'John Eldridge – Alresford'.

ELFES, Benjamin (also Elphs)   **London**
B.c. 1653, apr. Aug 1666 to Thomas Taylor of Holborn till 1674. Freed Jul 1674.

ELFES, Thomas   **London**
B.c. 1657, apr. Jul 1671 to George Hambleton (thro' L. Wythe) till 1678 but not freed.

ELLICOTT, John London
B.c. 1673. His parents are said to have come to London from Bodmin.
Apr. Sep 1687 to John Waters till 1694. Freed Jul 1696. Took as aprs.:
Mar 1698/99 **Robert Darwell** (son of Edward Darwell of Weston,
Buckinghamshire, yeoman) – free Jul 1708; Aug 1703 **James Brittain;**
1696 **William Elkins** – freed Mar 1709/10; Jun 1711 **William Kellaway;**
perhaps others after 1720. Reputedly died in 1733, but I have no data on
him after 1720. His son, John, b. 1706, became the more famous maker.
Said to have worked variously at Austin Friars, Swithin's Alley, Royal
Exchange and All Hallows, London Wall.

ELLIOTT, Henry London
Clockmaker. Made a Free Brother in CC Sep 1688. His son, Henry, was
apr. in 1704 to G. Tyler, at which time Henry senior was still alive,
though not heard of thereafter. Work known – at least two longcase
clocks are recorded signed 'Henry Elliott Londini fecit'. One bears the
name 'Raderiff' inside the movement, which may represent Redriff, the
old name for Rotherhithe, and may indicate that he worked there.

ELLIOTT, John London
B.c. 1667, apr. Sep 1681 to John Goode till 1688 but not freed. Took as
apr. Nov 1696 **William Elkins,** after which I have no record of him.
Prob. dead or gone by 1697-98. Work known – a watch is recorded.

ELLIS, David Aberdeen
Kept town clock 1560.

ELLIS, Jacob York
B. between 1609 and 1616, son of Brian Ellis, parchment maker, who
married in 1608. Free there 1636.

ELLIS, Henry (also Ells or Eyles or Egles) London
B.c. 1640, apr. Nov 1654 to Tobias Davis till 1661 but not freed.

ELLIS, James London
Apr. Jul 1658 to John Frowd, later transferred to Benjamin Bell. Freed
Oct 1667. Took as aprs.: Oct 1667 **William Beard;** Sep 1673 **Charles
Annott;** Jul 1674 **Aucher Gate.**

ELLIS, Paul London
Free Brother in CC Sep 1682. Alive in 1697, listed as dead in 1698, but

warned in 1701 to pay off his arrears of quarterage – perhaps evidence of the lengths to which the CC would go to get their dues.

ELLIS, Richard　　　　　　　　　　　　　　　　　**London**
Prob. an engraver. B.c. 1659, apr. Sep 1673 to George Deane, later transferred to James Wolverstone till 1680. Freed Jul 1683. Took as apr. Sep 1686 **Hugh Thomas**. Paid quarterage till c. 1687. Prob. dead by 1697/98. Work known – a bracket clock is recorded.

ELLIS, Thomas　　　　　　　　　　　　　　　　　**London**
B.c. 1658, apr. Aug 1672 to Thomas Taylor of Holborne till 1679. Freed May 1682 (after being threatened with prosecution by CC in Jan 1680/81 unless he took up his freedom). Took as apr. Apr 1687 **Amariah Cuthbert** – free Sep 1694. Prob. died before 1697/98.

ELLISON, Caleb　　　　　　　　　　　　　　　　　**London**
B.c. 1678, apr. Jan 1691 to Samuel Vernon till 1699, but not freed.

ELLORY, Walter　　　　　　　　　　　　　**Bodmin (Cornwall)**
Repaired town clock 1647.

ELLSON (see Elson)

ELMES, Joseph　　　　　　　　　　　　　　　　　**London**
B.c. 1659, apr. Jul 1673 thro' N. Coxeter to William Elmes, mat. inst. maker, till 1680, but not freed.

ELMES, William　　　　　　　　　　　　　　　　　**London**
Mat. inst. maker and a freeman of the Woodmongers' Co., admitted to CC as a free Brother Feb 1667/68. Took as aprs.: Jul 1668 **John Sambrook** (thro' T. Claxton); Oct 1669 **James Pullen** (thro' T. Claxton); Jul 1673 **Joseph Elmes** (thro' N. Coxeter); Jul 1682 **Thomas Cadgell**.

ELPHINGTON, W. M. (Wm?)　　　　　　　　　　　　**London**
Longcase clock recorded c. 1685. ?Not known to CC.

ELSON, David (also Ellson)　　　　　　　　　　　　**London**
Free Brother in CC May 1646. In Nov 1650 CC gave charity to his widow.

ELSTONE, George London
A springmaker (clock or watch) in Whitefriars in 1662.

ELTON, John London
B.c. 1654, apr. Jul 1668 (thro' N. Coxeter) to Jeremy Gregory till 1675.
Freed Sep 1675. In Mar 1692/93 bound an apr. for Charles Goode. Prob.
dead or gone by 1697/98.

ELTON, Thomas London
Freeman in CC by redemption Apr 1677 'being by trade an haberdasher
of small wares'. Took as aprs.: Sep 1687 **William Hall;** Mar 1696/97
Edward Horne – free Dec 1704; Apr 1700 **Alexander Le Roux** (son of
Theodore Le Roux of the Hague, late of London, merchant) – free Sep
1707; Sep 1702 **John Reason** (son of Alexander Reason, late of
Hammersmith, Middlesex, gent., deceased). Additionally he bound an
apr. in 1687 for Joseph Bates. In Apr 1693 being a freeman of the
Vintners' Co. and also of the CC by redemption (by means of his
father-in-law, Samuel Horne, *qv*, now deceased), he desired to be
acquitted of CC membership, but this was refused.

ELWOOD, John (also Ellwood) London
B.c. 1669, apr. Nov 1683 to John Saville junior till 1690. Freed Oct 1702
but paid no quarterage so prob. moved away.

ELWOOD, Martin London
Admitted to CC as a Free Brother, a Great Clockmaker, Jan 1687/88.
Paid quarterage till 1699. Work known – a longcase clock.

EMAN, John London
B.c. 1655, apr. Aug 1669 to Isaac Daniel (thro' S. Horne) till 1676.

EM(M)ERSON, Henry Newcastle-on-Tyne
Watchmaker, married at St. Nicholas in 1699.

EMERSON, Richard place not known
Lantern clock of c. 1690 recorded signed 'Richard Emerson fecit'. Place
of work unknown, but see Henry above?

ENEW, William London
B.c. 1673, apr. Jun 1687 to Thomas Wise till 1694 but not freed.

ENGLAND, John   **London**
B.c. 1678, apr. Feb 1692/93 to Thomas Taylor (thro' N. Russell) till
1699 but not freed.

ENGLOIS, George   **London**
B.c. 1635, apr. Oct 1648 to Edward Ward (thro' N. Payne) till 1656 but
not freed.

ENOU, Charles   **London**
B.c. 1655, apr. Jul 1667 to Jeremy East (thro' L. Wythe) till 1676 but not
freed.

ENTWISLE, Lawrence   **London**
B.c 1624, apr. Dec 1638 to Thomas Pace (thro' T. Dawson) till 1645 but
not freed.

ENWOOD, Samuel   **London**
B.c. 1648, apr. Aug 1662 to 'Mr.' Baxter (William?) till 1669 but not
freed.

ENYS, Edward senior (also Ennis and see Anis?)   **London**
B.c. 1637, apr. Jun 1650 to Thomas Lane (thro' N. Payne) till 1658.
Freed Jan 1658/59. Took as aprs.: Jul 1663 **Robert Doore,** later
transferred to R. Bowen; May 1673 **Elias Burgess;** Nov 1680 **Stephen
Bodham;** Sep 1683 **John Shaw;** Jan 1684/85 his son, **Edward Enys,**
freed by patrimony; Sep 1688 **William Napton** – free Mar 1695/96; Aug
1695 **Adam Compton** – free Oct 1716; Jul 1700 **Samuel Kisser** (son of
Stephen Kisser, late of Canterbury, woolcomber, deceased). In 1662
worked at 'ye Red Lyon, Fetter Lane'. Paid quarterage till 1705 at least.

ENYS, Edward junior   **London**
Son of Edward Enys senior. Freed in CC by patrimony Jan 1685/86. Paid
quarterage till 1705 at least.

ERBERY, Henry (also Erbury)   **London**
Apr. Jun 1642 (thro' O. Durant) to Thomas Howse, later transferred to
Robert Smith. Freed Jul 1650. Bound one apr. each for the following:
R. Smith, T. Platt, A. Blisse. In the 1656 rebellion against the CC he
supported both administrators and the rebels – after which he is not
heard of again.

ERLING, Jonathan   **Wigan (Lancashire)**
Clockmaker, fined in 1699 for working there when not a Freeman of the
town.

ESTE, William (East?)   **Oxford/Burford/Abingdon**
Master mason. At Abingdon 1505, Burford 1522, Oxford 1505-22. Died
1526. In 1505 with Louis Foose and Martin Williamson he agreed to
make a striking turret clock for Magdalen College for £10. Also in 1520
he made two sundials.

ESTER, Henry (also Esther – see Hester)

ESTON (see Eyston)

ETHERINGTON, George   **London**
Dec 1684 made a Free Brother in CC having been an apr. of Robert
Rooksby (who was not a CC member – there were clockmakers at York
called Rooksby and also Etherington?). Took as aprs.: Dec 1684 **John
Pepper** (thro' D. Stevens); Aug 1688 **William Hutchinson** (thro'
D. Stevens) – free Apr 1706; Sep 1691 **John Chamberlaine** (thro'
D. Stevens); Jul 1693 **Richard Voyce; John Manchester** (from
W. Haydon) – freed Apr 1700; Apr 1700 **Henry Curtis** (son of Robert
Curtis of Dublin, grocer); Aug 1701 **James Sheffield** (son of late
Christopher Sheffield of city of Durham, gent., deceased); Aug 1701
Joseph Rasher (from J. Edlin) – free Dec 1703; Dec 1708 **Anthony
Bannister** – free Jan 1715/16; Mar 1715-16 **Thomas Hayden,** and
perhaps others after 1720. An advertisement of 1689 records that 'George
Etherington, watchmaker, is removed from the Dial in Fleet Street over
against the New Church in the Strand, London, where all sorts of Jewel
Watches and others are made and sold'. Became CC Assistant 1701,
Warden 1706, Master 1709. Attended till at least 1720 and reputedly
died in 1729, when he was succ. by Thomas Hayden. Work known –
bracket and longcase clocks and watches, some signed 'George
Etherington, London', some simply 'Etherington, London'.

ETHERINGTON, Thomas I   **York**
A Quaker clock and watchmaker free there 1684. Chamberlain 1707/08.
Nominated Sheriff in 1718 and fined £70 for declining to take the office.
Died Apr 1728. Work known – a lantern clock signed 'Thomas
Etherington in Yorke'.

ETHERINGTON, Thomas II   **York**
Son of Thomas I. A Quaker watchmaker. Died (young?) 1693.

ETHERINGTON, Thomas III   **York**
Watchmaker and a Quaker, supposedly son of Thomas II. Freed 1740, died 1741.

EUSTACE, Richard (also Ewestasce)   **London**
B.c. 1673, apr. Jan 1687/88 to Withers Cheney till 1694 but not freed.

EVANS, David   London(?)
Sundial dated 1699. Place of work not known.

EVANS, George   **London**
B.c. 1678, apr. Jan 1692/93 to John Rant till 1699 but not freed.

EVANS, Henry   **London**
B.c. 1654, apr. Dec 1668 (thro' T. Bagley) to John Trippett, clockmaker of Kingston on Thames till 1675. Freed Jul 1682. Took as aprs.: Oct 1682 **Obediah Cluer** – free Jul 1709; Dec 1683 **Timothy Randell** (thro' F. Hill). Prob. dead or gone by 1697/98.

EVANS, Thomas   **London**
Apr. Jul 1648 to Samuel Davis. Free Sep 1673. Bound an apr. in 1687 for R. Browne. Paid quarterage till 1684. Prob. dead or gone by 1697/98.

EVEREST, Edward   **London**
B.c. 1660, apr. Aug 1674 to Henry Jones till 1681 but not freed. He died in 1680. His will, describing him as a watchmaker of St. Mary Matfellan parish, alias Whitechapel, mentions his mother, Audrey Curll. Apparently a young bachelor.

EVETT, Robert   **London**
Free Brother in CC Jan 1636/37. Prob. dead or gone by 1662/63.

EWER, John   **London**
B.c. 1673, apr. Jun 1687 to Luke Bird till 1694 but not freed. A watchmaker of this name lived at Plum Tree Street, Harlesden Green, parish of Willesden in 1721. Work known – longcase clocks and a watch.

EYRE, Richard   **London**
B.c. 1624, apr. Jul 1637 to Oswald Durant till 1645 but not freed. One of
this name still working in 1697, but if it was the same man he must have
been in his mid-70s.

EYSTON, Edward (also Eston)   **London**
Apr. Sep 1651 thro' J. North to Thomas Eyston. Free Jan 1659/60. Took
as aprs.: Jan 1663/64 **James Wightman**, later transferred to T. Fenn;
Dec 1674 **Bariah Pritchard; Samuel Marchant** (from R. Seigniour) –
free Mar 1677/78; Dec 1681 **John Fraser; Robert Thompson** (from
T. Fenn) – freed Feb 1681; Jun 1692 **Giles Bingley**; Mar 1697/98
Matthew Lampard. Paid quarterage till 1705 at least.

EYSTON, Thomas   **London**
Free Brother in CC Oct 1651, formerly apr. of William Partridge (not a
full freeman, as he was not apr. thro' CC?). Took as aprs.: Sep 1651
Edward Eyston (thro' J. North) – free Jan 1659/60; Feb 1653 **Thomas
Morrice** (thro' J. Matchett); Sep 1654 **William Cabot** as journeyman for
one year.

F

For makers' surnames sometimes spelt (or engraved) using the old double 'ff', see that name as listed under the single, capital 'F' (eg *Fox* – sometimes *ffox*).

FABER, Joseph   London
B.c. 1664, apr. Sep 1678 to Edward Whitfield till 1685 but not freed.

FAGE, Edward   London
Mat. inst. maker and freeman of another City Co. (which one not specified), made a Free Brother in CC Feb 1667/68. Took as aprs.: Jun 1669 **Richard Young** (thro' H. Wynne); Jul 1672 **John Warner** (thro' J. Curtis).

FAIRCLOUGH, Thomas (also Faircloth)   London
B.c. 1638, apr. Mar 1650/51 to Robert Smith (thro' H. Erbury) till 1659. Freed Mar 1660.

FAIRFAX, Thomas   Halifax
Repaired church clock 1694.

FAIRFAX, William   London
B.c. 1673, apr. Jan 1685/86 to John Warner till 1694 but not freed.

FALCONER (see Faulkner)

FAREWELL, John   London
B.c. 1672, apr. May 1686 to Isaac Nicholl, later transferred to Charles Gretton till 1693. Freed Sep 1697. Paid quarterage till at least 1705.

FARMBROUGH, Edward   **London**
Clockmaker, admitted into CC as a Free Brother Apr 1687. Paid no quarterage after that date. Prob. dead or gone by 1697-98.

FARMBOROUGH, Richard   **London**
B.c. 1671, apr. Jan 1685/86 to William Newton till 1692 but not freed.

FARMER, often written Ffarmer.

FARMER, Joseph   **London**
B.c. 1647, apr. May 1661 to Ralph Almond till 1668. Not freed (but paid quarterage in 1672?).

FARMER, John   **London**
Listed in Chancery Lane in 1662 – error for Thomas?

FARMER, Leonard   **London**
Supposedly repaired St. Margaret Westminster church clock in 1617, and a 'Mr.' Farmer worked on it in 1658.

FARMER, Richard   **London/Abingdon**
B.c. 1662, apr. May 1675 to Edward Norris, later transferred to Richard Browne till 1683. Freed Jul 1683. Took as apr. Nov 1684 **John Stanton** – freed Jan 1692/93. By Oct 1688 he had moved to Abingdon and then he took as aprs.: Oct 1688 **Henry Tey** from Deddington, Oxford; Dec 1695 **William Steptoe** – free Aug 1703; Feb 1703/04 **John Seymore** – free May 1711; Mar 1709/10 **John Sadler**; Mar 1716/17 **Stephen Durham**. Work known – lantern clocks, one signed 'Richard Farmer Londini fecit', one 'Richard Farmer Abingdon'. There is only one maker of this name, not two at the same time, as some authorities suggest.

FARMER, Thomas   **London**
In Apr 1640, Thomas, a maker of boxes for watches and keys, claimed he 'cannot subsist without the liberty of making both'. However the CC warned him he must not continue with box-making. In Nov 1646 he again promised to make no more watch work but only keys. In May 1653 he was admitted as a free Brother(?). It may be Thomas who is listed in error in 1662 as John.

FARMER, Thomas   **London**
B.c. 1668, apr. May 1682 to George Brackley later transferred to

Edmond Massey and then to Joseph Knibb till 1689. Freed Jul 1690. Paid quarterage till c. 1695. Work known – at least one longcase clock.

FARNHAM, John   **Winchester (Hampshire)**
Working 1428.

FARR, Robert   **Denbigh**
Made town clock in 1605.

FARRER, Abraham   **Pontefract (Yorkshire)**
Longcase clock known c. 1695. One clockmaker of this name had a son, Abraham, baptised there in 1728. One Abraham Farrer, clockmaker, died there 1753, but as several of this name worked there in succession, they are difficult to distinguish.

FARRER, Jonathan   **Halifax (Yorkshire)**
B. 1671 at Luddenden. Married 1695 Martha Acroyd. His son, Jonathan junior, was b.c. 1700. Record exists of his cleaning a watch in 1701 and 1702. Reputedly died in 1702. Work known – a longcase clock signed 'Jonathan Farrer fecit'.

FARRER, Samuel   **York**
Watchmaker, b. 1625, son of Roger Farrer, taylor. Free there 1648.

FAULKNER, Edward (also Falconer and Fulkener)   **London**
B.c. 1679, apr. May 1692 to Cornelius Herbert till 1700. Freed Sep 1702. Took as aprs.: May 1707 **William Shorter**; Sep 1711 **William Rigg**; perhaps others after 1720. Master in CC 1734. Work known – longcase clocks and watches.

FAULKINGHAM, ----   **London**
Cane-seller under the south-east corner of the Royal Exchange, who had faulty rulers confiscated by CC in 1671/72, supposedly made by John Nash. Paid search fees till 1674.

FAUX, John (also Fawkes)   **Warwick**
Clockmaker 1644-50. Made clock for St. Nicholas church and maintained it.

FAWCETT, William   **London**
B.c. 1626, apr. Apr 1638 to David Bouquett (thro' T. Dawson) till 1647 but not freed.

FEILDER, Thomas (signed Ffeilder but misspelt Fielder)   **London**
B.c 1664, apr. Sep 1678 to Withers Cheney till 1686. Free Sep 1687.
Took as aprs.: May 1693 **Edmund Baron;** Jun 1694 **Samuel Matthews;**
Apr 1698 **John Watts** – free Nov 1712; Mar 1700/01 **Edward Eston** (son
of John Eston, late of London, merchant, deceased) – free Apr 1708; Feb
1704/05 **Thomas Porter** (son of Thomas Porter, late of London, gent.
deceased); Jun 1707 **Thomas Bulkeley** – free Dec 1715; Jun 1710
Richard Gascoigne; Jan 1711-12 **Henry Hutchin;** Dec 1712 **Ambrose
Webb;** Mar 1719/20 **Mark Clarke;** perhaps others after 1720. Assistant
in CC 1708, Warden 1712, Master 1715. Attended till 1720, perhaps
longer.

FELLOWES, Thomas   **London**
B.c. 1665, apr. Nov 1679 to Richard Fennell till 1686 but not freed.

FELS, George   **London**
Watch recorded c. 1685. Not known to CC.

FENKMAN(?), William (writing unclear)   **London**
Freed in CC Sep 1661 having been apr. to Peter Closon.

FENN, John   **London**
Listed as working in Westminster in 1662 but this must be a slip for
Thomas Fenn, *qv.*

FENN, Robert (also Ffenn)   **London**
B.c. 1666, son of Thomas Fenn (not son of John, as sometimes stated).
Apr. to father Jun 1680 till 1687. Freed Dec 1687. Took as aprs.: Dec
1689 **Samuel Pitts;** Mar 1704/05 **Thomas Rewalling** (son of Thomas
Rewalling of parish of St. Giles Cripplegate, Middlesex, gold wire
drawer). Work known – one or two longcase clocks and a lantern clock
signed 'Robert Fenn, Westminster'.

FENN, Thomas   **London**
Apr. Aug 1647 to Thomas Claxton, transferred to William Bunting then
transferred in 1650 to John Cann, then again in 1652 to Gowen Langford.
Freed Jul 1657. Prob. worked in Westminster in 1662 'nr. the New
Exchange' (though listed in error as John Fenn). Took as aprs.: Jul 1660
Robert Wilkins; Apr 1666 **Robert Thompson** (transferred to Edward
Eyston); Nov 1668 **William Billinghurst; James Wightman** (from
E. Eyston) – freed Jan 1670/71; Mar 1679/80 **Isaac Whood;** Jun 1680 his

son, **Robert Fenn** – free Dec 1687; Jan 1682/83 **Joseph Gilbert**. Made CC Assistant 1673/74, but failed to attend meetings. Not heard of after 1682/83.

FENNELL, John   London
Recorded by some authorities but this is an error for Richard, *qv*.

FENNELL, Richard   London
B.c. 1656, apr. Sep 1669 to Matthew Crockford, later transferred to Thomas Bagley till 1677. Freed Nov 1679 after Bagley's death. Took as aprs.: Nov 1679 **Thomas Fellows**; Nov 1687 **John Browne**. Last heard of in Jan 1705/06 when he was much in arrears with his quarterage. Work known – several longcase and bracket clocks and a lantern clock signed 'Richard Fennell, Kensington'.

FENTON, John   London
Apr. Aug 1655 to Thomas Taylor – freed Jun 1662. Work known – at least one longcase clock.

FERMENT, John   London
Frenchman, a watchmaker, Free Brother in CC Sep 1679. Paid quarterage till c. 1683 but not later. Work known – a table clock and a watch. (There is a John Firman mentioned in the 1667 will of Simon Bartram, who leased a house from him in the parish of St. Anne Blackfriars, London; it is possible he is the same man).

FERMENT, Philipe (Baillie has Formant)   London
An engraver, made a Free Brother in CC Jul 1687. In Apr 1695 he admitted having an apr. who was illicitly bound to him and was fined. Paid quarterage till 1705.

FERRAR(S), John (also Ferrer(s) and Fferrar)   London
Clockmaker, freed in CC Aug 1693 by redemption by order of the Lord Mayor. Took as aprs.: Feb 1693/94 **Benjamin Wright** (thro' J. Wright); Aug 1694 **Joseph Robins**; Sep 1701 **John Simpson** (son of John Simpson of St. Margaret Westminster, co. Middlesex) – free Apr 1710; **Bartholomew Prestidge** – free Aug 1704; Dec 1705 **John Mason** (son of John Mason of Tottenham, Middlesex, gardiner) – free Jan 1712/13; Feb 1708/09 **William Goldsmith** (son of John Goldsmith of Barking, London, waterman) – free Jul 1719; Apr 1713 **Samuel Salter**; Mar 1715/16 **John Simpson**; maybe others later but I have no record of him

after 1715. Maybe connected with Vintners' Co. Work known – a longcase clock is recorded. See also Ferron.

FERRIS, Francis London
Servant of Thomas Tompion in 1695 and received on his behalf the sum of £60 for a gold repeating watch. No other trace of him but *cf* Francis Jervis.

FERRON, John London
Listed as CC 1692 by Baillie but prob. error for Ferrar, *qv*. Watch recorded.

FETTERS and **FITTERS** are prob. the same name.

FETTERS, Henry senior London
Supposedly free in Blacksmiths' Co. 1630. Never actually admitted into CC, but known to them. Worked in Westminster. Took as apr. Jun 1655 **William Robinson** (thro' L. Wythe) – free Oct 1667. Last heard of 1664.

FETTERS, Henry junior London
Free Brother in CC Nov 1654.

FETTERS, John (see Fitters)

FETTERS, Nicholas London
Free Brother in CC Oct 1632. Promised to bind his apr. **Thomas Taylor** thro' CC but did not. Taylor freed in CC Oct 1659. Worked in Westminster in 1662, after which not heard of again.

FETTERS, Richard London
Recorded as CC 1640 by Britten but this is prob. an error for Nicholas, *qv*.

FETTERS, William (see Fitter)

FIELD, James London
Citizen and waxchandler (ie member of the Waxchandlers' Co.). Never actually admitted into CC, but took as apr. thro' them Jul 1672 **John Calbeck** (thro' L. Wythe).

FIELD, Richard   **London**
Watch recorded c. 1690. Not known to CC.

FIELD, Samuel   **Hempstead**
Bracket clock recorded c. 1710.

FIELDER, Thomas (see Feilder)

FINCH, Daniel   **London**
B.c. 1653, apr. Apr 1667 to Nathaniel Barrow till 1674 but not freed.

FINCH, Jacob   **London**
B.c. 1672, apr. May 1686 to Isaac Carver, mat. inst. maker, (thro'
H. Wynne) till 1693, but not freed.

FINCH, John   **London**
B.c. 1654, apr. Oct 1668 to Nathaniel Barrow till 1675. Freed Jan
1675/76. Took as apr. Jul 1678 **Henry Parratt** – not freed. Made CC
Assistant from 1697, Warden 1705/06, Master 1707. Ceased to attend
early in 1710, when he prob. died. In Jun 1713 his widow, Mary, took as
apr. **Thomas Wilmshurst** – not freed. Work known – watches, at least
one longcase clock and a clock-watch.

FINCH, N.   **London**
Recorded by Baillie as apr. 1682, CC 1691 but this is an error for Robert
Finch.

FINCH, Robert   **London**
B.c. 1670, apr. Jul 1683 to James Markwick till 1691. Freed Jul 1691.
Took as apr. Nov 1711 **William Rapson**. Work known – at least one
watch.

FINCH, Simon   **London**
B.c. 1664, apr. Dec 1678 (thro' S. Davis senior) to Henry Kilminster, a
freeman of the Blacksmiths' Co., till 1685. Freed Dec 1706.

FINCH, Thomas   **London**
Clockmaker, made a Free Brother in CC Mar 1676/77. Worked in St.
Martins in Mar 1678/79 when he took as apr. **Joseph James** (thro'
S. Davis) – freed Jan 1689/90. Last heard of 1687. Said to be a possible

cousin of Tompion, on what authority not known. Work known – a watch and a longcase clock signed 'Thomas Finch London'.

FINCH, William   **London**
B.c. 1670, apr. Apr 1683 to Samuel Bowtell till 1691. Freed Jun 1691. Took as apr. Feb 1697/98 **John Love** – transferred Aug 1701 to Urian Berrington, perhaps because Finch had died, for he was not heard after 1701. Thought to have worked at Kingston. Work known – a watch and longcase clocks.

FINES (see Fynes)

FINLAW, Samuel   **Chester**
Son of Richard Finlaw, yeoman. Apr. 1640 to Thomas Wright of Chester, clockmaker.

FIRMAN (see Ferment)

FISHER, Charles   **London**
B.c. 1665, apr. Jul 1679 to Thomas Player till 1683 but not free.

FISHER, Ebenezer   **London**
B.c. 1673, apr. Apr 1687 to Solomon Bouquet (thro' N. Russell) till 1694 but not freed.

FITTER, F. R.   **London**
Mid-17th century watch recorded, maybe a mistake for John, *qv*.

FITTER, John (sometimes Fetter(s))   **London**
A watchmaker, initially at Battersea, and brother-in-law of Thomas Taylor of Holborn in whose will he is mentioned in 1690. Initially was not a member of CC but nevertheless took as aprs. thro' CC: Sep 1671 **Richard Browne** (thro' L. Wythe); Dec 1675 **Barnaby Whaley** (thro' Thomas Taylor of Holborn); Jul 1677 **John Wych** (thro' T. Taylor). Then in Aug 1685 was made a Free Brother in CC, at which time he was working at Fulham. Took as further aprs.: Aug 1685 **Lancaster Highmoor** (thro' D. Stevens); May 1687 **Henry Bullimore** (thro' E. Micklewright). Paid quarterage till c. 1691; dead by 1698. In Aug 1699 his son, Thomas Fitter, was apr. to Jasper Taylor. Work known – watches, signed 'John Fitter, Battersea'.

FITTER, William (sometimes Fetter(s))   **London**
Working 1697. Joined CC but for unexplained reasons his entry fee was returned to him Sep 1699.

FITTON, Charles   **London**
B.c. 1653, apr. Oct 1667 to Samuel Horne till 1674. Freed Oct 1674.

FITTON, Daniel   **London**
B.c. 1661, apr. Dec 1675 to John Bartholomew (thro' R. Smith) till 1682 but not freed.

FITTON, Thomas   **London**
B.c. 1624, apr. Apr 1638 to Thomas Land (thro' T. Dawson) till 1645, but not freed.

FITZGERALD, Edward   **Dublin**
Apr. 1693 to Walter Bingham. Working 1700 as watchmaker.

FITZJAMES, Thomas   **London**
B.c. 1635, apr. Apr 1648 to John Walters till 1656, but not freed.

FITZWALTER, John   **Beaulieu (Hampshire)**
Kept clock 1538-42.

FITZWALTER, Robert   **Exeter (Devon)**
Repaired organ clock at Exeter Cathedral in 1317.

FLETCHER, Bazil   **London**
B.c. 1678, apr. Sep 1692 to Thomas Wise till 1699 but not freed.

FLETCHER, Daniel   **London**
B.c. 1619, apr. Aug 1632 to Thomas Reeve till 1640. Free as a Brother Sep 1646. Took as aprs.: Jan 1646 **Thomas Daniell** (thro' T. Alcock) – free Dec 1656; Feb 1651 **Richard Viel** (thro' S. Davis). He died before 1653. His widow, Elizabeth, took as aprs.: Jul 1653 **Anthony Freeman** (thro' R. Beck) and also in 1653 **Richard Roberts**. By Jul 1664 she had re-married to a Mr. Smith and took her son, **Daniel Fletcher**, as apr. (thro' W. Godbed).

FLETCHER, Daniel London
B.c. 1651, son of Daniel Fletcher senior, apr. Jul 1664 to his widowed mother, now Elizabeth Smith, till 1672 but not freed.

FLETCHER, Edward London
A goldsmith. Apr. Jun 1679 to Thomas Fletcher (thro' S. Davis). Free Nov 1697. Took as aprs.: Aug 1698 **Thomas Fletcher,** Sep 1700 **William Boulton** (son of John Boulton of Roby, Lancashire, gent.); Sep 1705 **Thomas Goore** (son of Henry Goore late of Highton (Huyton?), Lancashire, husbandman) – free Aug 1716; Jan 1707/08 **Robert Owen.**

FLETCHER, John Chester
Watchmaker. His son, John, died 1659 and daughter, Mary, died 1660.

FLETCHER, John London
B.c. 1641, apr. Aug 1654 to Robert Robinson, transferred to John Savill, then again to Hugh Cooper but not freed. His will, dated 1659, proved 1661, names him as a watchmaker and leaves property to his sister Alice and brother Richard. Prob. a bachelor.

FLETCHER, Thomas London
Clockmaker and freeman of the Grocers' Co. Free Brother in CC Mar 1676/77. Took as aprs.: Jun 1679 **Edward Fletcher** (thro' S. Davis) – free Nov 1697; (May 1682?) **Wright Lamb;** Jun 1684 **John Parker;** Aug 1686 **Richard Wallitt** (thro' E. Norris) – free Aug 1693. In 1682 he worked in St. Martins. Bound aprs. for other masters (R. Baker, J. Hicks, and J. Howse of Croydon). Not heard of after c. 1693 and prob. died about then. Believed related to Robert Fletcher of Huyton who died 1743, *qv* and prob. also to Edward Fletcher above.

FLETCHER, Widow London
Widow of Daniel, *qv.*

FLEUREAU, Isaye (sometimes Esaye) London
Came from Orleans to work in Long Acre nr. St. Martin in the Fields. Married London 1694. Had son, Jacques, b. 1703. Apparently not known to CC. Work known – longcase clocks and watches.

FLEXNEY, Henry London
B.c. 1645, apr. May 1657 to Gowen Langford till 1663 but not freed.

FLINT, John   **Mansfield (Nottinghamshire)**
Lantern clock believed c. 1660 signed 'John Flint Mansfield'.

FLOOD, Humphrey (see Lloyd)

FLOYD, William (see Lloyd)

FLORIO, John   **Croydon(?)**
Workman of John House of Croydon in Nov 1687. Promised to join CC
at next court meeting, but he did not.

FLOWER, George   **London**
B.c. 1656, apr. Jul 1670 to James Atkinson (thro' L. Wythe), mat. inst.
maker, till 1677. Freed Jul 1682. Paid quarterage till c. 1695 but not
heard of after 1697. Work known – watches.

FLUE (see Flood)

FOLE, Robert (see Jole, for which this is prob. an error)

FOLLETT, Richard   **London**
B.c. 1639, apr. May 1653 to Thomas Wolverston till 1660 but not freed.

FONNEREAU, James   **London/St.Gluvias (Cornwall)**
A Frenchman (prob. one of the La Rochelle family) who was permitted
in 1653 by CC to work as journeyman to Mr. Bouquet whilst in England.
One of this name was a watchmaker in Truro Lane, St. Gluvias,
Cornwall, in 1676 – prob. same man.

FORCHIER, John   **London**
Recorded as 1694 by some authorities but I cannot confirm this.

FORD, Henry   **London**
B.c. 1633, apr. Jul 1647 to Nicholas Tomlins, transferred (maybe on
Tomlin's death?) to David Parry till 1654, but not freed.

FORD, James (Jacobus)   **Bedford**
Lantern clock supposedly c. 1690 signed 'Jacobus Ford de Bedford
fecit'.

FORD, John **Oxford** and **Aylesbury**

B.c. 1669, son of William Ford, cleric of Heyford, Oxon. Apr. to John Knibb of Oxford Apr 1682 till 1690. Freed at Oxford Jul 1691. Resident there till 1708 but by 1712 had moved to Aylesbury where a daughter was born. Insolvent there 1725. Work known – longcase clocks signed 'John Ford Bucks'.

FORD, Robert **London**

B.c. 1638, apr. Jan 1652/53 to Richard Record till 1659 but not freed.

FORD, Thomas **Buckingham**

Lantern clock c. 1680 signed 'Thomas Ford de Bucks fecit'. Another c.1705.

FORD, William **London**

B.c. 1678, apr. Jul 1692 to George Segner till 1699. Free Jan 1700/01. Took as apr. Dec 1701 **Edward Polling** (son of John Polling late of the parish of St. Mary Magdalen Milk Street, London, scrivener). Not heard of after 1701.

FORDHAM, John **Dunmow (Essex)**

Lantern clock recorded c. 1680.

FORDHAM, Joseph **Bocking (Essex)**

Said to be working there in 1700.

FORDHAM, Thomas **London**

Clockmaker, made a Free Brother in CC Aug 1687. Paid quarterage till at least 1705. Work known – a longcase clock and a watch signed 'Thomas Fordham, London'.

FOR(E)MAN, Francis **London**

Working from c. 1620. A 1622 petitioner for incorporation of CC. Believed worked at St. Paul's Gate. One of first CC Assistants in 1632, Warden 1634, after which he seems to have stopped attending meetings. Supposedly died 1649. Work known – lantern clocks, one signed 'Francis Forman at Paules' and one 'Francis Forman St. Paul's Gate'.

'FORGAT', ---- **London**

A classic howler! The *London Gazette* in 1680 records a lost watch, 'the name Forgat' (meaning forgotten), a name since recorded as Forgat the watchmaker!

FORMANT (see Ferment)

FORMBY, Richard   **Chester**
Serviced church clock 1652-59.

FORREST, Joseph   **London**
B.c. 1667, apr. Sep 1681 to Samuel Stevens till 1688. Freed Jan 1692-93
(signed with a mark as he could not write his own name). Paid no
quarterage after c. 1693. Prob. dead or gone by 1697/98.

FORREST, Matthew   **London**
B.c. 1658, apr. May 1672 to John Lowe, clockmaker, thro' L. Wythe till
1679, but not freed.

FORREST, Nathaniel   **London**
Recorded as apr. 1672 – error for Matthew, *qv*.

FORRETTE, John   **London**
Baillie has 1694, which I cannot confirm. Prob. a misreading of Forte,
qv.

FORSTER (see also Foster)

FORSTER, Clement   **London**
B.c. 1656, apr. Aug 1670 to Henry Wynne till 1677. Freed Jul 1682.
Took as aprs.: Jan 1682/83 **Robert Knott**; Dec 1686 **Job Netherwood**;
Jun 1689 **Edward Shaw**. Paid quarterage till 1689 but dead by 1697/98.

FORT(E), John   **London**
Apr. Dec 1660 to Richard Bowen, transferred to Evan Jones. Freed Nov
1672. Took as apr. Nov 1681 **John Higges,** later transferred to Luke
Bird – freed Nov 1688. Excused quarterage arrears in Sep 1699 and paid
them until late 1701, after which he is not heard of again. Work known –
a watch.

FORTUNA, Lawrence (see Foulston?)   **London**
B. in Normandy. Servant to Peter Dellamare. Working c.1560 – 71.

FOSTER (sometimes spelt Forster)

FOSTER, Jabez   **London**
Watch recorded c. 1660.

FOSTER, Jacob   **London**
B.c. 1676, apr. Jan 1690/91 to John Foster till 1698 but not freed.

FOSTER, James   **Leeds (Yorkshire)**
Watchmaker, b.c. 1642, married 1664 to Elizabeth Morris, both then
being 22 years old. Worked at Kirgait End. Wife and son William died in
1669. He died there in 1682.

FOSTER, John   **London**
B.c. 1666, apr. Aug 1680 to Daniel Quare (thro' S. Davis senior) till
1687. Freed Jan 1689/90, but refused to take the oath (prob. a Quaker).
Took as aprs.: Jan 1690-91 **Jacob Foster**; Oct 1694 **Edward Jagger** – free
Apr 1702. Not heard of after 1703.

FOSTER, John   **London**
One such listed by Baillie as apr. 1684 is an error for Joseph, *qv*.

FOSTER, John   **London**
B.c. 1680, apr. May 1693 to Nathaniel Smith till 1701. Freed Apr 1726.

FOSTER, Joseph   **London**
Apr. Sep 1684 to Francis Stamper (thro' S. Davis) – freed Feb 1691-92.
Took as aprs.: Dec 1694 **Greenaway Curtice**; Mar 1699-1700 **Benjamin
Hart** (son of late Benjamin Hart of St. Mary Magdalen Bermondsey,
cheesemonger); Mar 1703-04 **James Wyke** (son of Andrew Wyke,
Citizen and Loriner of London). Last heard of in 1704. Work known –
longcase clocks and watches signed 'Joseph Foster, Exchange Alley'.

FOSTER, William   **London**
Free in CC Jul 1660.

FOSTER, William   **London**
B.c. 1658, apr. Sep 1672 to Sutton Isaac, later transferred to Lawrence
Sindry. Made a Free Brother Aug 1681, but refused to take the oath
(maybe a Quaker?). Took as apr. Jun 1683 **John Gallaway**. Paid
quarterage till c. 1685, but not heard of thereafter.

FOTHERGAILE, James London
B.c. 1645, apr. Sep 1659 to Ralph Almond till 1666 but not freed.

FOULK, Humphrey London
B.c. 1632, apr. Jan 1646 to John Willow (thro' L. Wythe) till 1653 but
not freed.

FOULKS, ---- Salisbury
At the Three Lions – believed watchmaker and goldsmith. Advertised
for lost watch in *London Gazette* in 1701. See also next entry?

FOULKES, David London
B.c. 1657, apr. Jul 1671 to Peter Southworth till 1678 but not freed.
Summoned to CC court for infringements in 1680 and 1681.

FOULSTON, Lawrence London
Frenchman working 1568 according to Baillie (but see also Fortuna?).

FOWLE, Edward (also Fowell) London
B.c. 1644, son of Stephen Fowle, late of Whitechapel, Middlesex,
weaver. He was apr. thro' Merchant Taylors' Co. in Apr 1657 to Jacob
(or James) Smythurst of the Shambles till 1665. Freed Feb 1665.
Worked as a clockmaker in Whitechapel. Took as apr. in Merchant
Taylors' Co. Jun 1667 **John Longland** (son of William Longland of
Fulbeck, Lincolnshire, farmer) – free Jul 1674. Made a Free Brother in
CC Apr 1670. Took as apr. thro' CC Sep 1674 **Ezekiel Andrews** (thro' R.
Nicholls) – not freed. A 'Mr.' Fowles was a goldsmith at the Black Lyon
in Fleet Street in 1685, which may be him. Not heard of after 1674. May
perhaps have gone to East Indies with Andrews, *qv*.

FOWLER, D. London
Lantern clock recorded c. 1690. (Maybe error for Robert Fowler, *qv?*).

FOWLER, Robert London
Never actually admitted into CC but was recognised by them and in Oct
1654 bound as apr. **Joseph Atkins** (thro' J. Bayley). Prob. dead or gone
by 1662/63.

FOWLER, William Oxford
B.c. 1654, son of William Fowler, mason, of Oxford. Apr. Jun 1667 to
Richard Quelch, watchmaker, till 1675 but not freed.

FOWLES and PARTNER London
Goldsmiths in Fleet Street nr. Temple Bar in 1694, when advertised in
London Gazette for return of lost watch. May have been watch retailers.

FOX, ---- Thetford (Norfolk)
Repaired TC at the Cluniac Priory in 1530.

FOX, Charles London
Apr. Sep 1655 to John Pennock, later transferred to Robert Cosby.
Freed Oct 1662. Took as Apr. Jul 1663 **Samuel Southwood** (thro'
Tobias Davis). Work known – bracket clocks and lantern clocks, one
signed 'Charles Fox at the Fox, Lothbury, Londini, fecit'.

FOX, Mordecai (also ffox) London
A 'Great Clockmaker' who promised in Nov 1687 to join CC at next
court. Made a free Brother in CC Jan 1687/88. Took as apr. Jan 1687/88
William Grice. Paid quarterage till late 1699, when believed to have
died.

FRANK(E), Alexander Tiverton (Devon)
Worked on Halberton church clock 1619-36.

FRANK, Andrew Peebles (Scotland)
Kept town clock 1570.

FRANK, James Peebles (Scotland)
Kept church clock 1556 but dismissed.

FRANKLIN, Joseph London
B.c. 1666, apr. May 1679 to Henry Harper till 1687 but not freed. Work
known – one or two longcase clocks.

FRANKLIN, Thomas London
B.c. 1678, apr. May 1692 to Benjamin Merryman till 1699 but not freed.

FRASER, John (usually Frasor) London/Worcester
B.c. 1667, apr. Dec 1681 to Edward Eyston till 1688, but not freed.
Believed worked later at Worcester. Work known – at least one longcase
clock is recorded signed 'John Frasor', no town stated.

FRASER, Nicholas   **Haddington (nr. Edinburgh)**
Working 1636 according to Baillie.

FREARSON, John   **London**
Apr. Oct 1680 to Nathaniel Barrow. Freed Aug 1689. Paid quarterage till
c. 1691 but not later. Prob. dead or gone by 1697/98.

FREEBODY, John   **London**
B.c. 1657, apr. Dec 1671 to John Sweby till 1678 but not freed.

FREEMAN, Anthony   **London**
B.c. 1639, apr. Jul 1653 to Richard Beck, transferred to widow Fletcher.

FREEMAN, Edward   **London**
Baillie has 1697 but I cannot trace him.

FREEMAN, John   **London**
Free in CC (by redemption?) Jun 1646. Took as aprs.: Nov 1647 **Robert
Coster** – free Jan 1655/56; Oct 1648 **Hugh Dubbar** – not freed; Feb 1650
Bartholomew Powell – freed Oct 1668; Dec 1651 **Isaac Puzy** – free Jan
1658; Sep 1656 **Christopher Baldwin**. Made Assistant 1654. Died in
1678 or 1679. In Dec 1679 'being lately deceased' it was thought he had
left a will with a bequest to CC and investigation showed this to be so.
The legacy of £10 was paid over in Apr 1680.

FREEMAN, John   **London**
Evidently a second of this name was b.c. 1636, apr. Aug 1649 thro' James
Seaburne to Robert Whitwell, but not freed.

FREEMAN, Stafford   **London**
Apr. Dec 1656 to William North. Freed Jan 1663/64. Took as aprs.: Apr
1665 **Edward Brewer**; Jul 1679 **Nicholas Lancaster**. Excused
stewardship in 1678. Paid no quarterage after c. 1680. Dead by 1697/98.

FREEMAN, Thomas   **London**
B.c. 1673, apr. Sep 1686 to Cornelius Herbert till 1694. Freed Jul 1698.
(Prob. transferred to Thomas Meades May 1688). Not heard of after
1698.

FREKE, Daniel   **Bridport (Dorset)**
Longcase clock recorded c. 1705.

FRENCHAM, James — London
B.c. 1677, apr. Sep 1691 to John Wynne till 1698. Freed Sep 1698. Took as aprs.: Mar 1699/1700 **Thomas Williams** (son of Walter Williams late Citizen and Joyner of London, deceased); Sep 1701 **Thomas Dartnall** (son of Thomas Dartnall of Sutton, Kent, taylor) – freed Apr 1713; Jul 1703 **Thomas Howkins** – free Apr 1711; Jan 1707-08 **George Grove** – free Aug 1716; Sep 1710 **John Conny.**

FRE(E)THY, John — London
B.c. 1658, apr. Mar 1672 to Charles Rogers – not freed.

FREWEN, ---- — London
'Next the sign of the Naked Boy in Cheapside', a cane-seller. Had two sundials confiscated by CC 1671/72, supposedly made by widow Cater in Moorfields.

FROMANTEEL
The Fromanteel family were the most important, and until recently the least well-documented, family in the history of British horology. Their history is very long and involved. The following are brief details only. Much longer accounts of them, written by myself, may be found in: *Antiquarian Horology*, Mar 1975; *Country Clocks and their London Origins; Complete British Clocks; Clocks Magazine* (May, Jun, Jul 1980). See also R. A. Lee – *The First Twelve Years of the English Pendulum Clock.*

FROMANTEEL, Abraham — London/Newcastle-on-Tyne
B.c. 1646, son of Ahasuerus Fromanteel the elder. Apr. to father in CC Aug 1662 till 1669, but not freed (prob. because he went abroad with father). In Sep 1680 was freed when he came back to London, prob. to work in the family business. In Jul 1694 when called to be CC Steward he refused, as he was 'forthwith going to Holland', returning, he alleged, 'about Michaelmas 1697'. He was in London till about 1711, but prob. spent a lot of time in Newcastle-on-Tyne where he ultimately went to live. He died there in the winter of 1730, aged 84. Work known – one or two clocks signed 'A. Fromanteel, Newcastle' or even 'New Casteel', but prob. worked mostly under the general family trade name of 'Fromanteel, London'.

FROMANTEEL, Ahasuerus the elder — London/Amsterdam
B. 1607 at Norwich, prob. apr. there to Jacques van Barton. Came to London in 1631 where he joined the Blacksmiths' Co., then in 1632 CC

as a Brother, not becoming a full Freeman of the CC (and the City) till Jan 1655/56. This may well mean that his earlier life was spent working as a journeyman, and it is doubtful whether any work is known to survive bearing his name before 1655/56. One collaboration clock he made with East may suggest that he worked for him at this time. He is famous (*inter alia*) for having introduced the pendulum to England in 1658, but his work also shows other strong signs of original thinking and experimentation. He was constantly at odds with the CC who appear to have resented his talent. Took as aprs.: Dec 1637 **Jacob Hulst** thro' T. Dawson; Aug 1646 **Robert Collins** thro' J. Quash; Dec 1646 **John Mountage**; May 1651 **Stephen Smith** thro' J. Quash; Apr 1652 his son, **John Fromanteel**; Apr 1654 **Judah Cann** thro' W. Bunting but later passed over to A. Blisse; Jun 1660 **James Turgis**; Aug 1662 his son, **Abraham Fromanteel**; Sep 1663 his son, **Daniel Fromanteel**; Jun 1664 his stepson, **Joshua Winnock**. By 1668 he had set up a branch of his business in Amsterdam where he traded increasingly, though he died in England in 1693. Work known – his clocks and watches were sometimes signed with his full name, but later just his surname and town, which might be London or Amsterdam (see R. A. Lee in the bibliography).

FROMANTEEL, Ahasuerus the younger   **London/Amsterdam**
B. 1640, son of Ahasuerus the elder. Apr. to Simon Bartram, freed Jul 1663. Took as aprs.: Jan 1663/64 **Philip Gregson**; May 1668 **George Johnson**; **Jeremy Johnson** (from A. Beckner) – freed Dec 1668; Aug 1675 **Isaac Day** (thro' B. Rookes) but Day was re-bound thro' Weavers' Co. in Sep 1676 to Benjamin Graves). Prob. took over the business in Holland about 1675/76 for a short while. In Dec 1677 he took apr. **William Neighbar** (for B. Graves). Ultimately he lived in Amsterdam where he died in 1703. In his later years he was prob. in partnership with Christopher Clarke, *qv*, his son in law – see Fromanteel and Clarke. Work – part of the Fromanteel empire and not individually recognisable.

FROMANTEEL, Ahasuerus III   **London**
B. 1666, son of John Fromanteel, to whom he was apr. Jan 1679/80, but not freed. Still alive in 1698 but it is not known what became of him. No work is recognised as being by him.

FROMANTEEL and CLARKE   **Amsterdam**
A partnership between Christopher Clarke (an expatriate English clockmaker in Amsterdam, who married the daughter of Ahasuerus Fromanteel the younger) and *either* Ahasuerus the younger pre-1703 *or*

Abraham Fromanteel post-1703, or both. Work known – clocks and watches in the Dutch style signed 'Fromanteel & Clarke', usually without place name but sometimes incl. Amsterdam.

FROMANTEEL, Daniel   London

B.c. 1651, son of Ahasuerus Fromanteel the elder, to whom he was apr. Sep 1663 but not freed. Nothing further known about him but a wall clock came to light recently signed 'Daniel Fromanteel, London', which suggests he may well have survived.

FROMANTEEL, John   London

B. 1638, son of Ahasuerus the elder, to whom he was apr. Apr 1652, but prob. transferred to his brother-in-law, Thomas Loomes, and freed Jul 1663. Part of his apprenticeship was spent in the Hague with Salomon *(sic)* Coster working on the new pendulum clocks. Took as aprs.: Jul 1663 **Thomas Paul** – free Jan 1670/71; Apr 1670 **Thomas Cruttenden** – free Nov 1677; Dec 1673 **William Coward** – free Jul 1681; Jan 1679/80 his son, **Ahasuerus Fromanteel (III)**. Last heard of in 1682. Work known – a few clocks are recorded signed 'Johannes Fromanteel, Londini', but prob. mostly worked under the general Fromanteel company name.

FROMANTEEL, Samuel   London/Norwich

Apr. Jul 1653 in Blacksmiths' Co. to Andrew Prime (brother-in-law of Ahasuerus the elder). Not certain who Samuel was, but may have been a further son of Ahasuerus the elder. A clockmaker of this name at Norwich took as apr. May 1693 **Jonas Springfield**. (The Fromanteel and Prime clockmakers come from Norwich and care must be taken not to confuse this man with another Samuel Fromanteel, a turner – also from Norwich – and the brother of Ahasuerus the elder.)

FROWD(E), John (also Froude)   London

B.c. 1632, apr. Jan 1646 to Henry Wansey (thro' J. Waters) till 1653. Freed Oct 1654. Took as aprs.: Jul 1658 **James Ellis,** transferred to B. Bell and freed Oct 1667; Jun 1671 **Thomas Woodward; Thomas Player** (transferred from T. Weeks) – freed Sep 1672; Jul 1673 **Benjamin Stevens.** Became CC Assistant 1673 but did not attend after 1674.

FULLER, William   London

Bound apr. to Robert Silke, gunmaker, then transferred to Nathaniel Dike, then to John White. Freed Sep 1675. Took as apr. Sep 1677

Richard Hawkins; Sep 1683 **Samuel Carter;** Sep 1688 **Joshua Wilson;** Jul 1699 **James Mesniel** (son of James Mesniel senior of Tottenham, clockmaker). Also bound an apr. for Thomas Birch. Paid no quarterage after c. 1692 and received CC charity from 1711 to 1713, when prob. died.

FULLUM, George **London**
B.c. 1636, apr. Aug 1649 to William Clay thro' L. Wythe till 1657 – not freed.

FULWELL, Henry **London**
B.c. 1636, apr. Sep 1649 to John Bayes, transferred to Henry Child till 1657 but not freed.

FYNES, James (also Fines) **London**
B.c. 1674, apr. Sep 1688 to Henry Merryman (thro' R. Dent) till 1695 but not freed.

FYNES, John (details as above, but his name seems to have been James, not John).

G

GADLINGSTOCK, Samuel   **London**
Worked in Exchange Alley, prob. as a cane-seller. Had a faulty jointed
yard rule confiscated in 1671/72. There were two of this name – Samuel
senior of the Merchant Taylors' Co. was freed in 1637. His son, Samuel
junior, was made a freeman of the City of London by patrimony in 1668,
and it is prob. he who was the cane-seller.

GALLETT, Isaac (also Gallott)   **London**
B.c. 1641, apr. Jan 1655/56 to David Bouquet, transferred to Thomas
Weeks till 1662 but not freed.

GALLOWAY, John (also Gallaway)   **London**
B.c. 1669, apr. Jun 1683 to William Foster till 1690 but not freed. CC
records state 'son of Andrew Gallaway', but this has been crossed through(?).

GAMBEL, Thomas   **Walton by Kimcote (Leicestershire)**
Crude lantern clock survives dated 1704. Believed to have been the
village blacksmith. Could, perhaps, be the man below?

GAMBLE, Thomas   **London**
B.c. 1637, apr. May 1651 thro' N. Tomlins to John Nicasius till 1658.
Freed Apr 1657 'being released by the Plumbers' Co., of which his father
was a freeman'. Work known – none but see previous entry.

GAMMON, John   **London**
Lantern clock recorded signed 'John Gammon Londini fecit' said to be c.
1670 and a watch of c. 1680. No such person known to CC.

GANN(?), Daniel (name unclear)   **London**
Paid CC quarterage 1673.

GANY, Thomas   **London**
Recorded as CC 1699 by Britten but I cannot trace him.

GARANDER, Glande (also Garandeau)   **London**
Alien in Blackfriars in 1622. One Garandeau was clockmaker to the
Queen in Paris 1579-1600.

GARB(R)OUND, John (also Garbrand)   **London**
B.c. 1640, son of John Garbround, Citizen and Dyer. Apr. Nov 1654 to
Thomas Loomes till 1661 but not freed.

GARDNER – and all other variants.

GARDENER, Ambrose   **London**
Not a member of CC but in 1695 he was in the Tompion household with
wife Alice and son, Obadiah. In 1698 he took over apr. John Long from
John Sweby and then transferred him to George Wilson (and Long was
freed Jul 1698). In Dec 1700 one (Ambrose?) Gardner, goldsmith, of St.
Dunstan in the West, had son, Obadiah, bound to George Graham.
(Graham had joined the Tompion household in 1696).

GARD(E)NER, John   **London**
B.c. 1661, apr. May 1675 to John Wise till 1682. Freed Jul 1682. Paid no
quarterage after c. 1683. Work known – see John Garner and T. Garne.

GARDINER, John   **Croydon**
Watchmaker, prob. workman of John House of Croydon. In Nov 1687
promised to become a Brother in CC at next court and did so Jan 1687/88.
Paid quarterage till c. 1692.

GARDNER, Margaret   **London**
In Jun 1692 her apr., Elizabeth Boddily, bound thro' W. Cheney was
freed. Maybe widow of John?

GARDNER, Thomas   **London**
Watchmaker and member of the Blacksmiths' Co. Made a Free Brother
in CC May 1689/90. Took as apr. Jul 1693 **John Collins** – free Sep 1701.
Not heard of after 1704. Work known – longcase clock signed 'Thomas
Gardner London'.

GARFIELD, James London
Recorded as watchmaker by Baillie in 1698 – source unknown.

GARFOOT, William London
B.c. 1659, apr. Apr 1673 to John Cotsworth till 1680. Freed May 1680.
Took as apr. Jul 1687 **Aron Derby**. Paid quarterage till 1700. Work
known – watch, longcase clock and lantern clock, signed 'William
Garfott, Middle Temple'.

GARGRAVE, John London
In Sep 1656 he was accused of having taken an apr. from John Palfrey
when not entitled to, not being a free clockmaker. In same year he was
accused of not having paid his quarterage – so perhaps was a measure-
seller.

GARLE, Richard London
B.c. 1668, apr. Sep 1682 to Joseph Windmills (thro' E. Wilson) till 1689
but not freed.

GARNE, T. London
Bracket clock recorded c. 1680 (see John Gardner?).

GARNER, John London
Bracket clock recorded c. 1690 (see John Gardner?).

GARNET(T), Jeremy London
Error for Jeremy Gazuet, *qv*.

GARNETT, John Anthony London
B.c. 1658, apr. Mar 1672 to Charles Gretton till 1679, but not freed.
Believed went to France (prob. called Jean Anthoine).

GARNETT, William London
Watch recorded c. 1700 and bracket clock c. 1680. Not known to CC.
Prob. William Gurnett who was apr. in 1698.

GAR(R)ON, Peter London
B.c. 1673, apr. Apr 1687 to Richard Baker till 1694. In Jul 1694 'being an
alien and bound to R. Baker' and having been refused freedom by the
CC, he was granted freedom of the City by the Lord Mayor. He was then
made a Freeman of the CC in Aug 1694. In Oct 1696 he admitted

forging the name of Mr. Legrand on a watch of his own making. In 1697 he was warned about taking unofficial aprs. Took as aprs.: Jul 1697 **Joshua Parrs;** Nov 1699 **William Hall;** Apr 1705 **Henry Mesteyer** (son of Henry Mesteyer of Thorpe, Essex, clerk) – free Jun 1713; Feb 1709/10 **James Carington** – free May 1717; Dec 1713, his son, **Peter Garon;** Jul 1720 **John Burton** (from C. Lee). I have no data after 1720 but he supposedly became insolvent in 1723. Said to have worked at St. Bartholomew's Lane End and later at St. Giles Cripplegate. Work known – numerous watches, also bracket clocks and longcase clocks, some signed 'Garon, London', but usually 'Peter Garon London', or 'Peter Garon Londini'.

GARRETT, ----   Metfield(?) (Suffolk)
In 1628 was paid £5 for a new clock for Metfield church. In 1657 he repaired it. Prob. not a local man, as carriage was involved in supplying it. Could be Richard Garrett, *qv.*

GARRETT, Charles   London
B.c. 1669, apr. Nov 1683 to Abel Gould till 1690. Freed 1690/91. Took as aprs.: Sep 1695 **Daniel Dunster;** Sep 1714 **Jacob Hardman;** Oct 1720 his son, **Charles Garrett,** was admitted a freeman by patrimony. Not heard of after 1714.

GARRETT, Ferdinando   London
One of the first British clockmakers, said to be working by c. 1600 but unlikely to have worked before 1616. Freed in Grocers' Co. by redemption Nov 1618, then made free of the City of London. In 1622 had aliens **James Dudwitt** and **Isaac Perone** working for him 'in St. Martyns'. Was a 1622 petitioner for incorporation of CC but never actually joined CC and prob. died before 1632. Work known – two or three watches.

GARRETT, Richard   London
In Dec 1658 was told by CC to bring in proof of his training, which he never did. This suggests he was from the provinces and he may have been the Garrett of Metfield mentioned earlier.

GARSINE, John   London
In Dec 1657 he was working as journeyman to William Pettit without CC approval and was to be dismissed. Prob. French.

GARTON, Thomas   **London**
B.c. 1654, apr. Oct 1668 thro' L. Wythe to John Mann, a bodice-maker in the Strand, till 1675 – not freed.

GASCOIGNE, John (Johas Gaskoynes)   **Norwich**
Watchmaker, freed 8 Jun 1632. Believed Huguenot immigrant.

GASCOIGNE, Owen   **Newark**
B. 1647, son of William Gascoigne, *qv*. Died 1719. Succ. by son, William, till c. 1740. Work known – longcase clock.

GASCOIGNE, Richard (also Gascoyne)   **London**
B.c. 1662, apr. Jul 1676 to his brother, Samuel Gascoigne, till 1683, but not freed.

GASCOIGNE, Samuel   **London**
B.c. 1655, apr. Mar 1668/69 to Arthur Dove, after whose death he was transferred to Robert Seignior till 1676. Freed Apr 1676. Took as aprs.: Jul 1676 **Richard Gascoigne,** his brother; Jul 1681 **Henry Osmonde;** Apr 1686 **Matthew Nightingale.** Alive in 1697 but dead by 1698. Work known – watches.

GASCOIGNE, William   **Neward (Nottinghamshire)**
Working 1646/74. Succ. by his son, Owen, *qv*.

GATE, Aucher (Archer?)   **London**
B.c. 1660. Apr. Jun 1674 to James Ellis till 1681 but not freed.

GATEWOOD (see next entry)

GATWARD, Thomas   **London**
B.c. 1679, apr. Dec 1693 to Daniel Roofe (thro' E. Norris) till 1700 but not freed. Work known – lost watch signed 'Gatewood, London' prob. by him.

GAVEL(L)E, James   **London**
A clockmaker and alien, admitted to CC as a Free Brother Jan 1682/83. Paid quarterage till c. 1691. Work known – bracket clock and a longcase clock signed 'James Gavelle Londini'.

GAYFORD, John   **Great Yarmouth**
Free locksmith there 1664. Made turret clock for workhouse. Bailiff 1688. Died 1703 aged 69.

GAYFORT, Thomas   **Great Yarmouth**
Son of John to whom apr. 1676.

GAZUET, Jeremy (also Jérome)   **London**
B.c. 1658 in Geneva. A watchmaker and bachelor of St. Sepulchre, London, in May 1682 aged 24, when he was to marry Anne Rocher of Leicester Fields, spinster, aged 24. In Sep 1682 he was made a Free Brother in CC being a watch chain maker. However in Mar 1685, being a Brother but not a Freeman nor free of the City, he had goods confiscated (worktools, etc.) because he was accused of having made watches and signed them with his name on. He admitted having made one about two years earlier. He refused to attend CC court and the CC left it to the complaining watchmakers to sort it out. Took as apr.: Oct 1691 **John Shovell** (thro' D. Stevens). In 1699 he lived in the parish of St. James Clerkenwell when his son, Abraham David Gazuet, was apr. to J. Markwick. Paid quarterage till late in 1699, but not later. Work known – lantern and longcase clocks signed 'Jeremy Gazuet, St. Johns, London' and 'Jeremy Gazuet Londini fecit'.

GELDARTE, John (also Gildar?)   **York/Kings Lynn (Norfolk)**
Watchmaker, b. 1648 son of Joshua Geldarte, goldsmith of York. Free there in 1674. Nothing else known. Free at Kings Lynn 1685. (Inventory of John Gildar of Kings Lynn in Feb 1691 is prob. his.)

GELL, John senior   **York**
Watchmaker, son of Edward Gell, locksmith. Free 1634. Married firstly 1635 Jane Pawson of Leeds who died 1636. Married secondly 1636 Susan Mangie, widow, prob. one of the family of goldsmiths of this name. Son, John, b. 1636, died 1639. Presumably later had another son, John junior, *qv*.

GELL, John junior   **York**
Watchmaker, son of John senior. Free in 1663. Died 1698.

GEORGE, Andrew   **London**
Apr. Feb 1649-50 to John Cooke, transferred Oct 1650 to Peter de Lawne. Never actually admitted to CC but was recognised by them. Prob. dead by 1662-63.

GEORGE, Richard   **London**
B.c. 1661, apr. Aug 1674 to Charles Bonner till 1682 but freed Nov 1681.
Took many aprs., but as he was appointed Beadle in Jan 1697/98, many
of these may have been bound thro' him to serve other masters. Took:
Apr 1684 **Morris Oram**; Jul 1695 **Henry Guy** – free Jul 1702; Jan
1697-98 **William White**; May 1698 **John Dawkes** – free Sep 1707; Feb
1698/99 **William Martin** (son of Henry Martin, gent., of London); Jul
1699 **Samuel Mason**; Nov 1699 **Jonathan Browne** (son of James Browne
late of parish of St. Leonard Shoreditch, deceased); Sep 1700 **William
Ley** (son of Samuel Ley late of Sslyver or Fflyver, co. Worcestershire,
clerk, deceased); Mar 1701/02 **Stephen Rust** (son of Edward Rust
Citizen and Draper of London); Oct 1702 **Thomas Brookes** (son of
Charles Brookes late of parish of St. Dunstan in the West, London,
cabinetmaker, deceased) – free Nov 1709 (as **Edward Brookes**); Jul 1705
Samuel Lebow, a child in the care of parish of St. Mary le Bow; May
1708 **Richard Conyers** junior; Dec 1709 **John Walker** – free Dec 1717;
Jan 1709/10 **Bulmer Francis**; Dec 1710 **Walcot Hendy**; Jan 1710/11
Philip Greenly; Feb 1710/11 **Richard Barber**; May 1711 **Charles Henry
Forbes**; **Marmaduke Etty** – freed Dec 1716. Additionally he bound for
other masters: Jul 1700 **Kirkby Golton** (son of Edward Golton, Citizen
and Weaver) for Charles Harris; Apr 1704 **William Lens** (son of Bernard
Lens, Citizen and Haberdasher of London) for Sarah, widow of
Benjamin Harris – freed Apr 1712; Sep 1705 **William Rose** (son of John
Rose late Citizen and Clothworker of London, deceased) for John
Baptiste Hall, glazier; Jul 1706 **James Coombs** (son of James Coombs of
Kingston on Thames, Surrey, taylor) for Richard Tills – free Apr 1719;
Aug 1706 **John Parry** (son of Francis Parry late of Pembroke, co.
Pembroke, mercer, deceased) – for George Allatt.
   He was a poor man and in receipt of occasional CC charities from 1699
till he died in 1712. His widow, Isabella, was also a pensioner till she died
in Jun 1718, when they paid ten shillings to the daughter towards the
funeral. The new Beadle was John Drew. Work known – none; he was
prob. an engraver.

GEORGE, Thomas   **London**
Late 17th century longcase clock, c. 1685, is known signed 'Tho. George
in ye Strand Fecit'. Nothing is known about him – unknown to CC.

GERNON(S), Bernard (or Barnett?)   **London**
In Dec 1658 his work was judged by CC to be inadequate and was
ordered to be defaced and a fine imposed (though he had not yet become

a member or been permitted to trade). He was also ordered to produce proof of his training. In Jul 1659 he was made a Free Brother, as a former apr. of Solomon Wasson of Bristol. In Aug 1663 took as apr. **John Wigginton** (thro' N. Payne).

GERRARD/GHERRALD, Richard London
Listed by Baillie as 1689. I cannot trace him. Richard George?

GIBBS, Joshua London
Apr. Dec 1689 to Thomas Gibbs. Freed Jul 1700. Took as aprs.: Jul 1700 **George Francis** (son of Marmaduke Francis, Citizen and Tyler and Bricklayer of London); May 1707/08 **William King** – free Apr 1720; Nov 1710 **James Exelby** – free Sep 1718; Oct 1714 **John Sanders;** Jul 1717 **Thomas Bull.** Work known – longcase clocks signed 'Joshua Gibbs, London'.

GIBBS, Thomas London
B.c. 1659, apr. Nov 1672 to Henry Hester till 1680. Freed Jul 1681. Took as aprs.: Dec 1684 **Whitestone Littlemore,** later transferred to Tompion; Dec 1689 **Joshua Gibbs** – free Jul 1700; Oct 1695 **Richard Burnett** – free Apr 1706; Apr 1707 **Robert Serjant** – free Apr 1720; May 1708 **John Pepys** (junior?); Aug 1717 **Alexander Harvey.** Made CC Assistant 1701, Warden 1708, Master 1711. Last attended 1719. Work known – watches.

GIBB(E)S, Walter London
B.c. 1626, apr. Oct 1639 to Edward East (thro' O. Durant) till 1647. Freed May 1648. Worked in Fleet Street (prob. for East). Took as aprs.: Apr 1650 **James Greene** transferred Jan 1651/52 to John Dodsworth; Aug 1660 **Hugh Holland;** Jul 1663 **Charles Jones; Thomas Parrat** (from Edward Whitfield) – freed Jul 1702. Received regular CC charity from 1693 to Sep 1701, when believed died (paid from the gift of Edward East). Work known – none and prob. always worked as an engraver for East.

GIBSON, Benjamin London
Son of Benjamin Gibson, Citizen and Carpenter. Apr. Aug 1650 to Richard Masterson, transferred Dec 1653 to Masterson's widow, but not freed.

GIBSON, G. Thetford (Norfolk)
Recorded as c. 1690 but I have no data.

GIBSON, James London
Made a Free Brother in CC Nov 1669, a 'great clockmaker'. Paid no quarterage after c. 1670.

GIDEON, Robert London
B.c. 1670, apr. Apr 1684 to William Young, transferred later to Thomas Brayfield till 1691. Freed Mar 1691/92. Took as aprs.: May 1696 **Isaac Webb**; Nov 1703 **Roger Stone** – free Jan 1710/11; Aug 1709 **Thomas Timbrell** (son of Benjamin Timbrell of parish of St. James in Westminster); Jan 1715/16 **Benjamin Langford**. I have no data on him after 1716.

GIFFORD, John Exeter
Repaired cathedral clock 1376-95.

GIFFORD, Thomas London
B.c. 1671, apr. Sep 1685 to Robert Seigniour, later transferred to Robert Webster (prob. in 1687 when R.S. died) till 1692. Freed Oct 1692. Paid no quarterage after c. 1693.

GILBERT, Charles London
B.c. 1676, apr. May 1690 to Isaac Nicholl till 1697. Freed Jul 1700. Took as apr. Feb 1700/01 **Francis Ives** (son of Francis Ives late of Wellingborough, Northants, Esq. deceased) – free Apr 1709. Work known – watch.

GILBERT, Faustine (or Augustine) London
Apr. May 1653 to Nicholas Coxeter. Free Apr 1661. One F. Gilbert working at Angers, France, c. 1675 may be him.

GILBERT, Joseph London
B.c. 1668, apr. Jan 1682/83 to Thomas Fenn till 1689 but not freed.

GILBERT, Richard London/Bristol
B.c. 1652, apr. Oct 1664 to Thomas Hancorne till 1673 but not freed. One of this name worked at Bristol in 1711, prob. same man.

GILBERT, Thomas London
B.c. 1644, apr. May 1656 to Robert Coster till 1665 but not freed.

GILBERT, William London

B.c. 1672, apr. Apr 1685 to John Longland later transferred to Henry Kilminster till 1693. Freed Aug 1695. Took as apr. Aug 1696 **John Anderson.** Paid no quarterage after 1699.

GILGOUR, Thomas Elgin (Scotland)

Free watchmaker there 1697.

GILK(E)S, George London

Listed as apr. 1693 but this is an error for Robert, *qv.*

GILK(E)S, Richard London

B.c. 1664, apr. Jul 1678 to William Hancorne, later transferred to Benjamin Bell (as Hancorne had deserted and left Gilkes) till 1685. Freed Jul 1686. Took as aprs.: Jun 1695 **Richard Glover** – free Oct 1703; Jan 1698/99 **Stephen Rewis** (son of John Rewis of St. Mildred Poultry, London, plasterer). Also bound an apr. for George Cawdron. Not heard of after 1703.

GILKS, Robert London

B.c. 1679, apr. Apr 1693 to Richard Watts till 1700 but not freed.

GILK(E)S, Thomas Sibford Gower (Oxon)

Quaker clock- and watchmaker. B.c. 1665, son of Thomas and Mary Gilkes of Sibford Gower. Married Anne X, had issue 1702-15. Son Thomas b. 1704 set up in Charlbury as clockmaker and son Richard b. 1715 set up at Adderbury. Took as apr. **John Farndon** of Deddington. Still alive 1743. Work known – 30 hour longcase clock signed 'Thomas Gilkes, Sibford'.

GILLIARD, John London

Prob. French. Servant (journeyman?) of Lewes Billiard in St. Clementt Danes parish, London in 1551.

GILLIARD, Nicholas London

Prob. French. Servant (journeyman?) of Lewes Billiard in St. Clement Danes parish in 1549.

GILMORE, John senior Battle (Sussex)

B. 1660, son of James Gilmore. Died 1717. May have been an apr. of T. Punnett. Work known – lantern clock signed 'John Gilmore Battle fecit'.

GILMORE, John junior   **Battle (Sussex)**
B. 1677, son of John Gilmore senior. Died 1726. Clockmaker and also ran a gunpowder mill. Married 1700 Mary Cray of Lewes, the sister of Elizabeth, wife of clockmaker Abraham Weston of Lewes, whom she had married in 1699. Issue: Mary, John, William, James, Thomas, Henry and Elizabeth. John III was b. 1701. Work known – two longcase clocks and a lantern clock.

GILPIN, Edmund (sometimes Edward)   **London**
A Freeman of the Leathersellers' Co. Entered CC as a Free Brother in 1632. Took as aprs.: Jun 1638 **William Woodington** thro' R. Masterson; Oct 1648 **Michael Bird** thro' Thomas Taylor – freed in Oxford in 1654; Jul 1650 **Daniel Manley** thro' T. Taylor – freed Oct 1660; Jun 1656 **James Markwick** thro' T. Taylor – free Aug 1666; Aug 1666 **Joseph Duke** thro' J. Markwick – free Apr 1682; **Henry Shuttleworth** thro' T. Taylor – free Jan 1669/70; 1668 **James Wood** thro' J. Markwick; Jan 1671/72 **John Bradley** thro' J. Markwick. Made Assistant in 1646 but was away for some years (maybe in Oxford?) and then began to attend again from 1659 until 1672. Obviously closely associated with Thomas Taylor, who paid his quarterage for him in 1662. Last heard of in 1677 when much in arrears with quarterage. Work known – several watches.

GILSON, Henry   place not known
Watch hallmarked 1698.

GINN, William   **London**
In Jun 1697 'in the Little Old Bayly using the Art of a Boxmaker but by Trade a Turner, given one month's warning to cease the trade'. In Jan 1699/1700 he was admitted to CC. Last mentioned Jan 1719/20 when in arrears with his quarterage. One of this name at Perth in 1778 can hardly be the same man.

GIRLINGTON, John   **London**
B.c. 1667, apr. Sep 1681 to Erasmus Micklewright till 1688 but not freed.

GIROD, James (also Jasper)   **London**
Frenchman, a watchmaker. Made Free Brother in CC Oct 1692. In Apr 1695 was in trouble for keeping an unbound apr. who lived with Guiguer, *qv*, but he refused to pay a fine. Paid quarterage till c. 1698. Work known – watches and a bracket clock signed 'James Girod

London'. A Jacques Girod working at Copet, France, late in the 17th century may be the same man.

GITTER, John (not Gilbert as sometimes stated)   **London**
B.c. 1670, apr. Nov 1683 to Nathaniel Pyne till 1691 but not freed.

GLASS, John   **Edinburgh**
Working 1692.

GLAZIER, William   **London**
Apr. Aug 1658 to Thomas Mills thro' A. Grose. Freed Apr 1666. Took as aprs.: Feb 1669/70 **Simon Lambe**; Mar 1673/74 **William Cooke** – free Apr 1681; Jul 1682 **Thomas Tingley**. Work known – a longcase clock signed 'William Glazier Londini fecit'.

GLEAVE, John   **Nantwich (Cheshire)**
Watchmaker. Died Oct 1702.

GLOVER, Daniel   **London**
B.c. 1673, apr. 1687 to Charles Hougham till 1694. Freed Sep 1699. Paid quarterage till 1700. Work known – watch.

GLOVER, John   **London**
Free (Brother?) Jul 1700. Took as aprs.: Sep 1715 **Francis Wright; Robert Blackbourne** – free Nov 1720. In Apr 1717 one John Smith Glover, son of ---- Glover, late Citizen and Clockmaker deceased, to be given CC charity towards his apprenticeship as 'his mother hath 5 poor fatherless children now living and at present incapable of being disposed of'. He was apr. 1717 to Richard Andrews in CC.

GLOVER, Samuel   **London**
B.c. 1668, apr. Sep 1681 to Nathaniel Chamberlain till 1689. Freed Aug 1694. Took as apr. Oct 1701 **George Harle** (son of Richard Harle, late of S. Shields in co. Durham, mariner) – 'note this boy is both deaf and dumb'; Nov 1717 **Walter Bowen** – transferred Oct 1719 to Thomas Bradford.

GLUMMER, Peter   **London**
Baillie records him as 'Of the French Church – 1582, Clockmaker'.

GOALLON, James London
Alien journeyman with Cornelius Mellin in Blackfriars in 1622.

GOBART, James (see Goubert)

GOBERT, Peter (signs Pierre) London
French watchmaker, Free Brother in CC Sep 1687. Paid quarterage till early in 1703.

GODBED, Matthew (Mathias) London
B.c. 1644, apr. Nov 1657 to Henry Kent thro' B. Hill till 1665 but not freed.

GODBED, William (sometimes Godber) London
B.c. 1624, apr. Mar 1638/39 to Thomas Reeve thro' R. Masterson till 1645. Freed Aug 1646. Took as aprs.: Oct 1647 **Henry Harland** transferred Oct 1650 to Peter de Laune, free Nov 1654; Jun 1649 **Gabriel Dowse;** May 1653 **Thomas Moyser;** Feb 1655 **Edward Plant** – freed Apr 1664; Oct 1660 **James Egersley.** Also bound one apr. for widow Fletcher, and one for John White. Was a rebel in 1656 against CC administration. In 1662 worked in Cornhill. Last heard of in 1664. Work known – watches, one signed 'Gulielmus Godbed, Lombart Street, Londini'; another said to be dated 1665.

GODDARD, Benjamin London
B.c. 1678, apr. Feb 1692/93 to Isaac Goddard, but transferred to John Stanton till 1699. Freed Nov 1701. Took as aprs.: Jul 1705 **Philip Burchett** or **Burnett** (son of Richard Burchett of Kingston on Thames, Surrey) – free Oct 1715; Feb 1714/15 **Henry Berry** (who got a grant being the son of an impoverished freeman). I have no data on him after 1714.

GODDARD, Isaac London
B.c. 1661, apr. Aug 1675 to Thomas Grimes thro' S. Davis till 1682. Freed Dec 1684. Took as aprs.: Sep 1687 **William Lockin;** Feb 1692/93 **Benjamin Goddard,** transferred to John Stanton; Apr 1699 **Samuel Leach** (son of William Leach late of Colchester, milliner, deceased), transferred to Edward Stanton, then again in Dec 1701 to Michael Shields, clockmaker, of the Blacksmith Co. Maybe worked for the Stantons. Not heard of after 1699. Work known – longcase clocks signed 'Isaac Goddard Londini'.

GODDARD, John London
Native of Paris. In 1618 had been here three years, a Papist, lodger and servant with Isaac Sunes Hounsditch (prob. Isaac Symms, *qv*).

GODDARD, Thomas London
B.c. 1625, apr. Nov 1638 to Richard Child thro' R. Masterson till 1646 but not freed.

GODDARD, Thomas London
B.c. 1671, apr. Apr 1685 thro' D. Stevens to John Stasebey of the Clothworkers' Co. till 1692, but not freed. Said to work in Shoe Lane and bankrupt in 1723, but I cannot confirm this and I have no trace of him after 1685.

GODFREY, Henry Oxford/London
B.c. 1663. Son of George Godfrey yeoman of Hillend Berks. Apr. Jun 1676 to John Quelch watchmaker of Oxford till 1684, but not freed there. Made Free Brother in CC in London Jul 1685. Last heard of in 1704. Work known – watches and longcase clocks.

GODFREY, John London
B.c. 1668, apr. Mar 1682/83 to James Hatchman till 1689, but not freed.

GODIN, Louis Paris/London
A goldsmith in Paris, 1677-91. Watchmaker at Hand Alley Bishopsgate, London in 1701.

GODRONE, ---- London
An alien working in 1622 with John Canninge *(qv)* behind St. Clements Church, prob. a journeyman.

GOFFE, ---- London
In Sep 1700 was warned to take up his freedom but did not.

GOLD, Abel (see Gould) London

GOLDSMITH, John London
B.c. 1660, apr. Sep 1674 to Robert Williamson till 1681. Freed Sep 1681. Paid quarterage till 1699, when died.

GO(U)LDSMITH, Thomas London
Apr. Jul 1683 to William Brayfield. Freed Apr 1692. Took as apr. Jan
1703/04 **Mark Joseph Laworthy.**

GOMES, William Oxford
Kept St. Martins Church Clock, c. 1550-85.

GOOD(E), Charles London
Watchmaker. Free Brother in CC Sep 1686. Took as aprs.: Mar 1692/93
Mougham James thro' J. Elton; Jul 1714 **Lewen Bloomer.** I have no
dates on him after 1714, but reputedly died in 1730. In 1712 he contested
a patent application by John Hutchinson claiming that he had made a
watch 14 years earlier to do the same as Hutchinson's, ie wind without an
aperture in the case. Work known – several watches, also lantern,
bracket and longcase clocks(including month longcase) usually signed
'Chas. GoodeLondon'.

GOOD(E), John London
B.c. 1657, apr. Jun 1671 to John Matchett till 1678. Freed Jul 1678.
Took as apr. Sep 1681 **John Elliott.** Paid no quarterage after c. 1682.
Work known – longcase clock signed 'John Goode London'.

GOODBED, William (see Godbed)

GOODLAD, Richard London
In Jul 1688 he promised to join CC at next court. Admitted a Free
Brother Sep 1689, a 'Great Clockmaker', but paid no quarterage
thereafter.

GOODLIN, Peter London
Freed in CC Apr 1637.

GOODMAN, Timothy Towcester (Northamptonshire)
Lantern clock recorded c. 1680.

GOODO, Francis London
Watch dated 1705.

GOODRICH, William London
B.c. 1675, apr. Aug 1689 to Amos Winch thro' T. Hicks, till 1696, but
not freed.

GOODWIN, Thomas   **London**
Elected clerk to CC in 1662. Perhaps not a maker. Died and was replaced by Francis Speidell in Jul 1694. Widow Jane maintained 1706 and 1717.

GOODWIN, William   **London/Stowmarket (Suffolk)**
B.c. 1661, apr. Jun 1675 to John Harris till 1682 but not freed. Paid quarterage in Stowmarket 1681-87 and 1688-1734 in Market Place. In 1736 referred to as 'the late' William Goodwin. Work known – lantern clocks, a 30 hour longcase and a watch.

GOODYER, Robert (also Goodier)   **Bristol**
A smith who worked on a TC in 1583.

GORDIN, John (sometimes Gordon, but signed Gordin)   **London**
B.c. 1675, apr. 1689 to Benj. Graves till 1696. Freed Jul 1698. Took as aprs.: Mar 1700/01 **William Gasdon** (son of John Gasdon of Stretham, Surrey, yeoman) – free Jan 1713; Jul 1707 **Thomas Norton**. Worked at the Black Spread Eagle in Ludgate Street. I have no data on him later than 1707, but Baillie lists him till 1723. Work known – watches and a bracket clock signed 'John Gordin – London'.

GORDON, John (also Gordowne)   **Edinburgh**
Apr. 1680 to Richard Milne.

GORDON, Thomas   **Aberdeen**
Gunmaker who kept town clocks in 1595.

GORDON, Thomas   **Edinburgh**
Apr. Nov 1688 to Andrew Brown. Freed Sep 1703. Had as aprs.: 1706 **William Murray** – free 1712; 1739 **Robert Fairholm** transferred to Patrick Gordon on death of Thomas in 1743. Work known – longcase clocks.

GORSTOW, Richard   **London**
B.c. 1637, apr. Aug 1650 to Thomas Claxton till 1658, but not freed. Prob. dead or gone by 1662-63. Work known – lantern clock with alarm work signed 'Richard Gorsselow – London'.

GOSLING, Richard
Recorded by Britten, but this is an error for Gorslow.

GOSSE, Jeremiah **London**
Apr. Jul 1660 to Richard Bowen. Transferred to Thomas Holland transferred to Thomas Taylor of Holborn. Freed Jan 1667/68.

GOSSE, John **London**
B.c. 1649, apr. Oct 1662 to Richard Scrivener thro' T. Taylor, till 1670, but not freed.

GOUBERT, James **London**
Watchmaker and naturalised Frenchman. Free Brother in CC Sep 1690. Last heard of in 1701 when in arrears with quarterage. Work known – bracket clocks usually signed 'Jacobus Goubert – London'.

GOULD, Abel (sometimes Gold) **London**
B.c. 1659, apr. Jan 1673/74 thro' Charles Bonner to E. Clough of the Loriners' Co., till 1680. Freed Nov 1683. In Jun 1683 was involved in making watches with invented names for John Harman and 'did work in his own house'. In Nov 1683 'is to take an apr. when he has taken his freedom of the City' – he took **Charles Garrett** – freed Feb 1690/91. Paid no quarterage after c. 1686, when prob. died, and certainly before 1698. Work known – watches and longcase clocks.

GOULD, Christopher **London**
A 'Great Clockmaker' – made Free Brother in CC Apr 1682. Took as aprs.: May 1682 **Andrew Clarke** thro' D. Stevens; Apr 1687 **George Kippis** thro' D. Stevens; Dec 1693 **Thomas Cartwright** thro' R. Watts; Aug 1698 **Robert Osborne;** Dec 1701 **Charles Gould** (son of John Gould of Middlemarsh, co. Dorset, smith); Dec 1713 **John Gibbs;** Mar 1714/15 **Thomas Norris;** Aug 1715 **John Frederick Aleman;** Nov 1715 **Matthew Meadows;** Jan 1717/18 **Thomas Shorter.** Was made Beadle in Sep 1713 and may have bound some of the above aprs. for other masters. Died in 1718, when Charles Tolley replaced him as Beadle. Had received regular CC charity ('pension') from 1713 till he died, when his widow was chosen as pensioner in his place. Worked in 1701 'near the north east corner of the Royal Exchange'. Work known – several watches, longcase clocks, bracket and lantern clocks (incl. Turkish market examples) and hooded clocks. Usually signed 'Christopher Gould Londini fecit' or 'Christopher Gould, London'. Seems strange that such a prolific and competent worker should have been such a poor man.

GOULD, James   London

Not strictly a member of the CC but his apr. **John Wither** was freed, Sep 1699.

GOWETH, John   Oxford

B.c. 1669, son of John Goweth, gunsmith of Oxford. Apr. Oct 1686 to John Knibb. Freed Oct 1694. Believed still alive 1734. Work known – a watch.

GRACEBY, John   London

Lantern clock recorded c. 1680. This name unknown in CC records. Could this be a slip for John Staceby? (*qv*).

GRAHAM, George   London

Very famous maker, mentioned in most clock books. B.c. 1673 in Cumberland, the son of George Graham, farmer. Was a member of a Quaker family, though not thought to have followed that faith himself. Apr. Jul 1688 to Henry Aske till 1695. Freed Sep 1695. Believed to have gone to work for Tompion almost immediately, ie c. 1696. In 1704 married Elizabeth Tompion, niece of his master. Partner with Tompion c.1711 – 13, and when latter died and Graham succ. him. 'George Graham nephew of the late Mr. Thomas Thompion, who lived with him upwards of 17 years, and managed his trade for sometime before his death, and to whom he left all his stock and work, finished and unfinished, continues to carry on the said trade at the late dwellinghouse of the said Mr Tompion, at the sign of the Dial and Three Crowns, at the corner of Water Lane, and Fleet Street, London, where all persons maybe accommodated as formerly'. In 1720 he moved 'George Graham watchmaker is removed from the corner of Water Lane in Fleet Street to the Dial and One Crown on the other side of the way, a little nearer Fleet Bridge, a new house next door to the Globe and Duke of Marlborough's Head Tavern'. Made CC Assistant from 1716, Warden 1719, Master 1722. Took as aprs.: Dec 1697 **Joseph Ward**; Dec 1700 **Obadiah Gardner** (son of Ambrose Gardner, goldsmith, of St. Dunstans in the West – who worked for Tompion); May 1714 **Benjiman Flindell**; Jun 1715 **Samuel Barkley** (later Graham's successor); Sep 1719 **Daniel Cole**; Jul 1720 **Ephraim How** (from John Marshall); no doubt others after 1720 of which I have no records. Was a Fellow of the Royal Society and contributed many papers. Graham is credited with several inventions such as the dead-beat escapement in 1715, the mercury pendulum in

1726, the cylinder escapement for watches in 1726 – on what authority these are ascribed to him I do not know.

Work known – he was primarily a maker of watches, and is said to have produced approximately 3,000, as well as 170 clocks (mainly bracket clocks) and also lantern and a few longcase clocks. This output is calculated from the numbering system he carried on from Tompion, running from around 4,400 to around 6,600 for watches, with repeating watches from around 400 to 965.

Graham died 16 Nov 1751 and was buried in Tompion's grave in Westminster Abbey.

*For Graham's background see John B. Penfold's excellent study *The Cumbrian Background of George Graham, Clockmaker* (*Antiquarian Horology*, March 1974).

GRA(I)NGER, Richard   London
Not a member of CC but in Feb 1664/65 R. Granger 'a butcher in Southwark' (?) took as apr. in CC Edward Clark (thro' William Petty).

GRA(I)NGER, Richard   London
B.c. 1671, apr. Sep 1685 to Francis Munden, later transferred to Jonathan Rant till 1692. Freed Sep 1695. Took as aprs.: Sep 1698 **William Gurnett;** May 1702 **Samuel Jeanes** (son of Samuel Jeanes Citizen and Painter Stainer of London). Paid no quarterage after 1703.

GRANGER, Marc   London
Clock c. 1690.

GRAINGER, Marc   London
Longcase clock recorded c. 1690? One of this name listed in France c. 1650, a watchmaker. Not known to CC.

GRANT, William   London
Baillie lists him as CC 1660, which I cannot confirm, but a man of this name paid quarterage in 1672.

GRAPE, Richard   London
B.c. 1671, apr. Aug 1685 to John Wheeler thro' Robert Cosbey till 1692 but not freed.

GRAVE, Joseph   **London**
B.c. 1673, apr. May 1687 to Joseph Williamson thro' D. Stevens till
1694, but not freed.

GRAVER, Thomas   **Manchester**
In 1397 sued by Prior of Warrington for having made an unsatisfactory
clock for 100/-.

GRAVES, Benjamin   **London**
An engraver. B.c. 1654, apr. April 1668 in CC to Richard Nau till 1675.
Free as a Brother Jul 1675 (because he was already a Freeman of the
Weavers' Co.). Took as aprs.: Dec 1674 thro' Weavers' Co., **Joseph
Tanner,,** transferred to Isaac Day and freed in CC Apr 1684; Sep 1676
thro' Weavers' Co., **Isaac Day** (who had already been bound to
Ahasuerus Fromanteel junior in 1675(?)) – freed 1679 in CC; **William
Moseley** – freed Dec 1680; Feb 1689 **John Gordon** – freed Jul 1698; Sep
1691 **John Bull** (thro' Christopher Maynard); Nov 1694 **George
Waterer;** Feb 1697-98 **James Heton;** Dec 1700 **William Wood** (son of
William Wood, late of Gaston (Garstang?) co. Lancashire, yeoman,
deceased); May 1703 **George Watkins** (son of William Watkins of St.
Giles in Fields, Middlesex, coachman) – free May 1716; Nov 1712
Samuel Shaw; Jul 1716 **John Roden;** perhaps others after 1720.
Additionally bound in Jul 1705 **William Browne** (son of William Browne
late of the parish of St. Andrew Holborn, Blacksmith) for William
Barker gunsmith, and Sep 1705 **Richard Packe** for Thomas Cartwright.
Referred to as Captain Graves 1700-13. In 1719 was appointed Clerk to
the CC to replace Speidel, deceased. Made Assistant in CC 1697, Warden
1702, Master 1705. Believed died 1731. Work known – none. Prob.
purely an engraver or perhaps watch casemaker.

GRAVES, Benjamin   **London**
B.c. 1670, son of James Graves *qv*, apr. June 1684 thro' D. Stevens to his
father till 1691, but transferred (on father's death?) to G. Oversee – but
not freed. Some of the entries relating to Benjamin senior may perhaps
relate to Benjamin junior but this is unlikely.

GRAVES, James   **London**
An engraver and a Freeman of the Weavers' Co. Took as aprs.: in
Weavers' Co., May 1654 **Robert Holme** – free 1663; May 1658 **John
Serwin** – free Jun 1669; Dec 1668 **George Lowcock;** Jul 1673 **William
Moseley** freed 1680 in CC; Jun 1677 **Joseph Armiger** – freed Sep 1688 in

CC. Officially joined CC as a Free Brother in Jul 1676 and took as aprs. in CC: Aug 1676 **George Cawdron** (thro' J. Matchett) – freed Jan 1684/85; **John Wynne** (from William Watmore) – freed Sep 1678; May 1682 **John Clarke** (thro' N. Russell) – freed Jul 1691; Jun 1684 son **Benjamin Graves** thro' D. Stevens; Sep 1672 **Nicholas Shaller** (thro' L. Wythe). In Feb 1682-83 he accused Francis Dinnis of engraving a false name on a watch despite being warned on a previous occasion. In Feb 1682/83 he was warned by CC that he must return the gold shavings which he cut out when engraving cases etc., to those for whom he or his servants did the work, instead of keeping these shavings. Not heard of after c. 1684. Work known – prob. not recognisable (see James Grimes).

GRAY, John   London
B.c. 1666, apr. Jul 1680 to John Westoby till 1687 but not freed. Believed working till c. 1705 but not apparently known to CC. Work known – watch and longcase clock signed 'John Gray in Johnson's Court, Londini fecit'.

GRAY, Timothy   London
Free Brother in CC Sep 1633. Prob. dead or gone by 1662/63.

GRAY, William   London
B.c. 1677, apr. Jan 1691/92 to Peter Lodowick till 1698 but not freed. Watch recorded supposedly c. 1730, signed 'William Gray Bond Street, London'.

GREATOREX, Ralph (also Gratrix)   London
Apr. Mar 1639 thro' T. Dawson to Elias Allen, mathematician (mat. inst. maker). Freed Nov 1653. Took as aprs.: 1654 **Henry Wynne** – freed Oct 1662; Mar 1655 **Daniel Bulty** – freed Apr 1663; Jun 1656 **Francis Jervis;** Jan 1657/58 **Thomas King** – freed Apr 1669; Jun 1664 **Robert Okeshott**. Worked in Temple Bar in 1662. Must have been abroad for in May 1666 he was summoned to be CC Assistant as 'since the last count (he) is returned to England'. However he was excused in July 1666 as 'he shall agane goe to sea'. Not heard of thereafter.

GREBANT, ----   London
Alien in St. Bartholomews in 1622 with two aprs., but see Phillipe Grebay.

GREBAY, Phillipe (maybe Greban)   **London**
Watch recorded c. 1610. One such in Paris c. 1670 watchmaker. May be same as Grebant above.

GREBAUVAL, Guillaume (or Grebaunal)   **London**
Believed from Rouen. In Oct 1655 appointed with CC approval as journeyman to David Bouquet.

GREENE, Edward   **London**
B.c. 1668, apr. Aug 1682 to Thomas Davis till 1689 but not freed.

GREEN, Ernest   **Wallingford (Berkshire)**
c. 1700.

GREEN, George   **London**
B.c. 1647, apr. Apr 1661 to Matthew Crockford till 1668, but not freed.

GREENE, James   **London/Gloucester**
Apr. Apr 1650 to Walter Gibbs, transferred Jan 1651-52 to John Dodsworth. Freed Dec 1664. Work known – lantern clock signed 'James Green, Moorefield'. Dead or gone by 1697/98. Another maker of this name working at Gloucester c. 1685, maybe same man.

GREENE, James   **London**
B.c. 1664, apr. Jul 1678 to Henry Jones till 1685. Freed Sep 1685. Paid quarterage till at least 1705.

GREEN(E), John   **Shrewsbury**
Watchmaker there 1688.

GREEN, Nathaniel   **London**
B.c. 1674, apr. Sep 1688 to Daniel Beckman thro' T. Hancorne till 1695. Freed Sep 1695. Paid quarterage till at least 1705.

GREENAWAY, Curtice   **Oxford/London**
Son of Thomas Greenaway, joiner of Oxford. Apr. Feb 1688 to Michael Bird, watchmaker of Oxford – cancelled on death of master (Oct 1689). Transferred to Wright Lane of Oxford. Bound in London Dec 1694 to Joseph Foster, clockmaker. On death of father in Apr 1699 he returned to Oxford where freed in May 1699. Died Apr 1702. Work known – longcase clock and lantern clock signed 'Curtice Greenaway, Oxford'.

GREENBANCK, John place not known
30-hour longcase clock noted, c. 1690. Believed Northern England.

GREENHILL, John Ashford
Lantern clock c. 1660.

GREENHILL, Nathaniel London
B.c. 1660, apr. Oct 1674 to Edward Clough thro' C. Bonner till 1681 but
not freed.

GREENHILL, Richard Canterbury
Freed there 1676 by redemption. Still working in 1707 when son Samuel
was apr. to him. Work known – longcase clocks.

GREGG, Francis London
B.c. 1677, apr. Sep 1691 to John Clowes thro' T. Morgan till 1698, but
not freed. Prob. became free of another Co. Worked in Russell Street in
1711. In 1714 'Francis Gregg watchmaker is removed from the Dial in
Russell Street, Covent Garden to the Dial in James street over against the
Palace Gates'. Said to be later in York Street. Insolvent 1743. Work
known – longcase and bracket clocks and watches (incl. year longcase)
signed 'Francis Gregg London' and 'Francis Gregg Covent Garden'.

GREGORY, James London
B.c. 1636, apr. May 1650 to Benjamin Hill thro' L. Wythe till 1657.
Freed Jul 1657. In Nov 1657 he was accused with David Parry of illicitly
keeping **John Barton** as apr. and warned to dismiss him, ultimately
being fined in Mar 1658/59, presumably for this offence. Took as apr.
Jan 1659/60 **Robert Wood** – freed 1671.

GREGORY, Jeremy London
Free Brother in CC Oct 1652, but also some doubt whether he was made
a Free Brother in 1646. Before this however he was 'accepted' by CC and
took aprs. thro' them, perhaps because of his close connection with the
powerful East family. Said to have been apr. in the Goldsmiths' Co. to
Jeremy East (brother of Edward) and to have been closely influenced by
East. May well have worked some long time for the East company. Took
as aprs.: Aug 1647 **Henry Mason** thro' Henry (William?) Bunting; Mar
1648 **Thomas Moth** thro' W. Bunting – free Sep 1656; Apr 1652
Stephen Woolridge thro' J. Bayes; Jun 1653 **Markham Keyes** thro'

J.Bayes; Jul 1655 **John Thompson** thro' R. Beck – freed Sep 1662; Jun 1656 **John Wright** thro' R. Beck – freed Sep 1671; Oct 1664 **Richard Marchant** thro' S. Horne; Jul 1668 **John Elton** thro' N. Coxeter – freed Sep 1675; **John Cotsworth** thro' N. Coxeter – freed Jul 1669; **John Curtis** (from S. Bartram, prob. on Bartram's death) – freed Apr 1671; Feb 1671/72 **Thomas Jones** thro' B. Bell – freed Sep 1679; Dec 1674 **Nestor Helme** thro' N. Coxeter – he ran away in 1678; Feb 1675/76 **John Grevile** thro' S. Horne; May 1680 **Samuel Clay** thro' B. Bell – freed Dec 1687; Sep 1680 **Thomas Jackson** thro' T. Wheeler – freed Apr 1688 (after Gregory's death); **Robert Pattison** thro' T. Wolverstone – freed Apr 1688. Closely connected with Robert Grinkin in whose will of 1660 he is mentioned as a 'very loving friend'. Also connected with Simon Bartram in whose will of 1665 he is a 'loving friend' and executor. In Oct 1655 he employed **Jacob Renon** a foreigner as journeyman, and also employed then illicitly **Jacques Patte** from Geneva as journeyman (in collusion with Grinkin and Bartram). He was frequently complained about by several Freemen for employing foreigners, being 'abused' for this in 1657 by Thomas Weeks, in 1668 by John Nicasius and in 1685 by Daniel Beckman who accused him of employing a Frenchman (**J. Gazuett**). Became CC Assistant from 1656, Warden from 1660, Master 1665-68 and again in 1676. Supported CC in the 1656 rebellion. Last attended in 1685. Died between Apr and Jul 1686. Worked in Cornhill in 1662, in 1663 was a 'watchmaker near the Castle Tavern in Cornhill'; in 1678 he advertised for Nestor Helme his 18 year old run-away apr. In 1664/65 he gave as bondsmen his uncle Mr. Thomas Waplett and his brother-in-law Mr. Samuel Lloyd of Shrewsbury, draper. In 1686 he was father-in-law of Richard Jarratt. Presumably father of Jeremiah Gregory *qv*. Work known – surprisingly little – one longcase clock, one lantern, three table clocks, three watches. Signed sometimes 'Jeremie Gregory, near ye Royal Exchange, London' and 'Jeremie Gregorie at the Royal Exchange'. Said to be much influenced by work of East and Henry Jones, which is not surprising if, as seems likely, he worked largely for East.

GREGORY, Jeremiah   London

Name usually Jeremiah in full, believed son of Jeremy *qv*, but maybe his grandson ? B.c. 1673, apr. Sep 1686 to Samuel Stevens till 1694. Freed Dec 1694. Took as aprs.: Sep 1695 **John Draper** (son of John Draper Citizen and Cloth worker) – freed May 1703; Aug 1699 **John Ireland** (son of John Ireland of St. Olave, Hart Street, packer); Nov 1703 **Edward Hall** – freed Jan 1710/11; Jul 1715 **Richard Furnifull;** Jul 1720 **Jonathan**

Silson; no doubt others later. I have no record of him after 1720, but believed to have lived till at least 1734.

GREGORY, Robert   **London**
B.c. 1656, apr. Jul 1670 to Henry Crumpe (thro' E. Stanton) till 1677. Freed Apr 1678. Took as apr. Jul 1681 **Francis Rainsford.** Freed Apr 1689. Also took **Edward Brookes** from E. Whitfield and later transferred him to J. Stedman – freed Dec 1690. Alive 1697 but prob. dead by 1698.

GREGORY, Thomas   **London**
Apr. Jul 1650 to Francis Stephens (thro' J. Bayley). Freed Aug 1671. Paid quarterage till 1672. Maybe same man as next entry?

GREGORY, Thomas   **London**
A tallow chandler admitted Dec 1673 'a free clockmaker by redemption on orders of the Lord Mayor, having taken a house within 3 doors of the new buildings of this City'. Maybe same man as above?

GREGSBY, Edward (or Edmund)   **Sittingbourne**
Sometimes Grigsby. Dates estimated c.1673 – c.1685. Work known – a lantern clock.

GREGSON, John   **London**
B.c. 1675, apr. Dec 1689 to George Nau till 1696, but not freed.

GRENDON, Henry (sometimes Grindon)   **London**
Working by 1633. Entered CC as a Free Brother Mar 1640/41. Made Assistant 1646 but seems never to have attended after that. Work known – several watches signed eg 'Henry Grenden of ye Exchange'.

GRETTON, Charles   **London**
B.c. 1649, apr. Jun 1662 to Humfrey Downing (thro' L. Wythe) till 1670. Freed Jun 1672. Took as aprs.: Mar 1672-73 **John Anthony Garnett;** Dec 1678 **Thomas Clifton** – freed Sep 1687; May 1684 **Henry Barrett** – freed Apr 1692; **Charles Kemp** (from P. Sergeant) – freed Sep 1688; Jun 1690 **Ralph Mills** later passed to C. Lee and freed Sep 1697; Oct 1694 **Henry Sully** – freed Apr 1705; **John Farewell** (from I. Nichols) – freed Sep 1697; Jan 1697/98 **Joseph Antram** – free Oct 1706. Perhaps others after 1720. Also bound an apr. for Ben Johnson. Took as journeyman Feb 1674-75 **Henry Bradley,** though Bradley was not yet a freeman and was not therefore supposed to. Said to have worked at The

Ship, Fleet Street. In 1683 still in Fleet Street and in 1685 was 'in Fleet Street over against Sergeants Inn Gate'. In 1701 he arranged to give £50 to CC to form a charity to aid orphan children of deceased members if they would raise a further £50. Made Assistant from 1689, Warden from 1697, Master 1700. Still attending 1720 after which I have no information, but believed still working till 1733. Work known – a prolific worker by whom watches, lantern clocks, longcase clocks and bracket clocks known. Signed variously as 'Charles Gretton, London', 'Charles Gretton in Fleet Street' and 'Carolus Gretton in Fleet Street Londini Fecit'.

GRETTON, P. London
Fake name put on watch c. 1700 by Nicholas Vanstripe, *qv*.

GRETTON, William London
Quoted as a lantern clockmaker c. 1665 in 'Black Fryers'. I cannot confirm this. Seems not to have been known by the CC.

GREVILLE, John London
B.c. 1661, apr. Feb 1675/76 to Samuel Horne till 1682 but not Freed.

GREY, John Chester
Repaired St. Mary's clock 1547-48.

GREY, Richard Chester
Repaired St. Mary's clock 1551-52.

GRIBELIN, Simon London
An engraver and designer from Blois, who became a Free Brother in CC Jan 1686/87. Believed b. Paris or Blois 1661/62 and to have gone to London c. 1680. In Jul 1709 he gave a copperplate engraving of the Company Arms to the CC so as to be excused Stewardship. In 1715 he repaired the copperplate for which he was excused quarterage till 1723. Was listed as an engraver at St. Martins in the Fields in 1710 when his son Samuel was apr. as a goldsmith. Believed died 1733. Work known – only books. Published *A Book of Severall Ornaments Invented and Ingraved by Simon Gribelin*, 1682, *A Book of Ornaments Useful to Jewellers, Watchmakers and all other Artists*, 1697, and *Book of Ornaments* in 1704.

GRICE, Thomas London
B.c. 1654, apr. Apr 1667 to Richard Ames till 1675. Freed May 1675.

Work known – A sundial without town and dated 1705, has the legend 'Seize the present moment, the evening hour is nigh'.

GRICE, William   **London**
B.c. 1673 (rough book says he is son of Richard Grice Citizen) apr. Jan 1687/88 to Mordecai Fox (thro' D. Stevens) till 1694 but not freed.

GRICE, William   **Ormskirk**
Baillie has 1687 (which is apprenticeship date for William of London) but I do not know his reasoning behind the Ormskirk connection.

GRIELL, Samuel   **London**
B.c. 1635, apr. Feb 1649/50 to Peter Bellune till 1656 but not freed.

GRIFFITH, James   **London**
Mat. inst. maker free of another (unknown) Co. but made a Free Brother in CC Feb 1667/68.

GRIFFIN, George   **Cork**
Clockmaker 1694. Died 1726.

GRIFFIN, Thomas   **Warwick**
Blacksmith 1631-76, who repaired clock and bells at St. Nicholas Church.

GRIGG (see also Gregg)

GRIGG, John   **London**
B.c. 1670, apr. Nov 1684 to Edward Hunt (thro' D. Stevens) till 1691, but not freed.

GRIGGS, Richard   **London**
Never actually admitted into CC but known to them. Prob. dead by 1663 and not on 1662 list.

GRIGNION, Daniel   **London**
The data on him is confused and it is difficult to believe he worked before 1700. Supposedly b. 1684 in France and in England by 1688 (age 4?). Son Thomas b. 1713, worked with him at least up to 1748. Seems not to have been a member of the CC (before 1720 anyway). 'Thomas and Daniel Grignion finishers to the late Mr. Daniel Quare at the Kings Arms and

Dial in Russel Street, Covent Garden'. Work known – watches, longcase clocks, signed 'Daniel Grignion, London'.

GRIGSBY (see Gregsby)

GRIGSON, Philip   London
B.c. 1650, apr. Jan 1663/64 to Ahasuerus Fromanteel junior till 1671 but not freed.

GRIME, Thomas   place not known
Oval watch recorded c. 1625 – see Grimes?

GRIMES, Edward   London
B.c. 1626, apr. Mar 1640/41 to Elias Allen (thro' R. Masterson). A dispute arose in Jun 1651 about his apprenticeship. Never actually admitted to CC. Prob. dead by 1662/63.

GRIMES, James   London
Entered in CC records as free of Weavers' Co. and taking as apr. Sep 1672 **Nicholas Shaller** (thro' L. Wythe) but this is believed to be an error for James Graves, *qv*.

GRIMES, Thomas   London
Free of the City of London 1668, coming from Earl Shilton, Leicestershire, and having been the apr. of (blank). Made a Free Brother in CC Sep 1671 'a great clockmaker' – same day and same trade as Tompion. Took as aprs.: Aug 1675 **Isaac Goddard** (thro' S. Davis) – freed Dec 1684; Sep 1681 **George Wilson** (thro' D. Stevens) later passed on to Zachary Mountford and freed Sep 1692; **William Grimes** – freed Jul 1682. Not heard of after 1681. Work known – a month longcase clock signed 'Thomas Grimes, London', but name-plate of Edward Bird covering his signature (?).

GRIMES, William   London
Freed as Brother Jul 1682 'servant of Thomas Grimes', which means apr. or journeyman. Strange that he was not made a full Freeman. Took as aprs.: May 1683 **James Jenkins** (thro' D. Stevens) – freed Jul 1692 (also a Brother); Sep 1691 **John Topping** (thro' E. Norris). Working till at least 1705 but not heard of thereafter. Work known – three or four longcase clocks. Signed 'William Grimes, Londini fecit' or 'William Grimes, Londini'.

GRIMKIN, Richard   **London**
Recorded as pre-1658, watchmaker, but must surely be an error for
Robert Grinkin, *qv*.

GRIMLEY, William   **London**
B.c. 1673, apr. Aug 1687 to Robert Player ('a clock case maker and Free
Joyner') till 1694. Freed Sep 1694. Paid no quarterage after 1695, but
this may simply mean that he worked outside of the CC influence.
Almost certainly a wooden clock casemaker. Work known – none as yet
identified.

GRINDALL (see Grendon)

GRINDON (see Grendon)

GRINKIN, Edmund   **London**
Son of Robert Grinkin the elder and alive in 1626 when not yet 21. Free
of the Blacksmiths' Co. in 1637 by patrimony and listed till at least 1639
there. In 1640 was warned by the CC that he must join, but seems never
to have done so. Some authorities record him at the Hague 1650-80, on
what evidence I do not know. However he signed the CC counter petition
of 1656, although he was not a member. Prob. worked for and supported
his influential brother Robert, *qv*. Died before 1660. Work known – a
watch.

GRINKIN, Robert senior   **London**
Watchmaker. Member of the Blacksmiths' Co. of which he is believed to
have been Master in 1609. Had as aprs.: c. 1598 **Edmund Bull** – freed
1607; c. 1608 **John Willow** – freed 1617. Original petitioner for CC 1622.
Died 1626, leaving wife Ann and children William, Ralph, Robert and
Edmund, *qv* and daughters Hester and Katherine. Mentions brothers-
in-law, the Whitwells, *qv*. Witnesses were John Willow, *qv*, William
Clifton and Richard Craile, *qv*. Left his mathematics books and tools to
son Robert. Work known – watches, but some of them may be by Robert
junior (it is not generally realised that father and son were of the same
name).

GRINKIN, Robert junior   **London**
Son of Robert senior, b. post-1605, married post-1626. Member of
Blacksmiths' Co. before 1636 and became Assistant there in 1647.
Became Free Brother in CC in 1632. Assistant 1637, Warden from 1640,

Master 1648 and 1654. Gave CC a gift of £5 in 1634. Fined 1638 for not binding aprs. thro' CC. Took as aprs.: (thro' CC) Jul 1638 **Henry Tempest** (thro' T. Dawson); Jun 1642 **Robert Whitwell** (thro' O. Durant) – freed Jan 1649; Mar 1642 **Nicholas Ashwell** (thro' O. Durant) – freed Dec 1649; Apr 1647 **Thomas Smythe** (thro' J. Quash); Jan 1649 **William Jones** (thro' L. Wythe); Jan 1651 **Gregory Dossett** (thro' L. Wythe) – transferred to W. Rogers and freed Apr 1662; Jun 1655 **Nicholas Calvert** (thro' B. Hill); Jul 1659 **William Sandis.** Closely associated with Jeremy Gregory and Simon Bartram with whom in Oct 1655 he shared journeyman **Stephen Jarrey.** Inherited books and tools under his father's will in 1626. Supported CC administration in 1656 rebellion. His house was in Fleet Street 1645-58 and during his Mastership CC Courts were held there. He died in 1661, mentioning in his will his wife Elizabeth, late brother Edmund, *qv*, brothers Francis Hanslapp and Austine Bancks, and his 'very loving friends' John Benson, John Nicasious, Henry Dorsett, John Bayes, Jeremy Gregory, William Rogers. John Benson was a witness. Work known – watches, not many. Signed 'Robert Grinkin of Fleet Street'.

GRINKIN(G), Robert   Exeter (Devon)
Married 1632 Elizabeth Towgood. Issue baptised 1633-44. Was in St. Lawrence parish in 1660. Last heard of 1662/63. Maintained St Peter's church clock in 1649. Work known – none. Seems to have been a different man to Robert Grinkin of London though there are some odd similarities.

GRINKING, Thomas   Exeter
Kept local church clock 1690.

GRIZEL(L), John (signed Grizell)   London
B.c. 1665, apr. Dec 1679 to Alexander Warfield (a clockmaker of the Blacksmiths' Co.) thro' C. Bonner till 1686. Freed Feb 1687. Paid quarterage till 1693. Dead by 1697/98 and prob. died c. 1693.

GROOME, John   Colchester (Essex)
Working c. 1658. Believed died 1691. Work known – longcase clocks. A man of this name became journeyman in 1703 to Andrew Brown of Edinburgh, *qv*, but it hardly seems likely to be the same man.

GROS(SE), Anthony   London
Never officially joined CC but known to them and accepted by them

(unless it is he who is entered in 1632 as **Richard Grose** in error). Took as apr. Aug 1658 **Christopher Desborough** – free Feb 1665/66. Also bound an apr. for Thomas Mills. In 1663/64 refused to serve as Steward for which he was fined. Not heard of thereafter.

GROSE, Richard (or Grove?)   **London**
Admitted to CC 1632, prob. as a Brother.

GROUNDS, Gabriel   **Dutton (Cheshire)**
Married 1698 Mary Sutton of Newton. He died 1724.

GROUT, William   **London**
Apr. Aug 1648 to Joseph Quash. Freed Aug 1660. Took as apr. Feb 1660 **Cornelius Harbert** (alias Harbottle) (from or thro' Davis Mell) – freed Feb 1667/68. Worked in Cornhill.

GROVE, George   **London**
B.c. 1626, apr. Nov 1638 to Robert Parkinson thro' T. Dawson till 1647, but not freed.

GROVE, Richard (see Grose)

GUÉPIN, Abraham   **London**
Watchmaker in Spitalfields Market in 1702.

GUÉPIN, David   **London**
Longcase clock recorded c. 1690. Nothing known of the maker.

GUÉPIN, Isaac   **Lewes (Sussex)**
Married 1697. Working till 1718.

GUÉPIN, John   **London**
B.c. 1673, apr. Jun 1687 to David Minuell an engraver, thro' L. Sindry till 1694, but not freed.

GUÉPIN, Peter   **London**
Bracket clock recorded c. 1700 but another record says c. 1750(?).

GUIGUER, Anthony   **London**
Watchmaker. Made Free Brother in CC Dec 1687. Paid quarterage till c. 1692. In Apr 1695 had an illicit apr. **James Girod**. Work known – watch and bracket clock. Signed 'Anthony Guiguer, London'.

GUIL(L)IN, Ely/Elias (also Gwillin)   London
Free Brother in CC Jan 1647/48.

GURNEY, Ezekiel   London
B.c. 1678, apr. Jan 1692 to Edward Speakman till 1699, but not freed.

GUTCH, John   London
Watch casemaker. Free Brother in CC Apr 1673.

GUVANE, Patrick   Edinburgh
Kept church clock 1552.

GUY, Henry   London
B.c. 1646, apr. Jul 1660 to Lancelot Meredith till 1667 but not freed –
perhaps transferred to Benjamin Hill.

GUY, Samuel   London
B.c. 1678, apr. Sep 1692 to John Andrews of Leadenhall Street till 1699,
but not freed though apparently working till c. 1730. Work known – two
or three longcase clocks, signed 'Samuel Guy, London'.

GUYOTT, Abraham senior (also Gyott)   London
Free Brother in CC May 1648. Took as aprs.: Sep 1648 **Abraham Guyott**
junior (thro' T. Taylor); Nov 1648 **Richard Taylor** (thro' T. Taylor) –
freed Jan 1655; Apr 1653 **Humfrey Wortley** (thro' T. Taylor). In arrears
with quarterage 1664. Work known – none. Maybe worked for Taylor?

GUYOTT, Abraham junior   London
Presumably son of Abraham senior. B.c. 1634, apr. Sep 1648 to
Abraham senior thro' T. Taylor till 1655, but not freed.

GWILLIN (see Guillin)

H

HACK, Grace   **London**
A woman b.c. 1678, apr. Feb 1692 to James Jenkins till 1699 but not freed.

HACKETT, Simon (also Harkett)   **London**
A goldsmith and prob. son of Simon Hackett of the Goldsmiths' Co. who
died in 1620. Free Brother in CC Oct 1632. Took as aprs.: Nov 1631(?)
George Robinson; Nov 1637 **John Hide** (thro' O. Durant); Nov 1638
Thomas Taylor (thro' R. Masterson) – free Aug 1646; Aug 1645
Thomas Bruce (thro' R. Masterson); Sep 1651 **Thomas Wilson** (thro' J.
Bayes) – free Nov 1659; Jul 1654 **Thomas Rotherham** (thro' J. Bayes) –
free Jan 1622/23; May 1660 **Christopher Maynard** (thro' J. Bayes) – free
May 1667. Assistant in CC 1635, Warden from 1637, Master 1646 and
1659. Lived in Cornhill. Died 1664. Work known – various watches one
signed 'Simon Hacke' another 'Simon Hackett of the Royal Exchange
Fecit'.

HADDON, John   **Southam (Warwickshire)**
Clockmaker 1698-1718. Repaired turret clock at Southam and
Leamington Hastings.

HADLEY, Humphrey I   **Birmingham (Warwickshire)**
Blacksmith died 1698, father of Humphrey II.

HADLEY, Humphrey II   **Birmingham (Warwickshire)**
Son of Humphrey I. Working 1702-08. Made several turret clocks incl.
that for Aston church.

HAID, John   **London**
Apr. Mar 1659/60 to Thomas Taylor but not freed.

HAINES, John (also Haynes)   **London**
In Aug 1666 he was warned for practising the trade not having served an
apprenticeship of 7 years. Jul 1676 made a Free Brother.

HALEY, Michael   **Halifax (Yorkshire)**
Repaired church clock 1651.

HALEY, Samuel   **London**
B.c. 1643, apr. Apr 1657 to John Hilderson till 1664, but not freed.

HALL, Christopher   **London**
Apr. Mar 1646/47 to Simon Bartram (thro' T. Alcock) – freed Nov 1655.

HALL, John   **Monks Kirby (Warwickshire)**
Blacksmith? Repaired church clock 1673-1700.

HALL, John Baptist   **London**
B.c. 1656, apr. Nov 1669 to Edward Clough thro' C. Bonner till 1677 but
not freed. In 1680 summoned to CC court regarding infringements
(presumably failure to take up Freedom?). Took as apr. Sep 1705
William Rose (thro' R. George). Believed member of Glaziers' Co. Work
known – longcase clock signed 'John Hall London'.

HALL, Joseph   **London**
B.c. 1670, apr. Jul 1684 to Edward Norris till 1691, but not freed. Work
known – lantern clock signed 'Jos. Hall, London'.

HALL, Peter   **London**
Free Brother in CC Jan 1647/48.

HALL, Ralph   **London**
Free Brother in CC Oct 1638.

HALL, Samuel   **London**
Watch of c. 1680 recorded. Apparently not in CC records.

HALL, Thomas   **London**
B.c. 1662, apr. Mar 1675 to George Hambleton thro' C. Bonner till 1683.

Freed Sep 1695. Paid quarterage till at least 1704. Took as aprs.: Jul 1696 **Samuel Holman**; Mar 1698/99 **Thomas Jewson** (son of Robert Jewson late citizen and Weaver of London, deceased). Work known – longcase clocks signed 'Thomas Hall, London' and 'Thomas Hall, Londini, Fecit'.

HALL, William   London
B.c. 1666, apr. Dec 1680 to Cornelius Harbert till 1687, but not freed.

HALL, William   London
B.c. 1673, apr. Oct 1687 to Thomas Elton till 1694, but not freed.

HALLEWAY, ----   London
Clock and clock-watch recorded c. 1685. See Holloway?

HALLEY, William (see also Hatly?)   London
B.c. 1650, apr. Jul 1663 to Thomas Battin till 1671, but not freed.

HALLING, John   Colchester (Essex)
Repaired cathedral clock bells in 1670.

HALLY, Thomas (see Hatly?)   London
Bracket clock recorded c. 1660, watch c. 1675, and at least two longcase clocks c. 1720, yet apparently a maker not known in CC archives. But see Hatley.

HALSEY, George (*cf* Halshey)   London
B.c. 1666, apr. Aug 1680 to Sarah widow of Nicholas Payne till 1687. Freed Feb 1687/88. Took as apr. Aug 1692 **Joseph Pinder**. Paid quarterage till c. 1697 but dead by 1698.

HALSEY, Richard   London
Late 17th century watch recorded by Baillie. Apparently not in CC archives.

HALSHEY, Henry (*cf* Halsey)   Lancaster
Watchmaker. Died 1683.

HALSTAFFE, Peter   Exeter
Clockmaker 1657-80.

HALSTEAD, Charles   London
B.c. 1656, apr. Jul 1670 to Richard Halstead till 1677. Freed Sep 1677.
Took as aprs.: May 1678 **Henry Holdcroft;** Jun 1683 **Christopher
Egleton** later passed to C. Lee and freed Nov 1695; Feb 1688-89 **Walter
Watts** – freed Mar 1695/96; Apr 1692 **Daniel Delander** later passed to
T. Tompion and Freed Jul 1699; Feb 1697/98 **John Hitchcock** – freed
Jun 1718; Jul 1702 **Joseph Boult** (son of John Boult late of London,
leather seller, deceased) – freed Jun 1710; in Apr 1705 his widow
Dorothy took his son **William Halstead** – freed Nov 1715, died 1705.

HALSTEAD, John   London
Son of Robert. Free in CC by patrimony Jul 1698. Working till at least
1712. Work known – watches and longcase clocks.

HALSTEAD, Richard   London
B.c. 1647, apr. Nov 1661 to Nathaniel Chamberlain till 1668. Freed Mar
1669/70. Took as aprs.: Jul 1670 **Charles Halstead** – freed Sep 1677;
Dec 1671 **John Lagoe** – sent away in Aug 1673 and took instead **Henry
Street;** Sep 1676 **Benjamin Jones** passed on Apr 1678 to Edward East as
Richard Halstead had died.

HALSTEAD, Robert   London
Apr. to Richard Nau then transferred to Isaac Daniel, freed Jul 1668
(prob. not bound thro' CC). Took as aprs.: Apr 1670 **Amos Winch** –
freed Jul 1677; Jun 1671 **John Bell;** Feb 1671/72 **Samuel Conduitt;** May
1675 **Robert Saunders;** Sep 1679 **John Trubshaw** – freed Jan 1686/87;
Jun 1684 **Joseph Bell** later passed on to J. Trubshaw; Apr 1690 **Ralph
Miller** – freed Nov 1697; Dec 1691 **Francis Still** – freed Mar 1698/99;
May 1701 **Thomas Vernon** (son of Daniel Vernon late of Church
?Minchell, County Chester, farmer) – freed Aug 1708; Feb 1710/11 **John
Halstead;** Jul 1714 **Nathan Tilly.** His son John was freed by patrimony
in Jul 1698 and his son George (who had a right to Freedom in another
Company) was freed by patrimony Mar 1710/11. Was a goldsmith at the
Crown and Dial (or Golden Crown) in Fleet Street between Water Lane
and Salisbury Court where he sold watches, eg by Tompion. In 1684 he
was left a ring in the will of Thomas Taylor, *qv.* In Mar 1682/83 the CC
seized two bad watch movements from his shop. He denied they were his
work but claimed he took them in part exchange – they were smashed. By
1712 he was prosperous enough to buy some stocks from the CC. Became
Assistant 1698. Warden from 1696, Master 1699, and attended till 1720.
However, in Apr 1717 he advised the CC that he was

going to live in the country and was unlikely to attend future Courts, but notices for him could be left at his son's house. Work known – watches.

HALTON, ---- Carlisle (Cumberland)
Repaired cathedral clock in 1677 – may be Halling, *qv*.

HAM, John London
B.c. 1659, apr. Mar 1673/74 to George Stevens thro' Danield Stevens till 1680, but not freed.

HAMBLETON, George (sometimes Hamilton) London
Free Brother CC Mar 1669/70. Took as aprs.: Jul 1671 **Thomas Elfes** (thro' L. Wythe); Mar 1674/75 **Thomas Hall** (thro' C. Bonner). Free Sep 1695; Oct 1680 **James Smythies** (thro' C. Bonner). Died before Jan 1685/86 when his widow began to receive CC pension which she drew until 1694. Work known – a watch c. 1660 by 'George Hamilton'.

HAMDEN, John London
B.c. 1625, apr. Dec 1638 to John Charlton, thro' T. Dawson till 1644, but not freed.

HAMILTON, George (see Hambleton)

HAMILTON, George London
B.c. 1677, apr. Aug 1690 to Nathaniel Delander till 1698. But not freed.

HAMLIN, Richard London
Made a faulty watch seized by CC 1676/77. See also under John Parker and John Pinson.

HAMLYN, Thomas London
B.c. 1624, apr. Jul 1638 thro' T. Dawson to Edward Bisse a Freeman of the Coopers' Co., till 1645. Never actually admitted to CC but known to them. Prob. dead by 1662/63.

HAMMOND, Anthony London
B.c. 1667, apr. Nov 1681 to John North till 1688, but not freed.

HAMMOND, Henry London
Apr. Oct 1672 to Nathaniel Barrow. Freed Jul 1680. Took as aprs.: Mar

1686/87 **Nathaniel Beseley** later passed on to J. Willoughby; Dec 1691 **Morris Hughes** later passed on to T. Bates. Paid quarterage till at least 1705.

HAMMOND, John   **London**
B.c. 1663, apr. Apr 1676 to Henry Merryman till 1684 but not freed.

HAMMOND, Samuel   **Battle (Sussex)**
B. 1668 son of John Hammond, ironmonger and gunpowder manufacturer. Married 1691. Only child Mary b. 1694. Worked on church clock at Battle, and made new chiming clock for Rye church in 1718 with four tunes and six bells. Took as aprs.: 1712 **Samuel Jemmett**; 1719 **John Petter**; 1726 **John Brook**. Died 1736. Widow died 1750. Work known – several 30 hour longcase clocks.

HAMMOND, Valentine   **Dublin**
Apr. 1658 to G. Southwark. Working c. 1665.

HAMPSCHER, William   **Bungay (Suffolk)**
Paid for work on church clock in 1568.

HAMPTON, Edward (signed Hamptonne)   **London**
B.c. 1660, son of Nicholas Hampton of Jersey, County Hants, deceased, apr. in Vintners' Co. to Andrew Low till 1681. Freed there Oct 1681. Also apr. thro' CC Jul 1674 thro' Andrew Low of Vintners' Co., but to serve Abraham Thomeguez clockmaker. Agreed in 1677 to become a Brother in CC when apprenticeship ends – but never did. Work known – a watch is on record.

HAMPTON, John   **Norwich**
Free there Feb 1563 as a locksmith. Repaired St. Peter Mancroft church clock 1580.

HAMPTON, Joseph   place not known
Longcase clock on record c. 1700.

HANBURY, John   **London**
B.c. 1650 apr. 1664 to Henry Jones till 1671, but not freed.

HANCOCK, Edward London
Watch recorded c. 1680. Not known to CC. Perhaps an error for Hampton?

HANCORNE, James London
B.c. 1661, apr. Mar 1675/76 to Philip Buckner till 1682, but not freed.

HANCORNE, Thomas London
B.c. 1637, apr. Sep 1650 to Thomas Taylor (of Essex House Gate) till 1658. Freed Apr 1659. Took as aprs.: Oct 1664 **Richard Gilbert;** Jun 1696 **Francis Haines** – freed Jul 1707; Jun 1698 **James Reith** – freed Apr 1706. Also bound an apr. for Daniel Beckman (Taylor's son-in-law). In 1684 was left a ring in the will of Thomas Taylor. Made CC Assistant from 1676, but oddly never became Warden or Master. In 1709 was 'now sick and in want' and was given a CC pension of 5/– a week, which he kept till his death about 1716. It was then paid to his widow who died about Oct 1719. Work known – none. Prob. worked as a journeyman for Taylor.

HANCORNE, William London
B.c. 1655 (prob. son of Thomas), apr. Jul 1668 to Thomas Taylor (by Essex House Gate) till 1676. Freed Jul 1676. Took as apr. Jul 1678 **Richard Gilkes** who was transferred Dec 1678 to B. Bell as Hancorne 'absenteth' (had left), and not heard of again.

HANDE, Thomas (perhaps Hanen?) London
Two watches on record. Some confusion whether his name was Hande or Hanen, the latter listed as working at Chancery Lane in 1662.

HANDS, Richard Stretton-on-Dunsmore (Warwickshire)
Blacksmith who repaired Monks Kirby church clock 1697-1719.

HANEN, Thomas (see Hande)

HANSLAPP, Robert (also Hanslope) London
Apr. Oct 1646 to Edward East thro' T. Alcock. Freed Mar 1653/54. Took as aprs.: Jun 1654 **William Hanslapp** – freed Jul 1663; Jun 1659 **William Cornish.** Perhaps related to Robert Grinkin junior, *qv*.

HANSLAPP, William (alias Williams?) London
Apr. Jul 1654 to Robert Hanslapp. Freed Jul 1663. Buried 1690 at St.

Mary Abbots, Kensington 'William Hanslip alias Williams, clockmaker who died at his cousin Taylor's house, being ye Crown Inn Kensington'.

HANSON, George **London**
B.c. 1674, apr. Jul 1688 to John Clowes thro' D. Stevens till 1695. Freed Mar 1695/96. Took as apr. Dec 1697 **John Jackler.** In 1696 was to be punished 'for being admitted at Guildhall (as City Freeman?) without presentment of the Warden'. Dead by Feb 1718/19 when widow Mary took their son **George Hanson** as apr.

HANWELL, Zachariah **London**
B.c. 1672, apr. Jan 1686/87 to Richard Wise thro' T. Morgan till 1693. Freed Jul 1694. Took as aprs.: Feb 1695/96 **Samuel Mercer;** Sep 1702 **Edward Westbury** (son of John Westbury of Warwick City, cordwainer). Note the Wises and Hanwell had Warwick connection. Paid quarterage till at least 1705. Work known – longcase clocks signed 'Z. Hanwell, Londini'.

HARBAR, Jasper **London**
An invented name engraved on a watch by Jasper Harmer (*qv*) which the CC confiscated in 1682.

HARBERT, Cornelius senior (also Herbert) **London**
His real name was Harbert, misspelt as Harbottle, later often simplified further to Herbert and misspelt Harplett. B.c. 1645, apr. Apr 1659 to David Mell but re-apr. Feb 1660/61 to William Grout. Freed Feb 1667/68. Took as aprs.: Apr 1671 **Thomas Drew** – dismissed him May 1672 as he was 'incapable of learning his trade' and instead took **Thomas Campe;** Nov 1674 **Joshua Scott;** Oct 1675 **Richard Holloway;** Dec 1680 **William Hall;** Sep 1686 **Thomas Freeman** (later passed (1688) to Thomas Meades); Jan 1690/91 his son **Cornelius Harbert** – freed Mar 170/01; May 1692 **Edward Falconer** – freed Sep 1702; Sep 1695 **John Hawkins;** Sep 1700 **William Cleeter** (son of George Cleeter of St. Brides, London, Framework knitter) – freed Aug 1709; Nov 1702 **Edward Archer** (son of James Archer late of Shadwell, Middlesex, mariner, deceased). Thereafter it is difficult to tell whether aprs. are the father's or the son's though most were the son's. Worked at London Bridge. Still alive 1705. Work known – a watch.

HARBERT, Cornelius, junior　　　　　　　　**London**
Son of Cornelius senior. Name suffered same changes as father's. B.c.
1676, apr. Jan 1690-91 to father till 1697. Freed Mar 1700/01. Took as
aprs.: Aug 1701 **Robert Currier** (son of John Currier of Little Ravely,
County Hunts, yeoman); Jul 1702 **John Spencer** (son of Joseph Spencer
of Hadley, Suffolk, Gent.); Jun 1708 **Joseph Hinde**; Jul 1712 **John
Watson**; no doubt others after 1720. Believed lived till 1715. Took his
son Cornelius III apr. in 1727. Worked at London Bridge. Work known
– longcase clock.

HARBOTLE (see Harbert)

HARCOURT,　　　　　　　　**London**
Clock repairer near Westminster Abbey 1469.

HARDINGE, Francis　　　　　　　　**London/Portsmouth**
B.c. 1659, apr. Apr 1673 to Edward Clement till 1680. Freed Apr 1687.
Paid no quarterage after 1687. A maker of this name is recorded at Portsmouth c. 1700. Work known – longcase clock signed 'Francis Hardinge,
Portsmouth'.

HARDINGE, John　　　　　　　　**London**
B.c. 1662. Free Brother in CC Sep 1685 a **'great clockmaker'**. Paid no
quarterage after 1685. In Jan 1692/93 John Hardinge of St. Martin in the
Fields, clockmaker, Batchelor aged 31 married Mrs. Frances Wilmott of
St. James, Westminster, widow aged 30 at Putney. Still alive 1697, but
not heard of after that.

HAR(D)STAFF(E), Zachariah　　　　　　　　**London**
B.c. 1643, apr. Apr 1655 to John Sammon till 1664, but not freed.

HARFORD, John　　　　　　　　**Bath**
Data confused. A lantern clock is recorded supposedly dated 1658, but
perhaps this is a slip for 1758 as one of this name worked there in the
1730-70 period.

HARGROVE, William　　　　　　　　**London/Settle (Yorkshire)**
B.c. 1674, apr. Oct 1688 to Isaac Carver thro' J. Weeks till 1695, but not
freed. A William Hargreaves is recorded at Settle (Yorks) c. 1710-30, but
this may be too early a dating of a man who worked there from c. 1750.
Work known – longcase clocks are known by the Settle maker from c. 1750.

HARINGTON, Thomas (alias Clerke) **Henley-on-Thames (Oxfordshire)**
Clock-keeper, 1494-1515.

HARKAM(?), Thomas London
Working 1697. Prob. badly written for Hancorne, *qv*.

HARKETT (see Hacket)

HARLAND, Henry London
Apr. Oct 1647 to William Godbed, transferred Oct 1650 to Peter De
Laune. Freed Nov 1654. Took as aprs.: Jun 1656 **Wombwell
Wentworth**; Aug 1664 **Tobias Smeeton**. All these names, Harland,
Wentworth, Smeeton – have Yorkshire connections.

HARLEY, Joseph Wingrave (Buckinghamshire)
Late 17th century longcase clock recorded.

HARMAN, John Horsham (Sussex)
A lantern clock recorded. See under John Harmer?

HARMER, Jasper (also Harmar) (also James) London
An ironmonger nr. Smithfield Bars. In Mar 1682/83 some unfinished
watch movements were confiscated by CC from his shop as they had
suspect names (Ambrose Smith – Stamford, William Burges fecit and
Jasper Harbar, London) and also he had not served an apprenticeship.
He refused to acknowledge the authority of the CC and was to be
prosecuted. In Mar 1685/86 the CC again had complaints about him for
practising when not trained. One of this name is recorded in 1730 at
Islington. Work known – a watch and a month longcase clock, signed
'Jasper Harmer, London'.

HARMER, John (also Harman?) London
B.c. 1667 apr. Dec 1680 to Thomas Jenkins till 1688, but not freed.

HARPER, Henry (also Harpur) London
Apr. Jul 1657 to Humfrey Peirce. Freed Aug 1664. Took as aprs.: Apr
1667 **Thomas Bennett**; Sep 1671 **Thomas Whittle** – freed Jul 1683; Sep
1673 **Charles Huddlestone**; May 1679 **Joseph Franklin**; Dec 1682
Thomas Smith; Thomas Chamberlaine (from Samuel Rosse) – freed
Jan 1687-88; May 1691 **Thomas Hyde**; Aug 1696 **Richard Allen** (son of
John Allen of Pangbourne, Co. Berks. gent). Worked in Cornhill. In

1687 CC accused him of employing various Frenchmen and also a workman who had never been apr., but he accused the CC of doing the same themselves and they decided to prosecute him. In Apr 1688 he brought a law suit against them to question the legality of their enforcing quarterage. In Jul 1688 the CC confiscated 12 steel watch chains from his shop in Cornhill and destroyed them as inadequate work. He sued them for trespass in his shop. Made CC Assistant from 1682 but hardly ever attended and only then when forced to and after 1688 he did not attend at all. Paid his quarterage till 1703. Reputedly died in 1708, though I cannot confirm this. Work known – watches, longcase clocks signed 'Henry Harper, London' and sometimes 'Henry Harpur, London'.

HARPLETT, Cornelius (see Harbert)

HARRALD, Richard (sometimes Harold) London
B.c. 1668, apr. Nov 1682 to Richard Warren till 1689. Freed May 1690. Took as aprs.: May 1691 **Conan Mowtlow** – freed Jul 1700; Sep 1695 **William Fell** – freed Jan 1705/06; Feb 1703/04 **John Lee**. Working till at least 1704.

HARRIS (see also Harrys)

HARRIS, ---- London
An Ironmonger at the Maypole in the Strand – had faulty rulers seized by CC Mar 1672/73, one tenth of an inch too long on a two foot rule. Prob. not a clockmaker but a measure seller who came under CC control.

HARRIS, Anthony London
Great clockmaker. Free Brother Jan 1683/84.

HARRIS, Benjamin London
Apr. (prob. thro' Blacksmiths' Co.) to John Dyde, a Free Blacksmith, and then transferred to Thomas Tompion, freed Aug 1677. Took as apr. **Thomas Roycroft** from C. Lee – freed Nov 1699. Dead by Apr 1704 when his widow, Sarah, took apr. (thro' Richard George) **William Lens** (son of Barnard Lens, of London, Citizen and Haberdasher) – freed Apr 1712.

HARRIS, Charles London
B.c. 1673, apr. Aug 1686 to Robert Webster till 1694. Freed Aug 1695.

Took as aprs.: **Henry Cole** (thro' R. Webster), Jul 1700 **Kirby Golton** (son of Edward Golton, Citizen and Weaver) (thro' R. George).

HARRIS, Charles London
B.c. 1673, son of John Harris (I?) clockmaker, apr. to his father Jul 1687, but not freed. (This may perhaps be the same man as the previous entry.)

HARRIS, Ebenezer London
B.c. 1668, apr. Dec 1682 to Benjamin Bell till 1689, but not freed.

HARRIS, Francis William London
B.c. 1675, apr. Sep 1689 to Thomas East, transferred Sep 1691 to William Simcox till 1698. Freed Jul 1702. Last heard of in 1713 when he was excused arrears of quarterage on account of his poverty. Baillie records him in 1725, which I cannot confirm.

HARRIS, George Fritwell (Oxfordshire)
B.c. 1619, son of Jeffrey Harris of Fritwell. Issue by first marriage b. 1643-51. Married secondly 1654 Betteris Toms at Chipping Norton and has issue 1655-66. Died Jun 1694 leaving will. Succeeded by son Nicholas, *qv*. In 1669 and 1682 repaired local church clocks and made church clock for Hanwell in 1671. Work known – lantern clocks with unique key-wind feature signed 'George Harris in Fritwell, fecit' and 'George Harris of Fritwell, 1668'.

HARRIS, George London
B.c. 1654, apr. Aug 1668 to Thomas Long till 1675, but freed Jan 1674-75. (George Harris springmaker made a free clockmaker by redemption on order of the Lord Mayor!). Took as aprs.: Mar 1674-75 **William Young** – freed Apr 1682; **James Hatchman** (from T. Long) later transferred to John Harris. Dead by Jan 1680-81 when widow, Mary, took **William Mason** – freed Apr 1688. Work known – prob. not identifiable.

HARRIS, George London
Watchmaker in Cripplegate, married in 1699, according to Baillie but I do not know his source.

HARRIS, Jacob London
B.c. 1632, apr. Nov 1646 to David Bouquett, thro' J. Quash, till 1653, but not freed.

HARRIS, Jeffrey   **London**
Bracket clock recorded c. 1700 signed 'Jeffrey Harris, London'. No
other details. Apparently not recorded in CC archives.

HARRIS, John   **Burford (Oxfordshire)**
Working 1631. Nothing else known.

HARRIS, John (of Westminster)   **London**
Believed boxmaker (ie watch cases). An original 1622 petitioner for CC.
One of first Assistants in 1632. Warden from 1633 (but refused to serve),
Master 1641 and 1644-45. Apparently attended till c. 1651/52. Believed
still working 1662 at Westminster. (Baillie has 'died 1655' which must be
wrong). Had as aprs.: **John Champion** – freed by 1651; took Aug 1641
John Thorpe (thro' O. Durant) – freed Jul 1657; Oct 1658 **James Lello**
(thro' R. Williamson) – freed Oct 1666. Supported administration in
1656 rebellion.

HARRIS, John (of Holborne Bridge)   **London**
Clockmaker and Freeman of the Blacksmiths' Co. Apprenticed to
William Petty. Freed Jan 1659-60. Worked at Holborn Bridge. Took as
aprs.: Nov 1661 **Thomas Williamson** – freed Jan 1668-69; Jan 1666/67
Richard Pepys – freed Mar 1673/74; Apr 1669 **Francis Knollys;** May
1670 **Thomas East** – freed 1677; Sep **Henry Badger** (but dismissed him
Dec 1672); Jan 1672/73 **John Pepys** – freed Apr 1680; May 1675 **William
Goodwin;** Sep 1679 **Robert Clements** – freed Sep 1686; **Philip Browne** –
freed Apr 1688; Jul 1682 **Philip Lynam;** Jul 1687 son Charles Harris; his
nephew **John Harris** – (free of the Blacksmiths' Co.) was freed May
1690; 1691-92 **Thomas Shield.** Worked at Holborne Bridge. Assistant
from 1676, Warden 1684, Master 1689, attended till c. 1708. Was a
'cozen' of Thomas Dyde, watchmaker, in his 1686 will. Lent money to
CC. Work known – bracket clocks signed 'John Harris, London'. The
various John Harrises are very difficult to distinguish.

HARRIS, John (nephew)   **London**
Watchmaker, Freeman of the Blacksmiths' Co. and nephew of John
Harris of Holborne Bridge. Free Brother in CC May 1690. Paid
quarterage till 1697, but dead by 1698. Took as apr. Jul 1693 **James
Hayes** (thro' N. Russell). Work known – a longcase clock may be by this
man.

HARRIS, John **London**
B.c. 1678, apr. Nov 1692 to Humfrey Maysmor of the Blacksmiths' Co.
thro' N. Russell – not freed.

HARRIS, John **Oxford** and **London**
Son of John Harris, chandler of Oxford. B.c. 1656, apr. Jul 1668 to
Michael Bird till 1678. Freed Feb 1678 at Oxford but freed as a Brother
in CC Aug 1677. Paid quarterage to CC 1677 to 1682. Took as apr. in CC
Aug 1677 **John Spurrier** (thro' S. Davis) – freed 1684-85. Took as aprs.
at Oxford: 1680 **Hugh Broadwater**; 1682 **Robert Veasey**. Work known
– watch signed 'Harris – Oxon'.

HARRIS, Mary **London**
Widow of George, *qv*.

HARRIS, Nicholas **Fritwell (Oxfordshire)**
Whitesmith and clock- and watchmaker. B. 1657 third son of George
Harris of Fritwell. Succ. father and inherited his tools in 1694. Married
1695 Elizabeth X. Died 20 May 1738. Worked on several local church
clocks. Work known – a lantern clock.

HARRIS, Richard **London**
In 1641 said to have made clock for St. Paul's, Covent Garden with a
pendulum, but this seems to be unreliable and I cannot confirm his
existence. Apparently not known thro' CC archives. A late 17th century
bracket clock is recorded, but signed 'Richard Harris, London'. See next
entry.

HARRIS, Richard **London**
B.c. 1679, apr. Jul 1693 to Thomas Brafield till 1700, but not freed.

HARRIS, Robert **London**
Longcase clock recorded c. 1700. Nothing else known.

HARRIS, Thomas (sometimes Harrys) **London**
Member of the Blacksmiths' Co., apparently with little or no connection
with CC. Said to have worked in Water Lane (and a Mr. Harris in Water
Lane did pay search fee in 1671). Said to have made turret clock for St.
Dunstan's in the West, Fleet Street in 1671 with jacks (Gog and Magog)
to strike the quarters and a double dial. Took as apr. **Thomas Hickson**,
later passed to Thomas Speakman and freed Jan 1690/91. Work known –

longcase, lantern and bracket clocks signed 'Thomas Harris in ye Strand Londini'.

HARRISON, Anthony   **London**
B.c. 1679, apr. Apr 1693 to Joanna May, widow, till 1700. Freed Sep 1701. Took as aprs.: May 1706 **Thomas Cox** (son of William Cox late Citizen and Cooper, deceased); Sep 1716 **Edward Ellis** (or Ells); Jun 1717 son **Thomas Harrison**. Said to have still be working in 1726. Work known – a watch.

HARRISON, George   **London**
B.c. 1675, apr. Nov 1689 to Joanna May, widow, till 1696, but later (pre-1695) transferred to Thomas Tompion – freed Jul 1698. Took as aprs.: Jul 1699 **John Cogger** (son of John Cogger of (?) Great Anstale in co. (illegible, Cor....) – free Aug 1706; Dec 1704 **Samuel How** (son of Thomas How, late of London, bricklayer, deceased); Jan 1711/12 **William Johnson**; Sep 1713 **John Bunce**; Oct 1716 **Richard Dean**; Mar 1719/20 **Daniel Rosbotham** (Roebotham?). Work known – watch and longcase clock signed 'Harrison, London' prob. by him.

HARRISON, Thomas   **Chester**
Watchmaker. Buried Apr 1686.

HARRISON, William   **London**
B.c. 1678, apr. Jan 1692-93 to Richard Blundell thro' F. Raynsford till 1699. Freed Nov 1700. Took as aprs.: Nov 1700 **John Cheney** (son of Francis Cheney late of Newgate Street, gent., deceased); May 1703 **Robert Tonycliffe** (son of Ralph Tonycliffe late of parish of St. Andrew Undershaft, London, deceased).

HARRYS, Thomas (see Harris)

HARRYS, William   **Rye (Sussex)**
Clockmaker. Buried there May 1559.

HAR(T)FORD, John   **London**
Joined CC 1632 (as Brother?). In 1639 was a subscriber as Hardford. In 1649 was Assistant as Harford.

HARTLEY, ----   **London**
Recorded by Britten as trading in watches when untrained in New Street, Shoe Lane. I cannot confirm this (see Hatley).

HARTWELL, Francis   London
B.c. 1664, apr. Apr 1678 to D. Stevens till 1685, but not freed.

HARV(E)Y, Benjamin (also Munday)   London
B.c. 1650, apr. Jan 1661/62 to Joseph Munday till 1672, but not freed.

HARVEY, John   London
B.c. 1677, apr. Jan 1691/92 to Philip Corderoy (thro' E. Norris) till 1698, but not freed.

HARVEY, Robert   Oxford
Free there Sep 1588 as a clockmaker. One of this name went with the organ-builder Thomas Dallam to Constantinople to deliver his musical clock. Dallam also known to have made organs for Oxford Colleges. Work known – a balance wheel wall clock, early 17th century signed 'Robertus Harvie', dial engraving signed 'G.D.'.

HARVEY, Samuel   London
B.c. 1673, apr. Nov 1686 to Samuel Clyatt till 1694. Freed Jul 1696. Working till at least 1700. Work known – a watch.

HARVEY, Thomas   Colchester (Essex)
Clockmaker in St. Nicholas parish. Will dated 1678, proved 1679. Also ship-owner. No work known. Sons John, Thomas and William mentioned and daughter Hannah Brunton.

HARVIE, William   Wigan (Lancashire)
Repaired church clock 1651. Prob. a blacksmith.

HARWOOD, Benjamin   London
Supposedly in Blacksmiths' Co. 1626.

HASLUCK, Jacob   London
Watch of c. 1695 recorded – at 'St John Street'. I cannot confirm this.

HASSENIUS, James (signed Jacobus)   London
Alien watchmaker made a Free Brother in CC Jan 1682/83. In 1685 warned for not binding his apprentices thro' CC. Took in May **Samuel Bryan** (thro' D. Stevens). Paid quarterage till about 1697. Reputedly went in 1698 to Russia, his native country – I cannot confirm this. Work known – bracket clock and watches signed 'Jacobus Hassenius'. Late

17th century watches and longcase clocks signed 'I Hasius – Amsterdam' may be by him?

HATCH, George   **Hatfield**
Reputedly in CC c. 1690, but I cannot trace him.

HATCH, John   **London**
B.c. 1671, apr. Apr 1685 to Henry Wynne till 1692. Freed Jul 1693, though paid no quarterage thereafter.

HATCHMAN, James   **London**
B.c. 1659, apr. Sep 1673 to Thomas Long. Later passed to George Harris then to John Harris till 1680. Freed Jan 1680-81. Took as aprs.: Mar 1682/83 **John Godfrey;** Apr 1688 **Robert Trippet;** Jun 1693 **Robert Taylor** (son of blank Taylor of Reading, cutler, deceased); Mar 1694/95 **John Dercy** (thro' E. Burgess); Dec 1698 **John Haynes** (son of John Haynes, Citizen and girdler). Still working Dec 1719 when excused arrears of quarterage 'being very poor'.

HATLY, ----   **London**
'Sword cutler in New Street near Shoe Lane who maketh pin cases and tradeth in watches and clocks'. Accused in May 1680 for not having served an apprenticeship in the trade. Could this be Thomas or William Hally, *qv*.

HATTON, John   **London**
Never actually admitted into CC but known to them by 1646. Prob. dead or gone by 1662.

HAUGHTIN, Richard (also Haughton)   **London**
B.c. 1668, apr. Mar 1682-83 to Richard Wise till 1689. Freed Mar 1690/91. Took as aprs.: Jul 1692 **John Hill** (son of Richard Hill) – freed Apr 1703; Jul 1695 **John Hughes** – freed Apr 1704; Mar 1707/08 **Thomas Boswell.** Work known – longcase clock signed 'Richard Haughton, Londini fecit'.

HAVEN, Robert   **London**
Recorded as 1657 by Britten but I cannot confirm this.

HAVEN, Thomas   **Chelmsford/London**
Freed in CC Jan 1652/53 having been the servant of Thomas Chamberlayne at Chelmsford for 10 years.

HAVES, Peter   **London**
Baillie has 1662, which I cannot confirm.

HAWKE, Christopher (also Hocke)   **Bodmin (Cornwall)**
Married 1661 Eustes Blake at Bodmin. Repaired tower clock at
Lostwithiel in 1671. In 1673 made new clock for St. Naunter's chapel for
£6.

HAWKES, Susan   **London**
B.c. 1669, apr. Sep 1683 (thro' S. Davis) to John Lowe and Mary his wife
till 1690 but not freed. Prob. not engaged in clock trade.

HAWKINS, Ambrose   **Wells (Somerset)/Exeter (Devon)**
At Wells in 1690. Moved to Exeter between 1692-95. Set up shop in
Cathedral precincts. Repaired Cathedral clock, and made several other
local church clocks. He died there 1705. His widow, Anne, died some
time before 1711. Work known – four or five longcase clocks of
outstanding quality including two month longcases and a three train six
bell clock and a grande-sonnerie longcase, signed 'Ambrose Hawkins de
Exon fecit' and 'Amb. Hawkins, Exon'. A lantern clock recorded signed
'Ambrose Hawkins de Wells fecit'. A longcase signed 'Ann Hawkins
Exeter', maybe his widow?

HAWKINS, George   **London**
B.c. 1674, apr. May 1688 to Benjamin Wright till 1695, but not freed.

HAWKINS, John   **Exeter**
Recorded as c. 1680-1704, but I cannot confirm this. Perhaps an error for
Ambrose, *qv*.

HAWKINS, John   **London/Southampton**
B.c. 1681, apr. Sep 1695 to Cornelius Harbert till 1702, but not freed.
One of this name is recorded at Southampton later and see also previous
entry.

HAWKINS, Mark senior   **Newmarket/Bury St. Edmunds**
B. about 1674, Newmarket. Married 1700 at Bury Mary Deave. Various
issue there 1702-11 incl. 1703 William and 1707 Mark who became
clockmakers. Died at Nowton 11 Mar 1749/50 aged 76. Widow Mary
died 1752 aged 81. Work known – lantern and longcase clocks and
watches. Known to have made church clocks.

HAWKINS, Richard London
B.c. 1663, apr. Sep 1677 to William Fuller till 1684, but not freed.

HAWKINS, William London
B.c. 1662, apr. Aug 1676 to Francis Dinnis, engraver, till 1683. Freed Jun 1684. Took as apr. Sep 1685 **George Twell** – not freed. Not heard of after 1690. Work known – a longcase clock is on record.

HAWLEY, Henry London
Clockmaker. Free Brother in CC Mar 1671/72. In May 1680 'being sick and poor' was granted 30/- charity from CC and 30/- more in Jul, he being 'still under languishing sickness and in extreme want'. In Sep 1680 his widow got a further 10/-.

HAWTYEN, Samuel London
B.c. 1676, apr. Jan 1690/91 (thro' J. Papworth) to John Wise junior till 1697, but not freed.

HAYDEN, John (signed thus) Croydon
Watchmaker. In Sep 1687 promised to become a Brother in CC at next Court but not heard of again. Presumably connected with William.

HAYDON, John Exeter
Lanternmaker who kept local church clock 1585-1609. Died 1614.

HAYDON, William Croydon/London
Watchmaker of Croydon (with John Howes) made a Free Brother in CC Aug 1687. Took as apr. Jul 1691 **John Manchester** (thro' D. Stevens) – free Apr 1700. Paid quarterage till at least 1703. Work known – lantern clock signed 'William Haydon, London'.

HAYES, Edmond London
B.c. 1661, apr. Sep 1675 to Joshua Short till 1682. Freed Jan 1682/83.

HAYES, James London
B.c. 1679, apr. Jul 1693 to John Harris (a Freeman of the Blacksmiths' Co.) thro' N. Russell till 1700, but not freed.

HAYES, John London
B.c. 1662, apr. Sep 1676 to James Woverstone, an engraver, and Freeman of the Barber Chirurgeons' Co., thro' S. Davis, till 1683, but not freed.

HAYES, Walter London
A mat. inst. maker and Freeman of another Co. but made a Free Brother
in CC Feb 1667-68. Assistant from 1669, Warden from 1679, Master
1680. Last attended 1687. He was excused wardenship in 1677 as he is
'often and long out of town' on his affairs. In 1671/72 a Mr. Hayes
'ironmonger' paid search fee. Work known – a sundial dated 1670,
signed 'Walter Hayes at the Cross Daggers in Moorfields, Londini
Fecit'. (I cannot understand Baillie's 1654 date and his 'died 1685' is
clearly wrong.)

HAYES, William London
B.c. 1672, apr. Nov 1686 to Daniel Le Conte (Freeman of the
Haberdashers' Co.) thro' R. Williamson till 1693, but not freed.

HAYLE(S), ---- Ipswich (Suffolk)
Finished the Boroughgate clock in 1629 (ie the Old Goal Clock) – paid
40/-. See next entry?

HAYLE, ---- London
Watch recorded 'Th. Hayle in Popeshead Alley' c. 1650. May be
previous maker?

HAYNES, John (see Haines)

HAYNES, William Buckingham
Clockmaker. Son William bap. there in 1702 (died 1704). Perhaps the
man in the next entry.

HAYNES, William London
B.c. 1666, apr. Nov 1680 to Thomas Williamson, thro' E. Bridgeman till
1687. Freed Feb 1703. Prob. worked for Williamson till then. See also
previous entry.

HAYTER, William London
B.c. 1671, apr. Dec 1685 to John Parker till 1682. Freed Feb 1694. Paid
quarterage till 1699.

HEADY, George London
B.c. 1661, apr. Aug 1675 to Daniel Quare, thro' S. Davis till 1682. Freed
Sep 1682. In Jul 1685 bound an apr. for Samuel Bowtell.

HEARNE, ---- London
Supposedly a 1630 subscriber for incorporation of CC but I cannot trace him – see Helyn?

HEARN(E), Joseph (see also Herne) London
B.c. 1676, apr. Jul 1690 to Cornelius Jenkins, till 1697, but not freed.

HEATH, Benjamin London
B.c. 1647, apr. Sep 1661 to Charles Rogers till 1668, but not freed.

HEATHCOCK, Timothy London
Free Brother in CC Jul 1698. Paid quarterage till 1705 at least.

HEATHCOTE, Timothy (error for Heathcock, *qv*).

HEATHER, William London
Received 10 shillings charity from CC in 1701/02 but not clear whether he was a clockworker.

HEBAT (see Hebert)

HEBDITCH, Richard Bristol
Made clock for cathedral 1630.

HEBERT, Abraham (watch for Herbert) London
B.c. 1634, apr. Aug 1648 to David Bouquett till 1655, but not freed.

HEBERT, Anthoine London
Watchmaker at Moorfields 1670. Porter Street 1690, Horse Shoe Alley, Shoreditch 1701. One such in CC 1725, strangely late. Work known – longcase and bracket clock.

HEBERT, James (signed Hebat) London/Brighton
Watchmaker. Made a Free Brother Sep 1682. One such recorded at Brighton c. 1716.

HECHSTETTER, Joseph London
(also Heckstetter and Hockstetter)
B.c. 1674, apr. Jun 1687 to William Cattell till 1685. Freed Jan 1694/95. Took as aprs.: May 1697 **Samuel Bridges** (who served John Berry, engraver) – freed Aug 1704; Jun 1699 **Job Hobbins** from R. Thacke; Jan

1699/1700 **Edward Woollard** (son of John Woollard of Cambridge, grocer). Paid quarterage till 1702.

HECKET, John   Stratton (Cornwall)
Kept church clock 1584.

HECKETT/HICKETT, Thomas   Stratton (Cornwall)
Repaired church clock 1529. Married 1538 at Poughill. Died 1572.

HEDDON, ----   Stratton (Cornwall)
Repaired church clock 1603.

HEERMAN, John (signed Johannes)   London
Watchmaker, a Dutchman. Free Brother in CC Sep 1691: 'in a necessitous condition'. Paid no quarterage thereafter.

HELDEN, Cornelius   London
B.c. 1672, (perhaps son of Onisephorus, *qv*). Apr. May 1686 to Nathaniel Delander till 1693, but not freed. Married May 1692 a batchelor aged 22, watchmaker of St. Catherine's Creechurch, London, to Sarah Troughton of Maidstone, spinster, aged 21, at Maidstone. Not heard of again.

HELDEN, Onisephorus   London
Admitted to CC 1632. Prob. already a Freeman of the Goldsmiths' Co. In 1636 refused to be an Assistant but became one from 1639, Warden from 1646, but never became Master (perhaps by choice). Took as aprs.: Jul 1649 **Robert Marston** (thro' J. Bayes); Nov 1654 **William Brewer** (thro' L. Wythe); Aug 1655 **William Clopton** (thro' S. Horne). Stood surety for John Bayes in 1650. In 1656 was a counter rebel. Work known – none, but his name is well-known in the CC archives. Perhaps made watch cases.

HELLAM, James   London
B.c. 1668, apr. Jan 1682/83 to Evan Jones, a Freeman of the Goldsmiths' Co., thro' D. Stevens, later transferred to Henry Jones till 1689. Freed Apr 1690. Took as aprs.: Jan 1695/96 **William Jones**; Sep 1700 **Peter Rawson** son of Edward Rawson of (Broxted?) Essex, farmer. Paid quarterage till late in 1703. Prob. worked for Jones.

HELLIWELL, Richard   **Halifax (Yorkshire)**
Repaired church clock 1626 and 1632.

HELME, Nestor   **London**
B. 1660 'son of Nestor Helme late of Tewksbury, Glocester, gent.', but this description has been crossed through in the records(?). Apr. Dec 1674 thro' N. Coxeter to Jeremy Gregory till 1682. However in *London Gazette* of Oct 1678 Gregory announced that he was a runaway apr., aged 18.

HELYN, ----   **London**
Known to CC, but never actually a member. Prob. dead by 1662-63.

HEMINS, Edward senior   **Bicester (Oxfordshire)**
Late 17th century TC. No details known. Believed succ. by son of same name.

HEMMING, Charles   **London**
B.c. 1665, apr. May 1679 to James Wolverstone till 1686, but not freed.

HENCHE, Ulrich   **London**
Clockmaker. In 1605 the King bought from him a clock in the form of a branch for £100.

HENDERSON, John   **London**
Recorded in 1662 but this is a slip for Hilderson, *qv*.

HENDRICKSON, John   **London**
In Jun 1652 was given permission to work for John Champion for six months. This may perhaps be a misrendering of John Hilderson.

HENEY, Richard (see Honey)

HENSHAW, John   **London**
B.c. 1675, son of Walter, apr. Apr 1689 to his father till 1696. Freed Apr 1696. Took as aprs.: Sep 1698 **John Dobson** – freed Nov 1714; Jun 1704 **Benjamin Macy** (son of Richard Macy of Chilmarsh, in co. Wilts, mason); May 1706 **John Shippy** (son of John Shippy of The Old Artillery Ground, Spittle Fields, co. Middlesex, weaver); Jun 1713 **William Garner.**

HENSHAW, Walter   London
Mat. inst. maker and Freeman of another Co. (the Weavers' Co. where
he bound apr. **Robert Cooke** in Aug 1659 – freed Sep 1675). Freed as a
Brother in CC Feb 1667-68. Took as aprs.: Sep 1683 **Simon Scatliss;**
Apr 1689 son **John Henshaw;** Jun 1690 **Jeremiah Tarleton;** Mar
1697/98 **Samuel Dyer;** Feb 1700/01 **Henry Flint** (son of Henry Flint of
Towcester, co. Northants, draper, deceased); Feb 1703/04 **John
Browne.** Was Assistant from 1682, Warden from 1693, Master 1695.
Attended (irregularly at first) until late in 1712 when prob. died.

HERBERT, Cornelius (see under Harbert)

HERBERT, Edward   London
Apr. Aug 1657 to Humfrey Downing thro' L. Wythe. Freed Oct 1664.
In Jul 1676 was called for Stewardship but did not appear and not heard
of thereafter.

HERBERT, Evan   London
B.c. 1666, apr. Sep 1680 to Thomas Herbert, thro' R. Linch till 1687.
Freed Jan 1691-92. Paid quarterage till c. 1695. Still working 1697.
Work known – a watch.

HERBERT, John   London
(sometimes Harbert but signed Herbert)
B.c. 1657 – one record says 'son of Nicholas Payne' which may mean
stepson. Apr. May 1672 to Nicholas Payne till 1680. Freed Jul 1682. In
Nov 1686 as a clockmaker, batchelor, aged 29 of St. Bennett Fink parish
he married to Elizabeth Croxton of St. Margarets Lothbury parish,
spinster aged 20. Took as aprs.: Apr 1684 **Stephen Brittaine** transferred
to Sarah Payne – freed Apr 1692; Sep 1690 **Thomas Carter** for Joanna
May; Jul 1693 **John Parr;** Jul 1695 **George Stratford** (son of Thomas
Stratford); Sep 1697 **John Purnell;** Mar 1699-1700 **Thomas Brockless**
(son of Alborne Brockless, late of St. Andrew, Holborn, Clothworker,
deceased); Sep 1711 his son **Edward Herbert** was freed by patrimony;
Sep 1713 **Henry Hurt.** In Feb 1701/02 got CC charity of 10/- as being a
poor workman. Prob. still alive in 1718 – see William Herbert's burial.

HERBERT, Thomas   London
Made Brother in CC Nov 1676 – prob. already free of some other Co.
Described as the King's Clockmaker in Sep 1680 when he took as apr.
Evan Herbert (thro' R. Lynch) – freed Jan 1691/92. Described as the

Queen's Clockmaker Dec 1683 when he took as apr. **John Okey** (thro' R. Lyons) – not freed. Said to have worked at Whitehall. Still working 1698 after which I have no information on him. Seems to have had little contact with the CC. Work known – bracket clocks signed 'Thomas Herbert, London'.

HERBERT, William (sometimes Harbert)   **London**
B.c. 1649, apr. Jul 1663 to Henry Child, thro' R. Peirce, till 1670. Freed Apr 1671. Mentioned as a 'loving kinsman' in 1676 will of Nicholas Payne. Took as aprs.: Jun 1675 **John Shaw**; Jan 1679/80 **John Chapman**. Son Henry Herbert – freed by patrimony Dec 1714. Seems to have had little contact with CC. In 1711 said to be already the Queen's Clockmaker, having earlier restored Hampton Court Clock. In 1707 when Langley Bradley got the contract for St. Paul's clock he disputed Bradley's ability. Wren pointed out that Herbert was already a bankrupt. Received CC charity from 1710-16. Dead by Jul 1718 when CC paid 10/- to his brother John to bury him. Work known – a watch.

HERNE, Edward (see also Hearne)   **London**
B.c. 1666, apr. Jun 1680 to Cornelius Jenkins till 1687, but not freed.

HERON, Henry   **London**
Supposedly apr. 1632 in Blacksmiths' Co.

HERRIS, William   **London**
B.c. 1669, apr. Apr 1682 to Thomas East, thro' H. Roberts till 1690. Not freed.

HERWICK, Nicholas   **London**
Recorded in Cheapside in 1580 (Britten), but I cannot confirm this.

HESTER, Henry (1st)   **London**
CC list of 1662 lists a man of this name, but as the next man was not free till 1671, could this be a third of the same name? Or was it Henry senior who was simply late taking up his freedom?

HESTER, Henry senior   **London**
Apr. to John Light and transferred to Richard Morgan then to Thomas Morgan. Freed in CC Apr 1671. Took as aprs.: 1671 **William Bulstrode** – in Nov 1672 he was allowed to replace Bulstrode who was incapable of learning his trade; Nov 1672 **Thomas Gibbs** – free Jul 1681; Mar

297

1672/73 **John Dearmer** for Catherine Bestwick; Jul 1675 **Edmund Duxbury;** Jan 1697/80 son **Henry Hester** – free Apr 1689; Jul 1681 **John Berrington;** Apr 1686 **Thomas Price;** Jul 1695 son **William Hester;** Feb 1699/1700 **John Hiorne** (son of illegible Hiorne, late citizen and plumber of London, deceased) – free Nov 1707. His son Thomas Hester was apr. Jun 1702 to William Mason. Worked at Westminster, prob. for Thomas Morgan at least until 1675. He received charity from CC from Oct 1714 to 1716. Dead by dec 1717. Work known – longcase clocks signed 'Henry Hester, Westminster' and a lost watch is on record.

HESTER, Henry junior   London
B.c. 1665, son of Henry Hester senior. Apr. Jan 1679/80 to father till 1686. Freed Apr 1689. Took as aprs.: **Thomas Wightman** – free Jan 1701/02; Jun 1697 **Richard Purrier** – free Apr 1706. Still alive in 1714.

HETH, Robert   Thame (Oxfordshire)
In 1573 made church clock for St. Mary's.

HEWENER(?), George   London
Name very indistinctly written on 1697 oath roll.

For **HEWES** see under Hues and Hughes

HEWITT, Alexander   London
B.c. 1671, apr. Mar 1685/86 to Benjamin Bell till 1692, but not freed. Inherited tools from Bell in 1691. Work known – longcase clock.

HEWITT, Charles   Coventry or **Kenilworth (Warwickshire)**
Blacksmith? Repaired clock of St. Nicholas Kenilworth 1693-95.

HEWITT, Joseph   Coventry or **Monks Kirby (Warwickshire)**
(also Huet)
Blacksmith? Repaired church clock at Monks Kirby in 1675. Watch recorded pre-1678, Coventry.

HEWITT, Thomas   London
Listed by Baillie as apr. 1685, but I cannot trace him. Error for Alexander?

HEWSON, John   London
B.c. 1669, apr. Nov 1683 to John Sellars till 1690. Freed Jul 1699 (master

had died in 1697). Took as apr. Jul 1702 **Joseph South** (son of Joseph South of Shewill Green, co. Southampton, carpenter) – freed Nov 1709. Last heard of in 1706 when in arrears with quarterage.

HEYLINGE, Bernard (see also Hil(l)ings)   **London**
Admitted as Free Brother Jul 1652 – b. in Antwerp.

HEYRICKE, Samuel   **Leicestershire(?)**
Wooden portable sundial dated 1687.

HEYTON, Robert   **Oxford**
Younger son of Robert Heyten of Chadlington. Apr. May 1656 to Michael Bird of Oxford till 1664, but not freed.

HEYWOOD, ----   **London**
Supposed subscriber to incorporation of CC in 1632, but I cannot trace him.

HICCOCK, John (also Hiccox)   **London**
B.c. 1636, apr. Jun 1650 to Nicholas Ashwell till 1657. Freed Jul 1657. Tok as apr. Oct 1662 **Henry Wansey** – not freed. Work known – a watch signed and a bracket clock signed 'John Hiccock, London'.

HICCOCK, Samuel   **Chester**
Clockmaker freed there 1678-79.

HICKMAN, Henry   **London**
A Loriner. In Jan 1680/81 his apr. **David Jones** was allowed to be transferred to Isaac Day, and Hickman agreed to ensure that he took up his freedom.

HICKES, John   **London**
B.c. 1671, apr. Jul 1685 to Samuel Bowtell, thro' George Heady till 1692. Freed Jul 1694. Another entry says apr. Nov 1686 to Isaac Nicholl – maybe two of this name were apr. but apparently only one survived, who worked till at least 1700. In 1700 Mr. Cadell is mentioned 'who lodges at Mr Hicks in Fox Court Brook Street'. Took as aprs.: May 1697 **Samuel Wagstaffe;** Mar 1699/1700 **David Strater** (son of John Strater of Newington Butts, co. Sussex, gent.); **William Stone** (taken from Thomas Fletcher).

HICKS, Thomas London
Free Brother in CC Jul 1666, but paid fee Apr 1667 (Baillie has 1664 which seems wrong). Made Assistant 1682 but after initial attendance he never attended again, nor was any attempt made to force him to. Took as aprs.: Nov 1682/83 **Thomas Cooke** – later passed to W. May; Aug 1689 **William Goodrick** for Amos Winch. Work known – none but a lost watch was recorded in 1675 signed 'Thomas Hicks, Londini'.

HICKSON, Thomas London
Apr. (prob. thro' Blacksmiths' Co.) to Thomas Harris (a Free Blacksmith), later transferred to Thomas Speakman. Made a Free Brother in CC Jan 1690/91. Took as aprs.: Jul 1691 **Hewett Ram**; May 1706 **Samuel Burgess** (son of Humfrey Burgess of St. James, Westminster). Not heard of after 1706.

HIDE, John London
B.c. 1624, apr. Nov 1637 to Simon Hackett (thro' O. Durant) till 1645, but not freed.

HIGGINS, John (also Higings) Belfast(?)
Lantern clock recorded late 17th century – c. 1700.

HIGGINSON, Henry (and Higgenson) London/Liverpool
Freed in CC Jun 1662. Recorded at Liverpool as a watchmaker by 1675. Wife Martha died 1676. Second wife Elizabeth died 1679. He died there 1694.

HIGGINSON, John London
His apr. **William Bankes** (taken from Benjamin Bell c. 1691) was freed Sep 1698.

HIGGINSON, Nicholas London
Free in CC 1646. Rebelled against CC in 1656. Working in Chancery Lane in 1662. Paid search fee in 1671.

HIGGINSON, Samuel London
B.c. 1674, apr. Aug 1688 to Richard Watts till 1695. Freed Apr 1698 and not heard of thereafter.

HIGGS, John London
Apr. to Robert Robinson. Freed Oct 1661.

HIGGS, John London
B.c. 1667, apr. Nov 1681 to John Fort. Later passed to Luke Bird till 1688. Freed Dec 1688. Took as aprs.: Mar 1690-91 **Clay Whitton** – free Apr 1698; Mar 1693-94 **William Maysmoor;** May 1700 **Edward Ashe** (son of Jacob Ashe of Swansea, gent.); Jan 1706/07 his son **Thomas Higgs** passed over May 1709 to Ab. Dearmer – free Jan 1716/17; Oct 1713 **William Piper;** Jul 1715 **Simon Kello.**

HIGHMORE, Edward London
B.c. 1666, apr. May 1680 to John Miller till 1687. Freed Sep 1687. Paid no quarterage after 1688.

HIGHMORE, Lancaster London
B.c. 1671, apr. Aug 1685 to John Fitter thro' D. Stevens till 1692, but not freed.

HILDERSON, John London
Name misspelt variously as Hillersden, Hinderson, Henderson and even Hendrickson, *qv*. Apparently never officially admitted to CC but known to them. Took as aprs.: Apr 1657 **Samuel Hayley** – not free; Jun 1662 **Thomas Watson.** Believed to have been closely associated with East. Address thought to have been Cecil Street, Strand. Work known – lantern clock chiming quarters on four bells, night clock and bracket clocks signed 'John Hilderson in Chesell Street, Londini', and 'John Hilderson Londini'.

HILL, Abraham London
Baillie – patented idea of using pendulum clock for finding longitude at sea.

HILL, Benjamin London
Formerly in Blacksmiths' Co. c. 1640. Made Free Brother in CC Oct 1640. Worked in Fleet Street. Made Assistant 1651, Warden 1652, Master 1657-59. Attended till 1670, dead by Oct 1670. Took as aprs.: **James Seaborne** – freed May 1649; Aug 1648 **George Taylor** (thro' L. Wythe); May 1650 **James Gregory** (thro' L. Wythe) – free 1657; Mar 1651 **Nathaniel Chamberlaine** (thro' L. Wythe) – free Jun 1659; Jan 1655/56 had work done by **Philip Charter** and **Henry Marshall** who were not yet officially apr.; Feb 1656 **John Woodward;** Oct 1658 **John Croft** – free Feb 1665/66; **Michael Cornish** – freed Oct 1661; Oct 1658 **Henry Reve,** later passed to William Comford and freed Feb 1682/83; Mar 1660

HILL, Edward

Thomas Benn; Jul 1661 **Matthew Moy**; Nov 1661 **Robert Andrews;**
son, **John Hill** – freed Nov 1670 by patrimony. Also bound several aprs.
for other masters – one for Robert Grinkin, one for J. Pennock, one for
T. Chamberlaine, one for H. Kent, one for L. Meredith, one for
H. Child. Work known – watches.

HILL, Edward   London
B.c. 1676, apr. Apr 1690 to Thomas Walford (thro' D. Stevens) to 1697.
Freed Jul 1698. Took as aprs.: Jan 1698/99 **George Cartwright** (from
Ed. Crouch) – free Jan 1706/07; Jun 1701 **Benjamin Sidey** (son of John
Sidey of St. Peter's Colchester, woollen draper) – for Robert Creed – free
May 1711; Sep 1704 **John Waldran** (son of John Waldran of St. Giles
Cripplegate, Middlesex, labourer); May 1711 **Isaac Collman; Joseph
White** – freed Jan 1714/15; Nov 1718 **James Walford.**

HILL, Francis   London
B.c. 1650, apr. Dec 1664 to Nathan Dike till 1671. Freed Sep 1672
(Baillie has another such apr. 1672, which is wrong). Took as aprs.: Dec
1687 **James Drury** – free Apr 1695; May 1698 **William James; Matthew
Skinner** – free Apr 1713. Also bound an apr. for H. Evans and one for
S. Stevens. Believed died 1702.

HILL, John   London
Supposed 1630 petitioner for CC but I cannot confirm this, but see
Thomas Hill below.

HILL, John   London
Eldest son of Benjamin Hill, *qv*. Freed in CC by patrimony Nov 1670.

HILL, John   London
B.c. 1678, son of Richard Hill, apr. Jul 1692 to Richard Haughtin, till
1699. Freed Apr 1703. Took as aprs.: Sep 1706 **Thomas Lawrence** (son
of William Lawrence of St. Martin in the Fields, Middlesex, labourer);
Oct 1708 **Thomas Lawrence(?)**; May 1714 **Richard Highmore**; Apr
1715 son, **Thomas Hill.** Work known – longcase clock signed 'John Hill,
Kings Street, Covent Garden'.

HILL, John   **Risborough/Wendover(?) (Buckinghamshire)**
Longcase clock late 17th century signed 'John Hill Risborough'. John
Hill of Wendover, clockmaker, date unknown, may be same man.

HILL, Thomas   **London**
Entered CC 1632 prob. as a Brother. Had watches confiscated in 1635 –
'a dialmaker at ye (Tower?)'.

HILL, Thomas   **London**
Longcase clock recorded c. 1690 signed 'Thomas Hill and Henry
Harper'. Supposedly worked 'over against Chancery Lane, Fleet Street'.

HILL, William   **London**
B.c. 1669, apr. Nov 1682 to Samuel Clyatt till 1690, but not freed.

HILLERSDEN, John (see Hilderson)

HILLERY, John   **London**
B.c. 1667, apr. May 1681 to Richard Jarrett (thro' N. Russell) till 1688,
but not freed.

HILLIER, William (also Hiller and Hillyard)   **London**
B.c. 1656, apr. Jan 1669/70 to Thomas Creed (thro' Nicasius Russell) till
1677. Freed Sep 1679. Took as aprs.: Aug 1682 **John Wills;** Nov 1684
bound an apr. for John Wynne. Paid no quarterage after 1685.

HILLINGS, Bernard (see Heylings)

HILTON, Evan   **Wigan (Lancashire)**
Watchmaker there by 1667. Free 1670. Died 1699 (Hawkes).

HILTON, John   **London**
B.c. 1676, apr. Nov 1690 to Thomas Tompion (thro' William Morelley)
till 1697. Freed May 1698. Paid no quarterage after 1698.

HILTON, Thomas   **London**
B.c. 1660, apr. Jul 1674 to John Marke, mat. inst. maker thro' L. Wythe
till 1681, but not freed.

HINDE, John   **London**
Goldsmith at the Golden Ball in Fenchurch Street, also described as in
Cornhill 1663-90, in association with Thomas Kirkwood. CC lent money
to him at interest in 1680. Bankrupt in 1711. CC got paid 5d. in the
pound.

HINDERSON, John   London
In 1662 CC list, prob. a clerical slip for Hilderson *qv*.

HITCHCOCK, William   Oxford
Son of Thomas Hitchcock, husbandman of Ratley Warwickshire. Apr.
Sep 1675 to John Knibb, watchmaker of Oxford till 1683 but not freed.

HITCHMAN, Nicholas   London
B.c. 1663, apr. Feb 1677/78 to Richard Ames till 1684, but not freed.

HOBBS, William   London
B.c. 1659, apr. Jul 1672 to William Robinson till 1680, but not freed.

HOBSON, John   London
Petitioner for incorporation of CC in 1630.

HOCHENADEL, ----   London
Watch c. 1700. Prob. Pieter Hochnadel of Vienna.

HOCKSTETTER, Joseph (see Heckstetter)

HOCKE (see Hawke)

HOCKEN, John (see also Hawkin?)   Stratton (Cornwall)
Kept church clock 1612.

HOCKER, John   Reading
1682-88. Lantern clocks and watch – but see Hoddle, died 1729?

HODDLE, John   Reading
Lantern clocks recorded c. 1688 but one such was apr. in CC 1697. See
also Hocker?

HODGES, Anthony (or Hedges?)   Oxford
B.c. 1651, son of Anthony Hodges (or Hedges), cleric of Wytham,
Berkshire. Apr. Mar 1664 to Michael Bird of Oxford till 1672. Freed Jan
1672.

HODGES, Nathaniel   London
A 'Great Clockmaker'. Free Brother in CC Dec 1681. In arrears with
quarterage in 1687, and not heard of thereafter. Work known – several

bracket clocks and a lantern clock, the latter signed 'Nathaniel Hodges' without town, but usually signed 'Nathaniel Hodges, Londini' or 'Nathaniel Hodges, Wine Office Court in Fleet Street'.

HODGKINSON, Sarah   London
Mar 1700/01 made free in CC by redemption by order of the Court of Aldermen – but never paid any quarterage. Took as apr. May 1701 **Elizabeth Price** (daughter of ---- Price late of St. Andrew, Holborn, Middlesex, shoemaker). Prob. not a clockmaker.

HODGSON, Mark   York
Watchmaker. Free 1676. Buried 26 Feb 1709. Work known – watch signed 'Marcus Hodgson, Eboraci'.

HODIERNE, John   London
B.c. 1624, apr. Jan 1638/39 to (Thomas) Platt (thro' O. Durant) till 1646, but not freed.

HODSON, John   London
B.c. 1653, apr. Jul 1666 to Thomas Rotherham till 1674, but not freed.

HOLBOROUGH, Thomas   Colchester/Ipswich
Goldsmith, also clock and watchmaker. B.c. 1676. Opened shop in Colchester, St. Runwald's parish, 1698 and took same year **Tobias Searson** as apr. Married 1699 Jane Bateson. Issue – 1701 Hannah; 1706 Thomas. Moved to Ipswich 1706 in St. Mary le Tower parish. Died 1727 leaving will. Succ. by son Thomas. Watch recorded as Thomas Holbrook by Baillie. Watch signed 'Thomas Holborough, Ipswich', longcase clock signed 'Thomas Holborough, Colchester'.

HOLDCROFT, Henry   London
B.c. 1665, apr. May 1678 to Charles Halstead till 1686, but not freed.

HOLDER, William   London
Published in 1694 '*A Discourse concerning Time*' regarding the divisions of Time and the calendar (Baillie).

HOLLAND, George   London
Recorded by Baillie as 1630 petitioner for CC but prob. an error for Thomas or John *qv*.

HOLLAND, Hugh   **London**
B.c. 1646, apr. Aug 1660 to Walter Gibbs till 1667, but not freed.

HOLLAND, John   **London**
Failed to pay CC quarterage in 1635 – watchmaker.

HOLLAND, Lewis   **London**
B.c. 1677, apr. Nov 1691 to Thomas Birch till 1698. Freed Dec 1698.
Took as apr. Jul 1700 **Richard Bishop** (son of John Bishop of Gloucester,
mercer). Work known – watches.

HOLLAND, Thomas   **London**
Subscriber in 1630 and Free Brother 1632. Made CC Assistant 1650,
Master 1656, last attended 1660. Took as aprs.: Jul 1660 **Jeremiah
Gosse** (thro' R. Bowen), transferred to Thomas Taylor of Holborn –
freed Jan 1667-68. Commonly known from 1650 as 'Captain' Holland.
Borrowed money from CC 1659/60. Made Clerk and Beadle Jan 1659/60.
Received charitable payments from CC from 1660. Prob. in very poor
health from 1660. In 1662 was suspended from his job as Clerk and
Beadle for which he reapplied unsuccessfully in Feb 1665-66. Was given
various charities, 'being very poore and at present sick', the last one
being 10/– in Oct 1667 'in case he doe goe beyond the sea, as he saith he
intendeth to doe'. Never heard of thereafter. Work known – a lantern
clock. May have worked mostly as a journeyman. (Baillie records two of
this name which appears to be an error.)

HOLLIARD, Samuel   **London**
B.c. 1679, apr. Apr 1693 to John Barrow till 1700. Freed Apr 1705.
Work known – clock recorded c. 1710.

HOL(L)IDAY, Edward (also Hollidaie)   **London**
Made a Free Brother in CC Apr 1650. Took as apr. Mar 1653/54 **Vincent
Wheeler** (thro' D. Moody). Supported the administration in 1656 rebel-
lion. In 1662 worked in Chancery Lane.

HOLLIS, Thomas   **London**
Apr. Sep 1649 to James Seaburne. Free Sep 1656. Took as aprs.: **John
Watts** (from T. Claxton) – free Jan 1664-65; Sep 1677 **Richard Lankister**
(at a low rate because of Hollis's poverty) – transferred Jan 1680/81 to
Benjamin Bell; May 1682 **Thomas Crane** (later rebound Mar 1683/84 to

Issac Nicholl). In 1656 sided with rebels against CC administration. Baillie records two men of this name – one apr. in 1682 which is an error.

HOLLOWAY, John   **Devizes (Wiltshire)**
Winged lantern clock signed 'John Holloway, Devizes', and dated 1682. Was free there in 1684.

HOLLOWAY, John   **Lavington (Wiltshire)**
Iron lantern clock dated 1611.

HOLLOWAY, John   **London**
Listed in 1700. Prob. a clerical error for William, *qv*.

HOLLOWAY, John   **Newbury (Berkshire)**
Watch recorded signed 'John Holloway, Newbury'. Hooded clock c.1675 – 95. Son of Humphrey Holloway, clothier. Apr. to W. Haywood.

HOLLOWAY, John   **Stroud (Gloucestershire)**
Lantern clock noted c. 1700. Prob. son of William *qv*.

HOLLOWAY, Richard   **London**
B.c. 1661, apr. Oct 1675 to Cornelius Herbert till 1682, but not freed.

HOLLOWAY, Robert   **London**
Free Brother in CC Oct 1632. In Nov 1632 promised to bring his apr. to be bound. Promised to pay quarterage 1633 – not heard of thereafter.

HOLLOWAY, William   **Stroud (Gloucestershire)**
Various lantern clocks are known which bear a number, apparently relating to the year when made. Dated ones include, 1666, 1669, 1675, 1678, 1679. At least one longcase clock is known. Will dated Mar 1693/94, proved Jan 1694/95, mentions son William *qv*, son John *qv*, youngest son Arthur, daughters Elizabeth and Martha and Hester Aldridge. Also wife Hester.

HOLLOWAY, William junior   **London**
Son of William Holloway of Stroud, *qv*. Free Brother in CC Sep 1697. Took as aprs.: Jan 1697/98 **Arthur Holloway** (his brother?) – free Sep 1705; Mar 1698/99 **Richard Langcraft** (from Wiltshire) taken from H. Kilminster – free Oct 1718; Jul 1700 **Thomas Dale** (son of Richard Dale of St. Bottolph Aldgate, clothmaker; Jul 1707 **Daniel Window** –

free Jan 1718/19; Aug 1711 **John Berrow**; Aug 1717 **John Howle**. I have no data after 1717. Believed worked at Cullum Street. Work known – at least one watch and a longcase clock signed 'William Holloway, London'.

HOLLYER, John   London
Watchmaker in St. Saviour's, Southwark. Daughter Sarah died 1713.

HOLME and HOLMES are listed together below.

HOLME, James   Manchester (Lancashire)
Watchmaker of Newton. Married 1665 Mary Hayward of Rochdale.

HOLMES, John   London
Baillie has 1697, which is an error for Thomas *qv*.

HOLMES, Major   London
Published in 1665 an account of a trial of Huygens pendulum clocks at sea.

HOLMES, Nester
Error for Nester Helme *qv*.

HOLME, Robert   London
Son of John Holme of parish of Kerley? County Westmorland, mason, deceased. Apr. thro' Weavers' Co. Apr 1663, trade not known.

HOLMES, Thomas   London
B.c. 1673, apr. Jul 1686 to Peter Miller till 1694. Freed Sep 1697, but excused entry fee on account of his poverty. Dead by Apr 1698 when CC paid a single Charity of 10/- to his widow.

HONEY, Richard   London
B.c. 1633, apr. Oct 1646 to Isaac Law (thro' T. Alcock) till 1654, but not freed.

HOOKE, A.   place not known
A watch recorded dated 1661, place unknown.

HOOKE, Robert   London
Born 1635, died 1703. Professor of Geometry and Secretary of the Royal

Society. Sometimes credited with various inventions such as anchor escapement and a type of wheel-cutting engine. Claimed priority over Huygens in applying a balance spring. It is difficult to know which of his claims were true and exactly what his experiments were.

HOOKER, John   **London**
Free Brother in CC as a watchmaker Sep 1698. Paid no quarterage up to 1705 at least. Reputedly died in 1751 (Baillie).

HOOPER, John   **Wells/Dorchester**
Moved to Dorchester in 1631. From Wells (Somerset).

HOPKINS, John   **London**
Made a Brother in CC Oct 1640. Took as apr.: **Jude Morgan** – free Jul 1654 (as a Brother). This suggests Hopkins was connected with another City Co. In Aug 1641 he bound an apr. for Isaac Law.

HOPPIN, Charles   **Exeter (Devon)**
Repaired church clock at Woodbury nr. Exeter. Died Nov 1606, left widow Mary and believed son Matthew, *qv.*

HOPPIN, Mathew   **Exeter (Devon)**
Locksmith and turret clockmaker. Made St. Mary's church automata clock and maintained other local church clocks. Married 1608 Jone Pere. Died Oct 1625, leaving bequests to his brother William, *qv.*

HOPPIN, William   **Exeter (Devon)**
Son of Charles Hoppin, b. 1603. Free 1627 as a locksmith. Performed many metalworking tasks including servicing church clocks. Had as aprs.: **Joseph Branscombe,** locksmith; **Peter Halstaffe,** locksmith and **John Peryam,** gunsmith. Died 1643.

HORNE, Samuel   **London**
B.c. 1633, apr. May 1647 to Peter Bellune (thro' J. Quash) till 1654. Freed May 1654. Prob. a boxmaker. In 1662 worked in Chancery Lane. Took as aprs.: **William Seabourne** – freed Mar 1659/60; Aug 1655 **Andrew Durdent** – freed Sep 1662; May 1661 **Sampson Crooke** – freed Jul 1668; Jul 1661 **John Perkins;** Oct 1667 **Charles Fitton** – freed Oct 1674; Aug 1669 **Thomas Jenkins** – freed Nov 1677; Apr 1674 **Samuel Bowtell** – freed Jun 1691; May 1677 **William Bartram** transferred to S. Bowtell – freed Sep 1684. Bound aprs. for several other Masters incl.

J. Gregory, 2. E. Jones, 2. O. Heldon, T. Mills, I. Daniell, S. Bartram, J. Nicasius. Was father-in-law of Thomas Elton, *qv*. In 1668 Nathan Barrow stood bondsman for him. Became CC Assistant 1660, Warden 1668, Master 1672-74; last attended 1680. Believed died 1685, certainly before 1693.

HORROCKS, Christopher   **Warrington (Lancashire)**
Watchmaker. Died 1663 leaving will.

HORSLEY, Cornelius   **York**
Watchmaker. B.c. 1635 son of Edward Horsley, painter, free 1656. Married 1665 at Northampton to Elizabeth Hunt – Quakers. Issue in York 1665 Edward; 1666 Cornelius (died young); 1668 Benedick; 1669 Mary. He died 1681. Widow died 1693.

HOSKINS, Daniel   place unknown
A four bell chiming lantern clock of c. 1630 is known signed without place. Some authorities state London but this is not certain. Not a CC member.

HOSSE, William   **Walton-on-Trent (Derbyshire)**
Recorded as 1678 by Baillie – source unknown.

HOTHAM, Henry   **London**
B.c. 1652, apr. Mar 1664/65 to John Pennock (thro' N. Payne) till 1672. Free Apr 1673. Work known – winged lantern clock signed 'Henry Hotham at ye Black Spread Eagle at ye west end of St. Paules'.

HOUGHAM, Charles (signed thus)   **London**
Also wrongly Huffam and Houghman. B.c. 1659, apr. Jun 1672 to James Wolverstone (thro' L. Wythe) till 1680. Freed Jul 1680. Took as apr.: Aug 1687 **Daniel Glover** – freed Sep 1699. Paid quarterage till at least 1703.

HOUGHTON, Richard   **London**
Apr. Nov 1653 to Nicholas Payne, then passed to Abraham Beckner – but not freed.

HOUGHTON, William   **Preston (Lancashire)**
Late 17th century. Supposedly devised pinion-wire drawing.

HOULGATT, W(M)   **Ipswich (Suffolk)**
(also Holgate, Howldgate, etc.)
Married 1617 Margery Bassett. Issue 1619-29. Widow died 1644. He
died c. 1637-44. Work known – watch signed 'W. Houldgatt att
Ipswich'.

HOUSE (see Howes)

HOW – see also House, Howes, etc.

HOW, Benjamin (signed Benjamin How, junior?)   **London**
B.c. 1671, apr. Apr 1685 to Daniel Roof (thro' D. Stevens) till 1692.
Freed Sep 1691. Paid quarterage till c. 1692 only. Work known – a
watch.

HOW(E), Daniel   **London**
B.c. 1659, apr. Aug 1673 to John Lowe (thro' L. Wythe) till 1680, but
not freed.

HOW(E), Richard   **Dorchester**
Believed b. 1666, died 1713. Longcase clocks and watches recorded.
Succeeded by son, Richard.

HOW, Thomas   **London**
B.c. 1656, apr. Sep 1670 to Isaac Roumyeu (thro' S. Bouquet) passed
over Mar 1671/72 to Nathaniel Delander till 1677. Freed Sep 1677. Took
as apr.: Sep 1679 **John Willoughby** – freed Sep 1686. Still working in
1697, but paid no quarterage after c. 1683.

HOW, William   **London**
Mat. inst. maker and free of another Co., but made a Free Brother in CC
Feb 1667/68. In Jul 1697 made Assistant, but excused for unstated
mitigating reasons. Paid quarterage till 1701. Believed died 1701/02.

HOWARD, John (sometimes Heward)   **London**
B.c. 1672, apr. Jul 1687 to John Miller till 1694. Freed Aug 1694.
Married Feb 1693, a batchelor clockmaker, aged 21, of St. Dunston in
the West, to Sarah Bradgate of St. Gregory's, spinster aged 22. Not heard
of after 1697. Work known – a watch is on record.

HOWELL, Benjamin   **London**
Believed goldsmith and member of Goldsmith's Co. B.c. 1679, apr. Apr
1693 to George Mertins (thro' E. Norris) till 1700. Freed Jun 1700.
Believed worked from 1704 to his death in 1715 at the Peacocks Feathers
in Cornhill nr. Royal Exchange. Took as aprs.: Aug 1710 **Edward Cleve**;
Sep 1711 **Richard Cooper;** May 1714 **Thomas Nobbs.**

HOWELL, Daniel   **London**
Working by 1634. Free Brother in CC Dec 1637. Took as apr. 1638
William Petty (thro' R. Masterson) – free Apr 1646. In Nov 1650 CC
made a grant to his widow, and another in 1655.

HOWSE/HOUSE/HOWES all follow together.

HOWES, James   **London**
Working 1697.

HOUSE, John (also Howes and Howse)   **Croydon**
Already a watchmaker at Croydon when made a Free Brother in CC in
Aug 1687. In 1687 was a bondsman at marriage of Henry Van de Hague,
clockmaker. In Nov 1687 promised to enter his workman **John Florio,**
into CC. Took as aprs.: Sep 1693 **Thomas Wilkins** (thro' Thomas
Fletcher). Believed died 1698/99, but was succeeded by another of this
name, presumably his son.

HOWES, Joseph (and Howse)   **London**
May have been two of this name. B.c. 1677, apr. Jul 1691 to Henry
Adeane till 1698 – (but not freed?). A watchmaker of this name freed in
CC Sep 1698, being already a member of the Merchant Taylors' Co.
Took as apr. Jul 1700 **Thomas Wright** (son of Thomas Wright of St.
Anne, Blackfriars, London, victualler); May 1703 **Daniel Leake** (son of
Samuel Leake of Ashbourne, co. Derbyshire, clerk, deceased); Jun 1705
Samuel Bennett (son of Samuel Bennett of St. Andrew, Holborn,
Middlesex, brandy-seller) – free Oct 1716; May 1711 **Thomas Leeman;**
Sep 1714 **John Hocker.**

HOWSE, Thomas (also House)   **London**
Working by 1632 – by trade a clockmaker, but Free of the Bakers' Co.
(Brown Bakers). Took as aprs.: (in CC) 1631 **Samuel Berry;** Jul 1638
John Walter (thro' O. Durant) – free Dec 1645; Jun 1642 **Henry Erberry**
(thro' O. Durant), later passed over to Robert Smith, and freed 1650.

Made Assistant in 1640, Warden 1642, when last attended. Believed worked at the Sun in Pope's Head Alley. By 1655 his widow, Elizabeth, had already re-married to Robert Smith (qv) who had died and she too had died. She left property in Pope's Head Alley, Queen Street and Bell Alley – see under Robert Smith. Work known – two watches.

HOWLET, Stephen   **London**
B.c. 1644, apr. Jul 1657 to Peter Bellon till 1665, but not freed.

HOWSON, John   **London**
Recorded by Baillie as CC 1699. I do not known him. Maybe error for John Howse?

HOYLE, Henry   **London**
A merchant made free by redemption in CC Apr 1677.

HOYLE, James   **Halifax (Yorkshire)**
Repaired Church clock in 1693.

HOYLE (Thomas?)   **London**
Baillie records a mid-17th century watch but initial letter doubtful.

HUDDLESTON, Charles   **London**
B.c. 1660, apr. Sep 1673 to Henry Harper till 1681, but not freed.

HUDSON, John   **London**
B.c. 1670, apr. Dec 1684 to Edward Jackson (later passed to Charles Halstead) – not freed.

HUES, Peter (or Pierry) (also Hewes and Hughes)   **London**
In 1628 'English Forrin', which might be Welsh or French? Joined CC 1632. Several minor infringements till 1662. Made Assistant in 1658 and seems not to have attended after that.

HUES, Thomas   **London**
B.c. 1648, apr. Nov 1662 to John Pennock (thro' N. Coxeter) till 1669, but not freed.

HUET, Joseph (see Hewitt)   **Coventry (Warwickshire)**

HUFFAM, Charles (see Hougham)

HUGGEFORD, Francis   **London**
B.c. 1661, apr. Jul 1675 (thro' S. Davis) to James Wolverstone (an engraver and Freeman of the Barber Chirurgeons' Co.) till 1682. Not freed.

HUGGEFORD, Ignatius   **London/Florence**
Freeman of the Haberdashers' Co. Free Brother in CC Jul 1671. Took as aprs.: Oct 1686 **Peter Huggeford** (thro' J. Delander), though 'being then beyond the seas'. Paid no quarterage after c. 1697. Listed as dead by 1698. Believed one of the first to apply jewelling to the interior of watches. In May 1704/05 when the CC were opposing Debaufre's jewelling patent application, the CC bought for £2.10.0. as evidence of their case 'an old watch, the makers name Ignatious Huggeford that had a stone fixed in the cock and balance work'. He prob. worked in Florence where an English clockmaker of this name settled in the late 17th century as watchmaker to Grand Duke Cosimo III, and had a son, Enrico, b. 1695. Work known – watch and lantern clock. Also a winged lantern clock with an Italian inscription.

HUGGEFORD, Peter   **London**
B.c. 1672, apr. Oct 1686 (thro' J. Delander) to Ignatious Huggeford, *qv* (prob. his father) till 1693. Not freed.

HUGHES – watch for odd spellings such as Hues, Hewes, etc.

HUGHES, John   **London**
B.c. 1675, apr. Jul 1689 to Stephen Wilmott till 1696, but not freed. Died 1695 leaving will. Then of St. Andrew Holborn parish. Mentions father, Herbert, mother Mary, brother, Morris, *qv*, who got bequest of £50 and also 'my bed, bolster and blankets'. Brother, Thomas, received a house at Wapping.

HUGHES, Morris   **London**
B.c. 1677, apr. Dec 1691 to Henry Hammond, later passed to Thomas Bates till 1698. Freed Mar 1699/1700. Believed died soon after 1699. Mentioned in will of brother, John, *qv*.

HUGHES, Peter (see Hues)

HULL, Philip   **London**
B.c. 1680, apr. Dec 1693 to William Young till 1701. Not freed.

HULME, John   **Stretford (Lancashire)**
Clockmaker married Jan 1698/99 Alice Heys.

HULSE, Isaac   **London**
On CC list of 1662, but maybe a misrendering of some other name as he
seems otherwise unknown.

HULST, Jacob (maybe Halst?)   **London**
B.c. 1624, apr. Dec 1637 to Ahasuerus Fromateel (thro' T. Dawson) till
1645. Freed Apr 1646.

HULTON, Ralph   **Chester**
Watchmaker Free there in 1670.

HUME, Benjaminn   **London**
B.c. 1677, apr. Aug 1691 to John Barnett till 1698, but not freed.

HUMFREYS, Nicholas   **London**
B.c. 1675, apr. May 1689 to Thomas Wheeler till 1696, but not freed.

HUMFREYS, William   **London**
B.c. 1678, apr. Jun 1692 to Nathaniel Higginson (thro' W. Speakman)
till 1699. Freed Jul 1699. Paid no quarterage after 1702.

HUNT, Edward (also Huntt)   **London**
B.c. 1659 (-1663?) apr. Jun 1677 to Thomas Williamson till 1684. Freed
Jun 1684. Married Aug 1684, batchelor, supposed aged 25 of St. Giles
parish Middlesex, to Margaret Ash aged 30 of St. Pauls, Covent Garden.
Took as aprs.: Nov 1684 **John Grigg** (thro' D. Stevens); Jun 1686
Jonathan Waters; Jun 1692 **John Bayley** – passed on to W. Bartram; Jun
1699 **Henry Clarke** (son of Henry Clarke of Lutterworth, co. Leicester,
husbandman). In 1695 bound an apr. for Isaac Lowndes. Got occasional
CC Charities from 1701-02 till 1709, when prob. died. In 1706 asked for
aid 'as having care for his eyes which are very weak'. Work known –
watch.

HUNT, John   **London**
A clockmaker and a Brother of the Society of Tobacco Pipe Makers.
Made a Free Brother in CC Jul 1671. Paid no quarterage after 1672. Dead
by 1698 and maybe died c. 1672.

HUNT, John   **London**
B.c. 1662 apr. Nov 1676 (thro' S. Davis) to John Lowe (a Freeman of the
Clothworkers' Co.) till 1693. Freed Dec 1699. Paid quarterage till at least
1703. Took as apr. Nov 1707 **John Newey**. Work known – longcase
clock signed 'John Hunt, London'.

HUNT, John   **London**
B.c. 1671, apr. Sep 1685 to Richard Baker (thro' John Wise junior), till
1692, but not freed.

HUNT, Laurence   **London**
In Nov 1675 he was to be prosecuted as a clockmaker not conforming to
CC rules. Believed died 1681.

HUNT, Noe (see Hurt)

HUNT, Richard   **Bristol**
Longcase clock c. 1700 signed 'Richard Hunt, Bristol'.

HUNT, Robert   **London**
B.c. 1647, apr. Apr 1661 to Lawrence Sindry till 1668, but not freed.

HUNT, William   **Exeter**
Clockmaker 1697-1727.

HURST, Arthur   **Ashford (Kent)**
Lantern clock recorded c. 1690.

HURST, Isaac   **London**
B.c. 1645, apr. Sep 1668 to Nicholas Coxeter till 1676. Freed Apr 1677.
Paid no quarterage after 1677.

HURT, Noe (sometimes Hunt in error)   **London**
B.c. 1672, apr. Mar 1686/87 to Joseph Biddle till 1693. Freed Dec 1695.
Took as apr. Jun 1696 **Charles Coller**. Paid quarterage till 1702.

HUSSAM, Charles (error for Huffam *qv*)

HUSSEY, Francis   **London**
Member of Merchant Talors' Co. Took over **Joseph Hussey** (his son?) in

CC from J. Bartholmew, Jul 1676. Took over (in Merchant Taylors' Co.)
Benjamin Merriman from E. Marskell – freed Dec 1686.

HUSSEY, Joseph London
B.c. 1662, believed son of Francis Hussey, *qv*. Apr. in CC Jul 1676 to
John Bartholomew, then passed to Francis Hussey till 1683. Freed Sep
1685. Took as apr. Oct 1685 **Richard Lambden**. Paid no quarterage after
c. 1686. Dead by 1698 and prob. died c. 1686.

HUTCHIN, Francis London
Baillie has 1685. I cannot trace him. Maybe an error for James, *qv*.

HUTCHIN, James London
B.c. 1671, believed son of Joshua. Apr. Sep 1685 to Joshua Hutchin
(thro' D. Stevens) till 1692. Free Apr 1698. Took as apr. Sep 1700
Daniel Garshatt (son of Daniel Garshatt late of Stepney, Middlesex,
weaver, deceased). Paid quarterage till 1702.

HUTCHIN, Joshua Liverpool/London
Free Brother in CC Apr 1683, 'having served his time in Liverpool'.
Took as aprs.: Sep 1685 **James Hutchin** (his son?) (thro' D. Stevens –
freed Apr 1698; Jan 1686-87 **James Andrew** (thro' L. Sindry); Jun 1690
William Caster (thro' D. Stevens – freed Aug 1697. Paid quarterage till
1705 at least. Work known – a watch and a longcase clock.

HUTCHINSON, Benjamin London
Apr. Sep 1682 to Poulters' Co. to Edward Hutchinson (his father?).
Watch recorded pre-1716.

HUTCHINSON, Edward London
A Freeman of Poulters' Co., Sep 1682. Bound as aprs.: Sep 1682
Benjamin Hutchinson (his son?); Jan 1686/87 **John Milbourne** – free
Oct 1693. Bound thro' CC 1693 **John Smith** (thro' Robert Williamson) –
free Sep 1703. Work known – longcase clocks.

HUTCHINSON, John London
In 1622 worked as an alien apr. to Cornelius Mellin in Blackfriars.

HUTCHINSON, William London
B.c. 1674, apr. Aug 1688 to George Etherington (thro' D. Stevens) till
1695. Freed Apr 1706.

HUTTON, James Edinburgh
Son of Henry Hutton of Burntisland. Apr. Dec 1685 to Richard Mills, but not freed.

HUTTON, Richard London
B.c. 1677, apr. Jul 1691 to Thomas Brafield till 1698, but not freed.

HYDE, John London
Apr. 1637 (according to Baillie but I cannot trace him).

HYDE, Thomas Henley-on-Thames
Smith, freed Sep 1464. Worked till pre-1499. Believed maintained church clock.

HYDE, Thomas London
B.c. 1677, apr. May 1691 to Henry Harper till 1698, but not freed.

HYETT, Giles London
B.c. 1634, apr. Aug 1648 to Richard Morgan (thro' N. Tomlins) but transferred to Robert Wrothwood till 1655. Not freed.

HYGHMAN, ---- Stoke-on-Trent (Staffordshire)
Repaired church clock 1605.

HYNE, Peter de London(?)
In 1607 made clock for Westminster Abbey.

HYNES, William Grantham
1601.

I

INGRAM, Thomas (also Ingerham)   **London**
B.c. 1672, apr. Jul 1686 (thro' D. Stevens) to Alexander Warfield, watchmaker, free of the Blacksmiths' Co., till 1693. Freed Aug 1695. Took as aprs.: Aug 1695 **Ralph Clowes** – freed Dec 1703; Apr 1700 **Richard Sanderson** (son of Richard Sanderson of St. Leonard Shoredich, Middlesex, victualler). Believed had son, William, free in CC 1730. Work known – watches.

INWOOD, Samuel   **London**
Supposedly apr. 1662 according to Baillie. I cannot confirm this.

IRELAND, Francis   **London**
Apr. Feb 1660 to William Sammon, later passed over to Thomas Knifton. Free Jul 1668. Free of the City in 1668, being the son of William Ireland of co. Lancaster, yeoman and apr. of William Sammon. Took as aprs.: Jul 1671 **John Barrow** – free Jul 1681; Jan 1676-77 **Zachariah Mountford** (passed over to W. Speakman and free Apr 1684). Paid quarterage till c. 1684.

IRELAND, Henry   **London**
Free Brother in CC Jan 1654-55, but a practicing clockmaker before that. In 1653 William Selwood, of Lothbury, left a bequest of £10., to his eldest daughter. Took as aprs.: 1655 **William Jones** (thro' W. Godbed) – free Jul 1663; Dec 1655 **Francis James** (thro' R. Robinson); **John Palmer** (thro' W. Bunting); In 1656 was accused by Fromanteel of having too many aprs. In 1662 worked in Lothbury. Prob. died before Jul 1671. Work known – lantern clocks.

IRELAND, John **London**
Recorded as apr. 1660 by Baillie, but this is a slip for Francis *qv*.

IRELAND, William **London**
Supposedly worked in Lothbury as a lantern clockmaker in 17th century. I cannot confirm this.

IRVING, Alexander (also Ervin) **London**
B.c. 1674, apr. Sep 1688 to John Wells till 1695. Freed Sep 1695. Still working in 1697, but not heard of thereafter. Believed worked at Westminster. Work known – four longcase clocks recorded.

ISAAC, Sutton **London**
Apr. Dec 1655 to Thomas Knifton, later passed over to John Sammon. Freed Jan 1662/63. Took as aprs.: Jan 1664-65 **Joseph Abberley;** Sep 1672 **William Foster,** later passed to L. Sindry. Freed 1681.

ISMAY, John **Oulton, nr. Wigton (Cumberland)**
Clockmaker. Possibly late 17th century, and early 18th century. Several longcase clocks known. One by this name died in 1724.

IVE, Francis **London**
Son of Matthew, *qv*. Working c. 1640.

IVE, Matthew **London**
Polish refugee c. 1610. Work known – a watch.

IVE, Thomas **London**
Free Brother in CC Apr 1634.

IVERY, John **London**
Reputedly repaired St. Margaret Westminster clock in 1548.

IVES, Zacharia **London**
A keymaker and member of the Salters' Co. Free Brother in CC Sep 1682. Alive in 1697, dead by 1698. Work known – longcase clock recorded signed 'Zac Ives fecit for Thomas Sclater, Gentleman'.

IZOD, William **London**
B.c. 1628, apr. Aug 1641 to John Burges (thro' O. Durrant), till 1649. Freed May 1649. Took as apr. Nov 1649 **Nathaniel Powell.**

J

JACCARD, Joseph   **London**
Recorded as 1680 on London Bridge, but this must be an error for Joseph Jackman, *qv*.

JACKMAN, Joseph (also Jakeman)   **London**
In Sep 1682 he promised to join CC at next quarter court, but did not. Prob. did not work here for long. Baillie records him till 1716 but I cannot confirm this, and the only certain dates for him are 1682/83. Work known – watches, one dated 1683, signed 'Jos Jakeman on London Bridge'; lantern clock dated 1683 signed 'Joseph Jackman Londini'; longcase clock signed 'Joseph Jackman on London Bridge fecit' and 'Jos. Jackman on London Bridge'.

JACKSON, ----   **Newington (Surrey)**
Had watch confiscated by CC Apr 1677.

JACKSON, David   **London**
B.c. 1670, apr. Jul 1684 to Luke Bird (thro' W. Simcox) till 1691, but not freed.

JACKSON, Edward senior   **London**
Freed by redemption Dec 1669 by order of Lord Mayor. Took as apr. Dec 1675 **Francis Birdwhistle**, free Sep 1687.

JACKSON, Edward junior   **London**
B.c. 1658 son of Edward Jackson, citizen and Ironmonger but by trade an innholder. Apr. Dec 1672 to Robert Wilkins till 1679. Freed Apr 1680

(in Sep 1672 had been formerly fraudulently bound to Wilkins). Took as apr. Dec 1684 **John Hudson**. Still alive in 1697.

JACKSON, James   London
B.c. 1667, apr. Nov 1681 to Robert Cosby, till 1688, but passed over to Samuel Clyatt and freed Sep 1689. Took as aprs.: Jan 1689/90 **Jeremiah Downes** (thro' H. Roberts); Apr 1694 **Thomas Gladstone** – free Jul 1703; Nov 1689 **John Newbury**; Aug 1706 **Hassell Morley** (son of Charles Morley of St. Dunstan in the West, framework-knitter); Jun 1702 **Ralph Magee** (son of William Magee late of parish of St. Margaret, Westminster, Gent.). Paid quarterage till at least 1703.

JACKSON, John   London
B.c. 1661, apr. Mar 1675 to Joseph Windmills, later passed to Thomas Taylor of Holborn till 1682. Freed Apr 1682. Signed with his mark in 1682. In Nov 1688 bound an apr. for W. Slough. Not heard of after 1688 and prob. dead or gone by 1697.

JACKSON, Joseph   London
B.c. 1624, apr. Mar 1638/39 to William Bowyer (thro' T. Dawson) till 1645. Freed Mar 1646/47. Took as apr. Jun 1656 **Sampson Jackson**. Prob. dead or gone by 1662.

JACKSON, Martin   London
Free Brother in CC Nov 1697 having served his apr. at Durham. Took as aprs.: Jun 1710 **Joseph Knibb** (thro' Martin Jackson, not free of the City); Nov 1715 **Robert Kerby**; Jan 1717/18 **Richard Davis**. Made CC Assistant 1716, Warden 1718, Master 1721, after which I have no data on him. Work known – bracket and longcase clocks.

JACKSON, Richard   London
Free in CC Oct 1632 (Brother?). Not heard of again.

JACKSON, Sampson   London
B.c. 1642, apr. Jun 1656 to Joseph Jackson till 1663, but not freed. Work known – longcase clock by Sampson Jackson of Thorpe (?which Thorpe).

JACKSON, Thomas   London
B.c. 1632, apr. Jan 1646/47 to John Burgis (thro' Jos. Quash), till 1653, but not freed.

JACKSON, Thomas London
B.c. 1666, apr. Sep 1680 to Jeremy Gregory (thro' T. Wheeler) till 1687.
Freed Apr 1688 (though master had died in 1686). Paid quarterage till
1704.

JACOB, Benjamin London
B.c. 1673, apr. Oct 1687 to Thomas Birch (thro' W. Fuller) till 1694.
Free Sep 1706. Paid quarterage till 1711. Work known – longcase clock
signed 'B. Jacob – London'.

JACOB, John (Jean/Jan) London
In 1622 was an alien working at Mr. Smythe's, prob. an apr. of George
Smith, *qv*. Baillie lists a Jan Jacobs at Haarlem.

JACOB, Paule London
In 1622 an alien at Mr. Smythe's, prob. an apr. of George Smith, *qv*.

JADWIN, Robert London
B.c. 1633, apr. Jul 1647 to William North (thro' T. Alcock), till 1654,
but not freed.

JAMES, Benjamin Shaston (Shaftesbury)
Longcase clock recorded c. 1700 'Benj James – Shaston'.

JAMES, Francis London
B.c. 1642, apr. Dec 1655 to Robert Robinson, then passed over to Henry
Ireland till 1663, but not freed.

JAMES, John London
Apr. Nov 1653 to Nicholas Tomlin, then passed over to Thomas
Loomes. Freed Feb 1661/62. Not heard of thereafter.

JAMES, Joseph London
B.c. 1664, apr. Mar 1678/79 (thro' S. Davis) to Thomas Finch, clock-
maker in St. Martins till 1685. In Dec 1687 promised to take up his
Freedom as a watchmaker at the next court. Freed Jan 1689/90. Took as
aprs.: Nov 1696 **John Bell**; Sep 1702 **William** (or James?) **Perdue** (son of
Johnathan Perdue of St. Bride's parish London, upholster), transferred
Jul 1706 to James Walker. I have no trace of him after 1704, though
Baillie records him till 1723.

JAMES, Mougham London
B.c. 1678, apr. Mar 1692/93 to Charles Goode (thro' T. Elton) till 1699, but not freed.

JANAWAY, William London
Baillie says apr. 1675. I cannot trace him.

JANSON, Martin London
Alien Horologius in 1561 (Baillie).

JAQUES, James London
Apr. 1679 according to Baillie. Prob. an error for William, *qv.*

JAQUES, William (signed Will) London
B.c. 1665, apr. Dec 1679 to John Wright, transferred to Nathaniel Delander till 1686. Freed Sep 1687. Took as aprs.: Aug 1691 **William Achurch** – free Sep 1699; Jan 1692/93 **George Cutter;** Jun 1695 **Benjamin Fifield;** Jul 1698 **Thomas Nichols** – free Apr 1707; May 1700 **Henry Duck** (son of Henry Duck Citizen and Goldsmith of London); Apr 1709 **John Lee** (son of Joseph Lee, Citizen and Merchant Taylor of London) – free Mar 1719/20; May 1711 **John Lang** – free Apr 1720; Jan 1716/17 his son **William Jaques;** Sep 1717 **Robert Jaques** (son?); Jun 1719 **Jeremiah Davis.** Made Assistant in 1708, Warden 1713-15, Master 1716, attended till 1719 at least. Prob. a goldsmith – in 1713 he produced for CC a paper re- Goldsmiths' Co. orders.

JARMIN, John Long Melford (Suffolk)
Repaired church clock 1683.

JARRETT, Richard (sometimes Jarratt) London
Freeman of the Salters' Co., made free in CC Jan 1670/71. Took as aprs.: Dec 1678 **Charles Viell** – free Apr 1686; Nov 1679 **John Mole;** May 1681 **John Hillery** (thro' N. Russell); Sep 1684 **Edmund Day** – free Apr 1692; Dec 1690 **John Marriott** – free Jun 1715. Made CC Steward 1672; Assistant 1674; Warden 1681-83; Master 1686. Ceased to attend in 1693 due to sickness. From 1694 he received occasional CC charity. In Dec 1695/96 he got 18/- sent to him 'to Ludgate'. Quarterage paid till 1697, but believed dead by 1698. Said to have worked in Lothbury. In 1686 was stated to be son-in-law of Jeremy Gregory. Work known – a watch and bracket clock. (Maybe confused with Richard Garrett, *qv.*)

JARRATT, Richard London
One of this name admitted as a brother in 1632. Can hardly be the same man as above.

JARREY, Stephen (Etienne) London
In Oct 1655 appointed as journeyman to work for Grinkin, Bartram and Jeremy Gregory. Came from Santerry(?).

JARVIS, Joseph London
B.c. 1657, apr. Dec 1670 to Barthol Powell till 1687, but not freed.

JARVIS, Simon London
B.c. 1657, apr. Apr 1670 to Richard Ames till 1678, but not freed.

JAYNE, John London
Baillie has CC 1687 but I cannot trace this name. Prob. an error.

JEEYES, Samuel London
B.c. 1657, apr. Jul 1670 to Philip Smith, mat. inst. maker (thro' L. Wythe) till 1677, but not freed.

JEFFERIES, John London
Free Brother in CC Jul 1639.

JEFF(E)S, Benjamin London
B.c. 1679, apr. Apr 1693 to John Willoughby (thro' W. Neighbour) till 1700, freed Jul 1702.

JEFFS, James London
Took as apr. Dec 1700 **Thomas Lynes** (son of Richard Lynes of Sl...., Middlesex, shoemaker). This is prob. an error for John Jeffs, *qv*.

JEFFS, John Oxford
Bellhanger working there 1640-50.

JEFFS, John London
B.c. 1675, apr. May 1689 to John Waters till 1696 (thro' J. Bailey). Freed Jul 1697. In 1699 ordered to dismiss a gunsmith who was working at his house on watchmaking. Took as aprs.: May 1699 **William Barker** (son of John Barker late of Eston?, co. Northants, Baker); Nov 1704 **Walter Bendall** (son of Matthew Bendall of Queen? Cammell, co. Somerset,

clothier); Jul 1714 **John Sherwood**; Dec 1716 **John Armstrong**. See also James Jeffs.

JELLY, John London
Barnard Castle ward. Free in Merchant Taylors' Co. Took as apr. **Simon Bartram** Feb 1611/12, till 1619. Watchmaker?

JENEWAY, William London
B.c. 1661, apr. Mar 1675 to John Savill (thro' N. Coxeter), till 1682, but not freed.

JENKINS, Cornelius London
B.c. 1657, apr. Jun 1671 to Isaac Daniell (thro' T. Fenn), till 1678. Freed Sep 1678. Took as aprs.: Jun 1680 **Edward Herne**; Mar 1684/85 **Thomas Condy** – freed Jun 1692; after Aug 1692 **Samuel Marshall** (from Anne widow of Isaac Daniell) – freed Feb 1689/90; Jul 1690 **Joseph Herne**; May 1695 **John Jenkins**; Apr 1698 **Thomas Clarke** – freed Sep 1709. Believed a watch casemaker. Paid quarterage till 1704 when believed died.

JENKINS, James London
B.c. 1669, apr. May 1683 to William Grimes a clockmaker (thro' D. Stevens), till 1690. Freed Jul 1692 as a Brother. Took as aprs.: Feb 1692/93 **Grace Hack** (a girl); Sep 1694 **Elizabeth Morgan**; Sep 1696 **Miles Thistlethwaite**; Sep 1700 **Samuel Simcox** (son of Isaac Simcox late of parish of St. Bottolph, Bishopsgate, London, silk twister, deceased) – free Jul 1708; Apr 1704 **William King** (son of Richard King of the parish of St. Andrew, victualler). Paid quarterage till 1705. Work known – longcase clocks signed 'Jenkins – London', prob. him.

JENKINS, Nicholas Thornbury (Gloucestershire)
Made Bristol turret clock, 1610.

JENKINS, Thomas London
B.c. 1656, apr. Aug 1669 to Samuel Horne till 1677. Freed Nov 1677. Took as aprs.: Dec 1680 **John Harmer**; May 1682 **Isaac Birdwhistle** – freed Aug 1692. In will of John Batten (1686) Thomas Jenkins and wife received bequests of mourning rings.

JENKINSONNE, John   **Boston (Lincolnshire)**
Repaired St. Nicholas chapel clock, Kings Lynn, in 1630. Supplied new
clock for it in 1631.

JENNINGS, Emanuel   **London**
B.c. 1668, apr. Jul 1682 to John Colston till 1689, but not freed.

JENNINGS, Robert   **London**
B.c. 1677 son of William Jennings, late of Tewksbury, co. Glos.,
milliner, deceased. Apr. Aug 1691 to Robert Thacke till 1698; freed May
1703. Took as aprs.: Dec 1709 **John Constantine** – freed Feb 1716/17;
Jun 1714 **Edward Motley**; Jul 1716 **Charles Jennings**; Mar 1718/19
John Ellis.

JENNION, William   **Chester**
Free 1601/02, clocksmith.

JERVIS, Francis   **London**
B.c. 1643, apr. Jun 1656 to Ralph Gretorix till 1664, but not freed.

JESSON, ----   **London**
Ironmonger, 'nr. the Bars without Aldgate'. Had faulty rulers
confiscated by the CC 1671-72.

JEVON, Henry   **London**
Not a clockmaker but an 'attorney-at-law', made free in the CC by
redemption by order of the Lord Mayor in May 1673. 'He having taken a
house and inhabiting in the new buildings of this City.' Took as aprs.:
with his wife, Christine; Jul 1679 **Elizabeth Edmonds**; Sep 1685 **Anne
Wenday.** In Sep 1706 his daughter, Mary, was freed by patrimony. (She
later married a 'Mr. Lyon' and was in arrears of quarterage in 1712.) He
paid no quarterage after about 1690.

JEYES (see Jeeyes)

JOHNS, Richard   **Exeter (Devon)**
Clockmaker. Freed 1628. Apr. of John Savage and later married his
daughter. Working till at least 1648.

JOHNSON – see also Johnstone.

JOHNSON, Benjamin   **London**
Not officially a member of the CC but apparently accepted by them.
Took as aprs. thro' CC: Jul 1693 **William Moore** (thro' C. Gretton) –
freed Apr 1701; Dec 1704 **James Kempe** (son of Charles Kempe, Citizen
and clockmaker deceased, watchmaker). Work known – longcase clocks
(one with 1¼ seconds pendulum) signed 'Benjamin Johnson, London'.

JOHNSON, Cornelys   **London**
In 1551 was servant of Lewis Billiard in St. Clement Dane's parish.

JOHNSON, Cornelius (II)   **London**
B.c. 1636, apr. Mar 1650/51 to John Nicasius (thro' William (error for
Nicholas?) Tomlins) till 1657, but not freed.

JOHNSON, Cornelius (III)   **London**
B.c. 1680, apr. Mar 1686/87 to Joseph Duke till 1693. Freed Apr 1694.
Paid no quarterage after c. 1694. In 1712/13 was considered for
prosecution for arrears but excused 'being out of trade'.

JOHNSON, George   **London**
Apr. Apr 1641 to John Nicasius (thro' O. Durrant). Freed Dec 1649.
Took apr. **Tobias Calcott** – freed Jun 1664.

JOHNSON, George   **London**
B.c. 1655, apr. May 1668 to Ahasuerus Fromanteel junior till 1676, but
not freed.

JOHNSON, Jeremiah   **London**
B.c. 1646, son of Robert Johnson of (Chesham?), Bucks. Apr. Jul 1660
to Nicholas Payne, then passed on to Abraham Beckner, then to
Ahasuarus Fromanteel junior. Freed Dec 1668, also free of the City then.
Took as aprs.: Jul 1671 **Arthur Mousley**; Aug 1674 **John Smart** – free
Sep 1682; 1681 **Vaughan Breynton,** freed Sep 1693; Mar 1687 **George
Payne.** Also bound an apr. for James Delander. Had a son Jeremy apr.
1697, *qv.* Got CC charity from c. 1707 to late 1709 when died. Believed
worked in Exchange Alley. Work known – watches and longcase clocks.

JOHNSON, John   **London**
B.c. 1659, apr. Jul 1673 to Barlow Rookes till 1680. Freed Aug 1680
(after death of Master). Took as aprs.: Aug 1682 **Richard Wythe;** May
1688 **Richard Say;** Sep 1691 **Thomas Rider** – free Sep 1698; Jul 1693

Richard Mort; Nov 1697 **Bevis Yeo;** May 1699 **William Palmer** (son of William Palmer, Citizen and Feltmaker of London, deceased). Alive till 1704 and believed died soon after this. (One of this name said to have worked at the 'Flower de Luces, Cheapside', in 1682 was in fact a jeweller with unknown Christian name so may not have been John.)

JOHNSON, John   **London**
Clockmaker. Admitted to CC as a Brother Apr 1678. Paid quarterage till c. 1689, but not later.

JOHNSON, Leonard   **Nottingham**
Working in 1541 according to Baillie.

JOHNSON, Michael   **London**
B.c. 1663, apr. Jan 1677 to David Lloyd till 1684. Freed Sep 1687. Took as aprs.: Aug 1697 **John Barnett**; Dec 1704 **Thomas King** (son of late Thomas King of St. Albans, Herts., gent, deceased). Not heard of after 1704. Work known – watches signed 'Michael Johnson, London' (Baillie also records him at Barnard Castle, which is a confusion with a much later man of the same name).

JOHNSON, Roger   **London**
In 1630 petitioner for incorporation of CC, but not heard of thereafter.

JOHNSON, Thomas   **London**
B.c. 1678, apr. Oct 1692 to Robert Player, clock casemaker (wooden), till 1699. Freed Jul 1700. This can hardly be the same man as listed below, *qv*.

JOHNSON, Thomas   **London**
Several longcase clocks are recorded, including one with 1¼ seconds pendulum and a month one signed variously 'Thomas Johnson, Ratcliffe Cross' and 'Thomas Johnson, London'. These seem to date between c. 1680 and c. 1705. Oddly enough no one of this name appears in CC records at this period. In 1701 a clockmaker of this name lived in Southwark when his daughter Patience, was buried; might be same man.

JOHNSON, William   **York**
Watchmaker. B. 1642, son of William Johnson, locksmith. Free 1656. Believed still alive in 1713 when son William freed.

JOHNSTONE, William   **London**
B.c. 1677, apr. Nov 1690 to Daniel Quare till 1698. Freed Apr 1702.
Work known – a bracket clock. In Dec 1698 a watchmaker of this name
agreed to buy clothing for apr. Isaac Johnson, prob. a relative, when he
was bound to J. Williamson, and this may be the same William Johnson.

JOHNSTONE – (see also Johnson).

JOHNSTONE, Alexander   **Edinburgh**
Son of Alexander Johnstone, lister, Burgess of Edinburgh. Apr. May
1688 to Andrew Brown.

JOHNSTOUN, David   **Edinburgh**
Son of Robert Johnstoun, Burgess of Stirling, merchant. Apr. May 1679
to Andrew Brown.

JOHNSTOUN, John   **Edinburgh**
Apr. 1671 to Robert Smith.

JOLE, Robert (erroneously Fole)   **London**
Mat. inst. maker and Freeman of the Stationers' Co. Freed in CC as
Brother Feb 1667/68, but refused to take the oath. Took as aprs.: Oct
1668 **James Brickhill** (thro' L. Wythe); Apr 1680 **Thomas Jole** (thro'
S. Davis). In 1671/72 CC seized faulty rulers from his Fleet Street
premises, supposedly made by William Elmes or Joseph Wells. In 1687
was due to serve as Steward and in 1688 he was fined £5. for refusing the
office and all future offices. Paid quarterage till 1705.

JOLE, Thomas   **London**
B.c. 1666 (prob. son of Robert *qv*). Apr. April 1680 to Robert Jole till
1687, but not freed.

JOL(L)Y, Jaques   **London(?)**
Watches c. 1620/30. Believed worked in France (not London as some
suggest).

JOLLY, John   **Belfast**
Watchmaker in Castle Street 1657.

JOL(L)Y, Daniel (also Jolley)   **London**
B.c. 1623, apr. Oct 1637 to John Droshout (thro' O. Durrant) till 1644,
but not freed.

JONES, Benjamin   **London**
B.c. 1662 apr. Sep 1676 to Richard Halstead, and on whose death (Apr
1678) was passed over to Edward East till 1683, but not freed.

JONES, Charles   **London**
B.c. 1649, apr. Jul 1663 to Walter Gibbs till 1670, but not freed.

JONES, Daniel   **London**
B.c. 1659, apr. Jul 1672 to Edward Wilson till 1680, but not freed.
Warned for not taking up Freedom 1680/81.

JONES, David   **London**
Apr. Jan 1680-81 to Henry Hickman, but passed over to Isaac Day.
'Henry Hickman will ensure that David Jones will become a Freeman of
the CC in due course.' Sep 1687 made a Free Brother.

JONES, Edward   **London**
B.c. 1672, apr. Jul 1686 to William Bartram till 1693, but not freed.

JONES, Evan   **London**
Freeman of the Goldsmiths' Co. and working in Fleet Street by 1646 –
not then in CC, but joined by 1647. Believed related to Henry Jones and
prob. worked for Edward East. Took as aprs.: Jul 1652 **Phineas
Baddeley** (thro' D. Moody) – free Jan 1661; Jul 1652 **Marmaduke Jones**
(thro' D. Moody) – freed Jan 1661/62?; Jan 1662-63 **John Delaville**
(thro' S. Horne); Oct 1670 **Edward Chambers** (thro' S. Horne); **John
Fort** (thro' R. Bowen) – freed Nov 1672; Jan 1682/83 **James Hellam**
(thro' D. Stevens), later passed over to Henry Jones and freed Apr 1690.
In 1656 rebellion he supported the CC administration. In 1662 listed as
working at Westminster. Made Assistant 1660, but in 1666/67 was
excused office of Warden etc., by paying fine. In Sep 1684 'was sick weak
and confined to his bed' and was given charity by CC. Had died by Apr
1685 when his widow received regular charitable payments till 1694
consistently getting a higher charity than other widows, paid from
Edward East's own charity. Work known – none – prob. a casemaker or
engraver working for East.

JONES, Henry   **London**
B.c. 1642, allegedly son of William Jones, vicar of Boulder, Southampton. Apr. Aug 1654 to Benjamin Hill but passed over to Edward East. Freed Jul 1663. Took as aprs.: Aug 1664 **John Hanburg**; Jul 1670 **Richard Ayres** – free Sep 1680; Jul 1673 **Nicholas Annat**; Aug 1674 **Edward Everest** (died 1680); Sep 1678 **James Greene** – freed Sep 1685; Dec 1682 son **William Jones** – not freed; Mar 1684 **Richard Staples**; Oct 1685 **Francis Robinson** – free Apr 1707; Feb 1688-89 **William Cleave;** pre-1685 took over **James Hellam** from Evan Jones – freed Apr 1690; Dec 1690 son **Henry Jones** – free Apr 1698; Jan 1690-91 **John Sherwood; John Silvester** (from Thomas Bates) – free Sep 1693; Dec 1693 **Joseph Prestwood** – passed to David Wyche. Worked in Inner Temple Lane (1675). Became CC Assistant from 1676, Warden 1687-90, Master 1691; last attended 1694. In Jan 1673-74 he complained that Robert Seigniour had erased his name from a royal clock (or had caused Edward Stanton to do it). In Nov 1678 he was on a special meeting which suspended John Matchet for being a Catholic (but *cf* East's Catholicism?). In Jul 1679 he had a great quarrel with the fiery John Nicasius, in which the latter was judged to be wrong. In Oct 1692 gave CC £100 for the use of the poor. Will dated Feb 1692. Died Nov 1695. Left widow Hannah, and son Henry property in parish of St. Bottolph without Aldgate. Buried at St. Dunston's in the West, Fleet Street. Work known – a prolific maker, and highly thought of. Usually signed 'Henry Jones in ye Temple', sometimes 'Henry Jones London'. Work includes watches, lantern, bracket and longcase clocks. His widow, Hannah, took as apr. Mar 1696/97 **John Magson** – free Jan 1704/05.

JONES, Henry senior   **London**
B.c. 1655, apr. Jul 1668 to Charles Bonner till 1676, but not freed. Not heard of after 1668 and prob. died. (Baillie's date of 1698 for this man is an error for Henry Junior *qv.*) Not apparently connected with Henry Jones, previous entry.

JONES, Henry junior   **London**
B.c. 1676, son of Henry Jones (entry before last). Apr. Dec 1690 to father till 1697. Freed Apr 1698. Paid quarterage 1698-1704 when believed died. Took as aprs.: Jul 1700 **Thomas Good** (son of William Good, of Westminster, pipemaker); Jun 1704 **Ralph Magge** (son of William Magge, Gent. of City of Westminster). Work known – none. Perhaps his work would be mistaken for that of the father, or indistinguishable from it?

JONES, Henry   **London**
Baillie records one such free 1697, but this is an error for 1698, Henry junior.

JONES, James   **London**
B.c. 1673, apr. May 1687 to Philip Thacke till 1694, but not freed.

JONES, Jonathan   **London**
B.c. 1664, apr. Dec 1678 to Robert Smith, later passed over to Nathaniel Delander till 1685. Freed Sep 1687. Took as aprs.: Oct 1688 **John Wightman** – freed Nov 1696; Jul 1693 **Edward Stephens**; Dec 1694 **John Walker** (thro' D. Beckman). Apr 1698 **Thomas Peeres**; Aug 1703 **Evan Thomas.** Last heard of in 1712 when, being called to serve as a Steward he 'appeared, and being aquainted therewith, he was very rude, being indrinke and would not give any direct answers whether he would hold (the office)'. Later apologised!

JONES, Marmaduke   **London**
B.c. 1638, apr. Jul 1652 to Evan Jones (thro' D. Moody) till 1659. Believed freed Jan 1661/62.

JONES, Samuel   **London**
B.c. 1674, apr. Mar 1688/89 to Edmund Massey till 1695, but not freed.

JONES, Thomas   **London**
B.c. 1657, apr. Feb 1671/72 to Jeremy Gregory (thro' B. Bell) till 1678. Freed Sep 1679. In 1678 was witness to will of Thomas Whaplitt. Took as aprs.: Apr 1686 **John Stanford Clark** – freed Jan 1696/97; Nov 1691 **John Berault**; Aug 1700 **John Jones** (son of William Jones of Gosport, co. Southampton, apothecary). (Could be relative of THE Henry Jones.) Paid quarterage till 1702. Work known – a watch.

JONES, Valentine   **London**
B.c. 1679, apr. Oct 1693 to John Banbury till 1700. Free Jan 1704/05. Took as aprs.: Feb 1709/10 **Philip Palmer**; May 1712 **Thomas Babb**; Sep 1713 **Edward Preston**; Aug 1717 **Alexander Willard.** Baillie says bankrupt 1725.

JONES, William   **London**
B.c. 1635, apr. Jan 1649/50 to Robert Grinkin (thro' L. Wythe) till 1656, but not freed.

JONES, William London
Apr. Jun 1655 to Henry Ireland (thro' W. Godbed) freed Jul 1663.

JONES, William London
B.c. 1668, son of THE Henry Jones. Apr. Dec 1682 to his father till 1689, but not freed. Prob. died young.

JORDAIN(E) (see Jourdain) London

JORDAN, James Chatham (Kent)
Longcase clock known c.1700 – c.1710.

JOS(E)LIN, Edward London
B.c. 1676, apr. Mar 1690-91 to James Wolverston till 1697. Freed Mar 1697/98. Took as aprs.: Jan 1708/09 **George Davis** (son of John Davis of St. Martins-in-the-Fields, Middlesex, bricklayer) – freed Jun 1720; May 1715 **Charles Sampson;** Jun 1720 **John Hecker** from John Martin. Baillie records him as late as 1728.

JOURDAIN, William (also Guillaume Jordain) London
Apr. April 1646 to Robert Smith (thro' T. Alcock) but not freed. Can hardly be the same man as one of this name who was a Huguenot refugee to London in 1699. Listed at Stewart Street, Artillery Ground in 1700, Smack Street, Artillery Ground 1703, Dossett Street, Stepney 1704. Work known – longcase clocks signed 'Jourdain – London' and 'William Jourdain'.

JOVAT, ---- London
Baillie records him c. 1675. I cannot trace him.

JOYCE, George London/Bristol
B.c. 1670, apr. Aug 1684 to Nathaniel Pyne till 1691. Freed Aug 1692, after which he paid no subscriptions to CC. Almost certainly gone by 1697. In 1698 a watchmaker of this name appears at Bristol as bondsman to a marriage – must surely be the same man.

JOYCE, John Cockshutt (nr. Ellesmere, Shropshire)
With wife Elizabeth he lived at the Lodge and had son William, b. Feb 1691/92, who himself became a clockmaker. No example of his work appears to have survived today, but he is reputed to have been a clockmaker.

JOYCE, John William   **Wrexham, Denbighshire**
Clockmaker. Died 1717. Related to John Joyce, but relationship
uncertain.

JOYNE, John   **London**
B.c. 1647, apr. Aug 1660 to John Smith till 1668, but not freed till Sep
1687. Still working in 1697, but not heard of thereafter.

JOYNSON, Richard   **Wrexham (Denbighshire)**
Working by 1701. Died 1711.

JULIAN, Gregory   **London**
Apr. Aug 1656 to Tobias Davis. Freed Jun 1664, but not heard of thereafter.

K

KAMPE (see Campe)

KAY, David   Crail (Scotland)
In 1553 made church clock for Dundee, but left in 1554 before it was finished. In 1576 maintained Glasgow town clocks, one of which he had made.

KAY, John   Aberdeen (Scotland)
Loriner. In 1582 he repaired the town's three clocks and supplied a new one.

KEENE, John   London
Ironmonger. Paid CC search fee 1673.

KELL, John   London
Never actually admitted to CC but known to them. Prob. dead by 1662/63.

KELLETT, Thomas   London
Watchmaker in CC records 1635.

KELME, ----   London
Recorded by Britten c. 1670. Prob. an error for Helme *qv.*

KEMP, Charles (sometimes Keamp)   London
B.c. 1664, apr. Aug 1678 to Prettyman Sergeant, later passed over to Charles Gretton, till 1684. Freed Sep 1688. Watchmaker. Took as aprs.:

Apr 1694 **Thomas Tompion** (son of James Tompion) – freed Dec 1702. Died in 1696, in which year his widow received CC charity. In Apr 1704 his orphaned son James, aged 14 or more, assisted by CC to be bound as an apr. to Ben Johnson.

KEMP, Henry   London
Baillie says 1643 watchmaker. Prob. an error for Kent, *qv.*

KEMP, John   Chester
A smith who repaired Holy Trinity clock in 1600.

KEMP, Richard   London
B.c. 1672, apr. Nov 1686 to John Wyse, junior (thro' Joshua Winnock) till 1693. Later passed to John Westoby and freed Jul 1701. Prob. died or left soon after.

KEMPS, Anthony (see Matthew)

KEMPS, Matthew (or Kempe)   London
B.c. 1649, son of Anthony Kempe, a jeweller and Free Denizen. Apr. Oct 1663 to his father (thro' N. Russell) till 1670 (though father was not a CC member!), and freed Jan 1670/71. Paid no quarterage thereafter.

KEMYES, Joshua   London
B.c. 1660, apr. Sep 1673 to Daniel Stevens till 1681, but not freed.

KENDAL(L), John   London
Early 17th century watch recorded.

KENEY (see Kenney)

KENNETT, John   London
'A poore workman', who received CC charity in Oct 1651 – (see John Kent?).

KENNING, William (signed Kening)   Banbury/London
B. 1648 son of Martin and Alice Kenning of Banbury, where he worked til c. 1675. Went to London about 1682, where threatened with prosecution for practicing when not a member of CC. Several further threats resulted in his joining as a Brother, a Great Clockmaker in May 1685 (not 1684 as some say). Took as apr. **Edward Cooke** (thro'

D. Stevens). Paid quarterage till 1705 at least. Work known – lantern clock signed 'William Kenning – Banbury fecit, 1674'.

KEN(N)EY, Vincent   **London**
Clockmaker. Paid £19.12s.8d. by Henry VIII for 11 clocks and dials.

KENNEY, William (error for Kenning *qv*)

KENNON, William 1682–85 (error for Kenning *qv*)

KENNON, William (see also Kenyon)   **London**
Apr. Jan 1656 to Jacob Betts (thro' J. Bayes). Freed Mar 1674/75. Took as apr. Jan 1678/79 **John Price**. Believed died or left 1679/80.

KENT, Henry   **London**
Brother in CC Sep 1640. One of the rebels in 1656. Worked at Westminster 1662. Took as aprs.: Jul 1647 **Henry Daniell** (thro' T. Claxton); Nov 1657 **Mathias Godbed** (thro' B. Hill). Made Assistant from 1668. Last attended 1671 when prob. died. Always in arrears with quarterage. Work known – a watch is recorded.

KENT, John   **Congleton (Cheshire)**
Late 17th century lantern clock signed 'Johannes Kent – Congleton' – see Kennett?

KENT, William   **London**
B.c. 1668, apr. Jun 1681 to Samuel Marchant till 1689, but not freed (Baillie lists another of this name as free in CC in 1681 but this is an error for the above man).

KENTON, Joseph   **London**
B.c. 1665, apr. Jul 1679 to Richard Ames till 1686. Freed Sep 1686. Paid quarterage till about 1697, when died.

KERMON, William (error for Kennon, *qv*)

KENYON, William   **Liverpool (Lanchashire)**
Clockmaker. Believed b. 1667. Issue b. 1708-20. Perhaps connected with Kennons, *qv*.

KERNICKE, Christopher   **St. Neot (Cornwall)**
Worked on church clock 1622.

KERSLAW, William   **Stirling (Scotland)**
Kept town clock 1548.

KEWELL, Thomas   **London**
B.c. 1672, apr. Aug 1685 to Richard Colston till 1693, but not freed.

KEY, Josiah   **London**
Late 17th century. Made locks for Hampton Court Palace. Work known
– watch case.

KEY(E)S, Markham   **London**
B.c. 1640, apr. Jun 1653 to Jeremy Gregory (thro' J. Bayes), till 1661,
but not freed.

KEYS, William   **Monks Kirby (Warwickshire)**
Repaired church clock in 1699. Blacksmith?

KEYMES, Joshua (see under Kemyes)

KHELLER, Johann Michael   **London**
Watch recorded, first half of 17th century.

KIDD, John   **London**
B.c. 1641, apr. Oct 1655 to John Betts (thro' N. Payne) till 1662, but not
freed.

KIDSON, William   **York**
Clockmaker. Free 1614. The first maker to work there. Was associated
with John Newsome. Had as apr. **John Pennock.** Work known – watch
signed 'Wm. Kitson Att Yorke'.

KILGOUR, Patrick   **Aberdeen/Edinburgh (Scotland)**
In 1672 came to Aberdeen, a 'knockmaker and watchmaker' and agreed
to make an eight day pendulum clock free of charge in return for his
Freedom to trade there. In 1692 he agreed to repair town clocks and
convert one to pendulum and fit maintaining power. Was at Cannongate,
Edinburgh in 1702.

KILMI(N)STER, Henry (signed Killmister)   **London**
Free in Blacksmiths' Co. (as Kelmaster) 1676/77. Free Brother in CC Jul 1677. Took as aprs.: Dec 1678 **Simon Finch** (thro' S. Davis senior) – freed Dec 1706; Dec 1683 **Edward Parker; William Gilbert** (from J. Longland) – freed Aug 1695; Mar 1698-99 **Richard Longcraft** or **Langcraft** (son of Richard Longcraft of Wilsford, co. Wilts, yeoman) – later passed over to William Holloway – freed Oct 1718; Jun 1710 **Isaac Edwards,** later passed over to John Bailey. Also bound and apr. for Joshua Alsope. Work known – watch.

KINDER (?), William   **London**
Watchmaker of St. Olave's, Southwark. Died 1710.

KING, John   **London**
Ironmonger. Paid CC search fee in Feb 1671/72.

KING, John   **London**
Baillie says apr. 1686 – I cannot trace him.

KING, Jonathan   **London**
B.c. 1668, apr. Jul 1682 to Richard Watts till 1689. Freed Nov 1689. In Jun 1689 he married at St. Savior's, Southwark, being then a batchelor, watchmaker, aged 23 (he said) to Rebecca Dowson of Great St. Bartholomew, spinster, aged 21. Working till 1698 but no trace thereafter.

KING, Nehemiah   place not known
Lantern clock recorded dated 1693.

KING, Thomas   **London**
Apr. Jan 1657/58 to Ralph Greatorex. Freed Apr 1669.

KING, Thomas   **London**
B.c. 1678, apr. Apr 1692 to Joseph Moore till 1699. Freed Jan 1699/1700. Paid quarterage till 1702.

KINGSMILL, George (alias Wogan)   **London**
Apr. to William Smith (thro' N. Tomlinson). Freed Jul 1667. Took as apr. Jul 1672 **Edward Millet** (thro' L. Wythe) but in Mar 1672/73 he had 'absented' and deserted his apr. (A later record suggests that he paid quarterage till about 1693 which is prob. an error.)

KINGSNORTH, John   **London**
B.c. 1674, apr. Sep 1688 to Thomas Stubbs (thro' D. Stevens) till 1695, but not freed.

KINNING, John (see Kynning)

KIPPIS, George   **London**
B.c. 1673, apr. Apr 1687 to Christopher Gould (thro' D. Stevens) till 1694, but not freed.

KIRK, James   **Edinburgh (Scotland)**
Son of Robert Kirk, and his wife Helen (Ferguson) merchant Burgess of Edinburgh. Apr. Mar 1648 to Robert Smith, clockmaker. In Dec 1648 his mother complained that the master did not teach him nor maintain him properly.

KIRK, John   **London**
B.c. 1655, apr. Nov 1668 to George Crouch, later passed over to Edward Staunton till 1676. Freed Jan 1677/78. Work known – longcase clock.

KIRK(H)ALL, Thomas   **Bolton (Lancashire)**
Married 1625 Ann Bonfourne. Made turret clock for Brindle in 1637 (error in dating this as 1673?).

KIRKWOOD, Thomas   **London**
Goldsmith and banker (with John Hind, *qv*) 'over against the Exchange, Cornhill' 1670-81. Borrowed money at interest from CC. Not a maker.

KNAGG family   **Carlisle (Cumberland)**
Family of blacksmiths who maintained local turret clocks from 1604 to well into the 18th century.

KNAPP, John   **London/Reading (Berkshire)**
Bracket clock signed 'John Knapp, London', lantern clock signed at Reading.

KNIBB – for this family see R. A. Lee '*The Knibb Family, Clockmakers*' and C. F. C. Beeson '*Clockmaking in Oxfordshire*'.

KNIBB, Edward   **London**
Supposedly apr. to Joseph Knibb in 1693, but I cannot confirm this.

KNIBB, John   **Oxford**
B. 1650 brother of Joseph Knibb for whom he worked from about 1664.
Free there 1673. Continued to trade at Oxford after brother John had
moved to London. Had as aprs.: 1673 **Samuel Aldworth**; 1675 **William
Hitchcock**; 1679 **Thomas Lidbrook**; 1681 **Mathias Unite**; 1682 **John
Ford**; 1686 **John Goweth**; 1696 **John Free**; 1698 **Thomas Gillett**; 1706
George Wentworth; c. 1710 **Humphrey Brickland**. Died 1722. Work
known – prolific maker of all types of clocks, usually signed at Oxford,
but one is recorded signed at Hanslope and one signed at London – see
Beeson and Lee.

KNIBB, Joseph   **Oxford/London/Hanslope (Buckinghamshire)**
B. 1640, son of Thomas Knibb of Claydon. Not known where apr. but
may have served his cousin, Samuel. By 1665 was working in Oxford.
Took as aprs. there: 1668 **Peter Knibb** –freed Nov 1677; 1669 **Thomas
Smith**. Moved to London and became a free Brother in CC in Jan
1670/71. Took as aprs. there: May 1672 **Patrick Vans**; Dec 1673
Edmund Massey – freed Jan 1682/83; **John Miller** (thro' Isaac Puzy)
formerly apr. of Samuel Knibb – freed Nov 1674; Sep 1676 **John Drew** –
freed Sep 1684; Apr 1682 **Edward Wright**; Jan 1684/85 **Brouncker
Watts** – freed Feb 1693/94; **Thomas Farmer** (thro' or from Edward
Massey and George Brackley) – freed Jul 1690; May 1699 **James Hunt**
(son of Thomas Hunt tallow-chandler of Highworth(?) – illegible,
Northants) – freed Dec 1708. Said to work at the Dial in Fleet Street.
Became CC Assistant from 1689. Attended regularly till 1697 (when he is
said to have sold the London business). He would normally have been a
warden in that year (1697) but in view of his move then to Hanslope he
never was. Attended only once thereafter in 1699. Died Dec 1711. Work
known – for details see Lee and Beeson.

KNIBB, Peter   **Oxford/London/Farnborough (Warwickshire)**
B. 1651 son of George Knibb, yeoman of Farnborough. Apr. Jul 1668 to
Joseph Knibb of Oxford till Dec 1676. Freed in CC Nov 1677 having
moved to London with Joseph c. 1670. Took as apr. Nov 1679
Cadwalider Wise. Moved to Farnborough 1679 where married
Katherine Shrewsbury. Work known – a bracket clock and a watch.

KNIBB, Samuel   **Newport Pagnell (Buckinghamshire)/London**
B. 1625 son of John Knibb, yeoman of Claydon and cousin of John and
Joseph above. Working at Newport Pagnell by 1655 where he may have
had cousin Joseph Knibb as apr. Was in London (Westminster) by Apr

1662. Joined CC as a Freeman by redemption in Jul 1663. Took as aprs.: Jan 1664/65 **George Tipping** (freed after his master's death) Jun 1674 having been passed on to F. Bicknell; Jan 1667/68 took (as a second apr. being allowed to bend the rules) **John Miller** – freed (after master's death) Nov 1674 having been passed on to Isaac Puzy and then to Joseph Knibb. Was associated for a time at least with Henry Sutton (not in CC). Believed died about 1670. Work known – very little. A calculating machine made with Henry Sutton in 1664 for Henry Morland; a bracket clock and two or three longcase clocks, signed 'Samuel Knibb, Londini, fecit'.

KNIFTON, Thomas   London
Apr. Nov 1632 in Clothworkers' Co. to William Selwood. Never officially admitted into CC but took as aprs. there: Jan 1647/48 **Thomas Burgis** thro' W. Bunting; May 1651 **Thomas Ogden** (thro' N. Coxeter) – freed Jul 1659; **William Seaman** – freed Jan 1659/60; Feb 1660 **Francis Ireland** (thro' W. Seaman (or Sammon)) – freed Jul 1668. Also bound an apr. for John Salman. Worked in Lothbury, at the Cross Keys. May have been dead by mid-1663 (Baillie suggests death as Knifeton in 1667). Believed succ. by John Ebsworth *qv*. Work known – lantern clocks signed 'Thomas Knifton at ye Cross Keys in Lothbury'.

KNIGHT, Charles   London
B.c. 1664, apr. May 1678 to William Marston till 1685. Freed Jun 1685. Took as apr. Jun 1691 **John Parratt**. Not heard of after 1691.

KNIGHT, John   Kenilworth(?) (Warwickshire)
Blacksmith? Repaired St. Nicholas Kenilworth church clock in 1640-46.

KNIGHT, John   London
In 1684 made watch for King to give to Muley Hamet (Baillie).

KNIGHT, Michael   London
B.c. 1659, apr. Jan 1673/74 to Thomas Tompion (after latter had taken his Freedom by redemption) thro' L. Wythe, till 1680, warned to take up his Freedom Jan 1680/81 – freed Jul 1681. Took as aprs.: Feb 1682-83 **Thomas Day** – freed Apr 1691; Jul 1691 **Robert Youell** (thro' T. Tompion); Apr 1697 **John Barnardiston** – freed Sep 1714. Also bound an apr. for Tompion in 1691. Not heard of after early in 1699 and paid no quarterage after that. Work known – may have worked largely

for Tompion but a longcase clock and bracket clock are known signed 'Michael Knight, Londoni, fecit'.

KNIGHT, Richard   **London**
B.c. 1660, apr. Feb 1674/75 to John Wise till 1681. Freed Sep 1682 (signed with his mark!). Took as apr. Apr 1686 **John Pickering**. Also bound an apr. for Langley Bradley. Working till 1705 but not recorded after that.

KNIGHT, Thomas   **London**
B.c. 1672, apr. Jun 1688 to Dorcas Bouquett till 1693, but not freed.

KNIVETON, ----   **London**
Baillie records 'died 1667'. Prob. Thomas Knifton, *qv.*

KNOLLYS, Francis   **London**
B.c. 1655, apr. Apr 1669 to John Harris till 1676, but not freed.

KNOTT, Robert   **London**
B.c. 1668, apr. Jan 1682-83 to Clement Foster till 1689, but not freed.

KNOT(TE)SFORD, John   **London**
B.c. 1666, son of William Knotsford, *qv.* Apr. Mar 1680-81 to his father till 1687, but not freed. Prob. dead or gone by 1697. Work known – one or two longcase clocks signed 'John Knotsford, London'.

KNOT(TE)SFORD, William   **London**
Apr. Jan 1656-57 to Henry Child (thro' John Bayes). Freed Mar 1663-64. Took as apr. Mar 1680/81 son **John Knottesford**. Also bound an apr. for Benjamin Merryman. Assistant in CC from 1676, Warden from 1681, Master in 1693. Attended, at times, only when forced to. Alive 1697, but listed as dead in 1698. Work known – watches, bracket clock and longcase clock signed 'William Knottesford, London'.

KRATZER, Nicholas (also Cratzer and Kratzner)   **Oxford/London**
B. Bavaria 1487. Admitted Corpus Christi College 1516-22. Made an Oxford turret clock in 1520. Astronomer and clockmaker to Henry VIII in 1530s-40s. Said to have been unable to speak English. Once thought to have designed Hampton Court Palace clock – see Beeson.

KREVET, Hans **Bath (Somerset)**
C. 1645 made clockwork for exploding gunpowder.

KYFFIN, Edward **London**
B.c. 1668, apr. Nov 1682 to John Browne (thro' S. Davis) till 1689, but
not freed.

KYNNING, John (sometimes Kinning) **London**
B.c. 1679, apr. May 1693 to Peter Wise till 1700. Free May 1701. Took as
aprs.: Jun 1701 **David Doublett** (son of Gabriel Doublett of the Old
Artillery Ground, Middlesex, mariner); Apr 1706 **James Andrews** (son
of James Andrews, late of Plymouth, co. Devon, mariner, deceased) –
free Mar 1719-20. Received CC charity in 1716 and I have no record of
him after that.

KYNUIN or **KYNUYN, James** **London**
In 1584 'a fine workman' nr. St. Pauls. Work known – box
compass/sundial dated 1593. See next entry also.

KYNVIN, Jonas place not known
Maker of clock in 1593 according to Britten. Prob. an error for James
Kynuin, *qv.*

L

LABRU, ---- London
Table clock recorded c. 1680. But see De La Rue.

LADD, Samuel London
B.c. 1677, apr. Dec 1691 to Robert Nemes till 1698. Freed Jun 1710.

LA FOSSE, Samuel (see De La Fosse)

LAGOE, John London
B.c. 1657, apr. Dec 1671 to Richard Halstead till 1678, but in Aug 1673 was to be dismissed and a replacement found.

LAIGHTON (see under Layton)

LAINY, David London
Watch movement c. 1680 recorded by Baillie.

LAKE, Bryan London
B.c. 1653, apr. Jul 1667 to John Ebsworth till 1674. Freed Nov 1674. Paid quarterage till Mar 1674/75, but not later.

LAMB, Abraham London
Apr. about 1651 to William Pettit (thro' Thos. Taylor), but not freed. Prob. dead by 1662/63.

LAMB, Edmund London
Free in CC Mar 1675 having been apr. to (records blank). Took as apr.
Jun 1675 **George Walker** (thro' Jeffrey Bailey).

LAMB, Luke London
B.c. 1669, apr. Dec 1683 to Johnson Weekes till 1690, but not freed.

LAMB, Simon London/Rochester? (Kent)
B.c. 1655, apr. Feb 1669/70 to William Glazier till 1676, but not freed. A
longcase clock is recorded c. 1700 signed 'Simon Lamb – Rochester'
which is presumably the same man.

LAMB, Thomas London
Free Brother in CC Oct 1632.

LAMB, Wright London
In May 1682 he was already the (illicit) apr. of Thomas Fletcher.
Ordered to be bound officially through CC.

LAMBDEN, Richard London
B.c. 1671, apr. Oct 1685 to Joseph Hussey till 1692, but not freed.

LAMBERT, Robert London
French, a denizen clockmaker in 1544. Worked on a turret clock for
Norwich.

LAMB(E)Y, John Exeter
Married 1700. Worked until 1705.

LAMPE, Benedicke London?
A High German who supplied in 1610 'a coache of silver with a clocke
and other motions in it' to the first Earl of Salisbury for £40.00.

LAMPREY, Benjamin Banbury (Oxfordshire)
Clock and watchmaker who married 1st c. 1696 to Jane X who died 1708.
Married 2nd c. 1711 Elizabeth X who died 1715. Married 3rd c. 1719.
Had 13 children of which son John b. 1704, succ. him in the trade. Died
Sep 1721. Work known – a lantern clock signed 'Benjamin Lamprey,
Banbury'.

LAMUDE, Peter London
B.c. 1670, apr. Apr 1684 to Nathaniel Delander till 1691, but not freed.

LANCASTER, Nicholas London
B.c. 1665, apr. Sep 1679 to Stafford Freeman till 1686, but not freed.

LANCASTER, Richard (see Lankister)

LANCASTER, Richard London
B.c. 1664-70, apr. Sep 1684 to Henry Merryman till 1691, but not freed. Married in May 1687 (claiming aged 23 but prob. only 17) as a watchmaker of St. Martin's, bachelor to Elizabeth Free of same, age 23, spinster at St. Martin Ludgate Hill. This marriage prob. meant the end of his apprenticeship.

LAND, Thomas (erroneously Lane) London
Never officially admitted to CC but was known to them by 1635, and bound aprs. thro' them. Apr 1638 **Thomas Fitton** (thro' T. Dawson); Jul 1646 **Francis Parrey** (thro' T. Alcock); Jun 1650 **Edward Enys** (thro' N. Payne) – freed Jan 1658-59. Prob. dead or gone by 1662-63.

LANE, John London
B.c. 1665, apr. Jan 1679-80 to Samuel Vernon till 1686, but not freed. Work known – two watches on record.

LANE, Thomas Barnstaple (Devon)
Kept Kay Hall clock in 1611 (cf Lang William).

LANE, Thomas London
C. 1650, believed error for Land, qv.

LANE, Wright Oxford/London
B.c. 1662, son of Nathaniel Lane, cleric, late of Dolton, Devonshire. Apr. to Michael Bird, watchmaker, of Oxford in 1676 till 1683. In Jul 1687 summoned to appear before CC Court for transgressions. Free at Oxford 1689.

LANG, William Barnstable (Devon)
In 1614 kept Kay Hall clock (cf Lane, Thomas).

LANGFORD, Ellis   **London**
B.c. 1650, apr. Oct 1663 to Gowen Langford, later passed on to Francis
Bicknell then to Morgan Cave till 1671 – freed Sep 1672.

LANGFORD, Gowen (also Gooing)   **London**
B.c. 1623, son of William Langford of Garrett St. Andrew, Dorset, gent.
Apr. May 1637 to Robert Cordwell (thro' O. Durant) till 1644. Freed as a
Brother Oct 1652. Took as aprs.: Oct 1652 **Thomas Fenn** (thro'
J. Cann) – freed July 1657; May 1657 **Henry Flexney;** Oct 1663 **Ellis
Langford,** later passed on to F. Bicknell.

LANGLEY, Thomas   **London**
Apr. Jun 1655 to Samuel Davis – freed Oct 1664.

LANGLEY, Thomas   **Oxford**
B.c. 1660, son of Thomas Langley, mercer, of Stanford, Berkshire. Apr.
Apr 1673 to John Quelch, watchmaker of Oxford till 1681. Freed Dec
1687.

LANGLYE, William   **Liskeard (Cornwall)**
In 1605 made Market Hall clock for £2.18s.4d.

LANKISTER, Richard   **London**
Apr. Sep 1677 to Thomas Hollis, transferred Jan 1680/81 to Benjamin
Bell.

LARKIN, Edward   **Winchester (Hampshire)**
Recorded as 1681.

LARMETT, Abraham   **London**
Never actually entered CC but known to them. Prob. dead by 1662/63.

LASHBROOK, Thomas   **London**
B.c. 1647, apr. Mar 1661/62 to William Petty, boxmaker, till 1668, but
not freed.

LASHBROOK, Thomas   **London**
B.c. 1679, apr. Apr 1693 to Richard Conyers till 1700 – freed Sep 1701.
Took as aprs.: Oct 1701 **William Due** (son of Samuel Due of Reddion?
co. Berks, taylor); Sep 1703 **Henry Lashbrook** – freed May 1715; Feb
1709/10 **Thomas Paine.**

LATHAM, Henry   **London**
B.c. 1641, apr. Dec 1655 to Humfrey Downing (thro' L. Wythe) till 1662, but not freed. (A Mr. Latham paid quarterage in 1672).

LATHAM, John   **London**
B.c. 1679, apr. Aug 1693 to John Shaw till 1700. Freed Sep 1700. Took as aprs.: Feb 1706/07 **John Cole;** May 1712 **Thomas Griffith;** Jun 1717 **John Butler.** Baillie says died 1740. Work known – watches and bracket clock, signed 'John Latham London'.

LAUD, John   **London**
Baillie has 1662, but I cannot trace any such person.

LAUGHTON, William (also spelt Layton)   **London**
Freeman of the Grocers' Co., admitted as a Brother in CC 1683. Took as aprs.: Feb 1687/88 **Thomas Terrier** – freed Feb 1694/95; Sep 1690 **James Wheeler** (thro' D. Stevens); May 1703 his son, **William Layton** – free Sep 1710.

LAUNDY, John (see Lawndy)

LAURENCE, ----   **London**
Baillie has 1576 – I cannot trace this maker.

LAUSSINE, Esaius   **Edinburgh (Scotland)**
1595.

LAWRAYPIERE, William   **London**
(Much mis-spelt as eg Larapiere,, Lavrepier, Lavespeare, DeLavrespiere, etc.) Perhaps two of this name. In 1622 was an alien journeyman with Cornelius Mellin in Blackfriars. Brother in CC Jun 1650. Took as aprs.: Jun 1649 **John Rickard** or **Record** (thro' T. Wolverston) – free Mar 1657; Sep 1653 **Thomas Wyth** (thro' R. Record). In 1661 Benjamin Wolverstone paid part of his quarterage for him.

LAW, Isaac   **London**
In 1632 he was warned to bring evidence of his training to CC, then in Oct 1632 he 'was forbidden the trade, being an engraver not a clockmaker'. Though he never officially joined the CC he was tolerated by them and took as aprs.: Oct 1641 **John Cooke** (thro' J. Hopkins) –

freed Apr 1649; Oct 1646 **Richard Honey** (thro' T. Alcock); Dec 1651 **Thomas Carter** (thro' J. Cooke) – free Dec 1659; Apr 1655 **John Dodson** (thro' J. Cooke). In 1664 when called to be Steward he refused. In 1668 was excused Assistantship 'alledging the great losses that he hath susteyned' (in the fire?). In Jan 1676/77 he was in arrears but was excused partly due to his age and 'the discontentment of his trade'. Worked in Blackfriars.

LAW, Silvester   London
B.c. 1665, apr. Aug 1689 to Richard Baker (thro' T. Fletcher) till 1696, but not freed.

LAW, Timothy   London
B.c. 1676, apr. Mar 1690 to William Cam till 1697, but not freed.

LAWNDY, John   London
B.c. 1678, apr. Sep 1692 to Thomas Walford till 1699, but not freed.

LAWRENCE, Henry (also Laurence)   London
B.c. 1679, apr. Jan 1691/92 to Richard Colston till 1700 – freed Apr 1704. Took as aprs.: Aug 1706 **Edward Vaughton** (son of Thomas Vaughton of T - (illegible) in co. Warwick, shoemaker) – freed Apr 1715; Mar 1713-14 **Thomas Lake;** May 1715 **John Rogers;** Oct 1719 **Richard Hutchinson.** Baillie records him till 1724.

LAXTON, Thomas   London
B.c. 1620, son of John Laxton of Huntington(?), apr. Jan 1633 to Henry Archer, transferred to Richard Lord till 1641. Admitted (as Brother?) Apr 1642. Then admitted again (as a Freeman?) Nov 1653. These entries relate to same man (not as Baillie suggests two).

LAYTON, John (also Laighton, Leighton, etc.)   London
Brother in CC Mar 1653/54. Constantly in arrears with quarterage until in Jun 1679 Mr. Barrow (Nathaniel) lent him some money, which he will deduct gradually from the price of each movement that John Layton makes for him. Received CC charity from Apr 1682 till Jan 1683-84, when prob. died. Prob. worked for Barrow.

LEA (see also Lee)

LEA, John   **Lutterworth (Leicestershire)**
Clockmaker. Paid in 1602 to maintain the Harborough chimes at 6s.8d. a
year.

LEA, Roger   **Warwick**
Carpenter who repaired the wooden part of St. Nicholas clock 1617-18.

LEACH, Richard   **London**
Longcase clock recorded c. 1700.

LEACH, Robert   **London**
In March 1675 this name is written in CC records in error for Robert
Lynch, *qv*.

LEAF, John   **London**
Recorded by some authorities as apr. 1672, but this is an error for 1772.

LEAKE, Faith   **London**
B.c. 1663. A boy. Apr. Jan 1677 to John White, then transferred to
Daniel Quare till 1684. Freed Jan 1685-86.

LEAKE, George   **London**
B.c. 1671, apr. Jan 1685/86 to John Wright till 1692. Freed Sep 1693.
Paid quarterage till c. 1695. Work known – a lantern clock.

LEAVER (see Lever)

LE CAMUS (see De Camus)

LE COUNT, Daniel (also Le Compte and Le Conte)   **London**
Freeman of the Haberdashers' Co. and a clockmaker, made Free Brother
in CC Sep 1676. Took as aprs.: Aug 1677 **Charles Ekins** (thro'
N. Coxeter); Jan 1681/82 **James Way** (thro' W. Speakman); Aug 1686
Daniel Lefebure (thro' W. Speakman); Nov 1686 **William Hayes** (thro'
R. Williamson); Oct 1693 **George Vievar**. Said to be a refugee from
France. Paid quarterage till 1705 at least. Work known – several longcase
clocks and watches.

LE COUNT, James (also Le Comte)   **London**
Signed Jacques. A watchmaker. Promised in Feb 1686/87 to become a

353

Brother in CC, which he did in Apr 1687, but paid no quarterage after that date.

LEDEIRK, ----   London
Table clock recorded, 17th century. See Ledeur?

LEDEUR, R.   London
Watch c. 1620. See Ledeirk?

LEE, Christopher   London
B.c. 1678, apr. Nov 1691 to William Young till 1699, but not freed.

LEE, Cuthbert   London
B.c. 1654, apr. Aug 1668 to Robert Williamson till 1675. Freed Aug 1676. Took as aprs.: **Joseph Biddell** – freed Apr 1684; **Thomas Snelling** (from R. Williamson) – freed Sep 1680; Sep 1681 **Thomas Roycroft;** May 1685 **Thomas Ashbrooke;** Oct 1686 **John Sedley** (thro' B. Marshall) (Aug 1687 to be prosecuted for 'undue keeping of John Sedley); **Benjamin Brandon** (from B. Bell) – freed Dec 1689; Jul 1690 **Richard Newton** (from J. Saville who had departed) – freed Mar 1695-96; Jul 1690 **Edward Mercer** (later passed to T. Tompion) – freed Jul 1699; Sep 1693 **Ralph Toleson** (passed to R. Webster), Jun 1693 **Christopher Egleton** (from C. Halstead) – freed Nov 1695; **Ralph Mills** (from C. Gretton) – freed Sep 1697; **Thomas Vassiere** – freed Sep 1698; Nov 1698 **Thomas Sutton** (son of Robert Sutton late of parish of St. Giles, Cripplegate, porter, deceased) – freed Nov 1705; Jul 1705 **Henry Harris** (son of William Harris late of parish of St. Martin in the Fields, Middlesex, coach harnessmaker, deceased) – freed Sep 1712; Sep 1708 **James Freeman** – freed Feb 1718-19; Apr 1710 **William Baker;** Nov 1715 **William Parr;** Oct 1716 **Cuthbert Turbet;** Jan 1718-19 **John Burton** (passed over 1720 to P. Garron); **Thomas Partington** – freed 1720. Several times in trouble for 'employing foreigners and those not bred up in the trade' and his many apprenticeship movements may have been attempts at camouflaging this. I have no data on him after 1720. Work known – two bracket clocks.

LEE, Edward   London
B.c. 1655, apr. Feb 1668/69 to Jeffrey Bailey till 1676, but not freed.

LEE, John   **Leicester**
B.c. 1667, son of John Lee of Leicester, apr. May 1680 to John Wilkins
of Leicester, clockmaker, for eight years.

LEE, Richard   **Halifax (Yorkshire)**
Repaired church clock 1665.

LEE, Roger   **Leicester**
Prob. brother of John, *qv*, apr. of John Wilkins. Freed 1691. Work
known – lantern and longcase and watches. Succ. by son William.

LEE, Samuel   **London**
B.c. 1673, apr. Jun 1687 to Jeffrey Bailey till 1694. Freed Mar 1694-95.
Took as aprs.: Jan 1697-98 **Clement Collins** – freed Jan 1705-06; May
1714 **John Thornhill**; Jul 1719 **Thomas Blodwell**. Work known – three
longcase clocks, signed 'Samuel Lee, London'.

LEE, Underwood   **London**
B.c. 1674, apr. Jan 1688/89 to Edward Stanton (thro' E. Burgess) till
1695, but not freed.

LEES, James   **Ashton-under-Lyme (Lancashire)**
Clockmaker. Two of his children died in 1697 and 1706.

LEFEBURE, Charles   **London**
A Frenchman and a great clockmaker. Free Brother in CC Sep 1687.

LEFEBURE, Daniel   **London**
B.c. 1672, apr. Aug 1686 (thro' W. Speakman) to Daniel Le Conte (a
Freeman of the Haberdashers' Co.) till 1693, but not freed.

LE FLET, Petrus de Dessus   **London**
Baillie records him in 1562.

LEGRAND, Francis   **London**
Free Brother in CC Oct 1646.

LEGRAND, James senior (signed Jaques)   **London**
Brother in CC Oct 1640, a Frenchman. In Apr 1645 fined for employing
a journeyman 'that came out of France' without presenting him to CC.

Took as apr. Apr 1656 his son, **James Legrand** junior (thro' D. Moody) – freed Jan 1664/65. Last heard of in 1662.

LEGRAND, James junior   London
Son of James senior, apr. to his father (thro' D. Moody) Apr 1656. Freed Jan 1664-65. In Oct 1696 Peter Garon admitted forging the name Mr. Legrand on a watch.

LEIGHTON (see Layton)

LEIVE(S)LEY, George senior   Shrewsbury (Salop)
Watchmaker. Father of George junior. See also Liversay.

LEIVE(S)LEY, George junior   Shrewsbury (Salop)
Son of George senior. Working 1697.

LELLO, James   London
B.c. 1634, apr. Oct 1648 to Thomas Alcock till 1655. Freed Apr 1656 (having served Samuel Betts). Took as apr. Apr 1664 **John Peryer**. Also in 1658 bound an apr. for John Harris. Still working in 1675.

LEMAIRE, ----   London
Watch c. 1700.

LENWOOD, Samuel   London
B.c. 1648, apr. Aug 1662 to Thomas Claxton till 1669, but not freed.

LESSENEY (Lesene) **Sebastian**   London
Clockmaker to Henry VIII and a native of Normandy – 1538-42 (Baillie).

LESTER, Thomas   London
Clockmaker, made a Free Brother in CC Apr 1698. Paid quarterage till at least 1705. Possibly connected with the later Lister?

LESTOURGEON, David senior   Rouen/London
Baillie has married Rouen 1660, London 1681 (but I wonder whether he has confused the next man and whether there was only one of this name in London in 1681).

LESTOURGEON, David (junior?)   London
Watchmaker, admitted as a Brother in CC Apr 1698 (though Baillie says

he was in London by 1681 and was son of David senior). Took as aprs.: May 1700 **Peter Joyce** (son of Stephen Joyce of Spittlefields, Middlesex, weaver): Jun 1701 **James Blackborow** (son of late John Blackborow, late of Aldersgate Street, London, leatherseller, deceased) – freed Feb 1711-12; Apr 1704 his son, **David Lestourgeon** – freed 1721; Dec 1708 **Thomas Cordell; Aug 1712 Peter Camper;** Jul 1716 another apr. name illegible. Prob. a member of the French Church, Spitalfields. One of this name, a turner in silver was at Church Lane in St. Martins parish next door to the King Charles' Head 1702-04. Believed working till at least 1731, but I have no data on him after 1720. Work known – watches and bracket clocks signed 'David Lestourgeon, London' or 'Lestourgeon, London'.

LETTE, J.   **Yatton (Somerset)**
Kept turret clock, 1545.

LEVER, Nathaniel (also Leaver)   **London**
B.c. 1665, apr. Jan 1679/80 to John Wright senior, till 1686, but not freed. Work known – a bracket clock signed 'Leaver, London' c. 1730 may be by him?

LEVITT, John   **London**
B.c. 1667, apr. Jul 1681 to Robert Williamson till 1688, but not freed.

LEWIS, John   **Dublin**
Watchmaker in Goldsmiths' Co. there 1679. Died 1680. See Lewse?

LEWIS, Thomas   **Gloucester**
B. 1656, married Feb 1681/82. Watchmaker.

LEWIS, Winstanley   **London**
Recorded by Baillie as apr. 1632 in Blacksmiths' Co.

LEWSE, John   **London**
Working in 1662 in Chancery Lane, but I cannot trace any other reference to him. However, see John Lewis?

LEWTHWAITE, William (also Laithwaite)   **Liverpool**
Watch and watch casemaker. Children b. there 1696-1710. Still working 1725. In 1710 took **Thomas Barron** as apr.

LEYNS, John   **London**
Said to be journeyman to Nicholas Vallin and to have died in 1603.

LIDDALL, Dennis   **London**
Mat. inst. maker. In Aug 1673 faulty rulers were confiscated from his shop.

LIDBROOKE, Thomas (also Ladbrooke)   **Oxford**
B.c. 1665, son of Robert Lidbrooke yeoman of Dassett, Warwickshire. Apr. Jul 1679 to John Knibb (to whom he is believed to be related) till 1686.

LIETUIJT, John (also Lietuty, Johannes)   **Delft/London**
Invited to England 1368 by Edward III as one of three clockmakers (see Vriemans).

LIGHT, Benjamin   **London**
B.c. 1673, apr. Sep 1687 to George Cawdron (thro' R. Gilkes) till 1694, but not freed.

LIGHT, John   **London**
Free in CC 1646. Took as apr. (1650s?) **Henry Hester** (later passed over to Richard Morgan).

LIGHTFOOT, Petrus   **England(?)**
A monk, formerly thought to have made clock for Wells Cathedral in the 14th century, but now discredited.

LIMPARD, John   **London**
Watch recorded c. 1610-20.

LINAKER, Samuel   **London**
Working c. 1610. One of the original CC Assistants from 1632 but by 1635 had 'gone'. Baillie records his death as 1649, which I cannot confirm. Work known – a watch.

LINDD, Henry   **Farnham**
Lantern clock recorded said to be c. 1700.

LINDFORD, Henry   **London**
B.c. 1677, apr. Sep 1691 to Edward Orton, till 1698, but not freed (see also Linford).

LINDSAY, John   **Nayland (Suffolk)**
B. 1677, son of John Lindsey (who died 1723). In Town minutes 1723-33. Work known – a longcase 30-hour and an eight-day clock.

LINFORD, Thomas   **London**
Watch recorded 1626.

LIONELL, James   **London**
On CC list of 1662, but I can find no other reference to him.

LISTER? (see Lester)

LITHERLAND, John   **Liverpool (Lancashire)**
                                                 and **Badsworth (Yorkshire)**
Watchmaker at Liverpool. Children born there 1677-84. He died there 1687. However, in 1682 his daughter Elizabeth was buried at Badsworth (Yorks) – perhaps when he was staying there.

LITTLEMORE, Whitestone   **London**
B.c. 1671, apr. Dec 1684 to Thomas Gibbs till 1692. By 1695 was working for T. Tompion. Freed May 1698. Took as aprs.: May 1698 **Samuel Berry** – freed Jan 1705/06; Sep 1701 **William Dove** (son of John Dove, late Citizen and Mercer of London, deceased); Jul 1704 **Thomas Adams** (son of John Adams, Citizen and Blacksmith).

LIVERMORE, Philip   **Chardstock (Somerset)**
Engraver. From Devon. Married there 1686. Said to have 'designed' lantern clocks.

LIVERSAY, George   **Prescot (Lancashire)**
Watchmaker. Application for Freedom rejected 1666.

LLOYD, Charles   **London**
B.c. 1669, apr. Sep 1683 to Thomas Tompion till 1690. Freed Jul 1691. Took as aprs.: Dec 1696 **Thomas Cox** – freed Mar 1707/08; Jun 1699 **James Penny** (son of John Penny of London, Clothworker); Jan 1704/05 **Thomas Hayes** (son of James Hayes late of parish of St. Margarets,

Westminster, labourer, deceased); not heard of after 1704. In Jul 1712 mentioned as deceased (but this could be a slip in the records for William Lloyd).

LLOYD, David   London
Freed in CC Jan 1677/78 the apr. of Ambrose Blisse having been transferred from John Cooke. Took as apr. Jan 1677/78 **Michael Johnson** – freed Sep 1687.

LLOYD, Edward   London
B.c. 1648, apr. Jan 1662/63 to Thomas Morgan till 1670, but not freed.

LLOYD, Humphrey (sometimes Flood/Flue)   London
Goldsmith. In 1607 Royal accounts show purchase of a clock 'covered with gold and set with diamonds and rubies' at £200. Maybe he was the Mr. Flue, the clockmaker, who in 1609 was to leave his shop to make way for Mr. Clerck the apothecary – Earl of Salisbury's accounts.

LLOYD, James   London
B.c. 1677, apr. Nov 1691 to Thomas Bates till 1698. Freed Sep 1700. Took as aprs.: Sep 1700 **Richard Batson** (son of Richard Batson of Bybury, co. Gloucestershire, grazier); Feb 1713-14 his son **James Lloyd** – freed 1722.

LLOYD, Joseph   London
B.c. 1651, apr. Apr 1664 to John Pennock (thro' I. Puzy), till 1672. Freed Sep 1673.

LLOYD, Lewis   London
B.c. 1659, apr. Sep 1673 to William Lloyd till 1700.

LLOYD, Nathaniel   London
B.c. 1659, apr. Jan 1673/74 to Bartholomew Powell till 1700.

LLOYD, Richard   London
B.c. 1657, apr. Aug 1670 to Michael Cornish till 1678. Freed Sep 1681. Not heard of thereafter.

LLOYD, William (also Floyd)   London
B.c. 1646, son of Robert Lloyd of Clarinton, co. Monmouth, yeoman.

Apr. Oct 1660 to Richard Lyon till 1667. Freed May 1668 of CC (and of the City).

LLOYD, William   **London**
Apr. 1658? to Nicholas Coxeter, transferred to Thomas Daniel, then to Richard Bowen. Freed Apr 1671. Took as aprs.: Jan 1671/72 **Richard Bennett;** Sep 1673 **Lewis Lloyd.** In Jan 1696/97 'having been several years beyond the sea he is much in arrears of quarterage but is excused on payment of 30/-'. In Oct 1705 he requested from the CC a certificate to state that he had been about 40 years a Freeman. Maybe died 1712, but see Charles Lloyd.

LOCHARD, Robert (not John)   **London**
(Recorded sometimes as John in error) Apr. Aug 1647 to John Matchett. Freed Oct 1655. Joined the 1656 rebels against the CC. Took as apr. Jan 1655 **Edward Prosser.** Work known – a watch is recorded.

LOKEAR (Lockyer), **Richard**   **Warwick**
Prob. a Smith. Made new wheel for St. Nicholas turret clock 1593-94.

LOCKIN, William   **London**
B.c. 1673, apr. Sep 1687 to Isaac Goddard till 1694, but not freed.

LOCKWOOD, Robert   **London**
B.c. 1633, apr. Feb 1647-48 to Edward Taylor (thor' W. Bunting).

LODGE, Thomas   **London/Farnham**
B.c. 1663. Married May 1688 aged 25, a bachelor, watchmaker, of St. Dunstan's in the West to Dorothy Connyers, 21, spinster, of St. Giles in the Fields. Work known – bracket clock c. 1695. Also a longcase clock signed 'Thomas Lodge, Farnham', presumably the same man. Recorded as working still in 1713 and perhaps later. Appears not to have belonged to CC nor to have been known to them.

LOD(O)WICK, Peter (signed Lodwick)   **London**
B.c. 1667, apr. Mar 1680/81 to Daniel Beckman till 1688. Freed Jul 1689. Prob. an engraver. Took as apr. Jan 1691/92 **William Gray.** Paid no quarterage after c. 1694.

LONDON, John   **Bristol**
Clockmaker, married there 1678. One of this name a gunsmith, had
Robert Sainsbury as apr. 1675-82. Work known – a lantern clock.

LONERAPEAR/LONDRAPEAR, William   **London**
This is an error for La Wraypear *qv.*

LONG, John   **London**
Free Brother in CC Dec 1677. Dead or gone by 1677. Maybe a member of
the Stationers' Co. for a John Long, Stationer, had his son John junior
apr. to John Stanton in CC Dec 1698. Work known – not possible to
distinguish from that of the next man, *qv.*

LONG, John   **London**
B.c. 1676, apr. Nov 1690 to John Sweby, transferred to Ambrose
Gardiner then to George Wilson till 1697. Freed Jul 1698. Took as aprs.:
Jul 1701 **Robert Sadler** (son of William Sadler of ? Rotoine, Wiltshire,
Gent, deceased); Jun 1707 **Francis Green;** Apr 1712 **Charles Taylor;**
Aug 1717 **Stephen Bassett.** Believed working till at least 1725. Work
known – watches and longcase clocks signed 'John Long, London' (but
see previous entry).

LONG, John   **Nottingham**
Clock watch recorded c. 1692. (Britten).

LONG, Thomas   **London**
Prob. a spring maker. Apr. Mar 1646 to Richard Morgan (thro'
T. Alcock). Freed Jan 1654-54. Took as aprs.: Feb 1655/56 **Thomas
Shepherd;** Aug 1668 **George Harris** – free Jan 1674/75; Sep 1673 **James
Hatchman,** later transferred to G. Harris and freed Jan 1680/81. In 1672
excused stewardship due to illness and prob. died not long after.

LONGLAND, Francis   **London**
B.c. 1657, apr. Jul 1671 to Bartholomew Powell till 1678, but not freed.

LONGLAND, John   **London**
B.c. 1653, son of William Longland of Fulbeck, Lincolnshire, farmer.
Apr. in Merchant Taylors' Co., Jun 1667 to Edward Fowle, clockmaker
of Whitechapel. Free there Jul 1674. Free Brother in CC Sep 1677 as a
Great Clockmaker. In Oct 1675 worked in Leadenhall Street 'where Mr.
Paul was' (Thomas Paul?). Took as aprs.: Jul 1680 **John Dickens,** later

passed to W. Cattell and freed Sep 1688; Apr 1685 **William Gilbert**, later passed to H. Kilminster and freed Aug 1695. Work known – longcased clock signed 'Johannis Longland, Londini, fecit'.

LONGSTAFF, George   **Darlington (co. Durham)**
Kept church clock 1648.

LOOMES, Thomas   **London**
Apr. to John Selwood. Free in CC Dec 1649. Took over on Selwood's death The Mermaid in Lothbury 'nr. Bartholomew Lane End'. In 1648 was overseer of will of his friend Sampson Shelton. Rebelled against CC in 1656 protest. Took as aprs.: Jan 1651/52 **Richard Beck** (from late J. Selwood); Jan 1651/52 **Simon Dutson** (from late J. Selwood) – freed 1654; Nov 1653 **Thomas Wilmot**; Nov 1654 **John Ramsden**; Nov 1654 **John Garbound; John James** (from N. Tomlins) – freed Feb 1661; May 1656 **Thomas Bagley** – freed Oct 1664; Apr 1661 **Daniel Worlidge; John Fromanteel** – freed Jul 1663; Oct 1663 **John White** later transferred to T. Bagley; Sep 1664 **Samuel Revell; Edward Sedwell** – freed Oct 1664; 1660s **William Warden.** Also bound an apr. for Edward Ward. Frequently fined for unapproved taking of aprs. Served as CC Steward 1663. Not heard of after 1664 (Baillie's 1674 prob. an error) and believed died 1665 in plague. Married Mary daughter of Ahasuerus Fromanteel with whom he was closely associated. Work known – several lantern clocks usually signed 'at ye Mermayd in Lothbury'. A chiming bracket clock is recorded. For detailed biography see Loomes, B. *Complete British Clocks*, Loomes, B. *Country Clocks*, Loomes, B. article in *Clocks* magazine in Dec 1979.

LORD, Joseph   **London**
B.c. 1670, apr. Jan 1684/85 to Jonathan Puller (thro' J. Bailey), till 1691, but not freed.

LORD, Richard   **London**
Admitted to CC Oct 1632 as a Free Brother. Signed with a mark – could not write. Took as apr. Jan 1633/34 **Thomas Laxton** (thro' H. Archer) – free as Brother Apr 1642, as Freeman Nov 1653.

LORD, William   **London**
Fined by CC 1638 (perhaps a slip for Richard Lord *qv*).

LOUARTH (see Lowart)

363

LOUGH, Thomas London
B.c. 1666, apr. Jul 1680 to George Tomlinson till 1687, but not freed.

LOUGHTON, William (see Laughton)

LOVELL, Nathaniel London
B.c. 1642, apr. Aug 1655 to John Samon till 1663, but not freed. Maybe connected with the Lowells, *qv.*

LOVETT, Jonathan (may be Levett) London
B.c. 1678, apr. Sep 1692 to Henry Pigott till 1699, but not freed.

LOW and **LOWE** all follow together.

LOW, Andrew London
Member of Vintners' Co. Took as apr. (in CC and Vintners' Co.) Jul 1674 **Edward Hampton(ne)** for Abraham Thomeguez – freed 1681.

LOWE, Christopher Ilmington (Warwickshire)
Prob. a blacksmith. Repaired church clock and bells 1677/79.

LOW, John Ashton (Lancashire)
Watchmaker of parish of Winwick who married there Dec 1694 Elizabeth Hill of Colbourne, spinster.

LOWE, John (sometimes Loe) London
Son of Robert Lowe, apr. in CC Aug 1653 to Nicholas Coxeter, passed over to Francis Munden. Not freed. Freed in Clothworkers' Co. by patrimony in 1660. Took as aprs.: May 1672 **Matthew Forrest** (thro' L. Wythe); Aug 1673 **Daniel Howe** (thro' L. Wythe); Nov 1676 **John Hunt** (thro' S. Davis); Sep 1683 with his wife Mary, took **Susan Hawkes** (prob. as a servant) (thro' S. Davis); In 1662 worked in Cannon Street. I have no record of him after 1683 (though Baillie suggests working till 1728?). Work known – a watch and a longcase clock signed 'John Lowe, London'.

LOW, John London
Jul 1692 became a Free Brother in CC being a watch casemaker 'a branch of the art of clockmaking'. Believed died by 1697/98.

LOWE, Richard London
B.c. 1665, a watch casemaker, married Nov 1690, of the parish of All
Hallows the Wall, age 25, a bachelor, to Mary Ladyman of St. Stevens
Coleman Street, a spinster aged 22. Apparently he was not a member of
CC, not known to them (unless maybe recorded in error as John above).

LOWART, Jasper (also Louarth/Loward) London
Brother in CC Aug 1641. Still alive in 1646, but dead by Nov 1650, when
his widow got a grant from CC.

LOWCOCK, George London
Apr. Dec 1668 to James Graves, *qv*, in the Weavers' Co., but his trade
not known.

LOWELL, George London
Ordered to appear before CC Jun 1656 – never heard of again.

LOWELL, Paul senior London
Supposedly a High German in Blacksmiths' Co. from 1628. Subscribed
to CC in 1630. Believed connected with David Bouquett in 1633. In 1654
he gave a silver bowl to CC. Took as aprs.: Dec 1646 **Paul Lowell** junior
(his son) (thro' J. Nicasius) – freed Jan 1653; Feb 1653-54 **Robert
Pannell** (thro' R. Record). Not easy to distinguish from Paul junior. In
1662 they both worked together in Show Lane (Shoe Lane?). In Jan
1672-73 the CC gave 10/- towards his burial being 'a very indigent
member of the Co.'.

LOWELL, Paul junior London
B.c. 1632, son of Paul senior, apr. Dec 1646 to his father (thro'
J. Nicasius) – freed Jan 1653-54, as a Free Brother. Took as apr. Apr
1659 **Paul Dellung**. Last heard of in 1662.

LOUNDES (see Lowndes)

LOWNDES, Charles London
B.c. 1660 (prob. son of Jonathan, *qv*), apr. Jul 1674 to Thomas Player till
1681. Freed Dec 1682. Took as aprs.: Sep 1683 **John Cotton** – freed Jul
1695; Sep 1688 **John Pierce**; Dec 1691 **George Pley** (thro' J. Southworth); Dec 1691 **William Lowndes**; Aug 1699 **Ralph Williamston** –
freed Jan 1706-07. Worked at Pall Mall. In 1706 warned about arrears of

quarterage, after which I have no record of him. Work known – bracket clock, longcase clock and watch, signed 'Charles Lowndes, Pall Mall, London'.

LOWNDES, Isaac   **London**
Watchmaker, made a Free Brother in CC Sep 1682. Took as aprs.: Sep 1689 **William Coombes** (thro' N. Speakman); **H. Aske;** Sep 1691 **Robert Richards;** May 1695 **Michael Hall** (thro' E. Hunt). Last heard of in 1702 when CC refused to excuse him of Stewardship though he claims he is 'to go into the country very suddenly'. Work known – watches, longcase clocks and bracket clocks, signed 'Isaac Lowndes, Pall Mall Court'.

LOWNDES, Jonathan   **London**
B.c. 1657. In Sep 1679 he married as a bachelor watchmaker aged 23 of St. Martins in the Fields to Grace Allen of St. Giles in Fields, spinster, aged 22. In Jun 1680 was summoned to CC court for infringements; became a free Brother Jul 1680. Took as aprs.: Jul 1688 **Anthony Pluett** (thro' D. Stevens) – freed Jan 1697-98; Sep 1693 **Thomas Smith** (thro' H. Aske). I have no record of him after 1702. In 1683 worked at The Dial in Pall Mall. Work known – lantern, bracket and longcase clocks and watches. Signed 'Jonatt. Lowndes, London', 'Jonathan Lowndes in Pall Mall, London', or 'Jonathan Lounds, Londini, fecit'.

LOUNDES, Samuel   **London**
Not a member of CC but his apr. **John Beckman** was freed in CC Jul 1695. Prob. worked for one of the other Lowndes.

LOWNDES, William   **London**
B.c. 1677, apr. Dec 1691/92 to Charles Lowndes till 1698, but not freed.

LOWRY, Morgan   **Leeds (Yorkshire)**
B. 1682 son of Jeremy Morgan. Britten records him at Holborn in 1700, which I cannot confirm. Married Leeds 1703 Ann Boyes, widow, aged 20. Daughter Ann bap. 1715. Wife died 1726. Married secondly 1737 Mary Thwaites. Worked in Briggate and Boar Lane. In 1725 an advertisement refers to 'Morgan Lowry clockmaker over against Boar Lane'. In 1731 was paid 13/- for work on St. Johns church. Died Leeds 1757. Work known – includes a year clock now in Abbey House Museum, Leeds.

LUCAS, John   Carlisle (Cumberland)
Repaired clock chimes 1657.

LUCAS, William   Dublin
Goldsmith/watchmaker 1672-1700.

LUCAS, William   London/Amsterdam(?)
Free in CC Apr 1669 having been apr. to Reginald Staunton (of the
Founders' Co.), transferred to Robert Robinson then to Thomas Bagley.
In Apr 1670 the Wardens met concerning his (wrong?) admission to the
Co. One of this name is recorded in Amsterdam in 1681, brother of
Jaques of La Rochelle and later Amsterdam.

LUCE, David   London
One of this name at Rouen, France c. 1620. Supposedly in London 1698,
though I cannot trace him and not a member of CC. Work known – one
or two watches signed 'David Luce, London'.

LUCIE, John   London
Apr. Aug 1655 to John Bayes, then to Nicholas Parke, then Charles
Bonner. Freed Oct 1663.

LUDFORD, Ralph   London
B.c. 1642, apr. Aug 1656 to William Almond (thro' S. Davis) till 1663,
but not freed.

LUEB, Michael   London
B.c. 1642, apr. Jan 1655/56 to Isaac Daniell (thro' T. Claxton) till 1663,
but not freed.

LUGG, Jasper   Gloucester
Working 1656-85. Lantern clock recorded signed 'Jasper Lugg of
Glocester fecit'.

LUMPKIN, Thomas   London
Free Brother in CC Jan 1694-95. Took as aprs.: Apr 1705 **John Martin**
(son of Nicholas Martin of Franliston?, co. Suffolk, yeoman, deceased) –
freed Mar 1714/15; Jul 1707 **George Melmouth**; Jan 1709/10 his son
Thomas Lumpkin; Jul 1712 **Charles Palfrey**; Mar 1713/14 **John Hart;**
May 1718 **Obadiah Smith** (these latter two both transferred to John
Allen in May 1720 – when perhaps Lumpkin died?). Made Steward in

1719, not heard of thereafter. Work known – bracket and longcase clock signed 'Thomas Lumpkin, London.'

LUND, Mr.   London
Paid subscription to CC 1641.

LUNTLEY, Thomas   London
B.c. 1671, apr. May 1684 to William Dobson till 1692, but not freed.

LUPTON, William   York
Clock and watchmaker. Free 1645. Died 1680, administration 1681.

LUPTON, William junior   York
Clockmaker. Son of William senior. Free 1681. Believed died 1689.

LYDDIATT, Thomas   London
Recorded by Baillie as late 17th century watchmaker, but I do not know him.

LYNAM, Philip   London
B.c. 1668, apr. Jul 1682 to John Harris till 1689, but not freed.

LYNCH, Robert (signed Linch)   London
Only one of this name, not two as Baillie suggests. Apr. Aug 1651 to Thomas Taylor, transferred Apr 1654 to John Dodsworth. Free Apr 1670. Took as aprs.: Apr 1670 **Francis Skipworth**; Apr 1675 **William Bennett** – freed Jul 1692; Jul 1675 **Thomas Peytling** – freed Aug 1682; Sep 1680 bound an apr. for Thomas Herbert. Had died by Jan 1684/85 from which time his widow got a quarterly charity from CC till Jan 1688/89.

LYNDSAY, Alexander (Friar)   Aberdeen
Repaired town clock 1537, which others could not.

LYON, George   Liverpool (Lancashire)
Watchmaker at Castle Street. Children b. 1691-1700.

LYON, John   Warrington (Lancashire)
Supplied turret clock 1666, worked on it 1669/72. In 1678 must have taken Thomas Stubbs as apr. (Free in CC 1685).

LYON(S), Richard   **London**
Apr. Nov 1649 to William Almond (thro' Ralph Almond), freed Dec 1656. Took as aprs.: c. 1657 **Jonathan Parry;** Oct 1660 **William Floyd/ Lloyd** – freed May 1668; Also bound aprs. for other Masters, ie for N. Delander, T. Herbert, R. Warren, S. Clyatt. Made Assistant from 1674, Warden from 1679, Master 1683. Attended regularly till 1690 when prob. died. Worked in Blackfriars in 1662. Work known – watch and longcase clocks signed 'Richard Lyons, London'.

M

MABB, William   **London**
B.c. 1675, apr. Aug 1688 to George Cawdron till 1696, but not freed.

MABYN, Davye   **Stratton (Cornwall)**
Kept church clock 1601.

MABYN, John   **Stratton (Cornwall)**
Kept church clock 1563.

McCULLOUGH, Andrew   **Belfast**
Silversmith and prob. watchmaker 1660-66.

MACHAM, Samuel   **London**
Clock recorded but prob. an error for Marchant, *qv*.

MADDEN, Thomas   **London**
Apr. Aug 1647 to William Rogers (thro' T. Alcock), but not freed.

MADOX, George   **London**
Paid CC quarterage 1672-73.

MAILING, Robert   **Aberdeen (Scotland)**
Maintained town clocks 1630.

MAINWARING (see also Manwaring)

MAINWARING, Andrew   **Dublin**
Goldsmith (and watchmaker) there 1671. Gone by 1674.

MAINWARING, William   **Dublin**
Apr. 1678 to Adam Soret. Goldsmith and watchmaker in 1685.

MAJOR, John   **London**
B.c. 1623, apr. Jun 1637 to James Allen (thro' Thomas Dawson), but not
freed.

MAJOR, Nathaniel   **London**
B.c. 1672, apr. Aug 1686 to Thomas Player till 1693, but not freed.

MALCHET, John (error for Matchett)

MALLETT, Peter   **London (and Barnstaple, Devon?)**
Late 17th century longcase clock recorded signed 'Peter Mallett
London'. One of this name worked at Barnstaple in the early 18th
century, maybe same man. Not in CC and nothing known about him in
London.

MALLETT, Stephen   **London**
B.c. 1675, apr. Sep 1689 to John Trubshaw till 1696, but not freed.

MANCHESTER, John   **London**
B.c. 1677, apr. Jul 1691 to William Hayden (thro' D. Stevens) till 1698.
Freed Apr 1700, having been transferred to George Etherington. Took
as aprs.: Apr 1707 **William Hayden** – freed Jul 1717; Sep 1716 illegible
name.

MANGIE, Edward   **York**
Watchmaker and Goldsmith. B.c. 1640 son of Edward Mangie,
whitesmith. Freed 1659. Believed married 1667. One of this name was a
goldsmith at Hull c. 1680. A whole family of this name were goldsmiths
in this area.

MANILL, Vincent   **London**
Longcase clock recorded c. 1700. Not in CC.

MANL(E)Y, Daniel I   **London/Yarmouth (Norfolk)**
Apr. Jul 1650 to Edmund Gilpin (thro' Thomas Taylor). Freed in CC
Oct 1660. Moved to Yarmouth by 1686 when son John, *qv*, got married.
Died Jun 1701, buried Beccles. Work known – watches, longcase and
lantern clocks.

MANL(E)Y, Daniel II   **Yarmouth (Norfolk)**
Son of Daniel senior. Married at Redisham 1691 to Rose Adams. Prob.
succ. to father at Yarmouth by 1714. Had died by 1730 when Thomas
Utting had taken over the premises.

MANLEY, John   **Bury St. Edmunds (Suffolk)**
Son of Daniel senior. Married at Redisham Anannah Keeble. Lost watch
advertised for in 1697. Died at Bury 1721.

MANLEY, George   **London**
Jan 1659/60 applied unsuccessfully to be CC Clerk. Perhaps he was not a
maker.

MANN, John   **London**
'Bodies maker in the Strand', *(sic)*, in 1668, when he took as apr. in CC
Thomas Garton (thro' L. Wythe).

MANN, Joseph   **London**
B.c. 1674, apr. Jul 1687 to Thomas Davis till 1695, but not freed.

MANSFIELD, Francis   **Cork**
Watchmaker there 1687 – c.1740. Died 1748. Married Mary Thornton.
Daughter Catherine married 1718 Simon Curtain, watchmaker.

MANSWORTH, Miles (or Wansworth?)   **London**
In Oct 1632 he was forbidden to practice the clock trade which he had
followed for three years as he was really a haberdasher. Also warned to
dismiss his apr.

MANWAYRING, Thomas (Mainwaring)   **London**
B.c. 1672, apr. Feb 1686/87 to Jeffrey Stanes till 1693. Freed Sep 1694.
Paid no quarterage after 1694.

MARCHANT, Richard   **London**
B.c. 1650, apr. Oct 1664 to Jeremy Gregory (thro' S. Horne) till 1671,
but not freed.

MARCHANT, Samuel senior   **London**
(Erroneously Merchant and Macham)
B.c. 1656, apr. Feb 1670/71 to Robert Seignior, later passed over to
Edward Eyston till 1677. Freed Mar 1677/78. Took as aprs.: Jun 1681
William Kent; Mar 1685-86 **John Parson** – freed Jul 1696; Apr 1692
Francis Turbutt; Jan 1692-93 his son **Samuel Marchant** – freed Sep
1700. Became Assistant from 1697, Warden 1705, when prob. died for
he never attended after that. His request for excusal from office in 1704
was denied, although 'he lives so far off as at Barking in Essex'. Work
known – longcase clock and watch.

MARCHANT, Samuel junior   **London**
B.c. 1678, son of Samuel senior. Apr. to father Jan 1692/93 till 1699.
Freed Sep 1700. Still alive and prob. working with father in 1704, but not
heard of thereafter.

MAR(E), Peter   **London**
(Also Lamer(e) and Lamar(e) and De Lamare, etc). A denizen clockmaker b. Normandy. Worked here from 1544. Worked on clock for
Norwich, and gave a clock to Threadneedle Street Church. Believed here
till c. 1571.

MARESQ, Philip Du   **London**
Watch c. 1660 (Baillie).

MARFIELD, John   **London**
Fleet Street in 1662. Prob. an error for Warfield, *qv*.

MARGOT, Green   **London**
Supposedly in Pall Mall in 1700 (Britten) but I cannot trace him.

MARKE, John   **London**
Mat. inst. maker. Free of another Co. but made a Free Brother in CC Feb
1667/68. Took as aprs.: Jan 1670/71 **Edward Batten** (thro' L. Wythe);
Jul 1674 **Thomas Hilton** (thro' L. Wythe).

MARKE(S), Thomas   **Exeter**
Kept local TC 1540s-1550s.

MARKEYS, John   **Exeter**
Kept local TC 1539.

MARKHAM, James   **London**
Supposedly watchmaker 1697, but prob. confusion with Markwick.

MARKHAM, Robert   **London**
Cane seller over against St. Dunstans Church in Fleet Street in 1672
when CC confiscated faulty rulers.

MARKWICK, James senior (sometimes Marquet)   **London**
Apr. Jun 1656 to Edward Gilpin (thro' R. Taylor), freed Aug 1666. Took
as aprs.: Dec 1674 **William Simcox** – freed Jan 1682/83; Jul 1683 **Robert
Finch** – freed Jul 1691; Jul 1690 **Robert Parker**; Sep 1691 **John Wright**;
Jul 1699 **Abraham David Gazuett** (son of Jeremy Gazuett); Aug 1699
John Foster (son of late – Foster of Southwark). Also bound three aprs.
for Edward Gilpin. In Sep 1677 was fined for abuse of Master at the
Steward's Feast at which he was a Steward. In 1673 he succ. 'Mr. Samuel
Betts deceased at Back of Royal Exchange'. In May 1686 he refused to
pay fine for absence from CC court and left 'in a abrupt and angry
manner'. Became Assistant in 1682, but from 1691 attended very
irregularly for which he was repeatedly cautioned and finally after Jan
1699/1700 he ceased to attend at all. Working till 1704, perhaps 1706.
Work known – prob. worked mostly for Gilpin, but longcase clocks and
watches are known, signed 'James Markwick, London'.

MARKWICK, James junior   **London**
Son of James senior, made free in CC by patrimony Apr 1692. Took as
aprs.: **Robert Parker** (from father) – freed Jul 1698; Feb 1698/99 **John
Robinson** (son of the late Christopher Robinson, deceased, merchant
of Rapahanack River in Virginia. Made Assistant in 1716, Warden
1717, Master 1720. Believed died 1730. Later on believed partner with
Robert Markham, who succ. him. Work known – watches and longcase
clocks.

MARKWITH, James   **London**
Baillie has 1699. Prob. Markwick, *qv*.

MARR, James   **London**
Never actually entered CC but was known to them. Prob. dead by 1663
and not on 1662 list.

MARRIOTT, John   **London**
B.c. 1628, apr. Jun 1641 to John Midnall (thro' O. Durrant) till 1649.
Not freed.

MARRIOTT, John   **London**
B.c. 1676, apr. Dec 1690 to Richard Jarratt till 1697. Freed Jun 1715.

MARSDEN, John   **London**
Brother in CC Sep 1698, a watchmaker. Took as aprs.: May 1703
William Burgess, son of Richard Burgess late of Alker, co. Lancaster,
farmer, deceased. I have no data on him after 1720 though believed lived
till c. 1741.

MARSH, John   **London**
B.c. 1662, apr. May 1676 to Thomas Parker till 1683, but not freed.

MARSH, Jonathan   **London**
B.c. 1677, apr. Oct 1691 to Richard Symonds till 1698. Freed Jan
1698/99. Took as aprs.: Apr 1707 **Charles Cotton**; Jan 1709/10
Benjamin Grigson. Work known – longcase clocks.

MARSH, Richard   **Ipswich (Suffolk)**
B. 1636, son of Richard and Margaret Marsh. Married c. 1670 Margaret
X. Issue 1671-74 two daughters. Also had son Richard. In 1674 in St.
Lawrence parish. Will dated 1706 proved Jan 1706-07. Was a
watchmaker. Work known – a clock-watch signed 'Richardus Marsh de
Ipswich Fecit', and a longcase clock.

MARSHALL, Benjamin   **London**
B.c. 1659, apr. Apr 1672 to Thomas Paul, later (Aug 1676) passed to
Abraham Prime till 1680. Freed Jun 1680. Took as aprs.: Jul 1683 **Luke
Page**. Also bound an apr. in 1686 for Cuthbert Lee. My last record of
him is in 1720 when he paid off his quarterage arrears (but Baillie records
him till 1732).

MARSHALL, Henry   **London**
In Jan 1655-56 was ordered to finish the work in hand for Benjamin Hill
and then find a proper master. Not heard of again.

MARSHALL, John   **London**
B.c. 1668, apr. Sep 1682 to Samuel Rosse later passed to Daniel Quare

till 1689. Freed Jan 1689/90, but did not take the oath – he was prob. a Quaker. In 1694 he advertised as 'watchmaker at the Rainbow Coffee House in Cornhill nr. Birchin Lane'. In 1695 he was 'Watchmaker against the Royal Exchange in Cornhill'. Took as aprs.: Jan 1693-94 **Thomas Stephens** – free Sep 1702; Sep 1698 **Wasteneys Law** (son of Stephen Law). In Dec 1698 he and his wife, Rebecca took Elizabeth Symonds apr. (as a maid). Also bound an apr. in Jun 1720 for George Graham. Work known – longcase clocks and supposedly inventor of the 'Magic night watch' (according to Baillie).

MARSHALL, John   St. Columb (Cornwall)
Repaired Town clock in 1617.

MARSHALL, Matthew   London
B.c. 1663, apr. Apr 1677 to Henry Adeane till 1684, but not freed.

MARSHALL, Samuel   London
B.c. 1668, apr. Aug 1682 to Anne, widow of Isaac Daniell, later passed to Cornelius Jenkins till 1689. Freed Feb 1689/90. Took as aprs.: Sep 1692 **Thomas Stevens** – free Apr 1700; Jul 1698 **Nicholas Browne;** Sep 1700 **James Canaries** (son of William Canaries of King Stanton (Kingsteignton), Devon, clerk), transferred Aug 1704 to John Shaw; Dec 1704 **Peter Moon** (son of Peter Moon late of St. James West in co. Middlesex, brewer deceased); Aug 1709 **Henry Carus** (son of Thomas Carus of Holton, co. Lancaster, gent.); Jun 1719 his son **Samuel Marshall** was freed by patrimony; Jul 1719 son **William Marshall;** Oct 1720 **John Lewis;** Mar 1719/20 **Henry Fitzwalter;** Mar 1719/20 **John Jarman.**

MARSHALL, Thomas   Halifax (Yorkshire)
Repaired church clock 1659 and 1663. A Christopher Marshall did so in 1701.

MARSHAM(?), ----   London
Ironmonger who paid CC search fee Feb 1671/72.

MARSTON, John   London
Not admitted to CC but known to them. Prob. dead by 1663 and not in 1662 list. Maybe confusion with Robert Marston, *qv.*

MARSTON, Robert London
B.c. 1635, apr. Jul 1649 to John Bayes, then passed to Onisephorus Helden till 1656, but not freed.

MARSTON, William London
B.c. 1645, apr. Jun 1659 to Joseph Munday, then transferred (prob. when Munday died in 1663) to Edward Whitfield till 1666. Freed Jul 1669. In 1663 was a witness to master's will. Took as aprs.: May 1678 **Charles Knight** – free Jun 1685; Jul 1683 **George Riley**. Made Steward 1684. Not heard of thereafter.

MARTENOT, ---- London
A Frenchman working 1662. See also Matinot.

MARTIN – see also Martine and Martins.

MARTIN, Abraham London
An engraver from Geneva. Made a Free Brother in CC Sep 1682. Still working in 1700. According to Britten he was given about 1685 a month longcase clock by his friend John Street, *qv*.

MARTIN, Edward London
B.c. 1648, apr. Nov 1662 to John Nicasius (thro' S. Horne) till 1669, but not freed.

MARTIN, Francis London
B.c. 1670, apr. Aug 1683 to John Wells till 1690, but not freed.

MARTINS, George (usually Mertins) *qv*.

MARTIN, Jeremiah London
B.c. 1666, apr. Apr 1680 to Thomas Tompion (thro' W. Dent) till 1687. Freed Sep 1687. Took as aprs.: Jan 1689/90 **Clement Brice;** May 1692 **Thomas Martin;** Jul 1697 **Jonathan Akeres**. Working till at least 1716, when in arrears with quarterage. Work known – watches and longcase clocks signed 'Jeremiah Martin, Londini' and 'Jere Martin Tottenham High Cross', and 'Jeremiah Martin London'.

MARTIN, John London
B.c. 1670, apr. Jun 1684 to George Carey till 1691, but not freed.

MARTIN, John   **London**
B.c. 1659, apr. Aug 1672 to Joseph Norris, transferred to Edward Norris
till 1680. Freed Sep 1679. In 1681 he had a house and clockmaker's shop
in Whitegate Alley between Bishopsgate Street and Spitalfield, but was
alleged to have bound an apr. thro' the Merchant Taylors' Co. – which he
denied. In May 1682 he acknowledged that he kept his brother (not
named but prob. William Martin, *qv*) as his apr. who was bound to James
Metcalfe of the Haberdashers' Co. – promised to re-bind him thro' CC.
Took as aprs.: Dec 1681 **Richard Print** – free Sep 1698; May 1682
William Martin – freed Apr 1702; Nov 1687 **Samuel Clark**; Apr 1693
Edward Brookes; Jul 1699 son **William Martin** – freed by patrimony
Apr 1710; May 1701 **Thomas Redwood** (son of John Redwood of
Aldingham, co. Herts, parish clerk); Nov 1715 **John Hocker/Hecker**,
later transferred to Edward Joslin. Work known – watches, bracket,
lantern and longcase clocks, signed 'John Martin, London' and 'John
Martin Londini, Fecit'.

MARTIN, Richard   **Northampton**
Lantern clock recorded c. 1695.

MARTIN, Thomas   **London**
B.c. 1671 (though claimed when marrying c. 1666), apr. Dec 1685 to
Richard Warren (thro' R. Lyons), till 1692 – not freed. In Jun 1688 he
married as a watchmaker of Stepney ('aged 22') to Annie Hill, spinster,
20, of All Hallows in the Wall. In Jul 1693 his apr. **John Ring** (taken over
from Nicholas Beck) was freed. Prob. dead or gone by 1696/97.

MARTIN, Thomas   **London**
B.c. 1678, apr. May 1692 to Jeremiah Martin till 1699, but not freed.
Work known – a longcase clock signed 'Thomas Martin, London'.

MARTIN(E), Thomas   **Wigan (Lancashire)**
Free 1675, Burgess 1686; Mayor 1706. Died 1716, leaving will. Had son,
Thomas, b. 1688 and succ. him there. Had as apr. (1677?) **Samuel
Williamson** – freed 1684.

MARTIN, William   **Bristol**
Clockmaker, signed marriage bond there 1689. Baillie records one there
1703-39.

MARTIN, William   **London**
B.c. 1668, apr. May 1682 to his father John Martin till 1689. Freed Apr
1702. Work known – longcase clock, three train.

MARTINOT, Barnaby (Martineau?)   **London**
One such at Farringdon Within ward in 1618. B. in Paris and a Roman
Catholic. Prob. same as Martenot working 1662.

MARTMOTT, William (maybe Martinot?)   **London**
In 1622 was alien journeyman with Cornelius Mellin in Blackfriars.

MARY, Jean   **London**
Denizen clockmaker in 1544.

MASEY, Thomas   **Oxford**
Smith who repaired church clock in 1550.

MASON, Charles   **London**
In Jun 1687 was already the apr. of Michael Bird (II) being bound thro'
the Blacksmiths' Co. Ordered to be rebound thro' the CC – but was not.

MASON, Henry   **London**
B.c. 1633, apr. Aug 1647 to Jeremy Gregory (thro' H. Buntin) till 1654,
but not freed.

MASON, John   **Bristol**
A smith, working on turret clocks 1671-80. In 1673 made clock for
Alderley.

MASON, Richard (sometimes Masson)   **London**
Entered CC as Free Brother Oct 1632. Still working 1635. (Confused
with but not same man as Richard Masterson.)

MASON, Robert   **London**
B.c. 1647, apr. Nov 1658 to Peter Bellone (thro' D. Moody) till 1668, but
not freed.

MASON, William   **Gainsborough (Lincolnshire)**
Believed working 1695.

MASON, William   **London**
B.c. 1666, apr. Jan 1680-81 to Mary, widow of George Harris till 1687.
Freed Apr 1688. Took as aprs.: Mar 1691 **John Wescott** – freed Jun
1703; Oct 1693 **John Dowset;** Mar 1697/98 **John Welcome** – freed Apr
1705; Jun 1702 **Thomas Hester** (son of Henry Hester, clockmaker); Sep
1706 **Thomas Garle** (son of Thomas Garle, late of Barnewell, co.
Northants, grazier); Aug 1713 **Edmund Poole.**

MASSEY, Edmund   **London**
B.c. 1660, apr. Dec 1673 to Joseph Knibb till 1681. Freed Jan 1682/83.
Took as aprs.: Mar 1688 **Samuel Jones; Thomas Farmer** from
G. Brackley then transferred him to Joseph Knibb 1689-90.

MASSEY, Henry (sometimes Massy)   **London**
Son of Nicholas I. Brother in CC Apr 1692. Married Anne Brissett and
mentioned in father's will in 1698. In Jul 1695 he admitted having two
alien aprs. Working till at least 1704. Work known – numerous watches
and bracket clocks signed 'Henry Massey, London'. Baillie records him
till 1745 which seems incorrect. I have no details of him later than 1704.

MASSEY, Jacob   **London**
Son of Nicholas I. Mentioned in father's will in 1698. Apparently not a
member of CC. Supposedly worked at Cranbourn Street. Work known –
longcase and bracket clocks signed 'Jacob Massey in Leicester Fields'
and 'Jacob Massey, London'.

MASSEY, Nicholas senior   **London**
Free Brother in CC Apr 1682, a French Protestant watchmaker,
promising to pay quarterage if he stays for a full year. Believed to be the
elder son of Nicholas Massey of Blois who died between 1646 and 1658.
Worked at Cranborn Street in parish of St. Ann Westminster. Died 1698
leaving widow Susannah and sons Henry Nicholas and Jacob (*qv*). Work
known – bracket clocks and watches, signed 'Nicholas Massey,
London'.

MASSEY, Nicholas junior   **London**
Son of Nicholas senior. Free Brother in CC Jul 1693. One of this name
married Mary Roper. Prob. succ. father at Cranborn Street. Still
working in 1700. I have no details of him after 1700, but Baillie records
him till 1723. Work known – watches (but difficult to distinguish from
work of his father.

381

MASTER, W. Henshaw   **London**
Recorded as 1689 in CC, but this is a clerical error for W. Henshaw,
Master (ie of the CC).

MASTERMAN, Richard   **London**
Recorded as 'English Forrin' 1628 in Blacksmiths' Co. but this is
perhaps an error for Masterson *qv.*

MASTERS, Richard   **London**
(Not same as Richard Masterson *qv*). Never actually admitted to CC but
known to them. Prob. died before 1662/63.

MASTERS, William   **London**
B.c. 1659, apr. Dec 1672 to Henry Young till 1680, but not freed till Aug
1701.

MASTERSON, John (sometimes Maston)   **London**
B.c. 1635, apr. Aug 1648 to Richard Masterson till 1656, but never freed
(perhaps son of Richard who worked largely for his father?). Worked at
Westminster in 1662. In Jul 1661 he was fined for faulty workmanship of
a clock. From Sep 1693 he received occasional charity payments from CC
till 1705, then his widow had them till about 1707.

MASTERSON, Richard   **London**
(sometimes Masterton, Masterman, Maston)
A watchmaker but free in the Clothworkers' Co. Dec 1631, by redemption. Free Brother in CC Oct 1633 and also an Assistant. Officially
transferred from Clothworkers' Co. in 1636. From 1637 he became a
Warden, Master 1642, last attended 1648. Believed died Dec 1653 when
his widow took over his remaining aprs. She had occasional CC charities
from Oct 1659 to 1665. Acted (unofficially) in role of Beadle in binding
aprs. for other Masters, incl., P. Closon, J. Starnill (2), W. Bowyer,
E. Gilpin, C. Vernon, E. East, S. Hackett (2), T. Reeve (2), E. Allen,
D. Howell, R. Child (2), J. Vautrollier (2), J. Pennock, W. Selwood,
though no working connections is apparent with any of these Masters.
Bound apparently as his own aprs.: May 1650 **Abraham Burton** – freed
Oct 1657; Jul 1650 **Joseph Webb**; Aug 1650 **Benjamin Gibson** – all
transferred to his widow on his death. In Dec 1654 she complained that
Abraham Beckner had taken one of them and he was made to return him.
Work known – perhaps three watches signed 'Richard Masterson at the
dyall at Mooregate' and 'Richard Masterson, London'.

MASTON, John London
1662 (see Masterson).

MATCHETT, George London
B.c. 1637, apr. Mar 1651/52 to William Petty till 1658, but not freed. Prob. dead or gone by 1662/63.

MATCHETT, John London
Free in CC Aug 1647. Believed worked in Bedford Street, but certainly in Covent Garden in 1680 and Westminster in 1662. Took as aprs.: Aug 1647 **Robert Lochard** – freed Oct 1655; Jul 1655 **Edward Bridgeman** – freed Oct 1662; Oct 1660 **Basil Brand;** Feb 1667-68 **John Tyler;** Jan 1668-69 **John Southworth** – freed Sep 1689; Jun 1671 **John Good** – freed Jul 1678. Also bound an apr. each for J. Graves, W. Partridge and T. Eyston. In May 1666 summoned to be Assistant but claimed he could not afford to be one! Made Assistant 1668, Warden from 1675/76 and should have been Master, but was suspended from future meetings in Nov 1678 as he 'is well known to be a Popish Recusant' (ie a Roman Catholic). His suspension was lifted in Sep 1687 and 'he is restored to his former status'. Last attended CC in 1689. Paid quarterage till 1694, but dead by 1697/98. Work known – watches are on record but none known to still survive.

MATHER, Samuel London
Freeman of the Haberdashers' Co. having been apr. to blank Smith there and later transferred to Michael Bird. Brother in CC Jun 1691. Took as aprs. in CC (when he hath obtained his Freedom of the City): Jun 1691 **Thomas Bell** (thro' J. Norcott); Sep 1696 **Samuel Woodhams;** Nov 1699 **Caleb Scott** (son of Joshua Scott, clockmaker). I have no record of him after 1699, though Baillie records him till 1712.

MATSON, Richard London
Apr. Aug 1647 to William North (thro' N. Payne) till 1656, but not freed.

MATTHEW(S), Francis London
Apr. Nov 1647 to Sampson Shelton (thro' T. Alcock), then transferred in 1648 (when Shelton died) to John Bayes. Freed May 1656. Supported the CC Administration during the 1656 rebellion.

MATTHEWS, William   **London**
B.c. 1672, apr. Dec 1686 to George Cawdron till 1693, but not freed and not heard of again.

MAUBERT (see also Mobert)

MAUBERT, Peter   **London**
B.c. 1663, apr. Jan 1679/80 to David Megrett, jeweller (thro' Dorcas Bouquet) till 1686, but not freed. Some of the Mauberts were Goldsmiths.

MAVINE, Daniel   **Edinburgh**
Apr. to Paul Roumieu, Aug 1681.

MAY, Edward senior   **Henley-on-Thames**
Longcase clock said to be c. 1680 is probably mid-18th century and by a later man of this name.

MAY, Joanna
Widow of William, *qv*.

MAY, John   **London**
A Dutchman by birth and a watchmaker. Free Brother in CC Feb 1692/93. Paid quarterage till at least 1702, after which I have no data but Baillie records his death as 1738. Work known – a watch signed 'John May, London'.

MAY, William   **London**
B.c. 1657, apr. Jan 1671/72 to Benjamin Bell till 1678. Freed Mar 1679. Also Freeman of the City. Took as aprs.: Nov 1682 **Thomas Wasse;** Feb 1684/85 **Matthew Bunce; Thomas Cooke** (from T. Hicks) – freed Aug 1699. He died before Nov 1689 after which his widow, Joanna, carried on the business. She took as aprs.: Nov 1689 **George Harris** later passed over to T. Tompion and freed Jul 1698; Sep 1690 **Thomas Carter** (thro' J. Herbert) – freed Jul 1699; Apr 1693 **Anthony Harrison** – freed Sep 1701; Sep 1696 **George Stratford** – freed Jan 1704/05; May 1699 **William Slough** (son of John Slough late of parish of St. Mary Whitechapel, Middlesex, silk thrower); Sep 1702 **David Craft** (son of Geoge Craft late of Lenham, co. Kent, yeoman, deceased); Aug 1707 **William Ballard;** Sep 1710 **William Cowdell;** Jul 1712 **Matthew Parkinson** – freed Dec 1719.

MAYHEW, Henry   **Parham and Hacheston (Suffolk)**
In 1686 made St. Lawrence, Ipswich church clock for £30. Sons John (b. 1697) and William (b. 1699) baptised at Parham, where he worked in 1710. Will dated and proved 1720. Buried at Hacheston. Work known – longcase clock signed 'Henry Mayhew, at Parham, Hatcheston', another 'Henry Mayhew, Parham', also a lantern clock.

MAYLARD, Thomas   **London**
B.c. 1668, apr. Mar 1682 to Henry Reeve till 1689. Freed Sep 1698. Took as apr. Mar 1699/1700 **William Maylard** (son of Thomas Maylard late of Reading, Berks., Bodice-maker, deceased). Still working 1705.

MAYNARD, Christopher   **London**
B.c. 1646, apr. May 1660 to Simon Hackett (thro' J. Bayes) – freed May 1667. Took as aprs.: Sep 1669 **Joseph Plomer;** Dec 1671 **Richard Covell;** May 1675 **John Sudbury** – freed Sep 1686; Sep 1692 son **George Maynard.** In 1691 he bound an apr. for B. Graves. Made Assistant in CC 1682, but was always a reluctant attender at meetings. Repeatedly warned for failure to attend and fined in Mar 1690 begging leniency 'as he has noe servant to look to his shop' and he lives at Hackney 'to and from which he goes and comes daily'. In 1675 he advertised his shop as at the Royal Exchange. Last heard of 1692/93, after which he never attended again. Prob. dead by 1697/98. Work known – bracket clock signed 'Christopher Maynard, London', watch signed at Royal Exchange London.

MAYNARD, George   **London**
B.c. 1678, apr. Sep 1692 to his father, Christopher Maynard till 1699, but not freed. Baillie records his as insolvent in 1723 (at St. Martin in the Fields). Work known – longcase clock signed 'George Maynard, London'.

MAYNARD, John I   **Long Melford (Suffolk)**
Blacksmith, b. 1636. Married 1669 Grace Myles. Died 1689 leaving tools to son, John, *qv*. Said to have made church clock for Long Melford.

MAYNARD, John II   **Long Melford (Suffolk)**
B. 1670 son of John I. Ironmonger. Married 1692/93 Mary Lungley. Died 1720. Work known – two lantern clocks maybe by him or his son John (b. 1695).

MAYO, William London
B.c. 1663, apr. Apr 1676 to Robert Cawne till 1684, but not freed.

MAYSMOR, Humphrey London/Wrexham (Denbighshire)
Not officially admitted into CC but apparently recognised by them. A clockmaker and Freeman of the Blacksmiths' Co. In Nov 1692 took **John Harris** as apr. in CC (thro' N. Russell). Later at Wrexham, living at Town Hill c. 1715-30. Work known – watch signed 'Maysmoor, Wrexham'.

MAYSMOR, William London/Wrexham (Denbighshire)
B.c. 1679, apr. Mar 1693/94 to John Higgs till 1700, but not freed. Working at Wrexham c. 1720.

MEAD(E)S, Thomas London
B.c. 1665, apr. May 1679 to Thomas Browne till 1686. Freed Apr 1687. Took as apr. May 1688 **Thomas Freeman** (from C. Harbert). Still working in Jan 1719/20 when in arrears with quarterage.

MEAKIN (see Meekin)

MEARS, Isaac (also Meers) London
B.c. 1647, apr. Sep 1661 to Robert Whitwell till 1668 but not freed.

Mebert (see also Maubert and Mobert)

MEBERT, Isaac London
Diamond-cutter. Never actually admitted into CC but known to them and in 1656 took thro' CC as apr. **Hector Bouquet** thro' Solomon Bouquet. Prob. dead or gone by 1662/63.

MEDHURST, Richard Croydon
Watchmaker and Free Brother in CC Nov 1687 – 'of Croydon'. Took as aps.: Jul 1689 **Thomas Young** (thro' D. Stevens); Sep 1693 **John Warren** (thro' T. Birch). Still working in Oct 1716, when in arrears with quarterage. Baillie records him till 1724.

MEDNALL, ---- (see Midnall)

MEEBERRY, Elizabeth London
B.c. 1666, apr. Oct 1680 to Edward Norris and Sarah his wife till 1687, but not freed. Prob. a domestic servant.

MEEKING/MEAKINS, Thomas   Dublin
Clockmaker and Free Goldsmith 1699, but working from 1689 till death in 1709. Apr. 1681 to Walter Bingham. Work known – longcase clock.

MEEKIN, William   Dublin
Clockmaker 1697-99.

MEGRETT, David   London
Jeweller and not strictly a member of CC. Took as apr. thro' CC Jan 1679/80 **Peter Maubert** (thro' Dorcas Bouquet).

MEIREDAY, John (see Merreday)   London
1662.

MELL, Davis   London
Said to have been a famous violinist and bandmaster to Charles II. Free Brother in CC Oct 1655 – was to work for Richard Morgan (as journeyman?) one month at springmaking and two at watchwork. Took as aprs.: Apr 1659 **Cornelius Harbert** (later passed to W. Grout); **Thomas Crawley** (taken from R. Morgan) – freed Oct 1660. Made CC Assistant from 1659; last attended in 1660. Work known – lantern clock, three train quarter-chiming on 10 bells signed 'Davis Mell, Londini' (name of Thomas Crawley on base); another one quarter-chiming on three bells signed 'Davis Mell in Crutched Friars, Londini'.

MELLIN, Cornelius   London
Alien in 1622 with aprs.: **John Hutchinson, John Cooke, Peter Michell, Nathaniel Delawne** and journeymen: William Martmott, William LaWray Pierre, Isaac Romier, John de Mouchie, William Bull and James Goallon. All living in the same house in Blackfriars. Work known – two watches, one signed 'in Blackfriars'.

MELLIN, Gui (Guillaume?)   London
Baillie records early 17th century watch, but this may well be a slip for Cornelius Mellin, *qv*.

MELLIN, John du   London
(Spellings vary, eg, John Demolyn, Dewmelane, Dumoulin, etc.).
French, denizen clockmaker 1544. Kept Dulwich College clock 1553.
Clock keeper to Queen Elizabeth 1556. Still working 1568.

MELVILLE, Robert   Aberdeen
A stationer, son of the late David Melville. Kept town clocks from 1645 till his death in 1651.

MENIALL, James (see under Mesniel)

MER (see Mare)

MERCER, ----   London
In 1671/72 had faulty rulers confiscated by CC from his premises at The Feathers in Fleet Street – supposedly made by John Nash. Prob. was an ironmonger or measure-seller.

MERCER, Edward   London
B.c. 1676, apr. Jul 1690 to Cuthbert Lee till 1697. Was transferred to Thomas Tompion by 1695 and freed Jul 1699. Paid no quarterage from 1699-1705. In Jul 1709 widow Mercer (his widow?) received charity from CC. Work known – none, but a longcase clock c. 1710 is known signed 'Edward Mercer, Thrapstone' (Northants). It is not known whether this might be the same man.

MERCIER, James   London
A Frenchman who in Jan 1697/98 admitted having two journeymen, both French. Was ordered to dismiss them within two months or face prosecution. Not a CC member. May be same man as Jaques Mercier who was at Amsterdam in 1687 and a Huguenot refugee from Paris.

MEREDITH, John   London
B.c. 1640, son of Lancelot. Apr. to his father Sep 1654 (thro' B. Hill) till 1661. Freed Oct 1664. Prob. in Chancery Lane 1662 as Merreday, *qv.*

MEREDITH, Lancelot   London
Free in CC Dec 1637 (as Brother?). In 1656 joined rebels against CC administration. Took as aprs.: Nov 1651 **John Bradshaw** (thro' W. Petty) – freed Dec 1658; Sep 1654 his son, **John Meredith** (thro' B. Hill) – freed Oct 1664; **Joshua Short** (thro' R. Ash) – freed Jul 1665; Jul 1660 **Henry Guy**. In Jan 1659/60 he applied unsuccessfully to become CC Beadle. Not heard of after 1660 and prob. dead by 1662.

MERREDAY, John   London
Also Meireday. At Chancery Lane in 1662. Prob. a clerical error for John
Meredith, *qv*.

MERRYMAN, Benjamin (sometimes Merriman)   London
B.c. 1662, the son of John Merryman of Newbury, Berkshire, yeoman
(deceased in 1676). Apr. in Merchant Taylors' Co. Feb 1676/77 to
Edward Marskell of Sweeting Lane, scissors maker, till 1683, later
transferred to Francis Hussey. Freed Dec 1686, Livery Nov 1692.
Meantime he became a Free Brother in CC as a watchmaker Sep 1682.
Took as aprs. thro' CC: May 1684 **John White** – free Apr 1692; Jun 1691
Edward Stopforth (for Henry Merryman); May 1692 **Thomas Franklin**;
Nov 1692 **Thomas Merryman** (thro' W. Knotsford), later passed over to
Thomas (illegible); Nov 1701 **William Knight Jeffrey** (son of Edmund
Jeffrey of Cambridge town, gent.). In 1693 he was 'of St. Martins
Ludgate' when acted as a witness to marriage of Edward Line and Mary
Banger. Last heard of in 1708 when he was excused CC Stewardship as he
held offices in the Merchant Taylors' Co. (Baillie records him as late as
1734 but I cannot confirm this). Work known – watches and longcase
clocks, signed 'Benj. Merriman, London'. See also under Thomas
below.

MERRYMAN, Henry   London
B.c. 1655, apr. Jan 1667 to Richard Bowen till 1676. Freed Feb 1674/75.
Took as aprs.: Apr 1676 **John Hammond**; Jun 1681 **William Billop** –
freed Sep 1688; Sep 1684 **Richard Lancaster**; Mar 1686-87 **John
Webster** – free May 1695; Sep 1688 **James Fynes** (thro' R. Dent); Jun
1691 **Edward Stopforth** (thro' B. Merryman); c. 1683 (or later) **John
Pecket** over from H. Bradley – freed Mar 1691-92; Apr 1693 **John
Wright** (thro' J. Peckett) – free Apr 1715; Jun 1693 **William Mitchinalle**
– free Sep 1702; May 1694 **Nathaniel Newman** – free Jun 1703; Dec
1697 **John Merryman** (son of John Merryman) – free Feb 1711/12. Paid
quarterage till 1702, but I have no record of him alive after then. Work
known – watches. See also under Thomas below.

MERRYMAN, Thomas   London
B.c. 1678, apr. Nov 1692 thro' W. Knotsford to Benjamin Merryman till
1699, but later (Nov 1698) was transferred to Thomas X (illegible name).
A Mr. Merryman received CC charity 1715 – Dec 1717, after which his
widow, Elizabeth, got it. Not known whether this was Thomas or
Benjamin or Henry.

MERT(T)INS, George (also Mart(t)ins)   **London**
B.c. 1666, son of John Merttins, Merchant of London. Apr. Apr 1680 to
his father thro' Dorcas Bouquet till 1687 (she promised not to pass him
over to any makers of clocks). Freed Jan 1688/89. Took as aprs.: Jan
1691/92 **Thomas Rowe** – free Apr 1699; Apr 1693 **Benjamin Howell**
(thro' E. Norris) – free Jun 1700; Dec 1694 **Matthew Walker**; Sep 1699
Thomas Coster; Feb 1699/1700 **Beauchamp Otgher** (son of Justus
Otgher Citizen and Mercer of London); Apr 1702 **Henry Guy** (son of
Richard Guy, Citizen and Vintner of London); Sep 1703 **John Mitford;**
Jun 1711 **Robert Chambers.** Became CC Assistant from 1708, Warden
from 1711, Master 1713, ceased to attend 1715. In Jun 1713 he was
transferred by order of the Court of Aldermen to the Skinners' Co., by
now as Sir George Merttins. Was a Goldsmith and watchmaker at the
Peacock nr. Royal Exchange, Cornhill, from 1688 till 1727 when he died.
Believed to be also in Goldsmiths' Co. Was Lord Mayor of London
1724-25. His apr., John Mitford, is believed to have married his
daughter in 1714 and they later became partners as Merttins and
Mitford, but are recorded as bankrupt in 1720.

MESNIEL, James (also Meniall)   **London**
A Frenchman, prosecuted Apr 1682 for practising when not in the CC.
Admitted a Free Brother May 1682, a small clockmaker. Paid quarterage
till mid-1699. In Jul 1699 his son, James junior, was apr. to William
Fuller, James senior then being described as a clockmaker of the parish
of Tottenham, co. Middlesex.

METAR, Henry   **London**
Longcase clock recorded c. 1710. Strangely unrecorded hitherto.

METCALF, Edward   **London**
B.c. 1670, apr. Jan 1684/85 to Richard Blundell thro' Nicasius Russell
till 1691, but not freed.

METCALFE, James   **London**
Free in Haberdashers' Co. Sep 1676, having been apr. to Thomas
Wilcox. Took as apr. thro' CC the brother of John Martin, who was to
serve John Martin as apr. c. 1682. Not a member of CC however.

MEYLOR, Nicholas   **Dublin**
Watchmaker 1631.

MICABIUS, John   London
Recorded as 1632 subscriber to CC, but this must be a slip for John Nicasius.

MICHEL (see also Mitchell)

MICHEL, James   Chardstock (Somerset)
Lantern clocks c.1670 – c.1700.

MICHEL, James   London
Longcase clock recorded c. 1700. One Mr. Michell paid CC search fee 1673.

MICHEL, John   Bath (Somerset)
Lantern clock recorded c.1670 – c.1700.

MICHEL, Jo. (John)   Chardstock (Somerset)
Lantern clocks recorded c.1670 – c.1700.

MICHELL, Peter   London
Alien. In 1622 was already an apr. with Cornelius Mellin in Blackfriars.

MICKLEWRIGHT, Erasmus   London
B.c. 1652, apr. Jun 1666 to Richard Bestwick, a springmaker and Freeman of the Cutlers' Co., thro' L. Wythe till 1673. Freed Aug 1673. Took as aprs.: Sep 1673 **Charles Baxter** – freed Apr 1681; Mar 1674/75 **Thomas Brafield** – freed Sep 1682; Sep 1681 **John Girlington;** Apr 1685 **James Boyce** – free Jul 1692; Nov 1692 **Richard Speakman;** Dec 1698 **Abiel Whichello** (son of Peter Whichello, Citizen & Glover); Jun 1699 **William Walker** (son of Ralph Walker, late of Henley-on-Thames, deceased, husbandman); Aug 1700 his son, **Erasmus Micklewright** junior, free 1708. Also bound an apr. for John Fitter. Paid quarterage till at least 1705. Work known – none, but if a springmaker then prob. unidentifiable.

MIDDLETON, Timothy   London
B.c. 1666, apr. Jul 1680 to Robert Dingley till 1687. Freed Nov 1687.

MIDNALL, John (sometimes Mednall)   London
Working c. 1620, became one of first CC Assistants in 1632, Warden from 1635 when last attended. In May 1637 he had been arrested for debt

and his wife appeared at CC court on his behalf to apologize for non-payment of quarterage, promising to pay later. In Jun 1641 took as apr. **John Marriott** thro' O. Durrant. Work known – watch on record signed 'John Midnall, Fleet Street', supposedly made for Cromwell.

MIL(L)BOURNE, John London
B.c. 1672, apr. in Poulters' Co. Jan 1686/87 to Edward Hutchinson till 1693. Freed Oct 1693. Paid quarterage to Poulters' Co. till 1697. Admitted to CC 1698, by trade a watchmaker and a Freeman of the Poulters' Co. Took as apr. in CC May 1703 **Edward Morgan** (son of William Morgan of St. Leonard Eastcheap, London, Taylor). Paid quarterage till at least 1705. Baillie records his death between 1722 and 1735, which I cannot confirm.

MILLER, ---- London
In 1656 was accused by Ahasuerus Fromanteel of having too many aprs., but we do not know who he was.

MILLER, Henry Chester(?)
Watchmaker from Dublin. Married 1700 at Chester to Rebecca Chetwood.

MILLER, John London
B.c. 1653, apr. Jan 1666/67 to Samuel Knibb till 1674, but on Knibb's death (pre-1674) he was passed on to Isaac Puzy, then later to Joseph Knibb. Freed Nov 1674. Took as aprs.: Jul 1676 **Jeremiah Mills;** May 1680 **Edward Highmore** – free Sep 1687; **Jonathan Puller** (taken thro' N. Coxeter) – freed Sep 1683; Jul 1687 **John Howard** – free Aug 1694; Sep 1695 **Richard Smith;** Jan 1699/1700 **John Peters** (son of Thomas Peters of New Street, London, victualler). Paid quarterage till mid-1702. Work known – lantern, bracket and longcase clocks, signed 'John Miller, London', one signed 'John Miller Londini fecit, Charing Cross'. One reported as 'John Miller, Showe Lane' is prob. an error for Thomas Mills, *qv*.

MILLER, Peter London
B.c. 1659, apr. Dec 1673 to John Wright till 1680. Freed Mar 1681/82. Took as aprs.: Jul 1683 **Thomas Holmes** – free Sep 1697; Aug 1694 **Francis Sanderson.** Baillie records his death as 1733 but I have no record of him after 1697.

MILLER, Ralph   **London**
B.c. 1676, apr. Apr 1690 to Robert Halstead till 1697. Freed Nov 1697. Paid no quarterage after 1698.

MILLER, Thomas   **Gazeley (Suffolk)**
Lantern clock recorded. Children b. to Thomas and Mary Miller in 1690s. He died 1701.

MILLETT, Edward   **London**
B.c. 1658, apr. Jul 1672 'by his friends' (ie prob. and orphan) to George Kingsmill, they providing as a fee only 30 shillings in buttons (ie silver buttons). But Kingsmill 'absented' and he was re-apprenticed Apr 1673 to Nicholas Beck till 1680. Freed Nov 1680. Took as apr. Sep 1682 **Edward Plymley.** Described as a clockmaker of Hogsdon, Middlesex in Aug 1684 when, with John Millett (his brother?), he assaulted William Clement.

MILLETT, John   **London**
B.c. 1664 (prob. brother of Edward). Apr. Dec 1677 thro' S. Davis to William Clement (a Freeman of Blacksmiths' Co.) till 1685. However in Aug 1684 together with Edward Millett, as a clockmaker of Hogsdon, Middlesex, he assaulted William Clement. Never freed in CC.

MILLINGTON, Thomas   **Shrewsbury (Shropshire)**
Watchmaker there 1695.

MILLION, William (and Millian)   **London**
Freeman in Merchant Taylors' Co. Jul 1671 having been apr. to Silvester Guilder. Free Brother in CC as a great clockmaker Jan 1671/72. Paid quarterage till about 1674. Dead by 1698.

MILLS – see also Milne, which is a variant, esp. in Scotland.

MILLS, Jeremiah   **London**
B.c. 1663, apr. Jul 1676 to John Miller till 1684, but not freed.

MILLS, Ralph   **London**
B.c. 1676, apr. Jun 1690 to Charles Gretton, passed on to Cuthbert Lee till 1697. Freed Sep 1697. Took as aprs.: Nov 1700 **John Castens** (son of Orbert Castens *(sic)* late of parish of St. Leonard, Shoreditch, Middlesex, (watchmaker-erased) button-maker, deceased) – free Dec 1707; Feb 1715/16 **John Carpenter.**

MILLS, Thomas   London

Free Brother in CC Sep 1652, but was taking aprs. before then. Took as aprs.: Feb 1646 **Henry Passion** thro' N. Coxeter; Feb 1649/50 **Thomas Birch,** thro'N. Coxeter – free Mar 1658; Mar 1650 **Matthew Crockford** thro' N. Coxeter – free Apr 1658; Aug 1655 **Samuel Pepper** thro' S. Horne; Dec 1656 **Charles Cassway** thro' N. Coxeter; **William Glazier** thro' or from Anthony Grosse – freed Apr 1666; Jan 1662-63 **Samuel Skelton** thro' N. Coxeter. In 1662 worked in Westminster (at Shoe Lane?). Receipt for Aug 1662 reads:

	s.	d.
'Work done to my Lord of Salsbereyes klocke		
For a new pinnian to the woch parts	11.	00
for rounding flating and equallinge the krowne wheele	6.	00
for putting peaces to the ballance varge and brasinge it and new plomets	7.	00
for stopinge the hooles of the woch parte and makinge the wheeles to goe and of the klock	9.	00
for kleaninge the klocke	8.	00
for mendinge the fley of the strikinge parte and mendinge the strikinge	4.	00
(sic) £2	4.	00

But he accepted £2.0.0 straight.'

Work known – lantern clocks signed 'Thomas Milles, Shoe Lane, Londini fecit', (one has an hour hand and a quarter-hour hand which rotates once every quarter-hour).

MILNE, Gideon   Edinburgh

Apr. 1676 to Humphrey Milne.

MILNE, Humphrey (also Mylnes, etc.)   Edinburgh

Supposedly free there in 1660 but the page of the records was stolen and he was reinstated in 1687. Repaired town clock 1661. Took as aprs.: Jan 1676 **Gideon Milne;** Jan 1676 **George Myles** (or Mylne?); Aug 1692 **Hugh Campbell.** Prob. an Englishman in origin, maybe Staffordshire. Said to have died 1722, but perhaps died 1693. Widow (Jean Mathie) died c. 1725 at Craigwells. Work known – lantern clocks, four or five. See B. Loomes, *Complete British Clocks.*

MILNE, John   Edinburgh

Kept public clock 1648/49.

MILNE, Richard (sometimes Mills)   **Edinburgh**
Son of Thomas Mylne of Staffordshire, apr. Jul 1661 to Humphrey
Milne. Freed Sep 1678, having made a clock-watch as testpiece. Took as
aprs.: 1680 **John Goodoune** (or **Gordoune**); 1699 **Patrick Gordon** –
freed 1715; 1696 **James Thompson**; 1685 **James Hutton**; 1680
Matthew Bell. In 1703 was Boxmaster of the Guild of Hammermen,
though then suffering from old age and weakness. Believed lived with
sister(?) Esther Mills, wife of Robert Carstairs. In 1693 took a tenement
in Cannongate, east side of Leith Wynd, from Humphrey Mills of
Craigwell. Believed died about 1710.

MILNERNE, Henry   **Glovestone (Cheshire)**
Watchmaker. Buried Feb 1705 at Chester.

MINSHULL, William   **London**
B.c. 1652, apr. Aug 1666 to Nicasius Russell till 1673, but not freed.

MINUEL, Daniel   **London**
Error for David, *qv*.

MINUEL, David   **London**
An engraver (believed French) admitted to CC as Free Brother Apr 1683.
Took as aprs.: **John Tharles** (already working for him Sep 1686 and
promised to free him thro' CC in due time, ie Oct 1692); Jun 1687 **John
Guepin** thro' L. Sindry; Oct 1691 **James Shovell** thro' D. Stevens. In
Sep 1694 he was guilty of having two aprs., one legally bound, the other
an alien and bound by a Justice of the Peace. He was fined for this but
refused to pay. Still working in 1705.

MITCHELL – see also Michell and Mitzel.

MITCHELL, Joseph (prob. error for Stephen, *qv*).

MITCHELL, Myles   **London**
Brother in CC Jul 1640.

MITCHELL, Stephen   **London**
B.c. 1660, apr. Jul 1674 thro' R. Lyons to Nathan Delaunder till 1681,
but not freed.

MITCHINAL(L)E, William (and Mitchenell)   **London**
B.c. 1680, apr. Jun 1693 to Henry Merryman till 1701. Freed Sep 1702.
Took as aprs.: Jul 1703 **Joseph Wootton;** Aug 1716 **James Parkhurst.**

MITZELL, John   **London**
Watches recorded c. 1700, but information unreliable.

MOBERT – see Maubert and also Mebert.

MOBERT, Nicholas   **London**
Diamond-cutter. Took as apr. Apr 1676 **James Chavin** thro' Dorcas,
widow of Solomon Bouquet, till 1683, but not freed.

MOLE, John (also Moule)   **London**
B.c. 1665, apr. Nov 1679 to Richard Jarrett till 1686, but not freed.

MOLYNEUX, John   **Liverpool**
Watchmaker whose daughter was born there 1699.

MOLYNEUX, Thomas (see Mullinex)   **London**

MONCRIEF, John   **London**
B.c. 1674, apr. Sep 1688 to John Bellard thro' A. Wynch till 1695, but
not freed. Work known – clock-watch signed 'John Moncrief – London'.

MONDAY – see also Munday.

MONDAY, Benjamin (alias Harvey – see under Harvey)   **London**

MONDAY, Francis (error for Munden, *qv*)   **London**

MONDAY, Joseph (also Munday)   **London**
Son of Richard Monday of Chard, Somerset. Apr. Oct 1647 to Richard
Morgan thro' N. Tomlins, then passed over to Isaac Plovier. Freed Nov
1654. Sided with rebels against CC administration in 1656. Took as
aprs.: Sep 1655 **Edward Wilkinson;** Jun 1659 **William Marston,** later
passed to E. Whitfield and freed 1669; Jan 1661/62 **Benjamin Harvy**
(alias Munday). Will dated Aug 1663, proved Sep. Mentions wife Anne
and two children under 21 (Joseph and Anne) and 'such other child or
children as my wife now goeth withall'. Property at Chard. His wife to

keep 'the Rings, Jewells, Necklace and watch she useth to weare'. One witness was William Marston.

MONPAS/MONPAZ, Abel (maybe Maupas?)   **London**
In 1622 worked as an alien in Gunpowder Alley, Shoe Lane, at a smith's – same house as Lewis Votier, *qv*. Also recorded at Blois where marr. 1623 and where Votier also worked till death in 1638.

MONTFORT/MONTFORD – see Mountfort.

MOODY, David (also Mudie, Moude, etc.)   **London**
Apr. to William Partridge. Freed Oct 1649. Took as aprs.: 1651 **Walter Rhetorick;** bound aprs. for several other masters including two for E. East, two for E. Jones, and one each for E. Holliday, J. East, P. Bellone, W. Almond, J. Legrand (most of these have East connections). In 1656 he supported CC administration against rebels. In 1662 he worked in Fleet Street. Prob. worked for Edward East.

MOONE, Robert   **London**
B.c. 1650, apr. Mar 1663 to Samuel Davis till 1671, but not freed.

MOORE, Daniel   **London**
B.c. 1675, apr. Sep 1689 to Francis Stamper till 1696. Freed Feb 1697/98. Prob. a Quaker. Paid no quarterage after c. 1699.

MOORE, Joseph   **London**
B.c. 1669, apr. May 1683 to John Barrow till 1690. Freed Sep 1690. Took as apr. Apr 1692 **Thomas King** – free Jan 1699/1700. Paid quarterage till c. 1693. Dead by 1697/98.

MOORE, Roger   **Ipswich (Suffolk)**
Married 1687 Elizabeth Page. Issue: 1688 Roger; 1690 Thomas, *qv;* 1694 Elizabeth; 1697 Sarah; 1699 William; 1701 John. Died 1727. Repaired clocks of various local churches. Work known – three longcase and three lantern clocks, signed 'Roger Moore de Ipswich fecit'.

MOORE, William   **London**
B.c. 1679, apr. Jul 1693 thro' C. Gretton to Benjamin Johnson till 1700. Freed Apr 1701. Took as aprs.: Aug 1715 **George Riley;** Jan 1716/17 **Samuel Whichcote;** Mar 1719/20 **Thomas Butterfield.** Work known – longcase clocks.

MORAL(L)Y, William (sometimes Morelley)   **London**
B.c. 1666, apr. Feb 1680/81 thro' H. Child to Philip Corderoy till 1687.
Freed Dec 1688, having been transferred to Thomas Tompion. Prob.
always worked for Tompion. Took two aprs. for Tompion, and for
himself. Aug 1696 **Richard Driver**; Jan 1703/04 **Thomas Dodderidge.**
Working till at least 1704. *Cf.* W. M. Morley.

MORECOMBE, John   **Barnstaple (Devon)**
Made town clock at Hartland. Working 1622/58.

MOREHEAD, Robert   **Plymouth**
Married 1691.

MOREL(L), James (Jacques?)   **London**
B.c. 1662, apr Jun 1676 to Michael Rose till 1683, but not freed. Work
known – watch signed 'Jacques Morel'.

MOREY, S.   **London**
Lantern clock recorded c. 1700, but this name is not known through
records.

MORGAN, Henry   **London**
A keymaker, Free Brother in CC Jan 1677/78. Took as apr. Sep 1682
John Vipont thro' D. Stevens. Paid no quarterage after c. 1682 and prob.
dead or gone by 1697-98.

MORGAN, Humphrey   **Abergavenny (Wales)**
Late 17th century clock recorded.

MORGAN, John   **London**
B.c. 1678, apr Feb 1692-93 to John Wise junior till 1699. Freed Nov
1704. Took as aprs.: Jul 1707 **Anthony Donn** – free Dec 1719; May 1715
Lewis Williams. Reputedly worked in Chancery Lane. Work known –
longcase clocks, one signed 'Jon. Morgon – London'.

MORGAN, Jude   **London**
Son of Richard Morgan, *qv*, apr. to John Hopkins. Free Brother in CC
Jul 1654.

MORGAN, Richard   **London**
Springmaker. Free in Blacksmiths' Co. 1621. One of first CC Assistants

from 1632. Repeatedly warned for not binding aprs. thro' CC. Took as aprs. (in CC): Oct 1647 **Joseph Monday** thro' N. Tomlins, later passed over to Isaac Plovier; Aug 1648 **Giles Hyett** thro' N. Tomlins, later passed over to Robert Rothwood; Oct 1650 **Thomas Bagley** thro' N. Tomlins – free Nov 1658; Mar 1646 **Thomas Long** thro' T. Alcock – free Jan 1654-55; in Oct 1655 was ordered to teach his apr. (**Mr. Mell**) one month at springs and two at watchwork. Jan 1655-56 ordered to keep his servant, **Thomas Crawley,** one month at springs and one at clock and watchmaking, and warned to observe this again in March. Also had as apr. **Henry Hester,** later passed to Thomas Morgan. A 'Blacksmith' of this name stood surety for John Bayes in 1650. Work known – not recognisable in springs, but also made watches.

MORGAN, Robert   **London**
B.c. 1626 (could be son of Richard?), apr. Jan 1638/39 to Sampson Shelton thro' O. Durant till 1647. Freed May 1647. (CC lists show him as admitted in 1637 in error.)

MORGAN, Roger   **London**
B.c. 1644, apr. Feb 1658/59 to William Morgan till 1665, but not freed.

MORGAN, Thomas   **London**
Free in CC (as Brother?) Apr 1659. Took as aprs.: Jan 1662/63 **Edward Lloyd; Henry Hester** (from Richard Morgan) – freed Apr 1671; Jul 1675 **Stephen Cooper;** Sep 1679 **William Cue** – free Jan 1691/92; Jun 1689 his son, **William Morgan;** Also bound aprs. for other masters – 3 for James Clowes, 1 each for William Bridge, Richard Wise. In 1692 was called upon to hold Stewardship but he pleaded extreme poverty being 'not worth a quarter of £100' and was excused with a £2 fine. Paid quarterage till c. 1694, still alive 1697, but prob. dead by 1698 or shortly after.

MORGAN, William   **London**
B.c. 1637, apr. May 1650 to Simon Bartram thro' L. Wythe till 1658. Free Oct 1658. Repeatedly failed to appear when summoned to be Steward from 1678 to 1682, but finally appeared and claimed he could not hold office of Steward as he was 'the King's servant by patent in fee', but promised the Master a piece of venison instead! Took as apr. Feb 1658/59 **Roger Morgan.** Not known whether he made clocks or followed some quite different trade.

MORGAN, William   Londoı
B.c. 1675, son of Thomas Morgan, apr. to his father Jun 1689 till 1696
but not freed. Prob. dead or gone by 1697/98. See also next entry.

MORGAN, William   London (Southwark
Recorded at Southwark 1696. Might be the man above.

MOR(R)ICE, Thomas   Londoı
B.c. 1640, apr. Feb 1653/54 to John Matchett, transferred to Thoma
Eyston till 1661, but not freed.

MORLEY, William (but see also Morally)   Londoı
B.c. 1678, apr. Sep 1691 to John Willoughby till 1699, but not freed
(Unless he was the one freed Jan 1703/04.)

MORRELL, Vincent   Londoı
Longcase recorded c. 1700. No sign of him in records, but *cf* Vincen
Manill?

MORRIS, Edward   Londoı
B.c. 1651, apr. Jul 1664 thro' R. Nau to Peter Bellon till 1672. Freed Jaı
1672/73. Was a boxmaker (ie watch casemaker). Work known – none
Lantern clock recorded but this is prob. an error for Edward Norris, *qv*.

MORRIS, Samuel   Londoı
Prob. a measure-seller. In 1668 had faulty measures confiscated from hi
ironmonger's shop 'At the sign of the dripping pan nr. Charing Cross', aı
unforgettable address.

MORT, Richard   Londoı
B.c. 1679, apr. Jul 1693 to John Johnson till 1700, but not freed.

MOSELEY, William   Londoı
B.c. 1659/60, apr. Jul 1673 thro' Weavers' Co. to James Graves till 1681
but freed in CC as a Brother Dec 1680. In May 1684 as a bachelor, watch
maker, aged 25, of Newgate Street, London, he was to marry Ann
Cowse of the same, spinster, aged 17, at All Hallows in the Wall, but th
licence was cancelled. He was not heard of again and was marked off a
dead by 1697/98 and may well have died some years before.

MOSS, Tristram   **Londonderry (N. Ireland)**
'Maker of horologes' 1622.

MOTE, Garett (see also Moth/Mott?)   **London**
In Jan 1655/56 was a 'stranger' and was to serve Isaac Plovier as journey-man (not apr.) 'while in England'.

MOTH, Thomas (sometimes Mott)   **London**
Apr. Mar 1648/49 to William Bunting, then passed over to Jeremy Gregory. Freed Sep 1656. In 1656 supported the rebels against the CC administration. Never heard of thereafter.

MOTLEY, Richard   **London**
A clockmaker, became Free Brother in CC Jan 1682/83. Paid no quarterage after about 1683. Dead by 1697/98, prob. nearer to 1683. Work known – bracket clock signed 'Richard Motley, Wapping' believed early 18th century. Longcase clock signed 'Richard Motley at the Hand and Buckle nr. King Edward Stairs, Wapping'.

MOTT(E), Henry (*cf* Moth)   **London**
B.c. 1641, apr. Jan 1655/56 to John Palfrey, till 1662, but not freed. Nevertheless he was known to CC, listed as an 'outlier' in 1662, paid search fee 1673. In Nov 1675 he was noted as a clockmaker who was not conforming to the rules and was to be prosecuted. Work known – watch signed 'Henricus Mott in Drury Lane'.

MOTTEUX, Samuel   **London**
B.c. 1672, apr. Jul 1686 to Philip Corderoy till 1693. Freed Aug 1697. Took as apr. Apr 1698 **Robert Bryan**. Paid quarterage till mid-1698, then listed as 'dead'.

MOUCHIE, Jean de   **London (La Rochelle?)**
Listed as alien clockmaker in 1622 in London. One John de Mouchy listed at La Rochelle 1662 prob. same man.

MOULE, John – see Mole, John.

MOUND, Theophilus   **London**
B.c. 1679, apr. Feb 1693/94 to James Boyce till 1700, but not freed.

MOUNT, William   **London**
B.c. 1668, apr. Jul 1682 to Wither Cheney till 1689. Freed Sep 1692.
Alive 1697 but listed as dead by 1698.

MOUNTAGE, John   **London**
B.c. 1632, apr. Dec 1646 to Ahasuerus Fromanteel till 1653, but not
freed.

MOUNTFORD, Zachariah (also Mountfort)   **London/St. Albans/**
                                                          Oxford
B.c. 1662, apr. Jan 1676/77 to Francis Ireland till 1683, later transferred
to William Speakman and freed Apr 1684. Took as aprs.: Jul 1686 **John
Ashbrook; George Wilson** (from T. Grimes) – freed Sep 1692; Feb
1695/96 **Thomas Millett;** Mar 1704/05 **Edward Aldridge** (son of
Edward Aldridge, late of Sevenoaks, Kent, oatmeal maker, deceased).
Paid CC quarterage till 1704 (maybe later). Presumably moved to St.
Albans. Work known – one or two longcase clocks signed 'Zachariah
Mountford in St. Albans fecit'. Also a 30-hour longcase c. 1730 signed
'Zec Montfort, Glostr. Green, Oxon'.

MOUSELEY, Arthur   **London**
B.c. 1657, apr. Aug 1671 to Jeremiah Johnson till 1678, but not freed.

MOWTLOW, Conan (sometimes Montlow, Conon)   **London**
B.c. 1677, apr. May 1691 to Richard Harrald till 1698. Freed Jan
1700/01. However in Aug 1700 his entrance fee was refunded as he had
been obliged to take up his freedom in the Blacksmiths' Co. before he
could become free of the City. He promised to bind his aprs. thro' the CC
however. Paid quarterage till 1701, but not later.

MOWTLOW, Henry (sometimes Montlow in error)   **London**
B.c. 1664, apr. Aug 1678 to Richard Browne till 1685. Freed Nov 1685.
Took as aprs.: Jun 1694 **Abraham Acton** – freed Jul 1710; Dec 1700
Samuel Owen (son of Samuel Owen of Buckingham, co. Bucks,
husbandman); Sep 1705 **George Lee** (son of George Lee of St. Leonard
Shoreditch, Middlesex, labourer. In Mar 1717/18 a man of this name
took as apr. **Thomas Golder,** but as another Henry Mowtlow was apr. in
CC in 1707, it is not known which Henry this was. References after 1717
may refer to the second man of this name. I cannot positively pin down
the first man after 1705. Work known – longcase clocks apparently

signed 'Henry Montlow, London' but his handwritten signature was clearly 'Mowtlow'.

MOY, Matthew   London
B.c. 1647, apr. Jul 1661 to Benjamin Hill till 1668, but not freed.

MOYSER, Thomas   London
B.c. 1640, apr. May 1653 to William Godbed till 1661, but not freed.

MUDDLE, Edward   Chatham (Kent)
Longcase clock seen, prob. c. 1700 – c. 1710. Baillie records him as pre-1760.

MUDDLE, Thomas   Rotherfield
Lantern clock recorded c. 1700 – c. 1710.

MULFORD, William   London
B.c. 1669, apr. Jul 1682 to John Norcott till 1690, but not freed.

MULLINEX, Thomas (and other spellings)   London
B.c. 1680, apr. May 1693 to Edward Boone till 1700, but not freed.

MUNDAY, Benjamin (see Harvey, alias Munday)

MUNDAY, Thomas   London
B.c. 1671, apr. Jun 1685 to John Benson till 1692. Freed Nov 1692. Took as apr. May 1701 **George Somersall** (son of Richard Somersall of St. Martins in the Fields, Middlesex, gentleman) – freed Jul 1708. Not heard of after mid-1701 and believed died soon after. (Baillie lists a second of this name as apr. in 1688, but this must be a slip for 1685).

MUNDEN, Francis senior   London
Warned in Jun 1652 for practising the craft when not having served an apprenticeship. Became Free Brother in CC Jul 1653. Maybe worked for Nicholas Coxeter as both his aprs. were bound thro' him: Aug 1653 **John Lowe**; Oct 1655 **John Noon**. Prob. dead or gone by 1662. Later items refer to Francis junior, who must surely be his son.

MUNDEN, Francis junior   London
B.c. 1648 (prob. son of Francis senior), apr. Jun 1662 to John Savill thro' T. Claxton till 1669. Freed Jan 1670/71. Took as aprs.: May 1680

Jonathan Rant – free Sep 1687; Sep 1685 **Richard Grainger,** later passed over to Joathan Rant and freed Sep 1695. Prob. dead by 1695.

MUNDEN, Richard   **London**
Baillie records him as 1695, but this is a slip for Francis junior.

MURCH, John   **Exeter (Devon)**
Son of William Murch, lantern-maker. Free there as a watchmaker 1698.

MURE, Peter (see Mare and de le Mare, etc.)   **England**
French 1544.

MURRAY, Widow   **London**
Received charity from CC 1695/96 under Edward East's charity. Presumably widow of a clockworker, but whose?

MUSSARD, Daniel   **London**
Watchmaker from Geneva. Free Brother in CC Dec 1686. Alive 1697 but recorded as dead in 1698. Work known – watch and longcase clock.

MYSON, Jeremiah (also Mison)   **London**
Free in CC Sep 1698, the apr. of Thomas Darlow. Took as aprs.: Jun 1701 **Jeremiah Dowset** (son of Thomas Dowset of parish of Braffin, co. Herts., yeoman) – free Jul 1708; Sep 1704 **Thomas Leonard** (son of Anthony Leonard of St. Sepulchre, London, mason). Paid quarterage till 1704 and not heard of thereafter.

MYLES, George (maybe Milne?)   **Edinburgh**
Son of John Myles. Apr. Jan 1676/77 to Humphrey Milne.

N

NAPTON, William   **London**
B.c. 1674, apr. Sep 1688 to Edward Enys senior till 1695. Freed Mar
1695-96. Paid no quarterage after c. 1696. Prob. dead or gone by
1697/98.

NASH, John   **London**
Mat. inst. maker and a Freeman of the Grocers' Co. Free Brother in CC
Feb 1666-67. Took as aprs.: Mar 1667-68 **Simon Chapman** thro'
N. Coxeter; Jan 1674-75 **Nathaniel Upton** thro' S. Davis; Jan 1689-90
John Wood – free Apr 1701. In 1671-72 CC confiscated faulty rulers
supposedly made by him for Mr. Mercer and Mr. Faulkingham. Paid
quarterage till at least 1704.

NASH, William   **London**
Early 17th century watch recorded signed 'William Nash, London'.

NASH, William   **London**
B.c. 1650, apr. Jan 1663-64 to Thomas Birch till 1671, but not freed.

NAU – (A name much mis-spelt also appearing as Noe/Nod,
Naw/Nowe, Noway/Nowen, etc. See also under Noway, Nouwen)

NAU, George   **London**
A jeweller and watch casemaker, a freeman of another Co. but not known
which one. Free Brother in CC Jul 1675. Took as aprs.: Dec 1678 **John
Blundell; Richard Blundell** – free Jul 1682; **Cuthbert Weaver** – free Jul
1682 (these latter two were prob. his journyemen as they became

Brothers not Freeman); Dec 1683 **John Anstey**; Aug 1684 **John Cooke;**
May 1688 **Jacob Taylor;** Dec 1689 **John Gregson;** Dec 1695 **John
Maylard.** In 1695 he was warned for refusing to pay quarterage and to
allow CC search, but finally paid quarterage till mid-1698 when he died.
His widow, Margaret, continued till 1702 at least 'in ye Strand over
against Bedford House'. She took as apr. Jun 1702 **Anthony London**
(son of John London of parish of St. Clement Danes, Middlesex,
carpenter).

NAU, Richard (and other spellings)   **London**
Apr. Jan 1653/54 thro' S. Bouquet to Peter Bellone. Free Apr 1661.
Prob. a boxmaker. Took as aprs.: **Edward Wilson,** passed to Robert
Smith; **Edward Morris** passed to P. Bellone; **Robert Halstead,** passed to
Isaac Daniell; **Benjamin Graves** for himself in Apr 1668, after which not
heard of again. Also recorded as Nod, Noe, etc. Worked in Chancery
Lane in 1662.

NAWE, Francis   **London**
Many variants of his name include Francois Nawe, Francis Nauwe,
Francis Nouwen, Francis Noway, Francoy Nowe. Believed b. in
Brabant, a relative of Michael Nouwen. Came to London c. 1580. Died
in 1593 of the plague with some of his children. Work known – watches,
signed 'Francois Nawe, at London', three train lantern clock dated 1588
signed 'Francoy Nowe à London'.

NAYLOR, William   **Liverpool (Lancashire)**
Watchmaker, married there 1697.

NEDAM (see Needham)

NEEDHAM, Christopher (also Nedam)   **Leicester**
Repaired town clock 1568/69.

NEEDHAM, John   **London**
B.c. 1677, apr. Nov 1691 to Richard Parsons till 1698, but not freed.

NEELD, George   **Coventry or Kenilworth (Warwickshire)**
Prob. blacksmith, working 1687/1700. Repaired church clock of St.
Nicholas, Kenilworth.

NEIGHBOUR, William London
B.c. 1663, apr. Dec 1677 to Ahasuerus Fromanteel junior, then passed over to Benjamin Graves till 1684. Freed Sep 1685. Took as apr. Apr 1693 **Benjamin Jefferies** (for John Willoughby) – freed Jul 1702. Paid quarterage till at least 1704.

NEILE, John London
B.c. 1644, apr. Dec 1657 to Joseph Quash till 1665, but not freed.

NEILL, John Glasgow
Made new clock for Tollbooth 1627/28. Dead by 1657.

NELSON, James London
B.c. 1624, apr. Apr 1638 to Oswald Durant till 1645, but not freed. Prob. dead by 1662/63. Work known – an astronomical watch.

NELSON, John Durham
Listed as 1683/1742, but I have no facts on him.

NELSON, Robert London
B.c. 1670, apr. Sep 1684 to Joseph Tanner till 1691. Freed Apr 1698. Never paid any quarterage, which suggests he left soon after. One of this name worked in Amsterdam in the early 18th century.

NEMES, Robert (sometimes Neames) London
B.c. 1655, apr. in CC Oct 1669 to Bartholomew Powell till 1676. Freed Mar 1677/78. Was by trade a founder and also a member of the Founders' Co. Took as aprs. in CC: Apr 1678 **John Price,** passed over Jan 1678/79 to William Kennon; Oct 1679 **Aubrey Davis;** Jul 1682 **Thomas Wood** – free Apr 1691; Nov 1684 **Thomas Boad** – free Apr 1692; Oct 1687 **Moses Browne;** Mar 1690/91 **Christopher Casinghurst;** Dec 1691 **Samuel Ladd** – free Jun 1710; Sep 1695 **William Lyne** – free Sep 1703; Sep 1696 **Joseph Stanton** (on condition that RN, being a founder, does not turn him over to any clockmaker) – freed Sep 1703; Apr 1702 his son, **Robert Nemes** – free Oct 1717; Dec 1703 **William Millett** – free Apr 1715; Jun 1710 his son, **John Nemes;** Nov 1713 **John Briggs;** Dec 1716 **William Gardner;** Nov 1717 another one, name illegible. This entry makes clear that founders were regarded as a separate group within the CC and were not supposed to make clocks.

NETHERWOOD, Job London
B.c. 1672, apr. Dec 1686 to Clement Forster till 1693, but not freed.

NETTER, Robert London
B.c. 1668, apr. Nov 1681 to John Winn till 1689, but not freed.

NEVE, Henry (Neue?) London
Longcase and bracket clock recorded signed 'Henry Neve in ye Strand'
c. 1700 – c. 1705. Apparently not known to CC.

NEVILL, George London
B.c. 1640, apr. Oct 1653 to William Comford thro' R. Beck till 1661, but
not freed.

NEWALL, John Wigan (Lancashire)
Watchmaker. Freedom application rejected in 1666.

NEWELL, John London
B.c. 1667, apr. Apr 1681 to Robert Doore till 1688, but not freed.

NEWBON, William Chester
B.c. 1651. In 1706, aged about 45, sentenced to death for stealing
watches from employer, John Wrench, *qv*, but later pardoned.

NEWSAM, Bartholomew London
Reputedly a Yorkshireman, on what authority I do not know. From 1568
until his death he leased a property in the Strand nr. Somerset House. In
1572 was designated Clockmaker to the Queen to succeed Nicholas
Urseau, but not until latter's death. He did work for the Queen but was
not officially appointed until 1590. He died in 1593 mentioning in his will
John Newsam of York (his brother?) to whom he left certain tools. The
rest of his tools he left to his son, Edward, on condition he became a
clockmaker – otherwise they were to be sold. Also left a sundial, a jewel
with a watch in it, a watch-clock in a purse, a sundial for a pedestal, and a
chamber clock of five marks' price. Work known – one or two clocks
survive, one signed 'Bartilmewe Newsum', one 'Nusam'.

NEWSAM, John York
Clockmaker there, reputedly by 1568. His will is dated 1586, but
believed still alive in 1593 to inherit tools from Bartholomew Newsam,
qv.

NEWTON, George London
Recorded as 1680 but I cannot trace him and he does not appear in CC records. Lantern clock signed and dated 'George Newton, 1660'.

NEWTON, Herbert London
B.c. 1650, apr. Jan 1663/64 to Thomas Wheeler till 1671, but not freed.

NEWTON, Richard London
Originally apr. thro' Drapers' Co. thro' John Thompson to serve John Saville junior, who by Jul 1690 had 'absented', and he was then passed over to serve Cuthbert Lee, they having promised that he will take up his CC freedom in due time. Freed Mar 1695/96 (and also free of the Drapers' Co.). In Sep 1699 he took as apr. thro' CC **Thomas Achurch.** Paid quarterage till about 1699 when he died.

NEWTON, Thomas London
In Oct 1664 he was in arrears with CC quarterage – but in fact had never been officially admitted!

NEWTON, William London
B.c. 1659, apr. Jul 1673 to Richard Ames till 1680, but not freed.

NEWTON, William London
B.c. 1662, apr. Aug 1676 to Edward Stanton till 1683. Freed Jan 1685/86. Took as aprs.: Jan 1685/86 **Richard Farmborough;** Sep 1687 **Benjamin Owen** thro' Isaac Webb. Believed worked at East Smithfield. Paid no quarterage after about 1688.

NICASIUS, John London
Member of CC from 1632, Assistant from 1646, Warden from 1648, Master 1653 and 1655. Attended till c. 1679, not later. His shop was in Fleet Street by at least 1648. (There was prob. a second man of this name, maybe his son, for one such was apr. in Blacksmiths' Co. to John Willow and freed there Nov 1647.) Took as aprs.: 1641 **George Johnson** thro' O. Durant – free 1649; Dec 1646 **Paul Lowell** junior thro' P. Lowell senior – free Jan 1653; Mar 1650 **Cornelius Johnson** thro' N. Tomlins; Apr 1649 **John Clarkson** thro' T. Alcock – free Jul 1657; May 1651 **Thomas Gamble** thro' N. Tomlins – free Apr 1657; c. 1654-57 **Joseph Edwards;** Oct 1655 **John Russell** (as journeyman for one year only, being from Holland); Nov 1661 **Robert Andrews;** Oct 1662 **Edward**

409

Martin thro' S. Horne; **Robert Seigniour** – freed Apr 1667. In Dec 1657 he was transferred from the Blacksmiths' Co. to CC, being a watchmaker. In Aug 1650 he was about to 'depart the land into Holland', and was back by Oct. In Mar 1655/56 he again went to Holland but was back by Jun. In 1660 he was mentioned in the will of Robert Grinking as a 'very loving friend'. He was a man of fiery temperament and in constant trouble for it. In 1668 he abused the Master, Jeremy Gregory, but later apologised. He was fined for abuse of the Master in Apr 1673, again in Feb 1673/74, again in Mar 1679. In 1679 the CC tried to make allowances 'considering his usual temper too well known to all persons of the Court', but he had insulted Henry Jones and was suspended from the Co. at his instigation unless he apologised – which he did not, and he never attended again after that. Robert Seigniour, his late apr. and prob. a relative, later had similar differences of opinion with the CC. His connections with Holland at this time of the birth of the pendulum are very puzzling, as is his connection with the Russells – Nicasius Russell was surely named after him. Work known – a watch signed 'Nicasius, London' said to be c. 1605.

NICKLIS, Benjamin (prob. Nicholas)   **London**
B.c. 1668, apr. Feb 1682/83 to Thomas Taylor of Holborne till 1689, but not freed. (Nicklis had formerly been bound to a member of the Blacksmiths' Co.)

NICHOLAS, David   place not known
Lantern clock recorded c. 1680 signed 'David Nicholas fecit' (Britten).

NICHOL, NICHOLL and **NICHOLS, NICHOLLS** all entered together, but differentiated where possible.

NICHOLL, Isaac (signed Nicoll)   **London/Wells (? Norfolk)**
B.c. 1660, apr. in London thro' CC Mar 1674/75 to Withers Cheney till 1681. Freed Mar 1681/82. Took as aprs.: Mar 1683/84 **Thomas Grave;** May 1686 **John Farewell,** later passed over to C. Gretton; Nov 1686 **John Hicks;** May 1690 **Charles Gilbert** – free Jul 1700; Jul 1710 **Andrew Vaslet** – free Aug 1717. In Jul 1709 he appeared to pay arrears of quarterage 'having been several years out of town', the meaning of this not being very clear. A man of this name (surely the same man) worked at Wells (prob. the one in Norfolk) from the early 18th century till c. 1740 – Baillie says from 1697, which I cannot confirm. Work known – a verge

watch signed at London; several longcase clocks signed at Wells, some of exceptional quality. My latest date for him in London is 1710.

NICHOLLS, Roger (sometimes Nicholas)   **London**
Apr. Jan 1659/60 to Robert Robinson, then passed over to John Savill and freed Jan 1667/68. Took as aprs.: May 1675 **Francis Barnard** (and later passed him over illegally to Isaac Puzy, for which he was fined in Jul 1675; Sep 1687 **George Street;** May 1699 **Nicholas Howett** (son of Richard Howett of St. Buttolphs, Bishopsgate, London); **James Debaufre** (son of Peter Debaufre, clockmaker, of St. Anne's, Westminster) – free Jun 1713. From Jul 1707 he received CC charity till 1708, when prob. died. He also bound an apr. in 1674 for E. Fowell.

NIGHTINGALE, John   **London**
B.c. 1641, apr. Mar 1655/56 to Thomas Stayner thro' Thomas Wolverston till 1662, but not freed.

NIGHTINGALE, Matthew   **London**
B.c. 1673, apr. Apr 1686 to Samuel Gascoigne till 1694, but not freed.

NILOE, Hans   **London**
A Dutchman who made a clock with 'music and motions' for the King in 1609 for £300.

NIXON, Thomas   place not known
Watch recorded c. 1605. I cannot confirm this.

NOAKES, James   **London**
A seller of canes in Popes Head Alley. Had faulty rulers confiscated by CC in 1671/72.

NOBLE, John   **London**
Longcase clock recorded supposedly c. 1690, but I have no confirmation of such a person and not known in CC records.

NOBLE, Phineas   **London**
B.c. 1679, apr. Sep 1693 to Edward Whitfield till 1700, but not freed.

NOD, Richard   **London**
Listed in 1662 but error for Nau, *qv.*

NOE, Richard London
Chancery Lane in 1662 – error for Nau, *qv*. A boxmaker.

NOEL, Aymé London/France(?)
Watchmaker recorded c.1620 – c.1640. Prob. France and not London.

NOLSON, John (sometimes Nelson) London
B.c. 1675, apr. Sep 1689 thro' D. Stevens to John Pitcher (when latter has taken his City Freedom), but later passed over to D. Quare till 1696. Freed Dec 1697. Paid no quarterage after c. 1698.

NOON(E), JOHN London
B.c. 1642, apr. Oct 1655 to Francis Munden thro' N. Coxeter till 1663, but not freed.

NOONE, Thomas Leicester
Clockmaker there Mar 1663/64 when his son, Thomas junior (trade unknown) was freed there.

NORCELL, John London
Recorded by Baillie. Prob. error for Norcott, *qv*.

NORCOTT, John (sometimes Northcott) London
Prob. apr. thro' some other Co., having been bound to a clockmaker and passed over to Samuel Drossatt and admitted a CC Freeman Apr 1681. However had already been paying CC quarterage since 1672. He was a member of the Leathersellers' Co. by 1664/65 when his apr. **John Watts,** was freed in CC, having been passed over to Thomas Claxton, then to Thomas Hollis. (This 1664 entry might refer to a second John Norcott, senior?). Took as aprs. in CC: Jul 1682 **William Mumford;** Mar 1690/91 **Samuel Cragg;** Feb 1691/92 **Thomas Cary** – free Apr 1706. Also bound an apr. for S. Mather. Alive still in 1697 but marked as dead by 1698. Work known – watches and longcase clocks, signed 'Johannes Norcott Londini' and 'Johanne Norcott'.

NORRIS, Charles London
B.c. 1673, son of Edward Norris, clockmaker. Apr. Apr 1683 to his father till 1690 but freed 'by patrimony' after only four years' service in Jul 1687. (NB in that year his father was Master of the CC). Dead by 1697/98.

NORRIS, Edward senior   **London**
B.c. 1637, apr. Apr 1650 thro' S. Davis to William Selwood till 1658.
However Selwood died in 1653 leaving him a bequest of £6. Freed Jan
1658/59. Took as aprs.: Apr 1661 **John Sutton;** May 1661 **Nathaniel
Worlidge;** Nov 1661 **Joseph Norris** (relationship unknown) – freed Sep
1670; Dec 1664 **Samuel Ayres;** Jan 1669-70 **Henry Aske** – free Jan
1676/77; May 1675 **Richard Farmer,** later transferred to Richard
Browne; **Richard Browne** – free Jan 1675/76; **John Martin** (from Joseph
Norris) – free Sep 1679; Oct 1682 **Charles Vans;** Apr 1683 his son,
Charles Norris – free Jul 1687; Jun 1684 **Joseph Hall;** Jul 1694 his son,
Edward Norris – free Nov 1702; Mar 1698/99 **John Everill** (son of John
Everill, deceased, late grocer of Stilton, co. Hunts.). Also bound several
other aprs. for other masters in manner of the Beadle, which masters
were: P. Corderoy, G. Merttins, D. Roofe, J. Benson, T. Fletcher,
W. Warner, W. Grimes. In Sep 1680 he took with his wife, Sarah,
Elizabeth Meeberry as apr., prob. as a servant. Became CC Assistant
from 1674, Warden from 1683, Master 1687. Ceased to attend in 1707
when prob. died. Baillie records him working at Dove Court, which I
cannot confirm. In Sep 1675 his house was The White House in
Bartholomew Lane. Work known – lantern clocks, signed 'Edward
Norris at the Cross Keys in Bethlem fecit'.

NORRIS, Edward junior   **London**
B.c. 1680, son of Edward senior. Apr. to father Jul 1694 till 1701. Freed
Nov 1702. Not really applicable to this volume but included to
distinguish from his father.

NORRIS, Joseph   **London/Amsterdam/London**
B.c. 1649, apr. Nov 1661 to Edward Norris (who may well have been a
relative but could not have been his father) till 1670. Freed Sep 1670.
Took as apr. Aug 1672 **John Martin,** later transferred to Edward Norris
and freed Sep 1670. Went to Amsterdam c. 1675-77, perhaps with the
Fromanteels, and worked there for some years. Was back in England by
Mar 1695/96 when CC gave consent that 'Mr. Joseph Norris, who lives in
the country' may bind an apr. when he pays off his arrears of quarterage.
In Mar 1695/96 he bound **Francis Maine.** Paid quarterage till c. 1696
but prob. dead by 1697/98 (or gone away again). Work known – Haagse
clock signed 'Joseph Norris, Amsterdam'. Lantern clock signed
similarly. Almost certainly worked under the Fromateel flag at one time,
as his master, Edward Norris, finished his time under Thomas Loomes
and prob. also was part of the Fromanteel workforce initially.

NORRIS, William   **London**
Recorded by Baillie as late 17th century, but I think this must be a slip as I cannot trace him.

NORTH, John   **London**
Apr. Aug 1641 thro' O. Durant to Ralph Ash. Freed May 1650. Took as aprs.: May 1655 **Edward Whitfield** – free Oct 1663; 1651(?) **Edward Eyston** – freed Jan 1659/60; Aug 1656 **Joshua Short,** later passed over to R. Ash, then to Lancelot Meredith; Oct 1668 **John Bartholomew,** later passed over to B. Wolverstone then to Robert Smith; **Nicholas Beck** (taken from T. Webb) – freed Jul 1669; Jul 1674 **John Waters,** later passed over to N. Beck – freed Jan 1682/83; Nov 1681 **Anthony Hammond;** Jul 1696 **Caspar Braim** or **Braem** – free Jul 1716. Also bound several aprs. for other masters, which masters incl. P. Collins, R. Ash, J. Waters. In 1673/74 he was excused Assistantship on account of illness at the request of Robert Seigniour, and he seems to have been forgotten about for was never made Warden later. Last known alive 1697, but marked as dead by 1698.

NORTH, Lancelot   **York/London**
B.c. 1601, son of William North, innkeeper. Free at York 1623. Baillie records him at London 1639-64, which dates I cannot confirm, but he was certainly mentioned in CC minutes in 1654, and I have no other record of him in London. A grant by CC in Jan 1651/52 to 'Mr. North being in Ludgate' prob. refers to him.

NORTH, William   **Dublin**
Clockmaker there in 1656. Maybe the same man as at London before and after?

NORTH, William   **London**
Free Brother in CC Jan 1638-39. Took as aprs.: Jul 1647 **Robert Jadwin** thro' T. Alcock; Aug 1649 **Richard Matson** thro' N. Payne. In 1659 he appeared at CC and was cleared of all quarterage arrears, but was ordered to rebind his apr. to some free clockmaker. Took as apr. Jan 1663-64 **William Smith.** Refused to serve as Steward in 1664. Not heard of thereafter. Work known – a watch signed 'William North Londini'. Baillie gives his address as St. Paul's Churchyard, which I cannot confirm.

NORTHCOTT, John (but see also Norcott)   **London**
Never admitted to CC but known to them. Prob. dead by 1663 and not

on 1662 list. Not the same man as John Norcott, but the earliest entry under Norcott may relate to Northcott.

NORTON, Edward   **Warwick**
Clock and watchmaker there 1640 – c.1700. Made clock with 48 instead of 60 divisions in hour circle – *London Gazette* 12 Jun 1701. In 1680 repaired church clock at Berrington, Salop.

NOWAY, Andrew   **London**
Variant of Nouwen/Nauwe, etc. B. in Flanders, reputedly working in London in 1571 but I have no data on him.

NOUWEN, Michael   **London**
Name also appears as Nauwe, Noway, Neuwers. Baillie records him as working as early as 1582. In 1599 agreed to make a striking clock for Gilbert, Earl of Shrewsbury, in a brass case at a cost of £16. Appointed overseer in will of Nicholas Vallin, *qv*, proved 1608/09. Work known – drum watch with name as Nawen, watch dated 1609 with name as Nouwen, another signed 'Michael Nouwen fecit 1613'. Work very uncommon.

NOWELL, Matthew   **London**
Baillie records him as apr. in Blacksmiths' Co. 1628, but I do not know of him.

O

OAKEY, John　　　　　　　　　　　　　　　London
Listed by Baillie as apr. 1683, but see Okey.

OAKHAM, Edward (also Okum)　　　　　　London
Entered CC 1632. Last mentioned 1634.

OAKLEY, John　　　　　　　　　　London/Oxford
B.c. 1671, apr. Apr 1685 to William Dent till 1692, but not freed. Only one of this name, not two as Baillie suggests. One of this name repaired turret clocks at Oxford from 1704. Work known – lantern clock signed 'John Oakly Oxon', dated 1704.

OAKSHOTT, Thomas　　　　　　　　　　　London
Watch casemaker who died at St. Saviour's Southwark Jun 1713. See also Okeshott.

OALSKIRK, John (surname undecipherable)　　London
On CC list of 1662.

OGBORN, Samuel (or William?)　　　　　　London
Some records say William, but most say Samuel. Entered CC Feb 1698-99, by trade a clock or watchmaker. In Jul 1699 he was to have his fees refunded as he 'cannot be passed at Guildhall as of this Company'. However he paid quarterage till at least 1704. (Baillie records him till 1722, though on what evidence I do not know.)

OGDEN, Isaac   **Halifax (Yorkshire)**
Son of James Ogden senior of Soyland and brother of Samuel. B. in 1660s-1670s. Dates of working said to be c.1693 – 1700. One Isaac Ogden, clockmaker, married in 1729 at Halifax to Grace Iredale. Work known – lantern clock signed 'Isaac Ogden, Sowerby'.

OGDEN, James   **Soyland, nr. Halifax (Yorkshire)**
Reputedly died 1715. Uncertain whether he was a maker but his sons were.

OGDEN, John   **Askrigg (Yorkshire)**
Son of James of Soyland and brother of Samuel. B. about 1660. Was a Quaker. Moved to Askrigg c. 1680 where he lived at Bowbridge Hall. Issue by wife, Margaret, were: 1701 James; 1702 Margaret; 1704 John; 1706 Ann; 1707 Bernard. Later moved to Darlington where died 1741. Work known – longcase clocks, mainly 30 hour. One has date 1681 carved into case, another dated 1715.

OGDEN, Samuel   **Halifax (Yorkshire)**
Son of James Ogden of Soyland, baptised 1669. Lived at Ripponden, nr. Halifax. Issue: 1687 Maria; 1689 Samuel (later a clockmaker); 1693 Thomas (later a clockmaker); 1697 Patience; 1699 John; 1701 Isaac; 1704 Dorothy. Wife, Sara, died 1712 at Ripponden. Before 1727 he moved to Benwell, nr. Newcastle. Date of death unknown. Work known – longcase clocks signed 'Sam Ogden', 'Samuel Ogden in Ripponden fecit', later 'Samuel Ogden Benwell'.

OGDEN, Thomas   **London**
Apr. May 1651 to Thomas Knifton thro' N. Coxeter. Freed Jul 1659. Not heard of again and prob. dead or gone by 1662. He must surely have some connection with the Halifax Ogdens, but if so this is still unknown.

OGLE, Edward   **London**
In Feb 1697/98 he was granted permission to delay taking up his freedom in the CC till next court day – but never heard of again.

OKESHOTT, Robert   **London**
B.c. 1650, apr. Jun 1664 to Ralph Greatorix till 1671, but not freed. See also Oakshott.

OKEY, John **London**
B.c. 1669, apr. Dec 1683 thro' R. Lyons to Thomas Herbert, the Queen's Clockmaker, till 1690, but not freed.

OLIVER, Thomas **London**
Prob. an inst.-maker. Paid CC search fee Feb 1671/72.

ORTON, Edward **London**
B.c. 1665-66, Apr. Aug 1680 to Samuel Clyatt till 1687. Freed Sep 1687. Despite an entry which reads in Sep 1682 that he had 'gone from' Abraham (*sic*) Clyatt (error for Samuel?) as he was 'not able to do him any service by some infirmities in his limbs'. Feb 1690/91 Edward Orton clockmaker of St. Andrew Holborn, bachelor, aged 25, was to marry Mary Williamson, spinster, aged 19 (daughter of Robert Williamson of St. Bartolomew Exchange, clockmaker) at St. Bartholomew Exchange, St. Peter-le-Poor or St. Bottolphs Bishopsgate. In Oct 1692 Edward Orton of St. Sepulchre, clockmaker, widower, aged 27, was to marry Anne Hawkins of St. Clement Danes, spinster, 23, at St. Clement Danes. Took as aprs.: Sep 1691 **Henry Lindford**; Jun 1696 **James Knight**. In Jul 1708 he claimed he could not serve as Steward as he was going out of town on the Queen's business, and was still 'out of town' in 1709. Not heard of thereafter. Work known – a longcase clock signed 'Edward Orton, London'.

ORAM, Morris (also Orum) **London**
B.c. 1670, apr. Apr 1684 to Richard George till 1691, but not freed.

ORLOGGER, Walter **Norwich**
Free as 'orloger' in 1420 at Norwich. Made clock for Norwich Cathedral, date not known. Paid on an account by Guild of St. George 1458.

OSBORN, Humphrey **London**
Supposedly in Blacksmiths' Co. 1617 and maker of lantern clocks, but I have no data on him.

OSBORNE, Thomas **Bolton (Lancashire)**
Clockmaker, 'slayne' and buried there 1665.

OSBORNE, Thomas **Dublin**
Watchmaker 1656.

OSBORN, William London
B.c. 1680, apr. Sep 1693 to Samuel Vernon till 1701. Freed Sep 1700, having been transferred to server Samuel Sadleir. Took as aprs.: Sep 1702 **John Reeve** (son of late John Reeve of Watford, Herts., grocer, deceased); Aug 1704 **Henry Wood** (son of Henry Wood, mariner, of Sherborne, Dorset); Aug 1708 with his wife Mary took **Elizabeth Stewart**, prob. as maidservant or to follow his wife's trade. I have no data on him after 1708, though Baillie records him till 1721. Work known – longcase clock signed 'William Osborn, London'.

OSMOND, Henry London
B.c. 1667, apr. Jul 1681 to Samuel Gascoigne till 1688, but not freed.

OSMOND, James London
Baillie has one as apr. 1681, which is a slip for 1687. B.c. 1673, apr. Sep 1687 to James Clowes thro' D. Stevens till 1694, but not freed.

OUGHTRED, Benjamin (also Outred) London
Free Brother in CC Oct 1639.

OVERBURY, Henry London/Rotterdam
B.c. 1673, son of Thomas Overbury, *qv*. Apr. Jul 1687 thro' James Delander to his father till 1694, but not freed. Work known – none, but a watch of c. 1705 is recorded signed 'Henry Overbury Rotterdam' and one of c. 1718 signed 'Henry Overbury, Overschie'.

OVERBURY, Thomas London
A watchmaker but a freeman in the Haberdashers' Co. Freed in Haberdashers Sep 1668, having been apr. to Henry Overbury (his father?). His apr., **Thomas Warden**, transferred in CC Feb 1672/73 to Thomas Player and was made free in Haberdashers' Co. Aug 1677. Jul 1687 he took his son, **Henry Overbury**, apr. in CC thro' James Delander. In Jul 1688 was made a Free Brother in CC. (A bit late?).

OVERTON, Warren Warwick
Clockmaker and blacksmith 1632-80. Repaired St. Nicholas church clock.

OVERY, John London
Baillie says b. 1675, died 1767, watch casemaker. I have no data. Not in CC records.

OVERZEE, Gerard London
Sep 1678 a clockmaker, naturalised, as a Free Brother in CC. Took as
apr. Sep 1678 **Nicholas Pope** thro' Samuel Davis. In Jun 1690 he asks
excusal from Stewardship being 'scarce of money and having no servant'
and still working out of town. Believed worked at Isleworth. Paid no
quarterage after c. 1696. Believed dead by 1698. Work known – watches,
lantern clocks, longcase clocks.

OVERZEE, Timothy London
B.c. 1679, apr. Nov 1693 thro' D. Stevens to Thomas Whitehead, a
freeman of the Tin Plate Workers' Co. till 1700, but not freed.

OWEN, Benjamin London
B.c. 1673, apr. Sep 1687 thro' Isaac Webb to William Newton till 1694,
but not freed. (One record says he was the son of William, but this is then
crossed out.) I have no further facts on him but Baillie records him till the
1740s.

OWEN, John Denbigh
Repaired church clock 1679-1715.

OWEN, John London(?)
Sundials recorded dated 1683 and 1697.

OWEN, John Warwick
Worked on St. Nicholas church clock 1604-05.

P

PACE, Thomas   London
Free Brother in CC Sep 1634. Took as aprs.: Sep 1637 **Jeffrey Bayley**, thro' O. Durant – free Mar 1646-47; (in 1642 and 1646 CC intervened in a quarrel between master and apr. but both parties refused to disclose the cause of their quarrel); Dec 1638 **Laurence Entwisle** thro' T. Dawson. Worked 'at ye Crown in Fleet Street'. I have no record of him after 1646. Work known – lantern clocks.

PAGE, Edward   Oxford
Son of John Page, yeoman, of Goring, Berks. B.c. 1670, apr. Jul 1684 to John Quelch of Oxford, but not freed.

PAGE, Joseph   London
B.c. 1661, apr. Oct 1674 to Nicholas Coxeter, later transferred to Jeffrey Baily (prob. c. 1679 on death of Coxeter). Freed Apr 1683. Paid no quarterage after 1683.

PAGE, Luke   London
B.c. 1669, apr. Jul 1683 to Benjamin Marshall till 1690, but not freed.

PAGNES, William   London
Recorded as lantern clockmaker in Butcher's Row, East Smithfield, c. 1690 by Britten, but seems likely to be a slip for William Payne, *qv*.

PAIN(E) – see also Payne.

PAIN(E), Benjamin   **London**
B.c. 1659, apr. Jun 1672 to William Watmore thro' L. Wythe till 1680, but not freed. Maybe son of Nicholas Payne mentioned in his will proved 1676, *qv*. One of this name worked at Littlethorpe, Leicestershire c. 1720 as a clockmaker.

PAINE, Christopher   **London**
Maker of rules, compasses, etc. in 1584.

PAINE, Edward   **Warwick**
Son of Thomas, *qv*. Repaired St. Nicholas church clock 1583-91.

PAINE, Thomas   **Warwick**
Keeper of St. Nicholas church clock 1564-1618.

PALFREY, John   **London**
Apr. Sep 1646 to Richard Scrivener thro' T. Alcock. Freed Nov 1654. Tok as aprs.: Jan 1655/56 **Henry Mott**; also bound an apr. in 1656 for L. Wythe. In 1656 was in trouble for taking an apr. and turning him over to another master without consent, and in trouble again for the same thing in 1664. Worked at St. Martins in the Fields. Will written 1670, proved within a week. No relatives mentioned – prob. a bachelor.

PALMER, ----   **Wortham (Suffolk)**
Repaired Metfield church clock 1684 and 1686.

PALMER, David   **Barnstaple (Devon)**
Kept Kay Hall clock 1563.

PALMER, Henry   **London**
B.c. 1679, apr. Dec 1693 to Josiah Ridley till 1700, but not freed.

PALMER, John   **London**
B.c. 1634, apr. Jul 1647 to Henry Ireland thro' W. Bunting till 1655, but not freed.

PALMER, John   **London**
B.c. 1679, apr. Jul 1693 to Alexander Warfield till 1700, but not freed.

PALMER, Thomas   **London**
Baillie records him as in Blacksmiths' Co. 1672, but I do not know him.

PANCK, Ralph   **London**
B.c. 1663, apr. Nov 1677 to Thomas Bagley till 1684, but not freed.

PANNELL, ----   **Bath (Somerset)**
Kept church clock 1575.

PANNELL, Robert   **London**
B.c. 1640, apr. Feb 1653/54 to Paul Lowell senior, thro' R. Record till 1661, but not freed.

PANTIN, Nicholas (also Panton)   **London/Oxford/Dublin(?)**
B.c. 1638, apr. Oct 1651 to Humfrey Downing thro' L. Wythe till 1659, but not freed. In Mar 1663 attempted unsuccessfully to become a freeman of Oxford. Work known – two horizontal sundials signed 'Nicholas Pantin, Oxford'. (One Nicholas Pantain, b. in Rouen, became a freeman of Dublin Goldsmiths' Co. 1682, who might be the same man. He was the father of Samuel Pantin, goldsmith there).

PANTIN, Robert (also Panton)   **London**
B.c. 1660 (surely son of Nicholas?). Apr. Aug 1674 to William Robinson till 1681, but not freed.

PAPAVOINE, Isaac   **London**
In Jan 1687/88 became Free Brother in CC, a Frenchman and clockmaker, who was to pay special fees 'if he do not become a free Denizen by midsummer'. Said to have worked at Dukes Court. Last mentioned in CC records 1705-06 when much in arrears with subscriptions. Work known – several longcase clocks, signed 'Isaac Papavoine, London' or just 'Papavoine, London'. Also bracket clocks.

PAPWORTH, John   **London**
B.c. 1665, apr. Feb 1678/79 to Sarah, widow of Humfrey Peirce, till 1686. Free Jul 1688. Took as apr. Jan 1690/91 **Samuel Hawtyen** to serve John Wise, junior. Paid quarterage till 1699.

PARE, ----   **Exeter**
Worked on cathedral clock 1679.

PARE, Thomas (see Thomas Parre, but also Thomas Pace).

PARIS, Nicholas senior   **Warwick**
Blacksmith, gunsmith, clock and watchmaker, gate-maker, gilder.
Lived in Jury Street. Arrived in Warwick about 1669, perhaps from
Rutland or Leicestershire, where he had relatives. Married Mary X c.
1674/75. Issue: Nicholas 1681; John 1685; Thomas 1687/88. Has as apr.
Richard Rittle junior. Died 1716. Work known – longcase, lantern and
bracket clocks and maintained local church clocks.

PARIS, Nicholas junior   **Warwick**
Son of Nicholas senior, b. 1681. Succ. father in 1716. Married 1705
Elizabeth Meadows. Died 1740, succ. by his sons. Maintained and prob.
made local turret clocks.

PARIS, Samuel   **Warwick**
Blacksmith/clockmaker. Believed brother of Nicholas senior. Arrived
about 1680. Two daughters b. 1681 and 1685. Maintained local church
clocks. Died 1723.

PARIS, Thomas   **Warwick**
Son of Nicholas senior. Clockmaker. In 1740 made quarter-chiming
turret clock for Oxford university. Died 1753.

PARK(E) – watch also for Parker variations.

PARKE, John   **London**
B.c. 1646, apr. Mar 1659/60 to John Bayes till 1667, but not free. May be
son of Nicholas, *qv*.

PARKE, Nicholas   **London**
Brother in CC Oct 1640. Took as aprs.: Aug 1655 **John Lucie** thro' John
Bayes, later passed over to Charles Bonner and freed Oct 1663; Dec 1650
Charles Bonner thro' John Cooke – freed Mar 1659/60 as servant of
widow Parke, so Nicholas must have died by then. He may have been a
member of the Goldsmiths' Co. Nicholas was still alive in Jul 1659, when
he declined to serve as steward (for ill health?).

PARKER, Cuthbert   **London**
B.c. 1645, apr. Oct 1659 to William Petty till 1666, but not freed.

PARKER, Daniel   **London**
Longcase clock recorded signed 'Daniel Parker in Fleet Street, London'
c. 1690. Not known in CC archives.

PARKER, Edward   **London**
B.c. 1669, apr. Dec 1683 to Henry Kilminster till 1690, but not freed.
(Maybe in Blacksmiths' Co.?).

PARKER, John   **Dublin**
Watchmaker. A free Goldsmith 1694-1713.

PARKER, John   **London**
Apr. May 1656 to Richard Record. Freed Mar 1674/75. Took as aprs.:
Mar 1674/75 **John Pinson**; Dec 1685 **William Hayter** – free Feb
1694/95; (difficult to distinguish now from next man of same name); Sep
1695 his son, **John Parker**. Believed died 1699. (Christopher, son of the
late John Parker, was apr. in 1701 to John Andrews). In 1677 he
interceded with CC concerning a faulty watch made by Richard Hamlin,
with whom he prob. had connections.

PARKER, John   **London**
B.c. 1656, apr. May 1670 to Humfrey Clarke till 1677. Freed Apr 1678.
In Sep 1697 one John Parker took his son, **Christopher Parker** as apr.

PARKER, John   **London**
B.c. 1659, apr. Apr 1672 to Michael Cornish till 1680, but not freed.

PARKER, John   **London**
B.c. 1670, apr. Jun 1684 to Thomas Fletcher, but not freed.

PARKER, John   **London**
B.c. 1670, apr. Nov 1684 to John Shaw till 1691, but not freed.

PARKER, John   **London**
B.c. 1678, apr. Mar 1691/92 to James Delander till 1699. Freed Sep
1706. Sep 1712 one JP took as apr. **Thomas Knight.** One JP got CC
charity from 1710-16. Not possible to distinguish them all.

PARKER, Robert   **London**
Recorded by Baillie as apr. 1659. Prob. an error for John.

PARKER, Robert London
B.c. 1676, apr. Jul 1690 to James Markwick junior thro' James Markwick senior till 1697. Freed Jul 1698. Paid quarterage till 1699, not later.

PARKER, Stephen Ipswich (Suffolk)
Gunsmith. Repaired clock and chime of St. Lawrence church in 1683 and made new clock for the Old Westgate Gaol in 1684.

PARKER, Thomas Dublin
Watchmaker and Free Goldsmith there 1693 till death in 1751. Work known – a watch dated 1709, bracket clock c. 1710.

PARKER, Thomas London
Apr. Nov 1658 to William Almond thro' D. Moody. Freed Apr 1669. Took as aprs.: Jul 1669 **Andrew Savery** – free Sep 1676; May 1676 **John Marsh**; Jun 1684 **Caesar White**. Work known – lantern clocks, signed 'Thomas Parker in Ann's Lane neare Aldersgate' (or St. Anne's Lane), and 'Tho. Parker Londini fecit'.

PARKHURST, Michael London
B.c. 1669, apr. Nov 1683 to John Bellard thro' D. Stevens till 1690, but not freed.

PARKINSON, Robert London
Free in CC Apr 1637. Took as apr. Nov 1638 **George Grove** thro' T. Dawson.

PARKS (see Perkes)

PARR, John London
B.c. 1679, apr. Jul 1693 to John Herbert till 1700, but not freed.

PARRE, David London
At Cornhill in 1662. Sometimes wrongly listed as Farre, and see also Daniel Parker? See under David Parry.

PARRE, Thomas (also Pare) London
Brother in CC 1634. In 1635 gave a CC a chamber clock. Still mentioned in 1661 and 1662. Work known – longcase clocks c. 1690 signed 'Thomas Parr, London' and also some signed 'Thos. Pare Londini fecit', c. 1690.

These late 17th century clocks seem unlikely to be by the first man, but no biographical details are known of a second in CC records. The first man is not heard of after 1662.

PARRATT, Henry   **London**
B.c. 1664, apr. Jul 1678 to John Finch till 1685, but not freed.

PARRATT, John   **London**
B.c. 1677, apr. Jun 1691 to Charles Knight till 1698, but not freed.

PARRATT, Thomas   **London**
B.c. 1645, apr. Oct 1667 to Edward Whitfield, later passed over to Walter Gibbs till 1675. Freed Jul 1702.

PARTINGTON, Puleston   **Chester**
Free 1671. Steward of Goldsmiths and Clockmakers 1677. Mayor of Chester 1706-07. Working as watchmaker till 1711.

PARTINGTON, Puleston   **Chester**
Freed 1687.

PARRY, David (also Parre)   **London**
Free Brother in CC Oct 1646. Took as apr. Jul 1647 **Henry Ford** thro' N. Tomlins; Nov 1657 with James Gregory took **John Barton** and 'fraudulently kept him' (ie without CC permission). Last heard of in 1662 in Cornhill.

PARRY, Francis   **London**
B.c. 1632, apr. Jul 1646 to Thomas Land thro' T. Alcock till 1653, but not freed.

PARRY, Jonathan   **London**
Apr. c. 1657/59 to Richard Lyon thro' R. Almond, but not freed.

PARSONS, John   **London**
B.c. 1671, apr. Mar 1685/86 to Samuel Marchant till 1692. Freed Jul 1696. Took as apr. Oct 1718 his son, **George Parsons.** I have no data on him after this, but Baillie records him at Basinghall Street till 1729.

PARSONS, Richard   **London**
B.c. 1668, apr. Nov 1682 to Isaac Day till 1689. Freed Apr 1690. Took as

apr. Nov 1691 **John Needham**. Britten records him at 54 Goswell Street till 1730, but CC records suggest he died about 1696/97. Work known – longcase and bracket clocks.

PARTER, William London
Baillie has CC 1692 but I don't know him. Prob. a slip for some other name.

PARTRIDGE, William London
Brother in CC Sep 1640. Took as aprs.: **David Moody** – free Oct 1649; Apr 1651 **William Rumett** thro' John Matchett. In 1660 he petitioned the King that he 'did in 1645 attend the King as clockmaker when at Oxford and then served a year and a half in the Life Guard of Foot and later raised a Company at his own charge, himself as Captain, and hath been a great sufferer by plundering, imprisonment and explulsions. He begs to be restored as Royal Clockmaker'. Also a petition from his wife, Sarah, saying that he was 'bred under Mr. Esté' (Edward East) and spent much time improving himself in his trade in France and Flanders and only discontinued it when in arms or in prison. He was prob. a Catholic, as were those with whom he claimed connection. Not heard of after 1660, prob. dead or gone by 1662.

PASEY/PACEY, Thomas London
Baillie records him in 1646 – see Pace.

PASSHELER, William Carlton Rode (Norfolk)
In 1523 agreed to make a turret clock for Hoxne, Suffolk.

PASSION, Henry London
B.c. 1633, apr. Feb 1646/47 to Thomas Mills thro' N. Coxeter till 1654, but not freed.

PATTE, Jaques (or Patta) London
In Oct 1655 was appointed to work as journeyman to Jeremy Gregory, being from Geneva.

PATTISON, Robert (also Pattenson) London
B.c. 1648, apr. May 1661 to Thomas Wolverston, later passed over to Jeremy Gregory till 1668. Free Apr 1668. Also free of the City of London 1668, being the son of Thomas Pattinson of London, Vintner. Paid quarterage till 1672, but not heard of thereafter.

PATTISON, Robert   **London**
B.c. 1662, apr. Jun 1676 to Thomas Tompion till 1683, but not freed.
Work known – a longcase clock signed 'Robert Pattison, Greenwich'.

PAUL, Nowell   **London**
Recorded as an alien working here 1668, but this is prob. an error for
Paul Lowell, *qv*.

PAUL, Thomas   **London**
B.c. 1649, apr. Jul 1663 to John Fromanteel till 1670. Freed Jan 1670-71.
Took as apr. Apr 1672 **Benjamin Marshall,** later (Aug 1676) passed him
over to Abraham Prime – freed Jun 1680. Paid quarterage till 1675.
Earlier was in Leadenhall Street. Work known – a silver travelling clock.

PAYNE, George   **London**
B.c. 1673, apr. Mar 1687 to Jeremiah Johnson till 1694, but not freed.

PAYN, John   **Southwold (Suffolk)**
In 1495 received 6s. 8d. for Walberswick 'newe klocke', prob. for
repairing it, not making it.

PAYNE, Nicholas (also Paine)   **London**
B.c. 1628, apr. Apr 1641 to William Daniell thro' O. Durant till 1649.
Freed Apr 1648. Took many aprs. for other masters (prob. as Beadle) but
apparently only one for himself, his 'son', **John Harbert,** bound May
1672 – freed Jul 1682 (prob. means 'son-in-law'). In Jul 1666 he was
excused stewardship as he has no servant at present. Masters for whom
he bound aprs. were: J. Betts (3), A. Prime (2), A. Beckner (2), one each
for W. North, H. Ireland, T. Wolverston, P. Willierme, S. Betts.
J. Pennock, R. Smith, E. Ward, T. Lane. Will dated 1673, proved Apr
1676. Made CC Assistant from 1679, but did not attend after 1672. Left
widow Sarah, house in St. Nicholas Alley, in St. Michael's parish,
Cornhill. Mentioned sons William, Thomas and Benjamin. Overseer is
'my loving kinsman' William Herbert, prob. the clockmaker of that
name, *qv*. Widow, Sarah, took as aprs.: Apr 1676 **Jonathan Boole;** Aug
1680 **George Halsey** – free Feb 1687/88; Jan 1687 **Gamaliel Voyce** ('on
consideration of her widowhood and that she may have a servant able to
instruct another') – free Jan 1694/95; post Apr 1684 took over **Stephen
Brittaine** from John Harbert; Oct 1695 **Samuel Ludlow** – free Sep 1707.
Paid her quarterage till c. 1697 then died.

PAYNE, William London
Lantern clock, dated 1618, signed 'in East Smithfield'. Not in CC records. See also Pagnes, William.

PEARCE (see under Pierce).

PEARSON, Adam Carlisle
Kept school tower clock 1649-1660.

PEATLING, Thomas (also Peytling) London
B.c. 1661, apr. Jul 1675 to Robert Lynch till 1682. Freed Aug 1682.

PECKETT, John (sometimes Pickett) London
B.c. 1669, apr. Jun 1683 to Henry Bradley, later passed over to Henry Merryman till 1690. Free Mar 1691/92. Took as apr. Jun 1696 **Edward Whittaker** – free Apr 1712. Also bound an apr. for H. Merryman. Paid no quarterage after c. 1696-97, prob. dead or gone by 1697/98.

PEERS, John London
B.c. 1663, apr. Apr 1676 to Robert Cosby till 1684, but not freed.

PEIRAE, Pasquier London
Free Brother in CC May 1648. (Baillie has Perot.) See Peros.

PEIRCE – this was the normal spelling at the time for Pierce, but for convenience this name is listed under Pierce.

PELLIN, Andrew Whitehaven (Cumberland)
Supposedly made church clock between 1691 and 1696. Had children baptised there 1692-99.

PEN, William Edinburgh
Bound as apr. to Andrew Brown Nov 1696, but not freed. (See also Penn.)

PENARD, Isaac London
Listed by Baillie as watchmaker c. 1600, but I do not know him and feel this may be a misreading of another name.

PENELL, John London
Baptism at St. Mary Abbot's, Kensington in 1700 of John Peter, son of

John Penell and his wife, Lorice, watchmaker in St. Giles (in the fields?) 'from ye Gore'.

PENFORD, Joshua (sometimes Penfold)   **London**
B.c. 1670, apr. Jun 1684 to Francis Stamper till 1691. Freed Jan 1695/96. Paid no quarterage after 1696 and prob. died soon after.

PENKETHMAN, Thomas   **London**
B.c. 1668, apr. Sep 1682 to Thomas Tennant till 1689. Freed Sep 1692. Paid no quarterage after c. 1692/93.

PENN, Thomas   **London**
Jun 1689 married as watchmaker, bachelor, aged 35 of St. Clement Danes parish to Constant Manly of St. Paul's Bedford, spinster, 25 – at St. Paul's (therefore b. about 1654). Watch recorded in style of c. 1660 but presumably much later, signed 'Thomas Penn at Clements Inn'. (One of this name b.c. 1686, apr. 1700 to Jonathan Puller, must be a different man, perhaps his son?)

PENNINGTON, Bernard junior   **Bodmin (Cornwall)**
Repaired town clock 1662-63.

PENNOCK, John   **York/London**
Apr. of William Kidson of York. Brother of CC Jul 1638. Became Assistant from 1651, Warden from 1654, Master 1660 and 1663, last attended about 1672. Took as aprs.: Oct 1638 **Nicholas Coxeter** (thro' R. Masterson) – free Mar 1646; Aug 1645 **Robert Robinson** (thro' O. Durant) – free Sep 1652; Aug 1655 **Robert Crome** (thro' B. Hill); Jun 1662 **Robert Pitcher** (thro' T. Claxton); Nov 1662 **Thomas Hues** (thro' N. Coxeter); **Joseph Lloyd** (thro' I. Puzy) – free Sep 1673; Mar 1664/65 **Henry Hotham** (thro' N. Payne) – free Apr 1673; Sep 1673 **William Searle** (thro' N. Coxeter). Also bound Sep 1655 **Charles Fox** for R. Cosby – free Oct 1662. In 1652 he gave the CC a 'house clock' as payment for his Assistantship entry. In 1662 he worked in Lothbury. Died between late 1673 and Apr 1677, when his widow got CC charity which she received till Sep 1679, when presumably she also died. Work known – a lantern clock signed 'John Pennock within Bishopsgate' (ie York); several others signed at London, eg 'John Pennock, Lothbury', 'John Pennock at Petty France Gate in ye Moorfields'.

PENNOCK, William   London
Recorded by Baillie as a clockmaker in 1637, but I do not know him.

PENNY, Charles   Wells (Somerset)
Believed to have been a journeyman clockmaker there in 1699. Working 1715-20 as a watchmaker and goldsmith.

PENTON, Isaac   London(?)
Three or four longcase clocks are known, apparently late 17th century to c. 1715, signed 'Isaac Penton', no place mentioned. These are marquetry clocks, one with pewter inlay. He would appear to be a late 17th century London maker but I have no data on him and he was not a member of CC.

PEPPER, John   London
B.c. 1670, apr. Dec 1684 to George Etherington thro' D. Stevens till 1691, but not freed.

PEPPER, Samuel   London
B.c. 1641, apr. Aug 1655 to Thomas Mills thro' S. Horne till 1662, but not freed.

PEPYS, John   London
B.c. 1658, apr. Jan 1672/73 to John Harris till 1679. Freed Apr 1680. Took as aprs.: Sep 1683 **Daniel Bell;** Jul 1700 **Nathaniel Stephens** (son of Thomas Stephens of Coventry, cheesemonger); Aug 1708 his son, **John Pepys,** who had been bound to someone else earlier in the year – free Jan 1715/16; Dec 1713 his son, **Samuel Pepys;** Aug 1715 his son, **William Pepys;** Jul 1717 **Richard Weekes;** Nov 1720 **John Poole.** Made CC Assistant from 1697, Warden from 1705, Master 1707, still attending 1720, after which I have no data on him. Work known – a watch by him was advertised as having been stolen in 1698.

PEPYS, Peter   London
B.c. 1666, apr. Nov 1680 to Richard Pepys till 1687, but not freed.

PEPYS, Richard   London
B.c. 1652, apr. Jan 1666/67 to John Harris till 1673. Freed Apr 1674. Could well be brother of John Pepys, who had same master. Took as aprs.: Dec 1674 **John Berry** – free Jul 1688; Nov 1680 **Peter Pepys.** Not heard of after 1680.

PERES, Mark (actually Marcos)   **London**
Free Brother in CC Jun 1680, a clockmaker. Paid no quarterage after c.
1682. Work known – a lantern clock signed 'Marcos Peres, London'.

PERKES, Henry (Parks?)   **Walsall (Staffordshire)**
Repaired church clock 1649.

PERKINS, Eysum   **London**
B.c. 1656, apr. Sep 1670 to James Atkinson, mat. inst. maker, thro'
R. Ames till 1677, but not freed. In Apr 1682 was to be prosecuted for
practising the trade at 'Rederiffe' (Rotherhithe) when not a member of
CC, but in May he promised to take up his freedom before Nov, but did
not. Britten records him at 'Rederiffe, the end of Love Lane', which
sounds possible, but I do not know his source.

PERKINS, John   **London**
B.c. 1648, apr. Jul 1661 to Samuel Horne till 1669, but not freed.

PERO(O)NE, Isaac   **London**
In 1622 was an alien at Mr. Garratt's, *qv* in St. Martins. In 1632 was to be
given further time by CC to accede to their requests, ie to join – but did
not. However, see next entry.

PERONE, Richard   **London**
Listed at Fleet Street in 1662, but one wonders whether Richard is a slip
in records for Isaac. Not in CC.

PEROS, Pasque   **London**
In arrears with quarterage in 1664. Obviously same man as previously
recorded as Pasquier Peirae.

PERRIER, Peter   **London**
Recorded by Britten as apr. 1660 to James Lello, but I cannot trace him.
However see John Peryer. May have been a goldsmith.

PERRY, George   **London**
Dead by 1691, having been father and master of Henry, *qv*, watchmaker.
Not in CC however.

PERRY, Henry (also Perrey)   **London**
Watchmaker, made Free Brother in CC Dec 1691, 'who had served his

time in the country and in the City to his father, George Perry, now deceased'. Took as apr. Sep 1702 **William Jobson** (son of John Jobson, gent., late of Wood Street, London, deceased). In 1716 called for Steward but was 'out of town'. In 1718 likewise but he 'sent word by his maid that he was going to the Bath for his health'. Last heard of in 1719-20 when in arrears with quarterage. Believed worked in Soho. Work known – bracket clock signed 'Henry Perry, London'.

PERRY, John London

Baillie records him as son of George, CC 1691-1725, but I cannot trace him. Prob. a slip for Henry, *qv*.

PERRY, Richard London

B.c. 1642, apr. May 1656 to Samuel Davis till 1663, but not freed.

PERSE, Henry London

B.c. 1646, apr. Jul 1659 to Richard Scrivener till 1667, but not freed. See Pierce family group.

PERYER, John (also Perrier) London

B.c. 1650, apr. Apr 1664 to James Lello till 1671, but not freed.

PETTIT, William (Guillaume) London

Sometimes difficult to distinguish from William Petty, *qv*. In 1622 listed as an alien 'with Mr. Ramsay in Tutle Street, King's clockmaker', ie journeyman to David Ramsay. A boxmaker. Working in 1662 in Westminster. Entered CC 1632, as a Brother. In Jun 1655 he gave CC a silver boat. Took as aprs.: c. 1651 **Abraham Lamb**, thro' T. Taylor; Sep 1654 **John Richards**, thro' J. Bayley. In Dec 1657 ordered to dismiss **John Garsine,** whom he had taken as journeyman without sanction.

PETTY, William (also Pette) London

B.c. 1625, apr. Apr 1638 to Daniel Howell thro' R. Masterson till 1646. Freed Apr 1646. Took as aprs.: Jan 1649/50 **Thomas Cooke;** Mar 1651 **George Matchett;** Oct 1659 **Cuthbert Parker;** Jul 1654 **Nathaniel Crowe** – free Sep 1661; **John Harris** – free Jan 1659/60; Mar 1661/62 **Thomas Lashbrook.** Also bound several aprs. for other masters – two for T. Belson, one each for R. Scrivener, R. Grainger, L. Meredith, R. Craile, R. Copping.

PHILBERT, Daniel   **London**
Frenchman, summoned to CC court Jul 1695 for transgressions but
failed to appear. One of this name recorded at Paris 1675.

PHILLIPS, Peter   **London**
In 1633 had not completed his seven years – allowed more time by CC.

PHILLIPS, Samuel   **London (Chelmsford?)**
B.c. 1657, apr. Nov 1671 to Nathaniel Chamberlain till 1678, but not
freed. One of this name worked at Chelmsford, Essex, c. 1680.

PHILLIPS, Thomas   **London**
Nov 1680 apr. to Bernard Rainsford for seven years, but the entry has
been deleted from the book – cancelled?

PHILLIPS, William   **Chester**
Free as a clockmaker 1639-40.

PICKERING, John   **London**
B.c. 1672, apr. Apr 1686 to Richard Knight till 1693, but not freed.

PICKET, John (see Peckett).

PIDGEON, Thomas   **London**
B.c. 1646, apr. Jun 1660 to John Bayes till 1667, but not freed.

PIERCE (normally spelt Peirce at this time).

PIERCE, (illegible – is listed as Henry Perse, *qv*).

PIERCE, Adam (also Pearce)   **London**
Apr. Jun 1657 to Edward East thro' D. Moody. Freed Jun 1664.

PIERCE, Humphrey (many other variants)   **London**
Apr. Aug 1646 to Robert Smith thro' J. Walters. Freed Sep 1653. Took
as aprs.: **Richard Craggs** – free Oct 1660; May 1663 **Samuel Clyatt** – free
Apr 1672; Jul 1657 **Henry Harper** – free Aug 1664; Feb 1668/69 **John
White**; May 1673 **Richard Watts** – free Jul 1680, by which time master
had died. His widow, Sarah, continued and took as aprs.: Feb 1678-79
John Papworth – free 1688; **William Taylor** (from Isaac Webb) – freed

437

Apr 1682; Nov 1684 **William Watson** – free Jan 1691/92. Alive 1693, listed as dead by 1698.

PIERCE, John (also Peerce)   **London**
B.c. 1666, apr. Jul 1680 to George Tipping till 1687, but not freed.

PIERCE, John   **London**
B.c. 1674, apr. Sep 1688 to Charles Lowndes till 1695, but not freed.

PIERCE, Richard   **London**
B.c. 1634, apr. Jan 1646/47 to Thomas Reeve thro' T. Alcock till 1655. Freed Jul 1657. Took as aprs.: Oct 1661 **Robert Dingley** – free Dec 1668, by which time master had died; **Ralph Child** – free Jan 1661-62; also bound an apr. for Henry Child and one for J. Betts. Still alive Nov 1664, dead by Dec 1668.

PIERCE, Sarah (see under Humphrey, whose widow she was).

PIERCE, T.   **Caernarvon (Wales)**
Said to have been working c. 1680 – doubtful.

PIERCE, Thomas   **Berkley (Gloucestershire)**
Died 25 Feb 1665 aged 77. For epitaph see *Complete British Clocks*.

PIERAS, Pasquier   **London**
(also many doubtful spellings such as Piras, Piraas, Pieras, Peros, Peirae) In May 1654 Mr. East paid his quarterage for him – may have worked for East. See also under Peros and Peirae.

PIGG, Robert   **London**
B.c. 1660, apr. Dec 1674 to John White till 1681, but not freed. (See also Robert Pike?).

PIGGOTT, Mr.   **London**
Seller of canes in Fleet Street over against Chancery Lane. In 1671/72 had faulty rulers confiscated by CC, supposedly made by William Elmes.

PIGGOTT, Henry (also Pigot)   **London**
B.c. 1657, apr. Feb 1671/72 to Sampson Crooke till 1678. Freed Sep 1687. Took as apr. Sep 1692 **Jonathan Lovett**. Paid no quarterage after c. 1693 when he prob. died.

PIKE, Robert   **London**
Baillie records late 17th century clock, but I have no record of this man – unless he is recorded as Robert Pigg, *qv* from bad spelling.

PILKINGTON, George   **Dublin**
Clockmaker c.1700 – c.1713, when free Goldsmith. Apr. c. 1694 to Robert Rigmaiden. One of this name was later at Tynan, co. Armagh.

PILSON, Abraham   **Plymouth**
Recorded as c. 1700, but I have no data on him. Watchmaker.

PINCHBECK, Christopher   **London**
B. 1670, died 1732, buried at St. Dunstan's Fleet Street. Had sons Edward, Christopher and John. Maker of clocks but best known as inventor of the Pinchbeck alloy. In 1721 'inventor and maker of the famous Astronomico-Musical Clocks, is removed from St. George's Court, St. James's Lane, to the sign of the Astronomico-Musical clock in Fleet Street nr. the Leg Tavern . . . etc.'. He died in 1732 aged 62 and was buried at St. Dunstan's Fleet Street. Not a member of CC. For full study see R. Shenton.

PINKART, John   **London**
B.c. 1650, apr. Jun 1663 to Joseph Quash till 1671, but not freed.

PINDER, Joseph   **London**
B.c. 1678, apr. Aug 1692 to George Halsey till 1699, but not freed.

PINGO, Joseph   **London**
B.c. 1668-70, apr. Mar 1684/85 to Robert Thompson till 1691, but not freed. In Oct 1690 as a watchmaker, bachelor, aged 22 of St. Martins in the Fields he married Elizabeth Wells of St. Bride's, spinister, aged 19 – at St. Lawrence, Old Jewry.

PINSON, John   **London**
B.c. 1661, apr. Mar 1674/75 to John Parker till 1682, but not freed. In Apr 1677 he received back on behalf of John Parker a movement from CC allegedly faulty, made by R. Hamlin.

PITCHER, John   **London**
Free Brother in CC Sep 1689, as a watchmaker. Took as aprs.: Sep 1689 (after he has taken his City Freedom) **John Nolson** thro' D. Stevens –

later passed over to D. Quare; Sep 1692 **John Chetwood;** May 1695 **Joseph Grisley;** May 1697 **Stephen Chambers**. In Aug 1693 a clockmaker, bachelor, aged 34 of St. Andrews Holborn, he was to marry Susan Newland of St. Helens, spinster, 25, at St. Mary Newington or Lambeth. Paid quarterage till 1701, then died.

PITCHER, Robert   **London**
B.c. 1649, apr. Jun 1662 to John Pennock thro' T. Claxton till 1670, but not freed.

PITTS, Samuel   **London**
B.c. 1675, apr. Dec 1689 to Robert Fenn till 1696, but not freed.

PLANT, Edward   **London**
Apr. Feb 1655-56 to William Godbed. Freed Apr 1664. Paid quarterage in 1671, not heard of thereafter. In Sep 1686 CC paid a small charity to Widow Plant.

PLATT, Oliver   **Wigan (Lancashire)**
Watchmaker. Free 1674, former apr. of Roger Darbyshire.

PLATT, Thomas   **London**
Brother in CC Jul 1637. Took as aprs.: Jan 1638 **John Hodierne** thro' O. Durant; Nov 1650 **James Browning** thro' H. Erberry. In May 1652 he was warned by the Lord Mayor to bind his aprs. thro' the Clothmakers' Co. In 1662 listed as working in Cannon Street.

PLAYER, Robert senior   **London**
Apr. Oct 1664 in the Joyners' Co. to Robert Gerrard – freed there May 1671. Made Free Brother in CC Apr 1678, being a case and cabinet maker and Freeman of the Joyners' Co. Took as aprs. in CC: Jan 1680-81 **Thomas Edwards** thro' D. Stevens; Aug 1687 **William Grimley;** Sep 1691 his son, **Robert Player** junior – free Jul 1700; Oct 1692 **Thomas Johnson** – free Jul 1700. In Jul 1700 'being free of the Joyners the latter require him to free his three prentices in that Co. in about a year's time – then this Co. will return the monies they have paid for their admission'. In Jan 1702/03 he gave notice that his son, Robert, is being summoned to take his freedom in the Joyners' Co. In 1719 Widow Player got a small charity from the CC. He is one of the very first wooden clock case makers, but I know of no example that can be attributed to him.

PLAYER, Robert junior   **London**
B.c. 1677, apr. Sep 1691 to father, Robert senior, in CC till 1698. Free Jul 1700. In Jan 1702/03 summoned to take up his freedom in the Joyners' Co. Still alive in 1703, as was his father. One of this name (son?) took as apr. Dec 1716 **Samuel Petty,** and was called to be Steward in 1719. Work known – Baillie records longcase clock and watch.

PLAYER, Simon   **London**
B.c. 1658, apr. Sep 1671 to William Speakman till 1679, but not freed.

PLAYER, Thomas (sometimes Plaire)   **London**
B.c. 1651, apr. Nov 1664 to 'Mr. Williamson', later passed over to Thomas Weeks, then to John Froud till 1672 and freed Sep 1672. Took as aprs.: Feb 1672/73 **Thomas Warden** (passed on from Thomas Overbury, a watchmaker but free of the Haberdashers) – freed in Haberdashers' Co. Aug 1677; Jul 1674 **Charles Lowndes** – freed Dec 1682; Jul 1679 **Charles Fisher; Aug 1686 Nathaniel Major; Oct 1688 John Smith;** Nov 1697 Robert Arlandy; Nov 1698 **Joseph Smallwood** (from J. Andrews); Jul 1710 **Gideon Perigall.** Received CC charity Jul 1718. In 1719 Widow Player received it.

PLAYTERS, Lionell   **London**
B.c. 1666, apr. Apr 1680 to Samuel Drossat thro' S. Davis till 1687, but not freed.

PLEASANT, Henry   **Sudbury (Suffolk)/**
           Colchester (Essex)
Bellfounder and clock chimemaker. First wife, Catrina, died 1673. Worked at Colchester from about 1686, in which year he tuned the bells at Long Melford. Agreed to make a new clock and chimes for Sudbury in 1701. Died 1708, administration granted to widow, Millicent. Known for the ryhmes he cast on his bells, eg from St. Nicholas, Ipswich: 'Henry Pleasant here at last, Made me as good as can be cast'.

PLEWITT, Francis   **London**
In Feb 1671/72 was a 'cane-seller nr. the Kings Head nr. the Blue Bell nr. Charing Cross', when he paid CC search fee.

PLEY, George   **London**
B.c. 1677, apr. Dec 1691 to Charles Lowndes thro' J. Southworth till 1698, but not freed.

PLEYDELL, John (and Plydell)   **London**
B.c. 1652, apr. Jun 1666 to Thomas Bagley till 1673, but not freed. Work known – lantern clock signed 'Jno. Pleydell, London'.

PLUETT, Anthony   **London**
B.c. 1674, apr. Jul 1688 to Jonathan Lowndes thro' D. Stevens till 1695. Freed Jan 1697/98. Paid quarterage till 1701 at least. Longcase clock known c. 1710 signed 'Ant. Pluett, St. James's Street'.

PLUM(M)ER, Joseph (or Plomer)   **London**
B.c. 1656, apr. Sep 1669 to Christopher Maynard till 1677, but not freed.

PLUMERD, Isaac (see Pluvier)

PLUVIER, Isaac   **London**
His name is often mis-spelt and appears in records as Plumerd, Plunerd, Plovier, Pliner, Plinier, Plumiere. In Dec 1637 was admitted into CC as journeyman to Mr. Bouquett. Fined 1646. Made a freeman Jan 1651/52. Believed to be a Dutchman. Took as aprs.: c. 1649 **Joseph Munday** (from R. Morgan, perhaps when Morgan died) – freed Nov 1654; Jan 1655/56 **James Seddon** thro' J. Quash – freed Oct 1662; Jan 1655/56 **Garret Mote** as journeyman 'whilst in England; Jun 1664 took over **Michael Yates** thro' or from C. Bonner.

PLUMLEIGH, Thomas   **London/Exeter**
B.c. 1673, apr. Jul 1687 to Thomas Taylor till 1694, but not freed. One of this name was bankrupt at Exeter 1725, having been a watchmaker there from at least 1707. The Exeter man appears to have married there in 1697 to Anne Payne.

PLUMSTEAD, ----   **London**
Paid CC search fee 1674.

PLYDELL (see Pleydell)

PLUMLEY, Edward (also Plymley)   **London**
B.c. 1668, apr. Sep 1682 to Edward Millett till 1689, but not freed.

POARSON, Emanuel (maybe Pearson?)   **Edinburgh**
Apr. in 1700 to Paul Roumieu junior, but not freed.

POISSON, Henry London
Baillie records him c.1695 – c.1720. I have no trace of him.

POLING, Anthony Exeter
Worked on cathedral clock 1689.

POLING, John Exeter
Made local TC 1670.

POLLYCOTT, Thomas London
B.c. 1670, apr. May 1684 to John Browne thro' D. Stevens till 1691, but not freed.

POND, John London
B.c. 1659, apr. Feb 1673/74 to Joshua Winnock till 1680, but not freed.

POOLE, Anthony London
Ironmonger in Foster Lane in 1671/72 when had faulty rulers confiscated by CC. Prob. a measure-seller.

POOLE, George London
Free Brother in CC May 1654. Took as aprs.: **John Salmon** between 1646 and 1654 from N. Tomlins, then passed him back again; Aug 1654 **Thomas Trippet** thro' N. Coxeter.

POPE, Nicholas London
B.c. 1664, apr. Sep 1678 thro' S. Davis to Gerard Overzee till 1685, but not freed.

POPKINS, John Dublin
Goldsmith and watchmaker. Free Goldsmith there 1672-79. Took as apr. in 1675 **John Bennett**.

PORTER, John London
Baillie records him as apr. 1680, but I do not know him.

PORTER, Matthew London
B.c. 1669, apr. Oct 1682 to Thomas Taylor of the Strand till 1690. Freed Sep 1692, his master being then deceased. Paid no quarterage after about 1693.

PORTER, Robert London
B.c. 1673, apr. Apr 1687 to John Cotsworth till 1694, but not freed.

PORTER, Sebastian London
B.c. 1666, apr. Sep 1680 to Jeffrey Bayley till 1687, but not freed.

PORTSMOUTH, John London
B.c. 1646, apr. Jan 1660/61 to Isaac Puzy till 1667, but not freed.

POTTER, John London
Baillie records him as Blacksmiths' Co. 1628 as 'English Forrin'. One of
this name was CC Beadle in 1633.

POURVIS, James (see Purvis)

POWELL, Bartholomew London
Apr. Feb. 1650/51 to John Freeman. Freed Oct 1668. Took as aprs.: Oct
1669 **Robert Nemes** – free Mar 1677-78; Dec 1670 **Joseph Jarvis**; Jul
1671 **Francis Langland** (error for John?); Jan 1673/74 **Nathaniel Lloyd**.
In 1708 Widow Powell received CC charity.

POWELL, John London
B.c. 1652, apr. Jun 1665 to Isaac Daniell thro' H. Smith till 1675, but not
freed.

POWER, Thomas London(?)/**Wellingborough (Northants)**
Maker of lantern clocks from c. 1680, sometimes believed to be London
but these are prob. the work of the Wellingborough man who died in
1709, his widow, Sarah, dying later the same year. Work known –
lantern clocks, one signed 'Thomas Power hoc fabricavit'. See my book –
Complete British Clocks for more details including his inventory.

POWNALL, Nathaniel London
B.c. 1625, apr. Nov 1649 to William Izod till 1656, but not freed.

PREDY, Thomas London
Failed to pay CC quarterage in 1635, but see also Priddith.

PRESTON, Josias London
B.c. 1627, apr. Apr 1640, being son of Christopher Preston late of

Craven in Yorkshire, bound to Richard Masterson but to serve Christopher Vernon till 1648. Not freed.

PRESTWOOD, Joseph (not George)   **London**
Some records say George but he signed himself Joseph. Bc. 1679, apr. Dec 1693 to Henry Jones, later passed over to David Wyche till 1700. Freed Jul 1703. Took as apr. Sep 1710 **Thomas Simpson.**

PREVOST, William   **London/Newcastle on Tyne**
Sometimes written Provost in error. B.c. 1662. In Feb 1689/90 he was described as a clockmaker of Newcastle, bachelor, aged 27, to marry Margaret Badudouin of Stepney, spinster, 21, at St. Mary Magdalen, Old Fish Street. Was not a member of CC, and prob. worked mostly in Newcastle. In Jan 1698/99 some kind of contest was held between himself and Deodatus Threlkeld as to who was the better maker. Baillie records that Edw. Burgis and Sam Watson were to decide, and that Threlkeld won. CC records show that they declined to take any part in the judging of the contest. Baillie records that Prevost was French. Work known – several longcase clocks including a month clock mostly signed 'William Prevost, London'. I do not know of a Newcastle signed clock.

PRICE, Charles   **London**
B.c. 1667, apr. Mar 1680/81 to George Stevens thro' D. Stevens till 1688, but not freed.

PRICE, John   **Alcester(?) (Warwickshire)**
Clockmaker who made church clock there, three train, in 1682.

PRICE, John   **London**
B.c. 1664, apr. Apr 1678 to Robert Nemes, but passed over Jan 1678/79 to William Kennon till 1685, but not freed.

PRICE, John   **Olney (Buckinghamshire)**
Clockmaker, buried there 1713. Maybe the Londoner above?

PRICE, Thomas   **London**
B.c. 1672, apr. Apr 1686 to Henry Hester till 1695, but not freed.

PRIDDITH, Thomas (sometimes Predy, *qv*)   **London**
Free Brother in CC Oct 1639.

PRIGEON, John London
B.c. 1633, apr. May 1646 to Elias Allen thro' T. Alcock till 1654, but not freed.

PRIME, Abraham London
B. 1648, son of Andrew Prime, *qv*. Apr. Apr 1665 thro' Nicholas Payne to his father, Andrew Prime till 1672. Freed Jan 1672/73. Took as aprs.: Apr 1678 **Benjamin Wright** – free Jun 1685; Aug 1676 **Benjamin Marshall** (taken from T. Paul) – freed Jun 1680. Also bound an apr. for father Andrew Prime and another for B. Wright. In Jul 1685 he pleaded poverty and was excused Stewardship for that year. Paid no quarterage after c. 1686 and prob. died then or soon after; dead by 1697/98. Work known – bracket clock on turntable base signed 'Abraham Prime Londini fecit'. May have worked mostly for his father.

PRIME, Andrew London/Norwich
B. 1619. Closely connected with Ahasuerus Fromanteel in origins, family and work. Apr. in Blacksmiths' Co. Aug 1632 to Abraham Boyce, being the son of Andrew Prime of Norwich, weaver. Freed in Blacksmiths' Co. Oct 1641. Free Brother in CC Oct 1646. Married 1646 Elizabeth Fromanteel, sister of Ahasuerus. Had issue 1647 Andrew (became girdler), 1648 Abraham (became clockmaker, *qv*), 1656 Esther. Took as apr. Jul 1653 in Blacksmiths' Co. **Samuel Fromanteel**, then as aprs. in CC: Aug 1654 **David Smith** thro' N. Tomlins – freed Feb 1661; Apr 1665 son **Abraham Prime** thro' N. Payne – free Jan 1672/73; Apr 1670 **John Davall** thro' N. Payne – free Nov 1677; **Edward Clement** thro' T. Claxton – free Apr 1671; Oct 1681 **Richard Wither** thro' Abraham Prime, passed over to J. Wells; was amongst the 1656 rebels against CC administration. Several times fined for refusing to serve as CC steward. Mar 1674 made Assistant despite his protests, but he never attended meetings (prob. left London or would have been forced to attend). Died in Norwich in 1710, having spent his later life there. Work known – lantern clocks signed 'Andrew Prime, Londini fecit', longcase clocks including month longcase signed 'Andrew Prime London'. In Dec 1674 made turret clock for St. Andrews Hornchurch for £25, then being of Cree Church Parish, London. For fuller details see my book, *Country Clocks*, my book *Complete British Clocks* and article on the Fromanteels in *Clocks Magazine* May, Jun, Jul 1980.

PRINCE, Richard London
B.c. 1645, apr. Oct 1659 to John Clarkson thro' T. Claxton till 1666. Not

freed till Nov 1680. Took as aprs.: Sep 1674 **John Bindley** thro'
L. Wythe, but not until after he has taken up his freedom – freed Nov
1680; Jul 1682 **John Tussingham.**

PRINCE, Thomas   London
B.c. 1660, apr. Sep 1674 to John Bellard thro L. Wythe till 1681, but not
freed.

PRINT, Richard   London
B.c. 1667, apr. Dec 1681 to John Martin till 1688, but not freed on time.
In Nov 1697 he was called to Court and told to take up his freedom but he
did not. Finally freed Sep 1698. Paid quarterage till 1705 at least.

PRITCHARD, ----   London
Mat. inst. maker. Paid CC search fee 1674-75.

PRITCHARD, Bariah   London
B.c. 1661, apr. Dec 1674 to Edward Eyston till 1682, but not freed.

PRIT(T)CHARD, Phil   London
Never actually entered CC but was known to them. Prob. dead by 1663,
and not shown in 1662 list.

PROCTOR, Joseph   place not known
Lantern clock recorded c. 1670.

PROSSER, Edward   London
B.c. 1641, apr. Jan 1655/56 to Robert Lochard till 1662, but not freed.

PRUJEAN, John   Oxford
Mat. inst. maker at New College Lane. Work known – paper astrolabe
signed 'Joha. Prujean Fecit Oxon'. Painted mural sundials. Working
1676-88.

PRYOR, Joseph   Liverpool (Lancashire)
Watchmaker. Issue b. there to wife, Grace, 1676-88. Wife died 1709. He
died 1719, leaving inventory of his goods.

PULLEN, James   London
B.c. 1656, apr. Oct 1669 to William Elmes, mat. inst. maker, thro'
T. Claxton till 1677, but not freed.

PULLER, Jonathan London

B.c. 1662, apr. Aug 1676 to Nicholas Coxeter, then passed over to John Miller (maybe in 1679 on Coxeter's death) – freed Sep 1683. Took as aprs.: Jan 1684/85 **Joseph Lord** thro' J. Bayley; Sep 1687 **Edward Williamson;** Sep 1696 **Robert Desbrow** – free Sep 1705; Oct 1696 **Henry Batterson** from W. Davison – free Jul 1701; **William Davis** from Thomas Davis freed Sep 1699; May 1700 **Thomas Penn** (son of John Penn late of London, surgeon, deceased); Dec 1703 **William Presbury;** Dec 1705 **Thomas Warden** (son of Thomas Warden late of parish of St. Gregory, London, joiner, deceased). Made Assistant in 1701 and attended till 1707, when presumed died. Believed worked in Red Lion Court in Fleet Street in 1690. Work known – watches, longcase and bracket clocks, including month longcase. Signed usually 'Jonathan Puller, London'.

PUNCHARD, William London

B.c. 1663, apr. Jun 1676 to Robert Seignior till 1684, but not freed.

PUNNETT, Thomas Battle (later Rye, Sussex)

Made turret clock for Battle in 1656 for £10. Made Mayfield clock 1657 for £11. Then lived at Cranbrook 1657 to c. 1669. Then went to live at Rye in 1673 till died there 1711. Was also a gunsmith.

PURDOUNE, Andrew Glasgow

Kept town clocks 1657.

PURVES/PURVIS, James place not known

Name also spelt Pourvis and also Jemes. Maybe Scotland. Lantern clocks known dated 1657. Region not known but see next entry.

PURVES, William Edinburgh

In 1539 repaired Aberdeen town clock. Was a Burgess of Edinburgh. In 1540 he contracted to make a chiming turret clock for Dundee church, completed in 1543. In 1546 he sued council for non-payment. It was destroyed by fire in 1553. In 1546 he began to repair Stirling town clock and add a moon dial, completed 1548. Appears in Edinburgh Hammermen's records 1541-42. Believed died c. 1560.

PUZY, Isaac London

Other spellings including Puzzy, Pusse, etc. B.c. 1637, apr. Dec 1651 to John Freeman till 1658. Freed Jan 1658/59. Took as aprs.: Jun 1668

John Sands; Jul 1671 **Christopher Struggle; John Miller** (after death of S. Knibb, 1674, and before being passed on to Joseph Knibb; Jan 1660 **John Portsmouth.** Was frequently in arrears with quarterage and in Jul 1675 'being much in arrears with quarterage' he had conspired with Roger Nicholls to get an apr. (Francis Barnard) for which he was fined. Also bound an apr. for John Pennock and one for John Trippett. Received charity from CC from Apr 1681 to Apr 1685, when prob. died. Work known – lantern clocks signed 'Issak Puzzy, London' and 'Isaac Puzzy, London'.

PYNE, Nathaniel   **London**
B.c. 1653, apr. Apr 1667 to Thomas Wheeler till 1674. Freed Nov 1677. Took as aprs.: Apr 1680 **John Andrews** – passed over to Samuel Stanton; Oct 1683 **John Gitter;** Aug 1684 **George Joyce** – free Aug 1692; Sep 1695 **Thomas Williamson;** Sep 1696 **Edward Kempe;** Mar 1706-07 **John (Andrews?).** Received CC charity Jan 1714-15, and prob. died soon after that. Work known – a longcase clock is recorded.

Q

QUARE, Daniel   **London**
Believed b.c. 1647/48 in Somerset. Became Brother in CC Apr 1671, as a
Great Clockmaker. Was a Quaker and as such would not sign oaths and
perhaps for this reason when he took his first apr. he is described as a
'covenant servant' rather than an apr. Took as aprs.: Jun 1673 **John Beck**
thro' J. White – free Sep 1681; Aug 1675 **George Heady** thro' S. Davis –
free Sep 1682; 1677 **Faith Leake** thro' J. White – free Jan 1685/86; Aug
1680 **John Foster** thro' S. Davis – free Jan 1689/90; Mar 1684/85 **Robert
Todd**; Jul 1685 **John Davis** – free Aug 1697; **John Marshall** (from
S. Rosse) – free Jan 1689/90; Nov 1690 **William Johnson** – free Apr
1702; **John Zachary** (from W. Simcox) – free Mar 1694/95; Aug 1696
John Kirton – free Feb 1705/06; **John Nolson** (from J. Pitcher) – free
Dec 1697; Jan 1701 **Stephen Horseman** (son of Stephen Horseman of
Brayton, Yorkshire, wheelwright, deceased) – free Sep 1709; **Richard
Vick** (from F. Asseline and W. Speakman) – free Apr 1702; Oct 1705
Joseph Appleby (son of William Appleby late of Sunderland, co.
Durham, shoemaker, deceased) – free Feb 1719/20; Mar 1707/08 **Daniel
Quare** (son of Robert Quare). Worked at St. Martins le Grand, later (by
1680) at The Kings Arms, Exchange Alley.
    About 1680 Quare is said to have made repeating watches of his own
design and in the struggle between 1686 and 1688, in which the CC
opposed the application for a repeating watch patent by Edward Barlow,
Quare is said to have played a leading part. In 1695 Quare applied for a
patent for a portable weatherglass although the CC opposed its granting
and, when this was granted in Sep, the CC decreed that they would
defend any member who still made or sold such glasses in opposition to
Quare's patent and who might get into trouble as a result. He was made

Assistant in CC from 1700, Warden from 1705, Master in 1708 and attended till his death in 1724, being buried at the Quakers' Burial Ground at Bunhill Fields, though said to have died at Croydon. He had three daughters and a son, who does not appear to have followed the trade. In later years he took into partnership Stephen Horseman, his former apr., which must have been after 1709, and after his death Horseman carried on the business till bankrupt in 1733. He became a very famous clockmaker and his name is amongst the best-known of any. Work known – very varied incl. watches, longcase clocks with year example, barometers, bracket clocks. For fuller details see the standard textbooks, there being as yet no book devoted to Quare.

QUARREL, Richard   London
B.c. 1677, apr. Sep 1691 to Philip Corderoy till 1698, but not freed.

QUASH, Joseph   London
B.c. 1623, apr. Oct 1637 to George Smith thro' O. Durant till 1644. Freed May 1646. Took as aprs.: Aug 1646 **William Grout** – free Aug 1660; Dec 1657 **John Neile**; Mar 1659/60 **Thomas Savage**; Jun 1663 **John Pinckart**. Also bound several aprs. for other masters, which included Ahasuerus Fromanteel (two aprs.); D. Bouquet, P. Bellune, J. Burgis, I. Ploviere, R. Grinkin. In 1662 he worked in Blackfriars. Served as Steward 1664. Dec 1674 was runner-up for position of Beadle. Work known – watches, signed 'Josephus Quash, Londini'.

QUELCH, John   Oxford
Son of Richard Quelch, apr. to brother, Richard, Nov 1652. Freed Sep 1663. Issue b. 1668-77. Took as aprs.: 1673 **Thomas Langly**; 1676 **Henry Godfrey**; 1684 **Edward Page**; 1686 **Joseph Rustin**. Alive 1694, but believed dead before 1699. Work known – a watch recorded.

QUELCH, Joseph   Oxford
Watchmaker recorded there 1684. Perhaps a clerical slip for John?

QUELCH, Martin   Oxford
Prob. son of Richard senior and apr. to him Feb 1650, then transferred Sep 1652 to Richard junior.

QUELCH, Richard senior   Oxford
Son of Richard Quelch of Wallingford, Berkshire. Apr. Aug 1608 to Triumph de St. Paule. Freed Sep 1616. Took as apr. 1650 **Martin**

Quelch (passed on Richard's death to Richard junior, ie Sep 1652); was succeeded by sons John, Martin and Richard. Work known – a watch.

QUELCH, Richard junior   **Oxford**
Son of Richard senior to whom apr. Freed Nov 1652. Believed died c. 1667. Took as aprs.: 1652 brother **Martin Quelch;** 1652 brother **John Quelch;** 1657 **Thomas Creed;** 1663 **James Browne;** 1667 **William Fowler.**

QUESNAY, Vincent   **London**
At Rouen 1524, Hampton Court 1532. Made clock(s) for Henry VIII.

R

R, W. place not known
Monogram WR recorded with date 1697. No other details.

RADCLIFFE, Charles Liverpool
Watchmaker recorded by Baillie as early as 1677. Children b. there 1693-99. He died 1700.

RADERIFF (or Rederiffe?) London
This name engraved inside Henry Elliot of London movement. Maybe name of journeyman or could be intended as the old name for Rotherhithe (Redriffe).

RADFORD, Gilbert Carlisle (Cumberland)
Did minor repairs to cathedral clock 1678-96.

RAFE, Thomas place not known
Lantern clock recorded c. 1661.

RAINES, William (also Raynes) London/York
Apr. Nov 1653 to William Almond thro' Ralph Almond. Freed Jan 1660/61. Took as aprs.: Jan 1663/64 **Joseph Sumner;** Jan 1667/68 **William Beadle;** George Crouch from Edward Bayley – freed Jan 1668/69. Last recorded in London in 1672. Britten gives his address as Butcher Row, East Smithfield. Later worked in York where died 1694 in a fall from his horse when returning to his home at Gilling, nearby. Work known – longcase clock signed 'William Rayns, York'; lantern clock signed 'Wm. Raynes in Yorke'.

RAINSFORD, Bernard (also Ranceford and Raynesford)   **London**
B.c. 1653, apr. Nov 1667 to Edward Clough, a freeman of the Loriners' Co., thro' C. Bonner till 1674. Freed Jul 1677. Took as aprs.: Dec 1677 **Robert Beale,** but in Nov 1680 he was allowed to take a new apr. as Beale had gone away, 'being afflicted with the King's Evil' and he took **Thomas Phillips** instead; May 1681 **John Allaway** – free May 1695. Paid quarterage till c. 1681, not later. Dead by 1697-98.

RAINSFORD, Francis (also Raynsford)   **London**
B.c. 1667, apr. Jul 1681 to Robert Gregory till 1688. Freed Apr 1689. Took as apr. Sep 1696 **Thomas Trevor.** Also bound an apr. for R. Blundell. Supposedly worked at Charing Cross. Paid quarterage till 1704 after which I have no record of him. Work known – table clock and a watch.

RAITT, Alexander   **London**
Recorded by Britten c.1685 – c.1710. I cannot trace him.

RAM, Hewett   **London**
B.c. 1677, apr. Jul 1691 to Thomas Hickson till 1698, but not freed.

RAMSAY, David   **Scotland/France/London**
B. in Scotland, some say Dundee, around 1585. Went to work in France. Appointed Clockmaker to James I in 1613 at a much higher salary than his predecessor and was given other sinecures. Made first Master of CC in 1631, but did not attend for first time till late 1634, being away 'in the country'. Scarcely ever attended any meetings except in 1652/53/54 period when, having suffered under the Commonwealth regime, he voted himself a grant from CC funds. Known to the CC then as Squire Ramsay. In 1622 he had as journeyman **William Pettit,** an alien and prob. French, working at Tothill Street, Westminster. In 1653 Ramsay lived in Holborn within two doors of the 'Wounded Hart'. He died in 1660, leaving a widow, Sarah. Work known – watches (in 1612 he was paid £61 for three watches for the Prince of Wales) and a table clock in the French manner. Signed work 'David Ramsay Scotus me fecit'. One watch case is signed 'De Heck'. A very enigmatic figure. For further details see my books *Complete British Clocks* and *Country Clocks*.

RAMSAY, John   **Dundee**
Son of Patrick, working early 17th century. In 1646 he was old and no longer able to care for the church clock.

RAMSAY, John **London**
Free in CC. Apr. 1637 but not heard of again thereafter. Work known –
two watches, signed 'John Ramsay, Londres' and 'John Ramsay fecit'.

RAMSAY, Patrick **Dundee**
Smith and gunmaker. Kept church clock 1588-1612.

RAMSAY, Silvester **Dundee**
Son of Patrick. Kept town clock 1637.

RAMSDEN, John **London**
B.c. 1641, apr. Nov 1654 to Thomas Loomes till 1662, but not freed.

RAMSDEN, Thomas **London**
Free Brother in CC Oct 1647.

RANDALL (see also Randell)

RANDALL, Christopher **Taunton (Somerset)**
Watchmaker, dying there 1666.

RANDALL, Maris (prob. Morris) **London**
B.c. 1666, apr. Jul 1680 to John Dearmer thro' S. Davis senior till 1687,
but not freed.

RANDELL, Richard **London**
B.c. 1651, apr. Jun 1665 to Francis Bicknell till 1672, but not freed.

RANDELL, Timothy **London**
B.c. 1669, apr. Dec 1683 to Henry Evans thro' F. Hill till 1690, but not
freed.

RANDELL, William **Ladock (Cornwall)**
Watchmaker, died there 1647.

RANDOLPH, Henry (Randall in error) **London**
Apr. Aug 1660 to Mr. Dob (William Dobbe), but not freed.

RANEAGE, Isaac **London**
Free Brother in CC Jan 1635/36. Not heard of again.

RANKLYN, Thomas (also Ranckle and Franklin)   **Oxford**
Locksmith and turret clockmaker. Apr. to John Winckle, smith. Freed Aug 1604. Took as aprs.: c. 1605 **Richard Carter;** c. 1611 **Richard Bradford;** c. 1650 **John Shewell.** Worked on turret clocks, locks and armour. Died 1658.

RANSOM, Edward   **London**
Died 1612 according to Baillie. I don't know him.

RANT, John   **London**
B.c. 1662, apr. Jul 1676 to William Cattell till 1683. Freed Sep 1687. Took as aprs.: Jan 1692/93 **George Evans;** Jan 1697/98 **Thomas Riley** (son of Daniel Riley of London) as apr. for Jonathan Rant; Aug 1700 **Erasmus Micklewright** (son of Erasmus Micklewright clockmaker of London) – free Jan 1708/09. Paid quarterage till 1700 only.

RANT, Jonathan   **London**
B.c. 1666, apr. May 1680 to Francis Munden till 1687. Freed Sep 1687. Took as aprs.: Oct 1691 **Thomas Robinson** – free Jul 1703; Mar 1694/95 **Speed Wilkins** – free Sep 1704; Jan 1697-98 **Thomas Riley** (son of Daniel Riley) thro' John Rant – free Sep 1705; Nov 1699 **William Wareham** (son of John Wareham of Stepney); Jul 1713 **Robert Harward.** Work known – bracket clocks.

RAWFINGER, John   **London**
Alien at 'Detford' in 1622.

RAXHALL, Christopher   **London**
B.c. 1643, apr. Oct 1657 to James Seaborne till 1664, but not freed.

RAY, Daniel   **Sudbury (Suffolk)**
B.c. 1666, apr. as locksmith 1681. Married c. 1698 Mary X. Son, Daniel, b. 1701. Will dated 1723, left tools to son, Daniel.

RAYE, John (also Rayer/Reyer)   **Oxford**
Smith who worked on turret clocks. Free 1620. In 1640 made turret clock for £22. Working till 1648.

RAYMONT, John   **London**
In 1622 was an alien working 'in the country', ie outside London.

RAYNER, Dove London
B.c. 1679, apr. May 1693 to Thomas Darlow thro' R. Williamson till 1700. Freed Jul 1701. I have no record of him after this, but Baillie records him at Little Old Bailey till 1765.

RAYNER, John London
B.c. 1673, apr. Mar 1687/88 to John Sudbury till 1694. Freed Dec 1697. Took as aprs.: Dec 1697 **John Mallowes;** Dec 1702 **Jonas Blake** (son of John Blake, Citizen and Clothworker of London); May 1708 **John Toleson** – free May 1715; Jul 1711 **John Cotton.** I have no record of him after 1711, but Baillie records him till 1727. Work known – watches recorded.

RAYNER, Stephen London
In Mar 1687/88 he was already the unapproved apr. of John Sudbury, but he now promised to take up CC Brotherhood in due course. Became Brother in CC as watchmaker May 1691. Took as aprs.: May 1691 **John Baldwin;** Nov 1696 **Edward Paul.** Working till 1700 at least, supposedly at Ye Dial, Bishopsgate Within. Work known – watches and clocks.

RAYNOLDS, Albon London
B.c. 1656, apr. Apr 1670 to John Wise till 1677, but not freed.

RAYNS (see Rains)

READ, Jon (but see Reynolds, Jon?) London
In 1584 a highly-skilled worker in the making of rulers, compasses, etc.

READ, Thomas (also Reead) London
Recorded by Baillie as 1632, but I do not know him. See Recas, also Thomas Reeve.

RECAS, Thomas London
In CC 1632, but see also Thomas Reeve and Read above.

REEVE, Henry London
Apr. Oct 1658 to Benjamin Hill, passed over to William Comfort. Freed Mar 1682-83. Summoned to CC court for infringements 1680 and 1681 (prob. for not having taken up his freedom). Took as aprs.: Mar 1682/83 **Thomas Maylard** – free Sep 1698; Mar 1686/87 **John Aldred.** Received CC charity in 1711, prob. died soon after.

REEVE, Roger   **London**
Apr. Jun 1650 to his father, Thomas Reeve, thro' R. Masterson, but not
freed.

REEVE, Thomas   **Harlestone**
Recorded by Britten as 1660. Maybe the Londoner below?

REEVE, Thomas   **London**
Working by 1630, a subscriber to incorporation of CC. Became Assistant
1646 but was excused Wardenship May 1648 on account of his
'weakness'. Took as aprs.: Aug 1632 **Daniel Fletcher** – free Sep 1646;
Mar 1638/39 **William Godbed** thro' R. Masterson – free Aug 1646; Jan
1646 **Richard Pierce** thro' T. Alcock – free Jul 1657; Jun 1650 his son,
Roger Reeve, thro' R. Masterson; Sep 1656 his son, **Thomas Reeve.**
Supposedly worked in Popes Head Alley. Work known – watches.

REEVE, Thomas   **London**
Son of Thomas senior, apr. Sep 1656 to his father, but not freed.

REEVE, William   **Stonham (Suffolk)**
B. 1642 at Mellis. A watchmaker who died in 1714, believed a bachelor
who lived with his brother at the Magpie Inn. Work known – none, but
some survive by his nephew, Samuel Reeve, in the early 18th century.

REEVES, Robert (also Reaves)   **York**
Watchmaker, b. 1636, free 1660. Married 1666 Elizabeth Adamson.
Three children b. 1666/72 of which only the last, a daughter, survived.

REGARD, Remond (Raymond)   **London**
A clockmaker. Free Brother in CC Apr 1677. Was a Huguenot, became
denizened 1682. In Jul 1692 he failed to appear when called to be Steward
being 'sick in the country'. In 1692 he advertised for return of a lost
watch by William Brafield to be returned to him at 'the upper end of
Russell Street, nr. Drury Lane'. Still alive in 1697, but not heard of
thereafter.

REISBYE (see Risby)

REMCHING, Edward   **London**
B.c. 1645, apr. Sep 1659 to Robert Robinson till 1666, but not freed.

RENNEZ, Nowell   **London(?)**
Recorded by Baillie as late 16th century. I do not know him.

RENOU/RENON, Jacob   **London**
In Oct 1655 was sanctioned by CC to work for Jeremy Gregory as
journeyman during his time in England. Obviously a Frenchman. Later
Renous were goldsmiths in London.

REVELL, Samuel   **London**
B.c. 1651, apr. Sep 1664 to Thomas Loomes till 1672, but not freed.

REYNOLDS (see also Raynolds)

REYNOLDS, George   **York**
Watchmaker, freed 1641. Died 1680.

REYNOLDS, Jon   **London**
Maker of rulers, compasses, etc. 1584.

REYNOLDS, Joseph   **London**
B.c. 1669, apr. Sep 1683 to Richard Whitehead till 1690. Freed Apr
1691. Paid quarterage till c. 1693 only.

RHETORICK, Walter   **London**
B.c. 1637, apr. Jul 1651 to David Moody till 1658, but not freed.

RICAUT, Isaac (also Reco)   **London**
Paid CC subscription 1635. (In 1632 Mr. Reco had been forbidden to
work any longer in the trade – prob. the same man who was banned until
he joined the Co.)

RICCARD, Richard (see Ricord)

RICHARDS, Henry   **London**
B.c. 1674, apr. Oct 1688 to Joseph Armiger till 1695. Freed Sep 1699,
(having been transferred to George Cawdron?). Took as apr. May 1703
James Emerson (son of Peter Emerson late of Diddington,
Huntingdonshire, clerk, deceased).

RICHARDS, John   **London**
B.c. 1640, apr. Sep 1654 to William Pettit thro' J. Bayley till 1661, but
not freed. In 1662 described as 'an outlier'.

RICHARDS, Luke   **London**
In 1633 had not yet served his full seven years and was allowed more
time. Freed Dec 1646. Took as apr. Mar 1649 **John Somillier**. In 1662
worked in Whitefriars.

RICHARDS, Peter (signed Pierre)   **London**
A watchmaker, French, made free Brother in CC Sep 1679.

RICHARDS, Richard (see Ricord, Richard)

RICHARDS, Robert   **London**
B.c. 1675, apr. Sep 1691 to Isaac Lowndes thro' W. Speakman till 1698,
but not freed.

RICHARDSON, Hugh   **London**
B.c. 1677, apr. Sep 1691 to Henry Bradley till 1698, but not freed.

RICHARDSON, John   **Belfast**
Watchmaker there 1692.

RICHARDSON, John   **Bridlington (Yorkshire)**
A Quaker clockmaker from South Cave, 1690.

RICHARDSON, John   **Warwick**
Blacksmith who maintained clock and bells of St. Nicholas 1666-98.

RICHARDSON, Moses   **Belfast**
Watchmaker 'At ye sign of ye clock' in Skipper Street 1678-80. Maybe
later at Londonderry c. 1700. Work known – watches.

RICHARDSON, Richard   **London**
B.c. 1653, apr. Oct 1667 to Richard Ames till 1674. Freed Sep 1675.

RICHARDSON, Richard   **London**
B.c. 1664, apr. Nov 1677 to John Bellard thro' S. Davis senior till 1685,
but not freed.

RICHARDSON, William　　　　　　　　　　**London**
B.c. 1633, apr. Dec 1647 to James Starnell thro' R. Masterson till 1654, but not freed.

RICHE, Jean　　　　　　　　　　**London**
Denizen clockmaker 1544.

RICORD, John (also Rickard, Record, etc.)　　　**London**
B.c. 1635, apr. Jun 1649 to William Lavrespierre thro' T. Wolverston till 1656. Freed Mar 1657/58.

RICORD, Richard　　　　　　　　　　**London**
Name much misspelt as eg Rickard, Richards, Record, Ric(c)ard, etc. Free Brother in CC May 1649. Aug 1652 a Free Clockmaker of the City of London by redemption. In 1656 joined the rebels against the CC administration. Took as aprs.: May 1649 **Benjamin Wolverston** thro' J. Seaborne – free Mar 1656; Jan 1652 **Robert Ford; John Parker** – free Mar 1674/75; Jul 1664 **Andrew Wall.** Also bound an apr. for Paul Lowell senior and one for William Lavrespierre. Work known – watch signed 'Richard Riccorde, Londini'.

RIDER, Thomas　　　　　　　　　　**London**
B.c. 1677, apr. Sep 1691 to John Johnson till 1698. Free Sep 1698. Believed dead later same year, though Baillie records him till 1717.

RIGDALE, N.　　　　　　　　　　**London**
Watch recorded c. 1610.

RIDLEY, Josiah　　　　　　　　　　**London**
B.c. 1663, apr. May 1677 to John Clowes thro' S. Davis senior till 1684. Freed Jan 1685/86. Took as apr. Dec 1693 **Henry Palmer.** Still working 1697. Work known – longcase clock.

RIGHTON, Thomas　　　　　　　　　　**London**
Lantern clock recorded c. 1685 signed at Grays Inn Lane. I have no record of him. Maybe a misrendering of some other name?

RIGMAIDEN, Robert　　　　　　　　　　**Dublin**
Free goldsmith there 1686, died 1751. Took as apr. c. 1694 **George Pilkington.** Work known – watches.

RILEY (and other variants, see under Ryley).

RING, John London
B.c. 1672, apr. Jun 1686 to Nicholas Beck, passed on to Thomas Martin till 1693. Freed Jul 1693.

RIPLEY, John York
Free 1471.

RISBRIDGER, William Dorking (Surrey)
Lantern and longcase clocks c. 1700.

RISBROOKE, ---- Norwich
Watchmaker there in 1648 involved in Royalist riot.

RISBY, Anthony (also Reisbye) London
Watchmaker. Mentioned in 1617 will of Randolph Bull. Original petitioner for CC in 1622.

RITHE, John London
B.c. 1641, apr. Oct 1654 to Richard Scrivener thro' N. Coxeter till 1662, but not freed.

ROBBINS (see Robins)

ROBARTS (see Roberts)

ROBENE, John Peebles (Scotland)
Kept town clock 1632.

ROBERTS, Hugh London
Apr. Jun 1657 to Solomon Bouquet, passed over to David Bouquet. Freed Jun 1664. Took as apr. Jul 1665 **Alexander Sanders**. Also bound an apr. for Thomas East and one for James Jackson. Received CC charity from 1713 till 1716, when prob. died. Work known – watches.

ROBERTS. Richard London
B.c. 1642, apr. Aug 1656 to Elizabeth Fletcher till 1663, but not freed.

ROBERTS, William   **London**
Never admitted to CC but known to them. In Nov 1636 they warned him
not to practice the trade, not having served a seven year apr. He is
mentioned in minutes again in 1641 and in 1646. Prob. dead by 1662/63.
Work known – lantern clock dated 1637 and watch signed 'William
Roberts fecit'.

ROBERTS, William   **London**
B.c. 1678, apr. Oct 1692 to Mordecai Fox thro' William Clement till
1699, but not freed.

ROBERTSON, John   **Liverpool/Chester(?)**
Watchmaker with children b. there 1689/97. One of this name worked at
Chester c. 1712 as a watchmaker.

ROBIN/ROBYN, Walter   **Launceston (Cornwall)**
Clockmaker who worked on town clock 1460.

ROBINS, Fabian   **London**
No trace of him in CC records and I have no data on him. Work known –
several late 17th century longcase and bracket clocks signed eg 'Fab.
Robin Londini fecit' and 'Fabn. Robins, London'.

ROBINS, Josias (also Robbins)   place not known
Lantern clock late 17th century signed 'Josias Robbins fecit'.

ROBINSON, Daniel   **London**
B.c. 1667, apr. Dec 1681 to William Arthur till 1688, but not freed. Not
in any of the normal later records. Work known – longcase clocks and
ebonised bracket clock signed 'Daniel Robinson, London'.

ROBINSON, Francis   **London**
B.c. 1658, apr. Mar 1672/73 to Thomas Williamson. By Jun 1677 he had
been in trouble for misbehaving, but by Sep 1677 he was back with his
master, having been punished, though the master protested that he
wanted rid of him, he could get no other master to take him.

ROBINSON, Francis   **London**
B.c. 1671, apr. Oct 1685 to Henry Jones till 1692, but not freed till Apr
1707. Prob. worked purely for Jones in early life. Took as apr. Oct 1717
Thomas Morris. Made CC Assistant 1717. In 1748 he was a finisher in

the country, but this is the only information I have on him after 1720. Work known – bracket and longcase clocks, signed 'Francis Robinson in the Temple' or 'Francis Robinson, London'. Supposed worked early in his career at Inner Temple Lane.

ROBINSON, George   **London**
B.c. 1617, apr. Nov 1631 to Simon Hackett, goldsmith till 1638, but not freed.

ROBINSON, John   **London**
B.c. 1668, son of William Robinson, *qv*. Apr. Jan 1682-83 to his father till 1689, but not freed.

ROBINSON, Robert   **London**
B.c. 1631, apr. Aug 1645 to John Pennock thro' O. Durant till 1652. Freed Sep 1652. Supported CC during 1656 rebellion. In 1662 worked in Lothbury. Took as aprs.: Sep 1659 **Edmund Remching** (or **Benching**); Aug 1654 **William Sumner** – free Oct 1661; **John Higgs** – free Oct 1661; Oct 1662 **William Taylor**; Jan 1668/69 **Humphrey Clark** (from Peter Closon); **William Lucas** (from Reginald Stanton and passed on to Thomas Bagley – freed 1669. Also bound two aprs. for John Saville and one for Henry Ireland. Work known – lantern clocks, supposedly signed early 'in Red Cross Street, London' and later 'at the Style in Lothbury, London'.

ROBINSON, Thomas   **London**
B.c. 1677 apr. Oct 1691 to Jonathan Rant till 1698. Freed Jul 1703. Took an apr. in 1716 but name illegible.

ROBINSON, William   **London**
Apr. Jun 1655 to Henry Fetters thro' L. Wythe. Freed Oct 1667. Took as aprs.: Oct 1667 **Henry Bradley** (in Feb 1674/75 Robinson complained to CC that Bradley was working for Charles Gretton, although not a freeman) – freed Jun 1681; Jul 1672 **William Hobbs**; Jan 1670-71 **Henry Smith**; Aug 1674 **Robert Panton**; Sep 1681 **Edward Brooke**; Jan 1682-83 his son, **John Robinson**; Jul 1683 **William Copplestone**. In Jul 1682 he was chosen steward but was 'out of town', but later in Jul he was excused stewardship 'as he has not ten shillings to spare'. In Sep 1688 he was threatened with prosecution as he supported Henry Harper against the word of the Master, Thomas Taylor (for dispute see under Harper). He died in 1691 leaving a will, being a watchmaker in the parish of

St. Margaret's Westminster and leaving everything incl. his tools to his wife, Frances.

ROE, ----   **Goostrey (Cheshire)**
Paid for repairing church clock in 1658.

ROE, Joshua   **London**
B.c. 1673, apr. Aug 1687 to Edmund Appley thro' J. Bayley till 1694, but not freed.

ROGER, ----   **Barnstaple (Devon)**
Repaired Exeter cathedral clock 1424.

ROGER, William   **Liskeard (Cornwall)**
Repaired town clock 1650.

ROGERS, Charles   **London**
B.c. 1636, apr. Nov 1649 to William Almond thro' Ralph Almond till 1657. Freed Dec 1657. In 1662 worked in Blackfriars. Took as aprs.: Sep 1661 **Benjamin Heath**; Jul 1662 **Henry Atlee** – free Jul 1672; Mar 1665/66 **Charles Templer** – freed Mar 1672/73; Mar 1672/73 **John Frethy**; his son, **Charles Rogers** junior passed over Mar 1678/79 from William Cowper. Worked till late 1704 at least. Work known – longcase clocks, signed 'Charles Rogers Guildhall', 'Charles Rogers at Guild Hall' and 'Charles Rogers at Chareing Cross, Londini'.

ROGERS, Charles junior   **London**
Son of Charles Rogers senior, *qv*. Apr. Aug 1677 thro' S. Davis to William Cowper (a freeman of the Vintners' Co.) but passed over to his father Mar 1678/79. Not freed.

ROGERS, John   **Daventry (Northamptonshire)**
Working 1693.

ROGERS, William   **London**
Brother in CC Oct 1640. Took as aprs.: Aug 1650 **Edward Scott** thro' T. Claxton; Jul 1656 **Nicasius Russell** thro' J. Salmon – freed Jul 1663; **Gregory Dossett** – freed Apr 1662 (Dossett was apr. to Robert Grinkin and Rogers prob. took him after Grinkin's death in 1660); Aug 1647 **Thomas Madden**. Also took Oct 1655 **Abraham Vanacker** as journeyman for about four months at rate of five shillings a week. In 1662

he was working in Chancery Lane. In 1660 he was mentioned in Robert Grinkin's will as a very loving friend. In Aug 1662 he was appointed Beadle. In Feb 1665/66 the Beadle's place was vacant due to his death. His widow received a small charity from CC till 1667.

ROGERS, William   **London**
B.c. 1668, apr. Dec 1682 to Thomas Taylor of Holborn till 1689, but not freed.

ROLEWRIGHT, Thomas   **Oxford**
Apr. to Richard Cakebread of Oxford. Freed Jul 1584. A smith who repaired local turret clocks till about 1588.

ROLFE, Daniel (also Rofe and Roofe)   **London**
Free Brother in CC Feb 1676/77. Took as aprs.: Jul 1679 **James Thwing** thro' S. Davis – free Apr 1688; Apr 1685 **Benjamin How** thro' D. Stevens – free Sep 1691; Dec 1693 **Thomas Gatward** thro' E. Norris. (See also Rose.)

ROLFE, Samuel   **London**
Recorded by Baillie but error for Rosse, *qv*.

ROMIER, Isaac   **London**
A difficult name often miswritten as Romeau, Roumyeu, Roumier, Romer, etc. In 1622 was an alien journeyman with Cornelius Mellin in Blackfriars. Chosen CC steward 1641. Believed joined CC 1635.

ROMER, Isaac   **London**
Prob. a different man from above. Free Brother in CC 1661. Took as apr. Sep 1670 **Thomas How** thro' Solomon Bouquet, later How was passed over to N. Delander.

ROMETT (see Rumett)

ROMNEY, John   **London**
On 1697 roll but prob. clerical error for Joseph, *qv*.

ROMNEY, Joseph   **London**
Apr. Aug 1657 to Simon Bartram thro' L. Wythe. Freed Oct 1664.

ROOF(E), Daniel (see under Rolfe).

ROOKER, Richard (but see also under Booker)   **London**
B.c. 1671, apr. Jan 1685/86 to John Clowes thro' Thomas Wilson till 1692. Freed Apr 1694. Took as aprs.: Sep 1698 **John Harris;** Feb 1701/02 **Richard Crosse** (son of Richard Crosse of parish of St. Bartholomew the Great, London, weaver); Jan 1706/07 **Joseph Cooke** – free Jul 1715; Aug 1711 **John Langton;** Dec 1714 **Abner Elton;** Aug 1716 **Joseph Slack.** Still recorded at Chelsea in 1748 (at which time Richard Rooker junior was a grocer at Holborn Bridge).

ROOKES, Barlow   **London**
Name sometimes Roakes and was known as 'Barly'. Apr. Jan 1656/57 to Lionel Wythe – freed Apr 1665. Took as aprs.: Apr 1670 **Isaac Day** (who was rebound Aug 1675 to Ahasuerus Fromanteel junior); Jul 1673 **John Johnson** – free Aug 1680; Jul 1674 **John St. George;** Nov 1677 **Thomas Southworth.** In 1669 complained to CC about alien workers. In 1677 was fined for abuse of Master, Jeremy Gregory. Died after 1679 and before Aug 1680, leaving will, which describes him as a clockmaker of Fore Street in St. Giles Cripplegate, and owning 24 acres of land in Lambeth. He left a son, Robert, and widow, Mary, 'now pregnant'.

ROOKESBY, Robert   **London**
Apparently not a member of CC but his apr., **George Etherington,** was made a Free Brother in CC Dec 1684. Prob. some connection with York where there were clockmakers named both Rooksby and Etherington a little later.

ROOKSBY, John (sometimes Rousby)   **York/Hull**
Watchmaker, son of Miles Rooksby, baker. Free at York 1647. A John Rousby of York, watchmaker, had a son, James, freed there 1683. Work known – clock recorded signed 'J. Rooksby in Yorke' c. 1690. *London Gazette* of 1691 reports a watch stolen, made by Rooksby of Hull.

ROPER, ----   **London**
Paid search fee 1671 – prob. a measure-seller.

ROSE, Christopher   **London**
B.c. 1649, apr. Oct 1663 to Thomas Claxton till 1670, but not freed.

ROSE, Daniel   **London**
In Apr 1695 he was guilty of binding an apr. privately. Agreed to bring him in to CC to bind. This is prob. a slip for Daniel Rolfe, *qv.*

ROSE, Michael   **London**
Apr. Oct 1663 to Thomas Claxton. Freed Jun 1676. Took as apr. Jun 1676 **James Morell**. Work known – longcase clocks, one signed 'Rose and Son'.

ROSSE, Daniel (error for Rolfe, *qv*).

ROSSE, James   **Exeter**
Watchmaker 1687-1707.

ROSSE, Samuel   **London**
B.c. 1651, apr. Aug 1664 to Thomas Taylor till 1672. Freed Sep 1672. Took as aprs.: Jul 1676 **Thomas Chamberlain** (later passed to Henry Harper); Sep 1682 **John Marshall** (later passed to D. Quare); Sep 1687 **William Dighton**. In 1688 the CC searched his watchmaker's shop and confiscated certain inadequate movements, at which time his wife not only refused to pay the search fee but 'gave them very evil words' and 'he was to be prosecuted'. Later the movements were returned to him with the deficient parts removed. Paid quarterage till c. 1693, when believed died.

ROSSE, William   **London**
B.c. 1670, apr. May 1683 to Thomas Wheeler till 1691, but not freed.

ROTHERODD, Benjamin   **place not known**
17th century watch recorded, but I do not know him.

ROTH(E)R(H)AM, Thomas   **Lewes (Sussex)**
Clock recorded pre-1684. I have no data but see next entry.

ROTHERHAM, Thomas   **London**
Apr. Jul 1654 to Simon Hacket thro' J. Bayes. Freed Jan 1662/63. Took as apr. Jul 1666 **John Hodson**.

ROTHWOOD, Robert   **London**
Baillie records two such but prob. only one of this name. Made a Brother in CC 1632. Made full freeman 1646. Took as apr. Aug 1648 (from R. Morgan) **Giles Hyett**.

ROUDEN (see under Rowden).

ROUMIEU is spelt a number of ways, eg Roumyre, Roumyeu, Roumjeu, and even Romier, etc.

ROUMIEU, Adam   **London**
Prob. French and believed to have been a watch casemaker. In Apr 1657 the CC ordered him to find a master to work with or leave the country. Not heard of again till Nov 1687 when he promised to join the CC at next court. Became a Free Brother in CC Jan 1687/88 as a goldsmith and watchmaker (which prob. means he was in the Goldsmiths' Co.). Listed in 1697 roll, but marked dead by 1698.

ROUMIEU, Adam (II)   **London**
Made Free Brother in CC Jan 1695/96. Took as aprs.: Apr 1711 **John Roumieu** – free Oct 1720; Jan 1719/20 his son, **Adam Roumieu.** I have no data on him after 1720.

ROUMIEU, James   **London**
Watchmaker, bachelor, aged 24, of St. Anne's Blackfriars in Oct 1692 when he married at the French Church to Magdalen Marchant of St. Martins in the Fields, spinster, aged 20. In Oct 1692 became a Brother in CC being a watchmaker and goldsmith and naturalised. Took as aprs.: Apr 1700 **Lewis de Rumeau** (son of John de Rumeau of parish of St. Anne, Westminster, gent.); Dec 1702 **James Pitan,** a denizen, (son of Peter Pitan) – freed May 1711. I have no data on him after 1705.

ROUMIEU, Paul senior   **Edinburgh**
Supposed French, from Rouen where one of this name worked c. 1645-60. Jun 1677 presented a watch to Guild of Hammermen and was accepted as a freeman without being asked to make the customary lock too, which suggests he was already an accomplished watchmaker. Died Mar 1694, buried Greyfriars Churchyard. Took as apr. 1681 **Daniel Mavine.** Work known – three watches at least.

ROUMIEU, Paul junior   **Edinburgh**
Son of Paul Roumieu senior. Aug 1682 presented a watch and was allowed freedom of Guild of Hammermen. Took as aprs.: Aug 1694 **John Cousteill** – freed 1715; Apr 1695 **Jacques Thibou** as journeyman; Sep 1701 **John Frugard** as journeyman; 1700 **Emanuel Poarson** as apr.; 1704 **David Mackerson** – freed May 1711. Believed died 1711. Daughter, Anne, entered charitable home in 1712, both her parents being dead. Work known – one or two longcase clocks, one month going.

ROUSE, Robert London
B.c. 1669, apr. Jun 1683 to Charles Baxter till 1690, but not freed.

ROUS(S)EL(L) – see all variants under Russell.

ROUTH, Samuel London
Recorded by Baillie but error for Samuel Rosse, *qv*.

ROWDEN, John (also Rouden and Rawden) London
John Rouden was an invented name on a watch seized by CC from John Cotsworth in 1682, said to have been engraved by Francis Dinnis, who denied it. However in Jan 1683/84 **John Rowden** was bound apr. to Francis Dinnis till 1690. Freed Jan 1681/92. Still working in 1705, as he paid quarterage till at least then.

ROWE, Thomas London
B.c. 1677, apr. Jan 1691-92 to George Merttins till 1698. Freed Apr 1699. Paid quarterage till at least 1701.

ROWNTREE, Ralph (sometimes Rontree) York
B. 1673, married 1696 Catherine Bankes. Work known – at least two longcase clocks noted, signed 'R. Rowntree, Ebor'.

ROY, David London
Made Free Brother in CC Jul 1682, being a small clockmaker and a free denizen. Still working 1697, but died about 1698 or soon after.

ROYCROFT, Thomas London
B.c. 1667, apr. Sep 1681 to Cuthbert Lee, later passed over to (blank) Beck, then later again to Benjamin Harris till 1688. Freed Nov 1699. Took as aprs.: Jul 1701 his son, **Arthur Roycroft**; Mar 1709/10 **William Mollet**; Mar 1711/12 **Lancelot Bryan**; May 1713 **Thomas Parker**; Aug 1717 **Daniel Gosbel**; Feb 1718-19 **John Lewis**. I have no data after 1720. But see also Rycroft.

RUDKIN, Thomas London
B.c. 1659, apr. Aug 1673 to John Wright junior till 1680. Freed Apr 1683. Took as apr. (after he has taken his freedom of the city) Apr 1683 **Daniel Coverdall**. Paid no quarterage after c. 1683. One of this same name was later at Amsterdam.

RUMBALL, Bryan   **Newbury (Berkshire)**
Lantern clock recorded. Working 1645, died 1685.

RUMDUD/RINNDUD – error for Romieu, *qv*.

RUMMETT, William (sometimes Romett)   **London**
Son of John Rumett. Apr. Apr 1651 to William Partridge thro' John
Matchett, but not freed.

RUSTIN, Joseph   **Oxford**
Son of Henry Rustin of Laurence Hinksey, Berkshire. Apr. 1686 to John
Quelch of Oxford for seven years.

RUSSELL, including all variants and the Dutch version Rousel,
Roussel, etc., which was usually anglicised into Russell.

RUSSEL, Cornelius   **London/The Hague**
Believed b. London 1608. Watchmaker. Had son, John, b. 1633.

RUSSELL, Cornelius   **London**
B.c. 1672, son of Nicasius Russell, *qv*. Apr. Sep 1686 to Abraham Clyatt
till 1693, but not freed. In Jan 1701/02 he came to CC court with a gift of
£10 from estate of his late father for the poor of the Co. It seems odd that
he did not personally join the CC. Re-apr. 1689 Fishmongers' Co.

RUSSELL, John   **London/The Hague**
B. 1633, eldest son of Cornelius Russel, watchmaker, *qv*. In Oct 1655
was approved by CC to be journeyman to John Nicasius for one year.
Believed spent period 1655-57 in London. In Oct 1657 was in the Hague
(believed to be with John Fromanteel, *qv*). Never actually joined CC.

RUSSELL, John   **London**
In Apr 1682 CC gave him 10 shillings charity. It is not known who he was
unless same as the earlier John Russell above.

RUSSELL, Nicasius   **London**
Son of Cornelius Russell, *qv*. believed b. 1642 in The Hague. Apr. in CC
Jul 1656 to William Rogers thro' J. Sammon. Freed Jul 1663. Generally
known as Captain Russell. Clearly he was named after John Nicasius,
with whom the Russells had close ties. Took as aprs.: Aug 1666 **William
Minshull**; Sep 1670 **Henry Child** – free Jan 1677/78; **Prettyman**

Sergeant on death of Henry Child (1665) – freed 1671/72; Jul 1675 **Isaac Crooke;** Jul 1681 **John Bailey;** Nov 1700 **William Daynes** (son of William Daynes of London, weaver). Additionally he bound several aprs. for other masters, which were Anthony Kemps, R. Jarret, R. Blundell, S. Bouquet, B. Bell, J. Graves, H. Maysmor, T. Taylor, J. Harris (of Blacksmiths). Believed member of Weavers' Co. Had son, Cornelius, *qv.* Was CC Assistant from 1676, Warden from 1688, Master 1692, attended regularly till late 1701. Dead by Jan 1701/02. Believed married 1664 Anne Manning, and had children: 1665 Richard; 1672 Cornelius; 1674 Samuel, and three girls. Work known – watches.

RUSSELL, Nicholas   St. Neot (Cornwall)
Came to repair church clock 1609-16.

RUSSELL, Thomas   London/Wootton (Bedfordshire)
B.c. 1670, son of John Russell, apr. 1684 in Cooks' Co. to William Whittingham whose 'cousin' he was. Free 1691. Not in CC. Left London for Wootton c. 1700. Clockmaker and bellfounder. Died 1745.

RYCROFT, Thomas   London(?)
Lost watch recorded in *London Gazette* 1693 – see Roycroft.

RYLEY, incl. Riley, Rilley, etc.

RYLEY, George   London
Freeman of the Lorimers' Co. Had taken **Jeffrey Stanes** as apr. for S. Chapman – freed Jul 1686.

RYLEY, Laurence   London
B.c. 1648, apr. Jul 1662 to (blank).

S

SACHEVERELL, Ben Assir (signed thus)   **London**
B.c. 1666, apr. May 1680 to William Thorowgood then passed over to
Thomas Tompion till 1687. Freed Sep 1687. Paid quarterage till c. 1688.

SADLER, Hatton   **London**
B.c. 1663, apr. Jun 1676 to Thomas Williamson till 1684, but not freed.

SADLE(I)R, Samuel   **London**
B.c. 1673, apr. Apr 1687 to Samuel Vernon till 1694. Freed Sep 1694.
Took as aprs.: Sep 1696 **Thomas Aunger;** Aug 1698 **John Maberley** –
free Feb 1705/06; **William Osborne** (from S. Vernon) – free Sep 1700;
Jul 1701 **John Thomas** alias **Trethwell** (son of Abiel Thomas alias
Trethwell late of Yelvestoft, Northamptonshire, clerk, deceased); Jun
1708 **William Lutman** – free Nov 1720; Nov 1709 **Henry Horne** – free
Feb 1718-19; Dec 1720 **Edmond Butterfield**. Became CC Assistant in
1720 after which I have no data on him. Work known – longcase clocks.

SAER, Joseph   **London**
Made Free Brother in CC as a clockmaker Apr 1687. Paid quarterage till
at least 1704. Work known – several longcase clocks signed 'Joseph Saer,
London' and 'Jos. Saer Perpoole Lane, London'.

SAINSBURY, Robert   **Bristol**
Apr. to John London, gunsmith, Jul 1675. Free Nov 1682.

ST. GEORGE, John   **London**
B.c. 1660, apr. Jul 1674 to Barlow Rookes till 1681, but not freed.

ST. PAUL, John de   **Oxford**
Also known as John the Frenchman. Married 1576 Elizabeth Smith, who
died 1589. Married 2nd Nov 1590 Alice Jones. Died 1596. Worked on
several local turret clocks.

ST. PAUL, Richard de   **Oxford**
Apr. to his father, Triumph de St. Paul, in 1639, but not freed.

ST. PAUL, Triumph de   **Oxford**
Son of John, *qv.* Free 1601. Married pre-1610 Ursula Ewen, who died
1643. Had as aprs.: 1608 **Richard Quelch**; 1639 his son, **Richard de St.
Paul.** Still alive 1651. Worked on local turret clocks.

SALE, George   **Salford Priors (Warwickshire)**
Repaired church clock 1696. Blacksmith?

SALE, Henry   **Salford Priors (Warwickshire)**
Worked on church clock 1695-96. Blacksmith?

SALE, John   **Dublin**
Free Goldsmith and clockmaker there 1700. Died 1739. Work known –
longcase clock.

SALMON, John   **Bristol**
Longcase clock said to be c. 1700 (but a later man of this name worked
there 1732-69?).

SA(L)MON, John (and Sammon)   **London**
B.c. 1634, apr. Mar 1648 to Nicholas Tomlins, then passed to George
Poole, then back to Tomlins again till 1655. Freed May 1654. (This is
very odd because Poole himself was not freed till May 1654). Took as
aprs.: Apr 1655 **Zachariah Hardstaff**; Aug 1655 **Nathaniel Lovell**; Dec
1655 **Sutton Isaac** (from T. Knifton) – free Jan 1662/63; Jul 1656 bound
an apr. for William Rogers.

SALTER, Mr.   **London**
In 1679/80 the CC search party was to meet at his house 'at the sign of the
goat nr. Fleet Bridge'. May be a maker?

SAMBROOK, John (sometimes Sanbrook)   **London**
B.c. 1655, apr. thro' T. Claxton Jul 1668 to William Elmes, mat. inst.
maker and freeman of the Woodmongers till 1676. Freed Sep 1680.

SAMMON, William   **London**
This is almost certainly a clerical error for John Salmon, or perhaps for
William Seaman. Took as apr. Feb 1660 **Francis Ireland** for T. Knifton
– freed Jul 1668.

SAMPSON, Mr.   **London**
In 1622 had alien David Bouquet (Bowkett) and two aprs. at his house in
Blackfriars.

SAMPSON, Mr.   **Warwickshire**
Prob. from Stratford, a clocksmith who repaired St. Nicholas church
clock 1590-91.

SAMPSON, William (also Sansom)   **Yatton (Somerset)**
Believed working 1536-66. Made turret clock there 1566.

SAMPSON, William   **Chester**
Admitted a free clockmaker there Jan 1584-85 in return for making a
clock with chimes and a dial for St. Peter's church. Daughter, Ales,
buried at St. Oswalds 1585.

SAMUELL, John   **London**
On CC list of 1662, but apparently not a member. But see Samwell.

SAMWELL, John   place not known
Lantern clock recorded dated 1665. Prob. same man as above.

SANDE, Thomas   place not known
Watch recorded of c. 1620. I do not know him, but see Land.

SANDERS (see Saunders).

SANDIS/SANDYS, William   **London**
B.c 1645, apr. Jul 1659 to Robert Grinkin till 1666, but not freed.

SANDRIN, Daniel   **London**
French by birth, an engraver. Made Free Brother in CC Apr 1692.
Working till at least 1697.

SANDS, John   **London**
B.c. 1655, apr. Jun 1668 to Isaac Puzy till 1676, but not freed.

SANTON, ----   **London**
Late 17th century winged lantern clock signed 'Santon, Londini'. I
cannot trace this maker. *cf* Stanton?

SA(U)NDERS, Alexander   **London**
B.c. 1651, apr. Jul 1665 to Hugh Roberts till 1672, but not freed.

SA(U)NDERS, Charles   **London**
B.c. 1658, apr. Mar 1672 to Isaac Carver, mat. inst. maker, thro'
H. Wynne till 1679, but not freed.

SA(U)NDERS, Daniel   **London**
Petitioner of 1622. Admitted to CC Oct 1632.

SAUNDERS, Richard   **Oxford**
Son of Ralph Saunders. Apr. Dec 1674 to Michael Bird till 1681, but not
freed.

SAUNDERS, Robert   **London**
B.c. 1661, apr. May 1675 to Robert Halstead till 1682, but not freed.

SAVAGE – for the Exeter Savages see Ponsford's *Time in Exeter*.

SAVAGE, Abraham   **London/Exeter**
Said to be son of Peter Savage. B.c. 1635, apr. May 1648 to Henry Child
thro' T. Alcock till 1656, but not freed. At St. Stephen's parish, Exeter
by 1660 and in St. Mary's parish 1670.

SAVAGE, John I   **Exeter**
Free there 1609. Died 1627. Made and serviced local turret clocks. Left
sons, Thomas and Peter, *qv*.

SAVAGE, John II   **Exeter**
Free 1658, the son of Peter Savage, *qv*. In St. Stephen's parish 1660, then
St. Lawrence parish 1671.

SAVAGE, John   **London**
Said to be son of John I of Exeter (but without evidence) and to have been
apr. in 1613 in Blacksmiths' Co., but I have no facts on him.

SAVAGE, Peter   **Exeter**
Free there 1628, succ. his father, John I, *qv*. Died 1657.

SAVAGE, Thomas I   **Exeter**
Son of John Savage I, whom he succ. in 1628. Married 1640. Died 1679.

SAVAGE, Thomas II   **London/Exeter**
B.c. 1645, son of Thomas Savage I. Apr. in London Mar 1659/60 to
Joseph Quash till 1666, but not freed there. Back in Exeter by 1672. Put
in prison there 1692. Dead by 1739 when his son, Francis, was apr. in
London.

SAVAGE, Thomas   **Warwick**
Repaired St. Nicholas clock 1685-1703. Blacksmith?

SAVAGE, William   **Warwick**
Repaired St. Nicholas clock 1622-30. Blacksmith?

SAVERY, Andrew   **London**
B.c. 1654, apr. Jul 1669 to Thomas Parker till 1676. Freed Sep 1676.
Took as apr. Sep 1681 **Peter Walter**. Still alive 1697 but believed died
soon after. Work known – lantern, longcase and bracket clocks.

SAVILLE, John senior   **London**
Free Brother in CC Jan 1653-54. Took as aprs.: Aug 1654 **John Fletcher**
thro' H. Cooper, later passed to R. Robinson; Jan 1659/60 **Roger
Nichol(a)s** thro' R. Robinson ('his other man being dead') – freed Jan
1667/68 having been passed on to R. Robinson; Jun 1662 **Francis
Munden** thro' T. Claxton – freed Jan 1670/71; Jul 1671 his son, **John
Saville** thro' L. Wythe – freed Aug 1678; Dec 1671 **John Ashton** thro'
L. Wythe; Mar 1675/76 **William Jeneway** thro' N. Coxeter; Sep 1678
bound an apr. for his son, John. He was a member of the Vintners' Co.
Became CC Assistant from 1674, but did not attend after 1678 and in

1679 was excused wardenship. Prob. died soon after. Work known – watches on record, but hard to say whether by John senior or junior.

SAVILLE, John junior   **London**
B.c. 1657, apr. Jul 1671 thro' L. Wythe to his father, John Saville senior till 1678. Freed Aug 1678. Took as aprs.: Sep 1678 thro' his father took **James Tomes;** Nov 1683 **John Ellwood** – free Oct 1702. In Jan 1683/84 CC gave him a charity payment of £1 but was to have no more 'being a prisoner in Ludgate'. In fact in Apr 1685 he got another five shillings. In Jul 1690 he 'had absented', leaving his apr. **Richard Newton,** taken in Sep 1684 thro' John Thompson of the Drapers' Co., 'Newton now to be passed over to C. Lee'. Work known – difficult to be sure whether by the son or the father, but a lantern clock is known and longcase clocks, signed 'John Saville, London' and 'John Savile Cheap Side'.

SAVILLE, William   **London**
B.c. 1673, apr. Mar 1686/87 to James Wolverston, an engraver, till 1694, but not freed.

SAY, Nehemiah   **London**
Apr. May 1648 to Henry Child thro' B. Hill (or thro' T. Alcock). Freed Sep 1656.

SAY, Richard   **London**
B.c. 1674, apr. May 1688 to John Johnson till 1695, but not freed.

SCARDEVILLE, John   **London**
B.c. 1649, apr. Oct 1663 to Gregory Dorsett till 1670, but not freed.

SCARESBRICK, James   **Liverpool**
Clockmaker, married 1663 Anne Hayes.

SCATLISS, Simon   **London**
B.c. 1669, apr. Sep 1683 to Walter Henshaw till 1690, but not freed.

Sch – for all names beginning Sch see also under Sh.

SCHREBBYS, Nicholas   **Walberswick (Suffolk)**
Repaired church clock 1499.

SCHUTE, Jasper (see Shutt).

SCOBELL, John Bodmin (Cornwall)
Repaired town clock 1645-46.

SCOLES, Thomas London
Alias of Thomas Stones, *qv.*

SCOTT, Edward London
B.c. 1636, apr. Aug 1650 to William Rogers thro' T. Claxton till 1657,
but not freed.

SCOTT, Edward London
Baillie records one as dying 1654, which may be same man as above, but I
cannot confirm this.

SCOTT, Joshua London
B.c. 1660, apr. Nov 1674 to Cornelius Harbert till 1681, but not freed. In
Nov 1699, then being of St. Bottolph's parish Aldgate, he had his son,
Caleb Scott, bound apr. to Samuel Mather (but Britten records this son,
Caleb, as being bound apr. in the Cutlers' Co. in 1705 to E. How, cutler).

SCOTT, Simon London
B.c. 1634, apr. Oct 1647 to William Comfort thro' L. Wythe till 1655,
but not freed.

SCRIVENER, Richard London
Brother in CC Jan 1639/40. Took as aprs.: Sep 1646 **John Palfrey** thro'
T. Alcock – freed Nov 1654; Sep 1652 **John Thorowgood** thro' W. Petty
– free Jan 1660/61; Oct 1654 **John Rithe** thro' N. Coxeter; Jul 1659
Henry Perse; Oct 1662 **John Gosse** thro' T. Taylor; Aug 1667 **Henry
Adeane** – free Sep 1675. In 1662 he worked in Fleet Street as an
engraver. Made CC Assistant from 1660. Last attended 1668. Was dead
by 1675. Work known – a longcase clock is on record.

SEABORNE, James London
Apr. to Benjamin Hill, freed May 1649. Took as aprs.: Sep 1649
Thomas Hollis – free Sep 1656; Sep 1653 **Jeremy East;** Oct 1657
Christopher Raxhall. Also bound several aprs. for other masters, incl.
three for Robert Whitwell, one each for Francis Strelley, S. Horne,
R. Rickard. In 1662 worked in Chancery Lane. Evidently a poor man,
for was in arrears with quarterage in 1664, and in Jan 1674/75 was
runner-up for position of Beadle. In Sep 1689 CC gave him 10 shillings

'wherewith to buy him tooles', being 'a poore member', but he was not to become a regular pensioner.

SEABORNE, Richard   **London**
Supposedly working 1642.

SEABORNE, Thomas   **London**
Recorded by Baillie as 1649 CC, but this is an error for James, *qv.*

SEABORN, William   **London**
Apr. Jan 1651/52 to Samuel Horne thro' James Seaborne. Freed Mar 1659/60. Took as apr. Apr 1662 **Robert Brian.** In 1662 was a boxmaker in Chancery Lane. His will was dated 1667, proved Jan 1667-68, and describes him as a bachelor. He left to his 'very loving friend, Nathaniel Barrow my best black vest and the breeches that belong to them'. A witness was George Copping senior, clockmaker, *qv.* He mentions his brothers and sisters. Prob. aged about 32 at death.

SEAMAN, William   **London**
Apr. to Thomas Knifton. Freed Jan 1659/60.

SEAMER – sometimes appears as Seamore and even Semor.

SEAMER, Abel senior   **York**
Son of William Seamer, to whom he was apr. Freed 1649. Died 1682. Will mentions wife, Dorcas, daughters Hannah and Dorcas, son Abel still an apr. and son Joseph not yet old enough to be apr. Will dated 1677.

SEAMER, Abel junior   **York**
Still an apr. in 1677 when mentioned in will of father, Abel I. Free 1681. Married 1683 Ann Wood. Daughters b. 1684 and 1685. Son, Joseph, freed 1713, when Abel still thought to have been alive.

SEAMER, Joseph   **York**
Watchmaker, freed 1649. Son of William Seamer, watchmaker.

SEAMER, Peter   **York**
Watchmaker, apr. of William Seamer. Freed 1636.

SEAMER, William   **York**
Watchmaker, freed 1627. Still alive 1649. Work known – watch recorded signed 'W. Semor, York'.

SEARLE, William   **London**
B.c. 1659, apr. Sep 1673 to John Pennock thro' N. Coxeter till 1680, but not freed.

SEDDON, James   **London**
Apr. Jan 1655-56 to Isaac Plovier (thro' J. Quash?). Freed Jan 1662/63.

SEDDON, Nathaniel   **London**
Free Brother in CC as watchmaker Jan 1691/92. Still working 1705 (Baillie says died 1739). Work known – lantern and bracket clocks and watches, signed 'Nathaniel Seddon at St. James's, London', but also believed signed his earlier work at Pall Mall. Till 1720 at least he had no dealings with CC and not a single apr. thro' them.

SEDGWICK, Samuel   **London**
B.c. 1679, apr. Feb 1692/93 to Thomas Beasley till 1700, but not freed.

SEDLEY, John (sometimes Sidley)   **London**
B.c. 1672, apr. Oct 1686 to Cuthbert Lee thro' B. Marshall till 1693. Freed Sep 1701. Took as aprs.: Jan 1708/09 **James Wilson;** Nov 1712 **John Hills;** Mar 1714/15 **Samuel Davies;** Nov 1716 (illegible); Oct 1719 **Michael Taylor.** I have no data after 1720, but Baillie records him till 1732. Work known – longcase clock signed 'John Sedley, London'.

SEDWELL, Edward (sometimes Sidwell)   **London**
Apr. Nov 1656 to Thomas Loomes. Freed Oct 1664. Believed died 1665 (of plague?).

SEGNER, George   **London**
A jeweller and naturalised, made a Free Brother in CC Jan 1689-90 by order of the Lord Mayor and Court of Aldermen by redemption. (This can hardly be the same man as George Seignior, *qv.*) Took as aprs.: Jul 1692 **William Ford** – free Jan 1700/01; Jun 1694 **Henry Holt;** May 1698 **Charles Taylor;** Jul 1699 asked leave to bind an apr. in three months' time as his last two have gone and 'one just out of his time'; Jul 1700 **Lawrence Wilson** (son of Michael Wilson of Elland, Yorkshire, yeoman); Jun 1701 **Edward Sutton** (son of Thomas Sutton, Merchant

Taylor of London); Apr 1705 **Daniel Hilldon** (son of Edward Hilldon late of Astashed, Surrey, wheelwright, deceased). I have no record of him after 1705.

SE(I)GN(I)OR, George   **London**
Son of Robert, *qv*. Inherited father's estate 1687, but not known whether he was a clockmaker. Not in CC.

SEIGNIOUR, Robert (also Seignior, Senior, etc.)   **London**
Apr. (not thro' CC) to John Nicasius and freed in CC Apr 1667. Took as aprs.: Oct 1667 **Richard Wright**; Mar 1667-68 **Thomas Cruttenden** (then passed over to John Fromanteel?); May 1670 **Gabriel Stubbs** – freed Mar 1675; Feb 1670/71 **Samuel Marchant** (later passed over to E. Eyston); **Samuel Gascoigne** (from widow of Arthur Dove) – freed Apr 1676; Aug 1671 **Francis Draycott** (from S. Vernon) – free Jul 1678; Jul 1672 **Philip Corderoy** – free Jul 1679; Jun 1676 **William Punchard**; May 1679 **Robert Chipp**; Sep 1685 **Thomas Gifford** (passed over to R. Webster, prob. when Seigniour died) – freed Oct 1692.
Worked in Exchange Alley. Constantly at loggerheads with CC administration, as his master, Nicasius had always been. In Sep 1671 he was called to account for 'contemptible words' he had spoken to and about the master (T. Claxton) and in Oct 1671 was fined 20 shillings for calling them a 'company of cheating knaves'. In Jan 1673/74 Henry Jones complained that he had faked his name on a clock. In 1673/74 he requested excusal from office of Assistant of John North, who was sick. In Aug 1674 he was appointed King's Clock and Watchmaker 'without fee' until the death or surrender of office of Edward East, who in fact outlived him. In Apr 1682 he was due to be CC Assistant but was not called to hold office. In 1682 he got £20 for a clock for the Treasury Chambers. His will is dated 1685 and was proved in 1687. He left his estate to his son, George. Was to be buried in St. Peter's the Poor, Broad Street, nr. to the bodies of his wife and deceased son. Mentions his sister-in-law Johanna Nicasius, alias Jones (therefore prob. related to John Nicasius). His sister had married Robert Webster and had a son, George Webster, *qv*. His will was said to have been changed but as no new will could be found this one was proved. Seigniour is a very enigmatic maker with some elusive links with York (see under Cruttenden and Stubbs) and also with Eyston and North, *qv*. Work known – a few longcase clocks and bracket clocks and watches, signed 'Robert Seigniour, London'.

SELLER, John   **London**
B.c. 1631, son of Henry Seller of Wapping, cordwainer. Apr. in Merchant Taylors' Co. Sep 1644 to Edward Lowe of Whitechapel, cordwainer till 1652. Free Oct 1654, livery 1676. May have been a Quaker. In Feb 1667/68 made a Free Brother in CC as mat. inst. maker, though refused to take the oath. Was a mapmaker, cartographer, inst. maker and globe-seller. In Feb 1671/72 he had faulty rulers confiscated by CC from his Exchange Alley shop. In 1671 he was appointed Hydrographer to the King and granted a 30 year copyright for his sea-atlases and also protection against any foreign ones being imported during that time. He traded throughout his career at the Mariner's Compass in Hermitage Stairs in Wapping, but also during 1671-75 at Exchange Alley in Cornhill, 1678-81 at Pope's Head Alley in Cornhill, 1682-86 West Side of Royal Exchange, 1689-90 at Wapping only and with his son, John junior at West End of St. Pauls.

Took as apr. in CC Nov 1683 **John Hewson** – free Jul 1699. Was made CC Assistant from 1682 but seldom attended meetings. By 1693 his business had declined – CC records explain in Sep 1693 that he was excused duty as Warden 'being often, and now grievously, afflicted with the Gout'. In 1695 his 'indisposition of body and incapacity to serve' is again mentioned. In Oct 1696 he was appointed Master but was excused because of his infirmity. His will was dated and proved in 1697 and he left £500 to eldest son, John, one third of his goods to widow, Elizabeth, and two thirds to younger son, Jeremiah, who took over the Hermitage Stairs shop. Work known – many maps and charts.

SELLERS, William   **London**
B.c. 1668, apr. Feb 1682/83 to John Clowes thro' D. Stevens till 1689. Freed Nov 1691. Took as aprs.: Sep 1694 **George Cooke;** Sep 1700 **Edward Buckett** (son of Francis Buckett late of parish of (illegible – Jasawsby), Lincolnshire, innkeeper, deceased); Jul 1705 **Thomas Parker** (son of Jonathan Parker late of Utley(?), Somerset, stockingmaker, deceased); Jun 1708 **William Hickson;** May 1715 **John Curtis.** In Sep 1702 Mr. Jenkins appeared at CC on behalf of himself and Mr. Sellers and was given three guineas as encouragement towards their expenses in confiscating a (faulty) clock. I have no data on him after 1715, but Baillie records him as late as 1740. Work known – longcase clock, musical, signed 'William Sellers, Long Acre, London'.

SELWOOD, John   **London**
Made Free Brother in CC Jan 1640/41. Was the brother of William

Selwood of the Mermaid in Lothbury. Believed married 1642 Dorothy Brookes. Took as aprs.: May 1646 **Richard Beck** thro' T. Alcock; **Thomas Loomes** – freed Dec 1649; Dec 1647 **Simon Dudson** thro' T. Alcock. Beck and Dudson were passed over to Thomas Loomes when Selwood died in 1651, being at time of his death of the parish of All Hallows in the Wall. Was made CC Assistant in 1651, but then died. Work known – a lantern clock is recorded dated 1642, but prob. worked mainly for brother, William. For further details see my article on The Mermaid in Lothbury, *Clocks Magazine*, Dec 1979.

SELWOOD, William   London
Free Brother in CC Apr 1633, but prior to this he was a member of the Clothworkers' Co. in which he took as apr. in 1632 **Thomas Knifton.** Took as aprs. in CC: May 1640 **Tobias Davis** thro' T. Alcock – free May 1653; Feb 1640/41 **Samuel Davis** thro' R. Masterson – free Feb 1647; Feb 1647-48 **William Clark** thro' S. Davis – free Nov 1654; Apr 1650 **Edward Norris** thro' S. Davis – free Jan 1658. Prob. had other aprs. too as he was repeatedly warned to observe CC rules about binding them. His will was written and proved in April 1653 and suggests he was a bachelor, living in parish of St. Margaret Lothbury. Left most to his brother, Bartholomew Selwood, incl. property in Grantham Lane in Thames Street. His mother, Anne, was still alive. At time of death he had in his employ 'three men servants' Toby Davis, William Clarke and Edward Norris. Bequests to Thomas Smyth, engraver, and eldest daughter of Henry Ireland, *qv*. Work known – lantern clocks, only a few, signed 'at ye maremade in Lothbury' in various spellings. The Mermaid was later taken over by Thomas Loomes. See my article The Mermaid in Lothbury in *Clocks Magazine*, Dec 1979.

SEMOR, Robert   London
Watch recorded 1682. Prob. error for Robert Seigniour, *qv*.

SENDRE, Lawrence   London
Listed in 1662, but prob. error for Lawrence Sindry, *qv*.

SERES, Joseph   London
Frenchman, summoned to CC court Jul 1695 for transgressions, but dismissed.

SERGEANT, Prettyman (and Prittiman)   London
B.c. 1650, apr. Jan 1664/65 to Henry Child thro' N. Payne, but passed

over on Child's death by his widow to Nicasius Russell and freed Mar 1671/72. Took as aprs.: Aug 1678 **Charles Kemp** (later passed to C. Gretton); Sep 1701 **Edmund Greenway** (son of Richard Greenway, Citizen and Longbowstringmaker of London); Jun 1703 **Edward Golding** (son of Edward Golding of Malding, Essex, gent.).

SERMON, Joseph　　　　　　　　　　　　　　**London**
B.c. 1661, apr. Jan 1675/76 thro' S. Davis to Morgan Cave of the Blacksmiths' Co. till 1682, but not freed.

SEYNER, George　　　　　　　　　　　　　　**London**
Recorded by Baillie but prob. a misspelling of George Segner, *qv*.

SHACKLETON, John　　　　　　　**Heptonstall (Yorkshire)**
Clockmaker at Stoney Gate, Heptonstall. Married 1694 Judith Wadsworth, who died 1717. Later at Foulridge, Lancashire, where he died 1725, leaving inventory of his tools, etc.

SHALLER, Nicholas　　　　　　　　　　　　　**London**
B.c. 1659, apr. Sep 1672 thro' L. Wythe to James Grimes, engraver, a Freeman of the Weavers' Co. till 1680, but not freed.

SHARLEY, Thomas　　　　　　　　　　　　　**Warwick**
Believed assistant to Sampson 1590-91.

SHARPE, John　　　　　　　　　　　　　　　**London**
B.c. 1635, apr. Apr 1647 to Henry Child thro' T. Alcock till 1656, but not freed.

SHARPE, Thomas　　　　　　　　　　　　　**London**
B.c. 1653, apr. Jul 1667 to Robert Whitwell till 1674, but not freed.

SHARPE, William　　　　　　　　　　　　　**London**
B.c. 1658, apr. Jul 1672 to John Ebsworth till 1679. Freed Jul 1681. Paid quarterage till 1705 at least. Work known – watches and bracket clock, signed 'William Sharpe, London'.

SHAW, Edward　　　　　　　　　　　　　　**London**
B.c. 1675, apr. Jun 1689 to Clement Forster till 1696, but not freed.

SHAW, John   **Holborn, London**
B.c. 1661, apr. Jun 1675 to William Herbert, but then re-apr. (passed over?) Sep 1675 to Thomas Taylor of Holborn till 1682. Freed Sep 1682. Took as aprs.: Nov 1684 **John Parker**; Nov 1689 **Samuel Wallington**; Aug 1693 **John Latham** – free Sep 1700; May 1696 **John Clarke**; Dec 1696 **Robert Styles**; Jan 1700-01 his son, **John Shaw**; Dec 1704 **Richard Barnett** (son of John Barnett, late of (illegible) in Radnorshire, clerk); Aug 1704 **James Canaries** (from S. Marshall); Mar 1705/06 **Thomas Newman** (son of John Newman late Citizen and Joyner of London); Jul 1707 **John Shaw**; Apr 1711 **Joseph Brandreth** – free May 1718; Feb 1713/14 **Edward Astley**; Sep 1715 **Richard Smith**. Made CC Assistant from 1705, Warden from 1709, Master 1712, last attended 1718 and prob. died soon after. Work known – bracket clocks and longcase and watches, signed 'John Shaw, Holborn', but also 'near the Bars in Holborn' and 'at the Dyall in Holborne'.

SHAW, John   **London**
B.c. 1669, apr. Sep 1683 to Edward Enys till 1690, but not freed.

SHAW, William   **Diss (Norfolk)/Gislingham (Suffolk)**
Lantern clock signed 'William Shaw, Diss' dated 1676. Longcase clock signed 'William Shaw, Gislingham' early 18th century. Prob. the same, man, but nothing known of his life.

SHELLEY, John (see Strelly?)   **London**
Variously recorded as 1660 and 1636, but I do not know this man. Lantern clock on record.

SHELTON, John   **London**
Baillie records him as apr. 1662, which must be an error for Samuel Skelton(?). One of this name, brother of Samuel Shelton, was alive in 1648, but maybe not a clockmaker.

SHELTON, Sampson   **London**
Member of Blacksmiths' Co., in which free 1621, steward 1632. One of first wardens in CC 1632, Master 1634 and 1638. Took as aprs. in CC: Jan 1638 **Thomas Claxton** (thro' O. Durant) – free Jun 1646; Jan 1638/39 **Robert Morgan** thro' O. Durant – free May 1647; Oct 1644 **Edmund Crome**; Nov 1647 **Francis Matthews** thro' T. Alcock, passed over Jan 1648-49 on Shelton's death to John Bayes. Died 1648, being of St. Bride's parish, mentioning his only brother, John, and his two half-

sisters Catherine and Bridget Shelton. Left £50 to CC the interest on which to be used for benefit of poor members. Wife Sybil. Father John Porter (must be step-father). Friend Mr. Thomas Loomes, *qv*, was appointed overseer to will. Work known – watches.

SHELTON, Thomas   **London**
In 1635 petitioned CC but was refused. In 1635 was made Clerk to the Co.

SHENOON, ----   **London**
A Frenchman listed in 1662. Nothing else known.

SHEPHERD, John   **London**
B.c. 1660, apr. Dec 1674 to Robert Starr, math. inst. maker, thro' L. Wythe till 1681, but not freed.

SHEPHERD, Thomas   **London**
Free Brother in CC 1632, watchmaker.

SHEPHERD, Thomas   **London**
B.c. 1641, apr. Feb 1655/56 to Thomas Long till 1662, but not freed.

SHEPHERD, Thomas   **London**
B.c. 1675, apr. Aug 1689 to John Barnard thro' John Smart till 1696, but not freed.

SHEPHERD, William   **Kempston(?)**
Recorded by Baillie as watchmaker c. 1700.

SHERBURNE, Thomas   **Newcastle on Tyne**
Recorded as 1667. Nothing else known.

SHERWIN, John   **London**
Apr. in Weavers' Co. May 1658 to James Graves, free in same Co. Jun 1669. Trade not known, but see under Graves.

SHERWOOD, John   **London**
B.c. 1676, apr. Jan 1690/91 to Henry Jones till 1697, but not freed.

SHERWOOD, William   **London**
B.c. 1673, apr. May 1686 to James Delander till 1694. Freed Dec 1695.

Took as aprs.: Sep 1697 **James Whitlock** – free Sep 1704; Sep 1702 **George Dessessars** (son of Abraham Dessessars, watch chainmaker of St. Leonards Shoreditch); Jun 1710 **Francis Crayford** – free May 1718; Oct 1716 **John Science**; his son, **William Sherwood**, freed by patrimony Oct 1720.

SHEWELL/SHOWELLS, John   Oxford
Turret clock and lockmaker. B. 1632 at Whitfield, Worcester. Apr. to Thomas Ranklyn c. 1650, freed Sep 1657. Working till 1676.

SHIELD, John   London
Baillie has apr. 1691. I cannot trace him, but see next entry.

SHIELD, Thomas   London
B.c. 1678, apr. Jan 1691/92 (and also re-entered Dec 1692) to John Harris till 1699, but not freed. In 1695 was working for Tompion in his household.

SHIELDS, Michael   London
Late 17th century watch recorded. Was a freeman of the Blacksmiths' Co. but practised the art of clockmaking. Took as apr. in CC Dec 1701 **Samuel Leach** (from Edward Stanton).

SHIRLEY, James   London
B.c. 1667, apr. Sep 1680 to James Delander till 1688, but not freed.

SHORT, Joshua   London
Apr. Aug 1656 to John North, passed on to Ralph Ash, passed on to Lancelot Meredith. Freed Jul 1665. Took as apr. Sep 1675 **Edmund Hayes** – freed Jan 1682/83. From Jul 1688 widow Short received an occasional charitable payment from CC until in Mar 1709/10 she had 10 shillings 'towards removing widow Short to Ludgate'. In Oct 1717 she was dead and her pension was allocated elsewhere.

SHOVEL, James and John (see under Chauvell)

SHOYWELL, Henry   London
B.c. 1647, apr. Jul 1660 to Lionel Wythe till 1668, but not freed.

SHRUBB, Thomas   London
B.c. 1675, apr. Nov 1689 to Philip Browne till 1696, but not freed.

SHUTT, Caspar   **London**
Baillie has Jasper Schute. Free Brother in CC 1647.

SHUTTLEWORTH, Henry   **London**
Apr. May or Oct 1662 to Edmond Gilpin thro' T. Taylor. Freed Jan
1669/70. In Sep 1674 paid off arrears of quarterage.

SIGNIO/SYNEO, Richard   **Bodmin (Cornwall)**
Repaired town clock 1658. Died 1660 leaving inventory of tools, etc.
Clearly a maker of clocks.

SILESBY, Thomas   **Northampton**
Working 1658. No other details.

SILKE, Robert   **London**
Master of William Fuller before passing him over to Nathaniel Dike
(pre-1675). A gunmaker, but maybe made clocks too. Not in CC.

SILVER, Joseph   **London**
Recorded by Baillie but error for Joseph Silvester, *qv*.

SILVESTER, John   **London**
B.c. 1672, apr. Aug 1686 to Thomas Bates, passed over to Henry Jones
till 1693. Freed Sep 1693. Took as aprs.: Aug 1695 **Philip Silvester;** Jun
1698 **William Russell.** Paid quarterage till 1701.

SILVESTER, Joseph   **London**
In 1671/72 was an ironmonger at the sign of the Frying Pan within
Ludgate. Had faulty rulers confiscated by CC said to have been made by
Isaac Webb.

SIMCOX, Josiah   **London**
B.c. 1662, apr. Nov 1675 to Henry Adeane till 1683, but not freed.

SIMCOX, William   **London**
B.c. 1660, apr. Dec 1674 to James Markwick till 1681. Freed Jan
1682/83. Took as aprs.: May 1687 **John Zachary,** later passed on to
D. Quare; Sep 1691 **Francis William Harris** – free Jul 1702; Feb 1693/94
Joshua Simcox. Also bound an apr. for Luke Bird. Alive 1697 but
believed died soon after.

SIMES, Isaac (see Symms)

SIMMS, Isaac (see Symms)

SIMPSON, William   **London**
B.c. 1668, apr. Mar 1681/82 to George Brooke till 1689, but not freed.

SIMS, William   **London**
B.c. 1679, apr. Apr 1693 to Thomas Bradford senior till 1700, but not freed.

SINCLARE, ----   **Dublin**
Watch c. 1690.

SINDRY, Lawrence (also Sendre, Sendry, etc.)   **London**
Apr. Jun 1649 to Henry Ireland thro' N. Payne. Freed Apr 1661. Took as aprs.: Apr 1661 **Robert Hunt;** Nov 1668 **Richard Browne** (passed on to E. Norris); Mar 1669/70 **John Eldridge** – freed Mar 1677-78; Aug 1676 **George Thompson; William Foster** (from Sutton Isaac) – freed Aug 1681; Jul 1696 **Joseph Elliott;** Jan 1697/98 **Samuel Wichell** – free Jul 1705; Sep 1700 **Samuel Kenn** (son of Samuel Kenn, late of New Street, London, linen draper, deceased); also bound an apr. for Joshua Hutchen and one for D. Minuell. Was in almost constant receipt of CC charity from Apr 1686 till his death about 1707.

SKELTON, Samuel   **London**
B.c. 1648, apr. Jan 1662-63 to Thomas Mills thro' N. Coxeter till 1669, but not freed.

SKEPPER (see Skipper)

SKIPPER, Thomas   **London**
B.c. 1661, apr. May 1675 to Thomas Taylor of the Strand till 1682, but not freed.

SKIPWORTH, Francis   **London**
B.c. 1656, apr. May 1670-71 to Robert Lynch till 1677, but not freed. In Apr 1685 was to be prosecuted for working when not freeman.

SKITTLETHORPE, Richard   **London**
Recorded by Britten c. 1690 as lantern clockmaker in Southwark Road, but I do not know him.

SLEATH, Thomas London
B.c. 1670, apr. Jul 1683 to John Wheeler till 1691, but not freed.

SLOUGH, William (also Sloogh) London
B.c. 1662, apr. Aug 1676 to Benjamin Bell till 1683. Freed Aug 1687.
Took as aprs.: Aug 1687 **Henry Bradshaw** – free Sep 1695; Nov 1688
Thomas Andrews (thro' John Jackson) – free Sep 1705; Oct 1690 **John
Colliber** thro' John Wise junior – free Apr 1703; Apr 1696 **John Eyre**
(son of Robert Eyre of Cosham, Wiltshire, gent) – free May 1703. Still
alive 1697 but prob. died soon after.

SLY, Robert place not known
Late 17th century bracket clock recorded.

SMALL, William London
B.c. 1670, apr. Mar 1684/85 to John Barnard till 1691, but not freed. I
have nothing further on him but Baillie records him as a watchmaker till
1705.

SMALLE, Lewis London
Reputedly maintained Lambeth parish church clock 1585-1605.

SMALLEY, Thomas London
Great Clockmaker, admitted a Free Brother in CC Jan 1687/88. Paid
dues till c. 1689 only.

SMALLPAGE, Daniel Leeds/Wakefield
B. 1668. Whitesmith. Married at Leeds 1691 Elizabeth Walker.
Repaired Halifax church clock 1721-23. *Leeds Mercury* of 1729 reads:
'Daniel Smallpage, watchmaker, who formerly lived at the Black Swan
in the house where Mr. Goodfellow lately dwelt, next the Cliff in
Westgate, Wakefield, where all persons who have occasion to make use
of him in the way of watchmaking may be carefully served by him'.
Another notice of 1736 reads: 'Whereas it is falsely reported that Daniel
Smallpage of Wakefield has given over the business of watchmaker . . .
he is removed to the house where the late Mr. Cherriholm dwelt – over
against Mrs. Wrights in Wakefield'.

SMALLWOOD, ---- London
Recorded by Baillie as dying 1653, but this is an error for William
Selwood, *qv*.

SMALLWOOD, John   **Maxfield, ie Macclesfield (Cheshire)/ (Chelford ?)**

Longcase clock c. 1700 signed 'John Smallwood, Maxfield'. Another 'John Smallwood. Chelford' c. 1710. Baillie records his death as 1715.

SMART, John   **London**

B.c. 1660, apr. Aug 1674 to Jeremiah Johnson till 1681. Freed Sep 1682. Took as aprs.: Aug 1689 an apr. for John Barnard; Dec 1696 **Daniel Duxbury**. Paid quarterage till at least 1702.

SMEATON, John   **York**

Watchmaker, free 1646. Chamberlain 1665-66. Died 1686 at his estate at Austhorpe, nr. Leeds. Will dated 1686 mentions sons, John, Samuel, Edward and James and sisters Faith and Sarah and daughter, Hannah. Work known – watch.

SMEATON, Tobias   **London**

B.c. 1650, apr. Aug 1664 to Henry Harland till 1671, but not freed.

SMITH, ----   **London**

Free of Haberdashers' Co. Took as apr. c. 1684 **Samuel Mather**, later passed over to Michael Bird and freed in CC Jun 1691.

SMITH, Ambrose   **Stamford (Lincolnshire)**

Mar 1682/83 CC seized a watch signed 'Ambrose Smith, Stamford', which was suspected of being an invented name, from shop of its maker, Jasper Harmer, *qv*. An Ambrose Smith, widower, married Anne Swallwell in 1694, marriage witnessed by Abraham Fromanteel (possibly the Abraham Fromanteel?).

SMITH, Aurthur   **Wrexham (Denbighshire)**

Repaired town clock 1662, 1668, 1670.

SMITH, Benjamin   **London**

B.c. 1656, apr. Apr 1669 to Thomas Birch till 1677, but not freed.

SMITH, Benjamin   **London**

B.c. 1679, apr. Dec 1693 to Joseph Windmills till 1700, but not freed.

SMITH, David   **London**
B.c. 1640, apr. Aug 1654 to Andrew Prime thro' N. Tomlins (or passed
over from him) till 1661. Freed Feb 1661/62.

SMITH, Gabriel   **Barthomley/Nantwich (Cheshire)**
B. 1656, died there Apr 1743 aged 87, working at Barthomley. Work
known – longcase and bracket clocks signed 'Gabriel Smith, Barthomley'
and 'Gabriel Smith, Namptwich' *(sic)*.

SMITH, George   **London**
In 1622 worked with two aprs. (prob. John and Paul Jacob, qv), as an
alien 'next to the New Exchange'. Entered CC 1632. Took as apr. Oct
1637 **Joseph Quash** thro' O. Durant – freed May 1646. Work known –
watches.

SMITH, George   **Edinburgh**
Believed son of James Smith. Locksmith and clockmaker, freed Sep
1647. Stood surety for brother, Robert, Dec 1648 re. James Kirk, *qv*.

SMITH, Gersen (Ssmidt)   **London**
Petitioner for incorporation of CC 1630.

SMITH, Harry   **Norwich**
'Harrye the Smith' repaired St. Peter Mancroft clock in 1584 – maybe
not called Smith?

SMITH, Henry   **London**
B.c. 1637, apr. Apr 1650 to Nicholas Coxeter till 1658. Freed Apr 1658.
Took as apr. Jun 1665 **John Powell,** for Isaac Daniel.

SMITH, Henry   **London**
B.c. 1656, apr. Jan 1670/71 to William Robinson till 1677, but not freed.

SMITH, Henry   **London**
B.c. 1669, apr. Nov 1683 to Thomas Creed till 1690, but not freed.

SMITH, Imbrey (or Emery?)   **Barford (Warwickshire?)**
Repaired church clock 1689-1714. Blacksmith?

SMITH, James   **Edinburgh**
Locksmith and clockmaker in 1647, father of Robert and George. Prob. the same as Smythe 1641. Died 1660.

SMITH, Jasper   **London**
In CC minutes 1648, maybe not a maker.

SMITH, John – there are 13 of them and I cannot guarantee their details are always correct.

SMITH, John   **Edinburgh**
Cannongate c. 1680. Bracket clock recorded.

SMITH, John (Jean Shmith)   **London**
Recorded in 1622, one of first CC Assistants 1632, Warden from 1638, Master 1639.

SMITH, John   **London**
Apr. Nov 1647 to Edward Daniell thro' L. Wythe. Freed Nov 1654.

SMITH, John   **London**
Apr. Mar 1648 to Thomas Wolverstone thro' N. Payne. Freed Aug 1656. In Apr 1657 one JS was fined for putting name of Estienne Hubert of Rouen on a watch.

SMITH, John   **London**
Baillie says apr. 1654, but I cannot trace him.

SMITH, John   **London**
One JS took as apr. Aug 1660 **John Joyne** – freed Sep 1687.

SMITH, John   **London**
One JS working in Cornhill in 1662.

SMITH, John   **London**
One JS, Citizen and Clockmaker, was deponent in 1666 in a dispute concerning one Andrew, son of Susan Smith, his guardian.

SMITH, John   **London**
In 1662 worked in Rum (or Ram) Alley, Westminster. This same man was in arrears with quarterage in 1664. One JS took over **John**

Buckenhill from William Thorowgood after Jun 1664, but on his death he went back to Thorowgood (pre-1672).

SMITH, John   **London**
A clockmaker, admitted a freeman of CC by redemption on order of the Lord Mayor Sep 1674, having taken a house in the new buildings of the city. Not sure if this is the JS who published *Horological Dialogues*. One JS took as apr. Jul 1695 **Joseph Bleeke** for John Allaway. Said to reside at St. Augustines in the City. His widow believed to be Mary Smith who in 1730 was at the 'Fan and Flower-de-Luce over against Somerset House in the Strand'. Prob. this JS who paid quarterage to CC till 1704.

SMITH, John   **London**
B.c. 1673, apr. Dec 1687 to John Barnard till 1694, but not freed.

SMITH, John   **London**
B.c. 1674, apr. Oct 1688 to Thomas Player till 1695, but not freed.

SMITH, John   **London**
B.c. 1679, apr. Aug 1693 to Edward Hutchinson, freeman of the Poulters' Co., thro' R. Williamson till 1700. Freed Sep 1703.

SMITH, Maurice   **London**
B.c. 1680, apr. Sep 1693 to Robert Webster till 1701. Freed Jul 1702.

SMITH, Nathaniel   **London**
B.c. 1634, apr. Feb 1647/48 to William Bunting till 1655, but not freed. Baillie says he worked at Popes Head Alley.

SMITH, Nathaniel   **London**
B.c. 1667, apr. May 1680 thro' S. Davis senior to Isaac Carver, mat. inst. maker, till 1688. Freed Jul 1689. Took as aprs.: May 1693 **John Foster;** Mar 1698-99 **John Bell** (son of William Bell late of Tarraby, Cumberland, yeoman, deceased); Jun 1704 **Samuel Mason** (son of Joseph Mason late of St. Mary Magdalen Bermondsey, deceased); May 1707 **Ebenezer Farlam;** May 1711 **Thomas Ball;** Apr 1720 **Charles Manning.**

SMITH, Patrick   **Dublin**
Watchmaker and free Goldsmith 1698-1737.

SMITH, Philip London

Mat. inst. maker and freeman of another Co. but made Free Brother in CC Feb 1667/68. Took as apr. Jul 1670 **Samuel Jeeves** thro' L. Wythe. In Jul 1683 paid for excusal of stewardship.

SMITH, Ralph Brampton(?) (Cumberland?)

Repaired clocks for the Howards of Naworth, 1624-28. Prob. a smith.

SMITH, Richard Bristol

Free there 1674.

SMITH, Robert Dunstable (Bedfordshire)

Longcase clock recorded reputedly c.1680 – c.1700 signed 'Robert Smith, Dunstable'.

SMITH, Robert Edinburgh

Son of James Smith. Believed married 1660 Elspeth Alexander. Took as apr. Mar 1648 **James Kirk** but was complained against in Dec 1648 for not teaching him correctly. George Smith, his brother, stood surety that he would. Took as further aprs.: Dec 1667 **John Alexander** – freed Aug 1671; 1671 **John Johnstoun**.

SMITH, Robert London

Said to be working by 1630 but free in CC Dec 1646 (as Smythe). Took as aprs.: Apr 1646 **William Jordaine** thro' T. Alcock; Aug 1646 **Humphrey Pierce** thro' J. Walters – free Sep 1653; Jun 1647 **James Ashley** thro' T. Alcock – freed 1655; Mar 1650 **Thomas Faircloth** thro' H. Erbury – free Mar 1660; Sep 1650 **Richard Bowen** thro' N. Payne – freed Sep 1657; **Henry Erbury** from T. Howse – freed Jul 1650. Married the widow of Thomas Howse, *qv*. Made CC Assistant from 1649, should be Warden from 1650, but was in ill-health. Died 5 Oct 1652, living in Popes Head Alley. Executor was Francis Smith. Believed member of Sadlers' Co.

SMITH, Robert London

Baillie records one as CC 1659, but I cannot trace him.

SMITH, Robert London

Free Brother in CC Jan 1668-69. Took **James Bartholomew** apr. thro' B. Wolverston – free Dec 1675; **Edward Wilson** thro' R. Nau – freed Feb 1670/71; Apr 1669 **William Davenport** thro' T. Claxton; Dec 1675

Daniel Fitton – passed over to J. Bartholomew; Dec 1678 **Jonathan Jones** passed on to N. Delander. Paid no quarterage after about 1679.

SMITH, Robert   **London**
Free Brother in CC Apr 1697, being English and a clockmaker by trade.

SMITH, Robert   **Thame (Oxfordshire)**
Smith working on local turret clocks from 1442.

SMITH, Robert the   **Walsall (Staffordshire)**
Repaired turret clock 1466.

SMITH, Ruth   **London**
Apr. Dec 1674 to Thomas Birch and Jane his wife 'to learn the art the said Jane useth', ie to learn Jane's trade.

SMITH, Stephen   **London**
B.c. 1638, apr. May 1651 to Ahasuerus Fromanteel thro' J. Quash till 1659, but not freed.

SMITH, Thomas   **Corby (Cumberland)**
Repaired clock 1635 for Howard family. Prob. a smith.

SMITH, Thomas   **Liverpool**
Watchmaker from London, whose son b. there 1724 (which of several).

SMITH/SMYTH, Thomas   **London**
B.c. 1634, apr. Apr 1647 to Robert Grinkin thro' J. Quash till 1655, but not freed. In 1653 was left a bequest in will of William Selwood, *qv*, being an engraver, at which time he also had a son, Thomas. A lantern clock signed 'Thomas Smith me fecit 1663' might be by him.

SMITH, Thomas   **London**
B.c. 1650, apr. Nov 1664 to Nathaniel Barrow till 1671, but not freed.

SMITH, Thomas   **London**
B.c. 1669, apr. Dec 1682 to Henry Harper till 1690, but not freed.

SMITH, Thomas   **London**
B.c. 1676, apr. Jul 1690 to John Sowter till 1697, but not freed.

SMITH, Thomas   **London**
B.c. 1677, apr. Aug 1691 to Stephen Wilmott till 1698. Freed Jul 1700.

SMITH, Thomas   **London**
B.c. 1679, apr. Sep 1693 to Jonathan Lowndes thro' H. Aske till 1700,
but not freed.

SMITH, Thomas   **Oxford**
Son of John Smith, yeoman of Bloxham. Apr. Oct 1669 to Joseph Knibb,
with whom believed went to London.

SMITH, Walter   **London**
Brother in CC Jan 1640.

SMITH, widow   **London**
Formerly widow of Daniel Fletcher senior (1664).

SMITH, William   **Bristol**
Free there 1679. Married Sarah Browne.

SMITH, William   **Dundee**
Repaired church clock there 1664-68.

SMITH, William   **Leek(?)/Wootton (Warwickshire)**
Repaired church clock of St. Nicholas Kenilworth 1650-62.

SMITH, William   **London**
Fleet Street 1646. One WS took as apr. **George Bryant** Apr 1657 thro'
N. Tomlins; took **George Kingsmill** thro' N. Tomlins – freed Jul 1667.

SMITH, William   **London**
B.c. 1640, apr. Aug 1654 to Jeffrey Bayley till 1661, but not freed.

SMITH, William   **London**
B.c. 1649, apr. Jan 1663/64 to William North till 1670, but not freed.

SMITH, William   **London**
B.c. 1665, apr. Jun 1678 to James Wightman till 1686, but not freed.

SMITH, William   **London**
B.c. 1667, apr. Sep 1681 to Edmond Appley till 1688, but not freed.

SMITH, William **London**
B.c. 1678, apr. Sep 1692 to James Wolverstone till 1699, but not freed.

SMYTH, Joshua **Steyning (Sussex)**
Lantern clocks recorded c. 1690.

SMYTH(E), George **Glasgow**
Kept town clocks 1610.

SMYTHE, James **Edinburgh**
Clockmaker in 1641, asked to make town clock by council. Prob. same as Smith, *qv*.

SMYTHIES, James **London**
B.c. 1667, apr. Oct 1680 thro' Charles Bonner to George Hamilton till 1688, but not freed.

SMYTHURST, Jacob or James **London**
Prob. a clockmaker. Master of Edward Fowle 1657-65. Member of Merchant Taylors' Co. Worked at the Shambles. Not in CC.

SNARY, Robert **Malton (Yorkshire)**
B.c. 1664. Married 1666 Ann Bartendale.

SNATT, John **Ashford**
Clock recorded c. 1700.

SNELL, George **London**
Apr. Jan 1679/80 to Thomas East. Freed Sep 1688. Paid quarterage till c. 1690 only. Work known – longcase clock on record.

SNELLING, Thomas **London**
B.c. 1659, apr. Sep 1672 to Robert Williamson, then passed on* to Cuthbert Lee till 1680. Freed Sep 1680. (*Sep 1674 Snelling being 'now in the Compter(?)', RW was allowed a new apr.) Took as apr. Jan 1682/83 **Benjamin Corbitt**. Paid no quarterage after c. 1689.

SNOOKE, John (name doubtful) **London**
In CC 1632. Could this be John Snow, *qv*.

SNOW, Daniel   place not known
Lantern clock recorded 1664.

SNOWE, John   Lavington (Lincolnshire)
Clocks and watch c. 1660-80. Must be connected with John Holloway, *qv.*

SNOW, John   London(?)
Lantern clock dated 1630.

SNOW, John   Sarum, Salisbury (Wiltshire)
Lost watch, 1680.

SNOWE, Nicholas   place not known
Wall alarum dated 1638.

SNOW, W.   Marlborough (Wiltshire)
Mid-17th century watchmaker.

SOAMES, Thomas   London
Baillie has 1656 – error for Thomas Loomes, *qv.*

SOEUFEW, Isaac (alias Isaac Swale, *qv*)

SOFFLEUR, Thomas   London
Recorded as 1680 watchmaker. I do not know him. Maybe a misrendering of some other name?

SOMERSALL, Mandeville   London
Lantern clock recorded, but I do not know him.

SOMERVILL, Thomas   Dublin
Clockmaker and free goldsmith 1681-1710.

SOMILLIER, John   London
B.c. 1635, apr. Mar 1649/50 to Luke Richards till 1656, but not freed.

SORET, Abraham   Dublin
Watchmaker and free Goldsmith 1685. Died 1715. Prob. son of Adam.

SORET, Adam   **Dublin**
Watchmaker and free Goldsmith 1675. Died 1723. Has as aprs.: 1678
Will Mainwaring; 1675 Joseph Wesoncroft.

SOUTHCOTE, Josias   **London**
B.c. 1667, apr. Mar 1681 to Thomas Taylor of Holborn till 1688, but not
freed.

SOUTHEN, Thomas   **London**
B.c. 1667, apr. Feb 1681/82 to Henry Young till 1688, but not freed.
Widow Southern got charity from CC Apr 1706.

SOUTHWARCK/SOUTHWICK, George   **Dublin**
Watchmaker and goldsmith. Free 1657 in Goldsmiths' Co. Died 1683.
Had as aprs.: 1658 **Valentine Hammond;** c. 1670 **Edward Ashton;** 1678
Henry Chaboner.

SOUTHWOOD, Samuel   **London**
B.c. 1649, apr. Jul 1663 to Charles Fox thro' T. Davis till 1670, but not
freed.

SOUTHWORTH, John   **London**
B.c. 1656, apr. Jan 1668/69 to John Matchett till 1677. Freed Aug 1689.
In 1691 bound an apr. for Charles Lowndes. In Feb 1701/02 got CC
charity of 10 shillings, being a poor member. In Apr 1702 his widow
received it.

SOUTHWORTH, Peter   **London/Exeter(?)**
Apr. May 1656 to John Wythe thro' J. Palfrey, later passed over to
Jeremy East. Freed Jan 1664/65. Took as aprs.: Jul 1671 **David Foulkes;**
May 1675 **John Clark;** Jul 1692 **Daniel Webb.** In 1686 he together with
his wife and daughters received 10 shillings each under will of John
Batten, *qv*. Still alive 1697, but marked as dead by 1698. One of this
name working in Exeter as watchmaker 1705.

SOUTHWORTH, Thomas   **London**
B.c. 1664, apr. Nov 1677 to Barlow Rookes till 1685, but not freed.

SOWTER, John   **London**
B.c. 1657, apr. Mar 1671 to Solomon Bouquet till 1678. Freed Jul 1683
(master then deceased). Took as aprs.: Jul 1690 **Thomas Smith;** Mar

1692 **Agmondesham Vesey**; Dec 1693 **Thomas Burscough**; Jun 1694 **Samuel Crouch**. Prob. dead or gone before 1697-98.

SPACKMAN, Edward   London
B.c. 1659, apr. Jan 1673/74 thro' Lionel Wythe to James Wolverston, Citizen and Barber-Chirurgeon till 1680, but not freed. (Despite similarity of name, this appears not to be the same man as Edward Speakman, *qv.*)

SPARKE, SPARKES and SPARKS are listed together, but distinguished under each individual entry.

SPARKE, Christopher   Exeter (Devon)
Supposedly repaired Cathedral clock 1644-45 (but not in Ponsford).

SPARKES, Nicholas   London
Recorded by some authorities 1659 (Nicholas Sparkes and widow Sparkes) but these are slips for Parke, *qv.*

SPARKE, Robert   Cockfield (Suffolk)
Clockmaker, will dated 1647, proved 1648. Left all tools to his son, William, *qv.*

SPARKS, Thomas   London
B.c. 1676, apr. May 1689 to John Drew till 1697, but not freed. (Baillie records him till 1732?)

SPARKES, Thomas   Wapping
Longcase clock c. 1710. Prob. the London man, *qv.*

SPARKE, Walter   Exeter (Devon)
Free as locksmith 1688. Buried 1705. Worked on local turret clocks.

SPARKE, William   Cockfield (Suffolk?)
Inherited father's work tools (Robert, *qv*)in 1647, so presumed clockmaker.

SPEAKMAN, Edward   London
B.c. 1668, son of William, *qv.* Apr. to father Jan 1682/83 till 1689. Freed Jan 1691/92. Took as aprs.: Jan 1692/93 **Ezekiel Gurney**; Aug 1697 **John Buckel**; Oct 1701 **Thomas Brockles** (son of late Alborn Brockles of

parish of St. Andrew Holborn, Middlesex, clothworker); Sep 1703 **James Wats;** Mar 1707/08 **John Coles.** I have no later data, but Baillie records him till 1712. Work known – longcase clock.

SPEAKMAN, John   **London**
B.c. 1678, son of William, *qv*. Apr. to father Sep 1692 till 1699. Freed Jun 1707. Took as aprs.: Jun 1707 **Thomas Johnson** – free Jul 1714; Sep 1712 **Joseph Fossey.** Work known – longcase clocks.

SPEAKMAN, Richard   **London**
B.c. 1678 (parentage unknown). Apr. Nov 1692 to Erasmus Micklewright till 1699, but not freed.

SPEAKMAN, Thomas   **London**
B.c. 1661, son of William, *qv*. Apr. Jan 1675-76 to his father till 1682. Freed Sep 1685. Took as aprs.: Dec 1687 **John Wharton;** (from T. Harris, of Blacksmiths Co.) **Thomson Hickson** – free Jan 1690-91; Jul 1693 **Francis Dorrell** – free Sep 1702; Jun 1697 **John Burrows** – free Jul 1704; Apr 1707 **Joseph Lake;** Apr 1712 **Henry Wood** – free Apr 1720; Sep 1714 **William Brown; Thomas Seffin** (passed over to E. Pitcher and freed Aug 1720. Work known – wall clock.

SPEAKMAN, William senior (also Speckman)   **London**
Apr. Aug 1654 thro' N. Tomlins to Peter Closon or Andrew Prime(?) till 1661. Freed Sep 1661. Took as aprs.: Jan 1662-63 **John Sweby** – freed Nov 1671; Aug 1670 **Boaz Brittain** – free Mar 1679; Sep 1671 **Simon Player;** Jan 1675/76 son, **Thomas Speakman** – free Sep 1685; Jan 1682-83 son, **Edward Speakman** – free Jan 1691/92; **Zachariah Mountfort** (taken over from F. Ireland) – freed Apr 1684; Jul 1685 his kinsman, **Thomas Trowe;** Jun 1683 **Richard Bryan** – freed Apr 1686; Jul 1688 **William Speakman,** his son; Sep 1692 his son, **John Speakman** – free Jun 1707; Dec 1694 **Philip Vick;** Dec 1696 **Ralph Morton;** May 1699 **Henry Clanfield** (or Cranfield) (son of Henry Clanfield late of Stanton Harcourt, co. Oxford, yeoman, deceased) – free 1707; Aug 1702 **Benjamin Broadhead** (son of Parry Broadhead of St. Andrews Holborn, Middlesex, gentleman) – free Sep 1709; Sep 1710 **Richard Andrews;** Apr 1715 **Gilbert Trow; Robert Benn** – free Dec 1716. Also bound aprs. for certain other masters, incl. J. Windmills, E. Clough, D. LeConte, I. Lowndes, N. Higginson, F. Asseline. In Jul 1682 chosen CC Steward, 'after much arguing', then Assistant from 1691, Warden from 1698, Master 1701, last attended 1717; prob. died soon after. In 1662 worked

in Westminster, and later in Hatton Garden. Work known – clocks, longcase, lantern, bracket, signed sometimes 'Speakman, London' but more often 'William Speakman Londini fecit' or 'William Speakman in Hatton Garden fecit'. As his work is not uncommonly met with and that of his sons is negligible, it seems likely they all worked for him.

SPEAKMAN, William junior   London
B.c. 1674, apr. Jul 1688 to his father, William senior, *qv* till 1695, but not freed.

SPEIDELL, Francis   London
Prob. not a maker but chosen Clerk to CC Jul 1694 in place of Thomas Goodwin, deceased. Still Clerk in 1704, when he had failed to keep the books in proper order and had embezzled monies from them. Died 1718/19.

SPENCE, John   Leicester
A hitherto unrecorded make but I recently uncovered a lantern clock signed 'John Spence in Leicester, 1688'. No facts of his life are known, but see also next entry?

SPENCE, John   London
Britten records a watch c. 1650-70. Not a member of CC and not otherwise documented, but see previous entry?

SPENCER, Thomas   London
B.c. 1657, apr. May 1671 to Solomon Bouquet till 1678. Free Nov 1685. In Apr 1682 Thomas Spencer 'in the Strand' was to be prosecuted for not conforming to CC rules (ie prob. by trading when not a freeman), but promised to conform. Took as apr. Nov 1685 **Michael Churchman** – free Nov 1694. Work known – longcase clock signed 'Thomas Spencer Londini fecit'. Prob. dead or gone by 1697/98.

SPITTLE, Richard   London
B.c. 1677, apr. Mar 1691/92 to William Davison till 1698. Freed May 1699. Took as apr. Apr 1701 **Jonathan Miles** (son of Robert Miles of St. Martin in the Fields, coachman). Believed died soon after 1701.

SPRAG(G)(E), Roger   Chester
Blacksmith who kept St. Mary's church clock. Died 1556/57.

SPRAGGE, Thomas Chester
Repaired St. Mary's clock 1538-46.

SPRATT, Gregory London
In 1622 was an alien with two aprs. in St. Martins.

SPRIGG, Henry London
Recorded by Baillie as apr. 1637 but I cannot trace him.

SPRING, William London
Watchmaker who in Nov 1687 promised to join CC at next court meeting, but did not.

SPRINGFIELD, Jonas Norwich
Apr. 1693 to Samuel Fromanteel.

SPRY, Jacob Liskeard (Cornwall)
Repaired town clock 1634.

SPURGIN, Jeremy Colchester (Essex)
B. 1666, married 1690 Jane Davill. Issue: 1691-99. Was a Quaker. In 1693 took lease on the Castle Inn in High Street. In 1697 fined for trading when not a free burgess. Died Aug 1699 aged 33. Widow continued in business, till her death in 1739, when sold out to John Smorthwaite. Work known – one longcase and one lantern clock. Also longcase signed 'Jane Spurgin in Colchester'. (See Mason)

SPURRIER, John London
B.c. 1663, apr. Aug 1677 to John Harris of Oxford (a Brother) thro' S. Davis till 1684. Free Feb 1684/85. Took as apr. Jul 1686 **Samuel Stilleto.**

STAC(E)Y, John London
B.c. 1661, apr. Aug 1675 to Thomas Wheeler till 1682. Freed Sep 1683.

STAINSBURGH, Robert Chippenham (Wiltshire)
Lost watch recorded in 1698, but no other details.

STAMFORD, ---- London
Baillie records him as CC 1640, but I cannot trace him and there may be some confusion with next entry, *qv*.

STAMFORD, Richard   London
B.c. 1639, apr. Sep 1652 to Nicholas Payne, in 1653 transferred to (P. Willierme?), but not freed. In Jan 1654 his father complained that his master (Peter Willierme) was not teaching him the trade and was not providing his clothing.

STAMPER, Francis   London
B.c. 1661, apr. Aug 1675 to Samuel Davis junior thro' S. Davis senior till 1682. Freed Nov 1682. Was a Quaker. In 1687 called to task by CC for refusing to allow his workrooms to be searched. Took as aprs.: Jun 1684 **Joshua Penford** – free Jan 1695-96; Sep 1689 **Daniel Moore** – free Feb 1697/98; Sep 1684 **Joseph Foster** (from S. Davis senior) – freed Feb 1691/92; Dec 1696 **Thomas Hymons.** In 1695 will of Benjamin Bell (*qv*) he is forgiven his debt of £25. Was loving friend and overseer of will of Thomas Virgoe, *qv*. Married about 1682 Mary X. His will describes him as of Lumbard Street, parish of St. Edmund the King, being proved in Mar 1698-99. He mentions daughters Elizabeth and Mary and son, Josiah. Also sister Elizabeth Collard (maybe wife of Leonard Collard, *qv*). Had estate at Doncaster and Stamford, a cottage at Tottenham, lands in Pennsylvania bought from Thomas Virgoe deceased (*qv*) (died 1685 also at parish of St. Edmund the King), lands bought of William Penn, lead and copper mine shares in Cumberland and Lancashire, half share in the trade of East Country Co. with Daniel Quare, cottage at Torpenhow (Cumberland), where he was b., and the parish of Allhallows, Cumberland, nearby. Work known – a hooded wall clock and a quarter-striking lantern clock signed 'Fran. Stamper at ye Golden Ball in Lumbard Streete, London'. Name noted engraved behind dial of a Joseph Knibb, London, wall clock.

STANBURY, Robert   Coventry or Warwick
Believed blacksmith. Repaired St. Nicholas Kenilworth clock 1698-1703.

STANDISH, William   London
Son of Thomas Standish of Standish, co. Lancashire, gent. Apr. Mar 1660/61 to Jeffrey Bayley. Freed Jan 1668/69. Took as aprs.: Sep 1670 **Robert Danson** – free Jul 1678; Jan 1678/79 **Joseph Bates** (who in 1683 was of parish of St. Andrew Holborn) – free Apr 1687; In Jan 1687/88 widow Standish received five shillings CC charity, and another similar payment in Jul 1700.

STANES, Jeffrey (see Staynes)   **London**

STANTON, Edward (sometimes Staunton)   **London**
Apr. Dec 1655 to Nathaniel Allen. Freed Jan 1662/63. Took as aprs.: Jan 1664/65 **William Cattell** – freed Apr 1672; Apr 1667 **Stephen Wilmott** – freed Sep 1674; Sep 1671 **Samuel Stevens** – free Jun 1680; Aug 1676 **William Newton** – free Jan 1685/86; **John Kirk** (from G. Crouch) – free Jan 1677/78; Sep 1681 **Thomas Watts** – Mar 1681/82 **John Strangfellow** – free Apr 1691; Oct 1683 **Samuel Winter; Jul 1687 William Cottrill;** Jan 1688/89 (thro' E. Burgess) **Underwood Lee;** Mar 1695/96 **Thomas Whitby;** Jun 1698 **Alexander Reid** – free Apr 1707; Dec 1701 **Samuel Leach** (from Isaac Goddard), later transferred to Michael Shields; Jun 1705 **Thomas Healy** (son of William Healy of St. Buttolph Bishopsgate parish, London, founder); also bound an apr. for H. Crumpe.
    In 1699 was overseer to John Ebsworth's will. Jan 1673/74 his name was suggested as the one employed by Robert Seigniour to engrave latter's name on a clock made by Henry Jones. In Jan 1689/90 he offered to borrow the CCs £500 investment money at 4%, but was turned down by them. Was made CC Assistant from 1682, Warden from 1693, Master 1697. Attended regularly till early 1715 when suddenly ceased – prob. dying then. Had an illness Mar 1701-02. Work known – several clocks of lantern and longcase types and bracket, incl. month longcase signed 'Edward Stanton in Leaden Hall Streete, Londini' or 'Edward Stanton, London'. His work said to have similarities to that of Joseph Knibb (or to be by Knibb).

STANTON, John   **London**
B.c. 1670, apr. Nov 1684 to Richard Farmer till 1691. Freed Jan 1692/93. (Relationship to Edward unknown, but *could* be his son.) Took as aprs.: Jan 1695/96 **Thomas Childs;** Dec 1698 **John Long** (son of John Long late of St. Sepulchre parish, London, stationer, deceased); Jun 1700 **William Knight Jeffery** (son of Edmund Jeffery of Cambridge, gentleman) – this was cancelled Nov 1701, witnessed by Stanton's wife, as the boy was rebound to Benjamin Merriman; **Benjamin Goddard** (from Isaac Goddard) – free Nov 1701; Paid quarterage till mid-1700, then apparently ceased. In Jul 1712 he promised to pay his arrears – 'he has been several years out of England'. I have no further data but Baillie lists him till 1725.

STANTON, Originall   **London**
Listed as working in 1662, but this is either a clerical slip on the

document, or perhaps someone's idea of a joke. 'Originall' should, of course, be Reginald, *qv.*

STANTON, Reginald   **London**
Clockmaker but freeman of the Founders' Co. Listed as working 1662, but not heard of after 1669. Took as apr. **William Lucas**, later passed over to Robert Robinson. Not in CC but known to them.

STANTON, Samuel (I)   **London**
Not in CC but known to them. Took apr. **John Andrews** over from Nathaniel Pyne post-Apr 1680 – freed Sep 1688 in CC. In May 1674 he paid CC search fee and large arrears (but no official entry for him is recorded).

STANTON, Samuel (II)   **London**
B.c. 1678, apr. Jun 1692 to Benoni Tebbatt till 1699, but not freed. Another of this name was later apr. in 1703.

STAPLES, Richard   **London**
B.c. 1671, apr. Mar 1684 to Henry Jones till 1692, but not freed.

STAPLETON, George   **London**
Baillie has 1686 but I cannot trace him. Maybe a slip for Thomas?

STAPLETON, Thomas   **London**
B.c. 1672, apr. Jun 1686 to Michael Cornish, later transferred to Richard Watts and freed Jan 1693/94. Paid quarterage till 1705 at least.

STAPYLTON, Myles   **Armagh (N. Ireland)**
'Maker of horologes' 1622.

STARKIE, Edward   **Liverpool (Lancashire)**
Watchmaker. Children b. there 1683-88 to wife, Martha, who died 1689.

STARKY, Mr.   **London**
Was master of John Drake in Blacksmiths' Co. 1605.

STARLEY, Francis (maybe Sturley?)   **London**
In Sep 1641 admitted to CC that he had not served an apprenticeship but had only spent six weeks with Mr. Stillinger. Was banned from trading.

STARNILL, James (or Starnell)   **London**
Prob. an engraver. Not in CC but known to them and bound aprs. thro'
them. May have been in Weavers' Co. Took as aprs.: Dec 1647 **William
Richardson** (thro' R. Masterson); Apr 1650 **John Archer** (thro'
Masterson) – free Nov 1660; May 1652 **John Benson** (also thro'
Masterson) – freed May 1660. Not on 1662 list.

STARR, Robert   **London**
Freeman of Stationers' Co. A mat. inst. maker, admitted to CC Feb
1667/68. Took as aprs.: Aug 1669 **Thomas Benbridge** (thro' T. Claxton)
– free May 1683; Dec 1674 **John Shepherd** (thro' L. Wythe); Aug 1677
John Bellinger (thro' N. Coxeter) – freed Jul 1686; May 1682 **John
Coatsfield** (thro' T. Wheeler).

STAS(E)BEY, John (also Staceby)   **London**
Apr. to Joseph Webb in Clothworkers' Co. c. 1666, freed Dec 1673.
Took as apr. thro' CC Apr 1685 **Thomas Goddard** thro' D. Stevens.

STAYNER, Thomas   **London**
Name difficult; could be Staynes but also looks like Stianer and Baillie
even has Saynoe, which is wrong. Admitted to CC Sep 1654 (as Brother?)
then apparently as full freeman Mar 1658/59. Took as apr. Mar 1655
John Nightingale (thro' T. Wolverston). Was an engraver in Fleet Street
in 1662.

STAYNES, Jeffrey (also Stanes, Staines, etc.)   **London**
Apr. in Loriners Co. to George Ryley (a freeman of the Loriners Co.) but
transferred to Simon Chapman of the CC. Free Jul 1686. Took as apr.
Feb 1686/87 **Thomas Manwaring.** Paid quarterage till at least 1700, but
in 1712 was to be sued for arrears.

STAYNES, Thomas (see Stayner)

STEAD, Thomas   **London**
B.c. 1654, apr. Dec 1668 to Richard Bowen, transferred to Joseph Webb
(a clockmaker but a freeman of the Clothworkers' Co.) till 1675. Freed
Dec 1678. Took as apr. Jan 1678-79 **Henry Bestwick** (thro' S. Davis),
later passed over to serve his mother, Katherine Bestwick (widow of
Richard Bestwick who had been a clockmaker though a freeman of the
Cutlers' Co.) – freed Sep 1686. Stead paid no quarterage after about 1684

and prob. dead by 1697/98. Widow Stead received CC charity from Jan 1699/1700 till 1706.

STEDMAN, James London

Not a member of CC. Took apr. **Edward Brookes** over from Robert Gregory (via Edward Whitfield) – freed Dec 1690.

STEGAR, John London

Sep 1699 admitted free of CC by redemption. Took as aprs.: Mar 1699/1700 **Charles Lowder** (son of Alexander Lowder late of Broome(?) in co. of Stafford, deceased, Doctor of Divinity); **Robert Powell** – freed Nov 1710; Nov 1713 **Thomas Sterry** (with Elizabeth Stegar, his wife); Jul 1716 **John Claus**; Jun 1718 **George Peck**.

STEINSONNE, Robert Glasgow

Smith – 1690. (Prob. Stephenson?)

STEPHENS/STEPHENSON – see under Stevens and Stevenson.

STEVENS, Benjamin London

B.c. 1659, apr. Jul 1673 to John Froude till 1680, but not freed.

STEVENS, Daniel London

B.c. 1639, son of Francis Stevens (*qv?*). Apr. May 1653 to Jeffrey Bayley till 1660. Freed Apr 1661. Took as aprs.: Sep 1673 **Joshua Kemyes**; Apr 1678 **Francis Hartwell**. In Sep 1680 he was appointed Beadle to succeed Samuel Davis. This position was usually given to a poorer member. The many aprs. bound thro' him thereafter were almost certainly boys who were to serve other masters (usually those who were Brothers of the Co.). In Jul 1697 he received 10 shillings charity from CC. In Jan 1697/98 his widow received it regularly till after 1700.

STEVENS, Edward London

Not in CC but known to them. Prob. dead by 1662/63.

STEVENS, Edward London

B.c. 1679, apr. Jul 1693 to Jonathan Jones till 1700, but not freed.

STEPHENS, Francis London

Brother in CC 1632. Took as aprs.: Sep 1648 **Francis Stephens** (his son?) thro' J. Bayley; his son, **Daniel Stevens** — freed 1661; Jul 1650

Thomas Gregory (thro' J. Bayley) – freed Jul 1671. In 1658 he paid his full quarterage arrears, but not heard of thereafter. Prob. dead or gone by 1662.

STEPHENS, Francis   **London**
B.c. 1634, prob. son of Francis senior. Apr. Sep 1648 to Francis Stevens senior thro' J. Bayley till 1655, but not freed.

STEVENS, George   **London**
A clockmaker, free Brother in CC Mar 1673-74. Took as aprs.: Mar 1673-74 **John Ham** (thro' D. Stevens); Mar 1680-81 may take **Charles Price** (thro' D. Stevens) after he has taken up his freedom of the city. In Jul 1688 he was excused Stewardship as he was about to go overseas. Paid quarterage till c. 1693. Work known – bracket clock signed 'Geo. Stevens in Drury Lane, London'.

STEVENS, Giles   **London**
B.c. 1656, apr. Jan 1670/71 to Robert Wilkins till 1677, but not freed.

STEVENS, John   **London**
Baillie has apr. 1648, CC 1655, but this appears to be a slip for Francis junior, *qv*.

STEVENS, John   **London/Colchester (Essex)**
B.c. 1670, apr. Nov 1684 to John Wynne thro' W. Hillier till 1691. Freed Dec 1691. Believed to have come from Colchester and returned there 1691 to marry Elizabeth Munsey. Took as aprs.: Nov 1695 **Robert Jennings;** Apr 1697 **Francis Reynolds;** Mar 1697 **John Hawksworth** – free Jul 1710; **John Dawson** (from W. Wheatley) – free Jul 1698; Dec 1705 **John Shirley** (son of late Samuel Shirley of St. Bride's, London, carver, deceased) – free Apr 1720; Jul 1707 **Robert Cary.** Work known – longcase clock signed 'John Stevens London', but lantern clock recorded signed 'John Stevens Colchester'. Believed died c. 1725 at Colchester.

STEVENS, Ralph   **London**
B.c. 1675, apr. Sep 1688 to Richard Warren till 1696, but not freed.

STEVENS, Samuel   **London**
B.c. 1658, apr. Sep 1671 to Edward Stanton till 1679. Freed Jun 1680. Took as aprs.: Sep 1681 **Joseph Forest** – free Jan 1692/93; Sep 1686 **Jeremiah Gregory** – free Dec 1694; Jun 1692 **Henry Thornton** – free

Feb 1699/1700; Dec 1693 **Robert Ware** (from F. Hill) – free Nov 1701; May 1695 **John Uffington** (son of Thomas Uffington) – free Sep 1702; Nov 1698 **John Coppin** (from J. Benson); Jan 1699-1700 his son, **Samuel Stevens** – free Mar 1706/07; May 1700 **James Finch** (son of Francis Finch of Hitchin, Herts., shoemaker); Aug 1703 **Samuel Stanton** – free Apr 1715. In Apr 1682 when CC threatened him about undue binding of aprs. he was listed as of Grub Street.

STEVENS, Thomas   London
B.c. 1678, apr. Sep 1692 to Samuel Marshall till 1699. Freed Apr 1700. Took as aprs.: May 1702 **Charles Wall** (son of Samuel Wall of parish of St. Christ Church, London, joiner); Jan 1706/07 **Moses Meigh** – free Dec 1714; May 1709 **John Melsom** (son of George Melsom of Drury Lane, co. Middlesex, taylor); Jun 1713 **Joseph Green**; Jul 1720 **Thomas Wood.**

STEVENSON, Adam   Dunfermline
Called Adam junior. Kept church clock 1698. Converted it to pendulum 1723. Believed worked till 1752 but another of this name cared for clock after 1733.

STEVENSON, Robert (see Steinsonne)

STEWARD, ----   Ipswich (Suffolk)
Longcase clock recorded c. 1700.

STIFFE, William   London
Apr. Nov 1676 to Simon Chapman, but not freed.

STIL(E)MAN, John   London
Brother in CC Sep 1640.

STILL, Francis   London
B.c. 1677, apr. Dec 1691 to Robert Halstead till 1698. Freed Mar 1698/99. Took as apr. Jan 1700/01 **John Assom** (son of John Assom of St. Andrew Holborn, Middlesex, butcher). Paid quarterage till at least 1704. Work known – a bracket clock signed 'Francis Still, London'.

STILLETTO, Samuel (could be Shilletto?)   London
B.c. 1672, apr. Jul 1686 to John Spurrier till 1693, but not freed.

STILLINGER, ----　　　　　　　　　　　　　**London**
Practising 1641 but not in CC.

STOCK, Isaac (Jabez)　　　　　　　　　　　**London**
Bracket clock reported c. 1700. A Jabez Stock is recorded about this time
too, but clocks by the latter I have seen are prob. c. 1720-40.

STOCKDALE, Thomas　　　　　　　　　　　　**York**
Apr. to William Kidson post-1614.

STOCKIN, Charles　　　　　　　　　　**Northampton**
1658.

STOCKTON, Thomas　　　　　　　　　　　**Chester**
Serviced church clock 1637.

STOKES, Samuel　　　　　　　　　　　　　**London**
In Jun 1699 his case was deferred by CC till next court, but in Jul a watch
was seized at his premises (in the hands of Thomas Creed, bearing the
name of William Davison), as being deficient. In Jul Stokes was arrested
at the Chamberlain's Suite for making clocks and watches though not a
free man. He worked in Little Britain.

STOKES, W.　　　　　　　　　　　　place unknown
Longcase clock c. 1700 signed 'W. Stokes fecit'.

STONE, Andrew　　　　　　　　　　　　　**London**
Free by redemption in CC Mar 1698/99 by order of Court of Aldermen.
Paid quarterage till 1701.

STONE, Henry　　　　　　　　　　　　　　**London**
Recorded by Baillie as 1623 but I cannot trace him.

STONE, James　　　　　　　　　　　　　　**London**
B.c. 1678, apr. Apr 1692 thro' D. Stevens to Thomas Stubbs till 1699,
but not freed.

STONE, Thomas (see Stones)

STONE, William　　　　　　　　　　　　　**London**
B.c. 1678, apr. Apr 1692 to Thomas Fletcher till 1699. Freed Apr 1700

(having been transferred to Johnn Hicks). Took as aprs.: Apr 1701 **Roger Elmes** (son of Roger Elmes of West Monkton, Somerset, carpenter); Feb 1703/04 **Henry Greatorix.**

STONES, Simon   **Sheffield (Yorkshire)**
Believed made clock for Marston church 1654.

STONES, Thomas (alias Scoles)   **London**
B.c. 1670, apr. Sep 1684 to John Westoby till 1691. Freed Apr 1692. Took as aprs.: Jun 1695 **Philip Abbot** – free Oct 1704; Jun 1697 **John Lewis** – free Apr 1705; Mar 1702-03 **John Bull** (son of Seth Bull, Citizen and Merchant Taylor of London); Jun 1711 **Benjamin Cheeswright.** I have no data on him after 1720, but Baillie records him up to 1747. He did not use the name of Scoles, though perhaps Stones was his adopted name? Work known – month longcase clock signed 'Thomas Stones, Lothbury'.

STOPFORTH, Edward   **London**
B.c. 1677, apr. Jun 1691 thro' Benjamin Merryman to Henry Merryman till 1698, but not freed.

STOREY, John   **London**
Watchmaker. Daughter b. to wife, Ann, who died 1699. He died at Harrington Street in 1721. Not a member of CC.

STORR, Marmaduke   **Selby (Yorkshire)**
Believed to have been a clockmaker but no work recorded by him. B. 1667 at Owstwick, East Riding, a Quaker. Moved to Selby where in 1691 married Elizabeth daughter of George Canby, clockmaker, *qv*. She died that year and he remarried in 1695 to Elizabeth Batty. Several children included Marmaduke, b. 1702, later a clockmaker, Batty b. 1710, also later a clockmaker. Marmaduke senior died in 1747.

STRACHAN, Andrew (or Abraham)   **London**
In Jul 1691 CC complained about him being 'a Scot between 30 and 40 years and no freeman for several years past has worked here without consent and avoided prosecution by moving from place to place – hath this July bound himself for seven years to Thomas Warden (a free Haberdasher) to avoid redress'. The apprenticeship was then cancelled by the Chamberlain. Work known – a longcase clock signed at Newcastle.

STRANGFELLOW, John (also Stringfellow)   **London/Halifax**
Some authorities record him as Thomas, which is incorrect. Name sometimes spelt Stringfellow, but he signed his name Strangfellow. B.c. 1667, apr. thro' CC Mar 1681/82 to Edward Stanton till 1688. Freed Apr 1691. Paid quarterage till c. 1693. Married in 1694 at Halifax being described as from Rochdale to Elizabeth Bentley. Issue there includes 1695 John, 1716 James and at least seven others, five of whom died young. Wife died 1711. He died 2 Sep 1718. Work known – a lantern clock signed at London, but apparently no Halifax work on record.

STRAUGHAM, John   **London**
Jul 1687 to be summoned to CC court re transgressions (prob. for trading when not a freeman).

STREET, Edward   **London**
Baillie says apr. 1633 under Blacksmiths' Co. which I cannot confirm.

STREET, George   **London**
B.c. 1673, apr. Sep 1687 to Roger Nicholls till 1694, but not freed.

STREET, Henry   **London**
B.c. 1659, apr. Aug 1673 to Richard Halstead till 1680, but not freed.

STREET, John   **London**
May 1685 to be prosecuted by CC for working when not a freeman. Britten records a longcase clock signed 'John Street, Londres' c. 1685 which was reputedly presented to his friend Abraham Martin, engraver (from Geneva), *qv*.

STREET, Richard   **London**
Watchmaker. Free Brother in CC Sep 1687. Made Assistant 1713, Warden 1716 but was excused as he had 'urgent business on his hands', and in fact rarely attended CC and apparently took no aprs. thro' them. Said to have worked in Shoe Lane. In 1716 was described as of Fleet Street when involved with William Wright in taking over the running of St. Paul's clock from Langley Bradley. Work known – watches, bracket and longcase clocks. One watch has hour hand rotating every quarter hour, telling time in 10-second units. The famous longcase clock he made in 1708 for Trinity College Cambridge Observatory, commissioned by Sir Isaac Newton, shows seconds in the arch area, perhaps the first use of this feature.

STRELLY, ----   Windsor
Baillie says Windsor before 1660. Another source says 1655.

STRELLEY, Francis   London
Free in CC Jul 1666 (as Brother?) Took as apr. Jan 1669/70 **Richard Symonds** (thro' James Seabourne). In Jan 1679/80 CC gave him a charity payment of two shillings, being 'a prisoner'. Work known – bracket clock signed 'Francis Strelley, Londini'.

STRELLY, John (see Shelley ?)   London
Baillie records table clock pre-1684. I don't know him. Maybe error for Francis, *qv?*

STRETCH, Peter   Leek (Staffordshire)/Philadelphia
B.c. 1670, worked at Leek till about 1701, then emigrated to Philadelphia where he joined a fellow Quaker, Abel Cottey from Devon, to become the earliest makers there. Had shop on corner of Front Street and Chestnut Street there, which became known as 'Peter Stretch's Corner'. Work known – only two or three English-made longcases are recorded by him, signed 'Peter Stretch, Leek'. A handful of Philadelphia-made clocks are known, mostly simple 30-hour ones. (See *Clocks* magazine, Aug 1978 for an article on Stretch.)

STRETCH, Samuel   Birmingham/Bristol (Somerset)
Reputedly b. 1657. Quaker. Moved from Birmingham to Bristol in May 1714. Had son, Samuel, free there 1733. Believed died 1743. Work known – longcase and lantern clocks recorded, also a watch.

STRETCH, Samuel   Leek (Staffordshire)
Late 17th century lantern clock recorded. Obviously part of family of Peter Stretch but relationship unknown. One of this name went to Philadelphia to work with Peter Stretch from c. 1711; free there 1717.

STRIBLING, Benjamin   Stowmarket (Suffolk)
B.c. 1663, married 1693, single, aged 30, clockmaker, to Elizabeth Lucas, spinster, aged 20. Children b. 1695-1709. Died 1720. Widow died 1754. Work known – lantern clocks and longcase.

STRIGG, Henry   London
B.c. 1624, apr. Nov 1637 to Simon Bartram thro' O. Durant till 1645, but not freed.

STRIGNER, ---- **London(?)**
Watch recorded c. 1687 made for James II. May not be British?

STRINGFELLOW, John (see Strangfellow)

STRUGGLE, Christopher **London**
B.c. 1657, apr. Jul 1671 to Isaac Puzzy till 1678, but not freed.

STUBBS, Gabriel **London**
B.c. 1656, apr. May 1670 to Robert Seigniour till 1677, but admitted as a Brother Mar 1675 'a small clockmaker who served his apprenticeship in the city of York'. Took as apr. Jul 1676 **John Wilmot** thro' S. Davis – then of Westminster. His connection with York is intriguing, as Seigniour appears to have had several York connections, *qv*.

STUBBS, John **London**
Recorded as a clockmaker of St. Andrew Holborn in 1719 when his son Nathaniel was bound apr. to Job Worall of the Cutlers' Co. This may be a slip for Thomas Stubbs, *qv*.

STUBBS, Thomas **London**
Apr. to John Lyon of Warrington. Free Brother in CC Apr 1685 as a 'great clockmaker'. Took as aprs.: Aug 1686 **Robert Tarbuck** (thro' D. Stevens); Sep 1688 **John Kingsnorth** thro' D. Stevens; Apr 1692 **James Stone** thro' D. Stevens. Paid quarterage till 1698 at least (Baillie records him till death in 1738, but I have no data after 1698 on him). Work known – longcase clocks signed 'Thomas Stubbs, London'. See also John Stubbs.

STYLES, William **Belfast (N. Ireland)**
'Maker of horologes' 1622.

SUDBURY, John **London**
B.c. 1662, apr. May 1675 to Christopher Maynard till 1683. Free Sep 1686. Mar 1687/88 promised to make his apr. **Stephen Rayner,** taken illegally, a free Brother in due course – did so May 1691; Mar 1687/88 took **John Rayner** – free Dec 1697; Mar 1700/01 **Benjamin Needham** (son of Benjamin Needham of parish of St. Bartholomew the Less, London, stationer) – free Sep 1709.

SUDELL, John　　　　　　　　　　　　　　**London**
B.c. 1669, apr. Aug 1683 to Benjamin Bell till 1690, but not freed. John is correct, but some CC records erroniously have William.

SUDELL, William　　　　　　　　　　　　**London**
Error in CC records for John, *qv*.

SUMER, John　　　　　　　　　　　　　　**London**
Free in CC Apr 1634, but usually written as Surmoire or Surmoice, *qv*.

SUMERALL, Thomas　　　　　　　　　　　**Dublin**
Recorded as 1683 but I have no details.

SUMMER, Ralph　　　　　　　　　　**Tiverton (Devon)**
Repaired Blundell School clock 1651.

SUMNER, Joseph　　　　　　　　　　　　**London**
B.c. 1650, apr. Feb 1663/64 to William Raynes till 1671, but not freed.

SUMNER, William　　　　　　　**London/Boston, USA(?)**
Apr. Aug 1654 to Robert Robinson. Freed Oct 1661. One of this name at Boston, USA, 1684.

SUNES, Isaac　　　　　　　　　　　　　　**London**
Master of John Goddard at Hounsditch in 1618, a Frenchman. Prob. Isaac Symms, *qv*.

SURMOIRE, John (sometimes Surmoice/Sumer)　　　**London**
Free in CC Apr 1634. Given CC charity Jan 1648/49 'being a poore decayed member of this Co.'.

SUTTON, Henry　　　　　　　　　　　　　**London**
Prob. an inst. maker, not a member of CC. Work known – a sundial dated 1654 signed 'Henry Sutton Behind the Exchange'; a planisphere dated 1659; a calculating machine made with Samuel Knibb in 1664 for Samuel Morland.

SUTTON, Isaac　　　　　　　　　　　　　**London**
Recorded in CC books as free in 1662, but this is a slip for Sutton Isaac (not Isaac Sutton).

SUTTON, John   **London**
B.c. 1647, apr. Apr 1661 to Edward Norris till 1668, but not freed.

SWALE, Isaac (alias Soeufew)   **London**
Listed as alien 1668. One source has Jaques Swale. I do not know this maker.

SWAN, Edward   **London**
B.c. 1637, apr. May 1650 to Ralph Ash thro' J. Bayes till 1658, but not freed.

SWANN, William   **London**
B.c. 1678, apr. Dec 1692 to Thomas Tompion till 1699. Freed Apr 1703 (son of the late John Swann of Lewis, Sussex, malster, deceased by 1703). Took as apr. May 1703 **Henry Clarke** (son of John Clarke of Stroud nr. Rochester, Kent).

SWEBY, John   **London**
B.c. 1648, apr. Jan 1662-63 to William Speakman till 1669. Freed Nov 1671. Took as aprs.: Dec 1671 **John Freebody;** May 1683 **Jeffrey Davis** – free Jul 1690; Nov 1690 **John Long** (later transferred to Ambrose Gardiner then to George Wilson and freed Jul 1698). Work known – a longcase clock is on record.

SWETTENHAM/SWEETENHAM, Edward   **Macclesfield/Dublin**
Dec 1697, a clockmaker, married at Macclesfield to Mary Coleman of Chester, spinster. Free at Dublin as Goldsmith/clockmaker 1703-30.

SWINNERTON, John   **Newcastle under Lyme (Staffordshire)**
B. 1664, brother of Thomas, *qv.* Free 1701. Will proved 1712, a clockmaker.

SWINNERTON, Thomas   **Newcastle under Lyme (Staffordshire)**
Free 1674, brother of John, *qv.* Died 14 Jul 1708. Work known – a lantern clock is on record.

SYM(M)(E)S, Isaac   **London**
Many varied spellings, incl. Simes, Sunes, Simms. An original petitioner for CC in 1622. In 1618 was a Frenchman, master of John Goddard, *qv,* at Hounsditch. Work known – several watches, one signed 'Isaac Symmes at Aldgate'.

SYMONDS, Richard   **London**
B.c. 1655, apr. Jan 1669/70 to Francis Strelley thro' James Seabourne till 1676. Freed Oct 1691. Took as aprs.: Oct 1691 **Jonathan Marsh** – free Jan 1698-99; Jul 1696 John (**Pennell?**). Still working 1697 but not heard of thereafter.

SYMONDS, Thomas (also Simonds)   **London**
Apr. to Hugh Cooper. Freed Apr 1661. Prob. dead or gone by 1662.

SYXFORTHE, John   **Masham (Yorkshire)**
Paid four shillings in 1542 for keeping church clock.

T

TAILOR and TAILEOUR – see under Taylor.

TALBOT, C.   Tuxford (Nottinghamshire)
Made church clock there in 1670. (Could this be a slip for T. Talbot, *qv?*).

TALBOT, Thomas   Nantwich (Cheshire)
Working from about 1675. Died there 29 Jun 1717. Work known – lantern clock signed 'Thomas Talbot', longcase clock signed 'Thomas Talbot, Nantwich'.

TANNER, Joseph   London
Apr. thro' Weavers' Co. Dec 1674 to Benjamin Graves, later transferred to Isaac Day and freed in CC as a Brother Apr 1682. Took as apr. in CC Sep 1684 **Robert Nelson** – free Apr 1698. Paid no quarterage after c. 1684 and prob. dead or gone before 1697.

TANTUM, Dan   Derby
Britten records bracket clock c. 1700 signed 'Dan. Tantum in Derby fecit'.

TANTUM, Francis   Loscoe (Derbyshire)
Several longcase clocks known late 17th century and early 18th century, but I have no actual dates for him.

TAPP, George   London
B.c. 1678, apr. Nov 1691 to Samuel Boutel till 1698, but not freed.

TARBOCK, John   Manchester (Lancashire)
Watchmaker. Bondsman in 1699 to marriage of Michael Fletcher of Manchester.

TARBUCK, Robert   London
Apr. Aug 1686 thro' D. Stevens to Thomas Stubbs, but not freed.

TARLES, John   London
Also Tarless and Tharles. In 1686 was already the apr. of David Minuel (prob. thro' some other City Co.), due to be free in Oct 1692. An engraver. Free Brother in CC Apr 1690. Took as aprs.: May 1699 **John Chandler** (son of Henry Chandler late of Coventry, deceased); Mar 1699/1700 **Anthony Dowson** (son of John Dowson of Thorpe Under (illegible), Yorkshire, yeoman); Sep 1705 **John Mitchell** (son of John Mitchell late of parish of St. Sepulchres, London, watch casemaker, deceased) – free Jun 1713; Mar 1710/11 **William Tarles**; Aug 1715 **Benjamin Stevenson.**

TARLETON, Jeremiah   London
B.c. 1676, apr. Jun 1690 to Walter Henshaw till 1697, but not freed.

TAYLOR, Abraham   London
Joined CC Jul 1668 (as Brother?). Paid quarterage till c. 1681.

TAYLOR, Andrew (also Taileour)   Dundee
Kept town clocks 1646-48.

TAYLOR, Charles   London
B.c. 1665, apr. Jan 1679/80 to Thomas Taylor of Holborn till 1686, but not freed.

TAYLOR, Edward   London
Recorded by Baillie as apr. under Blacksmiths' Co. 1629.

TAYLOR, Edward   London
B.c. 1624, apr. Nov 1637 to William Almond thro' O. Durant till 1645, but not freed. Took as apr. Feb 1647 **Robert Lockwood** thro' W. Bunting. Prob. dead or gone by 1662/63.

TAYLOR, George   Liverpool (Lancashire)
Watchmaker. Lost watch reported in 1705. At Juggler Street in 1712

when his daughter was b. Died at High Street in 1722. Inventory is preserved.

TAYLOR, George   **London**
B.c. 1635, apr. Aug 1648 to Benjamin Hill thro' L. Wythe till 1656, but not freed.

TAYLOR, George   **London**
Recorded by Baillie as CC 1699, but this is an error for George Tyler, *qv*.

TAYLOR, Jacob   **London**
B.c. 1674, apr. May 1688 to George Nau, jeweller and watch casemaker, till 1695, but not freed.

TAYLOR, Jasper (sometimes James)   **London**
B.c. 1671, believed son of Thomas Taylor of Holborn, *qv*. Apr. Jan 1685/86 to his father till 1692. Freed Apr 1695 (ie after father's death). Took as aprs.: Jun 1696 **Henry Smith** – Sep 1703; Aug 1699 **Thomas Fitter** (son of John Fitter, clockmaker, *qv* – and therefore a relative) – free Apr 1710; Dec 1701 **William Handy** (son of Hugh Handy of Henley-in-Arden, Warwickshire); Jan 1705-06 **Christopher Morrison** (son of Robert Morrison late of parish of St. Andrew Holborn, Middlesex, Haberdasher of Hats, deceased); Aug 1711 **George Freeman**. In 1690 mentioned in his father's will, *qv*. Work known – several bracket clocks and a longcase, signed 'Jasper Taylor in Grais Inn', 'Jasper Taylor, London' and 'Jasper Taylor, Holborn'. (Though sometimes recorded as James, he seems to have been virtually always named as Jasper as far as I can see.)

TAYLOR, John   **Ashton-under-Lyne**
Working from at least 1713. Died 1744. Maybe from London?

TAYLOR, John   **London**
B.c. 1644, apr. Jul 1680 to George Deane till 1687. Free Sep 1687. Still working 1697, but I have no data on him after this date. Work known – longcase clocks and watches on record. (Baillie records a second man of this name apr. at this time, but CC records show only one).

TAYLOR, John   **Northampton**
Working 1698 supposedly, but I have no data on him.

TAYLOR, Richard   **London**
B.c. 1634, apr. Nov 1648 to Thomas Taylor but passed over to Abraham
Guyott till 1655. Freed Jan 1655-56. Was a boxmaker. In 1656 he joined
the rebels against the CC administration. Working till at least 1664. Took
an apr. Jun 1656 for Edward Gilpin.

TAYLOR, Richard (see under Richard Cakebread)   **Oxford**

TAYLOR, Robert   **London**
B.c. 1679, (son of blank Taylor of Reading, Berkshire, cutler, deceased),
apr. Jun 1693 to James Hatchman till 1700. Freed May 1703. Took as
apr. Dec 1708 **John Goldsmith**. Was dead by Jan 1716/17 when his son
applied to CC for help towards cost of his apr., being just 14 years old – he
was bound to his stepfather, John Lake, Citizen and Weaver.

TAYLOR, Thomas
The numerous Thomas Taylors of this period are so confusing that there
are occasions when it is almost impossible to be sure which
apprenticeship related to which Thomas Taylor. The following is the
best assessment I can make of them.

TAYLOR, Thomas   **London**
Known as Thomas Taylor 'of Essex House Gate' and sometimes as 'of
Strand'. B.c. 1625, apr. Nov 1638 to Simon Hacket thro' R. Masterson
till 1646. Freed Aug 1646. Bound several aprs. for other masters (which
incl. three for E. Gilpin, two for A. Guyott, one for H. Bedford and one
for J. Dodsworth. Took as his own aprs.: Sep 1650 **Thomas Hancorne** –
free Apr 1659; Aug 1655 **John Fenton** – free Jun 1662; Jul 1659 **Henry
Younge** – free Apr 1672; Aug 1664 **Samuel Rosse** – free Sep 1672; Jun
1668 **William Hancorne** – free Jul 1676; May 1675 **Thomas Skipper;** Oct
1682 **Mathew Porter** – free Sep 1692 (after death of master). Supported
CC administration against rebels in 1656. Became CC Assistant 1656,
Warden from 1662, Master 1668. Died 1684. Will describes him as of St.
Clement Danes parish. Mentions wife, Mary, daughter Mary, wife of
Daniel Beckman, *qv*, Thomas Hancorne and Robert Halstead, *qv*. Work
known – I cannot be sure which work was by this man.

TAYLOR, Thomas   **London**
Known as Thomas Taylor of Holborn (senior). Was already apr. of
Nicholas Fetters by 1654, when latter promised to bind him thro' CC.
Free in CC Oct 1659. Took as aprs.: Mar 1659/60 **John Ward;** Mar 1659

526

John Haid; Jan 1659 **John Waynd**; Jun 1666 **Benjamin Elfes** – free Jul 1674; **Jeremiah Gosse** – free Jan 1667/68 (taken from T. Holland); Apr 1670 **John Bennett** – free Jun 1678; Aug 1672 **Thomas Ellis** – free May 1682; Jan 1679/80 **Charles Taylor;** Mar 1680/81 **Josias Southcote;** Dec 1682 **William Rogers;** Feb 1682/83 **Benjamin Nicklis;** Sep 1675 **John Shaw** – free Sep 1682; Sep 1678 his son, **Thomas Taylor** junior – free Jan 1685/86; (from J. Windmills) **John Jackson** – free Apr 1684; Jan 1685/86 his son, **Jasper Taylor** – free Apr 1695; Jun 1686 **David Wyche** (later passed over to Thomas Taylor junior); Jul 1687 **Thomas Plumleigh.** Made CC Assistant 1676, Warden from 1683, Master 1688. Died 1690. Wished to be buried at Fulham, where he owned property, 'near to my uncle Wyche'. Mentioned son Thomas junior, son Jasper under 21, daughter Susanne, brother Jasper, brother-in-law John Fitters, *qv,* wife Patience. Lived in parish of St. Andrew Holborn. (One Tabitha Taylor of St. Andrew Holborn who married 1688 John Clowes, may have been his sister). Work known – bracket clocks and watches, signed 'Thomas Taylor, Holborn' (some said to show signs of Joseph Knibb's work). A lost watch recorded in 1692 was to be returned to TT 'at the Upper End of Fetter Lane in Holborn' (his son ?).

TAYLOR, Thomas junior   **London**
B.c. 1664/65, son of Thomas Taylor senior of Holborn, *qv.* Apr. Sep 1678 to father till 1685. Free Jan 1685/86. Married Mar 1688/89 aged 24, bachelor, of St. Andrew Holborn, to Mary Edwards of same, spinster, 17, at St. James Clerkenwell. Took as aprs.: Feb 1692/93 **John England** thro' N. Russell; Apr 1692 **Walter Cawdrey;** (from father), **David Wyche** – free Apr 1694; Jun 1694 **Thomas Simkins** – free Sep 1711; Jun 1696 **James Barnes;** Jul 1700 **Robert Bumstead** (son of Richard Bumstead of Aspley, Bedfordshire, yeoman) – free Nov 1707; Aug 1702 **Jason Cox** (son of John Cox, Citizen and Haberdasher of London); Jul 1705 his son, **Thomas Taylor;** Mar 1707/08 **Thomas Rayment** (later transferred to John Winsmore); Aug 1711, his son, **Richard Taylor** (but he was also bound again Apr 1713?); Nov 1712 **William Laughton;** Apr 1717 **John Legg.** Became CC Assistant from 1701, Warden from 1707, Master 1720. I have no data on him after 1720. Work known – prob. not dstinguishable from that of his father.

TAYLOR, William   **Leeds (Yorkshire)**
Watchmaker. B.c. 1660. Married 1684 Alice Noble of Leeds, he then being 24, she only 17.

TAYLOR, William London
B.c. 1648, apr. Oct 1662 to Robert Robinson till 1669, but not freed.

TAYLOR, William London
B.c. 1660, apr. Dec 1674 to John Wright, mat. inst. maker, then passed over to Isaac Webb, then to widow Peirce till 1681. Free Apr 1682. Paid no quarterage after c. 1682.

TEADE/TEEDE, Thomas Warwick
Repaired St. Nicholas clock 1564-67. Died 1577. (But see next entry?).

TEAGE, Thomas St. Columb (Cornwall)
1585-94, repaired town clock. (This looks very like same man as previous entry).

TEASE, John (or Teare?) Dublin
Watchmaker 1696-1703.

TEBBATT, Benoni London
Sometimes Benjamin but usually Benoni. B.c. 1662, apr. Apr 1676 to Robert Dore till 1683. Freed Sep 1683. In Sep 1688 CC seized an inadequate gold watch case from his shop in Little Old Bailey – said to belong to Thomas Brafield, *qv*, but in fact William Brafield later admitted to having made it. Took as aprs.: Jun 1692 **Samuel Stanton;** May 1700 **John Partridge** (son of John Partridge of St. Clement Danes, Middlesex, ironmonger). Paid quarterage till at least 1703.

TEDMAN, James London
Baillie records watch of 1688. Error for James Stedman?

TEMPEST, Henry London
B.c. 1625, apr. Jul 1638 to Robert Grinkin thro' T. Dawson till 1646, but not freed.

TEMPLER, Charles London
B.c. 1651, apr. Mar 1665/66 to Charles Rogers till 1672. Freed Mar 1672/73. Paid quarterage till c. 1674 at least.

TEN(N)ANT, Leonard London
Clockmaker. Maintained clock at Salisbury House, Strand, for the Earl

of Salisbury between 1610 and 1628. Made clock for St. Margaret Westminster in 1617, with chime, for £37.

TENNANT, Thomas London
B.c. 1646, apr. Jul 1660 to Carr Coventry till 1667. Freed Apr 1668. Took as apr. Sep 1682 **Thomas Penkethman** – free Sep 1692. Not heard of after 1682. Prob. dead or gone by 1697/98.

TEROLD, Henry Bury St. Edmunds/Ipswich (Suffolk)
(also Tirrel and Thorald)
Free at Bury 1621-22. Watch known signed at Bury and another signed at Ipswich. A further one signed 'Henry Terold fecit'.

TERRIER, James London
B.c. 1672, apr. Aug 1685 to Isaac Day till 1693. Freed Sep 1694. Took as aprs.: Sep 1698 **Richard Weatherill**; Dec 1706 **Mary Terrier** – free Dec 1714.

TERRIER, Thomas (also Tirrier?) London
B.c. 1673, apr. Feb 1687/88 to William Laughton till 1694. Freed Feb 1694/95. Took as aprs.: Sep 1695 **Nathaniel Chiswell**; Jul 1696 **John Garrett**; Jul 1699 **Richard Weatherill** (son of Richard Weatherill of Stepney, Middlesex, weaver, deceased); **John Cobb** (from A. Yeatman) – free Jul 1703; Jan 1715-16 **Peter Bergeo**.

TERVEEN, Gerrit (sometimes Jarrat) London (and Haarlem)
Free Brother in CC Apr 1688 as watchmaker. Paid no quarterage after 1688 and prob. dead or gone by 1697/98. Baillie records him at Haarlem in 1700.

TERRY, John Banbury (Oxfordshire)
Clockmaker, married there 1700 Patience X. Died May 1736.

TERRY, John York
Clockmaker, b. before 1673. Made clock for York market in 1706, another for the castle 1716. Took as apr. his son, **Thomas**, in 1720. Son, **John**, a watchmaker, b.c. 1696; son, **Reuben**, b.c. 1693. Died 17 Feb 1757.

TEW, Thomas (but see also Tue) London
B.c. 1660, apr. Aug 1674 thro' Thomas Taylor of Holborn to William

Watmore, engraver (who was a freeman of the Barber Chirurgeons Co.) till 1681, but not freed. (Maybe related to Thomas Tue, *qv?*)

TEY, Henry   **London**
B.c. 1674 (son of Henry Tey, yeoman, of Deddington, Oxford – but this parentage crossed out in records?), apr. Oct 1688 to Richard Farmer (of Abingdon) till 1695, but not freed.

THACHE, Philip   **London**
Often written Thacke but signed his name Thache. B.c. 1663, apr. May 1676 to Thomas Wheeler till 1684. Free Sep 1685. Took as apr. May 1687 **James Jones.** In Mar 1701-02 he was in arrears with his quarterage but was dealt with tolerantly due to his circumstances. Work known – longcase clock and lantern clock, signed 'Philip Thacke, London'.

THACKE, Robert (or maybe Thache?)   **London**
B.c. 1667, apr. Aug 1681 thro' E. Norris to John Benson, engraver (and freeman of the Weavers' Co.) till 1688. Free Jan 1689/90. Marriage licence Sep 1688 to marry Ursula Smith. Took as aprs.: Aug 1691 **Robert Jennings** from Tewkesbury – free May 1703; Jul 1695 **Job Hobbins** – free Jun 1699; Nov 1702 **James Buchanan** (son of Charles Buchanan of parish of St. Margarets, Westminster, clerk); Mar 1708/09 **John Green** (son of John Green, late of London, chirurgeon, deceased) – free Sep 1716. Prob. an engraver and work not identifiable.

THARLES, John   **London**
Apr. of David Minuel, but see under Tarles.

THATCHE, Robert (see Thacke).

THEMAN, David   **Aberdeen**
Goldsmith who kept town clock 1493.

THEODRICKE, Henry   **London**
B.c. 1665, apr. Jul 1679 to John Curtis till 1686, but not freed.

THIBOU, Jacques   **Edinburgh**
Became journeyman to Paul Romieu junior Apr 1695.

THICK, Robert   **Frome (Somerset)**
Repaired town clock 1567.

THIRKILL (see Threlkeld).

THOMAS, Daniel   London
B.c. 1661, apr. Aug 1675 thro' S. Davis to John Browne, mat. inst.
maker, till 1682. Free Aug 1682. Took as aprs.: Mar 1694/95 **Elizabeth
Newman;** May 1702 **Hannah Pickes** (daughter of Isaac Pickes of
Plymouth, Devon, mercer) to serve Mary, his wife, in the trade of a
milliner; Sep 1704 **Sarah Stretton** – to serve Mary his wife – free Mar
1716-17 (being daughter of William Stretton, late Citizen and Grocer of
London). In 1708 he was excused stewardship on grounds of ill health.
(Obviously these apr. girls were all to carry on his wife's trade.)

THOMAS, Hugh   London
B.c. 1673, apr. Sep 1686 to Richard Elliss till 1693, but not freed.

THOMEGUEZ, Abraham   London
Free Brother in CC Jan 1675/76, a clockmaker 'being Naturalised'. In
1677 his two aprs. **Edward Hampton** (bound 1674 thro' Andrew Low in
the Vintners' Co.) and **John Cola Berson,** both agreed to become
Brothers of the CC in due course. By Apr 1682 his widow had already
remarried to John Arlandy, *qv*.

THOMLINSON, Richard   London
Apr. Apr 1669 to Thomas Bagley, but not freed.

THOMLINSON (see also Tomlinson).

THOMPSON/THOMSON are listed together.

THOMPSON, George   London
B.c. 1663, apr. Aug 1676 to Lawrence Sindry till 1684, but not freed.

THOMPSON, Isaac senior   London
Father of Isaac junior, *qv*, obviously working 1689 but not a member of
CC, not apparently known to them.

THOMPSON, Isaac junior   London
B.c. 1675, apr. Mar 1689/90 thro' H. Wynne to his father, Isaac
Thompson senior till 1696. Free Jul 1699. Paid no quarterage after 1699.

THOMPSON, John   **London**
Apr. Jul 1655 thro' R. Beck to Jeremy Gregory. Freed Sep 1662.

THOMPSON, John   **London**
Freeman of the Drapers' Co. In Sep 1684 he had bound **Richard Newton**
as apr. but he served with John Saville Junior.

THOMPSON, John   Truro (Cornwall)
Kept town clock 1698.

THOMPSON, John senior   **York**
Watchmaker and goldsmith. B. 1614, son of Thomas Thompson,
blacksmith. Free 1633. Fined for not taking up office of Sheriff in 1671.
Died 17 Jul 1692 aged 78. Will proved 1693.

THOMPSON, John junior   **York**
B. 1639, second son of John senior. Watchmaker. Died 1714.

THOMPSON, Robert   **London**
B.c. 1652, apr. Apr 1666 to Thomas Fenn, later transferred to Edward
Eyston till 1673. Free Feb 1681/82. Took as apr.: Mar 1684-85 **John
Pingo**. Prob. dead or gone by 1697/98.

THOMPSON, Rowland   **London**
B.c. 1660, apr. Jun 1674 thro' L. Wythe to Katherine Bestwick, widow,
till 1681, but not freed.

THOMS, William   Grampound (Cornwall)
Kept town clock 1663.

THORALD, ----   Ipswich (Suffolk)
Lost watch recorded 1683. Prob. error for Terrold, *qv*.

THORELET, David   **London**
Baillie records him as 1626, later at Rouen 1630-61. I do not know him.

THORESBY, Peter (sometimes Thearsby)   **York**
Watchmaker. B. 1646, prob. at Hull, son of William Thoresby, baker.
Free at York 1666. Married there 1668 Martha Briggs of Halifax. Still
alive 1680.

THORNHILL, Bryan   **London**
B.c. 1670, apr. Jun 1683 to Thomas Bradford till 1691, but not freed.

THORNTON, Henry   **London**
B.c. 1678, apr. Jun 1692 to Samuel Stevens till 1699. Free Feb 1699-
1700. Took as aprs.: Aug 1704 **Edward Greene** (son of Jacob Greene late
of city of Coventry, parchmentmaker); Feb 1708/09 **Philip Walton;** Mar
1712/13 **Robert Faulks;** Mar 1716/17 his son, **John Thornton;** Mar
1716/17 **John Gowland;** Dec 1719 **James Rolphe.** Supposedly working
at Basing Lane in 1723 and Royal Exchange in 1730, but I have no data
on him after 1720. Work known – several longcase clocks and octagonal
silver table clock, signed 'Henry Thornton, London'.

THORNTON, John   **London**
Paid CC search fee in 1671. Prob. a measure-seller.

THOROWGOOD, Edward   **London**
Mat. inst. maker and freeman of the Plumbers' Co. Brother in CC Jan
1668/69. Took as apr. **Cornelius Beard** Oct 1670 thro. L. Wythe, later
transferred to J. Atkinson, mat. inst. maker. Paid no quarterage after
about 1690. Prob. dead or gone by 1697-98.

THOROWGOOD, James   **London**
B.c. 1647, apr. Oct 1661 to John Thorowgood till 1668, but not freed.

THOROWGOOD, John   **London**
B.c. 1638, apr. Sep 1652 to William Petty, passed over to Richard
Scrivener till 1659. Free Jan 1660/61. Worked in Fleet Street as an
engraver in 1662. Took as apr. Oct 1661 **James Thorowgood.**

THOROWGOOD, Thomas   **London**
On CC list as at Fleet Street in 1662, but prob. a slip for William, *qv.*

THOROWGOOD, William   **London**
B.c. 1638, apr. 1652 to William Petty, then passed over to Thomas
Belson till 1659. Free Jan 1660/61. Believed worked in Fleet Street in
1662. Took as aprs.: Jun 1664 **John Buckenhill** (passed him over to John
Smith then on Smith's death took him back again) – free Sep 1672; Dec
1671 **John Wainwright** – free Sep 1679; Sep 1672 **Edward Buckenhill**
(for James Delander?) – free Feb 1687/88; May 1680 **Ben Assir**

Sacheverell (passed over to T. Tompion) – free Sep 1687. In Jan 1674/75 CC gave him a charity of 7s. 6d. being 'now a prisoner in Ludgate'.

THORPE, John London

B.c. 1628, apr. Aug 1641 thro' O. Durant to John Harris till 1649. Free Jul 1657. In Mar 1669/70 CC gave him a charity of 6s. 0d. from poor box, being 'a poor member of the Company who is blind' (though in 1676 he is referred to as 'almost blind'). Received regular charity from CC till Sep 1679, when presumably died.

THRELKELD, ---- London

Christian name believed William, but this is not certain. Not a member of CC but was known to them. In Jul 1638 took as apr. thro' T. Dawson in CC **Lionel Wythe** – free Dec 1645. Was prob. dead or gone by 1662/63. Not to be confused with later William Threlkelds. (This man may well be the William Threlkeld who was father of Deodatus, *qv*. He married Thomasine X and had first child, Thomasine, b. about 1620. Was at one time in France, later became curate of Brancepeth, co. Durham, where he died in 1675).

THRELKELD, Deodatus Newcastle on Tyne
(sometimes Thirkeld, etc.)

B.c. 1657, perhaps in France, son of William Threlkeld who became curate of Brancepeth. He died at Tritlington 1 Mar 1732/33. Married three times, 1 Dec 1684 Hannah Anderson of Newburn who died 1698; 2 Jan 1698/99 Margaret Ilderton (believed sister of Robert Ilderton, clockmaker), who died 1699; 3 Oct 1701 Margaret Moor of Whickham, who died 1758. Had several children amongst whom was Deodatus, who went to Virginia and was disinherited. Worked on All Saints Newcastle clock 1691, and made a new one c. 1705. In 1698 was challenged to a contest by William Prevost as to who could make the best clock – he won. Work known – bracket clock and watch, signed 'D. Threlkeld, Newcastle'.

THRELKELD, Ralph London

Son of Henry Threlkeld of London (later parish clerk of Brancepeth, co. Durham), and brother of William Threlkeld, below. Became goldsmith at the Sign of the Oyl Jar in the Strand. Work known – bracket clock and watch. (Watch c. 1710, clock c. 1740.)

THRELKELD, William   **London**
Believed son of Henry Threlkeld of London, later of Brancepeth, co.
Durham. B. 1674, died 1750. Watchmaker and goldsmith. Married 1st
1706 Lois Watson of London, who died 1731; 2nd 1741 Mary Roode.
Worked at the Sign of the Ring, Minories. Work known – longcase
clocks and watches signed 'William Threlkeld, London' and 'Wm.
Threlkeld in ye Strand'. (There might perhaps be two men of this name,
as his family relationships are very complex.)

THWING, James (but signed Twhing)   **London**
B.c. 1665, apr. Jul 1679 thro; S. Davis senior to Daniel Rofe till 1686.
Free Apr 1688. Excused stewardship in Jul 1712 on account of 'losses in
trade and great charges'. Steward 1718, after which I have no record of
him.

TIESE, John   **London**
Watches recorded c. 1610/20, one signed 'John Tiese at London'.

TILS, Richard (also Tills and Tillis)   **London**
Recorded from late 17th century. Not a member of CC but took as apr. in
CC Nov 1715 **James Coombs** from (or thro') R. George – free Apr 1719.

TINGLEY, Thomas   **London**
B.c. 1669, apr. Jul 1682 to William Glazier till 1690, but not freed.
(Baillie records another of this name as apr. 1686, but I cannot trace such
a one.)

TINHAM, Samuel   **New Sarum, Salisbury (Wiltshire)**
Longcase clocks known c. 1680-85.

TIPLING, William   **Leeds (Yorkshire)**
Clockmaker. Married 1692 Ruth Norton. Believed apr. of Williamson,
qv. Three children b. 1693-1700, died young. Worked on bells of St.
John's 1694, 1699, 1700 and 1701. In latter years was paid 10s. for
maintaining clock. Working in Kirkgait when died 1712. Widow
remarried 1713. Work known – three longcase clocks, usually signed
'William Tipling in Leeds fecit'.

TIPPING, Edward   **Warwick**
Blacksmith? Children b. 1662-77. Maintained church clock at St. Marys,
Warwick, 1663-87. (See also under George below.)

TIPPING, George London
B.c. 1650, apr. Jan 1664/65 to Samuel Knibb on whose death he was passed on to Francis Bicknell till 1671. Free Jun 1674. Took as apr. Jul 1680 **John Pierce**. Paid quarterage till c. 1685. Prob. dead or gone by 1697/98. In 1688 one Tipping repaired clock at Hatfield House, Herts, but see also Edward above.

TIRRELL (see Terold)

TITHERTON, John London
At least one longcase clock recorded signed 'John Titherton Londini fecit', believed late 17th century – c. 1700, but I have no record of such a maker. Not a member of CC. nor apparently known to them.

TODD, John York
Clockmaker, free there 1665.

TODD, Robert London
B.c. 1670, apr. Mar 1684/85 to Daniel Quare till 1691, but not freed.

TODD, Samuel York
Watchmaker. Son of Samuel Todd, milliner. Free 1686.

TOLESON, Ralph (also Tolson, Tollison) **London**
B.c. 1679, apr. Sep 1693 to Cuthbert Lee till 1700. Free Sep 1701, having been passed over to Robert Webster. Took as aprs.: Oct 1706 **Robert Ericke** (hardly legible) – free Mar 1719/20; Dec 1713 **John Ormond**. Work known – watch signed 'Ralph Toleson, London'.

TOLLEY, Charles (sometimes Talley) **London**
B.c. 1663, apr. May 1676 to Joseph Ashby till 1684, however in Jul 1678 was believed to have 'gone to be a soldier'. Freed Dec 1683 having been re-(?) apr. to John Brewer. Took as aprs.: Aug 1685 **William Martin;** May 1699 **William Mansfield** (son of Andrew Mansfield of St. Bottolph Aldgate, mariner); Apr 1701 **John Tyler** (son of Robert Tyler of Hatfield, Berkshire, farmer); May 1704 **Peter Dennis** (son of Henry Dennis of Warrington, Lancashire, innkeeper, deceased); Nov 1710 **John Nurse** – free Oct 1718; Jan 1711/12 **William Miles;** Sep 1714 **John Rainsford;** Sep 1717 **Benjamin King;** son **Charles Tolley** – freed Aug 1720 by patrimony. Received CC charity regularly from 1710-1719, after which his widow received it. Must have died in 1720 (alive still in Mar

1719/20). In Jan 1718/19 was appointed CC Beadle to replace Christopher Gould, deceased. This office normally given to a poor member. Work known – longcase clocks.

TOMAGUEZ (see Thomeguez and also John Arlandy)

TOMBS, Dan. London
Late 17th century longcase clock recorded, but no-one of this name appears in CC records. Maybe misreading of a name? Or perhaps James Tomes, *qv*, abbreviated as Jam.

TOMES, James London
B.c. 1664, apr. Oct 1678 to John Savill junior till 1685, but not freed. See also previous entry (Dan. Tombs).

TOMLINS, Nicholas London
Apr. Mar 1639 thro' O. Durant to Peter Closon. Free Oct 1646. Prob. worked for Closon throughout. Took as aprs.: Nov 1653 **John James** (passed over to Thomas Loomes on Tomlin's death, and freed Feb 1661/62); Mar 1648 **John Salmon** (passed over to George Poole then back again to Tomlins) – freed May 1654; **John Tyms** (passed over May 1658 to Richard Beck, Tomlins being dead). Also bound several aprs. for other masters incl. three for R. Morgan, two for J. Nicasius, one each for J. White, P. Closon, A. Prime, D. Parry, W. Smith. (See also under Nicholas Tomlinson).

TOMLINS, William London
CC records state he bound an apr. Mar 1650/51 for J. Nicasius, but this is prob. a slip for *Nicholas* Tomlins, *qv*.

TOMLINSON, George (signed Thomlinson) London
Free Brother in CC Mar 1673/74. Took as aprs.: Jun 1674 **Thomas Carter** thro' L. Wythe; Jul 1680 **Thomas Lough**. Paid no quarterage after c. 1681. Work known – lantern clock signed 'Geo. Thomlinson in George Yard in Lumbard Street fecit'.

TOMLINSON, Richard (see Thomlinson)

TOMLINSON, Nicholas London
His apr. **George Kingsmill** was transferred to William Smith from

whom he was freed Jul 1667. This is what CC records state but must surely be a slip for Nicholas Tomlins, *qv*.

TOMLINSON, Thomas   **London**
Free Brother in CC Nov 1646. In arrears with quarterage Oct 1664. In 1662 worked in Chancery Lane.

TOMLINSON, William   **Colchester (Essex)**
Watchmaker and goldsmith, b.c. 1654. Married Jane X by whom four daughters up to 1690. Took as apr. **John Rotherham** in 1701. Died 25 Apr 1710.

TOMLINSON, William   **London**
Watchmaker, Free Brother in CC Jul 1699. Took as aprs.: Nov 1703 **James Snelling;** Jan 1708/09 **Jonathan Newton** (son of Anthony Newton of Croydon, Surrey, wheelwright); Feb 1710-11 **Devereux Bowly** – free Nov 1718; Dec 1714 **Joseph Taylor.** Believed to have been a Quaker, supposedly dying in 1750, but I have no data on him after 1720 except that in 1748 he worked as a Finisher at Stoke Newington. Said to have worked at the Dial and Three Crowns in Birchin Lane nr. the Royal Exchange, and later in White Hart Court, Gracechurch Street. Work known – longcase clocks and bracket clocks, and watches on record.

TOMPION, Thomas   **London**
B. Jul 1639 at Northill, Bedfordshire, son of Thomas Tompion senior, blacksmith. Apr. unknown. May have worked in Buckinghamshire before London. In Jul 1671 he paid a search fee to the CC, though he was not made a Free Brother, as Great Clockmaker, till 4 Sep 1671. A bell cast for St. Lawrence church, Willington, nr. Northill in 1671 and signed 'Thomas Tompion Fecit 1671' suggests that Tompion may have moved to London in that year before Jul. Became a full freeman in CC by redemption Apr 1674. Took as aprs.: Jan 1673/74 **Michael Knight** (thro' L. Wythe); Jun 1676 **Robert Pattison;** Sep 1676 **John Webster;** Sep 1677 **Benjamin Harris** (thro' J. Dyde of Blacksmiths' Co.); Sep 1683 **Charles Lloyd** – free Jul 1691; Dec 1683 **Joseph Audley;** c. 1685 **Jeremiah Martin** (from W. Dent) – free Sep 1687; **Ben Assir Sacheverell** (from W. Thorowgood) – free Sep 1687; **William Morally** (from H. Child) – free Dec 1688; May 1689 **Robert Creed** – free Mar 1699/1700; Nov 1690 **John Hilton** (thro' W. Morally); **George Allatt** (from S. Bouquet) – free Jul 1691; May 1691 **Robert Anderson** (thro' M. Knight); Jul 1691 **Edward Boone** (from R. Dent) – free Jul 1691;

Dec 1692 **William Swann** (son of John Swann of Lewes, Sussex, maltster) – free May 1703; Jun 1694 **Thomas Davis** (thro' W. Moraly); Dec 1694 **Nicholas Heather; Edward Banger** (thro' J. Ashby) – free Jul 1695; **Whitestone Littlemore** (from T. Gibbs) – free May 1698; **George Harrison** (from Joanna May) – free Jul 1698; Nov 1698 **William Thompson** (son of Thomas Thompson, Citizen and Butcher) – free Feb 1708/09; **Edward Mercer** (from Cuthbert Lee) – free Jul 1699; **Daniel Delander** (from C. Halstead) – free Jul 1699; Mar 1699/1700 **Anthony Walraven** (son of John Walraven late of St. Martins in the Fields, goldsmith, deceased). Also employed Abrose Gardner, William Smith, Thomas Shields, Henry Callot, *qv*. In Jul 1684 he claimed he was sick and was also 'repairing and altering his house' when called to be Steward. Made CC Assistant 1691, Warden from 1700, Master 1703, attended till 1713, when died. Took into partnership Edward Banger, then took George Graham into partnership about 1711. Graham succ. him on his death in 1713. Work known – very prolific maker and perhaps the most famous of all time. For a detailed study see R. W. Symonds *'Thomas Tompion his life and work'*.

Tompion, Thomas junior   **London**
Nephew of Thomas senior, apr. Apr 1694 to Charles Kempe till 1701. Free Dec 1702. Married Feb 1699/1700, being a bachelor of St. Bride's parish aged 23, to Jane English, widow. Later was imprisoned as a criminal – again, see R. W. Symonds *'Thomas Tompion his life and work'*.

TOOLEY, John   **Warwick**
Serviced St. Nicholas church clock 1590-95.

TOPPIN(G), John   **London**
B.c. 1677, apr. Sep 1691 thro' E. Norris to William Grimes till 1698, but not freed. Baillie records his death as 1747. Work known – longcase and bracket clocks, signed 'John Toppin, London', but sometimes also signed himself 'John Toppin, Memory Master, London' – just what is intended by that I do not know.

TOPPING, William   **Liverpool (Lancashire)**
Watch springmaker. Sons b. there 1640/41. He died 1717 at Cooke Street.

TORADO, Francis senior   **London**
Free Brother in CC Apr 1633. Working 1662 alongside son, Francis junior, *qv*.

TORADO, Francis junior   **London**
First recorded 1662 alongside father, *qv*. Received CC charity with his wife from Jul 1682 till his death about Aug-Sep 1683, after which his widow received a pension till Jan 1692/93 when they paid five shillings towards her burial.

TORNIQUE, J.   **London**
Watch recorded c. 1670, but I do not know this name. Not apparently in CC.

TORPORLEY, Nathaniel   **England(?), London(?)**
Baillie records his as 1593, but I do not know him.

TORY, Sarah   **London**
B.c. 1646, apr. Dec 1660 to Richard Bowen and Mary his wife, till 1667, but not freed.

TOVEY, William   **London**
B.c. 1641, apr. Nov 1655 to Simon Dudson till 1662, but not freed.

TOWELL, Nicholas   **London**
B.c. 1657, apr. Apr 1669 to Samuel Davis till 1678, but not freed.

TOWNE, Joseph   **Horncastle (Lincolnshire)**
Watch recorded c. 1700.

TOWNSEND, John   **London**
Servant to Mr. Clarke (prob. Humphrey) in 1632 when forbidden by CC to work any longer at the trade.

TOWNSEND, Joseph   **Helmdon (Northamptonshire)**
Supposedly working c. 1700 but I have no data on him.

TRACY, Richard   **London**
B.c. 1648, apr. Mar 1661 to Nicholas Coxeter till 1669, but not freed.

TRACY, Stephen   **Rotterdam/London**
One such recorded at Rotterdam 1683. London watches known c.1700 – c. 1720.

TRAFFORD, Thomas London(?)
Lantern clock recorded signed 'Thomas Trafford fecit' prob. c. 1660-70. Place not known, supposed London, but no such person known to CC.

TRAPENCHEERE, John London
Engraver who in Jul 1678 engraved first copperplate of CC coat of arms – said to have been paid short. In Sep 1678 he appeared and claimed Nicasius gave him only 5s. out of 15s. due, but latter claimed to have given him the rest in clothing, etc.

TRASILLION, Anthony London
Worked at Hampton Court 1528-34.

TRAVIS, Samuel Sheffield (Yorkshire)
Watchmaker, children b. there 1699-1701. One daughter died 1723.

TREGOSSE, Stephen Grampound (Cornwall)
Kept town clock 1686.

TRENERRY, John Penryn (Cornwall)
Repaired town clock 1652.

TREVEEN, Jarrett (see Terveen).

TREVOR, Thomas (or John) London
Apr. Sep 1654 to Peter Delander thro' H. Cooper, but not freed.

TRIGG, Thomas London
B.c. 1679, apr. Sep 1692 to John Westoby till 1700. Free Jul 1701. Took as apr. Jan 1711/12 **Henry Barnes**. Believed worked in Bread Street. Work known – watch and longcase clock.

TRIPPETT, John Kingston-on-Thames (Surrey)
B. 1646, son of Richard Trippett of Kingston on Thames. Made Kingston church clock 1668 for £22. Daughter, Elizabeth died there 1694. He died there 1 Jan 1700/01. Admitted to CC Dec 1668 as Free Brother, a clockmaker. Took as aprs.: Dec 1668 **Henry Evans** (thro' T. Bagley) – free Jul 1682; Jul 1671 **Francis Wastnesse** (thro' I. Puzy). In arrears with quarterage 1687.

TRIPPETT, Robert London
B.c. 1674, apr. Apr 1688 to James Hatchman till 1695. Free May 1700.
Took as aprs.: Dec 1706 **William Hutchinson;** Dec 1706 his son,
William Trippet freed; Nov 1711 **Gersham Butcher;** Sep 1715 his son,
Robert Trippett. Believed worked at Wapping and insolvent 1723.

TRIPPETT, Thomas London
B.c. 1640, apr. Aug 1654 to Nicholas Coxeter, then passed over to
George Poole till 1661, but not freed. Prob. dead or gone by 1662.

TRIPPETT, William Bristol/Hull (Yorkshire)
Married at Bristol Feb 1660/61, a clockmaker. One such at Hull 1670-71
when he repaired Beverley Minster clock for £3 with salary of £10 yearly
to maintain it.

TROUT, Walter Exeter
Clockmaker 1697.

TROWE, John London
Recorded by Baillie as apr. 1685 but this must be a slip for Thomas, *qv.*

TROWE, Thomas London
B.c. 1671, apr. Jul 1685 to William Speakman (being his kinsman) till
1692, but not freed. Baillie records him as of St. Bride's parish and being
insolvent in 1729.

TRUBSHAW, John London
B.c. 1665, apr. Sep 1679 to Robert Halstead till 1686. Free Jan 1686/87.
Took as aprs.: Sep 1689 **Stephen Mallett;** from R. Halstead; **Joseph
Bell** – free Nov 1691; Jul 1695 **John Parsons;** Jul 1696 **Joseph Tilly** –
free Oct 1704; Jul 1704 **Thomas Grace** (son of Thomas Grace Citizen
and Joyner, but his clothes to be bought by John Grace, Citizen and
Joyner). Made CC Assistant from 1710, Warden pre-Nov 1714 but died
before he actually held Warden's office. May have been connected with
Cutlers' Co. Work known – longcase and bracket clocks, and watches.

TRUMBALL, P(eter) London/York
London marquetry clock supposedly c. 1700. Watch signed at York
hallmarked 1730.

TUCKEY, Edward   **London**
B.c. 1667, apr. Sep 1681 to Richard Ayres till 1688, but not freed.

TUDMAN, James   **London**
Apparently not in CC. One of this name married Jan 1686/87 Elizabeth Tunewell or Tinewell. Reputedly worked at The Crown, Lombard Street. Work known – longcase and bracket clocks, signed 'Jacobus Tudman Londini fecit'.

TUE, Thomas (but see also Tew)   **Kings Lynn (Lincolnshire)**
Lantern clock dated 1663 signed 'Tho. Tue de L'inn fecit', and another one dated 1697. Believed died in 1710 aged 97.

TUNN, James   **London**
Not in CC. Bracket clocks known c. 1700-1715 said to show Graham influence.

TURBUTT, Francis   **London**
B.c. 1678, apr. Apr 1692 to Samuel Marchant till 1699, but not freed.

TURGES/TURGIS, James   **London**
B.c. 1646, apr. Jun 1660 to Ahasuerus Fromanteel till 1667, but not freed.

TURKEY, Thomas   **London**
In Oct 1646 promised to bind his apr. thro' CC.

TURNBULL, Charles   **Oxford**
B. Lincolnshire, admitted Corpus Christi College 1573. Wrote treatise on globes and designed College sundial in 1581.

TURNER, John   **Dublin**
Watchmaker/goldsmith, free there 1685-1711, having been apr. in 1677 to John Martin.

TURNER, Samuel   place not known
Lantern clock, mid-17th century, signed 'Samuel Turner'.

TURNER, Thomas   **London**
In 1654 was servant to Peter de Landre.

TUSSINGHAM, John   London
B. between 1664 and 1668. Apr. Jul 1682 to Richard Prince till 1689, but
not freed. In May 1687 married as bachelor, watchmaker, aged 23 (but
prob. younger) of Bishopsgate Street, to Mary Freake of St. Mary
Aldermansbury, spinster, 24.

TUTELL, Thomas (also Tuttle)   London
B.c. 1674, apr. Apr 1688 to Henry Wynne till 1695. Free Jul 1695. Took
as aprs.: Jun 1697 **Thomas Barnaby;** Apr 1699 **William Collier** (son of
Richard Collier, late Citizen and Goldsmith of London); Aug 1699 **John
Coleson** (son of Caleb Coleson of Stretham, co. Surrey, yeoman). Paid
quarterage till 1701, when believed died. In 1709 his widow received CC
charity.

TUTON, Laurence   Bristol
Longcase clocks known c. 1690-1720.

TWELL, George   London
B.c. 1671, apr. Sep 1685 to William Hawkins till 1691, but not freed.

TWHING, James (see Thwing).

TYLER, George   London
B.c. 1678, apr. Nov 1692 to Robert Dingley till 1699. Free Dec 1699.
Took as apr. Jan 1704/05 **Henry Elliott** (son of Henry Elliott, Citizen and
Clockmaker) – free Dec 1720. Also took with Lucy his wife the following
girls: Dec 1714 **Mary Darby;** Apr 1716 **Rebecca Fisher;** Apr 1718
Eleanor Moseley; Jan 1719-20 **Catherine Jackson.** Work known –
longcase and bracket clocks signed 'George Tyler, Popes Head Alley,
London'.

TYLER, John   London
B.c. 1653, apr. Feb 1667/68 to John Matchett till 1674, but not freed.

TYMMS, John   London
Son of Edward Tymms, apr. Sep 1656 to Nicholas Tomlins, then from
May 1658 to Richard Beck, Tomlins having died. Not freed.

TYRER, Edward   Chester/Manchester
Clockmaker, free at Chester 1637/38. A watchmaker of this name had a
son baptised at Manchester 1644.

U

UNDERHILL, Cave   **London**
B.c. 1634, apr. Jul 1647 to Isaac Daniell thro' T. Claxton till 1655. Free Oct 1655. Paid no quarterage after c. 1668.

UNDERWOODE, William   **Bristol/London**
Apr. to John Clarke in Bristol, free Apr 1667. One of this name working in London from c. 1705 (believed died 1754 – maybe two of this name?)

UNEMAN, John and **William**   **England**
Dutch clockmakers working in England in 1368.

UNETT, William   **London**
B.c. 1678, apr. Sep 1692 to Richard Chilcott till 1699, but not freed.

UNITE, Matthias   **Oxford**
Son of Matthias Unite, minister of Fenny Compton, Warwickshire. Apr. Oct 1681 to John Knibb. Work known – lantern clocks signed 'Matthias Unite' and 'Matthias Unite fecit', without place name.

UPTON, Nathaniel   **London**
B.c. 1661, apr. 1674/75 thro' S. Davis to John Nash till 1682, but not freed.

URSEAU, Nicholas London
Many spelling variants incl. Oursian. Possibly of French origin. Working here by 1531, Denizen clockmaker 1544. Working initially at Hampton Court, then Westminster in 1568, Charing Cross 1565. Clockmaker to Edward VI and Queen Elizabeth. Died 1590. See Loomes *'Country Clocks and their London Origins'*.

V

VALE, Charles   **London**
Clockmaker at St. Saviours Southwark. Daughter Susanna died there
1711.

VALLIN, John   **London**
Many spelling variants incl. Vallen, Valeyn, etc. B. Ryssell, Flanders (ie
Lille) c. 1535. A Huguenot immigrant. In 1567 made an astronomical
clock in Brussels. In London by 1590. Made his will 1593. Died 1603
leaving issue John, Margaret and Nicholas. Work known – table clock.

VALLIN, Nicholas   **London**
Son of John Vallin, *qv*. Married 1590 at Austin Friars Dutch Church,
London to Elizabeth Rendtmeesters. B.c. 1565. Came from Brussels.
Lived in parish of St. Ann, Blackfriars. Had three daughters. Said to
have had as journeymen **John Archer** and **John Leyns**. Died 1603 soon
after father. Widow, Elizabeth, married 1604 Gerart Cosin, tailor. Work
known – a few clocks, two dated 1598 and 1600. See article in *Connoisseur
Year Book 1955*.

VANACKER, Abraham   **London**
In Oct 1655 bound to William Rogers as journeyman for about four
months at five shillings weekly, later six shillings weekly.

VANBROF, James   **place not known**
Recorded by Britten c. 1605.

VAN DE HAGUE, Henry   Croydon
B.c. 1664. Clockmaker, bachelor, aged 23, married Oct 1687 to Jane
Hayden of Croyden, spinster, 19 (prob. sister of John Haydon, *qv*) –
proposed by John House of same, clockmaker, *qv*. Not in CC.

VANDOOGANE, Awdryan   London
Dutch, came here for religion, 1570 – according to Baillie.

VANGALAND, Giles (also Vangale, Vangande)   London
Working 1568-85 'clockmaker, borne under the obedyence of the King
of Spain, payeth tribute to no companye and is of the Dutche Church'.

VANS, Charles   London
B.c. 1668, apr. Oct 1682 to Edward Norris till 1689, but not freed.

VANS, Patrick   London
B.c. 1659, apr. May 1672 to Joseph Knibb till 1680, but not freed. In
1680 twice summoned to CC court for infringements (prob. for not
taking up freedom).

VANSTRIPE, Nicholas   London
C. 1680-1701. A Dutchman, watchmaker, not free of CC. In 1701 he was
to be prosecuted for setting the Master's name (Gretton) on a new watch.

VARIER, George (also Verier)   Pont Nedd Fechan (Wales)
Recorded as working 1673, but one of this name did work there much
later, dying in 1782?

VARNAN, Samuel   London
Recorded by Baillie 1656, but must be a slip for Samuel Vernon, *qv*.

VASSIERE, Thomas   London
Free in CC Sep 1698 being the apr. of Cuthbert Lee (but not bound thro'
CC).

VAUGHAN, Robert   London
B.c. 1642, apr. Jun 1655 to Thomas Broome thro' H. Cooper till 1663,
but not freed.

VAULOUE, Mathew (also Vauloie/Vaulove/Vanlove)   **London**
French watchmaker. Free Brother in CC Sep 1692. Paid quarterage till
1698. Believed worked in St. Martins Lane.

VAUS, Patrick   **London**
Recorded by Baillie but prob. a slip for Vans, *qv*.

VAUSSEAU, Jacob   **London**
From Gien. In 1655 was to work as journeyman, but only for Grinkin,
Gregory and Bartram. Not in CC.

VAUTROLIER, James (sometimes Vautroler)   **London**
An alien working 'without Temple Bar' in 1622 and had Lewes Cuper
working with him. Was a 1622 petitioner and one of first Assistants in
CC. Took as aprs.: Sep 1637 **John Colson** thro' R. Masterson – free Nov
1646; Apr 1639 **William Dobbe** thro' R. Masterson – free (as Brother)
Sep 1646; Aug 1641 **Robert Wynne** thro' O. Durant. Work known –
watches.

VEALE, ----   **Bodmin (Cornwall)**
Late 16th century clockmaker.

VEALE, John   **Bristol**
Free there Feb 1680-1713.

VEALE, Thomas   **Bristol**
Free Feb 1652.

VECUE, Thomas   **London**
Baillie records him as 1632 but I cannot trace him.

VERBACK, William   **London**
B.c. 1667, apr. Apr 1681 to Dorcas Bouquet (later passed over to a
jeweller?), but not freed.

VERNON, Christopher   **London**
Free in CC Apr 1639. In 1639/40 took as apr. **Josias Preston** thro'
R. Masterson. Work known – lantern clocks recorded signed 'at ye Great
Turnstyle, Holbourne'.

VERNON, Samuel senior   **London**
Free Brother in CC Oct 1648. With Fromanteel was a ringleader in 1656 rebellion against CC administration. Took as aprs.: **William Bayley** thro' R. Ash and later passed him over to B. Wolverston; Aug 1671 had taken **Francis Draycott** (without consent) and then passed him on to Robert Seigniour; Feb 1677-78 son, **Samuel Vernon** – free Jan 1685/86; Jan 1679/80 **John Lane**. Made CC Assistant from 1668, Warden from 1677 but initially was excused due to 'inability of body', Master 1680, but in Oct 1680 was sick and J. Gregory deputised. Last attended 1681. Died before Jan 1685/86. Work known – watches.

VERNON, Samuel junior   **London**
B.c. 1663, son of Samuel Vernon senior, apr. Feb 1677/78 to his father till 1684. Free Jan 1685/86. Took as aprs.: Apr 1687 **Samuel Sadler** – free Sep 1694; Apr 1698 **Richard Barnwell** – free May 1705; Jan 1691/92 **Caleb Ellison;** Sep 1693 **William Osborn** (passed over to Samuel Sadlier; Oct 1696 **Richard Lamb;** Aug 1701 **William Blakey** (son of late Nicholas Blakey, Citizen and Clothworker of London, deceased); Aug 1701 **Edward Caddey** (son of one Caddey, Citizen and Gunmaker of London, deceased) – this latter entry is altered in rough books and is suspect. Paid quarterage till mid-1702 then died. Widow paid till late 1704, then died.

VESEY, Agmondesham   **London**
B.c. 1678, apr. Mar 1692 to John Sowter till 1699, but not freed.

VESEY, Robert   **Oxford**
Son of Robert Vesey, tailor, of Oxford. Apr. Mar 1682 to John Harris – free Sep 1691. Issue b. 1691-94.

VICARY, George   **London**
B.c. 1672, apr. Nov 1685 to Thomas Brafield till 1693, but not freed. (Baillie records two by this name, but there was only one).

VICK, Richard   **London**
B.c. 1678, son of Richard Vick. Apr. Jan 1692-93 thro' W. Speakman to Francis Asseline, a Freeman of the Haberdashers' Co. till 1699. But was later turned over to Daniel Quare and freed Apr 1702. Took as aprs.: Jun 1710 **John Johnson;** Jan 1711/12 **Thomas Gladman;** Mar 1716/17 **Richard Blinco;** Aug 1719 **Samuel Noyes.** I have no data on him after 1720 but is reputed to have lived on till 1750. Worked at the Seven Dials

in 1748. Reputedly keeper of clocks in the King's Palace. Work known – watches signed 'Richard Vick, London' but some include 'watchmaker to his late Majesty'. Also bracket clocks.

VIELL, Charles   **London**
B.c. 1664, apr. Dec 1678 to Richard Jarret till 1685. Free Apr 1686. Still working 1697. Work known — watches.

VIELL, Richard   **London**
B.c. 1637, apr. Feb 1651/52 to Daniel Fletcher thro' S. Davis till 1658, but not freed.

VIET, Ch.   **London**
Recorded by Baillie but error for Cl. (Claude), *qv*.

VIET, Claude   **London**
Watchmaker, believed from Orleans and married at Crispin Street Oct 1696 Marianne de la Neufmaison. Children incl. son. Abraham Claude, b. 1700, youngest child, Susanne, b. 1722 at Threadneedle Street. Free in CC Dec 1698. In Jun 1699 summoned by CC for keeping an apr. bound to a Dyer in the Mint. Took as aprs.: Sep 1701 **Adam Dhinsseau** (son of Isaac Dhinsseau of Southampton); Oct 1710 **Claude Renou**; Jan 1714/15 daughter **Marianne Viet** – free 1738. Daughter later became partner with Thomas Mitchell, hence Mitchell and Viet (after 1738). Work known – watches and bracket clocks, sometimes signed 'Viet, London' or 'Claude Viet, London' plus 'Watchmaker to her Majesty'.

VIET, Etienne (also Viette)   **London**
Huguenot and master clockmaker 1699 when daughter, Marianne, b. to wife, Ester. Not in CC.

VIET, Henry   **London**
Longcase clock noted c. 1705.

VIEVAR, George   **London**
B.c. 1679, apr. Oct 1693 to Daniel Le Count till 1700, but not freed.

VIGNEAU, Peter (or Daniel?) (also Vinio)   **London**
B.c. 1677, apr. Nov 1691 as Daniel to Richard Baker till 1698. Free Nov 1709 as Peter. Not certain which is his correct name.

VIPONT, John **London**
B.c. 1668, apr. Sep 1682 thro' D. Stevens to Henry Morgan till 1689, but
not freed.

VIRGOE, Thomas **London**
B.c. 1660, son of Michael or Nicholas (writing bad). Apr. Jan 1674/75 to
Samuel Davis till 1681. Free Jun 1682. Took as apr. Jul 1682 **Robert
Baldwin**. May have been a Quaker. Will dated 1683 records him as
clockmaker of parish of St. Edmund the King. He mentions property in
Bridgegate Street, Thetford, Norfolk to his mother, Mary Virgoe. His
'loving friend' Francis Stamper, *qv*, to be overseer. Also his loving friend
Robert King, goldsmith. Will proved 1685. Prob. a bachelor.

VOLANT, Elias **London**
Name also appears as Voland, Vollant, Volunt, and as Elie and Ely. A
Frenchman. In 1622 working with two aprs. 'att holboern att a baker's
house'. Admitted into CC 1632 (supposedly also in Blacksmiths' Co.)
had **Edward Ambrose** as an unapproved apr. and handed him back in
1634 to Josias Cuper.

VOTIER, John (prob. also Vautier) **London**
French clockmaker, supposedly here by 1532. Denizen 1544.

VOTIER, Lewis (also Vautier, Vowtere) **London**
An alien in 1622 in same house as Abel Monpas 'in gunpowder alley,
show lane, at a smythes' (Louis Vautier of Blois b. 1581, died 1638,
married 1617 Rachel Maupas – may be same man).

VOYCE, Gamaliel **London**
B.c. 1673, apr. Jan 1687/88 to Sarah Payne till 1694. Free Jan 1694/95.
Took as aprs.: Jan 1696/97 **William James**; Mar 1705/06 **William Wix**
(son of John Wix, Citizen and Cordwainer of London). Work known –
bracket clocks.

VOYCE, Richard **London**
B.c. 1680, apr. Jul 1693 to George Etherington till 1701, but not freed.

VRIEMAN, Johannes and **Willilmus** **London/Delft(?)**
Came to England 1368 at invitation of Edward III with Lietuty, *qv*. See
also Uneman.

W

WADE, John London
Received regular CC charity from Jan 1679/80 till Jan 1692/93, when 'being lately dead there was given to his sister wherewith to bury him 12s.'.

WAFFIELD, John London
Error for Warfield, *qv*.

WAGSTAFFE, Edward London
B.c. 1637, apr. Jan 1650/51 thro' R. Masterson to Edward East till 1658, but not freed.

WAINWRIGHT, John London
B.c. 1657, apr. Dec 1671 to William Thorowgood till 1678. Freed Sep 1679. Paid no quarterage after c. 1680.

WALDEN, Thomas Dorchester (Dorset)
Kept town clock 1620-39.

WALDIGRAVE, Thomas (also Waldegrave) London
B.c. 1641, apr. Nov 1654 to William Petty, transferred to Thomas Belson till 1662, but not freed.

WALDOE, John London
Clockmaker, free Brother in CC Apr 1677. Paid no quarterage after c. 1688.

WALFORD, Thomas   London
Engraver and watchmaker. Apr. c. 1683 thro' Weavers' Co. to Elisha
Dodd (a freeman of the Weavers' Co.). Free brother in CC Apr 1690.
Took as aprs.: Apr 1690 **Edward Hill** thro' D. Stevens (but only after
TW has taken his freedom of the City) – free Jul 1698; Sep 1692 **John
Lawndy;** Dec 1694 **John Innever;** May 1697 **John Stiles** – free Jan
1704/05; Mar 1704/05 **John Green** (son of Roger Green of St. Martins in
the Fields, mariner) – free Aug 1712; Nov 1706 **Charles Shuckburgh,**
later passed on to W. Camden and freed Dec 1719; Jul 1716 **John
Anderton.** Prob. died between 1716 and 1719.

WALKDEN, Thomas   London
B.c. 1668, apr. May 1682 to Solomon Bouquet thro' Dorcas Bouquet till
1689. Freed Jul 1694. Took as aprs.: Dec 1695 **Thomas Triggs** – free
Dec 1708; Mar 1696/97 **Richard Owen;** Aug 1701 **Robert Pack** (son of
Robert Pack late of Hixworth, Suffolk, farmer, deceased); Apr 1720
William Gomm. In 1719 worked in Grays Inn Lane.

WALKER, George   London
B.c. 1661, apr. Jun 1675 to Jeffrey Bayley, transferred to Edmund Lamb
till 1682, but not freed.

WALKER, George   London
B.c. 1662, apr. Aug 1676 to Thomas Creed till 1683. Freed Apr 1684.
Paid no quarterage after c. 1685.

WALKER, George   London
Baillie records another one apr. 1684, but this is a slip for the previous
maker, freed 1684.

WALKER, George   Oxford
Lantern clock signed 'George Walker, Oxon'. Working 1689.

WALKER, James   London
Britten records one of this name in CC 1632 (which I cannot trace)*.
Early 17th century lantern clocks are recorded signed 'James Walker in
Lowthbery fecit' and also in 'Louthbury'. In 1706 one of this name took
apr. **James** (or William – records uncertain) **Perdue.** Perhaps two
separate men of the same name? (*see John Walker, 1632.)

WALKER, Jonadab   **London**
B.c. 1665, apr. Apr 1678 to **Michael Cornish** till 1686. Free Jan 1687/88.
Took as apr. Jun 1719 **William Chew.**

WALKER, John   **London**
Entered CC 1632 as a Brother. Lantern clock recorded.

WALKER, Peter (also Waker)   **London**
Apr. Sep 1656 to Samuel Betts thro' N. Payne. Freed Oct 1663. Not
heard of thereafter.

WALKER, Peter   **London**
Recorded as apr. 1681 but record clearly says Wal*t*er. However longcase
clocks are known signed 'Peter Walker, London' up to about 1730.
Supposedly worked at Wild Street End. This name fails to occur in CC
records during this period however.

WALKER, Samuel   **London**
Baillie records him as 1699, but this is a slip for Samuel Mather.

WALKER, Thomas   **London**
Baillie records him as 1689 CC, but I cannot confirm this. One of this
name was mentioned as 'cozen' of John Ebsworth in his 1699 will, but
not known if he was a clockmaker.

WALKER, Thomas   **Oxford**
Blacksmith and locksmith, working on local turret clocks from 1665. His
apr. **George Haddocke,** freed 1685. Died between 1715 and 1726.

WALKER, Walter   **London**
Baillie has apr. 1681, but I cannot trace him.

WALL, Andrew   **London**
B.c. 1650, apr. Jul 1664 to Richard Riccord till 1671, but not freed.

WALL, John   **London**
B.c. 1662, apr. Feb 1676/77 to Thomas Davis till 1683, but not freed.

WALLACE, John   **Paisley (Scotland)**
Smith who kept town clock 1603.

WALLACE, William   **Aberdeen (Scotland)**
Repaired town clock 1533, but by 1535 it was in disrepair again and townsmen sent to Flanders to have it repaired or renewed.

WALLEY, Robert   **Bolton (Lancashire)**
Clockmaker. Died 7 Jan 1675.

WALLINGTON, Samuel   **London**
B.c. 1675, apr. Nov 1689 to John Shaw till 1696, but not freed.

WALLIS, Jacob   **London**
Lantern clock signed 'Jacob Wallis, London' and longcase clock on record but I cannot trace any data on him. Not known in CC records.

WALLIS, Richard   **London**
Recorded as 1686 by Baillie but this is a slip for Wallitt, *qv.*

WALLIT(T), Richard   **London**
B.c. 1672, apr. Aug 1686 thro' E. Norris to Thomas Fletcher, a freeman of the Grocers' Co. till 1693. Freed Aug 1693. Took as apr. Aug 1695 **John Cheeseman**. Still alive 1697 but dead by Dec 1709 when his widow, Katherine, took as aprs.: **Samuel Bennet;** Jan 1710/11 **Thomas Bennett;** Oct 1714 **Andrew Stevenson;** Sep 1716 **Samuel Wallit.**

WALSH, Robert   **Dublin**
Free Goldsmith there 1662-77 and watchmaker.

WALTER and **WALTERS** recorded together but distinguished where possible.

WALTER, ----   **London**
Baillie records him as late 17th century. This is prob. John Walter, *qv.*

WALTER(S), John   **London**
B.c. 1624, apr. Jul 1638 to Thomas Howse thro' T. Dawson till 1645. Free Dec 1645. Took as aprs.: Aug 1648 **Humphrey Pierce** – free Sep 1653; Apr 1648 **Thomas Fitzjames.** He is not heard of after 1648, but then one of this name appears again May 1689 when he took as apr. **John Jeffs** thro' J. Bayley – free Jun 1697. It could well be that these were two different men of the same name. Work known – bracket clocks, late 17th century, signed 'John Walter, London' and 'Jno. Walter, London'.

WALTERS, Nicholas   **London**
An original 1622 petitioner for CC. Work known – watch dated 1610
signed 'Nicholas Walter' (or Waller).

WALTER, Peter   **London**
Apr. Sep 1681 to Andrew Savery, but this must be Peter Walker, though
written clearly as Walter.

WALTER, Richard   **Nayland (Suffolk)**
Paid 14s. 1d. in 1565 for repairing church clock.

WALTHALL, John   **London/Bishop Hatfield**
B.c. 1670, apr. Jun 1684 to William Coward till 1691, but not freed.
Work known – longcase clock signed 'John Walthall, Bishop Hatfield'.

WANACKRON, Abraham   **London**
Apr. 1655 according to Baillie, but this is Abraham Vanacker, *qv*.

WANDESFORD, Miles   **London**
Fined by CC 1633.

WANFIELD, Edmund   **London**
Recorded by Baillie as apr. 1655, but prob. a slip for Edmund Wansell,
qv.

WANFORD, John   **London**
B.c. 1672, apr. Jun 1686 to Edward Whitfield till 1693, but not freed.

WANHAGAN, Patrick   **Aberdeen**
Kept town clocks with William Cook, *qv* in 1651.

WANSELL, Edmund   **London**
B.c. 1641, apr. May 1655 to Nicholas Coxeter till 1662, but not freed.

WANSEY, Henry senior   **London**
Sometimes Wanse. Took as apr. Jan 1646 **John Frowd** thro' John Waters
– free Oct 1654. Prob. dead by 1662.

WANSEY, Henry junior   London
B.c. 1649, apr. Oct 1662 to John Hiccock till 1670, but not freed. His
widow received regular CC charity from Oct 1682 till 1697.

WANSWORTH (see Mansworth)

WARBURTON, William London
B.c. 1672, apr. Sep 1685 to Thomas Beseley till 1693. Freed Nov 1693. Took as apr. Mar 1697/98 **Francis Bedford**. From Feb 1701/02 he received occasional CC charity payments. In 1718 appointed porter for CC (whatever that was).

WARD, Edward London
Free Brother in CC May 1638. Took as apr. Oct 1638 (or 1648?) **George Englois** thro' N. Payne; May 1654 **Thomas Battin** thro' T. Loomes – free Jul 1661.

WARD, John London
Apr. 1659/60 to Thomas Taylor. Work known – lantern clocks, one dated 1699.

WARD, Thomas London
CC 1632-35.

WARDE, William Skipwith (Yorkshire)
B.c. 1582, married 1640 to Susan Jackson, aged 34. Clockmaker. Not known where he was from, but prob. not local.

WARDEN, Thomas London
Apr. to Thomas Overbury, watchmaker, freeman of the Haberdashers' Co., transferred Feb 1672/73 to Thomas Player, clockmaker. Free in Haberdashers' Co. Aug 1677. In Jul 1691 CC accused him of binding A. Strachan, aged between 30 and 40 to avoid the prosecution of Strachan, and this was cancelled as an illegal apprenticeship by the Lord Chamberlain. Work known – longcase clocks signed 'Thomas Warden, London'. Prob. gone by 1697.

WARDEN, William London
Apr. in 1660s to Thomas Loomes, but not freed.

WARE, Robert (sometimes Warr) London
B.c. 1679, apr. Dec 1693 to Samuel Stevens thro' F. Hill till 1700. Freed Nov 1701. Took as aprs. for self and his wife, Mary: Apr 1704 **Jane Bridger** (daughter of Richard Bridger of Godalming, Surrey, gent); Oct

1705 **Mary Barnett** (daughter of Thomas Barnett of Wrexham, Denbighshire, deceased). Took May 1713 **Henry Mason.**

WARFIELD, Alexander senior   **London**
Watchmaker, freeman of the Blacksmiths' Co. Took as aprs. in CC: Dec 1679 **John Grizell** thro' C. Bonner – free Feb 1687/88; Sep 1683 his son, **Alexander Warfield,** thro' T. Taylor of Holborne – free Jan 1692/93; Jul 1686 **Thomas Ingram** thro' D. Stevens – free Aug 1695. Believed died between 1693-98.

WARFIELD, Alexander junior   **London**
B.c. 1669 son of Alexander Warfield senior, apr. Sep 1683 thro' T. Taylor of Holborn to his father till 1692. Free Jan 1692-93. Took as aprs.: Jul 1693 **John Palmer;** Aug 1698 **Samuel Ken;** Aug 1699 **Edward Jenkins** (son of Joseph Jenkins, deceased, late of St. Leonards Shoreditch, weaver – Rebecca Jenkins, widow, to pay for his clothes); Sep 1702 **Jacob Crouch** (son of Jacob Crouch of New Shoreham, Sussex, carver); Jul 1705 **William Cartwright** (son of Richard Cartwright late of Laughton, Cheshire, gent., deceased) – free Jan 1714/15; Aug 1710 **Shelton Barrett;** Nov 1713 **John Phipps;** Nov 1718 (blank) **King;** Aug 1719 **Thomas Lyney.**

WARFIELD, John   **London**
Sometimes known erroneously as Marfield and Waffield. Supposedly apr. 1629 under Blacksmiths' Co. Working in Fleet Street. 1646-62. Not a member of CC but known to them. One of rebels against CC administration in 1656.

WARING, Thomas   **Waringstown (Ireland)**
Clockmaker working 1686. Died 1733.

WARNE, Nicholas   **London**
B.c. 1667, apr. Aug 1680 to Henry Adeane till 1688, but not freed.

WARNER, John   **Draycott/Chipping Camden (Gloucestershire)**
Made church clock for Chipping Camden in 1695 for £8.

WARNER, John   **London**
B.c. 1658, apr. Jul 1672 thro' J. Curtis to Edward Fage, mat. inst. maker till 1679, but not freed.

WARNER, John London

B.c. 1660/61, apr. Mar 1675 to Henry Wynne till 1682. Freed Apr 1682. One John Warner, Citizen and Clockmaker of St. Clement Danes, bachelor, 28, married Elizabeth Watkins, spinster, 23, of Islington. Took as aprs.: Jan 1685/86 **William Fairfax;** Feb 1689/90 **Robert Watson;** Sep 1705 (being of St. Dunstan's in the West) **Richard Hamilton** (son of James Hamilton, farmer, deceased, late of Standhurst, co. Cumberland?). One of this name worked at the Golden Anchor nr. Temple Bar, according to Britten.

WARNER, John London

B.c. 1675, son of William Warner, dyer (which may mean of the Dyers' Co.). Apr. Nov 1689 thro' E. Norris to his father till 1696. Freed Jan 1696/97. CC Steward 1718. Took as apr. Jan 1717/18 his son, **Samuel Warner.**

WARNER, William London

Father of John above, *qv.* Took son, **John Warner,** as apr. thro' E. Norris Nov 1689 – free Jan 1696/97. Not a member of CC, may have been member of Dyers' Co.

WARTER, Robert York

Clocksmith. Made clock for minster in 1515.

WARREN, John London

B.c. 1679, apr. Sep 1693 to Richard Medhurst of Croydon thro' T. Birch till 1700, but not freed.

WARREN, Richard London

Apr. Feb 1659/60 to Richard Bowen. Free May 1668. Took as aprs.: Sep 1672 **John Burton;** May 1675 **Henry Bridgen** – free May 1682; Nov 1682 **Richard Harrald** – free May 1690; Dec 1685 **Thomas Martin** thro' R. Lyons; Sep 1688 **Ralph Stevens;** May 1695 **Thomas Dowsett;** Aug 1700 **Henry Webster** (son of Henry Webster of parish of St. Giles Cripplegate, London, brewer) – free Jun 1710. A watchmaker, he died in 1700, buried 29 Aug at St. Albans Wood Street. Widow, Elizabeth, carried on taking as aprs.: Sep 1700 **Daniel Dowsett** (son of Thomas Dowsett of Braughin?, co. Hertfordshire, yeoman); Jul 1706 his son, **Jeremiah Warren;** May 1709 **Edward Smith** (son of Robert Smith of St. Bennets Paul Wharfe, Citizen and Joyner of London – but parish then erased); Jul 1711 illegible, but could be **Thomas Clarke,** who was freed Aug 1720; Jan 1715/16 **Robert Body.**

WARREN, Thomas   **London**
B.c. 1653, apr. Jul 1667 to Benjamin Bell till 1674, but not freed.

WARWICK, James   **London**
B.c. 1642, apr. Jun 1656 to Thomas Taylor, transferred to Edmond Gilpin till 1663, but not freed.

WAS(H)BOURNE, John   **Gloucester**
Clockmaker working c. 1689. His son, Daniel, was apr. in Bristol 1702-09 to Benjamin Willoughby.

WASHINGTON, John   **Kirkby Stephen (Westmoreland)/**
                                                                          Penrith (Cumberland)
Paid in 1665 for examining church clock at Kirkby Stephen and believed to have supplied the new one in 1665 for £6. Worked on Penrith clock 1664-92. Died 1708 in Penrith, a clocksmith, leaving a will.

WASHINGTON, Mark   **London**
B.c. 1673, apr. Jul 1687 to Richard Browne thro' T. Evans till 1694, but not freed.

WASHINGTON, Richard   **Kendal**
Lantern clock and two longcase clocks recorded from the 1690s, signed 'Richard Washington, Kendal'. One of this name was mayor of Kendal in or about 1694.

WASON (see Wasson)

WASSE, Thomas   **London**
B.c. 1668, apr. Nov 1682 to William May till 1689, but not freed.

WASSON, David   **Bristol**
Son of Solomon Wasson, *qv.* Free there Aug 1670.

WASSON, Solomon   **Bristol**
Free 1642. Took **John Clarke** as apr. 1643-50. Work known – at least one lantern clock, balance wheel type, signed 'Solomon Wasson of Bristoll'.

WAS(S)ON, William **Belfast**
Blacksmith and clocksmith. Made first clock for Old Corporation
Church in High Street. Working 1693.

WASTNESSE, Francis **London**
B.c. 1657, apr. Jul 1671 to John Trippett thro' I. Puzy till 1678, but not
freed.

WATERMAN, William **London**
B.c. 1668, apr. Sep 1682 to Amos Winch till 1689, but not freed.

WATERS, (widow) **London**
Paid search fee in 1671 – maybe a measure-seller.

WATERS, John **London**
Apr. Jul 1674 to John North, but in Sep 1674 passed over to Nicholas
Beck. Freed Jan 1682/83. Took as aprs.: Sep 1687 **John Ellicot** – free Jul
1696; May 1689 **John Jeffs** thro' J. Bayley; Aug 1695 **Thomas Wallis**
thro' J. North; Nov 1693 **Samuel Barrett** – free Sep 1701; Nov 1698
William Cater (son of late Joseph Cater of St. Margaret Lothbury, book-
binder, deceased); Jul 1704 his son, **Daniel Waters,** to be passed over to
Thomas Bletsoe, a cooper. Made CC Assistant from 1705. Ceased to
attend 1706, when prob. died.

WATERS, John **London**
In Jan 1646 took **John Frowd** apr. for Henry Wansey. Not heard of again
and not a member of CC.

WATERS, Jonathan **London**
B.c. 1672, apr. Jun 1686 to Edward Hunt till 1693, but not freed.

WATERTON, William **London**
Recorded by Baillie as apr. 1685 but I cannot trace any such. Maybe a slip
for William Waterman?

WATKINS, John **Ripley (Surrey)**
Sundial recorded dated 1695. Maker or owner?

WATMORE, William **London**
Engraver and Goldsmith and freeman of the Barber Chirurgeons' Co. in
which he took Nov 1663 **James Wolverstone** as apr. (free Aug 1672).

Not a member of CC, but took as aprs. thro' them: Feb 1670/71 **John Wynne,** thro' R. Bowen; Jun 1672 **Benjamin Paine** thro' L. Wythe; Aug 1674 **Thomas Tew** thro' T. Taylor of Holborn.

WATSON, ----   **Truro (Cornwall)**
Maintained town clock 1681.

WATSON, Robert   **London**
B.c. 1675, apr. Feb 1689/90 to John Warner till 1696, but not freed.

WATSON, Samuel   **Coventry/London**
Enigmatic maker, a mathematician and designer of many complicated devices more than a regular clockmaker. Worked at Coventry from c. 1680 and supposedly moved to Long Acre, London c. 1691. Became free Brother in CC Sep 1692. Took as aprs.: Apr 1694 **William Billinghurst** thro' T. Wheeler; Dec 1701 **George Evett** (son of George Evett late of parish of St. Clement Danes, Citizen and Vintner, deceased). Was Sheriff of Coventry 1686. In Nov 1712 offered to sell to CC an instrument 'to discover the houre of the day at sea and several other useful mathematical matters' but the CC were not interested. Work known – was supposedly 'Mathematician in Ordinary' to Charles II and to have sold him a clock with sunrise and sunset motions in 1682 at £215, and also a highly-complicated astronomical clock completed in 1690 for £1,000. Also made two complex clocks, astronomical, for Isaac Newton. Several bracket clocks and longcase clocks known and watches of a more conventional type, usually signed 'Samuel Watson, London' or 'Samuel Watson Londini fecit'. A bracket clock known signed 'Samuel Watson Coventriae', and a Coventry period watch. See also under Edward Burgis. (See *Clocks Magazine* – Nov 1980.)

WATSON, Thomas (not John as some believe)   **London**
B.c. 1648, apr. Jun 1662 to John Henderson (Hilderson) till 1669, but not freed.

WATSON, William   **London**
B.c. 1670, apr. Nov 1684 to Sarah, widow of Humphrey Peirce till 1691. Free Jan 1691/92. Took as aprs.: Mar 1693/94 **Benjamin Horsley;** Nov 1699 **Thomas Dixon** (son of Samuel Dixon, late of St. Bridgets, London, Ironmonger, deceased). Prob. died soon after 1699. Work known – longcase clock recorded signed 'William Watson, Angel Alley in Leadenhall Street'.

WATTS, Brounker   **London**
B.c. 1670, apr. Jan 1684/85 to Joseph Knibb till 1691. Free Feb 1693/94.
Took as aprs.: Sep 1696 **Benjamin Rainsford** – free Mar 1708/09; May
1703 **John Batger or Badger** (son of Francis Badger of Middle Aston?,
Oxfordshire, yeoman) – free Oct 1720; Jul 1709 **Edward Bodenham** (son
of Roger Bodenham of Ramsbury, Wiltshire, gent., deceased) – free Jun
1719. In 1711 avoided CC stewardship as he was 'out of town', and I have
no data on him later than this. Baillie records his death as 1719, on what
evidence I do not know. Working in Fleet Street 1696. Work known –
longcase and bracket clocks and watches signed 'Brounker Watts,
London' or 'Brounker Watts, Fleet Street, London'.

WATTS, James   **Taunton Dean (Somerset)**
Watchmaker. Marriage bond there 20 Sep 1697.

WATTS, John   **London**
B.c. 1638, apr. Dec 1651 to Ralph Almond till 1659, but not freed.

WATTS, John   **London**
Free in CC Jan 1664/65 being apr. of John Norcott, leatherseller, later
transferred to T. Claxton then to T. Hollis.

WATTS, John   **Northampton**
Working 1673.

WATTS, John   **Stamford (Lincolnshire)**
Working c. 1690. Died 1719 leaving will. Work known – at least two
eight-day clocks.

WATTS, Richard   **London**
B.c. 1659, apr. May 1673 to Humfrey Peirce till 1680. Free Jul 1680
(Peirce then deceased). Took as aprs.: Jul 1682 **Jonathan King** – free
Nov 1689; Aug 1688 **Samuel Higginson** – free Apr 1698; Apr 1693
Robert Gilks; Dec 1693 **Thomas Cartwright** (for C. Gould); **Thomas
Stapleton** (from M. Cornish) – free Jan 1693-94. Paid no quarterage after
c. 1694. Prob. dead or gone by 1697/98. Work known – watches, signed
'Ricardus Watts, Londini fecit'.

WATTS, Thomas   **London**
B.c. 1668, apr. Sep 1681 to Edward Stanton till 1689, but not freed.

WATTS, Walter London
B.c. 1674, apr. Feb 1688/89 to Charles Halstead till 1695. Free Mar 1695/96. Took as apr. Dec 1698 **Robert King** (son of Robert King, deceased, late of parish of St. Margaret New Fish Street, goldsmith). Paid no quarterage after c. 1698.

WAWEN, Gervas London
B.c. 1676, apr. Nov 1689 to Richard Conyers till 1697, but not freed.

WAY, James London
B.c. 1667, apr. Jan 1681/82 thro' D. Stevens to Daniel Le Conte, a freeman of the Haberdashers' Co. till 1688, but not freed.

WAYND, John London
B.c. 1646, apr. Jan 1659/60 to Thomas Taylor, but not freed. But see next entry.

WAYND, Richard York
Watchmaker, free there 1667. (This would just fit age of John Waynd in previous entry. Perhaps there was a clerical slip in the records.)

WEAVER, Cuthbert London
Servant to George Nau, made a free Brother in CC Jul 1682. Paid quarterage till c. 1694 but prob. dead by 1697/98.

WEAVER, Simon London
B.c. 1671, apr. May 1684 to James Wightman till 1692, but not freed.

WEBB, Daniel London
B.c. 1678, apr. Jul 1692 to Peter Southworth till 1699, but not freed.

WEBB, Edward Church Stoke (Somerset)
Several lantern clocks recorded, some dated between 1681 and 1688, but believed to be working by 1676. Also 30-hour musical longcase clock, signed 'Edward Webb of Chew Stoke'. Lantern clocks usually signed at 'Church Stoke', which is said to be the old name for Chardstock (but is it perhaps Chewstoke?). See Mathew Webb.

WEBB, Elizabeth London
Widow of Thomas, *qv*.

WEBB, Isaac London
Mat. inst. maker, made a free Brother in CC Feb 1667/68. Took as aprs.:
Jan 1668/69 **Thomas Bassett** thro' L. Wythe; Sep 1687 took an apr. for
W. Newton; Apr 1695 **Adam Lodwick.** In Mar 1671/72 made faulty
rulers for Joseph Silvester. Paid quarterage (irregularly) till mid-1704
when died. (Britten records him as apr. to R. Masterson, which is an
error for Joseph Webb, *qv.*)

WEBB, James Bristol
Lantern clock recorded signed 'Jas. Webb Bristol fecit' c. 1680.

WEBB, Joseph London
Son of William Webb. Apr. in CC Jul 1650 to Richard Masterson (who
was also a Clothiers' Co. freeman), transferred Dec 1653 to Masterson's
widow. Free in Clothiers' Co. Apr 1663 by patrimony, and in that Co.
took as apr. 1666 **John Stasebey** – free 1673; then took in CC, being 'a
professed clockmaker' though free of the Clothiers' Co. Aug 1677 **John
Cother** thro' L. Wythe; Dec 1668 **Thomas Stead** – free Dec 1678. On
CC list of 1662 as an 'outlier' whatever that might mean.

WEBB, Mathew Chewstoke (Somerset)
Lantern clock recorded dated 1688. But see Edward Webb.

WEBB, Thomas London
In 1660 'one Webb' who tried to get into CC admitted that he had served
only four years – later was admitted on paying a fine. His apr. **Nicholas
Beck** freed Jul 1669, having been transferred to John North. (Perhaps
Webb died before 1669?) In Jun 1672 Elizabeth, widow of Thomas
Webb, clockmaker, took as apr. **Joan Deacle.**

WEBB, William Dublin
Watchmaker there 1649.

WEBB, William Wells (Somerset)
Repaired chimes of clock 1706.

WEBSTER, Anne London
Daughter of Robert, *qv.*

WEBSTER, George London
Son of Robert Webster who married the sister of Robert Seigniour and in

whose will he is mentioned as a minor in 1685. Apr. 1696 to father, but not covered by this volume.

WEBSTER, John Carlisle (Cumberland)
Maintained town clock 1651-69.

WEBSTER, John London
B.c. 1662, apr. Sep 1676 to Thomas Tompion, but not freed and not heard of thereafter.

WEBSTER, John London
B.c. 1672, apr. Mar 1686/87 to Henry Merryman till 1693. Freed May 1695. Took as aprs.: May 1695 **Richard Andrews** thro' D. Stevens – free Apr 1703; Nov 1696 **Simon Parish;** Apr 1700 **Charles Jones** (son of William Jones of Haverfordwest, Pembrokeshire, carpenter); Jun 1703 **Thomas Jennings** (son of Andrew Jennings, Citizen and Draper of London).

WEBSTER, Mary London
Daughter of Robert, *qv.*

WEBSTER, Robert London
Free Brother in CC Aug 1675. Believed this was the Webster who married the sister of Robert Seigniour, *qv.* Took as aprs.: May 1676 **John Edlin** thro' C. Bonner – free Sep 1687; Jun 1681 **Jasper Bonner** thro' C. Bonner; Aug 1686 **Charles Harris** – free Aug 1695; Feb 1688/89 daughter **Sarah Webster;** 1687 from R. Seigniour (on his death?) **Thomas Gifford** – free Oct 1692; Sep 1693 (or 1694) **Morris Smith** – free May 1702; Sep 1695 an apr. **Henry Cole,** for C. Harris; Jul 1696 his son, **George Webster** – free Jul 1703; May 1698 his daughters, **Mary** and **Ann Webster;** Feb 1700/01 **Peter Heather** (son of Peter Heather of St. Giles in the Fields, Middlesex, smith); **Ralph Toleson** (taken over from C. Lee – free Sep 1701; Jul 1707 **John Malson;** Feb 1711/12 his daughter, Margaret Webster, was freed by patrimony. Made CC Assistant from 1697, Warden from 1702, Master 1705, still attending 1720. May well have worked for Seigniour in his earlier years. Work known – watch and clock on record.

WEBSTER, Sarah London
Daughter of Robert, *qv.*

WEBSTER, Thomas   **Dundee**
Supposedly working 1689.

WEEDON, Samuel   **London**
Ironmonger, paid CC fee 1672. Was Jonas Barber's man, *qv*.

WEEDON, William   **London**
B.c. 1672, apr. Oct 1686 to Nathaniel Barrow till 1693. Freed Jul 1695.
Still working 1697 but not heard of thereafter.

WEEKES, Johnson   **London**
B.c. 1658 (prob. son of Thomas Weekes, *qv*), apr. Jun 1671 to Robert
Cooke, mat. inst. maker and freeman of the Weavers' Co., till 1679. Free
Dec 1683. Took as aprs.: Dec 1683 **Luke Lambe**; Oct 1688 an apr. for
Isaac Carver. Paid quarterage till 1704 at least.

WEEKES, Thomas senior   **London**
Free Brother in CC Oct 1654. Took as aprs.: Jan 1655/56 **Isaac Gallott**
thro' D. Bouquet; Feb 1655/56 **William Williamson** thro' L. Wythe –
free Oct 1663; **Thomas Player** from William Williamson and passed him
over by 1672 to John Froud (perhaps on his death). In 1654 he was
summoned before CC for trading when not a member, being then 'of St.
Olaves, Southwark'. Joined the rebels against the CC administration in
1656. In Apr 1657 fined for abusing the Wardens. In 1662 worked in
Chancery Lane. Dead by 1688 when his son, Thomas junior, was made a
freeman.

WEEKES, Thomas junior   **London**
Son of Thomas senior, made a freeman in CC (by patrimony?) Sep 1688,
by which time his father was dead. Took as aprs.: Apr 1703 his son,
Thomas Weekes; Dec 1713 his son, **Charles Weekes**, freed by
patrimony.

WEIR, David   **Glasgow**
Working 1690.

WELCH, John (see Welsh)

WELLER, George   **Wells (Somerset)**
Repaired clocks 1700/01.

WELLS, John London
B.c. 1658, apr. Mar 1672-73 to John White till 1679. Freed Sep 1682.
Took as aprs.: Aug 1673 **Francis Martin;** Jun 1686 **Richard Wither**
(transferred from Abraham Prime); Sep 1688 **Alexander Irving** – free
Sep 1695. Working till at least 1705.

WELLS, Jonathan London
B.c. 1662, apr. Jun 1676 thro' H. Wynne to Isaac Carver, mat. inst.
maker, till 1683, but not freed.

WELLS, Joseph London
Mat. inst. maker and freeman of the Joyners' Co. Free Brother in CC Feb
1667/68. Took as apr. Jul 1668 **Simon Barrett** thro' T. Claxton – free
Apr 1678. Faulty rulers, supposedly made by him for Robert Jole, were
confiscated by CC 1671/72.

WELLS, William London
A keymaker (for watches?), made a Free Brother in CC Apr 1689. In
1691 was a clockmaker with his wife, Mary, in parish of St. Saviour's
Southwark when his son, John, was bap. Still working till 1697.

WELSH, John (sometimes Welch) **Chesham (Buckinghamshire)**
Longcase and bracket clock recorded c. 1700.

WENDAY, Anne London
B.c. 1671, apr. Sep 1685 to Henry Jevon and Christian, his wife, till
1692, but not freed. Prob. a servant-girl.

WENT, Daniel (see Wint, Daniel)

WENTWORTH, Thomas Salisbury **(Wiltshire)**
(sometimes Wintworth)
Watch and clockmaker, working there by 1675, still there 1692. One of
his name there 1727 might be Thomas junior. His son, George, became a
clockmaker at Oxford. Work known – bracket clocks and longcase
clocks known, signed 'Thomas Wintworth, Sarum'.

WENTWORTH, Wombwell London
B.c. 1642, apr. Jun 1656 to Henry Harland till 1663, but not freed.

WESONCRAFT, Joseph (sometimes Wesoncroft)   **Dublin**
Goldsmith/watchmaker. Free there 1685, having been apr. 1675 to
Adam Soret. Died 1692.

WEST, Thomas   **London**
B.c. 1673, apr. Oct 1687 thro' D. Stevens to Thomas White till 1694.
Freed Mar 1695/96. Took as aprs.: May 1697 **Robert Hollingworth;**
Nov 1699 **John Davis** (son of Moses Davis of Deddington, Oxford,
salesman); Jan 1699/1700 **Henry Page** (son of John Page of Basing, co.
illegible, husbandman) – free Jan 1714/15; **James Hill** (son of John Hill
late of parish of St. Martins in the Fields, Middlesex, cutler, deceased);
John Arding (son of John Arding of St. Giles without Cripplegate,
London, tobacconist); Sep 1706 **Charles Wales** (son of John Wales, late
of Little Ba (illegible) Hall, Essex, Esqr., deceased); **Thomas Rewalling**
– free Oct 1715. Work known – lantern and longcase clocks and watches
are known signed 'Thomas West, London', but it is not clear whether
these are by this man or the next one.

WEST, Thomas (sometimes Weast)   **London**
B.c. 1674 (one note says son of either Richard or Robert West, but has
been erased), apr. Feb 1688/89 to John Edlin till 1695. Freed Aug 1698.
Paid quarterage till at least 1703. I am unable to distinguish this man
from the preceding either in his apprentices or his work.

WEST, William   **London**
A freeman of the Blacksmiths' Co., admitted into CC (prob. as a Brother)
Apr 1698. Took as apr. Jul 1706 **Ruhamah Robinson** (son of Ebenezer
Robinson of parish of Stepney, Middlesex, weaver) – free Aug 1713.

WESTCOTT, John   **London**
B.c. 1677, apr. Mar 1691 to William Mason till 1698. Free Jun 1703.

WESTMORELAND, Walter   **London**
Not in CC but known to them. Prob. dead by 1662/63.

WESTOBY, John   **London**
B.c. 1655, apr. Nov 1669 to Thomas Wheeler till 1676. Freed Apr 1677.
Took as aprs.: Jul 1680 **John Gray;** Sep 1684 **Thomas Stones** – freed
Apr 1692; Sep 1692 **Thomas Trigg** – free Jul 1701; Jun 1694 **Thomas
Carter,** thro' W. Clements; May 1697 **William Woster; Richard Kemp**
(from John Wise junior) – free Jul 1701. Believed died 1703. In Jun 1690

sent word to CC about his stewardship thro' Mr. Wheeler, and was prob. still working for him then. Work known – watches and longcase clocks, signed 'John Westoby, Londini fecit'.

WESTON, Abraham   **Lewes (Sussex)**
Married 1699 Elizabeth Cray (whose sister, Mary, married 1700 John Gilmore, clockmaker of Battle). His daughter, Mary, married 1731 Obadiah Body of Battle, clockmaker. Body prob. worked for Weston. Cared for town clock 1699-1707 incl. conversion to pendulum.

WESTWOOD, Richard   **London**
B.c. 1670, apr. Nov 1684 to Thomas Birch till 1691. Free Jan 1691/92. Took as aprs.: Jun 1694 **Henry Turner;** Nov 1710 **John Pyke.** Work known – lantern and longcase clocks and watches.

WETHERED, George   **London**
B.c. 1663, apr. Sep 1677 to Henry Wynne till 1684, but not freed.

WHALEY, Barnaby   **London**
B.c. 1661, apr. Dec 1675 thro' T. Taylor of Holborn to John Fitter of Battersea, watchmaker, till 1682, but not freed.

WHAPLITT, Thomas   **London**
Not known who he was but appears in CC court books as he gave CC a tankard in his will, dated Jan 1678. He died 5 Aug 1679. One witness was Richard Wise.

WHARTON, John   **London**
B.c. 1673, apr. Dec 1687 to Thomas Speakman till 1694, but not freed.

WHEATLEY, Henry   **London**
Not apparently in CC but passed over Oct 1702 apr. John Jacob, to James (Brinley?) thro' CC.

WHEATLEY, John   **London**
Son of Ralph Wheatley, Citizen and Cordwainer of London. Apr. Apr 1657 to Jeffrey Bailey. Free May 1668. Also free of the City 1668.

WHEATLEY, William   **London**
B.c. 1676, apr. Nov 1690 to John Dawson, later transferred to John

Stevens till 1697. Free Jul 1698. Took as apr. May 1700 **William Walker** (son of William Walker, Citizen and Haberdasher of London).

WHEELER, James   Colchester (Essex)
B. 1604, apr. to George Wheeler, locksmith. Married 1625 Mary Lamb. Various children include James b. 1625. Free Burgess there 1627. In 1635 was persecuted for his religion and escaped abroad, believed dying soon after. Work known – lantern clocks and watches are on record, but none known to have survived today.

WHEELER, James   London
B.c. 1676, apr. Sep 1690 thro' D. Stevens to William Laughton, a freeman of the Grocers' Co. till 1697, but not freed.

WHEELER, John   London
Free in CC by Patrimony Jul 1680. Took as aprs.: Jul 1683 **Thomas Sleath; ** Aug 1685 **Richard Grape** thro' R. Cosby; Aug 1687 **James Winstanley; John Eagle** – free Jul 1690. He was the son of Thomas Wheeler, *qv*.

WHEELER, Thomas   London
Apr. Jan 1647-48 to Nicholas Coxeter. Free Feb 1655/56. Took as aprs.: Apr 1656 **Nathaniel Dike** – free Jul 1663; Jan 1663/64 **Herbert Newton;** Apr 1667 **Nathaniel Pyne** – free Nov 1677; Nov 1669 **John Westoby** – free Apr 1677; son, **John Wheeler** – freed by patrimony Jul 1680; Aug 1675 **John Stacy** – free Sep 1683; May 1676 **Philip Thache** – free Sep 1685; Sep 1680 **Edward Bagshaw** – free Sep 1691; May 1683 **William Rosse;** May 1689 **Nicholas Humfreys;** Nov 1693 **James Charnock;** May 1695 **Samuel Townson** (son of Robert Townson) – free May 1702. Made CC Assistant from 1674, Warden from 1680, Master 1684, last attended about 1694, but did not die then (as some state), but died between 1695 and Jun 1701 when his widow received CC charity, and was almost certainly dead by 1697/98. Bound additional aprs. for Jeremy Gregory and R. Starr, and S. Watson. Work known – longcase clocks and lantern clocks, usually signed 'near ye French Church in London'.

WHEELER, Vincent   London
B.c. 1639, apr. Mar 1653/54 to Edward Holliday thro' D. Moody till 1660, but not freed.

WHELLAN, Thomas **London**
Britten records a lantern clock c. 1680 signed 'Thomas Whellan in Bishops Gate Street, Londini', but I can trace no such person.

WHETHALL, Thomas **London**
Not Wetherell as sometimes stated. B.c. 1650, apr. May 1664 to John Clarkson till 1671, but not freed.

WHINFIELD, Philip **London**
B.c. 1638, apr. Sep 1651 to Samuel Davis till 1659, but not freed.

WHITE, Caesar **London**
B.c. 1670, apr. Jun 1684 to Thomas Parker till 1691, but not freed.

WHITE, Edward **London**
B.c. 1633, apr. Sep 1647 to John White thro' N. Tomlins till 1654, but not freed.

WHITE, John **London**
Free in CC 1646. Took as aprs.: Sep 1647 **Edward White** thro' N. Tomlins; Jul 1651 **George Wilmot** thro' J. Bayley – free Jan 1670; Sep 1656 **William Young** thro' W. Godbed – free Jan 1668-69. He was also a freeman of the Grocers' Co.

WHITE, John **London/Richmond (Surrey)**
B.c. 1649, apr. Oct 1663 to Thomas Bagley thro' T. Loomes till 1670. Free Oct 1670. Took as aprs.: Mar 1672/73 **John Wells** – free Sep 1682; Dec 1674 **Robert Pigg; William Fuller** (from N. Dike) – free Sep 1675; Dec 1677 **Faith Leake** – free Jan 1685/86 (having been transferred to D. Quare); Sep 1671 **John Brooksted.** Also bound another apr. **John Beck,** for D. Quare. By 1677 was described as living at Richmond, but paid his quarterage in case he might come to work in London. Paid no quarterage after c. 1678.

WHITE, John **London**
B.c. 1656, Apr. Feb 1668/69 to Humfrey Peirce till 1677, but not freed.

WHITE, John **London**
B.c. 1670, apr. May 1684 to Benjamin Merryman till 1691. Free Apr 1692. Paid no quarterage after c. 1693.

WHITE, Joseph London
Paid CC search fee 1673, though not a member. Prob. a measure-seller.

WHITE, Thomas Fairford (Gloucestershire)
Longcase clock recorded c. 1700.

WHITE, Thomas London
Free Brother in CC Jan 1683/84. Took as apr. Oct 1687 **Thomas West** thro' D. Stevens – free Mar 1695-96. Dead by 1697/98, but prob. not till after 1692.

WHITEHEAD, Charles London
Recorded as apr. Oct 1663 to Henry Wynne, but this is prob. an error for Richard Whitehead, *qv*.

WHITEHEAD, Charles London
B.c. 1679, son of Richard Whitehead. Apr. Jul 1693 to his father till 1700, but not freed.

WHITEHEAD, Richard London
Recorded as 1647/48 but this is really Whiteheard, *qv*.

WHITEHEAD, Richard London
Apr. Oct 1663 to Henry Wynne. Free Sep 1671. Took as aprs.: Jan 1677/78 **Simon Whitehead;** Sep 1683 **Joseph Reynolds** – free Apr 1691; Jul 1693 his son, **Charles Whitehead.** Prob. dead or gone by 1697/98.

WHITEHEAD, Simon London
B.c. 1663, apr. Jan 1677/78 to Richard Whitehead till 1684, but not freed.

WHITEHEAD, Thomas London
Not a freeman of CC but known to them. Was a freeman of the Tinplate Workers' Co. Took as apr. thro' CC Nov 1693 **Timothy Overzee** thro' D. Stevens. Recorded as insolvent in 1725 (which I have not confirmed).

WHIT(E)HEAR(D), Richard London/Reading
Sometimes Whitehaire. Free Brother in CC Dec 1647. Work known – a lantern clock is recorded.

WHITFIELD, Edward   **London**
Apr. May 1655 to John North. Free Oct 1663. Took as aprs.: Oct 1667
Thomas Parratt (transferred to Walter Gibbs); **William Marston** (from
J. Monday, who died 1663) – free Jul 1669; Sep 1673 **Samuel Bennett;**
Sep 1678 **Joseph Faber;** Sep 1683 **Edward Brookes** (later passed over to
R. Gregory); Jun 1686 **John Wanford;** Sep 1693 **Phineas Noble.** In Jun
1701 he received charity from CC. In Mar 1704/05 they paid towards his
burial, and later paid charity to his widow, who was 'in great want' until
Dec 1704.

WHITFIELD, James   **Liverpool (Lancashire)**
Watchmaker, died. 1674.

WHITFIELD, John   **Liverpool (Lancashire)**
Watchmaker. Daughter b. there 1677. Work known – watch showing
hour by a revolving disc signed 'John Whitfield, Wavertry' (Wavertree
nr. Liverpool).

WHITFIELD, Robert   **Liverpool (Lancashire)**
Watchmaker. Children b. 1678-88. Died 1726 leaving will.

WHITFIELD, Samuel   **London**
Feb 1681-82 a watchmaker, bachelor, aged 30, of St. Clements
Eastcheap, marrying Elizabeth Ashton, spinster, 27, of St. Catherine's
Creechurch. Not a member of CC, so prob. did not work in London.
Maybe Whitfield of Shrewsbury – see next entry.

WHITFIELD, Samuel   **Shrewsbury**
Watchmaker there 1695-97. Maybe the London Whitfield – see previous
entry.

WHITFIELD, William   **London**
In CC records as receiving charity 1701-02, but this is an obvious error
for Edward Whitfield, *qv.*

WHITLACH, John   **London**
Free Brother in CC 1637. Took as apr. Jan 1639 **Edward Carpenter** thro'
T. Dawson. Gave CC a silver drinking cup.

WHITMAN, James   **London**
Paid CC quarterage 1672, but not a member.

WHITTAKER, James   Stoke-on-Trent (Staffordshire)
Spelt Whittycar. Repaired town clock 1615-32.

WHITTAKER, Roger   Stoke-on-Trent (Staffordshire)
Repaired town clock 1633-62. Died 1673 leaving widow, Elizabeth.

Whittingham, William   London
Listed in error as Richard, but was evidently called William. B.c. 1625, son of Robert Whittingham of Bradford, Yorkshire. A clockmaker but free in Cooks' Co. Had as apr. 1684 **Thomas Russell** – free 1691. CC threatened to prosecute him for trading when not a member in Apr 1682, May 1682, Apr 1685 and Apr 1688 – but he never did join. Died 1692.

WHITTLE, Angil   London
Lost watch recorded 1688, but not a member of CC and I know nothing else about him.

WHITTLE, Thomas   London
B.c. 1658, apr. Sep 1671 to Henry Harper till 1679. Freed Jul 1683. Took as aprs.: Nov 1684 **William Davenport**; May 1691 **Benoni Dunn**. Paid quarterage till at least 1705. Work known – watches recorded.

WHITTON, Clay   London
B.c. 1676, apr. May 1690/91 to John Higgs till 1697. Free Apr 1698. In Jun 1708 the CC held a 'Court of Conscience' about him (whatever that might mean – perhaps to do with his religion, or it might simply have been to consider leniency at his great arrears of quarterage, for he was ordered to pay off 26 shillings arrears at one shilling a week).

WHITWELL, Car   London
Baillie records him as 1593-1606. Perhaps brother-in-law to Robert Grinkin senior, *qv*.

WHITWELL, Robert   London
Apr. Jun 1642 to Robert Grinkin thro' O. Durant. Free Jan 1649-50, and gave CC a silver wine cup for his admittance. Prob. a relative (cousin?) of Grinkin. Took as aprs.: May 1649 **William Whitwell** thro' J. Seaborne; Aug 1649 **John Freeman** thro' same; Dec 1649 **Henry Apjohn** thro' same; Apr 1651 **Nathaniel Brickenden**; Sep 1661 **Isaac Meers**; Jan 1663-64 **Thomas Allen**; Jul 1667 **Thomas Sharp**. In 1662 he worked in Whitefriars. In Jan 1673/74 was given 10 shillings charity by CC for

'relief in his sickness'. Was dead by 1678 when his son, Hugh, was bound apr. to Edmond Whitfield, cutler. Work known – watches.

WHITWELL, William   London
B.c. 1635, apr. May 1649 to Robert Whitwell thro' James Seaborne till 1656, but not freed.

WHOOD, Isaac   London
Apr. Apr 1680 to Thomas Fenn, but not freed.

WICKES, William   London
Britten records him at Threadneedle Street 1680 (with his son, George?), but I don't know him. Not in CC.

WIFE, John   London
Late 17th century lantern clock recorded, but this must surely be an error for John Wise, *qv*.

WIGGINTON, John   London
B.c. 1649, apr. Aug 1663 to Bernard Gernons thro' N. Payne till 1670, but not freed.

WHITMAN, James   London
B.c. 1649, apr. Jan 1663/64 to Edward Eyston, transferred to Thomas Fenn till 1670. Freed Jan 1670/71. Took as aprs.: Sep 1672 **Thomas Dennis**; Mar 1678 **William Smith**; May 1684 **Simon Weaver**. Work known – longcase clock signed 'James Wightman in Lombard Street, Londini'.

WIGHTMAN, John   London
B.c. 1675, apr. Oct 1688 to Jonathan Jones till 1696 – free Nov 1696 (as Wrightman in error). Took as aprs.: Jun 1699 **Thomas Baldwin** (son of Thomas Baldwin of Henley-on-Thames, maltster) – free Sep 1699; May 1701 **Edward Webster** (son of Benjamin Webster of London, stationer); Feb 1708/09 **Daniel Burgess** (son of Obediah Burgess of Marlborough ?, Wiltshire, gent.); Sep 1712 **William Hodges** – free Oct 1719; Sep 1717 **Edward Chandler**.

WIGHTMAN, William   London
B.c. 1673, apr. Aug 1686 to Joseph Windmills till 1694. Free Feb 1696/97. Took as aprs.: Jul 1700 **Benjamin Maberley** (son of Joseph

Maberley late of Ramsbury, Wiltshire, farmer); Feb 1708/09 **John North** (son of John North of Harrow on the Hill, Middlesex, husbandman) – free Oct 1720; Jun 1714 **Edward Hopcraft**. Baillie records his death as 1744.

WILKES, John   Brackley (Northamptonshire)
Longcase clock c. 1715.

WILKINS, John senior   Leicester/Oakham(?)
Took as aprs.: May 1680 **John Lee; Roger Lee** – free 1691; **Edward Alcock** – free Sep 1692; **William Bates** – free Sep 1692; his eldest son, **Thomas Wilkins** – freed Jul 1698; second son, **John Wilkins** – freed 1698; **Josiah Ashwell** – freed 1702. Believed made new town clock 1688 (and took old one in for scrap). Was mayor in 1692. Believed died 1720/21. One of this name at Oakham in early 18th century might have been him?

WILKINS, John junior   Leicester/Oakham(?)
Son of John senior, free 1698. Recorded as insolvent 1729. Died before 1741/42. One by this name at Oakham in early 18th century might be this man.

WILKINS, John   Glapthorne (Northamptonshire)
B. 1673. Married there 1701, a clockmaker. Might be John junior, above?

WILKINS, Robert   London
B.c. 1646, apr. Jul 1660 to Thomas Fenn till 1667. Free Jan 1670/71. Took as apr. Dec 1672 **Edward Jackson** – free Apr 1680. Chosen Steward 1686 but excused the fine still outstanding in Sep 1687 because he had suffered 'great losses' and expenses (presumably in the Stewards' Feast). Still alive 1705 but reputedly died 1706. Work known – watches, one signed at 'Ludgat Street', another signed 'Robertus Wilkins Londini'. Baillie says he worked at Royal Exchange.

WILKINS, Thomas   Leicester
Eldest son of John senior. Free as watchmaker there Jul 1698. Died before 1743. Work known – longcase clock noted.

WILKINS, Thomas   London
B.c. 1679, apr. Sep 1693 thro' T. Fletcher to John Howse, watchmaker, of Croydon, till 1700, but not freed.

WILKINSON, Edward   **London**
B.c. 1642, apr. Sep 1655 to Joseph Munday till 1663, but not freed.

WILLIAMS, Peter (see Peter Willierme)   **London**

WILLIAMS, Thomas   **London**
B.c. 1676, apr. Sep 1689 to Isaac Day till 1697, but not freed.

WILLIAMS, William   **London**
Alias William Hanslapp, *qv*.

WILLIAMSON, Alexander   **Peebles (Scotland)**
Kept town clock 1650.

WILLIAMSON, Edward   **London**
B.c. 1673, apr. Sep 1687 to Jonathan Puller till 1694, but not freed.
Work known – at least two longcase clocks noted.

WILLIAMSON, John   **London/Leeds (Yorkshire)**
Admitted a Free Brother in CC Dec 1682 as a Great Clockmaker (at the same court as Jonas Barber, also a Yorkshireman), but paid no quarterage after 1682. Married Rebecca Whalley in Leeds 1683, and remained there, having 10 children by 1704 when his wife died. At this time John lived at Hillhousebank. In 1707 he then married Mary Kitching, by whom he had one child, he then married in 1712 Hannah Hudson by whom there were three more children. Hannah died 1747. John died in the workhouse in 1748, and must then have been about 86 years old. Work known – 30 hour clock signed 'near Temple Bar, Londini, fecit'. Of his Leeds work at least one watch survives and several longcase clocks incl. two of month duration and one year clock, all signed 'Jno. Williamson in Leeds, fecit'. The year-duration striking clock incorporates a pull quarter ting-tang repeater.

WILLIAMSON, John   **Liverpool (Lancashire)**
Watch and watch casemaker at Chapel Street 1710/16, when he died.

WILLIAMSON, John   **London**
B.c. 1678, apr. Feb 1692/93 to Thomas Day till 1699, but not freed.

WILLIAMSON, Joseph   **London**
Prob. a Quaker. Made a Free Brother in CC Apr 1686, a Great Clockmaker who served his time in Ireland. Took as aprs.: May 1687

Joseph Grave thro' D. Stevens; Dec 1698 **Isaac Johnson** (son of William Johnson late of Great Yarmouth, deceased, mariner) – free Jan 1705/06; Dec 1712 **Samuel Jenkins;** May 1717 **William Williamson.** Made CC Assistant from 1717, Master 1724, believed died 1725. Said to work in Clements Lane. Claimed to have invented equation clocks. Said to have been watchmaker to the king of Spain. Work known – longcase clocks.

WILLIAMSON, Robert   **London**
Apr. Oct 1658 to John Harris thro' J. Lello. Free Oct 1666. Took as aprs.: Aug 1668 **Cuthbert Lee** – free Aug 1676; Sep 1672 **Thomas Snelling** – free Sep 1680; Sep 1674 **John Goldsmith** (allowed, since T. Snelling is now 'in the Compter'(?)) – free Sep 1681; Jul 1681 **John Levitt;** Jul 1693 **Thomas Halhead** – Jul 1702; Sep 1695 **John How;** Apr 1696 **Erasmus Marriott;** Mar 1698/99 **Michael Cheltenham** (son of Peter Cheltenham senior, Citizen and Joiner); Mar 1699/1700 **John Smallpiece** (son of John Smallpiece of St. Ann's, London, plumber); his son, **Michael Williamson,** freed by patrimony Oct 1714. Also bound three aprs. for other masters. Working at 'St. Bartholomew Exchange' in 1691 when his daughter, Mary, married Edward Orton, clockmaker, *qv.* Became CC Assistant from 1682, Warden from 1695, Master 1698, ceased to attend suddenly in Jan 1704-05 when Prob. died. Work known – longcase clocks, signed 'Robert Williamson London', also watches at 'St. Bartholomew's Lane'.

WILLIAMSON, Samuel   **Wigan/Cronton (Lancashire)**
Free at Wigan 1684, formerly apr. of Thomas Martine. Prob. moved to Cronton, where died 1726 leaving will.

WILLIAMSON, Thomas   **London**
Son of Dove Williamson of Fulbank, Lincolnshire, clerk. Apr. to John Harris Nov 1661. Freed in CC Jan 1668/69, freeman of City 1669. Took as aprs.: Jun 1671 **William Brafield** – free Sep 1678; Mar 1672/73 **Francis Robinson,** but in 1677 Robinson 'has misdemeanoured' and he was allowed to take in his place **Edward Hunt** (free Jun 1684), but in Sep 1677 he was fined for having Robinson back again, though he professed he wanted rid of him but could get no-one else to take him; Jun 1676 **Hatton Sadler;** Nov 1680 **William Haynes** thro' Edward Bridgeman – free Feb 1703/04; Jun 1683 **Titus Chapman.** Paid no quarterage after about 1689 and prob. died about then. Work known – watches on record.

WILLIAMSON, William Banff (Scotland)
Maintained church clock 1626, but was not to be paid if the clock varied by more than a quarter of an hour.

WILLIAMSON, William London
Apr. Feb 1655/56 to Thomas Weekes thro' L. Wythe. Freed Oct 1663. Tok as apr. Sep 1664 **Thomas Player** (later transferred to T. Weekes). Jul 1679 was due to be steward but 'is dead'.

WILLIAMSON, William London
Clockmaker, free Brother in CC Jul 1689. Took as apr. Jun 1689 **William Davenport** (son of Charles Davenport) thro' W. Clement – free Feb 1706/07. Paid no quarterage after c. 1696 and prob. died or left soon after. Work known – watches and longcase clocks.

WILLIARME, Pierre London
(also misspelt as Williams and Wiellerme)
Believed a native of Geneva. In 1635 was at Aldersgate Ward, a stranger, watchmaker, in parish of St. Botolph, having been then 12 years in England. When asked for quarterage by CC in 1633 he claimed his wife had already paid. Not made a Free Brother till May 1648. Took as aprs.: Sep 1652 **Richard Stamford** thro' N. Payne, but in 1654 was complained against by boy's father for not teaching him the trade or providing him with clothing.

WILLIS, Ambrose London
B.c. 1673, apr. Feb 1687/88 to Thomas Baldwin till 1694, but not freed.

WILLIS, Richard London
Member of Blacksmiths' Co. In Dec 1656 presented **William Clements** (but he was represented Mar 1656/57 by Thomas Chapman). In 1669 his apr., **Humphrey Burrowes,** was made free of the City.

WILLOUGHBY, Benjamin London/Bristol
B.c. 1662, apr. Dec 1676 to Robert Dingley till 1683, but not freed. Supposedly at High Cross. Free at Bristol Mar 1691/92. Married pre-1693 Bridget, then pre-1699 Elizabeth. Took as aprs.: 1699 **John Masters** – free 1707; 1702 **Daniel Waisbourne/Washbourne** – free 1709; 1693 **John Yarrington** – free 1700. Work known – longcase clocks signed 'Benjamin Willoughby in Bristol', bracket clocks, watches, one signed at 'Small Street, Bristol'. (A Benjamin junior recorded c. 1705-65 might be an error for Benjamin senior?)

WILLOUGHBY, JOHN London

B.c. 1665, apr. Sep 1679 to Thomas How till 1686. Free Sep 1686. Took as aprs.: Sep 1691 **William Morley;** Apr 1693 **Benjamin Jeffes** thro' W. Neighbour – free Jul 1702; Jan 1694/95 **William Morley** (rebound?) – free Jan 1703/04; **Nathaniel Baseley** (from H. Hammond) – free Mar 1694/95; Sep 1699 **Richard Prestidge** (son of Bartholomew Prestidge, Citizen and Vintner); **Thomas Jemmett** (from C. Cutting) – free Jan 1704/05; Jul 1704 his son, **John Willoughby** – free by patrimony Jan 1711/12; May 1709 **Joseph Duck** (son of James Duck, Citizen); Dec 1710 **Richard Stratton;** Sep 1715 **Elias Wilkes.** John Willoughby senior was still alive in 1719, after which I have no details of him.

WILLOW, John (sometimes Wellow) London

Son of Christopher Willow (of Leominster?) and apr. in Blacksmiths' Co. 1609 to Robert Grinkin. Freed Aug 1617 as a clockmaker. Was a 1622 petitioner for CC as Wellowe. Prob. worked for Grinkin and was a witness to his will in 1626. Serviced clocks and watches for second Earl of Salisbury between 1625 and 1629, and supplied a new watch case of silver at 20 shillings. Believed worked in Fleet Street. One of first Wardens of CC from 1632, Master 1635-36. Took as apr. Jan 1646 **Humphrey Foulk** thro' L. Wythe (in CC). Took as apr. in B.C. c. 1638 **John Nicasius** – free 1647. Last attended CC Nov 1652. CC gave charity to his widow from Apr 1655 to Sep 1669. Work known – watches.

WILLOX, Alexander Aberdeen (Scotland)

A wright, who kept town clocks 1632-45.

WILLS, John London

B.c. 1668, apr. Aug 1682 to William Hilliar till 1689, but not freed.

WILLMOT, Thomas Dinder (Somerset)

Kept Wells clock in 1591.

WILMOT, George London

B.c. 1637, apr. Jul 1651 to Jeffrey Bailey, then pased over to John White till 1658. Free Jan 1670/71.

WILMOT, Isaac London

B.c. 1649, apr. Mar 1662/63 to John Bayes till 1670, but not freed.

WILMOT, John London
B.c. 1663, apr. 1676 thro' S. Davis to Gabriel Stubbs of Westminster, clockmaker, till 1684, but not freed.

WILMOT, John London
Baillie records a watch by him in 1679, but this can hardly be the one who was still apr.?

WILMOT(T), Stephen London
Apr. Apr 1667 to Edward Stanton. Free Sep 1674. Took as aprs.: Jul 1683 **John Eagle** (passed to other masters); Jun 1684 **Benjamin Collier** – free Jul 1693; Jul 1689 **John Hughes;** Aug 1691 **Thomas Smith** – free Jul 1700; Feb 1695/96 **Thomas Bardolph;** Apr 1710 **Aaron Tallis;** his son, **Thomas Wilmott,** – freed Apr 1716. Work known – longcase clocks.

WILMOT, Thomas London/The Hague(?)
B.c. 1639, apr. Nov 1653 to Thomas Loomes till 1660, but not freed. A ded made at the Hague in 1668 by Ahasuerus Fromanteel was witnessed by Thomas Wilmot, with others.

WILSON, Edward London
B.c. 1650, apr. Feb 1663/64 to Richard Nau till 1671. Freed Feb 1670/71 (having been transferred to Robert Smith?). Took as aprs.: Jul 1672 **Daniel Jones;** Sep 1682 bound an apr. for Joseph Windmills. Believed died or left between 1693 and 1697.

WILSON, George London
B.c. 1667, apr. Sep 1681 to Thomas Grimes thro' D. Stevens – free Sep 1692. Took as aprs.: Jul 1696 **Charles Molyns** – free Jul 1709; **John Long** (from Ambrose Gardiner) – free Jul 1698; May 1700 **William Ryley** (son of William Ryley late of St. Margaret Westminster, glazier, deceased); May 1703 **Samuel Whitehead** (son of Samuel Whitehead of Braintree, Essex, ironmonger); Mar 1705-06 **Henry Elliott** (son of Walter Elliott of St. Martin le Grand, victualler); Jul 1707 **William Geary;** May 1714 **James Englefield.** Was in arrears with quarterage in 1719-20, after which I have no data. Work known – longcase clocks, signed 'George Wilson, London'.

WILSON, John London
Baillie records him as mid-17th century. I do not know him, but in 1637 CC fined a 'Mr. Wilson' for not binding his aprs. thro' CC.

WILSON, Joshua London
B.c. 1675, apr. Sep 1688 to William Fuller till 1696, but not freed. However was obviously regarded as a member. Took as aprs.: Dec 1698 **Benjamin Rowe** (son of John Rowe, late Citizen and Loriner of London, deceased) – free Apr 1708; Sep 1702 **Joseph Reckless** (son of Joseph Reckless of Nottingham, gent.). Paid quarterage till 1702. Work known – lantern and longcase clocks, signed 'Joshua Wilson, London'. Also a watch by him hallmarked 1707.

WILSON, Joseph London
Mentioned in CC minutes Jan 1686/87, but prob. nothing to do with clockmaking but just present to attend to affairs of brother, Thomas, *qv*.

WILSON, Nathaniel London
B.c. 1644, apr. Nov 1658 to Jeremie East thro' D. Moody till 1665, but not freed.

WILSON, Richard London
Ironmonger within Newgate. Had faulty rulers confiscated 1672 by CC.

WILSON, Richard York
Clockmaker, free there 1586.

WILSON, Robert Manchester (Lancashire)
Watchmaker, died 1638.

WILSON, Thomas London
Apr. Sep 1651 to Simon Hackett thro' J. Bayes. Free Nov 1659. Took as aprs.: Jan 1663 **James Ashbourne** ('for a basket maker', which might mean to be a maker of basket tops for bracket clocks); also bound an apr. in 1685 for John Clowes. Jul 1674 excused stewardship for second year as he already held several 'troublesome and chargeable offices' in his own parish. Made Assistant from 1682, but attended only very infrequently and then only when forced to. In Sep 1686 (after which he never again attended) his Assistant's fee was returned to him 'being now in a meane condition'. In Jan 1686/87 he brought with him his brother, Joseph, concerning the financial arrangements to refund his fee. Work known – Baillie records watches.

WILSON, William London
B.c. 1672, apr. Jun 1686 to William Ames till 1693. Free Dec 1693. Paid

quarterage till c. 1695. In Feb 1712/13 he was sued for arrears of quarterage, but then was excused 'being out of the trade'. In Jul 1713 took as apr. **Humphrey Price.**

WILSON, William   **York**
Clockmaker, son of Richard Wilson, clockmaker. Free 1607.

WINCH, Amos   **London**
B.c. 1656, apr. Apr 1670 to Robert Halstead till 1677. Free Jul 1677. Took as aprs.: Sep 1682 **William Waterman;** Aug 1689 **William Goodrick** thro' T. Hicks; also bound an apr. for John Bellard. Called to serve as steward in 1690 but failed to appear as he 'hath betaken himself to White Fryers'.

WINCH, Joseph   **Uxbridge (Middlesex)**
Longcase clock recorded c. 1700.

WINDMILLS, Joseph   **London**
Free Brother in CC Sep 1671, a Great Clockmaker (by Jul 1671 he already had a journeyman, name unknown). Took as aprs.: Mar 1675 **John Jackson** (passed on to Thomas Taylor of Holborn); Apr 1680 **Samuel Brooks;** Sep 1673 **Thomas Bradford** thro' W. Speakman – free Sep 1680; Sep 1682 **Richard Garle** thro' E. Wilson; Aug 1686 **William Wightman** – free Feb 1696/97; Jan 1686/87 his son, **Thomas Windmills** – free Jan 1695-96; Jul 1691 **Samuel Bedford;** Dec 1693 **Benjamin Smith;** Sep 1695 **William Grimes;** Aug 1700 **Ralph Sherratt** (son of John Sherratt, late of Wem, Shropshire, ironmonger, deceased, his widow, Margaret, 'to buy his clothes'). Worked initially at St. Martins le Grand, later by 1687 at Mark Lane End, Tower Street. Made CC Assistant from 1691, Warden from 1699, Master 1702, attended till at least 1720. By 1714 was in partnership with son, Thomas. Work known – a considerable output of lantern clocks, some signed at 'St. Martins le Grand', watches, bracket and longcase clocks, usually signed 'Joseph Windmills, London', sometimes 'Joseph Windmills at Mark Lane End next Tower Street, Londini fecit'. Later work, with son, signed 'J.&T. Windmills of London' or just 'Windmills, London'. A printed label published by him in 1714 is found in Edwardes' *The Grandfather Clock*, advising how to set up a clock. A prolific and highly-regarded maker.

WINDMILLS, Thomas   **London**
B.c. 1672, son of Joseph Windmills. Apr. to father Jan 1686/87 till 1693.

Free Jan 1695/96. Took as aprs.: Dec 1696 **Thomas Bennett** – free Apr 1720; Aug 1703 **Thomas Charlwood;** May 1708 **Thomas Bezely;** Jun 1713 **William Dowse;** Jan 1716/17 **Manton Noone.** Made CC Assistant from 1713, Warden 1716, Master 1718. I have no data after 1720. Later in partnership with Bennett (presumably after 1720). Baillie records him till 1732. Worked in partnership with father initially, *qv.* Work known – watches, bracket and lantern and longcase clocks signed 'Windmills, London' or 'Thomas Windmills, London'.

WING, Henry   **London**
Working 1671, but prob. error for Wynne, *qv.*

WINN, John   **London**
Prob. Wynne, *qv.*

WINNOCK, Joshua (sometimes Wennock)   **Colchester/London**
B. 1650, son of Samuel Winnock of Colchester (for pedigree, see my books *Country Clocks* and *Complete British Clocks*). Apr. Jun 1664 to his step-father, Ahasuerus Fromanteel the elder, till 1671. Free Jan 1672/73. Took as aprs.: Feb 1673/74 **John Pond;** Apr 1695 his son, **Daniel Winnock** – free Apr 1708; Jul 1716 **Joshua Winnock.** In 1718 worked at Halfmoon Alley, Bishopsgate Street. Also bound an apr. for John Wise junior. He died in 1718. (See my article in *Antiquarian Horology*, March 1975.)

WINSTANLEY, James   Liverpool (Lancashire)/Wigan(?)
Watchsmith. Daughter b. there 1675. One of this name made clock dial at Wigan in 1700 and died 1715 there.

WINSTANLEY, James   **London**
B.c. 1673, apr. Aug 1687 to John Wheeler till 1694, but not freed.

WINSTANLEY, William   **Liverpool (Lancashire)**
Watchsmith and watch-springmaker. Children b. there 1675-80.

WINT, Daniel   **London**
B.c. 1679, apr. Mar 1693/94 to Thomas Morgan transferred to (blank) Clowes till 1700, but not freed.

WINTER, Samuel   **London**
B.c. 1669, apr. Nov 1683 to Edward Stanton till 1690, but not freed.

WINTER, William   **London**
B.c. 1672, apr. May 1686 to Robert Dingley till 1693, but not freed.

WINTLE, David   **London**
Recorded by Britten as c. 1680, but prob. a slip for Daniel Wint, *qv*.

WINTWORTH, Thomas (see under Wentworth)   **Sarum**

WIRRALL, Copley (sometimes Wyrall)   **London**
B.c. 1623, apr. Feb 1637/38 thro' O. Durant to Thomas Alcock till 1646.
Freed Feb 1647/48.

WISE, Cadwalider   **London**
(Not Cadwallder). B.c. 1665, apr. Nov 1679 to Peter Knibb (of whom
believed to be a relative) till 1686, but not freed.

WISE, John senior   **London/Warwick**
B.c. 1625, apr. Jul 1638 to Peter Closon thro' T. Dawson till 1646. Freed
Oct 1646. Apparently lived in Warwick 1653-68, where he repaired
clocks of St. Nicholas and St. Mary's church, at latter of which his
children were baptised, incl.: 1658 John, 1661 Joseph, 1663 Thomas,
1666 Robert. Free in CC in London again Mar 1669/70 by redemption
(though he was already a freeman?). Took as aprs.: Apr 1670 **Albon
Raynolds;** Sep 1671 his son, **Richard Wise** – free 1679; Feb 1674/75
Richard Knight – free Sep 1682; May 1675 **John Gardner** – free Jul
1682; Jan 1675/76 his son, **John Wise** – free Apr 1683; Jul 1678 his son,
Thomas Wise – free Feb 1686/87; Jan 1678/79 his son, **Joseph Wise** –
free Apr 1687; his son, **Peter Wise** – free by patrimony Apr 1693; son,
Luke Wise – free by patrimony Dec 1694; Jul 1680, his son, **Robert
Wise** – freed Sep 1695. In 1693/94 a John Wise clockmaker 'neere the
popeshead in Moorfields' stood surety for one Richard Wise in the
Cutlers' Co. Still alive in 1690 but dead by Apr 1693. Work known –
lantern clocks, signed 'John Wise fecit' and 'John Wise, Londini'. Also
longcase clocks but latter difficult to distinguish from his son's. Also
bracket clocks by him, or son.

WISE, John junior   **London/Bodicote (Oxfordshire)**
·B. 1658, son of John Wise senior, to whom he was apr. Jan 1675/76 till
1682. Freed Apr 1683. Bound an apr. each for R. Baker and W. Slough,
but took for his own aprs.: Nov 1686 **Richard Kemp** thro' J. Winnock,
later passed on to J. Westoby; Jan 1690/91 **Samuel Hawtyen** thro'

J. Papworth; Apr 1698 **Richard Penny;** Feb 1692/93 **John Morgan** – Nov 1704; Apr 1698 his son, **John Wise** (the third) – free Jan 1710/11; Mar 1699/1700 **John Morrell** (son of Nicholas Morrell of Warwick, smith); Nov 1703 **George Farr;** May 1718 **Samuel Bryan.** I have no data after 1720. Work known – difficult to distinguish from his father's, *qv.* A clock made for Bodicote church, inscribed 'John Wise, Londini, 1700' must have been made by this man.

WISE, Joseph London
B. 1661, son of John Wise senior to whom apr. Jan 1678/79 till 1685. Freed Apr 1687. Took as aprs.: Feb 1687/88 **Langley Bradley** – free Apr 1695; Sep 1695 **Joseph Cawkitt.** Prob. dead or gone by 1697/98.

WISE, Luke London/Reading
Free in CC by patrimony Dec 1694, being son of John Wise senior, deceased. Took as aprs.: Aug 1695 **Robert Coster;** Aug 1698 his son, **Luke Wise** junior; May 1703 his son, **Mark Wise** – free Feb 1719/20. In 1720 lived at Minster Street, Reading as watchmaker and gent. Work known – watches and longcase clocks signed 'Luke Wise, Reading', one also engraved 'God Save Queen Anne'.

WISE, Peter London
Free in CC by patrimony Apr 1693 being son of John Wise of London, clockmaker, deceased. Took as aprs.: May 1693 **John Kyning** – free May 1701; Apr 1697 **John Evans;** Sep 1701 **Christopher Lissamen** (or **Lassiman**) (son of Christopher L., late Citizen and Cook, of London, deceased); May 1703 **John Draycott** (son of James Draycott of Hartingfordbury, co. Herts., gent.). Believed worked in Cheapside. Made CC Assistant from 1720, Master 1725. Believed worked on till 1741 but I have no data after 1720. Work known – longcase clocks, signed 'Peter Wise, London', also watches.

WISE, Richard London
Son of John Wise senior, to whom he was apr. Sep 1671 till 1678. Freed Jul 1679. Took as aprs.: Mar 1682/83 **Richard Haughtin** – free Mar 1690/91; Jan 1686/87 **Zachariah Hanwell** thro' T. Morgan – free Jul 1694. Died before Mar 1690/91. Was witness to 1678 will of Thomas Whaplitt, *qv.* Work known – longcase clock.

WISE, Robert London
B. 1666, son of John Wise senior to whom apr. Jul 1680 till 1687. Free

Sep 1695. In 1705-06 he was in arrears of quarterage. Not heard of again. Work known – watches recorded.

WISE, Thomas   London
B. 1663, son of John Wise senior, to whom apr. Jul 1678 till 1685. Free Feb 1686/87. Thomas Wise, of St. Gabriel Fanchurch, clockmaker, bachelor, 24, to marry Mary Goddard of St. Martins Iremonger Lane, spinster, 23, in Jul 1689. In Jun 1693 Thomas Wise of St. Gabriel Fanchurch, clockmaker, widower, 29, married Anne Ravenscroft of Westham, Essex, spinster, 22, at Little Ilford, Essex. Took as aprs.: Jun 1687 **William Enew;** Sep 1692 **Basil Fletcher;** Jul 1695 **James Story** – free Apr 1704. Still alive 1697 but believed died soon after. Work known – bracket clock, watch, longcase clock, signed 'Thomas Wise Londini fecit', and 'Thomas Wise, Fenchurch Street'.

WISEMAN, John   London
Recorded as free in CC Oct 1646, but this is an error for John Wise (senior) *qv*.

WITHAM, Nathaniel   London
Sundial signed 'Nathaniel Witham Londini fecit, 1716'.

WITHE, John   London
Prob. same as Wyeth, *qv*.

WITHE, Leonall (see Lionel Wythe)   London

WITHER, James   London
Recorded by Baillie as apr. 1637, but I do not know such a man.

WITHER, John   London
Free in CC Sep 1699, apr. of James Gould.

WITHER, Richard   London
B.c. 1668, apr. Oct 1681 to Andrew Prime, a freeman of the Blacksmiths' Co. thro' Abraham Prime. In Jun 1686 was transferred to John Wells, but not freed. Baillie records another of this name, apr. 1682 which is incorrect.

WITHER, William   London
Free in CC Sep 1699, but paid no quarterage in period 1698-1705.

WITHERSTON, J.   Hereford
Bracket clock recorded c. 1690.

WITNES, Francis   London
B.c. 1639, apr. Nov 1653 to Job Betts thro' N. Payne till 1660, but not
freed.

WITT, Richard   London
On 1662 CC list but I can find no other record of him. Maybe a
misrendering of some other name.

WITTE, Samuel   London
Believed apr. Jan 1651 to John Champion. Free Jan 1660/61.

WITTAM, James   Dublin
Recorded as clockmaker 1695, but thought to be error for John, *qv*.

WITTAM, John   Dublin
Clockmaker there 1670, believed father of Lestrange, *qv*. See also James
Wittam.

WITTAM, Lestrange   Dublin
Believed son of John. Clockmaker there 1686.

WOGAN, George (alias Kingsmill, George, *qv*).

WOLFALL, William (or Wolsall?)   London
(Name uncertain, maybe Walpole?). Watchmaker of St. Martins in the
Fields who took as apr. in 1701 **John Bamber** (son of John Bamber of
Aughton, Lancashire).

WOLFORNE, Robert   London
Listed as at Fleet Street in 1662, but I find no other record of him.

WOLVERSTONE (includes such variants as Wofriston, Wolfrston,
etc.).

WOLVERSTONE, Benjamin   London
B.c. 1635, apr. May 1649 to Richard Rickard thro' James Seaborne till
1656. Free Mar 1656. In 1662 worked at Cornhill. Took as aprs.: **William
Bayley** (from Samuel Vernon) – free Apr 1663; Jul 1659 **William**

Dawson; Apr 1663 **Edward Berrisford;** Oct 1663 **Miles Ashton;** Jan 1667/68 **Thomas Wolverstone;** Jun 1668 and apr. for Hilkiah Bedford; **John Bartholomew** (from John North, later passed on to Robert Smith). In 1661 paid part of quarterage for William Delavrespierre.

WOLVERSTONE, Benjamin   **London**
B.c. 1679, son of James Wolverstone, to whom apr. Jun 1693, but not freed.

WOLVERSTONE, James   **London**
Son of Henry Wolverstone of Clifton, Staffordshire. Apr. in Barber Surgeons' Co. Nov 1663 to William Watmore, engraver and goldsmith – free Aug 1672. Was an engraver. Apparently not free in CC till Apr 1677 as a Brother, but was known to them by 1672. (There might perhaps be two contemporaries of the same name?). Took as aprs.: Jun 1672 **Charles Hougham** thro' L. Wythe – free Jul 1680; Jan 1673/74 **Edward Spackman** thro' L. Wythe; Jul 1675 **Francis Huggeford** thro' S. Davis; Sep 1676 **John Hayes** thro' S. Davis; **Richard Ellis** (from G. Deane) – free Jul 1683; Apr 1684 **Andrew Yateman** – free Nov 1692; May 1679 **Charles Hemming;** Mar 1686/87 **William Saville;** Jun 1693 his son, **Benjamin Wolverstone.** Paid no quarterage after c. 1694. In Jan 1682/83 he was accused of engraving fictitious names on works, which he denied, but accused the Assistants of the same thing. Feb 1682/83 he refused to submit to CC ruling, but claims if a workmaster brings him such a task, then it is *he* who should be punished first.

WOLVERSTONE, James   **London**
Son of Thomas Wolverstone, deceased. Freed by patrimony Jan 1690/91. Took as aprs.: Mar 1690/91 **Edward Joselin** – free Mar 1697/98; Sep 1692 **William Smith;** Oct 1697 **Joseph Starkey** – free Oct 1706. The two men of this same name are difficult to distinguish in the records.

WOLVERSTONE, Thomas   **London**
Apr. Sep 1643 to Edward East thro' O. Durant. Free Sep 1650. Had as aprs.: Mar 1648 **John Smith** – free Aug 1656; May 1653 **Richard Follett;** Feb 1651 **Joshua Bunting** thro' W. Bunting; Nov 1654 **Ralph Child** later passed over to R. Peirce; 1661 **Robert Pattison,** later passed over to J. Gregory. Also bound an apr. each for W. Dobb, T. Stayner, W. Lavrespierre. Several times in trouble for not binding his aprs. thro' CC.

WOLVERSTONE, Thomas London
B.c. 1653, apr. Jan 1667/68 to Benjamin Wolverstone till 1674, but not freed.

WOLVERSTONE, Thomas London
Free Brother in CC Dec 1670. This man, or one of the preceding two of this name, had son, James, freed in CC by patrimony Jan 1690/91.

WOMFIELD, Alexander London
This is a spelling slip for Warfield, *qv.*

WOOD, G. Exeter (Devon)
Lantern clock recorded c. 1660. This might be a slip for John Wood who is known to have been working there in 1727 and perhaps earlier.

WOOD, James London
B.c. 1655, apr. Oct 1668 to Edmond Gilpin thro' James Markwick (effective midsummer last) till 1676, but not freed.

WOOD, John London
B.c. 1675, apr. Jan 1689/90 to John North till 1696. Freed Apr 1701. Prob. a mat. inst. maker, which North was. Took as aprs.: Jan 1701/02 **John Barroll** (son of late William Barroll of Hereford, baker, deceased); Jun 1704 **Edmund Bell** (son of Henry Bell of Clerkenwell, Middlesex, gent.); Dec 1709 **Joseph Langthorne;** Jul 1713 **John Walton.**

WOOD, Richard London
B.c. 1637, apr. May 1651 to John Cooke till 1658, but not freed.

WOOD, Robert London
B.c. 1643, apr. Jan 1659/60 to James Gregory till 1667. Free Apr 1671. A boxmaker. Took as apr. May 1675 **John Banbury** – free Apr 1686. Supposedly worked at St. Dunstans.

WOOD, Samuel Sutton, nr. Prescot (Lancashire)
Married Jul 1698 to Margaret Woods of same.

WOOD, Thomas London
B.c. 1668, apr. Jul 1682 to Robert Nemes till 1689. Free Apr 1691. Took as aprs.: Apr 1691 **Arthur Wyke;** Dec 1695 **Joseph Winshurst;** Feb 1698/99 **Timothy Vancourt** (son of Timothy Vancourt of New Windsor,

Buckinghamshire, yeoman); Feb 1703/04 **James Kaus** (actually was prob. *John* Kaus) – free Nov 1712; Mar 1707/08 **John Downes;** Nov 1713 **John Morris;** Dec 1714 **James Rowley.**

WOODFORD, Jonathan   **London**
B.c. 1670, apr. Dec 1684 to John Ebsworth till 1691, but not free.

WOODINGTON, William   **London**
B.c. 1625, apr. Jun 1638 to Edward Gilpin thro' R. Masterson till 1646, but not freed.

WOODWARD, Henry   **Colchester (Essex)**
Clockmaker, with wife, Anne. Bought land in St. Helens Lane in 1679. Children incl. Jemima (baptised 1684 aged 6) and Mary b. 1692.

WOODWARD, John   **London**
B.c. 1642, apr. Feb 1656 to Benjamin Hill till 1663, but not freed.

WOODWARD, Thomas   **London**
B.c. 1657, apr. Jun 1671 to John Froude till 1678, but not freed.

WOOLRIDGE, Stephen   **London**
Apr. Apr 1652 to Jeremy Gregory thro' J. Bayes, but not freed.

WORGAN, John   **London**
Recorded as 1696 but I do not know him. Prob. a misrendering of some other name.

WORLEY, Simon   **Starton (Warwickshire)**
Longcase clock c. 1700 signed 'Simon Worley, Starton fecit'.

WORLIDGE, Daniel   **London**
B.c. 1648, apr. Apr 1661 to Thomas Loomes till 1669, but not freed.

WORLIDGE, Nathaniel   **London**
B.c. 1647, apr. May 1661 to Edward Norris till 1668, but not freed.

WORRALL, John   **London/Liverpool(?)**
Clockmaker in St. Andrews Holborn pre-1719. One of this name at Liverpool, married 1708, there till 1711, maybe same man.

WORTHINGTON, Edward   **London**
B.c. 1641, apr. Sep 1655 to James Cowpe thro' J. Bayley till 1662, but not
free.

WORTLEY, Humphrey   **London**
B.c. 1639, apr. Apr 1653 to Abraham Guyott thro' T. Taylor till 1660,
but not free.

WRAYPIERRE, William (see La Wraypierre, William).

WRENCH, Edward   **Chester**
Free there 1694. Believed married 1694, died 1714. Worked in
Gloverstone. Work known – watch and longcase clock.

WRENCH, John senior   **Chester**
Free there 1690. Died 1739. Took as apr. **Joshua Yoxon/Joxon.** His
employee, William Newbon, stole watches from him. Made Bluecoat
School clock 1720.

WREN, William   **London**
In 1697 a partner with Christopher Cutting, who agreed to dismiss him at
instigation of CC as he was a foreigner.

WRIGHT, ----   **London**
Longcase clock c. 1680, 1¼ seconds pendulum, but uncertain which of
the numerous Wrights this was.

WRIGHT, Benjamin   **London**
B.c. 1664, apr. Apr 1678 to Abraham Prime till 1685. Free Jul 1685.
Took as aprs.: Oct 1685 **John Doddington** thro' Abraham Prime; May
1688 **George Hawkins;** Feb 1691/92 **Daniel Cheeseman** – free Sep
1699; Jun 1696 **William Sanders;** Aug 1700 **Robert King** (son of Robert
King late of parish of St. Magnus, London, goldsmith, deceased). Died
before Jan 1709/10 when his widow, Mary, took as apr. **George Wright.**
Believed worked in Bell Alley, Coleman Street.

WRIGHT, Benjamin   **London**
B.c. 1679, apr. Feb 1693/94 to John Ferrer thro' J. Wright till 1700, but
not freed.

WRIGHT, Edmund   **London**
B.c. 1668, apr. Apr 1682 to Joseph Knibb till 1689, but not freed. Work

known – single-handed year clock giving one-minute time readings, signed 'Edm. Wright, Londini fecit'.

WRIGHT, Edward I   **Norwich**
Goldsmith. Took **Elias Browne** apr. in 1619.

WRIGHT, Edward II   **Norwich**
Could be same man as Edward I. Son, Timothy, free as clockmaker Mar 1650/51.

WRIGHT, Edward III   **Norwich**
Watchmaker, whose son, William, was apr. to a tailor in 1685.

WRIGHT, John   **Liverpool (Lancashire)**
Watchmaker of Comman Garden. Died 1701.

WRIGHT, John senior   **London**
Apr. Jan 1653/54 to Thomas Claxton. Free Nov 1661. Took as aprs.: Dec 1679 **William Jaques** (passed over to N. Delander); Jan 1679/80 **Nathaniel Lever**; Jan 1685/86 **George Leake** – free Sep 1693; perhaps Feb 1693/94 **Benjamin Wright**. Got CC charity from Sep 1694 to Sep 1697 and believed died later in 1697, certainly by 1698. Work known – longcase clock.

WRIGHT, John junior   **London**
Apr. Jun 1656 to Jeremy Gregory thro' R. Beck. Free Sep 1671. Took as aprs.: Aug 1673 **Thomas Rudkin** – free Apr 1683; Dec 1673 **Peter Miller** – free Mar 1681; Dec 1674 **William Taylor**. Believed died soon after 1684. Work known – longcase clock, but not known whether by JW senior or junior.

WRIGHT, John   **London**
B.c. 1677, apr. Sep 1691 to James Markwick till 1698. Free Apr 1700. Paid quarterage till 1702 when he received CC charity.

WRIGHT, John   **London**
B.c. 1679, apr. Apr 1693 to Henry Merryman thro' J. Picket till 1700. Free Apr 1715. Took as aprs.: Nov 1716 **John Snow**; Jan 1716/17 **John Dawle**.

WRIGHT, John   **Mansfield (Nottinghamshire)**
Lantern clock recorded, believed late 17th century. Believed died 1708.

WRIGHT, John Norwich
Son of Thomas Wright. B. 1580 at Bungay (Suffolk). Apr. in 1595 to a
Norwich grocer. Free as a clockmaker Sep 1613. His son, Isaac, was apr.
to a baker in 1631; his son, Robert, apr. to him in 1621.

WRIGHT, Richard London
B.c. 1653, apr. Oct 1667 to Robert Seignior till 1674, but not freed.

WRIGHT, Robert London
Free Brother in CC Apr 1634. Maybe Wright of Norwich.

WRIGHT, Robert Norwich
Son of John. Apr. to his father as clockmaker 1621, but not free.

WRIGHT, Robert Warwick
Repaired St. Nicholas church clock 1579/80.

WRIGHT, Thomas Chester
Free 1613. His apr., **Dutton Bunbery,** freed 1636. Also took **Samuel
Finlaw** apr. 1640-47; **William Bickerstaffe** 1633-42. Witness in 1664 to
stewardship of John Buck.

WRIGHT, Timothy senior Norwich
Son of Edward Wright, free at Norwich as clockmaker Mar 1650/51. His
son, Timothy, free as watchmaker 1677.

WRIGHT, Timothy junior Norwich
Son of Timothy senior. Free as watchmaker Jan 1677/78.

WRIGHT, William London
B.c. 1670, apr. Dec 1684 to Henry Brigden till 1691, but not freed.
Worked at Crown Street, Southwark by 1716 when involved with
Richard Street in taking over running of St. Paul's clock from Langley
Bradley. Still at Crown Street 1731. Died by 1719, succ. by son, William.
Seems to have had little to do with CC. Work known – bracket clocks and
longcases, signed 'Wm. Wright, Crown Court, Southwark'.

WYCHE, David London
B.c. 1672, apr. Jun 1686 to Thomas Taylor senior, passed over to his son,
Thomas Taylor junior till 1693. Free Apr 1694. Took as aprs.: Dec 1697
James Bunn; Jan 1700/01 **William Chubb** (son of Edward Chubb of

Fulham, butcher); **Joseph Prestwood** (from Henry Jones) – free Jul 1703; Sep 1705 **George Hay** (son of Alexander Hay of Hitchingfield, Sussex, clerk); Jun 1713 **John Titford;** Sep 1717 another one, name illegible. Work known – watches. Believed worked next to the Cross Keys Tavern, Strand.

WYCH, John   **London**
B.c. 1663, apr. Jul 1677 thro' Thomas Taylor of Holborn to his brother-in-law, John Fitter of Battersea, watchmaker, till 1684, but not freed. Wych was a relative of Taylor.

WYETH (see also Wythe).

WYETH, George   **London**
Free in CC Oct 1646.

WYETH, John (also Withe)   **London**
Free Brother in CC Apr 1656. Took as apr. May 1656 **Peter Southworth** thro' J. Palfrey, later passed over to Jeremy East. In 1657 ordered to turn away one of his aprs. In 1662 worked in Westminster. Last heard of in 1664 when in arrears of quarterage. In Jul 1656 he showed the CC a 'spelter metal' boxed watch, which the CC disliked, considering it deceitful 'being in imitation of Gould' and they ordered that no more must be made in the fashion of 'watch boxes or cases'.

WYKE, Arthur   **London**
B.c. 1678, apr. Apr 1691 to Thomas Wood till 1699, but not freed.

WYNN, Edward   **London**
Watch recorded c. 1630.

WYNNE, Ellis   **Harlech (Wales)**
Sundial recorded dated 1711. (Ellis Wynne, 1670/1734, was a writer – prob. owner, not maker.)

WYNNE, Henry (erroneously Wing)   **London**
Maker of mat. insts., etc. Free in CC Oct 1662 having been apr. of Ralph Gretorix. In 1671 CC recorded him as an 'ironmonger'. Took as aprs.: Oct 1663 **Richard Whitehead** – free Sep 1671; Jun 1669 an apr. for Ed. Fage; Aug 1670 **Clement Forster** – free Jul 1682; Mar 1675 **John Warner** – free Apr 1682; Sep 1677 **George Wethered;** Apr 1680 **Simon**

Cade – free Apr 1688; Apr 1685 **John Hatch** – free Jul 1693; Apr 1688 **Thomas Tutell** – free Jul 1695; Apr 1696 **Richard Glynne** – free Sep 1705. Also bound several aprs. for other masters, incl. 3 for Isaac Carver, 1 for Isaac Thompson, 1 for J. Atkinson. Became CC Assistant from 1676, Warden from 1686, Master 1690, attended till 1708. Work known – mainly sundials, usually signed 'Henry Wynne Lond. fecit', one erected by Charles II at Windsor signed 'Henricus Wynne Londini fecit'.

WYNNE, John (sometimes Winn)   **London**
B.c. 1656, apr. Feb 1670/71 thro' R. Bowen to William Watmore, engraver, then to James Graves, engraver, till 1677. Free Sep 1678. Took as aprs.: Nov 1681 **Robert Netter;** Nov 1684 **John Stevens** thro' W. Hillier – free Dec 1691; Sep 1691 **James Frencham** – free Sep 1698; Aug 1695 **William Hall;** Dec 1697 **Benjamin Collier.** Paid quarterage till at least 1704.

WYNNE, Robert   **London**
B.c. 1628, apr. Aug 1641 thro' O. Durant to James Vautrollier till 1649, but not freed.

WYRALL, Copley (see Wirrall).

WYTH, John
See Wyeth, but also sometimes Withe and Wither.

WYTHE, Joan   **London**
Widow of Lionel, *qv*.

WYTHE, Lionel   **London**
B.c. 1626, apr. Jul 1638 to (blank) Threlkeld thro' T. Dawson till 1647. Free Dec 1645. Worked in Fleet Street in 1662. May have been in Waxchandlers' Co. Was appointed Beadle to CC from Feb 1665/66, but even before that he had bound several aprs. for other (non-freemen) masters, in all binding very many aprs. Prob. took as his own aprs.: Jan 1656/57 **Barlow Rookes** – free Apr 1665; Jul 1660 **Henry Shoywell.** In Mar 1669/70 he borrowed £10 from CC 'he having taken a house'. Died after 22 Dec 1674 but before 18 Jan 1675. Widow, Joan, received CC charity infrequently from 1675 but regularly after Dec 1691 till Jul 1694. Joan bound as apr. Mar 1678 **Elizabeth Ayloffe,** but prob. not to do with clockmaking. Work known – none. Was prob. a part-maker.

WYTHE, Richard   **London**
B.c. 1668, apr. Aug 1682 to John Johnson till 1689, but not free. Said to be son of Lionel, but on what authority I do not know.

WYTHE, Thomas   **London**
B.c. 1639, apr. Sep 1653 to William Lavrespierre thro' R. Record till 1660, but not freed.

WYTHER, James   **London**
Apr. Apr 1638 thro' R. Masterson to Richard Child, but not freed.

Y

YARDE, Thomas   **London**
Watch recorded c. 1580, but I cannot trace this man.

YARRINGTON, John   **Bristol**
Apr. 1693/94 to Benjamin Willoughby. Free Dec 1700.

YATE, Cornelius   **London**
Petitioner for CC in 1622. Watch known c. 1625.

YATE, William (sometimes Yates)   **London**
Petitioner for CC in 1622. One of this name was free of the City of London Jan 1610/11 thro' Joiners' Co., which might be him. Bound an apr. thro' CC 1640. Work known – watches.

YATES – watch also for Yate.

YATES, John   **Kenilworth (Warwickshire)**
Blacksmith, who repaired St. Nicholas, Kenilworth, clock 1687-1702.

YATES, Michael   **London**
B.c. 1651, apr. Jun 1664 to Isaac Plovier thro' C. Bonner till 1672, but not freed.

YATES, Samuel   **Kenilworth (Warwickshire)**
Clockmaker there, who repaired St. Nicholas church clock in 1687. May be the London Yates below.

YATES, Samuel London
Free Brother in CC Jul 1647.

YATES, Samuel London
Clockmaker but freeman of the Clothworkers' Co. Free Brother in CC
Jan 1685. Paid quarterage till c. 1693, but not later.

YEARES(?), Peter Chester
Serviced church clock 1623.

YEATMAN, Andrew London
B.c. 1670, apr. Apr 1684 to James Wolverstone till 1691. Free Nov 1692.
Took as aprs.: Nov 1692 **John Cobb** (later passed over to T. Terrier);
Apr 1694 with Mary, his wife, took **Elizabeth Rowley**. Still working in
1697.

YOUELL, Robert London
B.c. 1677, apr. Jul 1691 to Michael Knight thro' T. Tompion.

YOUNG, Francis London
B.c. 1666, apr. May 1680 to Henry Young till 1687, but not freed.

YOUNG, G. London
Baillie records him as working at Charing Cross c. 1685, as watchmaker,
but I cannot trace him.

YOUNG, Henry London
Apr. Jul 1659 to Thomas Taylor (of Strand?). Free Apr 1672, when he
paid arrears of quarterage (prob. because he had delayed taking up
freedom over-long). Took as aprs.: Dec 1672 **William Masters** – free
Aug 1701; May 1680 **Francis Young;** Dec 1680 **Daniel Aldridge;** Feb
1681-82 **Thomas Southen.** In Jul 1689 he was called to serve as steward
but did not appear and was said to have gone to Portsmouth. Believed
worked 'near the Wine House in the Strand'. Work known – longcase
clocks usually signed 'Henry Young in ye Strand, London'.

YOUNG, Richard London
B.c. 1655, apr. Jun 1669 to Henry Wynne to serve Edward Fage, mat.
inst. maker, till 1676, but not freed.

YOUNG, Thomas **London**
B.c. 1675, apr. Jul 1689 thro' D. Stevens to Richard Medhurst of Croydon, watchmaker, till 1696. Free Sep 1699. Paid quarterage till at least 1704.

YOUNG, William senior **London**
Apr. Sep 1656 thro' William Godbed to John White, a freeman of the Grocers' Co. Free in CC Jan 1668-69, and free of the City 1669. Took as aprs.: Apr 1684 **Robert Gideon** (later passed on to T. Brayfield); Nov 1691 **Christopher Lee**. In Jul 1681 was called to be steward but sent word he could not as his wife was dying. Made Assistant 1691, but excused Wardenship 1699 and seems never to have attended CC thereafter. Paid no quarterage after 1700 and may have died soon after but one of this name (senior or junior?) received CC charity Jan 1705-06. Work known – watches (and some clocks?) signed 'William Young at Charing Cross'.

YOUNG, William junior **London**
B.c. 1660, apr. Mar 1674/75 to George Harris till 1681. Free Apr 1682. Took as aprs.: Dec 1693 **Philip Hull**; Aug 1696 **Richard Cooke**; Sep 1701 **Benjamin Stevens** (son of Thomas Stevens of Coventry, Warwickshire, cheesemonger); Feb 1713/14 **Tobias Cleer**. Work known – difficult to distinguish from that of William Young senior.

YOUNG, William **Oxford**
Turret clock-worker/maker and smith. Working 1656-95 on local church clocks and in 1680 made clock for St. Lawrence, Reading for £30.

Z

ZACHARY, John   **London**
B.c. 1674, apr. May 1687 to Daniel Quare thro' W. Simcox till 1695.
Free Mar 1694/95. Took as aprs.: Jun 1696 **John Beck**; Aug 1713 **John Huntley.**

ZINZANTH, Henry   **London**
Recorded by Baillie as apr. 1656, but I cannot trace such a person and this is prob. a misreading of some other name.

BIBLIOGRAPHY
Detailed studies in regional clockmaking

Baillie, G. H.: *Watchmakers and Clockmakers of the World, Volume One.* (N.A.G. Press, 1969 – see also Volume Two under Loomes).

Beeson, C. F. C.: *Clockmaking in Oxfordshire.* Antiquarian Horological Society, 1967.

Bellchambers, J. K.: *Devonshire Clockmakers.* Torquay, 1962.

Bellchambers, J. K.: *Somerset Clockmakers.* Antiquarian Horological Society, 1969.

Brown, H. Miles: *Cornish Clocks and Clockmakers.* David & Charles, 1970.

Daniel, John: *Leicestershire Clockmakers.* Leicester, 1975.

Elliott, D. J.: *Shropshire Clock and Watchmakers.* Chichester, 1979.

Haggar, A. L. and Miller, L. F.: *Suffolk Clocks and Clockmakers.* Antiquarian Horological Society, 1974.

Hughes, R. G.: *Derbyshire Clock and Watchmakers.* Derby Museums, 1976.

Lee, R. A.: *The Knibb Family Clockmakers.* Byfleet, 1964.

Legg, E.: *Clock and Watchmakers of Buckinghamshire.* Fenny Stratford, 1975.

Loomes, Brian: *Lancashire Clocks and Clockmakers.* David & Charles, 1975.

Loomes, Brian: *Westmorland Clocks and Clockmakers.* David & Charles, 1974.

Loomes, Brian: *Yorkshire Clockmakers.* Clapham, 1972.

Loomes, Brian: *Watchmakers and Clockmakers of the World, Volume Two.* N.A.G. Press 1976 – see also under Baillie, G. H.

Mason, Bernard: *Clock and Watchmaking in Colchester.* 1969.

Mather, Harold H.: *Clock and Watchmakers of Nottinghamshire.* Nottingham Museum, 1979.

Moore, Nicholas: *Chester Clocks and Clockmakers*. Chester, 1976.

Peate, Iorweth C.: *Clock and Watchmakers in Wales*. Cardiff, 1960.

Penfold, John B.: *The Clockmakers of Cumberland*. Brant Wright Associates, 1977.

Ponsford, Clive N.: *Time in Exeter*. Exeter, 1978.

Ponsford, C. N., Scott, J. G. M. and Authers, W. P.: *Clocks and Clockmakers of Tiverton*. Tiverton, 1977.

Seaby, W. A.: *Clockmakers of Warwick and Leamington*. Warwickshire Museum, 1981.

Smith, John: *Old Scottish Clockmakers 1921*, E. P. re-published 1975.

Symonds, R. W.: *Thomas Tompion, his life and work*. 1951, re-published Antique Collectors' Club 1969.

Tebbutt, Laurence: *Stamford Clocks and Watches*. Stamford, 1975.